Peasant Economy,

Culture, and Politics of

European Russia,

1800–1921

PEASANTS IN A NON-BLACK-EARTH VILLAGE DURING *RASPUTITSA* (THE WASHING AWAY OF THE
ROADS DURING THE SPRING OR AUTUMN THAW OR RAINY SEASON), C. 1896, BY B. W. KILBURN
(CALIFORNIA MUSEUM OF PHOTOGRAPHY, KEYSTONE-MAST COLLECTION,
UNIVERSITY OF CALIFORNIA, RIVERSIDE).

Peasant Economy, Culture, and Politics of European Russia, 1800–1921

Edited by

ESTHER KINGSTON-MANN

AND TIMOTHY MIXTER

With the Assistance of

JEFFREY BURDS

PRINCETON UNIVERSITY PRESS

PRINCETON, NEW JERSEY

Library of Congress Cataloging-in-Publication Data

Peasant economy, culture, and politics of European Russia,
1800–1921 / edited by Esther Kingston-Mann and Timothy Mixter
with the assistance of Jeffrey Burds.
p.   cm.
Includes index.
ISBN 0-691-05595-5 (alk. paper)—ISBN 0-691-00849-3
(pbk. : alk. paper)
1. Peasantry—Soviet Union—History—Congresses.
2. Peasantry—Political aspects—Soviet Union—History—Congresses.
3. Soviet Union—Social life and customs—Congresses.
I. Kingston-Mann, Esther. II. Mixter, Timothy, 1949–
III. Burds, Jeffrey.
HD1536.S65P43   1990
305.5'633—dc20   90–8643

This book has been composed in Linotron Palatino

1   3   5   7   9   10   8   6   4   2

1   3   5   7   9   10   8   6   4   2
(Pbk.)

To the members of our conference *skhod*,
August, 1986, Boston, Massachusetts

Contents

List of Illustrations

Frontispiece. Peasants in a Non-Black-Earth Village During *Rasputitsa* (the washing away of the roads during the spring or autumn thaw or rainy season), c. 1896, by B. W. Kilburn (California Museum of Photography, Keystone-Mast Collection, University of California, Riverside).

List of Maps and Figures

Preface

THIS COLLECTION of essays was generated by the first international conference ever held on the history of the Russian peasantry. Funded by the National Endowment for the Humanities, it took place in August 1986 at the University of Massachusetts at Boston and was generously supported by the university administration and in particular by Provost Robert Greene.

The conference itself represented an important breakthrough in the field of peasant studies. For the first time, the majority of the Russian population was being discussed by a wide range of junior and senior scholars on the basis of archival research which reflected the regional variations of the Russian empire, permitting comparisons between Russian peasants and those in other parts of the world which were far more solidly based than had ever been possible before. The intellectual excitement generated by the research findings presented and by the impact of conceptual insights from other geographic areas and disciplines was fostered by the profoundly insightful commentaries of Teodor Shanin, James Scott, and Kevin O'Neill. The responses and suggestions made by Evsey Domar, George Yaney, Allan Wildman, and Tom Gleason were extremely useful as well. We hope that our questions and our "answers," as reflected in this book, will generate further research and questions and even, at a not too distant date, a second international conference on the Russian peasantry which will extend into the Soviet period.

Although David Christian was not part of the initial conference, he was willing to contribute a paper based upon his research into the pre-Emancipation period; the essays by Christine Worobec, Scott Seregny, and Rodney Bohac are substantially different from their original conference presentations. Conference papers that have appeared elsewhere, sometimes with titles slightly altered from those presented in Boston, include:

Rodney Bohac, "The Mir and the Military Draft," *Slavic Review* 47, no. 4 (Winter 1988): 652–66.

Ben Eklof, "World in Conflict? Corporal Punishment, School and Village Culture in Russia, 1881–1914," *Slavic Review*, forthcoming.

Beatrice Farnsworth, "The Soldatka: Folklore and Court Record," *Slavic Review* 48, no. 1 (Spring 1990): 58–73.

Stephen P. Frank, "Popular Justice, Community and Culture Among the Russian Peasantry, 1870–1900," *Russian Review* 46, no. 3 (July 1987): 239–65.

Maureen Perrie, "Folklore as Evidence of Peasant Mentalité: Social Attitudes and Values in Russian Popular Culture," *Russian Review* 48, no. 2 (April 1989): 119–43.

David Ransel, "The Foundling Market: Children of the Russian Foundling Homes in a Network of Exchange between Town and Village," in *Mothers of Misery: Child Abandonment in Russia* (Princeton, 1989).

Scott Seregny, "A Different Type of Peasant Movement: The Peasant Unions in the Russian Revolution of 1905," *Slavic Review* 47, no. 1 (Spring 1988): 51–67.

Christine D. Worobec, "Patterns of Property Devolution Among Ukrainian Peasants in Kiev and Kharkiv Provinces," in *Occasional Papers of the Kennan Institute for Advanced Russian Studies*, no. 206 (1986).

The other papers, which contributed significantly to the success of the conference, were:

Robert Edelman, "Parties, Agitators and the Spread of Rebellion: 1905 in the Right-Bank Ukraine."

Cathy A. Frierson, "Official Culture and Peasant Counter-Culture Within the Village: *Volost* Court Activity at the End of the Nineteenth Century."

Steven L. Hoch, "Sharecropping and Peasant Tenancy Relations in Post-Emancipation Russia."

Robert Eugene Johnson, "Kinship and Non-Agricultural Earnings in Kostroma: A Preliminary Communication."

James H. Krukones, "Throw the Rascals Out!" Criticism of Peasant Officials in the Newspaper *Sel'skii Vestnik* ("Village Herald"), 1881–1889.

Carol Leonard, "Industry and Agriculture in Pre-Emancipation Russia: Iaroslavl' Guberniia."

Thomas S. Pearson, "Authority and Self-Government in Russian Peasant Village Administration (1881–1917): Problems and Perceptions."

Robert Rothstein "*Zhenskaia Dolia* and the Russian Folk Song."

Richard Rudolph, "The Russian Peasant Family and the Economy."

Andrew M. Verner, "Peasant Petitions to Nicholas II and the First State Duma: Some Methodological Observations and Preliminary Conclusions."

Special thanks are due to Jeffrey Burds for help with organization, preparation of the conference program, and preliminary editing, as well as to Tom Gleason for his helpful advice and encouragement.

The assistance in preparing photography and maps of Edward Kasinec and Natalia Zitszelsberger (of the New York Public Library) and of Mark T. Mattson, Dennis Leeper, Jocelyn Clapp and John Lupo, is much appreciated, as is the work of Princeton University Press's Gail Ullman, Cindy Hirschfeld, and Molan Chun Goldstein, and of Barbara Grenquist..

The most essential kind of moral support, without which projects like this are never completed, came from Wendy Fearing, Mary Jane Rupert, Bill Freeman, Franny Osman, Erica Ackerman, David Wootton, Chris Cotton, Choon-Heng Leong, Heather Hogan, Rochelle Ruthchild, Roberta Thompson Manning, Frank Wcislo, Lucille Wilmot, and above all from Jim Mann, who now knows more about the Russian peasantry than any composer of contemporary music in the world.

—E. K.-M. AND T. M.

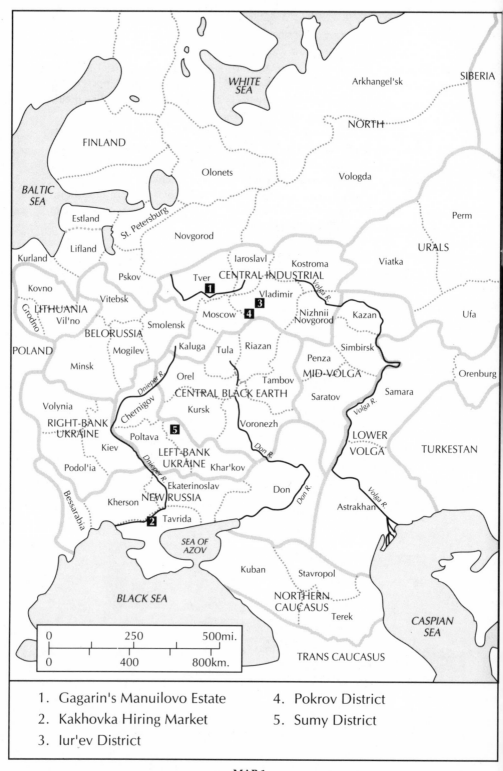

1. Gagarin's Manuilovo Estate
2. Kakhovka Hiring Market
3. Iur'ev District
4. Pokrov District
5. Sumy District

MAP 1.
Regions and Provinces of European Russia

Geographic Regions

Baltic Area: Region composed of the provinces of Estland, Lifland, and Kurland, approximately equivalent to modern Estonia and Latvia.

Belorussia: (White Russia) Area composed of the provinces of Mogilev, Vitebsk, Smolensk, and Minsk.

Central Agricultural Region: See Central-Black-Earth Zone.

Central-Black-Earth Zone: Includes the provinces of Orel, Kursk, Tambov, Voronezh, Tula, and Riazan. Sometimes called the Central Black Earth Region or Central Agricultural Region. Some definitions include the provinces of Saratov, Penza, Simbirsk, and Samara; others include only the southern districts of Riazan.

Central Industrial Region: Unless otherwise noted, includes the provinces of Iaroslavl, Tver, Kostroma, Kaluga, Moscow, Vladimir, and Nizhnii Novgorod (and sometimes Riazan and Tula). At times, used interchangeably with Non-Black-Earth Region, or Zone.

Left-Bank Ukraine: Provinces on the eastern bank of the Dnieper River, including Poltava, Chernigov, and Khar'kov. Sometimes referred to as Little Russia.

Lithuania: Area comprising the provinces of Kovno, Vil'no, and Grodno.

Little Russia: See Left-Bank Ukraine.

Lower Volga: Region composed of the provinces of Samara, Astrakhan, Ufa, and Orenburg.

Mid-Volga: Region composed of the provinces of Saratov, Simbirsk, Penza, and Kazan.

New Russia: Region comprising the provinces of Tavrida, Kherson, and Ekaterinoslav. Sometimes, all or part of Bessarabia Province and/or the Don Oblast are included.

Non-Black-Earth Zone: See Central Industrial Region. Occasionally used as a synonym for north Russia and may include the provinces of Olonets, Vologda, Arkhangel'sk, Novgorod, St. Petersburg, and Pskov and almost always the provinces of the Central Industrial Region noted above.

Northern Caucasus: Region north of the Caucasus Mountains, comprising the Kuban Oblast and the province of Terek. Sometimes includes the province of Stavropol and the Black Sea Province.

Right-Bank Ukraine: Provinces on the western bank of the Dnieper River, including the provinces of Kiev, Podol'ia and Volynia. Sometimes used interchangeably with the term Southwest.

Ukraine: Area composed of the Left-Bank Ukraine, Right-Bank Ukraine, Ekaterinoslav, Kherson and Tavrida provinces. Although there is disagreement over definitions and linguistic usage, we have chosen to use Russian terms for all provinces. This was done for reasons of consistency and not to indicate agreement with one or another political interpretation.

Peasant Economy,

Culture, and Politics of

European Russia,

1800–1921

Breaking the Silence: An Introduction

Esther Kingston-Mann*

THE RESEARCH CONTEXT

From the mid-nineteenth century until the 1920s, educated Russians passionately and rancorously debated the "peasant question." To policymakers, reformers, revolutionaries, and academics, painfully aware that the penalties that backwardness had imposed upon peasant societies from China to Ireland ranged from a loss of autonomy to national extinction, the realities of peasant life and its potential for change became a matter of urgent scholarly and practical concern.[1] It was important to determine, for example, whether peasants were tradition-bound and rigid. It was necessary to discover whether peasant institutions were strong or weak. And perhaps most important of all to the seldom disinterested observers of the Russian countryside, were peasants the *objects* of change—that is, were they the receivers, the victims, the mute and stubborn obstacles to progress? Or were they the *subjects*—the shapers, contributors, and even, at times, the principal actors upon the historical stage? The rise of Stalin put an abrupt and violent end to such debates and questions, not least in the area of scholarship.

In the West, there was less controversy and far less research. Until recently, historians of Russia did not study the peasant majority of the population. The only significant exception was Geroid Robinson's *Rural Russia Under the Old Regime* (1932), a book that portrayed peasants as an increasingly impoverished social element, shattering into kulak and proletarian fragments in their encounter with the modern capitalist world. Unfortunately, Robin-

* I am deeply indebted to the work of the anthropologists Robert LeVine and Merry White, whose conceptual frameworks have served as a point of departure for my discussion. They are not, of course, responsible for the substantial revisions and amendments which I have made. See LeVine and White, *Human Conditions: The Cultural Basis of Educational Developments* (New York, 1986), pp. 13–15.

[1] Such fears were further exacerbated by the experience of military defeat at the hands of the Japanese in 1905 and by the Germans in 1918. See discussion in E. Kingston-Mann, "Marxism and Russian Rural Development: Problems of Experience, Evidence, and Culture," *The American Historical Review* 86, no. 4 (October 1981): 731–52.

son's landmark study did not serve to stimulate further research. Instead, it had the unforeseen consequence of closing the peasant question in Western scholarship for over thirty years. Not a single major English-language investigation of the topic appeared until 1968, which saw the publication of *The Peasant in Nineteenth Century Russia*, edited by W. S. Vucinich. But neither the appearance of this valuable collection, nor the publication of Teodor Shanin's *The Awkward Class* (1972), a study which explicitly called attention to peasantry as a conceptual challenge to the assumptions of modern scholarship, would move a significant number of researchers in the field of Russian history to attend to the peasant question in the post-Emancipation era.[2]

Only in the 1980s, as historians of Russia began to investigate issues of social history (and well after the urban factory worker gained recognition as a major historical topic), did the peasantry begin to attract widespread scholarly attention.[3] It was in this emerging context that in 1986, participants at the first international conference ever to focus on the peasantry of European Russia produced the essays contained in this volume.[4] For the first time, scholarly research in the field had advanced to the point that it became possible to publish a collection of essays dealing with peasant economy, culture, and politics based upon local, provincial, and regional investigations, many the result of archival research.

[2] In the late 1960s, Soviet scholarship on the peasantry began to flourish once more. Western historians would eventually take their cue from the valuable investigations carried out by V. A. Alexandrov, Boris Mironov, A. M. Anfimov, A. S. Nifontov, M. M. Gromyko, Viktor Danilov, and a number of other historians, economists, sociologists, and ethnographers. However, on a methodological level, their immensely useful work was sometimes marred by an overreliance on statistics alone and a hasty grouping of data derived from several, distinctly different, locales. Ideological constraints were also troubling; a tendency to omit arguments and evidence contained in the data when they challenged prevailing "Leninist" assumptions on occasion resulted in an extremely selective use of economics and statistics. See discussion of Zyrianov, Anfimov, and N. K. Karataev in Kingston-Mann, chapter 1, n. 19.

[3] The Seminar on the History of Russian Society in the Twentieth Century: Colloquium on Rural Society, 1905–1930, organized by Moshe Lewin and Alfred Rieber at the University of Pennsylvania in 1982 was particularly important in charting the contours of future research, and important questions were raised in *The Politics of Rural Russia, 1905–1914*, ed. Leopold Haimson (Bloomington, 1979), George Yaney, *The Urge to Mobilize: Agrarian Reform in Russia, 1861–1930* (Urbana, 1982), and Dorothy Atkinson, *The End of the Russian Land Commune* (Stanford, 1983).

[4] The Peasantry of European Russia, 1800–1917 (Boston, 1986). It is important to note that our efforts reflect a general quickening of interest in this topic, manifest as well in the 1986 conference on the Russian peasant commune, organized at the University of London by Professor Roger Bartlett. See Roger Bartlett, ed., *Land Commune and Peasant Community in Russia* (New York, 1990). Some important recent studies include Moshe Lewin, *The Making of the Soviet System* (New York, 1985) and Teodor Shanin, *Russia as a Developing Society*, 2 vols.: 1, *The Roots of Otherness: Russia's Turn of Century*; 2, *Russia 1905–07: Revolution as a Moment of Truth* (New Haven, 1986).

The curious and lengthy "silence" of Western Russianists on the peasant question was not due to the disappearance of the rural populace from the historical scene; well over 40 percent of the Soviet population continue to live outside of urban locales. But there were objective difficulties and cultural presuppositions that posed serious obstacles to scholars in the field.[5] Some were of the sort routinely confronted by historians of other geographic areas who study populations that are predominantly illiterate; others were specific to the Russian historical situation. In the words of a scholar at a recent conference of Russianists, since peasants seldom managed to exert power on a national scale, were they in fact the historian's legitimate business, or were they more appropriately the subject matter for anthropologists and collectors of folklore? Since peasants provided relatively little in the way of written records, how were historians to assess data filtered through the accounts of bailiffs, estate managers, policemen, landlords, and officials, or the findings of economists, statisticians, teachers, doctors, and the various activists who made their way to the countryside in the decades after the Emancipation of 1861? As we shall see, officials, scholars, and "do-gooders" of various sorts did not carry out their work in isolation from the political fray or from the cultural assumptions of their time. Their preconceptions became their working hypotheses, and would serve to illuminate some important aspects of peasant life, while leaving others in shadow or, at times, in utter darkness.

THE LADDER HYPOTHESIS

Many progressive-minded Russians—both Marxist and non-Marxist—took their cue from the Enlightenment values of Voltaire and Diderot, who claimed that untutored peasants dwelt in a stagnant, isolated, and unchanging world of irrational tradition. To these eighteenth-century thinkers, peasants were truly "prehistoric." Only after they somehow acquired the knowledge and the values possessed by enlightened men like themselves would peasants become rational and "human," and make their entrance onto the historical stage.[6] Warmhearted Russian Westernizers of the 1840s, like Vissarion Belinskii and the young Alexander Herzen, wrote sympathetically of "pre-human" serfs, capable of reason only after they were freed, protected by the rule of law, and enabled to shed their ignorance and their prejudices. According to Anthony Netting's brilliant characterization of the "Westernizer" view of the peasantry: "The folk would become truly Russian only when they became human, human only as they acquired one by one enlight-

---

[5] A similar "silence," broken somewhat earlier, characterized the field of German historical scholarship. See Robert Moeller, ed., *Peasants and Lords in Modern Germany* (New York, 1986), pp. 1–10 and *The German Peasantry*, ed. Richard Evans and W. R. Lee (New York, 1987), pp. 1–36.

[6] See discussion in Harvey Chisick, *The Limits of Reform in the Enlightenment* (Princeton, 1981), p. 70, and Harry Payne, *The Philosophes and the People* (New Haven, 1976), p. 96.

1. GENRE PHOTOGRAPH OF PEASANTS FROM OREL PROVINCE STRESSING THE QUAINT AND EXOTIC ASPECTS OF VILLAGE LIFE POPULAR AMONG URBAN AUDIENCES, C. 1877 (J. X. RAOULT, *NESKOL'KO NARODNYKH TIPOV ROSSII* [ODESSA: LITH. N. BECKEL, 1878?]).

enment and the fruits of Western culture."[7] Raising the peasantry out of the degradation of serfdom and the barbarisms of village life was a common theme for mid-nineteenth-century proponents of emancipation; in later decades, revolutionary "uplift" blended with elements of racism in the Marxist G. V. Plekhanov's description of the Russian peasants as "Chinese, barbarian-tillers of the soil, cruel and merciless, beasts of burden whose lives provided no opportunities for the luxury of thought."[8]

The powerful bonds that linked members of the peasant "herd" (the livestock image was used both by the tsarist Minister of Agriculture A. S. Ermolov and by the Marxist Leon Trotsky) bred an ignorant hostility to outsid-

[7] Anthony Netting, "Russian Liberalism: The Years of Promise: 1842–1855 (Ph.D. diss., Columbia University, 1967), p. 612.

[8] G. V. Plekhanov, *Sochineniia*, 10 (Moscow, 1923), p. 29.

ers, which erupted in pogroms against Jews and the lynching of doctors suspected of being the carriers of the diseases they came to cure. Loyalties to family and community were described as "chains" and "fetters" which prevented peasants from exploring the opportunities available to them in the world outside. In order to destroy the ties between peasant children and their primitive parents and neighbors, a leading progressive educator of the 1880s demanded that peasant children be physically removed from their homes. In his words, "the longer children, under the prevailing way of life, are separated from the domestic hearth, the better for both children and parent."[9] From such a perspective, it was clear that only after backward peasants ascended the rungs of civilization's ladder, leaving every aspect of their hideous and repellent world behind, could their culture deficit at last be made good. The distinguishing marks of "civilization" were not difficult to recognize. According to Ermolov, once Russian peasants attained a higher stage of human development, they would want nothing better than to live "rationally" on separate homesteads instead of in "herdlike" communes.[10]

In the Soviet period, peasants were reproached for a variety of rather contradictory failings. In the *ABC of Communism* (1918), E. P. Preobrazhenskii and N. I. Bukharin decried petty-bourgeois individualism and peasant ignorance of any notion of collective action or cooperation. In contrast, Trotsky regretted the peasantry's herdlike behavior. According to Lenin, even the urban proletariat was "brought low" by its "semi-peasant" character. Whether peasants were assessed as economic or political actors, or simply as human beings, they were found to function at an inferior level. In the Stalin era, policies emphasizing the need to move peasants to what were defined as ever-higher stages of economic and political development were implemented in a particularly coercive and brutal fashion in the policy of forced collectivization. In Stalin's own terms, this policy was a progressive step forward, a move that many peasants were tragically incapable of comprehending.[11]

Variations of Western-style "modernization theory," complete with scenarios of unilinear change and rigid distinctions between "subhuman" peasants and the civilized, rational, and progressive inhabitants of the city have been influential among both Western and Soviet scholars. As Shanin has suggested, the conception of progress as the industrialization of backward hinterlands would have troubling implications for non-Russianist liberal and socialist thinkers, particularly as they grappled with the impact of racist notions

---

[9] *Quoted in* Ben Eklof, *Russian Peasant Schools: Officialdom, Village Culture and Popular Pedagogy, 1861–1914* (Berkeley, 1986), p. 73.

[10] A. S. Ermolov, *Nash zemel'nyi vopros* (St. Petersburg, 1906), pp. 187–91.

[11] In World War II, Stalin himself described "forced collectivization" as a progressive measure which was made necessary by the peasantry's stubborn backwardness. See Richard Lauterbach, "Stalin at 65," *Life*, 1 January 1945, p. 67.

of colonialism in the nineteenth and twentieth centuries.[12] Were the newly freed peoples of Africa and India like Plekhanov's aforementioned "barbarian-tillers of the soil, cruel and merciless, beasts of burden whose lives provided no opportunities for the luxury of thought"?

Rather uncritical conceptions of the modernization perspective continue to hold sway within the Soviet Union today. Gorbachev makes the link to Stalin quite explicit, when he denounces Stalinist *methods* but argues that Stalin's collectivization *policies* were nonetheless necessary because of the "medieval backwardness" of the Russian countryside.[13] The sociologist Tatiana Zaslavskaia, a leading proponent of perestroika, argues that reform is now essential in the Soviet Union because Soviet citizens are no longer primitives. Unlike the men and women who inhabited Russia's villages in earlier decades, who were in her words simply "cogs" in a bureaucratic machine, peasants have at last become human beings with dignity, rational demands, and rights to freedom of action.[14]

This approach to understanding peasants possesses both strengths and weaknesses. Clearly, it possesses the virtue of illuminating the cruelty, violence, and deprivation of peasant life, its internecine conflicts, the subjugation of women and ill-treatment of children.[15] Influential turn-of-the-century studies, like the physician A. I. Shingarev's *The Dying Village*, documented the prevalence of infectious disease, high rates of infant mortality, and premature death among the peasantry of Voronezh Province. As Samuel Ramer's essay in our collection indicates, trained physicians who made their way to the Russian countryside in the late nineteenth century were sensitive to the abundant evidence that peasants were ignorant and skeptical about modern medical achievements. Troubled and sometimes demoralized by

---

[12] There is an extensive literature on the subject of modernization theory. See discussion in Shanin, *Russia as a Developing Society* 1, pp. 179–80 and J. E. Golthorpe, *The Sociology of the Third World* (Cambridge, 1975) in contrast to G. Kay, *Development and Underdevelopment: A Marxist Analysis* (London, 1975). Particularly useful accounts of some of the research problems generated by "modernization theory" perspectives are contained in Joseph Gusfield, "Tradition and Modernity: Misplaced Polarities in the Study of Social Change," *The American Journal of Sociology* 72, no. 4 (January 1967): 351–61, and the insightful essay by Ian Farr, "Tradition and Modernity in German Historiography," *The German Peasantry*, ed. Richard Evans and W. R. Lee, pp. 1–36. A recent defense of modernization theory can be found in Ian Roxborough, "Modernization Theory Revisited," *Comparative Studies in Society and History* 30, no. 4 (October 1988): 753–61.

[13] M. S. Gorbachev, *Perestroika: New Thinking for Our Country and the World* (New York, 1987), p. 40.

[14] See Zaslavskaia's views and writings, as expressed in *Sovetskaia Kultura*, 23 January 1986; *Pravda*, 6 February 1987; and *Moscow News*, 8–15 March 1987.

[15] Although the exploitation of women and abandonment of children was in no sense a uniquely peasant phenomenon, see David Ransel's devastating account of child abandonment among the Russian peasantry in *Mothers of Misery: Child Abandonment in Russia* (Princeton, 1988).

their encounter with the life-threatening consequences of peasant deficiencies in scientific understanding, literacy, and technology,[16] many of those most devoted to helping the peasantry called attention to the miseries of village life.

At the same time, it is significant that observer/benefactors of this sort were frequently incapable of imagining that peasants were not simply ignorant and foolish, but that peasant attitudes were in fact part of a complex system of beliefs about disease, health, and literacy that was deeply rooted and sometimes effective. It was, for example, a commonplace of gentry debates on education in the nineteenth century that peasants resisted having their children taught to read and write. But in reality, peasants organized and maintained their own "free schools" to teach reading and writing independent of government aid or supervision,[17] and their efforts went unremarked by leading policymakers and by their Marxist critics. As proponents of much-needed change in the countryside, physicians, agronomists, and reforming officials were sensitive to some aspects of peasant life but blind to others. They frequently wrote in language so heavily laden with value judgments reflecting their frustration, anger, and, often, their contempt and hatred for the primitive that they cannot be seen as impartial.[18] When observers of this sort contemplated the peasantry, they managed to find what no anthropologist then or since has ever been able to discover—a people without values, institutions, or a culture.

THE UNIVERSALIST HYPOTHESIS

Educated Russians influenced by neoclassical economics or by Marxist analysis were quite at home with the "ladder" hypotheses,[19] but when they devised strategies for change, they shifted emphasis and focused upon what they considered to be the universal characteristics of peasants in the modern

[16] The literature documenting peasant ignorance and brutality is too extensive to be cited here. For a useful recent discussion of peasant resistance to rational medical procedures, see Rose Glickman, "The Peasant Woman as Healer" (Paper presented at the First Conference on Women in the History of the Russian Empire, Akron, Ohio, August 13, 1988).

[17] See, for example, N. V. Chekhov, *Tipy russkoi shkoly v ikh istoricheskom razvitii* (Moscow, 1923), p. 35 and general discussion in A. S. Prugavin, *Zaprosy naroda i obiazannosti intelligentsii v oblasti prosvehshcheniia i vospitaniia* (St. Petersburg, 1895), pp. 31–52.

[18] In his discussion of "traditional" and "modern" societies, the sociologist Ralf Dahrendorff has suggested the use of terms that are more dispassionate in tone. In describing the life chances available in peasant and nonpeasant societies, Dahrendorff distinguishes between *options*—choices, opportunities for change, transformation, etc., and *ligatures*, or connections that provide continuity and a measure of permanence. He suggests that while modern societies are rich in options, peasant societies are rich in ligatures. See Dahrendorff, *Life Chances* (Chicago, 1978).

[19] The peculiar similarity between Russian Marxist and capitalist assumptions about progress, reason, and change is discussed in detail in Esther Kingston-Mann, "Marxism and Russian Rural Development," pp. 731–52.

world. There was a certain democratic and egalitarian impulse behind the neoclassical argument that peasants were not fundamentally different from other people, that each peasant was at least potentially a profit-maximizer, as capable as any other individual of pursuing rational self-interest which could be measured in monetary terms. From such a perspective, the challenge was to diminish existing restrictions on this natural impulse, provide opportunities for it to flourish, and unlock the human potential which every individual possessed.[20]

Progressive-minded reformers who took this view urged the implementation of programs aimed at destroying what were taken to be the reactionary constraints (family and community ties, ignorance, lawlessness, etc.) that kept the universal urge for profit-maximization from manifesting itself.[21] Once these constraints were gone, they saw Russia's prospects as unlimited—as Finance Minister Sergei Witte wrote in 1899, an awakening of the "spirit of enterprise" could transform an ignorant peasant into a railway financier. Alert to evidence that such phenomena were actually occurring, Witte was particularly fond of "rags to riches" success stories of individuals who became rich and respected by taking charge of their lives and breaking away from their conservative and ignorant village communities. When he and his supporters interpreted the findings of the Special Conference on the Needs of Agriculture, which met from 1902 to 1904, they paid particular attention to examples of "profitable separation," and downplayed the fact that most conference delegates made no reference to the issue of peasant efforts to break with their communities.[22]

Marxists, certain that class conflict was a universal feature of the modern world,[23] were particularly sensitive to the very real manifestations of capitalism in the Russian countryside. G. V. Plekhanov and V. I. Lenin carefully documented the antagonism they discovered between an increasingly proletarianized peasantry and an ever more powerful host of village kulaks, gentry capitalists, and government officials. Their research provided valuable

---

[20] Today such views are particularly prevalent among adherents of the human capital school of economics. See discussion in Lester Thurow, *Dangerous Currents: The State of Economics* (New York, 1983), p. 216.

[21] In the nineteenth and early twentieth centuries, both Marxists and neoclassical economists assumed that, in the short run at least, capitalist practices and private-property rights represented a progressive stage in historical development. See discussion in Kingston-Mann, "Marxism and Russian Rural Development," pp. 731–40.

[22] See A. A. Rittikh, *Krest'ianskoe zemlepolzovanie* 2, in *Svod trudov mestnykh komitetov po 49 guberniiam evropeiskoi Rossii* (St. Petersburg, 1903) and P. P. Semenov, *Printsipal'nye voprosy po krest'ianskomu delu s otvetami mestnykh sel'skokhoziaistvennykh komitetov* (St. Petersburg, 1904), pp. 14–15.

[23] Lenin's narrow focus on conflict models for analyzing the peasant question is discussed in Esther Kingston-Mann, *Lenin and the Problem of Marxist Peasant Revolution* (Oxford, 1983), pp. 38–54.

evidence about peasant indebtedness, rents, and tax rates and documented the economic pressures that led peasants to leave the village to become hired agricultural laborers or factory workers (*otkhodniki*) in the urban centers of the empire. This process was described as inexorable, painful, and progressive in economic and political terms. Just as Witte hoped that peasant entrepreneurs would become the mainstay of an enlightened autocracy, Lenin hoped that peasant proletarians would hasten the outbreak of socialist revolution.

Universalists of this sort were less sensitive to the fact that most Russians were in reality neither proletarians nor entrepreneurs, but small producers who farmed the land with the help of their families and communities and paid taxes, rents, and other fees to the privileged elements in society. Viewing the commonalities of rural life as superficial in comparison with the evidence of competition, profit seeking, and the omnipresent manifestations of class struggle and immiseration, they discounted as "romantic" and "populist" the evidence that economic and political habits of acting in common were fostered by the repartitional land communes to which most peasants belonged. To A. A. Rittikh, a leading administrator of the Stolypin reforms, the commune simply masked the struggle of individual peasants for prosperity and rational self-assertion; Lenin for his part inaccurately described commune peasants in 1895 as individuals farming "single-handed" on their own strips of land, "isolated producers" in search of profit.[24] Certain that most peasants were becoming proletarianized and increasingly impoverished, they were indifferent to evidence detailing the coping mechanisms by which, as Elvira Wilbur has shown, peasants survived rather than perished.

THE ROMANTIC AND POPULIST HYPOTHESIS

While Marxists and neoclassical economists moved freely back and forth between evolutionary and universalist approaches, Slavophiles and populists of the nineteenth and twentieth centuries rejected Enlightenment notions of progress and were equally skeptical about profit-maximizer and class-conflict hypotheses. Instead, the Slavophiles A. S. Khomiakov and Ivan Aksakov celebrated local context, and the integrity of a social order and culture created by peasants. Alongside the idealizations and the hypocrisy which scholars have generally seen as their hallmark,[25] it should be noted that Slavophiles

---

[24] V. I. Lenin, *Polnoe sobranie sochinenii*, 5th ed., 1 (Moscow, 1971–1975), p. 451.

[25] The Slavophiles, as patriarchal admirers of an idealized tsar-protector, had no desire to join the peasant communes which they so admired, and saw its guarantees of security as a bulwark against the outbreak of a revolution that might destroy their privileged position. However, it is also true that by taking Nicholas I's slogan of "Autocracy, Orthodoxy and Nationality" far more seriously than it was intended, they became a particularly disquieting challenge to the Baltic German officials entrusted by the tsar with the task of establishing a Prussian-style bureaucracy on Russian soil. See discussion in Andrzej Walicki, *The Slavophile Controversy* (Oxford, 1975).

were among the first folklorists and ethnographers of the Russian rural scene.[26] Distrusting the notion of universal laws of historical development, they considered the specificity of Russian national and "folk" traditions eminently worthy of study, and sought a path toward a more prosperous and industrialized future which was not based upon the obliteration of these traditions.[27]

In later decades, empirically minded scholars influenced by populist notions, like the economist Alexander Chuprov and the statistician F. A. Shcherbina, would deny that peasants were either featureless barbarians suffering from a "culture deficit" or embryonic J. P. Morgans or Alfred Krupps. Unlike the adherents of the "ladder" or the "universalist" hypotheses, they believed that a vast body of evidence indicated beyond question that peasants already possessed a culture—a way of life and a "way of seeing" which deserved careful investigation. With varying degrees of tough-mindedness, some sought to discover the peasantry's "golden hearts," while others set themselves to follow the relativist teachings of Wilhelm Roscher and the German Historical School. What they shared was an agreement that (1) indigenous peasant values and institutions were not illusory but real, and (2) existing peasant beliefs and practices possessed rational and progressive potential as well as a host of weaknesses.

Soviet and Western scholars, intensely skeptical about the claims of populism and concerned to avoid any romanticization of peasant life, have tended to dismiss the writings of investigators described as "populist." Emphasis has been placed above all upon the foolishness of enthusiasts—the name of I. I. Kablits comes immediately to mind—whose insistence on the uniqueness and specificity of peasant culture transformed them into fanatic nationalists or sentimental utopians.[28] In this process, the more complex and broad-ranging perspectives of late-nineteenth-century "populistic" economists and statisticians like V. I. Orlov, N. A. Kablukov, A. S. Posnikov and A. I. Chuprov faded from view.

[26] An intriguing discussion of the link between romantic traditions and anthropological research may be found in Richard Schweder, "Anthropology's Romantic Rebellion Against the Enlightenment," *Culture Theory*, eds. R. A. Schweder and Robert A. LeVine (Cambridge, 1984), pp. 32, 48. See also Clifford Geertz, " 'From the Native's Point of View': On the Nature of Anthropological Understanding," *Local Knowledge: Further Essays in Interpretive Anthropology* (New York, 1983), pp. 55–70.

[27] Although their writings on this topic have been neglected, both the Slavophiles and the Populists of the post-Emancipation era devised strategies for industrial as well as agricultural development. See, for example, A. S. Khomiakov, *Polnoe sobranie sochinenii*, 3 (Moscow, 1914), p. 468.

[28] See general discussion in Richard Wortman, *The Crisis of Russian Populism* (Cambridge, 1967) and Arthur Mendel, *Dilemmas of Progress in Tsarist Russia* (Cambridge, Mass., 1961).

As we have seen, the "ladder" hypothesis, universalist notions, and romantic/populist approaches serve to illuminate different aspects of the peasant "picture." It is not the intention of our contributors to replace these perspectives with an equally unconditional and opposite set. The realities of peasant life are too rich to be squeezed into a single-factor explanation. Nor do we want to assert that peasants were "primitives," proto-capitalists and proletarians, or a vague "something in between."[29] Well aware of the questions and the answers of their predecessors, our contributors take their place as students of the peasant question along an extended continuum of observers. Like the scholars who have preceded them, they are confronting evidence and balancing their own preconceptions against the impulse to learn and to "see" more clearly the realities of peasant life. This continuum also includes the peasantry, who had much to lose if they were unable to balance their preconceptions against impulses toward flexibility and pragmatism in the insecure world they inhabited.

In even more ambitious terms, Clifford Geertz has described what I have called a continuum as a process of recognizing ourselves as scholars "among others," that is, as not different in nature from those who are observed or studied. In his words: "To see ourselves as others see us can be eye-opening. To see others as sharing a nature with ourselves is the merest decency. But it is from the far more difficult achievement of seeing ourselves among others, as a local example of the forms human life has locally taken, a case among cases, a world among worlds, that the largeness of mind, without which objectivity is self-congratulation and tolerance a sham, comes."[30]

MORAL ECONOMY

In general, the investigations included in this volume suggest that before and after their emancipation from serfdom, Russian peasants who survived the demands of a difficult climate and the more or less importunate claims of landlords, tax collectors, and military recruiters, possessed what James Scott has called a "moral economy" which shaped both their economic and noneconomic behavior.[31] Serfs on the Gagarin estate described by Rodney Bohac

[29] This judgment owes much to theoretical approaches set out by Teodor Shanin. However, since his analysis does not focus on the same issues I raise, he should not be held responsible for my recasting and revisions. See discussion in Teodor Shanin, *Rules of the Game* (London, 1972); *Russia as a Developing Society* (1986); and my critical review of his work, "Revolution and Russian Rural Development: The 'Awkward Class' Social, Economic and Political Context," *Peasant Studies* 15, no. 4 (Winter 1988): 129–36.

[30] *Local Knowledge*, p. 16.

[31] See James Scott, *Moral Economy of the Peasant* (New Haven, 1976).

strove persistently to protect their interests, appealing to masters not in the name of equality, but in defense of their own notion of "real" paternalism rather than a brutal extraction of income. Acting on a belief that "unjust" prices were unacceptable, the peasants studied by David Christian poured out their vodka in protest against price increases that went beyond what they considered a fair standard and, at other times, ritualized its use for the sealing of transactions and court decisions. Scott Seregny has shown that in Vladimir Province, peasants asserted their subsistence claims to forest resources in opposition to landlords who were attempting to use the forests for private profit. And like the mid-Volga peasants studied by Orlando Figes, the villagers of Khar'kov and Vladimir insisted on the principle that land belonged to those who worked it.

The wide range of "shaming" devices and *charivari* devised in the hiring markets researched by Timothy Mixter indicate as well that peasants were not without a culture, value systems, and standards. In search of survival, material well-being, wealth, prestige, power, security, respect and continuity, peasants were like peoples elsewhere who busily pursued potentials that were richly symbolized in their rituals and traditions. They did not need to wait for outsiders to fill the void in their lives with meaning. Despite widespread illiteracy and the low level of their technological achievements, peasants did not seem to lack useful and practical knowledge, motivation, or images of well-being and public virtue.

On the most immediate level, the social identities of peasants were organized by local age and sex hierarchies which subjugated young people to the authority of the household head (*bol'shak*) or to the elder (*starosta*) of the village community's assembly (*skhod*). As Christine Worobec has shown, the female spheres of activity were kept rigidly separate from those of the male members of the household. Women were subjugated to the authority of fathers, husbands, and elder sons, and deprived of the best rewards and privileges, although they received a measure of respect for their labor contribution. The value of their labor was assessed according to conventions and moral standards that defined virtue and vice and created both the basis for positive self-regard and hopes for the possibility of advance—not toward equality and full partnership but toward greater increments of security, prestige, and power for the woman as mother and eventually as mother-in-law and wife of the head of the household (*khoziain*).

The labor of children was key to the survival of the family, since the peasant household was a team in which each member was responsible for task performance in one or more areas of the productive process. In such a context, reproduction was in no sense optional; it was a need given the highest priority. The rejection of filial loyalty or fertility was viewed as immoral, irrational, lunatic, and deserving of social ostracism. As Worobec and Wilbur have shown, to be without children was not only God's punishment but the greatest of human disasters. Sons were of particular importance, because a family of daughters who each went out to marry and live elsewhere (*na chuzhaia storona*) would eventually cease to exist. In the words of an ancient proverb: "One son is not a son; two sons is a half-son, but three sons is a son."

REGIONAL DIFFERENCES, LOCALISM, AND MAKING THE WORLD "RODNOI"

In the Russian context, generalizations about peasants are particularly difficult to make because the degree of variation in geographic and historical factors at work in different regions and provinces, and even on a sub-provincial level, produced such a rich variety of behaviors. In the past, Western scholars tended to generalize about Russia as a whole; insufficient emphasis was placed upon the degree to which economic and social conditions, patterns and practices varied from region to region. As Stephen Wheatcroft has shown, peasant living standards were improving in the economy as a whole between 1891 and 1913, but conditions in the Central Producing Region were far more bleak. Christine Worobec demonstrates that the fieldwork of women in the Central Industrial Region gained them more autonomy than it did elsewhere. As Elvira Wilbur's research indicates, rates and definitions of poverty differed even within the single province of Voronezh. In Moscow Province, the division of labor according to gender varied widely; in one district, the mowing of young grass was women's work; but in others, it was an exclusively male occupation.[32] Esther Kingston-Mann's data suggests that communal practices were inconsistent as well; in one region, communes granted allotments to their members according to family size; elsewhere, the number of able-bodied laborers per household served as the basic criterion.

Adding to the difficulty of generalizing about Russian peasants as a whole was the enormous emphasis that peasants placed upon what was *rodnoi*, native, or one's own—the unique practice of one's household, village, *volost'* or *krai*. We find an abundance of local and regional names for particular flowers and trees, and for the particular strips of land which comprised a household allotment. The language of peasants was filled with words, phrases, and proverbs describing the uniqueness of one's own "place," where, as it was said, "birds sing differently and flowers bloom more brightly." Equally rich was the peasant store of epithets to describe those who were not *rodnoi*—the "white-eyed fools" from Perm, and the "big-ears" from Iaroslavl—the outsiders.

[32] According to a contemporary Soviet observer, an informant reported that "where he lives [*u nego na rodine*], in Solvychegodskii district," women were not permitted to engage in the mowing of young grass. See Vasilii Belov's sensitive discussion of the issue of peasant rootedness in particular locales and relationships. *Lad: Ocherki o narodnoi estetike* (Moscow, 1984), pp. 14, 94–97, and Kathleen Parthe, " 'Time, Backward!' Memory and the Past in Soviet Village Prose," *Occasional Papers of the Kennan Institute*, no. 224.

Although this sort of local particularism served to isolate and fragment the loyalties of the peasants from various regions, provinces, and districts, it also served another purpose. In a world that their lowly social status and insecure material position rendered so uncertain, the creation of local rituals, relationships, and economic and social distinctions served as well to establish a circle of trust and control, a sort of moral community within which responsibility was shared. What was *rodnoi* stood for what was locally known and accepted as normal, in contrast to the practices, appearance, and characteristics of the outsider and the outside world. At the same time, the boundaries peasants established to define what was *rodnoi* were by no means static; they were often hotly contested and they changed over time.[33] To make a new place *rodnoi* was the task and the challenge of every young girl who married, even in a neighboring village. Because she had gone "to the other side," to a new family and village, she had to create new ties; for it was only with the help of supporters in her new locale that she could hope for greater respect and status in the future as a mother and later as a mother-in-law.

In the course of the nineteenth century, when peasants in increasing numbers sought to meet their financial burdens by leaving their households, villages, and regions to become hired laborers, the evidence suggests that they made their new living space *rodnoi* by establishing strategic relationships grounded in networks of kin and neighbors. As Timothy Mixter's essay demonstrates, peasants attempted to transform hiring markets into their "turf," by creating enclaves made up of peasants from their home province or district.[34] Confronted by the risks as well as the opportunities, institutions, and values of the hiring market, they did not give up their traditional aspirations. As Jeffrey Burds indicates, when peasants became hired laborers in distant provinces, they did not abandon their villages; they "raided the cash economy" in order to strengthen their "home" community. In this complex process of departure and return, peasants did not retain the "old ways" unchanged. Instead, they infused them with new combinations of indigenous and imported meanings. Peasants created a "hiring-market" culture; new rituals and traditions combined in novel ways the elements of village and non-village life.

FLEXIBILITY AND RISK TAKING

Peasant behavior, as described by our contributors, reveals the existence of a moral economy rooted in filial loyalty, fertility, social supports, and a mea-

---

[33] I am indebted to James Scott for this suggestion. See Kingston-Mann, "Russian Peasant Communalism" (paper presented at Rockefeller Foundation–sponsored conference, Peasant Culture and Consciousness, Bellagio, Italy, January 1990).

[34] See Robert Johnson's discussion of this issue in *Peasant and Proletarian: The Working Class of Moscow in the Late 19th Century* (New Brunswick, N.J., 1979).

2. MAKING HAY AT VOLKHOVO (PROKUDIN-GORSKII COLLECTION, LIBRARY OF CONGRESS).

3. PEASANT MUSICIANS AND AUDIENCE, POLTAVA PROVINCE, C. 1877 (J. X. RAOULT, *NESKOL'KO NARODNYKH TIPOV ROSSII* [ODESSA: LITH. N. BECKEL, 1878?]).

4. STARVING CHILDREN IN SAMARA PROVINCE, 1921 (BETTMANN/HULTON).

5. PLOWING A FIELD IN NIZHNII NOVGOROD PROVINCE AS RECOVERY FROM THE CIVIL WAR AND
FAMINE BEGAN, SEPTEMBER 1923 (BETTMANN/HULTON).

sure of opportunity within the norms established by the community. Peasant culture reflected aspirations toward continuity and control within a world that was often arbitrary and insecure. The vagaries of the Russian land and climate, the burden of low technology, and the shifting and unequal burdens imposed by their social superiors made flexibility, audacity, and risk taking mandatory for those who would survive. Whether we consider the risks of farming the Russian land or those assumed by young married peasant women who were obliged to create a new place for themselves as family members on "the other side" or the potential for a disastrous outcome which faced a young man or woman who chanced the uncertainties of a hiring market thousands of miles away from their native villages, it is clear that peasant cultural norms were a source of stability within an uncertain, shifting, and potentially dangerous material and social context.

Alongside the isolation, rigid adherence to custom, and aversion to risk and to outsiders, which have already been recognized as important aspects of nineteenth-century Russian rural life, our contributors have found much evidence of the flexibility and pragmatism that scholars like Robert Edelman have documented among Ukrainian peasants who, despite their reputation for blind anti-Semitism, distinguished between Jews who were exploiters and those who were not,[35] or the peasants described by Teodor Shanin, whose thirst for information in 1905 led them to send out messengers in search of "a student or a Jew" to read them the latest news.[36] However much peasants may have sought continuity or freedom from outside interference, it was also true that on occasion, flexibility and selective change represented their only hope of survival at the margins of subsistence. Samuel Ramer's nineteenth-century village healers learned selectively from physicians; they began to make use of quinine for malaria, for example, but continued to act as village "therapists" and counselors. And according to my own investigations, peasants were not usually irrational opponents of economic innovation; under certain circumstances, they devised ingenious mechanisms to reward individual innovators even within the framework of their repartitional land communes.[37]

Peasants did not simply follow elite leadership or reject it, nor did they always resist the incursions of outsiders. Their attachment to their own world did not preclude a recognition that they needed the help of outsiders—who were at such times conveniently redefined as "insiders." As Scott Seregny has shown, peasants in 1905 acted to form complex coalitions with

[35] See Robert Edelman, *Proletarian Peasants: The Revolution of 1905 in Russia's Southwest* (Ithaca, N.Y., 1987), pp. 39–40, 100–101.

[36] Teodor Shanin, *Russia, 1905–1907: Revolution as a Moment of Truth*, p. 131.

[37] A useful discussion of peasant engagement with the culture of the world beyond the village is contained in Jeffrey Brooks, *When Russia Learned to Read: Literacy and Popular Literature, 1861–1917* (Princeton, 1985).

radical schoolteachers and gentry radicals in Sumy and Vladimir, and made sure that such alliances corresponded to their own notions of social justice. On occasion, these values were overshadowed by fears of gentry power and privilege. As Seregny points out, *volost* elders in Vladimir fearfully voted in 1905 to support local gentry conservatives, but at the same time they were careful to apologize to the radical reformer S. V. Bunin for their actions, and to thank him for his willingness to defend peasant interests.[38] Orlando Figes demonstrates that in 1917, when the weakness of state authority confronted peasants of the middle Volga region with unprecedented freedom of action, their behavior was not rigid but quite pragmatic, as they constructed an intricate social circle of "insiders" which included nonpeasant carpenters, teachers, and sympathetic village priests. Urban workers who contributed nothing to the local economy were excluded; local squires were welcomed and granted allotments; but the estates of landlords most notorious as agents of repressive actions were put to the torch.

The work of our contributors suggests that the economics, politics, and sociology of nineteenth-century and early-twentieth-century Russian peasant life formed part of a complex culture which in turn was part of history. Peasant life contained—along with elements of self-defense, stability, and class struggle—a record of historical efforts at constructive engagement with institutions, values, and social elements which many observers have tended to define as irretrievably alien to peasants. Our exploration of Russia's peasant question thus challenges some accepted interpretations and raises new questions which we hope will stimulate further research, particularly into the aspects of peasant life that are underrepresented in our collection. The history of peasant/landlord relations in the post-Emancipation period, the development of cottage industry and proto-industrialization, the emergence of peasant cooperatives, the institutions of village self-government and peasant culture—in particular, the role of peasant religion and folklore—are only a few of the most obvious topics for further exploration. It is our hope that this collection will encourage other scholars in the field to discover the specific historical relationships between defensive reaction and xenophobic outbreaks on the one hand, and on the other the elements of flexibility, risk taking, and patterns of change which do not repudiate tradition.

Over a century ago, the novelist Ivan Turgenev set out the challenge that peasants have always posed for their observers in his influential collection *A Sportsman's Sketches*. In his story of a master and a peasant who had both managed to escape from the clutches of bloodthirsty brigands, Turgenev describes the master's dismay at his peasant's failure to express normal and

---

[38] A particularly useful account of the limits and the extent of outside influences upon Russian peasant-soldiers in 1905–1906 is contained in John Bushnell's *Mutiny Amid Repression: Russian Soldiers in the Revolution of 1905–1906* (Bloomington, 1985).

decent human feelings. When they were both in danger, facing the threat of violent death, why, asks the master, did the peasant regret the loss of his horse, but say nothing at all about the much more tragic prospect of being parted from his wife and children? In Turgenev's words, the peasant replies, "Why should I have grieved over them? They weren't in the hands of the robbers. And besides, I always hold them in my mind, as I am holding them now." Filofei [the peasant] then fell silent.[39] As researchers, we may well learn from Turgenev that the depth of our understanding will depend upon an awareness of the shaping power of our expectations, and upon our willingness to pursue the questions that disturb them.

[39] I. S. Turgenev, "Stuchit!" *Zapiski okhotnika* (Leningrad, 1945), p. 328.

PART I

Peasant Economy

Although we have divided the book into three sections in order to provide helpful signposts, and to provide the reader with some idea of the way that the collected essays fit together, it is our belief that a major strength of this volume lies in its clear demonstration of the way that peasants linked and, at times, blurred the distinctions between economy, culture, and politics.

Within this section, Esther Kingston-Mann provides a picture of the multiple roles played by the traditional peasant village community (*mir*, or *obshchina*). Drawing upon data from very different regions of the Russian empire, she describes communal efforts to accommodate both economic innovation and individual initiative. Calling into question the assumptions about commune backwardness held by many commentators in the late imperial period and by a number of present-day historians, Kingston-Mann provides evidence that suggests that communes may have led the way in initiating or adopting certain forms of innovation. At the same time, she stresses that tenure issues were in all likelihood less important as an explanation of the problems of Russian rural development than the general lack of a rural infrastructure and the inadequacy of state and nonpeasant commercial services.

Important aspects of the impact of developing capitalism in the Russian countryside are examined by Jeffrey Burds. In the first English-language study ever to examine labor migration from the village perspective, Burds emphasizes the conflicting and complicated economic and social roles played by leading members of village society in the Central Industrial Region. Commune elders in search of increased income to meet state-imposed fiscal exactions thus promoted labor migration, while restricting migrant labor autonomy in order to ensure that wages earned would in fact be sent back to the village. The kulak, usually portrayed by historians as the "villainous" moneylenders of the Russian countryside, appears in Burds's account as the preferred creditor, considered by peasants to be more vulnerable to the influence of community norms and kinship relationships than outside officials or contractors. Burds's description of the peasant village reveals both the power of peasant communal institutions and the ambiguities of class struggle in the Russian countryside.

Elvira Wilbur approaches the controversial question of Russia's late-nineteenth-century agrarian crisis by examining the province of Voronezh, generally agreed to be one of the "poorest" in the Russian empire. Her examination of family histories and detailed statistical records indicates that even in the most poverty-stricken regions of Voronezh, living standards were not in a state of steady decline. Poverty was cyclical, and its primary causes were not class conflict, but (1) family demographic failure, (2) chronic illness/permanent disability, (3) a household's initial lack of economic resources, and (4) family disputes. Wilbur's data suggest that the capacity for survival in the short or long run was facilitated by the flexibility of the peasant household and the efforts of the peasant commune.

Stephen Wheatcroft advances the contemporary debate on the issue of agrarian crisis by taking a comparative regional approach. His careful and detailed examination of grain production figures, per capita peasant ownership of livestock, changing levels of direct and indirect taxation, and fluctuation in the real wages of agricultural laborers demonstrates that while many indicators suggest that peasant economic and living standards were rising in the empire as a whole during the period 1891–1913, advances were uneven and, in some regions, close to nonexistent. Although no "general" crisis existed, particular regions were in serious straits.

—T. M. AND E. K.-M.

CHAPTER 1

PEASANT COMMUNES AND ECONOMIC INNOVATION:
A PRELIMINARY INQUIRY

Esther Kingston-Mann[*]

> Property! A sacred right!
> The Soul of Society!
> The source of laws.
> Where you are respected,
>   where you are inviolable,
> That country is blessed,
>   the citizen is tranquil and well off.
> —*Ivan Pnin, 1802*

LONG before widespread empirical investigations had been conducted on the subject, most educated Russians had come to believe that private economic effort was superior to any economic activity that individuals could carry out in common.[1] Sanctioned and supported by the most prestigious economic authorities of the day, journalists and experts celebrated what they called the "magic of property."[2] In the words of Ivan Vernadskii, the leading Russian professional economist of the 1850s:

[*] I wish to thank John Bushnell, Tim Mixter, and Stephen Wheatcroft for their helpful suggestions and comments.

[1] The prevalence of this type of thinking among economists and economic reformers is discussed in N. K. Karataev, *Ekonomicheskie nauki v Moskovskom universitete (1755–1955)* (Moscow, 1956), pp. 94–113; V. A. Kitaev, *Ot frondy k okhranitel'stvu: Iz istorii Russkoi liberal'noi mysli 50–60 godov xix veka* (Moscow, 1972), pp. 188–99; and S. S. Shashkov, "Russkaia obshchina i ee vragi," *Delo*, no. 1 (January 1881), pp. 129–54. In recent scholarship, Zack Deal refers to the "fixation on private property" among agricultural reformers in the pre-Reform era in "Serf and State Peasant Agriculture: Kharkov Province, 1842–1861," (Ph.D.diss., Vanderbilt University, 1955), pp. 78, 88, as does Moshe Lewin, "Customary Law and Russian Rural Society in the Post-Reform Era," *Russian Review* 44, no. 1 (January 1985): 11.

[2] Such phrases were common in the work of August Comte, Frederic Bastiat and Henry Carey, whose writings became required reading for students of political economy at the universities of St. Petersburg and Moscow in the 1850s. See the essay in praise of Henry

It is stubborn to think that one must not imitate Europe but continually work out in everything one's own independent principles, including the exchange of private for communal ownership, just as if someone began believing it unnecessary to walk on two feet as the Europeans do and for the sake of working out national principles, one should walk on all fours.[3]

Neither Vernadskii's enthusiasm nor his certainty were uniquely Russian; leading mid-nineteenth-century economists the world over shared his optimistic faith in the universal efficacy of private property rights, with England as the model for progress and development.[4] In later years, Russian officials from Minister of Finance N. Kh. Bunge to Sergei Witte quoted enthusiastically from the economic dictum of John Stuart Mill: "If you guarantee to a man the rights of property in the desert, he will turn it into a smiling garden, but if you lease the garden to the same man for nine years, he will turn it into a howling desert."[5]

Carey by the economist and future Minister of Finance N. Kh. Bunge, "Garmoniia khoziaistvennykh otnoshenii: Pervaia politiko-ekonomicheskaia sistema keri," *Otechestvennye Zapiski* 11 (November 1859): 1–42, and the general discussion in Kitaev, *Ot frondy*, pp. 190–95.

[3] "Rech'," *Trudy Imperatorskago Volnago Ekonomicheskago Obshchestva* (cited hereafter as TIVEO) 4 (October 1865): 328. Vernadskii was a professor of economics and statistics, first at Kiev and then at Moscow, a translator of the economist Frederic Bastiat, an official of the Ministry of the Interior after 1856, chair of the political economy committee of the Imperial Free Economic Society, and publisher and contributor to the journals *Ekonomicheskii ukazatel'* and *Ekonomist*.

[4] Vernadskii's confident universalism owed much to Comte and to John Stuart Mill's *Principles of Economics* (1848), the classic mid-nineteenth-century statement of the conventional economic wisdom of the day. In Mill's words: "whoever knows the political economy of England, or even of Yorkshire, knows that of all nations, actual or possible." In 1885, the English economist Henry Sidgwick wrote of the certainties of the 1850s: "Some 35 years ago, both the theory of political economy and its main outlines, and the most important practical applications of it, were considered as finally settled by the great number of educated persons in England." This consensus would be broken by such disquieting events as the Irish famine and the decline of English agriculture, and by the emergence of the German Historical School of economics. Practical and theoretical challenges to the axiomatic faith in unrestricted markets and unconditional private property rights set off a *"Methodenstreit"* among professional economists which lasted until the triumph of Alfred Marshall and the "marginalist" school of economics in the 1880s. It was significant that Russian empirical researchers studied, and began their work, in the decades of challenge to neoclassical economics. Mill's statement occurs in *System of Logic* 2 (London, 1872), p. 499. See also, Clive Dewey, "The Rehabilitation of the Peasant Proprietor in 19th Century Economic Thought," *History of Political Economy* 6, no. 1 (Spring, 1974): 42; Gerard Koot, "English Historical Economics and the Emergence of Economic History in England, *History of Political Economy* 12, no. 2 (Summer, 1980): 170–205; J. C. Wood, *British Economists and Empire* (New York, 1983), pp. 183–94. See Esther Kingston-Mann, *The Majority as an Obstacle to Progress: Problems of Russian Rural Development, 1800–1917* (forthcoming, 1991), and "In Search of the True West: Western Models and Russian Rural Development," *Journal of Historical Sociology* (Spring 1990).

[5] See general discussion in I. V. Chernyshev, *Agrarno-krest'ianskaia politika Rossii za 150 let* (Petrograd, 1918), pp. 65–67. Bunge was, of course, a former professor of economics and

Such economic truths seemed to lay bare the root cause of Russia's agricultural problems. In a countryside where the peasant majority of the population held allotments in communal tenure,[6] how could innovation and productivity increase be fostered? According to the conventional economic wisdom of the time, it was axiomatic that peasants would not invest capital or labor in agricultural improvement if they believed that they would lose their investment at the next commune repartition. On the eve of Emancipation, writings which emphasized the failings of the commune and the virtues of private tenure accumulated steadily. But it is worth noting that in the 1870s, when the indefatigable researcher E. I. Iakushkin examined the available literature on the subject, he found that out of 150 articles and books on the commune published before 1861, virtually all were theoretical in character.[7]

It was not until the last third of the nineteenth century that the assumptions of educated Russians were tested by wide-ranging empirical investigation. In a massive and historically unprecedented effort to base their researches on direct peasant testimony, statisticians hired by local zemstvo organizations went out to the countryside to interview some 4.5 million peasant families in thirty-four provinces of the empire (a number equivalent to the combined populations of Spain and Portugal!).[8] In the discussion that follows, the findings reported in a wide range of statistical and economic

---

statistics, and an author of widely used textbooks on these topics. See general discussion in E. Kingston-Mann, "Russian Economists and the Magic of Property" (Paper presented at the Midwest Conference of the American Association for the Advancement of Slavic Studies, Ann Arbor, April 1987).

[6] With the exception of the western regions of the Russian empire and some parts of the south, where hereditary (*podvornoe*) tenure prevailed, most peasants were members of re-partitional land communes, which periodically redistributed the strips of land allotted to each member household on the basis of collective social principles (family size, number of adult males per household, etc.). The peasant term for this institution was *mir*, a designation which was significant because *mir* was also the Russian word for both "peace" and "world." The other term commonly used to refer to the commune was *obshchina*. Distinctions between communal and *podvornoe* tenure were frequently difficult to make, because even *podvornoe* regions were characterized by common usage of pasture and forest lands and a variety of other collectivist activities. See discussion of peasant and nonpeasant terminology in Steven Grant, "Obshchina i Mir," *Slavic Review* 35, no. 4 (December 1976): 636–51.

[7] Cited in P. S. Efimenko, "Programma dlia sobiranii svedeniia ob obshchinnom zemle-vladenii," *Slovo*, no. 6 (June 1878): 4.

[8] An important, but less-direct empirical investigation of peasant commune activities was undertaken between 1878 and 1880, when the Imperial Free Economic Society and the Russian Geographical Society organized a survey of 816 communes in twenty Russian, two Ukrainian, and two Belorussian provinces. The standardized questionnaires they prepared were not given to peasants but to local administrative officials, landlords, priests, and justices of the peace. See discussion in L. I. Kuchumova, "Iz istorii obsledovaniia sel'skoi po-zemel'noi obshchiny v 1877–1880 godakh," *Istoriia SSSR*, no. 3 (May–June 1978): 115–27, and a recent discussion in Boris Mironov, "The Russian Peasant Commune After the Reforms of the 1860s," *Slavic Review* 44, no. 2 (Summer 1985): 438–67.

data published between the 1870s and 1900 will be set out as they relate to the question of communes and rural innovation.[9] My goal is to provide an overview of the range, variety, and impact of efforts at innovation in areas that practiced communal repartition. In other words, if peasants opted for the commune, did the evidence indicate that they were also accepting economic backwardness, low productivity, and a primitive, authoritarian collectivism? It is worth noting that such questions were first raised by scholars influenced by populism, who sought Russia's salvation in the development of indigenous institutions and values, and were therefore, quite understandably, in the forefront of empirical research into the mechanisms by which grass-roots economic change took place.[10]

PROBLEMS OF EVIDENCE

The complexities of this topic were many, and they continue to pose difficulties for contemporary scholars: problems of culture bias, evidence, and methodology have always complicated the task of conceptualizing the process of peasant innovation. The literature on innovation was extensive, and embedded in a wide range of statistical accounts that did not always focus on comparable factors. Efforts at consistent definition, measurement, evaluation, and generalization were made more difficult by the enormous varia-

---

[9] I have examined data from diverse regions of the empire, ranging from Siberia to Moscow and to the Volga provinces from Kazan to Saratov. In addition, I have taken seriously the scholarly judgments of A. I. Chuprov, the dean of turn-of-the-century Russian professional economists, and of F. G. Terner, who began work as an assistant to the pre-Reform economist Ludwig Tengoborskii and served in later years as a respected government consultant and as assistant minister of finance under N. Kh. Bunge.

[10] The provincial and regional studies that best reveal the geographic range, diversity, and problems involved in peasant efforts at innovation in commune districts include: V. I. Orlov, *Formy krest'ianskogo zemlevladenii v Moskovskoi gubernii*, 4, pt. 1 of *Sbornik statisticheskikh svedenii po Moskovskoi gubernii* (Moscow, 1879); A. A. Kaufman, *Obshchina i uspekhi sel'skogo khoziaistva v Sibiri* (St. Petersburg, 1894); V. E. Postnikov, *Iuzhno-russkoe krest'ianskoe khoziaistvo* (Moscow, 1891); F. A. Shcherbina, "Russkaia zemel'naia obshchina," *Russkaia Mysl'*, no. 5 (May 1880): 1–32, no. 6 (June 1880): 72–122, no. 7 (July 1880): 1–36, no. 8 (July 1880): 85–118, no. 10 (October 1880): 34–63, no. 12 (December 1880): 44–60; and "Solvychegodskaia zemel'naia obshchina," *Otechestvennye Zapiski*, no. 7 (July 1879): 60–89; N. Raevskii, *Ocherk Saratovskoi gubernii* (Saratov, 1873); N. N. Chernenkov, *K Kharakteristike krest'ianskogo khoziaistva* (Moscow, 1905); L. S. Lichkov, "Intenzivnaia kultura i obshchinnoe zemlevladenie," *Russkaia Mysl'*, no. 6 (June 1887): 33–47; A. S. L[alo]sh, "Sel'skaia obshchina v Olonetskoi gubernii," *Otechestvennye Zapiski*, no. 2 (February 1874): 218–37; V. N. Grigoriev, "Zemsko-statisticheskie issledovanii po Kurskoi gubernii," *Russkaia Mysl'*, no. 12 (December 1884): 56–73; "Zemsko-statisticheskie issledovania po Smolenskoi gubernii," *Russkaia Mysl'*, no. 9 (September 1886): 1–11; N. Romanov, *Statisticheskie opisanie Orlovskago uezda* (Viatka, 1876); S. N. Iuzhakov, "Formy zemledel'cheskago proizvodstva v Rossii," *Otechestvennye Zapiski*, no. 7 (July 1882): 1–56; "Statisticheskii zakon zemlevladenii v Rossii: Etiud," *Severnyi Vestnik*, no. 7 (July 1886): 167–88.

tion in ecological, geographic, and historical influences at work in the disparate regions of the Russian empire.

It is also significant that within the Russian context, the acquisition of knowledge had never been a politically harmless or neutral exercise. In the pre-Reform era, statistics were frequently treated as a state secret, and debates of the 1860s on research methods and goals for economic investigation frequently took on political overtones. The Grand Duke Konstantin and his associates in the Royal Geographic Society were accused of "planning a revolution," while P. A. Valuev, the future minister of the interior, darkly noted that meetings to debate statistical and economic issues were a "symptom of our [Russian society's] disorganization."[11] Economic research was routinely censored and at times prohibited by a bureaucracy ever fearful of subversive activity. As early as 1867, the government had decreed that no zemstvo documents or newspapers could be published without prior government approval; inter-provincial research projects were also prohibited.[12]

On the provincial and local level, the abysmal ignorance of the officials and the politics of the data-gathering process imposed severe limits on the quantity and quality of the information received. In one particularly notorious incident, an *ispravnik* ordered by the authorities to provide all possible data on climate reported six months later that although "no stone had been left unturned," he was unable to locate *"Klimat"* anywhere in the district! Such idiot zeal contrasted sharply with the suspicion that local officials frequently showed toward government fact-finders from St. Petersburg. It was not unusual for investigators to report that they were lavishly wined and dined, and then accompanied on their rounds by a multitude of unwanted "advisers" whose real task it was to report back to the town official who employed them.[13] Viewed as spies for the central authorities, such researchers experienced precisely the sort of distrust and fear reserved by the provinces for outsiders ever since Gogol's "Inspector General" first visited the town of N———.

Although government policymakers recognized that reliable data was needed for fiscal and other purposes, once the zemstvo statistical investigations began, authorities on every level came to see its field-workers as a set of even more dangerous intruders. Such fears were not unfounded; many zemstvo statisticians belonged to the generation that joined in the "movement to go to the people" and made use of their investigative opportunities to engage in subversive agitation. Evading restrictions on travel and free

[11] *Quoted in* S. Frederick Starr, *Decentralization and Self-Government in Russia, 1830–70* (Princeton, 1972), p. 261.

[12] Vera Romanova Leikina-Svirskaia, *Intelligentsiia v Rossii vo vtoroi polovine xix veka* (Moscow, 1971), pp. 209–10 and P. P. Semenov Tian-shanskii, *Istoriia poluvekovoi deiatel'nosti Imperatorskago russkago geograficheskago obschestva 1845–1895* 1 (St. Petersburg, 1896), p. 172.

[13] N. Raevskii, "Ocherki Saratovskoi gubernii," *Delo*, no. 3 (March 1873): 180.

speech, researchers like I. A. Verner, V. N. Grigoriev, and P. S. Efimenko questioned peasants about political as well as economic issues, and were imprisoned and exiled for their illegal activities. Gentry hostility to the radical behavior of plebian researchers was exacerbated by the discovery of widespread gentry tax evasion—apparently some 30 million *desiatiny* (desiatina = 2.7 acres) of estate property were not being taxed in the 1870s and 1880s.[14] The fear that such exposés might lead to increased taxation combined easily with the notion of statisticians as dangerous anarchists. In the 1880s and 1890s, government officials cut off funds to zemstvo organizations, prohibited the publication of zemstvo findings, and closed down statistical bureaus in Vladimir, Petersburg, and Poltava.[15]

Research efforts were also hampered by questions related to the reliability of data. Before 1861, Russian statistics were drawn primarily from the reports of provincial officials who summarized the observations of the gentry and the local police. To some extent, this practice continued throughout the nineteenth century; even the hearings of the influential Valuev Commission of 1873 contained only three instances of peasant testimony. But during the post-Emancipation period, researchers widened their sights to include the peasant population; farmstead censuses based upon the reports of village elders were compiled for Samara (1869), Moscow (1871), and Arkhangel'sk (1872). In 1871, N. N. Romanov published a study of the value and income of peasant allotments in Viatka Province, making use of direct peasant testimony, and V. I. Pokrovskii carried out a household survey in Tver which became a model for the work of V. I. Orlov, the most eminent of the the early zemstvo investigators. In 1876, Orlov was invited by the Moscow provincial zemstvo to organize a statistical bureau for the study of agricultural conditions. Abandoning his academic post, he and the assistants he gathered together managed to interview the inhabitants of 5,500 villages in every *uezd* in Moscow province. Their findings, published in a massive eight-volume series in 1877, became a model for other studies of the Russian countryside.

Orlov's energy and dedication were legendary among contemporary fieldworkers and academics. Before dying of overwork at the age of thirty-seven, he had sponsored dozens of publications based on local research. In addition, he established research programs for the study of Kursk, Voronezh, Samara, and Tambov provinces, and recruited equally idealistic and gifted

---

[14] See Robert Johnson, "Liberal Professionals and Professional Liberals: The Zemstvo Statisticians and Their Work," in *The Zemstvo and Russia: An Experiment in Local Self-Government*, ed. Terence Emmons and Wayne Vucinich (Cambridge, 1982), pp. 343–49 and E. Kingston-Mann, "Understanding Peasants, Understanding the Experts: Zemstvo Statisticians in Pre-Revolutionary Russia" (Paper presented at the American Association for the Advancement of Slavic Studies national conference, November 1989).

[15] Z. Tverdova-Svavitskaia, *Zemskie podvornye perepisi 1880–1913* (Moscow, 1926), pp. 117–18.

young statisticians like N. A. Kablukov, N. N. Chernenkov, and A. F. Fortunatov, who organized investigations of other provinces. Innovators like N. F. Annenskii and P. P. Chervinskii tried to devise strategies for obtaining reliable data from peasants who invariably reported that each harvest was the worst yet, fearing—with good reason—that any reports of success would encourage landlords to raise rents and officials to raise taxes.

As zemstvo specialists came to better understand the workings of the peasant village, they refined their research techniques. Increasingly sophisticated about the difficulty that outsiders might encounter in obtaining reliable data from peasants with no reason to trust them, they recognized the problem of what twentieth-century social scientists would much later describe as "negotiating entry" into unfamiliar group settings.[16] It was suggested, for example, that investigators attempt to win the peasant's trust and elicit reasonably honest responses by (1) asking questions in relaxed and informal settings (preferably out-of-doors), (2) telling the respondents exactly what was being written down, and (3) taking notes only in pencil, on pieces of paper that were small, a bit smudged, and altogether unofficial-looking. Preference was given to public rather than private questionings, since it was thought that other members of the village *skhod* could then have the opportunity to criticize or correct imprecise or inaccurate statements of their neighbors.[17]

The formidable methodological problems encountered by field investigators may not have been as peculiarly Russian as the politics of economic investigation. However great the frustration of experts like F. G. Terner, S. Ia. Kapustin, and P. S. Efimenko about the inconsistency and contradictoriness of the questions and classifications used by Russian field investigators, similar complaints were made by the organizers of the *Enquête Agricole* and by the staff of the British Royal Commissions of the 1870s. During this period, statistics was everywhere in the process of becoming a more systematic and regularized set of procedures, and like Efimenko, European statisticians of this period frequently criticized field-workers for proceeding without adequate theoretical preparation while academics constructed elaborate theoretical models without benefit of empirical data.[18] Russian research organiza-

[16] See, for example, Chris Argyris, "Diagnosing Defenses Against the Outsider," *Issues in Participant Observation*, ed. George McCall and J. L. Simmons (New York, 1969), pp. 114–27 and Leonard Schatzman and Anselm Strauss, "Strategies for Seeing," in *Field Research: Strategies for a Natural Sociology* (New York, 1973), pp. 18–33.

[17] See, for example, the discussion of investigation methods in P. P. Chervinskii (Chernigovets), "Tri programmy dlia izucheniia obshchiny," *Nedelia* no. 36 (1878), cols. 1164–73; N. M. Astyrev, "K voprosu ob organizatsii tekushchei zemskoi statistiki," *Russkaia Mysl'*, no. 5 (May 1887): 43–60; and S. M. Bleklov, *Travaux statistique des zemstvo russes* (Paris, 1893), pp. 21–22.

[18] See Theodore Porter, *The Rise of Statistical Thinking, 1820–1900* (Princeton, 1986), and the

tions responded to such complaints (when they were not being closed down by government fiat) by attempting to develop clearer standards (for investigation, and formulas for the combination of economic variables that would permit the systematic categorization of peasant households. Under Kablukov, who came to head the Statistical Division of the Moscow University Juridical Society in the 1880s, much energy was applied to the task of making the various statistical projects then under way more consistent with one another, so that a reliable basis for comparison could be established.

GENERAL FINDINGS: POVERTY AND THE QUESTION OF RURAL DIFFERENTIATION

Historical accounts of late-nineteenth-century Russia frequently emphasize the conflict between populist romantics who idealized village life and more tough-minded government officials and Marxists who focused on the issues of poverty and class differentiation.[19] But in fact, idyllic representations of Russian village life were seldom to be met with in the decades after 1861, even from the writers most optimistic about the future of peasants and peasant institutions. Romanov in the northeastern province of Viatka, V. E. Postnikov in Ekaterinoslav to the south and V. N. Grigoriev in the north-central province of Kursk documented the plight of commune peasants whose poverty forced them to sell their allotments. In three *uezdy* (*uezd* = district) of Saratov Province, the statistician Romanov found peasant death rates to be twice the level found among Swedish peasants of the 1870s and 1880s.[20] Statistical investigations of village life which presented evidence suggesting that the commune was a viable institution, capable of development and change, invariably included data indicating that mounting financial burdens were

discussion of Russian and European statisticians and economists in Kingston-Mann, *The Majority as an Obstacle to Progress: Problems of Russian Rural Development.*

[19] My own view is that both critics and admirers of Lenin's *The Development of Capitalism in Russia* have all too often accepted his assessment of the populists and have not sufficiently questioned either his extremely selective use of their work, or his failure to refer to evidence or conclusions contained in zemstvo statistical investigations that did not coincide with his own view. See discussion of Lenin's economics in Esther Kingston-Mann, *Lenin and the Problem of Marxist Peasant Revolution* (New York, 1983), pp. 38–54. Lenin's faulty reading of the investigation of Shcherbina is discussed by Elvira Wilbur in chapter 3 of this volume. Recent Soviet scholarship provides a more nuanced picture of the intellectual debates of the period—see especially, V. A. Alexandrov, *Sel'skaia obshchina v Rossii* (Moscow, 1978) and *Obychnoe pravo krepostnoi derevni Rossii* (Moscow, 1984). But the "Leninist" tradition has, unfortunately, persisted. See, for example, the selective use of V. P. Vorontsov's work contained in A. M. Anfimov and P. N. Zyrianov's "Nekotorye cherty evoliutsii russkoi krest'ianskoi obshchiny v poreformennyi period," translated in *Soviet Studies in History* 21: no. 3 (Winter 1982–3): 74–76, and note 22 below.

[20] N. Romanov, *Statisticheskie opisanie orlovskago uezdy viatksoi guernii* (Viatka, 1876), pp. 1–2.

threatening the peasantry as a whole with economic disaster. Even the statistician V. S. Prugavin, who wrote of the peasantry's "golden hearts," did not claim that they were prospering.[21]

Despite Marxist claims to the contrary, most field investigators and professional economists of the late nineteenth century were well aware of the existence of economic differences within and outside of the peasant commune. No serious economist or statistician of the time ever claimed that commune members were equal either in income or resources. According to commune practice, tools and livestock were privately owned, and it was widely recognized that the more prosperous could manipulate the decision-making process of village assemblies so as to exclude the poor and even deprive them of land. Even the economist V. P. Vorontsov, the foremost nineteenth-century investigator of progressive economic activities within the peasant commune, insisted as well on the existence of inequalities within and outside of the commune.[22]

While the existence of inequality was not disputed, there was bitter disagreement over its possible cause. In the view of some observers, the peasant proletarians of the post-Emancipation era were created as a result of earlier gentry machinations. The statisticians N. Karyshev and P. Osadchii noted that before 1861, serfowners, aware that the coming reforms would include land grants to peasants, quickly acted to convert "possessional" into domestic, that is, landless, serfs. F. A. Shcherbina documented the actions of wealthy serfowners who emancipated their peasants before 1861 with "beggarly" allotments of 1/4 *desiatina* per male.[23] N. N. Chernenkov drew from his investigations of Saratov Province the conclusion that rural economic differences were a cyclical feature of commune life. His figures indicated that allotment size rose and fell with the various phases of a family's life cycle, particularly in the commune, which frequently distributed land according to family size. Thus, parents rich in land were those with many children, while

---

[21] V. S. Prugavin, "Sel'skaia zemelnaia obshchina v povolzhskom krae," *Iuridicheskii Vestnik*, no. 5 (May 1885): 91–119, and *Russkaia zemel'naia obshchina v trudakh ee mestnykh issledovatelei* (Moscow, 1888). See also V. P. Vorontsov, "Ocherki obshchinnago zemlevladeniia v Rossii," *Otechestvennye Zapiski*, no. 1 (January 1882): 211–50; no. 3 (March 1882): 83–111; no. 4 (April 1882): 331–64.

[22] Vorontsov, *Progressivnye techeniia*, pp. 25–27. Although the Soviet scholar Karataev cites Lenin's claim that Vorontsov ignored evidence of unequal distribution of tools among the commune peasantry, Vorontsov in fact included several statistical tables which revealed the unequal distribution of farm machinery. Karataev then goes on to describe zemstvo statistics as "scanty" material gathered by "undeservedly" well-known authors. N. K. Karataev, "Liberalnye narodniki," *Istoriia russkoi ekonomicheskoi mysli*, ed. A. I. Pashkov and N. A. Tsagalov, 2 (Moscow, 1960), pp. 276–79.

[23] This data is cited in N. Karyshev, "Krest'ianskoe zemledelie i obshchina v Khersonskoi gubernii," *Russkoe Bogatstvo*, no. 2 (February 1895): 40, and Shcherbina, *Russkaia Mysl'*, no. 12 (December 1880): 58.

the "wealthy" became land poor when their children married and claimed their own allotments. According to Chernenkov, inequalities were not signs of class formation but part of the cycle of growth and decline in the peasant household.[24] Some statisticians, like V. E. Postnikov, emphasized the emergence of the kulak moneylender, who hired his indebted neighbors to work for him on rented land. Postnikov attributed rural inequality to the development of capitalism, and his work was cited with particular approval by Russian Marxists.[25]

Each of these explanations carried significantly different implications for the future of Russia's rural development. All but the last suggested that when inequalities were either imposed from above or cyclical in character, they could not be taken as proof that *internal* contradictions and tensions were destroying the peasant commune. Shcherbina and Chernenkov were certain that the commune's fate was not preordained; they believed that if government policy were less biased in favor of Russia's privileged elite and if peasant financial burdens were lightened, innovation and improvement could take place on a village level. In contrast, Marxists who praised the work of Postnikov (in contradistinction to Postnikov himself), considered rural differentiation and communal disintegration a brutal sign of progress, an indication that the Russian countryside was experiencing the combination of economic growth and social dislocation that had occurred much earlier in Western agricultural and industrial revolutions.[26]

Controversies over rural inequality were difficult to resolve for technical as well as ideological reasons. In most cases, reliable data had not been collected for a long-enough time to permit meaningful generalizations about the dynamics and direction of change. Since statistical projects could take up to ten years to complete, economic conditions could significantly change before the research was finished. Data gathered at the outset might thus not be accurate by the time the project ended. Cycles of family growth and division, and the practice of periodic repartition also complicated the task of interpreting the significance of economic differences, since an investigator who took a cross-section of a village at a given time might come away with a misleading and superficial picture of the actual socioeconomic relations of its members. In this problematic context, judgments on the evidence were frequently shaped by prevailing historical assumptions about peasants and progress.

[24] Chernenkov is cited as the first to focus on this cyclical process by K. R. Kachorovskii, "The Russian Land Commune in History and Today," *Slavonic and East European Review* 7, no. 21 (March 1929): 565–76. This theory became the basis for the cyclical models developed by A. V. Chaianov, and later elaborated by Teodor Shanin in *The Awkward Class* (Oxford, 1972).

[25] See, for example, Postnikov, *Iuzhno-russkoe*, p. 369.

[26] See general discussion in Kingston-Mann, *Lenin and the Problem of Marxist Peasant Revolution*, pp. 38–54.

The pitfalls of this approach were particularly evident in Lenin's influential *The Development of Capitalism in Russia*, an economic study which included few statistics reflecting the dynamics of rural differentiation. Instead, Lenin's certainty about increasing rural differentiation led him to use figures indicating the *existence* of inequality at a particular time as proof of the *growth* of inequality.[27]

The data on poverty and inequality contained in zemstvo statistical investigations was considered by turn-of-the-century Marxists and by other social critics to be incontrovertible proof that the commune was in a state of rapid and steady decline. But here, too, the story was more complex. Available evidence indicated that after a decade of decline in rates of repartition during the 1870s, a kind of chain reaction of repartitions took place in the 1880s, with the establishment of repartitional communes in villages that were previously under more privatized forms of tenure.[28] The statistician Lichkov documented peasant efforts to introduce the commune in every *uezd* of Saratov province where it did not already exist, most notably among the German colonists who were the most prosperous of Saratov's peasant inhabitants.[29]

6. THE VILLAGE OF KOROBOVO (PROKUDIN-GORSKII COLLECTION, LIBRARY OF CONGRESS).

[27] Kingston-Mann, *Lenin*, pp. 48–54. Lenin's research was more convincing to his fellow Marxists and even to "state capitalist" government reformers than it was to professional statisticians. K. R. Kachorovskii, one of the most eminent statistician-economists of the early 1900s, found that Lenin's work reflected only the sketchiest degree of knowledge of primary sources, and was characterized by an arbitrary selection of data in order to support a priori conclusions. Kachorovskii, *Bor'ba za zemliu* (St. Petersburg, 1908), p. xlviii.

[28] See Vorontsov, *Progressivnye techeniia*, p. 134; V. Prugavin, *Russkaia zemel'naia obshchina*, pp. 46–51; and Anfimov and Zyrianov, *Nekotorye*, pp. 75–76.

[29] L. S. Lichkov, "Eshchë k voprosu ob obshchine," *Iuridicheskii Vestnik* 1, no. 9 (September

When the statistician V. Trirogov studied a Ukrainian settlement in Saratov, he expected to find evidence of the "Ukrainian," Western-oriented tradition of holding on to private household allotments at all costs. Instead, he
discovered that the burdensome terms of the Emancipation made it impossible for peasants to maintain their own pastureland, and led them to see the
commune's common land as their only chance to preserve their livestock.[30]
In contrast to Western economic theories which assumed that private property represented the only reliable source of economic and social security,
Shcherbina discovered that in Solvychegodskii *uezd* in the northeastern province of Vologda, peasant proprietors claimed to find their security in the
transfer of their land to the repartitional land commune in return for rights
to common land.[31] The peasant Chervochkin argued that it was private property that was risky and unreliable; looking out for one's self and one's family
meant opting for the commune; in his words, "I need to think of my children
and my future."[32]

In response to the empirical evidence of peasant loyalty to the commune,
Kapustin suggested that educated Russians might need to reevaluate some
of their economic assumptions. "Perhaps," he reflected, "there is some feature of communal ownership which at present completely escapes us!"[33] In
the *Tübingen Zeitschrift* of 1876, the scholar K. D. Kavelin wrote that he could
not comprehend "what is behind the predisposition of our simple people
toward communal ownership."[34] Equally puzzled, the Marxist G. V. Plekhanov would complain in the 1880s of the commune peasant's "inability" to
understand the advantages of private ownership even when they were explained "ten times over in ten different ways."[35] Certain that the commune
was a hopelessly backward institution where greedy kulaks entrapped their
unfortunate neighbors, Plekhanov could only interpret its attraction for the
majority of the peasantry as an illustration of peasant ignorance and backwardness.

1887): 226, and Shashkov, "Russkaia obshchina i ee vragi," *Delo*, no. 1 (January 1881): 150–
53.

[30] V. Trirogov, "Nashi obshchiny," *Otechestvennye Zapiski*, 1879:3, pp. 96–98, and see also
Lichkov, "K voprosu o razlozhenii pozem. ob.," *Russkoe Bogatstvo*, no. 3 (March 1886): 491.
This would be a persistent theme among peasants who returned to their communes in the
aftermath of the Stolypin Reforms. See Judith Pallot, "Khutora and Otruba in Stolypin's
Program of Farm Individualization," *Slavic Review* 43, no. 2 (Summer 1984): 242–56.

[31] Shcherbina, "Solvychegodskaia zemel'naia obshchina," *Otechestvennye Zapiski* no. 7
(1879), p. 60. The need for common pastureland would have a similar impact on peasants
who left their communes during the Stolypin Reforms, and rejoined them in later years. See
discussion in Judith Pallot, "Khutora," pp. 242–56.

[32] Shcherbina, "Solvychegodskaia zemel'naia obshchina," p. 60.

[33] S. Ia. Kapustin, *Formy zemlevladeniia u russkago naroda, v zavisimosti ot prirody, klimata i
etnograficheskikh osobennostei* (St. Petersburg, 1877), p. 24.

[34] *Quoted in* Kapustin, p. 24.

[35] G. V. Plekhanov, *Sochineniia* 10 (Moscow 1923), p. 129.

THE REALITIES OF COMMUNAL TENURE

Before 1861, many critics of the commune tended to see it either as a sort of autocracy writ small, ruled by a rigid and ignorant village elder, or as a deplorably egalitarian embodiment of Tocqueville's "tyranny of the majority." In later years, gentry and bureaucratic critics were joined by Marxists like Lenin and Plekhanov, who argued that the commune was disintegrating due to the increasing power of kulak minorities over the village poor. Throughout these wide-ranging judgments, a recurrent theme was discernible: it was generally agreed that there was an inherent conflict between the interests of the innovative individual and the claims of collectivist institutions which were conservative at best, and at worst, imbued with "the idiocy of rural life."[36] The evidence collected by zemstvo statisticians in the 1870s and 1880s soon revealed the abstractness of these images of a wholly collectivist commune which engulfed the individual and swallowed up all natural impulses toward innovation, and of private property institutions which everywhere ensured completely independent, constructive, and creative individual decision making.

Statisticians of the post-Emancipation period established beyond any question that village life in commune districts had never been completely collectivist; individual, household, and commune-wide rights and obligations had always coexisted. Within and outside of communes, individuals owned their personal belongings, and the "woman's box" represented the adult female's claim to unconditional ownership of the product of her work at poultry raising, weaving, and other activities. Member households owned their houses and garden plots and possessed exclusive but temporary claims to allotments of scattered strips of land whose product could be disposed of without asking permission of the commune *skhod*. Common rights to the use of pasture, forests, and rivers were managed according to complicated and flexible rules which varied according to changing environmental and social pressures.

In Saratov, for example, it was a common practice for large villages to use their meadows in common and divide the hay according to the number of adult laborers in each commune household.[37] In Smolensk, Grigoriev documented the division of meadows into shares used by various member households according to family size.[38] While the specifics of collectivist practice varied from province to province, the tradition of acting in common to decide land-use questions was widespread. Modes of repartition were extremely varied. Among the more common were the *pereverstka*, a limited exchange of

---

[36] See discussion in Kingston-Mann, "Marxism and Russian Rural Development," pp. 731–52.

[37] Cited in Kapustin, *Formy*, p. 45.

[38] See discussion in Grigoriev, "Zemsko-statisticheskie issledovaniia po Smolenskoi gubernii," pp. 1–11.

7. CARRYING HAY HOME FROM THE FIELDS NEAR THE VILLAGE OF BOGORODSKOE, CHERNIGOV PROVINCE, 1895 (ALEXANDER IVANOVITCH PETRUNKEVITCH PAPERS, MANUSCRIPTS AND ARCHIVES, YALE UNIVERSITY LIBRARY).

strips which applied only to those households whose size had changed since the last repartition, the *zherebevka*, which required peasants to exchange by lot the previously marked-off strips, and the *korennoi peredel'*, a radical redistribution which involved a change in both the number and size of the strips into which commune land was divided.[39]

Nevertheless, as flexible and complicated as the repartitional practices may have been, they clearly limited the individual peasant's freedom to treat communal allotments as a profit-making enterprise. Our discussion will now turn to the evidence on peasant introduction of grass cultivation, improved systems of crop rotation, the use of fertilizer, and related changes aimed at raising agricultural productivity.

COMMUNE-BASED INNOVATION: GRASS CULTIVATION, IMPROVED CROP ROTATION, INTENSIVE CULTIVATION

Within and outside the peasant commune, most late-nineteenth-century Russian peasants cultivated their scattered strips of land according to some

---

[39] These are only a few of the many terms that peasants used for the multitude of variations on the three major kinds of repartition. See the detailed discussion in Steven A. Grant, "Obshchina i Mir," pp. 636–51.

form of the three-field system, a farming practice that left one field fallow every three years in order to guard against soil exhaustion. Among the three fields and within each of them, land was subdivided further according to the soil's fertility and moisture content, with strips of land in each area allotted to heads of commune households. Although this system of field use is now recognized as compatible with modern techniques and practices, nineteenth-century agricultural specialists considered it irretrievably backward.[40] High priority was given to the introduction of more complex patterns of field use and crop rotation, with the land kept fallow under a traditional three-field system sown with grass or fodder-crop mixtures. By following this system, it was possible to obtain all the results that fallowing achieved, while providing more food for livestock. In England's Agricultural Revolution, such changes resulted in a vast increase in agricultural productivity and livestock husbandry, thus creating the material basis for the growth of England's industrial power and national wealth.

In Moscow Province, the first reports of grass cultivation dated back to the 1870s, when several groups of commune villages in various *uezdy* introduced the use of clover. This innovation aroused heated debate in surrounding areas, and despite the reputed isolation of the Russian village, statisticians documented peasant deliberations over the new crop as far as thirty *versty* away from the innovating communes.[41] In these early instances, communes seem to have been acting on their initiative, although in many later cases there were indications of zemstvo influence and guidance, and the specialist A. A. Zubrilin was praised in the 1880s and 1890s as the "first obstetrician of Volokolamsk *travoseianie* (grass cultivation)."[42]

[40] Recent scholarship has revised the view that strip cultivation and the three-field system were inherently backward as agricultural practices. According to George Mingay, a leading historian of the Agricultural Revolution, "Modern research has shown that open fields were far more flexible and progressive than used to be supposed. There might, for instance, be periodic reorganization of holdings to achieve a more compact or more equitable distribution of the strips; piecemeal enclosures were made from time to time in order to procure more land for breeding, fattening, dairying, and other purposes; the number of fields was increased (or existing ones were subdivided) in order to allow for more complex rotations. . . . The old picture of an extremely conservative, rigid and inefficient system which persisted unchanged over the centuries has therefore to be considerably modified." *Arthur Young and His Times* (London, 1975), p. 99. According to Donald McCloskey, the argument that scattered strips were inefficient because of the time required to travel from one plot to another did not hold when plowing was carried out jointly, and an entire area serviced by one plow became the equivalent to a large consolidated plot. With joint effort, little time was in fact wasted. If the plowing of a plot took one day of plowing, oxen or horses would have to be brought back to the village at night to be fed and housed in any case, and the loss of time was minimal. "The Persistence of English Common Fields," in *European Peasants and Their Markets*, ed. William Parker and E. L. Jones (Princeton, 1975), pp. 78–79. See discussion of Russian practices in N. Karyshev, *Trud: Ego rol i usloviia prilozhenii v proizvodstva* (St. Petersburg, 1897), p. 68 and Terner, "Obshchinnoe vladenie," pp. 36–37.

[41] V. P. Vorontsov, *Progressivnye techeniia*, p. 49.

[42] *Quoted in* Hiroshi Okuda, "On Some Aspects of the Final Stages of the Russian Peasant

In general, evidence is scanty on the subject of change rates, but there were indications that on occasion, communes could move quite rapidly. In Tver Province, for example, grass cultivation was practiced on 3,973 *desiatiny* of commune land in 1877; by 1894, it had spread to 14,152 *desiatiny*.[43] In Volokolamsk *uezd* in Moscow Province, forage crops and a four-field crop rotation were introduced in two villages by 1892; by 1900, 127 were using the new system, and by 1903 (under Zubrilin's guidance) 245 out of 368 villages in the *uezd* were participating.[44] In Novgorod, the beginnings of grass cultivation were reported in 1898; by 1902, it was being practiced in 149 commune villages. In response to such initiatives, the Moscow agronomist I. P. Stepanov concluded that in Moscow Province, communes were not obstacles to progress, but "pioneers" in the transition to grass cultivation.[45]

The change process seemed to vary not so much according to tenure considerations as it did in response to the severity of environmental constraints and financial burdens prevalent in a given area. The sowing of clover might first appear in the peasant's garden plot (*usad'ba*) or on land leased by the whole commune. V. I. Orlov found that in Moscow Province, communes only imposed the introduction of grass cultivation on all members after several successful years of trial on special "experimental" or garden plots.[46] Once begun, the transition process might take anywhere from three to four years. Delays did not necessarily indicate opposition to change or fear of risk; they were also efforts to ensure that the cost of innovation did not drive peasants across the boundaries dividing subsistence from disaster. In Volokolamsk, for example, after a successful two-year experiment with clover on private garden plots, one commune decided to postpone its decision to sow clover on the common lands because some members could not afford to buy the improved seeds that year.[47]

Elsewhere, delays were occasioned not by psychological attitudes toward change on the part of peasant commune members, but by other practical considerations. If for example, a commune decided to plant clover, it had to work out alternative methods of crop rotation because clover could not be planted again on the same field for six years, and was therefore incompatible with a traditional three-field rotation. In the Sychevskii *uezd* of Smolensk Province, Grigoriev noted that commune peasants set up special fields for

Commune: Village Ramen'e and the Strategy of Collectivization" (paper presented at the Conference on the Russian Commune, University of London, July 1986), p. 1.

[43] Vorontsov, *Progressivnye techeniia*, p. 196.

[44] B. G. Bazhaev, *Travopol'noe khoziaistvo v nechernozemnoi polose Evropeiskoi Rossii* (St. Petersburg, 1903), pp. 260, 331.

[45] I. P. Stepanov, *Neskol'ko dannykh o sostoianii sel'skogo khoziaistva v Moskovskoi gubernii* 1 (Moscow, 1922), pp. 112, 116.

[46] Vorontsov, *Progressivnye techeniia*, p. 192.

[47] Ibid., p. 193. See reports on grass cultivation in Tavrida Province in Postnikov, *Iuzhnorusskoe*, p. 361.

fodder crops outside the regular three-field system until they were able to devise an orderly procedure for transition to the new rotation. Eventually, in Smolensk, Iaroslavl, and Tver, commune peasants began to introduce a four-field system with clover on two fields.[48] In 1889, in the Kashinskii *uezd* of Tver Province, each phase of the communal change process was in evidence, with striking indications of both the caution and the deliberateness of incremental peasant innovation. Seventy communes practiced a degree of grass cultivation. In nineteen, grass was being cultivated on the garden plots of member households; in twenty-five, it was grown on special parcels which were not part of the regular crop rotation; in sixteen it was planted in one of the fields of the regular rotation. Only in ten communes had grass cultivation already become part of the regular crop-rotation system.[49]

Whatever the role of individual peasant incentive or of tenure arrangements, it was clear that peasant innovations were carried out within a general context of geographic and political constraints. In contrast to England's eight-month growing season, Russia's was, in general four, and Russian winters were so severe that livestock had to be kept indoors for six months in the black-earth district and seven months in the areas farther to the north. This cut by roughly a third the number of animals that could be fed from a season's forage crops. Without access to labor-saving tools suitable for farming the soil of the non-black-earth regions, the planting and harvesting of forage crops would have increased by a third the demand for man-hours at the two peak seasons for farm labor if the same land area were cultivated.

As former serfs, most peasants, within and outside the commune, were freed by the Emancipation of 1861 with less land than they had formerly cultivated; they were also burdened with redemption payments set far above the market value of the land they received. And it was they rather than the gentry or the entrepreneurs who financed with their tax contributions the state's burgeoning commercial and industrial programs. For peasants faced with substantial financial burdens in the last decades of the nineteenth century,[50] the financial risks entailed by certain forms of agricultural innovation could become prohibitive. As the economist A. I. Chuprov noted, when grain prices covered only the costs of an extensive system and the gentry of a given district practiced extensive cultivation, enjoyed lower production costs, and marketed goods more cheaply, small producers who took the risk of engaging in the more costly process of intensive cultivation were courting

[48] Grigoriev, "Zemsko-statisticheskie issledovaniia po Smolenskoi gubernii," *Russkaia Mysl'*, no. 9 (September 1886): 10–11, and see also F. G. Terner, "Obshchinnoe vladenie i chastnaia sobstvennost'," *Vestnik Evropy*, no. 5 (May 1895): 41–42.

[49] Terner, "Obshchinnoe vladenie," p. 42.

[50] Both the nature and the precise impact of the state's financial exactions are a subject of much controversy and debate. See essays by Elvira Wilbur and Stephen Wheatcroft (chapters 3 and 4) in this volume.

disaster. Under such circumstances, when peasants preferred to rent land at high prices to the option of investing more labor and capital in their own allotments, they were not demonstrating a lack of initiative. Instead, they were recognizing that the costs of innovation bore more heavily on peasants than on the large landowner.[51] To economists and statisticians who documented the difficulties facing would-be innovators, the disproportionate cost of innovation to the peasantry suggested that intensive cultivation may not have been the best measure of the economic rationality of peasants or their communes.[52]

FERTILIZER USE

Zemstvo statistics of the 1880s and 1890s indicated that fertilizer use was most widespread in the "capitalist" Baltic regions of western Russia and among the predominantly commune peasants of the north-central province of Iaroslavl. In general, commune peasants outside the black-earth zone used fertilizer more intensively than either the gentry or the noncommune peasantry.[53] In the black-earth region to the south, where the need for fertilizer had only recently become apparent in some districts, a more complex picture emerged. In this area, zemstvo statisticians reported that peasants blamed the commune for their failure to use fertilizer, claiming that it made no sense to fertilize the land if they could lose their improved strips to a lazy neighbor in the next repartition. But the statisticians who investigated the provinces of Tambov and Saratov, where such assertions were most common, did not in fact discover a higher degree of fertilizer use in noncommune districts. And in Samara, most villages that did not carry out periodic repartitions *also* *failed* to fertilize their lands. In these instances, subjective assessments made by peasants were apparently at odds with the statistics on fertilizer use.[54]

 This sort of contradictory evidence suggested to some researchers that fertilizer use, like the use of new field systems, might not be a useful indicator of whether or not peasants were "willing to innovate," and that peasant attitudes were not always the decisive factor. In the south, L. S. Lichkov found that however well aware Saratov peasants were of the benefits of fertilizer, the poorest nevertheless sold whatever livestock manure they possessed to their richer neighbors in order to meet tax payments, or mixed dung with

---

[51] A. I. Chuprov, *Krest'ianskii vopros* (Moscow, 1909), p. 22.

[52] "Vnutrenee obozrenie," *Delo*, no. 6 (June 1874): 68–73. For a careful discussion of the concrete advantages and disadvantages of intensive cultivation for serfs and state peasants in Khar'kov Province, see Zack Deal, "Serf and State Peasant Agriculture," pp. 278–97.

[53] Vorontsov, *Progressivnye techeniia*, p. 190.

[54] Vorontsov, *Krest'ianskaia obshchina* (Moscow, 1892), p. 415. See also Grigoriev, "Zemsko-statisticheskie issledovanii po Samarskoi gubernii," *Russkaia Mysl'*, no. 8 (August 1885): 16–37.

straw to use for the fuel they needed in order to survive the winter months. Lichkov's data also revealed that the rapaciousness of local landlords created significant economic disincentives for would-be peasant innovators who rented land in addition to their commune allotment. In Riazan, for example, landlords demanded that tenants fertilize the land they leased with four to six *puds* per *desiatina—as a condition of the rental contract*. In these areas, where peasant renters were forced to fertilize the landlord's land before they fertilized their own, the statistical data unsurprisingly revealed that the use of fertilizer on peasant allotments was rare to nonexistent.[55]

On occasion, peasants defended their interests against such gentry tactics by enacting commune prohibitions on the transfer or sale of manure outside of its confines. In Moscow Province in the 1870s, communes in one district required their members to place a certain quantity of manure on each allotment annually; the use of fertilizer on noncommune land was permitted only *after* the commune's requirements were met.[56] In such instances, the use of fertilizer seemed more related to gentry/commune power relationships than to issues of tenure or to conservative peasant attitudes. In any case, as the scholar N. Bervi had noted some years before, the quality of soil within a single commune might vary so greatly that peasants might need to use 200 *puds* on one strip, 15 on another, and none at all on a third.[57] Given such varied circumstances, zemstvo statisticians could not easily use data on peasant use and nonuse of fertilizer on their allotments as a measure of rural innovation.

UNCONDITIONAL PROGRESS: EFFORTS AT LAND IMPROVEMENT

As we have seen, neither grass cultivation nor the use of fertilizer was a panacea for the ills that plagued Russian agriculture. But there were some improvements that seemed unarguably positive in their impact. From Moscow to the southern provinces of Tambov and Ekaterinoslav, zemstvo statisticians documented the dramatic benefits of swamp drainage, irrigation, and land-clearing projects which required much labor but relatively little in the way of expensive machinery. Although no claims were made that commune-sponsored measures were adequate to the needs of the region studied, V. I. Orlov found that Moscow peasant efforts at swamp drainage were less frequent in noncommune districts. In Dmitrovskii *uezd*, for example, most of the forty-five villages in one *volost* (county) participated in a swamp-drainage

---

[55] Lichkov, "Intenzivnaia," pp. 33–47.

[56] Vorontsov, *Krest'ianskaia obshchina*, p. 415, and Kapustin, *Formy*. See also Iakushkin's discussion of prohibitions on the sale of manure outside the commune in Tula Province in *Sbornik materialov dlia izuchenii sel'skoi pozemel'noi obshchiny*, ed. F. G. Barykov, A. V. Polovtsov, and P. A. Sokolovskii (St. Petersburg, 1880), p. 202.

[57] V. V. Bervi, *Polozhenie rabochago klassa v Rossii* (St. Petersburg, 1860), p. 199.

project in the 1870s which turned its heavy and infertile soil into productive, relatively valuable arable land. In Bogorodskii *uezd*, thousands of *sazheny* of drainage ditches were dug by communes acting in common. In some cases, special machinery was used, with rental payments raised by means of levies that the communes imposed on their members. As peasants in this district put it, "the commune has the power, and then does its best." In Klinskii *uezd*, which possessed the worst soil in the province, peasants were able to create the best agricultural conditions of all. Orlov found that communal efforts had transformed much of the land; along the Moscow *chausée*, villages of former state peasants had organized themselves in a massive and successful swamp-drainage effort. In this particular project, Orlov found no evidence of guidance by outside experts or by the authorities. Peasants were apparently themselves responsible for creating a plan for improvement and implementing it through a series of agreements among local communes.[58]

Reports of commune-based land improvements were quite common in zemstvo publications of the 1880s and 1890s, and in journals like *Delo, Russkaia Mysl'*, and *Russkoe Bogatstvo*. In the thickly forested terrain of Vologda, for example, A. I. Efimenko and A. S. Lalosh documented efforts at land clearing through the communal organization of tree cutting, digging up of roots, and the burning of stubble. Further south and east in Tambov and Saratov, where land was relatively fertile and already cleared, L. S. Lichkov reported that communes had organized irrigation projects including the digging of ditches, wells, and ponds and the use of primitive but effective peasant-designed and built water-raising machines. Lichkov noted that such efforts were characterized by extremely careful and complicated calculations intended to ensure that the supply of water would be distributed according to the labor investment of each household. Similar efforts were reported in Ekaterinoslav, where over a three- to four-year period, communes in one *uezd* built a water-supply system which extended over a distance of three *versts*.[59] Although no claim was made that most commune peasants in the provinces studied were engaged in such activities, statisticians like Lichkov contended that their data indicated that the commune did not necessarily block economic change or improvement.

COMPULSION AND REWARDS FOR INDIVIDUAL EFFORT: THE COMMUNE'S ROLE

There are people who are ready to die for their fatherland, but there aren't any who would work their whole life in order to accumulate a fortune for their neighbors.

—*Evropeets* (1871)

---

[58] Orlov, *Formy*, pp. 263–67.

[59] Lichkov, "Intensivnaia," pp. 43–44, and see also reports of land-clearing projects in Smolensk Province in Grigoriev, *Russkaia Mysl*, no. 8 (August 1885): 16–37.

In general, Russian peasant communities did not permit their members uninhibited freedom to make economic decisions as they chose; the agricultural cycle was governed by rules that were mandatory for each household. But the compulsory powers of the repartitional land commune extended much further than the common rights and obligations that village communities had claimed in earlier periods of Western European history. In areas where communes prevailed, once a majority agreed to a particular innovation it was binding on all members; no individual or group could refuse to participate in a communal swamp-drainage or irrigation project.[60] On the other hand, an individual could not act independently; improving an allotment frequently depended on a peasant's ability to convince neighbors to do the same. Such a prospect could dampen the enthusiasm of an innovator impatient to carry ideas for change into practice; however, in other situations, the social pressure of the commune could produce quite positive results. Commune peasants in Tula told the statistician S. N. Iuzhakov that within the commune no one wanted to be left behind and be publicly labeled "lazy" or "negligent" by meetings of the village *skhod*, while E. I. Iakushkin reported on peasants who claimed that in comparison with private owners who competed with their neighbors and rejoiced over each other's downfall, commune peasants were glad to see friends and neighbors prosper; their joint projects made it possible that they all would "do well together."[61]

There was general agreement among statisticians who investigated the topic of innovation that change was usually initiated by individuals in areas under private tenure, but spread more rapidly in commune districts.[62] On private land, individuals engaged in a variety of experiments, and if they possessed sufficient capital to sustain their improvements, they established farms that stood like oases in a desert of backwardness. In contrast, communes were slower to introduce new agricultural practices, but once accepted their innovations were adopted by the village as a whole. In some areas, communes voted against change. In others, they served as a mechanism that obliged members to maintain or improve the land, and imposed limits on the fragmentation of allotments. The compulsory manuring of allotment land and prohibitions on the sale of manure in Riazan Province have already been noted, but commune efforts to preserve soil quality were also documented in Moscow Province—where commune assemblies (*skhody*), which recognized that the cultivation of flax rapidly exhausted the soil, went on to set compulsory limits to the quantity of flax that could be planted on

---

[60] Vorontsov, *Progressivnye techeniia*, pp. 178–79.

[61] E. I. Iakushkin in *Sbornik*, ed. Barykov et al., p. 200. Mironov notes that the 1878–1880 survey documented commune efforts to encourage the better use of fertilizer and field methods, with "indolent peasants" first "reproved" by the commune *skhod* and then temporarily deprived of their land allotments if they persisted in their economically retrograde behavior. Mironov, "The Russian Peasant Commune," p. 441.

[62] Vorontsov, *Progressivnye techeniia*, p. 179.

each allotment.[63] In similar fashion, three commune *uezdy* in Kursk Province prohibited the degeneration of allotments into waste, claiming that such neglect injured the interests of any household that might receive them in the next repartition.[64]

In the late nineteenth century, as tax burdens combined with mounting population pressure and the usual environmental disasters took their toll, peasants in areas under private tenure found it particularly difficult to resist the temptation to fragment their allotments. In the Ukrainian provinces of Kiev and Poltava, noncommune peasants attempted to protect their private and short-term interests regardless of the future consequences of their actions for themselves, for the land, or for the community. Whole villages disintegrated as peasants fled in search of lucrative employment. In the Don region, allotments degenerated into waste as peasants exhausted the soil in fruitless attempts to meet their financial obligations and ended by selling their allotments to the village kulak.[65] Although fragmentation and too-frequent repartition were serious problems in commune districts as well, the statistician Fortunatov's survey of thirty-four provinces of European Russia indicated that the communes protected peasants against land loss better than systems of more private tenure.[66] In areas where more privatized property relationships were dominant, no local decision-making body possessed the power to halt fragmentation and too frequent repartition. State action was required, and in fact, the government finally acted in 1893 to prohibit the fragmentation of peasant allotments.

Examples of peasant apathy and lack of incentive abounded in the writings of gifted observers like Gleb Uspenskii, Skaldin (F. P. Elenev), and Engel'-gardt, who undertook no systematic empirical studies but carefully observed some of the more poverty-stricken commune villages of the post-Emancipation era and feared that they were typical.[67] In contrast, field-workers of the 1880s and 1890s documented an almost fanatic peasant concern that investments of labor or capital be justly rewarded. In the northern provinces, A. I. Efimenko reported that investments of labor were so highly valued that if a peasant discovered a beehive, the compensation received from the commune would vary according to whether or not the discovery was accidental or was

[63] Orlov, *Formy*, p. 266.

[64] Grigoriev, *Russkaia Mysl'*, no. 12 (December 1884): 70.

[65] See discussion in L. Kotelianskii, "Ocherki podvornoi Rossii," *Otechestvennye Zapiski*, no. 2 (February 1878): 124–63; no. 8 (August 1878): 13–44; no. 9 (September 1878): 40–73.

[66] A. F. Fortunatov, "Raspredelenie pozemel'noi sobstvennosti v Evropeiskoi Rossii," *Russkaia Mysl'*, no. 7 (July 1886): 110–35. See also A. A. Karelin, *Obshchinnoe vladenie v Rossii* (St. Petersburg, 1893).

[67] See, for example, Gleb Uspenskii, *Polnoe sobranie sochinenii* 5 (Moscow, 1940), pp. 124–50; Skaldin (F. P. Elenev) *V zakholust'i i v stolitse* (St. Petersburg, 1870); and A. M. Engel'gardt, *Iz derevni: 11 pisem (1872–1882 gg)* (St. Petersburg, 1882), pp. 125–31, 133–38, 145–47, 231–33, 239–42.

the product of a deliberate and laborious search. Peasant courts in the provinces of Vologda and Olonets routinely demanded that the successful litigant in a property conflict be paid by his or her adversary for labor time lost due to participation in court proceedings.[68]

In areas as diverse as Tambov and Tula provinces, peasants who fertilized their plots either received special monetary payments at the time of repartition, or a similar plot, or the right to retain their original allotments.[69] In Kazan, "improvers" exchanged strips only with each other so that no family would be forced to exchange an allotment sown with clover for an ordinary plot.[70] In Western Siberia, the statistician-economist A. A. Kaufman was unable to discover a *single* instance in which peasants failed to receive compensation at the time of repartition for any investments of labor or capital that were out of the ordinary. In Northern Tobolsk, for example, he documented the ingenious and complicated arrangements that peasants had devised in order to balance out the competing claims of the innovative individual and the survival of the community as a whole. When a repartition was scheduled, commune strips were divided into three categories on the basis of such factors as soil quality, location, and degree of improvement. In order to avoid penalizing the more innovative peasants, all "improvers" were permitted either first choice of the best-quality land or, in some cases, the option of retaining their original allotments. In order to prevent the emergence of a self-perpetuating monopoly of all good land by the initial improvers, all the "nonimprovers" received first priority in the allotment of second-quality land. Land in the third category was distributed on an equal basis to all commune members on the basis of labor needs.[71]

In this connection, it is useful to recall the insights of A. M. Engel'gardt, an observer famous for his tough-minded judgments on the weakness of the commune and the egoism of its members (and much quoted on this score by Plekhanov and Lenin). When Engel'gardt wrote of peasant incentive, he was careful to distinguish between what he called the abstract ideal of "pure" collectivism and the realities of peasant interaction. Engel'gardt suggested that if acting in common was interpreted in "mechanical" fashion, with observers attempting to discover peasants who eagerly invested their labor or capital without any hope of personal reward, they would search in vain for peasant collectivism (except in cases of hay mowing and certain other specific tasks). But if collectivism was understood as a variety of joint procedures for apportioning work in which specific and personal contributions of labor or

[68] A. I. Efimenko, *Issledovaniia narodnoi zhizni* (Moscow, 1883), pp. 12–14.

[69] Terner, "Obshchinnoe vladenie," p. 35. Orlov's evidence on commune compensation for innovation is cited in Kapustin, *Formy*, p. 50.

[70] Terner, pp. 35–36.

[71] Kaufman, *Obshchina i uspekhi*, pp. 133–42, and see also evidence cited by Trirogov from Saratov Province in *Otechestvennye Zapiski*, no. 11 (November 1878): 125.

capital were recognized and compensated, then innumerable instances could be found of peasants uniting for constructive action. Engelgardt went on to claim that educated Russians of good will, who were committed in principle to cooperative populist/socialist endeavors, often found it difficult to understand the "messy" realities of peasant collectivism. For peasants within and outside the commune, mutual aid and reward within a collective framework was a relatively ordinary fact of life—although for Engelgardt, these virtues did not necessarily outweigh the greed, apathy, dishonesty, violence, and other notable and widely documented features of peasant behavior.[72]

PEASANT COLLECTIVISM

Among zemstvo statisticians of the late nineteenth century, peasant collectivism was not described in idealized terms. There was general agreement that in the very worst situations, collectivist practices did not survive. Gross examples of greed, competition, and callousness abounded under such conditions and were graphically described by Engelgardt, Skaldin, Postnikov, and Orlov.[73] The novelist Uspenskii wrote of a brutalized and apathetic Samara village where the commune *skhod* excluded the poor from the use of common lands or forests. Uspenskii despaired at the "complete absence of moral bonds among members of the village commune . . . In place of the old arbitrary rule [of feudal masters] has come neither knowledge, nor development, nor even a kind word between neighbors."[74]

While many educated Russians at the turn of the century believed that such experiences were universal, in reality, zemstvo statisticians documented a wide variety of collectivist economic and social practices in areas where peasants were not in a state of utter ruin. In addition to the agricultural improvements already mentioned, F.A. Shcherbina wrote of the collective cultivation of land purchased or rented by peasants in Poltava, Tambov, and Bessarabia in the 1870s.[75] By the last decade of the nineteenth century, this practice had been documented in twenty-six provinces of European Russia. In Penza Province, some 14,000 *desiatiny* of allotment land were farmed collectively in over a thousand communes, while over 60 percent of the communes in two districts of Voronezh Province farmed a portion of their lands in this manner. In response to such data, Engelgardt made the unheard of proposal that communal cultivation practices be used as a device to *promote* the more rapid spread of improved methods of field use.[76]

[72] Engel'gardt, *Iz derevni*, pp. 76, 94, 258.

[73] Orlov's data on Moscow Province indicated that cooperative measures did not prevail in the most desperately poor or economically polarized districts. Orlov, *Formy*, pp. 50, 269.

[74] Uspenskii, *Polnoe sobranie sochinenii*, pp. 124–50.

[75] F. A. Shcherbina, *Ocherki iuzhno-russkikh artelei i obshchinnykh form* (Odessa, 1881), p. 37.

[76] Engel'gardt's proposal is discussed in A. A. Karelin, *Obshchinnoe vladenie v Rossii* (St.

In Vologda Province, Kapustin described the efforts of commune peasants to construct their own mills and organize a division of labor according to the labor capacity of member households.[77] In Moscow Province, Orlov documented the collective renting of quarries, peat bogs, and mills by communes or groups of communes.[78] In Simbirsk, Tula, and Moscow provinces, there were reports of communal organization of timber-cutting activities. Wood was apportioned by the decision of the village *skhod* (taking into account the type of wood, the height of the trees, their width, and the number of branches each possessed, and according to the number of members of each household). According to the economist F. G. Terner, peasants on enclosed farms, however free they were to make use of their foresight, thrift, intelligence, and individual initiative, did not possess in the same measure as their commune counterparts the institutional mechanisms that fostered community-wide improvements.[79]

In Tambov, Lichkov documented the arrangements made by commune assemblies for child care for peasant women during the ripening of the harvest.[80] Moscow communes aided fire victims by allotting a certain amount of timber for each burned-out household, with obligations for cartage of wood divided among villages within five *versty* of the area where the fire occurred.[81] In one district of Bessarabia Province where land was farmed in common, the grain harvested was divided according to the labor capacity of member households, with a portion set aside beforehand to build and maintain a school.[82]

In widely documented cases of *pomoch* (help, aid), it was evident that peasant families did not reach out to help a faceless and unknown poor, or arrange child care for anonymous and needy families. Ordinarily, peasants ex-

---

Petersburg, 1893), pp. 178–93. According to Orlando Figes, the practice of collective cultivation played a significant role in the peasant agricultural economy at least until the civil war which followed the Bolshevik Revolution. Figes, "Collective Farming and the 19th Century Russian Land Commune: A Research Note," *Soviet Studies* 38, no. 1 (January 1986): 89–91.

[77] Kapustin, *Formy*, p. 71.

[78] Orlov, *Formy*, pp. 271–75; see also reports on collective cultivation using improved methods in Poltava province in *Nedelia*, no. 27 (1876): 34–35.

[79] Terner, "Obshchinnoe vladenie," pp. 24, 43.

[80] Lichkov, "Intensivnaia," pp. 43–44, and see general discussion of *pomoch'* in M. M. Gromyko, "Obychai pomochei u russkikh krest'ian v xix v.," *Sovetskaia etnografiia*, no. 4 (1981): 26–38; no. 5 (1981): 32–46.

[81] Orlov, *Formy*, p. 268. According to Iakushkin's report on *Starukhinskaia obshchina* in Tula province, a peasant who could not complete farm work for a reason the *skhod* considered "good" would have his work completed by his neighbors—on condition that he treated them with food and liquor. Iakushkin, in *Sbornik*, ed. Barykov et al., p. 201, and see also I. Kh., "Pomoch' (iz obychno-obshchinnykh otnoshenii," *Russkoe Bogatstvo*, no. 1 (January 1879): 66–74.

[82] F. A. Shcherbina, *Ocherki*, p. 290.

tending aid through commune decisions were acquainted with and in daily contact with those they helped. From a Western perspective, which often assumes an inherent conflict of interest between the individual and an abstract and faceless "collective," Russian peasant collectivism appears extraordinarily personal; commune peasants did not submit themselves to the demands of alien institutions in order to help unfamiliar people. Help was given to neighbors, whose ruin might directly increase the financial obligations of each commune member and whose plight was frequently attributed not to character defects but to the burdens imposed by officials, by landlords, or by the ever-threatening Russian land and climate.

TENURE, PRODUCTIVITY, AND RUSSIAN RURAL DEVELOPMENT

As we have seen, peasant notions of property and ownership were not always easy to categorize and classify. Individual members of communes practicing periodic repartition did not relinquish various forms of more or less private property (personal belongings, the "woman's box," etc.). In noncommune areas, peasants mowed hay in common and coordinated many of the tasks that were part of the annual agricultural cycle. As Orlov noted, even the most independent of Moscow peasant proprietors were eager to retain common meadow, forest, and pasture land.[83] Comparisons between the economic virtues of communal and private tenure were thus easiest to make at very high levels of abstraction. In general, peasants with land sufficient to permit them to set aside special parcels for pasturing livestock so that they could engage in intensive cultivation without diminishing the size of their arable land, that is, peasants with larger allotments, tended to be more productive than their land-poor counterparts among the commune peasantry.

Efforts at innovation in commune and freehold villages were particularly difficult to compare according to productivity rates. Statisticians attempting to record seed/yield ratios in the northern, communal regions of the empire found that the abandonment of the least-fertile land could improve yields even without any change in agricultural practice. In contrast, yields rose in a number of areas in the south because new and fertile land was brought into cultivation, again *irrespective* of efforts at innovation.[84] Using a single measure—like the use of fertilizer or improved plows—as an indicator of innovative agricultural activity by peasant communes was equally problematic, because the problems facing the would-be innovator differed so greatly in the fertile black-earth regions of the Ukraine and the areas of thin gray soil

[83] See I. V. Mozzukhin, *Agrarnyi vopros v tsifrakh i faktakh* deistvitel'nosti (Moscow, 1917), p. 237 and Judith Pallot, "Agrarian Modernization on Peasant Farms in the Era of Capitalism," *Studies in Russian Historical Geography* 2, ed. James Bater and R. P. French (London, 1983), pp. 444–45.

[84] Some of these caveats were greatly clarified for me in discussions with John Bushnell.

to the north, or in areas distant from or close to markets,[85] or to urban centers where agricultural tools were produced. For the pioneering statisticians of the 1870s and 1880s, manifestations of improvement were hard to discern because the "old ways" were seldom completely replaced; peasants usually devised a variety of combinations of the old and the new. As we have seen, the time-honored three-field system might also incorporate the planting of nontraditional crops which enriched the soil.

For staunch believers in the progressive benefits of private property rights and for adherents of the commune, the Russian rural scene posed challenges that could not easily be explained away. In 1873, the district secretary of the Moscow Agricultural Society, an enthusiastic critic of the commune, was confronted with a request for information on the feasibility of establishing enclosed private farms in Moscow Province. As he considered the conditions of the Moscow countryside, he found himself forced to confess that such measures for privatization were as yet inappropriate. Despite the advantages that the enclosed private farm (the *khutor*) possessed in principle, if fire, theft, or serious illness occurred, a Moscow peasant family on its own would suffer irreparable harm because of the inadequacy of roads or any nearby sources of aid and supply. These deficiencies made the introduction of private property systems for peasant farming an unrealistic option.[86]

In contrast to the daunting prospects that faced the peasant individualist, S. Ia. Kapustin described the activities of peasants in the Don *oblast* who pooled their resources and rented some 200 *desiatiny* in common. According to Kapustin, these families were successful in that they were able to farm the land without having to hire themselves out to work for others. But theirs was no peasant idyll; neither common sense nor a willingness to cooperate had brought them an even minimally decent material life. The Don "collective" lived in mud huts, too few in number to secure their needs for medical care, clothing, or the replacement of tools or other necessities, and with no hope for help from other, equally impoverished and distant villages.[87]

According to Kapustin, neither the commune nor the *khutor* was a panacea for the problems that plagued subsistence peasants in an economically back-

---

[85] This point is emphasized in the work of Elvira Wilbur (chapter 3 in this volume).

[86] Cited in Kapustin, *TIVEO* 2 (1877): 343–44. A similar point was made by peasants in Tula Province who claimed that the commune allowed them access to pastureland, use of the ponds, and various other forms of mutual aid in case of illness, snowstorms, and so forth. See discussion by Iakushkin in *Sbornik*, ed., Barykov et al., p. 200.

[87] As Timothy Mixter has indicated, late-nineteenth-century Russian peasants could not rely on patrons, the state, or the emergence of capitalism to deal with issues of theft, fire, fuel, and grain stores. Medical, educational, and police arrangements were provided most reliably—but by no means efficiently—by the commune. See Mixter, "The Politics of Relief Stations for Migrant Agricultural Laborers in Russia, 1875–1915" (paper presented at National Conference of the American Association for the Advancement of Slavic Studies, Boston, November 1988).

ward society. Peasants everywhere needed roads, schools, access to medical care, and tools, and more hands to share in the economic and social tasks that faced them.[88] These were not tenure issues. As A. I. Chuprov observed, peasants without education, capital, or sufficient numbers to carry on modern farming would not be miraculously supplied with these necessities by the simple act of leaving the commune and establishing themselves as owners of isolated plots of land.[89]

CONCLUSION

Late-nineteenth-century zemstvo data suggest that there was no inherent contradiction between comunal repartition and the introduction of a variety of improvements that required a substantial investment of labor, capital, and intelligence. Our preliminary inquiry suggests that communes pioneered certain forms of land improvement, particularly in the form of swamp drainage and irrigation. As economic institutions, they were capable of flexibility and responsiveness to changing circumstances as well as conservatism. Although collectivist traditions did not seem to imbue peasants with such character defects as laziness and apathy, the evidence of commune innovation gathered by zemstvo statisticians indicates that communal innovation was in no sense an exercise in collectivist self-sacrifice. Instead, as we have seen, peasant communes managed to devise for themselves a number of ingenious systems of reward and compensation for the expenditure of labor within the process of periodic repartition.[90]

The commune sometimes provided a convenient mechanism for the implementation of community-wide innovation; its powers of compulsion were used to compel change as well as to block it. Although innovations were most frequently initiated among freehold peasants, the evidence that I have thus far examined suggests that they spread more quickly in commune dis-

---

[88] Kapustin's analysis prefigures the contemporary analysis provided by James Scott, who has focused upon the elemental character of the choices and values available to the rural poor in a premodern or "modernizing" society. In the Don collective, we find similarities to James Scott's Vietnamese peasants who lived so close to the margin of subsistence that any setback meant less food, humiliating dependence, or the sale of land or livestock—necessities that reduced the already difficult odds of achieving an adequate level of subsistence in the following year. See James Scott, *The Moral Economy of the Peasantry* (New Haven, 1976).

[89] Chuprov, *Rechi i stat'i*, p. 50.

[90] Peasant efforts to reconcile the interests of the commune and rewards for individual effort were apparently unknown to the scholar A. A. Manuilov, who hoped that Irish traditions of "tenant right" could show Russian peasants how to reward innovation under conditions of temporary land occupancy or to K. R. Kachorovskii, who discussed the conflict between *pravo na trud* (the unconditional right to land, i.e., to the means of survival) and *pravo truda* (the right to land based upon individual investments of labor). See A. A. Manuilov, *Arenda v Irlandii* (Moscow, 1895), p. 221, and K. R. Kachorovskii, *Russkaia obshchina, vozmozhno li, zhelatel'no li ee sokranenie i razvitie* 1 (St. Petersburg, 1900), pp. 3–21.

tricts. If this data meets the test of further research, it holds some interesting implications for theorists and historians of technological development, who suggest that the introduction of innovations does not in itself raise the general level of development unless large numbers of prospective users (in this case, peasants were the "users") decide to adopt, modify, and alter the new tool or technique in order to make it appropriate to the specifics of their situation.[91] In the Russian context, the village-wide mechanisms capable of fostering the spread of new techniques and increased use of new tools were clearly stronger in areas of communal tenure.

As I have suggested, in the late-nineteenth-century data on communal and *podvornoe* villages, it is difficult to find figures that are reasonably comparable and where changes in productivity rates can be systematically traced. Where statistical parallels have been drawn, there is no clear-cut evidence that the efforts associated with either form of tenure were consistently more successful.[92] Further village, provincial, and regional studies need to be carried out in order to establish the degree of relative economic advances made in commune and noncommune villages. But at this point, it seems likely that neither tenure issues nor peasant attitudes toward change weighed as heavily in questions of innovation and productivity increase as a number of other factors. In late-nineteenth-century rural Russia, the amount of land a peasant household cultivated, the specifics of landowner coercion in a given area, the peasantry's competitive disadvantages in comparison with the gentry, state-imposed financial burdens, lack of access to credit and education, and the strikingly different requirements dictated by the extreme variations in land and climate everywhere weakened and undermined whatever "magic" the institution of private property may have possessed. The commune's clear advantage—and on this issue the evidence is substantial—was that it permitted a sharing of the numerous risks and dangers involved in a grass-roots rural development.

[91] See Stuart MacDonald's intriguing discussion of the importance of the user and of "user modification" in the course of England's Agricultural Revolution, "Agricultural Improvement and the Neglected Laborer," *Agricultural History Review* 31, part 2 (1981): 81–90.

[92] See S. A. Klepikov, diagrams 20a, 20b, in A. V. Chaianov, *Atlas diagramm i kartogramm po agrarnomu voprosu* (Moscow, 1917), pp. 25, 39 n. 7, and N. A. Karyshev, "Podvornoe i obshchinnoe khoziaistvo. Statisticheskie paralleli," *Russkoe Bogatstvo*, no. 1 (January 1894): 45–67; and no. 6 (June 1894): 102–35.

CHAPTER 2

THE SOCIAL CONTROL OF PEASANT LABOR IN RUSSIA: THE RESPONSE OF VILLAGE COMMUNITIES TO LABOR MIGRATION IN THE CENTRAL INDUSTRIAL REGION, 1861–1905

Jeffrey Burds

THIS article is an investigation of the Russian peasant commune in the Central Industrial Region (see map 1) from the Emancipation of the serfs in 1861 to the dawn of the Stolypin reforms in 1906.[1] All over European Russia, the peasant commune served in varying degrees and permutations three distinct, yet often overlapping and conflicting, roles: (1) the commune functioned as an extension of the state *apparatus*, responsible as a collective for the fulfillment of dues and obligations, and for the general maintenance of order according to the norms of peasant customary law; (2) the commune was a *mitigator*, an organization of families associated by proximity, tradition, kinship, religious, and cultural bonds which *in practice* served and protected the interests of villagers from the inroads of outsiders, both distinct (such as state agents, creditors, market middlemen) and amorphous (such as commoditization and wage labor); and (3) the commune was a *broker*, the principal mediator (with *volost'* authorities) between locally controlled resources (in labor, raw materials, land) and outside agents.[2]

In the Central Industrial Region, in particular, a very high rate of peasant labor migration for non-agricultural side earnings became the chief catalyst which bonded these three elements together in a distinct regional form. The convergence of forces had three key components. The Russian state sought

---

[1] I am grateful to a number of individuals who shared with me their work, ideas, criticisms, and support during the course of preparing this article: Mark von Hagen, Esther Kingston-Mann, John Merriman, James Scott, A. J. Segal, and Richard Stites. Very special thanks to Gregory Freeze and Timothy Mixter.

[2] This *operational* definition of the peasant commune (mir, *obshchina, obshchestvo*) may be contrasted to the more detailed exposition in the excellent article by Boris Mironov, "The Russian Peasant Commune After the Reforms of the 1860s," *Slavic Review* 44, no. 3 (Fall 1985): 441–42.

to coopt the peasant commune in order to expropriate the cash earnings of peasant workers through state taxation and redemption dues, while avoiding the pitfalls of Western-style proletarianization. In its efforts to subordinate the peasant commune to state control, the state followed a carrot-and-stick strategy: while vigorously pursuing the impossible task of imposing a rule of law in the countryside, state policy also upheld and extended the status of village patriarchal authorities, who were likewise threatened yet dependent upon the vital lifeline provided by the departure of household members for outside earnings to the urban and industrial centers. The attitude of the village hierarchy was one of ambivalence: migration for earnings was an "inescapable evil, which appears as the necessary consequence of the absence of local industry and the insufficient size of allotment lands."[3]

This was the essential ingredient in the regional crisis of peasant economy: The overriding task of primary village institutions (commune, household, family) was somehow to integrate into a *changing conception of community* a large proportion of village members who would spend most of their adult lives in wage-earning positions outside of the village. In the West, these forces had led to a clear social division of labor between peasants and proletarians, while in Russia, all the way up to the time of the Revolution of 1917, the ranks of the non-agricultural workforce continued to be filled to a large degree by labor recruits from the countryside. In the interregnum which marked the period, opportunists—cognizant of their capacity to exploit the breach to their advantage—stepped in to assist cash-hungry villages fending off state tax agents on the one hand, and peasant families threatened by a pervasive sense of insecurity in the commodity economy, on the other.

CHANGING PATTERNS IN PEASANT SUBSISTENCE STRATEGIES

Russia's fiscal system during the last half of the nineteenth century was founded on a critical contradiction. Despite the presence of a well-developed industry and the predominance of non-farm earnings among peasant households in the Central Industrial Region, taxes were most often based on land, on the size of peasant allotments.[4] While imposing a tax based primarily on land, the state nonetheless recognized that peasants in the Non-Black-Earth Zone would migrate for outside earnings in order to fulfill those obligations. This policy was in keeping with procedures established in the pre-Emancipation era, when noble landlords in the northern forest region by and large imposed cash dues on their serfs, thereby generating a system of estate ad-

---

[3] *Sel'skokhoziaistvennyi obzor Tverskoi gubernii za 1894-i god* (Tver, 1895), pt. II, p. 7.

[4] Ministerstvo finansov, Departament okladnykh sborov, *Sushchestvuiushchii poriadok vzimaniia okladnykh sborov s krest'ian. Po svedeniiam, dostavlennym podatnymi inspektorami za 1887–1893 gg. (Materialy dlia peresmotra uzakonenii o vzimanii okladnykh sborov)* (hereafter, *SP*), 2 vols., II (St. Petersburg, 1894–1895), p. 48.

ministration that was virtually indifferent to alternative *forms* of peasant labor. All over European Russia, the cost of redeeming the land far exceeded
its real market value: the size of allotments was reduced, the best land was
held back by landlords or sold at a profit to outside buyers. Peasant families
could not make a living off their allotments, and were compelled therefore
to rent additional land or work as wage laborers in the agricultural and non-
agricultural sectors. In the Central Agricultural Region, such terms were imposed deliberately, so as to ensure a large, inexpensive pool of wage laborers
for demesne agriculture. In the Non-Chernozem (Non-Black-Earth) zone to
the North, however, the terms of redemption were a direct reflection of the
comparatively poor quality of land: noble income had long been derived not
so much from demesne agriculture, but from serf labor in non-agricultural
occupations. Artificially high redemption costs were a reimbursement to the
landed nobility for their lost labor income (*obrok*, or quitrent payments). In
twelve Moscow districts, for instance, the average obligation on an individual parcel was 10.45 rubles, while the mean rent for the same size and quality
parcel was 3.6 rubles.[5] The Soviet historian P. A. Zaionchkovskii found that
the typical redemption price for land in central Non-Black-Earth districts was
one to two times its actual value among former state peasants, and two to
two and a half times for former manorial peasants. In this way, the Russian
fiscal system operated on the presumption that peasants in the non-chernozem areas would turn to sources outside agriculture to supplement their
earnings and fulfill state obligations. Three other factors—a steady increase
in rural tax burdens throughout most of the last half of the nineteenth century, the peasant's growing reliance on the market as a purveyor of needed
items, and a rapid population growth—gave further impetus to peasant migration for supplemental earnings.

For estate administrators before Emancipation, and for the state agents
who supplanted them after 1861, the principal concern in The Non-Black-
Earth Zone was not the land, but the payments for it. To compensate for the
inevitable discrepancy between land values and labor power, the reward of
allotments was as a rule determined by the "economic significance of the
allotment," in connection with the "greater or lesser side-earnings of locals."
In this way, communes in Non-Black-Earth districts translated state exactions
on village land into a modified village-based income tax. Rarely were land-
distribution or tax-assessment schemes founded on the number of revised
souls or even according to the number of souls actually present.[6] The system
left enormous room for arbitrariness.

To meet the excessive obligations of state tax and redemption dues, peas-

[5] P. A. Zaionchkovskii, *Otmena krepostnogo prava v Rossii*, 3rd ed. (Moscow, 1968), pp. 301–
2.

[6] *SP*, II, pp. 48-49.

ants in the Central Industrial Region were compelled to depart for earnings outside of their native villages. (Tables 2-1 and 2-2 contain data on the rapid growth of peasant labor migration from 1861-1910.) Taking European Russia as a whole, the number of issued passports grew in inverse proportion to the distance from the center, with the percentage of issued passports declining in definite concentric rings as one moved away from Moscow. The Central Industrial Region—Moscow and six surrounding provinces—held the absolute and proportionally highest number of issued passports. In the mid-1890s, for every 100 souls (both sexes) of the general village population, there were issued in Kaluga Province—20.5 passports; in Vladimir—20.4; Tver—18.4; Riazan—17.9; Iaroslavl—17.0; Moscow—16.6; and Tula—14.4.[7] This central high-migration core was bordered on the east by Kostroma and Nizhnii Novgorod, and to the West, Smolensk, where there was an average of 10 to 13 passports per hundred.

While it is difficult to determine with precision the total number of *otkhodniki*, most estimates for the 1890s (based on issued passports) agree on a figure near 2 million for the nine provinces in the Central Industrial Region, more than 6 million for the whole of European Russia.[8] This corresponded in the Central Industrial Region to more than 14 percent of the total rural population: more than a third of all adult peasant males, at least one member of every peasant household, were involved in some form of work that took them away from their villages.

The sheer magnitude of the migration phenomenon not only reflected a profound transformation of the traditional village world, but eventually did itself also become a major agent of change in the Russian countryside. D. N. Zhbankov, a statistician and zemstvo physician commenting on the impact of migration throughout the Central Industrial Region, concluded that the growing networks of peasant-workers traveling to and from the village exerted a "powerful influence on the entire life of the rural population, on its economic and social conditions, family relations, development, habits, customs, and finally, on health—both for the migrants and for that part of the population which is left at home."[9] The growth and persistence of a large number of peasant households based simultaneously in the farm and non-farm economies generated a "third" culture—neither fully traditional, nor

[7] P. Vikhliaev, "Ob ustoichivosti vnezemledel'cheskikh otkhozhepromyslovykh zarabotkov sel'skogo naseleniia," *Narodnoe Khoziaistvo*, no. 3 (1900): 74–76. Also, see L. E. Mints, *Otkhod krest'ianskogo naseleniia na zarabotki v SSSR* (Moscow, 1925), pp. 10–11, 16–18, 22–24.

[8] To avoid confusion with migrant labor as it is more popularly understood in the West, the original Russian terms will be used throughout this article. *Otkhod* or *otkhodnichestvo* refers to the phenomenon of a peasant worker's departure for outside earnings. *Otkhodnik* refers to the peasant worker who departs.

[9] "Vliianie otkhozhikh promyslov na dvizheniia naseleniia za 1866–1890 gg.," *Vrach* 16, no. 24 (1895): 636.

TABLE 2-1.
Peasant Labor Migration in 43 Provinces of European Russia, 1861–1910

Regions and Provinces	Average Annual Number of Issued Passports (in Thousands)					
	1861–1870	1871–1880	1881–1890	1891–1900	1902	1906–1910
I. Non-Agricultural/Industrial	850.7	2,060.9	2,455.1	3,203.9	3,871.4	4,572.5
North and Northwest	296.4	669.5	740.6	1,037.2	1,293.7	1,443.5
Arkhangel'sk	14.0	34.1	33.0	42.9	49.0	52.1
Vologda	16.2	63.0	70.4	109.0	140.2	160.2
Olonets	8.9	27.6	32.5	46.3	48.1	51.9
St. Petersburg	40.3	84.0	104.5	151.2	193.3	175.2
Novgorod	34.1	95.9	98.0	141.7	182.6	214.1
Pskov	13.4	25.8	32.1	64.0	98.3	128.3
Smolensk	58.6	115.6	123.5	157.2	191.2	219.6
Tver	110.9	223.5	246.6	324.9	391.0	442.1
Central Industrial Region	510.2	1,281.8	1,541.0	1,902.9	2,225.4	2,684.7
Iaroslavl	71.9	142.4	149.7	188.7	233.9	239.8
Moscow	108.1	199.9	236.9	374.9	458.0	536.9
Vladimir	54.9	200.3	231.2	294.7	368.9	388.7
Kostroma	39.7	138.4	171.8	183.5	10.9	282.1
Kaluga	78.1	172.3	205.4	257.2	284.2	313.5
Nizhnii Novgorod	37.2	116.1	143.4	18.7	203.0	210.6
Tula	46.1	109.3	139.8	221.7	267.1	293.8
Riazan	74.2	203.1	262.8	363.5	399.4	419.3
Belorussia	44.1	109.6	173.5	263.8	352.3	444.3
Vitebsk	22.7	39.2	57.5	97.0	148.4	166.7
Minsk	8.7	27.6	57.5	77.8	94.7	99.3
Mogilev	12.7	42.8	58.5	89.0	109.2	178.3
II. Southern Agricultural	117.1	421.3	816.9	1,204.2	1,398.9	1,551.7
Ukraine	116.4	413.2	796.9	1,152.9	1,306.3	1,439.3
Poltava	24.6	83.7	139.0	193.8	221.4	195.5
Khar'kov	18.6	63.9	122.9	175.7	231.2	244.4
Chernigov	19.4	65.1	102.7	149.5	188.1	201.1
Kiev	10.1	46.8	138.6	235.9	244.4	295.1
Volynia	8.0	31.6	61.2	85.7	15.5	110.5
Podol'ia	6.4	30.6	78.8	109.0	117.9	132.6
Kherson	12.1	40.3	65.8	89.5	103.3	113.9
Ekaterinoslav	11.5	29.7	56.1	71.0	135.5	80.8
Tavrida	5.7	21.5	31.8	42.8	49.0	65.4
North Caucasus	0.7	8.1	20.0	51.3	92.6	112.6
Don Oblast	0.7	8.1	20.0	51.3	92.6	112.6
III. Central Agricultural	244.7	969.9	1,297.1	1,572.2	2,213.8	2,319.3
Central Chernozem	126.8	412.0	558.8	620.4	952.7	1,011.6
Voronezh	24.3	127.7	155.8	14.4	222.5	252.4
Kursk	32.1	110.1	165.0	245.4	272.7	240.0
Orel	35.5	85.3	122.7	193.3	221.6	267.9
Tambov	34.9	88.9	115.3	167.3	235.9	251.3
Volga	117.9	556.9	738.3	951.8	1,261.1	1,307.7
Astrakhan	4.2	29.0	53.6	71.9	77.3	90.8

TABLE 2-1 (cont.)

Regions and Provinces	Average Annual Number of Issued Passports (in Thousands)					
	1861–1870	1871–1880	1881–1890	1891–1900	1902	1906–1910
Saratov	14.4	69.4	107.3	143.9	176.1	143.7
Samara	6.8	31.6	34.6	51.4	129.6	111.0
Penza	24.0	77.9	91.1	123.8	153.3	147.9
Simbirsk	15.6	92.5	133.5	137.8	166.1	171.5
Kazan	15.0	89.4	108.9	145.6	199.5	219.2
Viatka	31.8	143.6	174.1	220.2	268.4	310.7
Ufa	6.1	23.5	35.2	57.2	90.8	112.9
IV. Eastern Agricultural	20.9	119.6	161.3	231.1	291.5	328.1
Ural	20.9	119.6	161.3	231.1	291.5	328.1
Perm	13.8	80.8	121.0	192.0	228.9	252.4
Orenburg	7.1	38.8	40.3	39.1	62.6	75.7
Total	1233.4	3570.7	4730.4	6211.4	7775.6	8771.6

Source: Adapted from L. E. Mints, *Otkhod krest'ianskogo naseleniia na. Zarabotki V SSSR* (Moscow, 1925), pp. 16–18.

fully urbanized—to a large degree unparalleled in other European peasant societies, where the absence of mutually reinforcing legal and cultural bonds to the land facilitated a more rapid and complete division of labor into peasants and proletarians.

The impact of migration on regional peasant agriculture was enormous. A study conducted at the turn of the century in five districts of Vladimir Province—inventories of 100,000 households consisting of more than one-half million peasants—noted the following patterns: "Only 16.2 percent of men of working age are employed in agriculture alone and more than half of all [male] workers have broken from the land. And among those 16 percent who are employed only in agriculture, a full half are aged 51–60—that is, peasants who have been rejected from industrial activity."[10] The tensions created by this growing dichotomy between village and workplace intersected at three key junctures, each of which underscored the growing insecurity of dependent family members who remained in the village: (1) *old versus young*, as the growth of wage labor undermined the foundations of the traditional patriarchal economy; (2) *male versus female*, since labor migration in the Central Industrial Region was primarily a male phenomenon, with males outnumbering females by almost six to one in hired labor as late as 1897;[11] and (3)

[10] A. V. Smirnov, "Zemledelie i zemledelets tsentral'noi promyshlennoi gubernii," *Russkaia Mysl'*, no. 7 (1901): 174.

[11] S. N. Prokopovich, "Krest'ianstvo i poreformennaia fabrika," *Velikaia reforma*, VI (Moscow, 1911), p. 270. While the rate of growth of men's *otkhod* had more or less stabilized by the 1890s, women's *otkhod* showed a marked increase near the end of the century—reflecting greater restrictions on child labor, increased mechanization, and a fundamental shift in village social structure.

TABLE 2-2.
Peasant Labor Migration as a Proportion of Village Population, 1861–1910

Regions and Provinces	Proportion of Issued Passports to Local Peasant Population					
	1861–1870	*1871–1880*	*1881–1890*	*1891–1900*	*1902*	*1906–1910*
I. Non-Agricultural/Industrial						
North and Northwest						
Arkhangel'sk	5.9	13.0	11.3	12.6	14.7	13.8
Vologda	1.8	6.1	6.0	8.2	10.4	10.7
Olonets	3.2	9.1	9.6	12.4	13.4	13.2
St. Petersburg	8.6	17.9	21.8	28.9	27.6	23.0
Novgorod	4.5	11.6	10.5	13.1	13.4	14.2
Pskov	2.0	3.3	3.6	6.2	8.7	10.4
Smolensk	6.3	11.2	10.3	11.2	12.6	13.0
Tver	8.0	14.6	14.4	16.7	22.6	23.0
Central Industrial Region						
Iaroslavl	9.1	17.0	16.4	18.9	24.1	23.1
Moscow	10.0	18.0	20.4	29.9	33.9	34.2
Vladimir	4.8	16.0	16.7	19.1	26.1	24.2
Kostroma	3.9	12.3	13.8	13.1	7.6	20.0
Kaluga	8.8	17.2	18.3	20.5	25.8	25.4
Nizhnii Novgorod	3.1	8.8	9.6	11.0	13.1	12.0
Tula	4.2	8.8	9.9	14.3	20.1	20.0
Riazan	5.4	12.7	14.3	17.5	22.7	20.5
Belorussia						
Vitebsk	3.5	5.0	6.0	8.3	10.8	10.9
Minsk	1.1	2.8	4.6	4.9	10.0	4.1
Mogilev	1.6	4.5	5.0	6.0	6.5	9.1
II. Southern Agricultural						
Ukraine						
Poltava	1.4	4.2	5.9	7.0	8.2	6.3
Khar'kov	1.2	3.6	5.9	7.2	9.9	9.2
Chernigov	1.4	4.2	5.7	6.9	8.3	8.0
Kiev	0.6	2.5	6.1	8.5	7.2	7.8
Volynia	0.6	2.0	3.2	3.7	0.5	3.2
Podol'ia	0.4	1.7	3.6	4.2	3.9	4.1
Kherson	1.2	3.3	4.4	4.8	4.8	5.0
Ekaterinoslav	1.2	2.4	3.7	3.9	6.3	3.2
Tavrida	1.4	4.2	4.8	4.9	3.8	5.0
North Caucasus						
Don Oblast	0.1	0.5	1.1	2.3	3.7	4.0
III. Central Agricultural						
Central Chernozem						
Voronezh	1.3	5.7	6.1	7.4	8.5	8.0
Kursk	1.8	5.3	7.0	9.2	11.9	10.0
Orel	2.6	5.3	6.7	9.2	11.6	12.2
Tambov	1.9	4.2	4.7	5.9	8.8	8.2
Volga						
Astrakhan	1.9	10.8	15.9	17.6	8.3	9.0

TABLE 2-2 (cont.)

	Proportion of Issued Passports to Local Peasant Population					
Regions and Provinces	1861–1870	1871–1880	1881–1890	1891–1900	1902	1906–1910
Saratov	0.9	3.8	5.2	6.1	7.7	6.0
Samara	0.4	1.6	1.5	1.9	4.6	3.4
Penza	2.1	6.1	6.2	7.6	10.6	10.0
Simbirsk	1.4	7.5	9.3	8.6	10.8	10.0
Kazan	1.0	5.3	5.6	6.7	9.2	9.2
Viatka	1.5	5.8	6.1	6.9	8.5	8.8
Ufa	0.5	1.7	3.2	3.0	3.9	4.3
IV. Eastern Agricultural						
Ural						
Perm	0.6	3.2	4.3	6.1	7.5	7.0
Orenburg	1.2	5.6	4.9	4.1	3.9	4.3

Source: Adapted from L. E. Mints, *Otkhod krest'ianskogo naseleniia na. Zarabotki V SSSR* (Moscow, 1925), pp. 22–24.

community versus household, since growing strains on smaller and weakened peasant households in the Central Industrial Region led families to rely increasingly on the village commune for redistributing the products of wage labor back to the village.

Essential as it was for popular well-being and industrial development, peasant labor migration posed a serious challenge to institutions at all levels: the state, the community, and the migrant's household. For the state, a more mobile population hindered efforts to gain information about, control, and tax the rural population, upon whom the overwhelming burden of fiscal solvency fell. As a district tax inspector from Moscow Province complained: "Work in factories and shops, significantly raising the tax-paying ability of the population, in actuality exerts an unfavorable influence on tax receipts. . . . The earnings received, with rare exceptions, are left in the inns and factory stores; only a negligible part of those earnings reach home, which scarcely suffice for keeping a family."[12] For state tax authorities, the primary task lay in expropriating the product of peasant labor, a task that became extremely complicated when the bulk of peasant income was derived from cash wages earned outside of the village. The outmoded tax system therefore placed an enormous, unforeseen burden on the local village administration and the police. Theirs was the unenviable task of keeping track of labor migrants, and assuring that they fulfilled their fiscal responsibilities.

However, the difficulty of keeping track of *otkhodniki* was not merely a matter for state concern. Migration posed a direct threat to whole communities in two ways. First, it fundamentally altered the internal dynamics of the patriarchal peasant household, challenging the traditional capacity of elders

[12] *SP*, II, p. 100. Also, see *SP*, II, pp. 55, 71.

and family chiefs to reallocate the labor products of junior family members. Second, unrestricted whole-family departures increased the proportion of fixed state dues for the households that remained, threatening to plunge villagers into greater hardship.

As the primary foundation of family subsistence in the Central Industrial Region gradually shifted from local and household-based production to non-local wage labor, the hierarchical structure of the traditional peasant family was undermined. A report from Vladimir Province in 1899 vividly illustrates the tension:

> With the change in the form of obtaining a means for living, family relations are also changing in the countryside. When the whole family works together, earnings are likewise made together. When only individual members of the household begin to acquire a means independently, each on his own, then naturally there appears the desire to retain hold of that which has been earned for oneself personally and only for one's own [immediate] family. Hence, there are constant complaints on the part of elders about [household] divisions, about the fact that the young forget the home. When the junior members of the family become the main bread winners in the peasant household, their role in the family also changes. Elders have already ceased to enjoy the absolute authority they wielded in earlier times. "When the young grow up," laments one correspondent, "they don't obey their elders [any more], but only behave defiantly."[13]

Families remaining at home expressed an uneasy confidence in those household members who left the village for earnings: particularly the youth "who become accustomed to the easy, wild life" away from the village and who were, it was feared, all too ready to abandon their responsibilities at home.[14] As villagers in Pokrov District, Vladimir Province complained: "Outside labor tears the people away from agriculture; . . . young people, working in the factories, have completely lost touch with agriculture and they don't even know how to handle a plough or a scythe."[15]

Observers noted the growing preference among village youths to break permanently with the village:

> Several members of the [peasant] family—sons, brothers, nephews—who have returned from military service or work outside the village, where they have been on several occasions, having become habituated to a more independent life, with easier work, are beginning to feel bur-

[13] *Obzor Vladimirskoi gubernii v sel'skokhoziaistvennom otnoshenii za 1899 god*, pt. III (Vladimir, 1900), p. 34.

[14] Smirnov, "Zemledelie i zemledelets," p. 184.

[15] *Obzor Vladimirskoi gubernii . . . za 1899 god*, pt. III, pp. 33–34.

dened by heavy peasant labor and their subordinate status as younger members of the family, and [therefore] work poorly, obey poorly, and are dissatisfied with everything. Finally, they declare directly that they do not want to live at home anymore, and will accordingly leave for "the side" and not return if only they are given their share.[16]

The threat of abandonment was great, the fate of families left in the village particularly precarious: "with the abandonment of the farm and with the sale of the farming implements comes the decline [of the household], and those who remain in the village, who often sit without even a piece of bread, receive no assistance from those living on the side."[17] Villagers offered a number of explanations for this abandonment, but almost all of these came down to the temptations associated with industrial and urban life, and the corruption of traditional values, the decadence and wastefulness it engendered.

Charges of spiritual laxness, decadence, and immorality were inseparably linked in popular perceptions of *otkhodniki*. The "free atmosphere, the easy, high–paying work" in the town or factory enticed all *otkhodniki*.[18] A village priest from Vladimir Province complained:

> Migration to the factory exerts a corrupting influence on the workers and their families. A departing youth, lacking any of the supervision of family elders and having for himself a steady flow of money and free time, does not concern himself with the household, gets into the habit of undesirable vices, debauchery, a loss of morality, indifference to religion and to the rites of the Church. On Good Friday, a worker thinks nothing about duty until [he is] disgracefully drunk, gorging himself with sausage, playing the accordion, dancing and singing various songs. It's a fact! Of course, this exists in a minority [of cases], but it exists. . . . For several years they do not go to confession and do not partake of the blessed Sacraments; nineteen, twenty, twenty-two year olds refuse to get married, but instead prefer to live together conjugally outside the law. . . .[19]

For those dependents who remained in the village, the alleged moral degeneration of young peasant-workers was directly reflected in their carelessness with money. *Otkhodniki* were said to "spend a lot on clothes and in general live wastefully." It was generally believed that their "Side-earnings would

---

[16] Z. N., "O krest'ianskikh semeinykh razdelakh," *Pravo* no. 12 (1901): 638. Also, see V. Dadonov, " 'Russkii Manchestr' (Pis'mo ob Ivanovo-Voznesenske)," *Russkoe Bogatstvo*, no. 12 (1900): 58; and D. N. Zhbankov, *Bab'ia storona: Statistiko–etnograficheskii ocherk* (Kostroma, 1891), pp. 25–27.

[17] *Obzor Vladimirskoi gubernii . . . za 1897 god* (Vladimir, 1898), p. 499.

[18] Ibid., p. 37.

[19] Quoted by Smirnov, "Zemledelie i zemledelets," p. 184.

suffice to make every peasant rich, if [they were spent] on a peasant's budget. . . . Every *otkhodnik* wastes 6 rubles a month just on food—at home this money would feed a whole family." "They drink tea with wheat bread twice a day, while for the *muzhik*"—who must save his money—"lentil cake is better than wheat." *Otkhodniki* "waste a lot on clothes, watches, accordions and other 'appurtenances of the toilet.' "[20] Time and again, the same sad story was heard: money that should have been sent back to the village was being wasted on vodka, gambling, and other seductions.

Regardless of whether the growing independence of *otkhodniki* posed any real threat to the livelihood of family members in the village, the *perception* of their vulnerability was sufficient to dictate a policy of strict control over migrants. Such regulation was regarded as both a moral and an economic imperative. Family members who lived in the village, dependent on the steady flow of cash from peasant-worker earnings, were threatened by a pervasive sense of insecurity.

The evidence of a growing cultural crisis was the marked proliferation in the rate of peasant household divisions in the decades immediately following the Emancipation. As the Valuev commission report concluded in the 1870s: "Family divisions have increased with each year [since the Emancipation] and it has reached the point that not only two brothers, but even a father and son break off into separate households."[21] According to data from the Ministry of Internal Affairs, during the years 1861–1882, there was an average of 116,229 household divisions annually. In the years 1874–1884, the average annual number of divisions had jumped to 140,355, so that by 1884, 52.4 percent of all peasant households in 37 provinces of European Russia had only one or no adult male worker in the family.[22]

The accelerated splintering of large, multiple-family households after 1861 was confirmed by the 1897 census. A regional analysis of household size, available in Table 2-3, shows the relative impact of household divisions on peasant families in the Central Industrial Region. On the whole, peasant households in the Central Industrial Region had an average of one to two fewer member-workers than households in any other region of European Russia, excluding the north and notheast. The earlier picture of the elder-patriarch managing a multiple-family unit gave way to the simple family head as chief in his own household of five or six members: "given the fre-

---

[20] *Obzor Vladimirskoi gubernii v . . . za 1899 god*, pt. III, pp. 34–35.

[21] See N. K. Brzheskii, *Ocherki iuridicheskogo byta krest'ian* (St. Petersburg, 1902), p. 112.

[22] Ibid., p. 156; V. A. Fedorov, "Semeinye razdely v Russkoi poreformennoi derevne," *Sel'skoe khoziaistvo i krest'ianstvo severo-zapada RSFSR v dorevoliutsionnyi period* (Smolensk, 1979), p. 30; "Razdely semeinye," *Entsiklopedicheskii slovar'*, F. A. Brokgauz and I. A. Efron, eds., 82 vols. (St. Petersburg, 1890–1904). Also, see the discussion in Cathy A. Frierson, "*Razdel*: The Peasant Family Divided," *The Russian Review* 46, no. 1 (January 1987): 35–52.

quency of family divisions, the authority of the father has been rendered too weak to prevent children from living any way they like."[23]

Weakened by divisions and by increasing, long-term departure of adult male workers for outside earnings, peasant households in the Central Industrial Region became more dependent than ever on the village commune to ensure family security: only the village commune could harness the resources necessary to redistribute peasant-workers' wage earnings from the workplace back to the village.

A separate cause for concern was the trend toward whole-family resettlement. Since fiscal obligations were imposed collectively on whole communities, not individuals or households, each departure from the community threatened to raise the already excessive obligations of the households that remained. This report from Moscow Province in 1882 delineated the trend:

TABLE 2-3.
Peasant Household Size in European Russia, 1897

Zone/Region	Distribution of Peasant Households (Based on Proportion to Total in European Russia)	Average No. Inhabitants per Household
Non-Agricultural Zone	18.94	6.2
Moscow	5.09	6.04
Northwest	5.66	6.9
Upper Volga	8.19	5.8
Middle Agricultural Zone	35.03	6.7
Oka river	6.37	6.8
Central Agricultural	11.16	6.9
Middle Volga	7.90	6.3
Left-Bank Ukraine	9.60	6.9
Western Zone	16.48	9.5
Baltic	0.51	13.5
Belorussia-Litkuania	6.90	9.5
Right-Bank Ukraine	9.07	7.7
Steppe Zone	18.48	7.8
South Steppe	10.69	8.8
Southeast Steppe	7.79	9.1
North and Northeast Zone	11.07	6.1
Northeast	8.17	6.0
North	2.90	6.2

Source: P. G. Ryndziunskii, *Krest'iane i gorod v kapitalisticheskoi Rossii vtoroi poloviny XIX veka* (Moscow, 1983), pp. 22–23 (Based on the 1897 census).

[23] A. A. Isaev, "V Iaroslavskoi gubernii (iz putevykh zametok)," *Otechestvennye Zapiski*, ser. 3, 251, no. 8 (August 1880): 179.

Such *Riazan'tsy*, who—in their own words—have come "for earnings," are met rather more frequently in the factories of Moscow District than they were in former times. The workers themselves explain that this influx of workers from Smolensk and Kaluga Provinces to Moscow factories [is due to] the poor quality of land in those provinces and the insufficient size of allotments—as a result of which, had they remained home, they would not have had the means for the payment of taxes. Overwhelmed by concerns about their "daily bread," they emigrate with their entire families and settle somewhere near a factory. Meanwhile, the land—in the best cases—is worked by some members of the family who have remained home. And not infrequently it is hired out for a negligible price or simply given back to the village commune. On the whole, the desire to relinquish the land completely is found rather frequently among these workers, since the land is giving them no profits whatsoever and only augments the items of expense in their extremely modest budgets, keeping them completely under its burden.[24]

Particularly in the 1870s and 1880s, the burden of the land and the enticements of urban life were sufficient to encourage widespread whole-family resettlement. As tax reforms in the mid-1880s reduced land expenses—especially in the Central Industrial Region, where annual fiscal obligations declined by at least 20–30 percent per household—and the cost of urban living skyrocketed, it became impossible to live either wholly off the land or entirely from outside earnings.[25]

While the rate of growth of whole-family departures therefore declined by the 1890s, whole-family migration nonetheless showed a strong and steady increase. In Tver Province, for instance, the number of issued family passports increased from 16,808 families in 1893 to 18,046 families in 1896.[26] This growth in whole-family departures was directly associated with abandonment of village ties. For example, of the 47,376 peasant families with family passports in Moscow Province during the late 1890s, 35,177 had no cottage in the village: this represented 14.3 percent or one in seven of all peasant households in the province.[27] Communes were therefore faced with the con-

---

[24] *Sbornik statisticheskikh svedenii po Moskovskoi gubernii: Otdel sanitarnoi statistiki* III, pt. 4 (Moscow, 1882), p. 124.

[25] For a chronology of the rate of divestment and reinvestment into peasant agriculture in the Central Industrial Region, see Vikhliaev, "Ob ustoichivosti," pp. 89–90. On reductions of land obligations, see Ministerstvo Vnutrennykh Del, Tsentral'nyi Statisticheskii Komitet, *Ponizhenie vykupnogo platezhi* (St. Petersburg, 1885), appendix, pp. 82–111.

[26] *Statisticheskii ezhegodnik Tverskoi gubernii za 1897 god*, pt. II (Tver, 1898), p. 28.

[27] A. A. Bulgakov, *Sovremennyia peredvizheniia krest'ianstva. Napravleniia, razmery i usloviia krest' ianskikh dvizhenii Moskovskoi gubernii po novym tsifrovym dannym za desiatiletie 1894–1903 gg.* (St. Petersburg, 1905), pp. 15–16.

siderable challenge of extracting dues from whole families absent from the village.

IN DEFENSE OF PEASANT PATRIARCHALISM: INSTITUTIONAL RESPONSES TO PEASANT MIGRATION

The threats to household and village security posed by migration for earnings generated a communally sanctioned policy of strict control over *otkhodniki*. In this way, village interests in high-migration districts were unexpectedly aligned with those of state officials: communes shared with the state the concern surrounding potential abandonment by wayward migrants. Both faced the difficult task of expropriating non-village earnings through existing village institutions.

The thrust of state policy throughout the post-reform period (prior to the Stolypin reforms in 1906) was therefore to support communal efforts to regulate *otkhodniki*. Essentially, the state sought to coopt communal forms of social control by aligning its own initiatives with the interests of the traditional village hierarchy. The gist of these shared interests was reflected in a *volost'* court resolution in Moscow Province during the 1860s:

> the father is the total master in the home; the sons have no kind of individual property outside of the life of the father, and only with his blessing are they able to separate. Frequently, the *volost'* court receives a petition from the son requesting apportionment of part of the property of the father, but such petitions are always ignored. Parental power must be observed and upheld, and besides, while the sons live with the father they pay their taxes more punctually.[28]

Patriarchalism was the cultural and legal basis that endowed village communities with considerable leverage over departing members. This tactic of implementing legal solutions to strengthen the vitality of traditional hierarchies was applied throughout European Russia. Only in the Central Industrial Region, however, did regionally specific conditions facilitate the development of an apparatus sufficiently powerful and far-reaching to enforce such regulations.

In their efforts to empower communal institutions, state officials, on the one hand, vigorously pursued the collection of taxes and arrears, convinced of the "stubbornness and unwillingness of peasants to pay dues without co-

[28] Quoted in S. V. Pakhman, *Obychnoe grazhdanskoe pravo v Rossii: iuridicheskie ocherki*, 2 vols., II (St. Petersburg, 1877–1879), pp. 142–43. For an excellent survey of state efforts to uphold peasant patriarchal authority in the Russian countryside, see James I. Mandel, "Paternalistic Authority in the Russian Countryside, 1856–1906" (Ph.D. diss., Columbia University, 1978).

ercive measures."[29] On the other, they endowed peasant communal institutions with powerful sanctions for expropriating those obligations from community members. These sanctions were listed in article 188 of the Emancipation statute: (1) compensate for arrears through the seizure of the delinquent's personal immovable property; (2) hire out the delinquent, or his family members, for work, deducting the wages for communal use; (3) designate a guardian for the delinquent household; (4) sell the delinquent's movable property; (5) sell part of the delinquent's immovable property, which is not considered to be essential to the farmstead; (6) seize the delinquent's allotment.[30]

In practice, these enhanced sanctions—intended for use in rural tax collection—were wielded in equal measure by communal authorities to coerce the fulfillment of an *otkhodnik's* family obligations. The appartus evolved into an imperfect hybrid of bureaucratic initiative and cooptation of "little community" norms founded on concerns about subsistence and family security. In this lay both the principal strength and weakness of state fiscal policy. The key tension consisted of the commune's conflicting roles as both an extension of the state apparatus *and* a cultural entity. The gist of this tension was best expressed by N. K. Brzheskii, the leading contemporary authority on peasant taxation in Russia:

> Village authorities, who are inclined as a general rule to be over-indulgent towards taxpayers, do not bring in taxes until [there is] an insistence on the part of the police; but once the police have started to act, the sternest measures are employed, quite often at a time when peasants have no money for paying taxes. . . .[31]

In the context of the Russian fiscal system, non-fulfillment of obligations by some households threatened to increase the already excessive dues of every other household in the village. In their efforts to prevent or alleviate such developments, all villagers—rich and poor, solvent and delinquent—collectively pursued a wide variety of manipulative schemes to keep *otkhodniki* tied to the village, and to redistribute migrant earnings from the workplace to the village.

Very frequently, peasant-workers completely break every connection with their homes, living at the factory by themselves, away from their

[29] From a memorandum in the state revenue office of Tver Province dated 13 July 1896, quoted in *Statisticheskii ezhegodnik Tverskoi gubernii za 1897 god*, pt. II, p. 106.

[30] Summary of Paragraph 188, 19 February 1861, *Polnoe Sobranie Zakonov* (hereafter, *PSZ*), 2nd ser., no. 36,657. *SP*, II, p. 51. *Volost'* court rights and responsibilities were defined in article 102.

[31] *Nedoimochnost' i krugovaia poruka sel'skikh obschestv. Istoriko-kriticheskii obzor deistvuiushchego zakonodatel'stva, v sviazi s praktikoiu krest'ianskogo podatnogo dela* (St. Petersburg, 1897), p. 411.

families. Those fellow villagers who remain in the village are perfectly cognizant that their situation is most unfavorable, and begin a subtle struggle with departing workers, in order to compel them to part with their good earnings. . . . Assessing such workers certain duties which are to the advantage of the community is practiced extensively.[32]

The pressure was particularly great in Non-Black-Earth areas, where there was a disproportionate relation between land income and state dues. In the Central Industrial Region, the Emancipation settlement and state fiscal policies since the 1860s had redefined the status of the repartitional commune: excessive dues had transformed its purpose into a mechanism for the redistribution of burden.

As a result, there was a marked aversion to accumulating allotment lands among peasants on Non-Black-Earth districts. "Cases of the use of supplementary reapportionments (*krugovaia poruka*) do not take place, nor are there cases of the deprivation of delinquents of land, nor does one find anyone desiring to take this land for themselves, [since this would mean] taking on all of the taxes belonging to it."[33] This aversion to taking on additional allotments—those given up to the commune (*upalye nadely*) and those seized for non-payment of dues (*otobrannye nadely*)—may be contrasted to procedures in areas where agriculture was more profitable: in the Central Agricultural Region, for instance, fellow-villagers were often eager to expand landholdings through the communal right of expropriation.[34]

Meanwhile, communes in the Central Industrial Region aggressively fought to bind peasant-workers to the land. As the governor from Vladimir Province reported at the beginning of the 1880s: in Non-Black-Earth regions, "resettlement is made particularly inconvenient until the end of the redemption operation, since on poor land, after having released working hands, the village commune frequently proves to be incapable of liquidating redemption debts."[35] Communes in the Central Industrial Region were generally unwilling to permit families to break their connections with the village completely. As one commune in Moscow Province reasoned in a resolution from late in the century: "if peasants were [permitted to] leave the commune, then there would no longer be a sufficient number of persons for the payment of state taxes and arrears."[36]

[32] *Obzor Vladimirskoi gubernii . . . za 1899 god*, pt. III, p. 34.

[33] Based on a report in V. I. Barykov, A. V. Polovstev, and P. A. Sokolovskii, eds., *Sbornik materialov dlia izucheniia sel'skoi pozemel'noi obshchiny*, I (St. Petersburg, 1880), p. 236.

[34] See the example in ibid., I, p. 192.

[35] Quoted in B. V. Tikhonov, *Pereseleniia v Rossii vo vtoroi polovine XIX v. (po materialam perepisi 1897 g. i pasportnoi statistika)* (Moscow, 1978), p. 115.

[36] Ibid., p. 134. For comparable cases, see A. P. Svirshchevskii, ed., *Otkhozhie promysly krest'ian Iaroslavskoi gubernii* (Iaroslavl, 1896), p. 23; *Otkhozhie promysly krest'ianskogo naseleniia Iaroslavskoi gubernii (po dannym o pasportakh za 1896–1902 gg.)* (Iaroslavl, 1907), pp. 23, 38, 75.

Given the inevitable difficulty of finding others to take land at prices that exceeded its productive value, tenancy agreements developed a distinct regional form. The typical procedure was one in which the allotment's owner, unable to work the land profitably, tried to minimize his own losses by sharing the fees with renters. Normally, the *otkhodnik* simply signed over the land to a family member, another member of the community, or to the disposition of the entire commune. The migrant usually agreed to pay the difference between the taxes (and redemption payments and the actual market price that could be obtained through land utilization. The logic was obvious: in Non-Black-Earth districts "it is more advantageous to pay part of the taxes, and be without any allotment, than it is to take the land and carry all of the taxes."[37] As a rule, to guarantee fulfillment of obligations, communes insisted that land be given up for village use, and that the *otkhodnik* pay the annual dues—a departure fee which was known in the village as an *otpusknoe* or *spusta*. Typical was this case in Vladimir Province during the late-nineteenth century:

> One village in Suzdal District, where land income exceeds the payments attached to it and where those leaving for the factory previously gave their land up for rent and even received for it an insignificant payment, there was recently passed a resolution whereby no one could give his allotment up for rent without the permission of the mir. In this way, peasant-workers have been kept from exploiting their land, having been coerced either to pay all the taxes or to give it up to the commune, paying for it seven rubles per year. Likewise, the commune will not give its authorization for the [complete] redemption of the allotment. In such a way, the village commune does with great success extract kopecks from its members.[38]

This procedure was founded on the commune's right—granted in paragraph 130 of the Emancipation statute—to restrict any household's dispossession of the land.

Despite the emergence of a wide variety of local innovations, existing sources reveal that the procedures for temporarily giving up one's allotment were quite similar throughout the Central Industrial Region. V. Dadonov ob-

---

[37] F. G. Terner, "Krest'ianskie platezhi i sposoby ikh vzyskaniia," *Vestnik Evropy*, no. 10 (1895): 474. Also, see V. Vorontsov, *Progressivnyia techeniia v krest'ianskom khoziaistve* (St. Petersburg, 1892).

[38] *Obzor Vladimirskoi gubernii . . . za 1899 god*, pt. III, p. 34. See also Smirnov, "Zemledelie i zemledelets," pp. 177–79; A. V. Smirnov, "Iz nabliudenii zemskogo statistika," *Russkoe Bogatstvo*, no. 4 (1904): 8, 10–11. On the conditions for a household's complete withdrawal from the commune and registration as a private landholder, see *PSZ*, II, no. 36, 657, 19 February 1861: chapter 5, paragraph 130. For evidence of the support among state officials for such exactions, see *SP*, II, p. 95.

served similar schemes among peasant-workers from villages around Ivanovo-Voznesensk during the 1890s, where the departing adult male worker
as a rule remained responsible for the payment of obligations on the land:
"the commune obliges the departing member to pay 3 rubles annually as a
'departure fee,' and if the departing member leaves a hut in the village, even
if it is boarded up, he adds 1–2 rubles more."[39] In Suzdal District, this departure fee measured 7–10 rubles annually per one-soul allotment, versus 8–16
rubles plus natural labor duties if the *otkhodnik* worked the land himself.[40] In
Nizhnii Novgorod Province and Dmitrov District, Moscow, this charge was
dubbed the *guliatskii obrok*—or "wanderer's tax."[41] In Nizhnii Novgorod, the
guliatskii obrok ranged from 38–63 percent of the annual assessment for a single-soul allotment. Sometimes, however, the *guliatskii obrok* exceeded annual
obligations on the land, a charge that villagers usually encouraged, since an
otkhodnik's absence freed him from onerous *natural duties* (such as road work,
police duty, etc.).[42] Typically, such a departure fee was designated in a written agreement with the commune signed prior to the *otkhodnik's* departure.[43]

8. AN ARTEL OF MIGRANT LABORERS ON THEIR WAY INTO NON-AGRICULTURAL WORK (COMPARE
THE BETTER QUALITY OF FOOTWEAR WORN BY *OTKHODNIKI* HERE WITH THAT WORN BY MIGRANT
LABORERS IN ILLUSTRATION 14) (JOHN FOSTER FRASER, *RUSSIA OF TO-DAY* [LONDON: CASSELL AND
COMPANY, LTD., 1915], FOLLOWING P. 104).

[39] Dadonov, " 'Russkii Manchestr'," p. 58.

[40] Smirnov, "Zemledelie i zemledelets," p. 178.

[41] *SP*, II, p. 96.

[42] *SP*, II, p. 57. The data is based on eighty-seven villages in Nizhnii Novgorod Province.

[43] For an example of such a written agreement, see Zaionchkovskii, *Otmena*, pp. 301–2. On
the requirement of preliminary signed contracts among migrants with tax arrears, see *SP*, II,
p. 77.

The written contract was an important assurance both to the commune as well as to the migrant, for whom the guarantee of a right to his allotment was a safety net during economic downturns, illness, and old age: "The farmstead ordinarily remains in the ownership of the departing adult worker, since he gives up the field land only for a time, and not forever."[44] The legal standing of such written agreements was amply demonstrated in the years following the Stolypin reforms. Even among peasant families in Moscow Province who had for 15–35 years lived and worked outside of their villages, a large number returned to their native communities and successfully reclaimed their long-neglected allotments as private disposable property.[45]

Available data suggest that the majority of peasants departing for side-earnings gave their land up to the commune rather than in private rental agreements with individual fellow-villagers. In Dorogobuzh District, Smolensk, from a cross-sample of 500 heads of peasant households working "on the side" in 1889, 339 gave their land up to the commune, while 161 peasant household heads transferred it to other individuals in the village.[46] Communes encouraged written and formal legal procedures so as to protect the village from inevitable disputes over who was responsible for paying dues on the land. In the majority of districts, rental contracts had to be approved by the commune.[47] In Sychëvka District, Smolensk, in extreme cases where delinquent allotments were seized, communes refused to recognize transactions in which tax delinquents had given the land over to someone else, and seized the allotments for the commune, with the renter of the land suffering damages.[48] Likely tenants were in this way urged to secure prior approval of the commune, while otkhodniki were encouraged to pay the departure fees and then turn the land over to the disposition of the commune. Land was then rented at reduced rates (more closely reflecting the actual productive value of the land) or—in the absence of interested renters—it was redistributed among selected households. In this way, villages in the Non-Black-Earth Zone raided the cash economy for receipts which were used to subsidize the ailing village economy.

Communes imposed the terms of full or partial fulfillment of land obligations on otkhodniki through their power—shared with volost' authorities—to manipulate the issuing of needed internal passports. This vestige of serfdom, strengthened after Emancipation, was a powerful mechanism which ex-

---

[44] SP, II, p. 96.

[45] On the enormous number of legal battles surrounding such claims to the land during the years 1908–1910, see the fascinating discussion in "Nishchenstvo," Statisticheskoe ezhegodnik Moskovskoi gubernii za 1910 god (Moscow, 1911), pp. 89–91.

[46] SP, II, p. 110.

[47] Smirnov, "Sostoianie mestnykh . . . 1899 goda," p. 34.

[48] SP, II, p. 109.

tended the control of local authorities far beyond the village boundaries. The passport system placed the power to allocate peasant labor firmly in the hands of village and household chiefs. As the Governing Senate, the highest body responsible for interpreting legal precedent in autocratic Russia, resolved on 3 March 1892:

> To the peasant household chief, as the person who is responsible for the punctual payment of the taxes of the household, belongs the right to give his consent or refusal for the issuing of passports to an inseparable member of the family or to make an agreement conditional upon the fulfillment of certain obligations.[49]

For many administrators, such a sanction was the only guarantee for the prompt fulfillment of taxes and communal dues, "the sole connecting link, the sole basis for the preservation of the authority of the household chief."[50]

State efforts to uphold the legal authority of household patriarchs and to preserve the principle of the "indivisible family unit" was nothing more than the confirmation of peasant customary law. In his analysis of *volost'* court proceedings in the area around Iaroslavl, the famed ethnographer E. I. Iakushkin summarized the general pattern that he observed:

> An adult son is able to leave the home for earnings. The passport, however, is issued each time only with the permission of the father, the household elder or chief, under conditions which oblige payment of a fixed sum of money to the family (father) for the payment of taxes and for the fulfillment of needs. In the event of carelessness [on the part] of the son who has departed for earnings, if he stops sending money home because of negligence, or because he has himself received little compensation, the *volost'* court recognizes the right of the father to demand the return of the son to the native village.[51]

By and large, peasant courts upheld the authority of the household chiefs over household labor power, recognizing that to issue a son a passport without the father's authorization only "encourages . . . the young peasant gen-

---

[49] Resheniia Pravitel'stvuiushchego Senata, no. 1392. Cited in I. L. Goremykin, *Svod uzakonenii i rasporiazhenii pravitel'stva ob ustroistve sel'skogo sostoianiia i uchrezhdenii po krest'ianskim delam,* I, pt. 1 (St. Petersburg, 1900), p. 344. A law dated 3 June 1894 (*PSZ,* no. 10,709) raised this widely accepted principle of peasant customary law to the statutory level.

[50] See the discussion in M. S. Simonova, *Krizis agrarnoi politiki tsarizma nakanune pervoi rossiiskoi revoliutsii* (Moscow, 1987), pp. 117–18. The law that officially abolished parental control over peasant passports appeared as part of the Stolypin reform initiative, dated 5 October 1906.

[51] E. I. Iakushkin, with S. P. Nikonov, *Grazhdanskoe pravo po resheniiam Krestobogorodskogo volost'nogo suda Iaroslavskoi gubernii i uezda* (Iaroslavl, 1902), p. 179.

eration towards non-payment of duties and toward disobedience of parental power."[52]

The restriction of passports was extensive throughout the Central Industrial Region, common in all but one district each in Moscow and Vladimir provinces, the majority of districts in Riazan, Tver, Kaluga, Iaroslavl, and Kostroma, and large parts of the remaining provinces in the region.[53] Usually, *otkhodniki* were required as a condition for the issuing of a passport, to pay the current year's tax, or part of the arrears.[54] As we have seen, many communes simply merged passport fees with taxes (and bribes) into a single "departure fee" which had to be paid before an *otkhodnik's* passport could be issued or renewed. Very often, communes or *volost'* officials demanded a written agreement or leave-contract in which the departing worker formally identified his responsibilities, and provided a schedule of payment.[55]

Passport restrictions were applied differently from district to district. In Iaroslavl Province, for example, where accumulated arrears were low, payment of all or part of the arrears was a strict condition for the release of a passport in five districts. In Iaroslavl District, however, this demand was strictly applied only to those who would be away from the village for long periods of time; officials were more lenient toward those leaving for shorter periods, durations of less than a year.[56] In some districts, the use of passport restrictions as a means of extracting taxes and arrears required a formal resolution from the communal assembly, "depending on the person."[57] In several districts, the restrictions on passports applied not only to the heads of peasant households, but also to family members.[58]

Local officials were lenient in most cases; those peasant-workers who failed to come up with the requisite funds were often granted passports for shorter periods, from one to six months, the renewal of which would depend on the *otkhodnik's* payment from earnings sent back to the village.[59] Such short-term passports would, it was hoped, keep *otkhodniki* on a tighter rein, so as to encourage more responsible behavior. By and large, passport restrictions were imposed subjectively, depending on the perceived character of the person departing for earnings. A *volost'* elder in Moscow Province reasoned this way: he issued short-term passports principally to "unreliable

---

[52] Tikhonov, *Pereseleniia v Rossii*, p. 122.

[53] The following list contains areas specifically cited where passport restrictions of one form or another were applied: *SP*, II, pp. 38, 44–45, 52, 60, 67–68, 77–78, 88–89, 98, 105, 110.

[54] *SP*, II, pp. 38, 60, 67–68, 88–89, 98, 105, 110.

[55] For examples, see *SP*, II, pp. 77–78, 67.

[56] *SP*, II, pp. 67–68.

[57] *SP*, II, pp. 88, 60.

[58] *SP*, II, pp. 53, 67–68, 77, 88, 98.

[59] On short-term passports, see *SP*, II, pp. 44, 67–68. On the procedures for renewal, see pp. 44, 68, 88–89, 105, 110. On imposed restrictions, see pp. 60, 67–68, 77.

persons who have shown themselves to be careless in the payment of duties and who had lost his trust."[60]

The widespread use of short-term passports as a means for encouraging fulfillment of obligations is reflected in the data on passports issued in the Central Industrial Region during the late-nineteenth century. For the whole of European Russia, despite the fact that even in agricultural areas average *otkhod* was two to six months annually, the overwhelming majority of passports were short-term: an average of 49.5 percent of all passports issued in the years 1890–1896 were for three months or less; while one in four (26.9 percent) was for six months; and slightly less than one in four (23.7 percent) was for a year or more.[61] In the Central Industrial Region, where *otkhod* played a particularly significant role in gross peasant incomes, and where migrants' absence for earnings was increasingly year-round, the proportion of long-term passports was even lower. The data from Kostroma Province in 1887 were typical: just over half (50.3 percent) of all issued passports were for periods of three months or less; a third (31.58 percent) were for six months; and fewer than one in five (18.12 percent) of all passports were for a year or more. The growing awareness among *volost'* and village authorities of the need to restrict passports was reflected in the changing proportion of long- versus short-term passports: between 1869 and 1887, the proportion of passports for a year or more declined from less than one in four (23.8 percent) to less than one in five (18.2 percent); in the same period, the proportion of one-month passports rose from 38.73 percent to 46.84 percent.[62] Evidently, during this period communes had learned the efficacy of restricting passports to regulate *otkhodnik* behavior and to encourage the prompt fulfillment of obligations. (For a comparative summary of the data on passport duration between 1861 and 1910, see Table 2-4.)

Of course, communal authorities were not unaware that the rigid enforcement of a policy that deprived passports to those in arrears could be self-defeating in a context where peasant income relied overwhelmingly on cash sent from wages earned outside of the village. In parts of Kaluga Province, therefore, "passports were issued without hindrance: otherwise, due to the absence of local earnings, arrears would only increase. The renewal of passports for those absent is sometimes delayed due to their non-payment of assessed taxes."[63] In some areas, the need for outside earnings exceeded the risk of desertion, and communes did not restrict passports. The reasoning behind such decisions reveals, however, that such cases did not represent a rejection, but rather a reorientation of the commune's basic coercive strategy.

[60] Tikhonov, *Pereseleniia v Rossii*, p. 118.

[61] From Vikhliaev, "Ob ustoichivosti," p. 81.

[62] N. N. Vladimirskii, *Otkhod krest'ianstva Kostromskoi gubernii na zarabotki* (Kostroma, 1927), p. 84. Also, see Mints, *Otkhod krest'ianskogo naseleniia*, p. 29.

[63] *SP*, II, p. 105.

TABLE 2-4.

Passport Term in 43 Provinces of European Russia, 1861–1890

Regions and Provinces	1861–1870 (in percent)			1871–1880 (in percent)			1881–1890 (in percent)		
	1–3 Months	6 Months	One Year	1–3 Months	6 Months	One Year	1–3 Months	6 Months	One Year
I. Non-Agricultural/Industrial	12.5	43.4	44.1	36.9	29.9	33.1	38.7	29.9	31.
North and Northwest	17.1	41.5	41.4	38.2	30.1	31.7	38.1	29.0	32.
Arkhangel'sk	17.4	35.6	47.0	39.7	26.2	34.1	38.7	28.6	32.
Vologda	30.0	34.2	35.8	67.6	17.2	15.2	65.2	19.6	15.
Olonets	12.5	46.2	41.3	48.0	25.6	26.4	57.4	21.7	20.
St. Petersburg	2.3	36.7	61.0	21.2	29.7	49.1	20.2	26.8	53.
Novgorod	32.2	42.8	25.0	49.5	29.0	21.5	44.5	27.7	27.
Pskov	2.0	38.8	59.2	14.1	34.5	51.4	19.4	29.3	51.
Smolensk	24.5	48.4	27.1	32.0	42.9	25.1	28.9	42.7	28.
Tver	15.8	49.2	35.0	33.7	35.4	30.9	30.6	35.4	34.
Central Industrial Region	13.6	44.9	41.6	40.3	32.4	27.3	38.5	34.2	27.
Iaroslavl	7.3	29.3	63.4	27.3	23.7	49.0	26.9	23.9	49.
Moscow	10.8	44.1	45.1	22.1	39.7	38.2	17.6	43.3	39.
Vladimir	21.1	47.6	31.3	58.9	27.8	13.3	54.3	30.8	14.
Kostroma	23.6	40.6	35.8	63.1	21.4	15.5	66.0	21.8	12.
Kaluga	9.2	50.8	40.0	32.2	40.1	27.7	30.9	42.4	26.
Nizhnii Novgorod	15.4	49.7	34.9	55.8	27.9	16.3	55.0	27.6	17.
Tula	7.6	55.0	37.4	23.3	46.6	30.1	19.6	48.1	32.
Riazan	13.6	41.8	44.6	39.9	32.0	28.1	37.8	35.7	26.
Belorussia	6.9	43.8	49.3	32.2	27.4	40.4	39.6	26.5	34.
Vitebsk	0.2	51.9	47.9	20.0	34.1	45.9	29.5	32.2	38.
Minsk	8.2	37.6	54.2	38.2	19.6	42.2	50.1	18.6	31.
Mogilev	12.3	41.8	45.9	38.4	28.4	33.2	39.1	28.6	32.
II. Southern Agricultural	7.9	47.6	44.5	48.4	22.6	29.0	57.9	19.4	22.8
Ukraine	6.2	42.4	51.5	43.1	23.7	33.2	56.9	19.6	23.5
Poltava	13.8	59.1	27.1	58.3	27.5	14.2	67.7	19.1	13.2
Khar'kov	3.6	62.2	34.2	59.3	24.8	15.9	70.5	16.1	13.4
Chernigov	0.4	58.6	41.0	44.1	33.8	22.1	48.1	31.9	20.0
Kiev	1.6	36.4	62.0	35.0	22.5	42.5	64.0	16.2	19.8
Volynia	0.6	21.7	77.7	38.5	8.9	52.6	54.2	11.3	34.5
Podol'ia	0.3	31.0	68.8	24.6	23.4	52.0	54.6	16.8	28.6
Kherson	15.6	40.9	43.5	42.6	27.9	29.5	51.9	21.4	26.7
Ekaterinoslav	1.7	43.8	54.5	37.3	25.5	37.2	50.3	24.6	25.1
Tavrida	17.8	27.7	54.5	48.2	18.6	33.2	50.7	19.1	30.2
North Caucasus	9.7	52.8	37.5	53.7	21.5	24.8	58.9	19.1	22.0
Don Oblast	9.7	52.8	37.5	53.7	21.5	24.8	58.9	19.1	22.0
III. Central Agricultural	22.1	44.5	33.4	62.0	22.7	15.3	63.1	21.9	14.9
Central Chernozem	18.0	46.7	35.3	53.7	27.3	19.1	55.4	26.0	18.4
Voronezh	14.5	52.7	32.8	73.2	15.8	11.0	74.1	14.0	11.9
Kursk	20.3	50.5	29.2	52.7	32.1	15.2	58.2	25.6	16.2
Orel	20.9	45.4	33.7	41.7	33.9	24.4	41.3	36.3	21.4
Tambov	16.3	38.2	45.5	47.0	27.3	25.7	48.1	28.0	23.9
Volga	26.2	42.3	31.6	70.3	18.1	11.6	70.8	17.8	11.4

TABLE 2-4 (cont.)

	1861–1870 (in percent)			1871–1880 (in percent)			1881–1890 (in percent)		
Regions and Provinces	1 – 3 Months	6 Months	One Year	1 – 3 Months	6 Months	One Year	1 – 3 Months	6 Months	One Year
Astrakhan	29.3	42.0	28.7	79.8	10.5	9.7	82.2	8.3	9.5
Saratov	12.9	43.0	44.1	64.5	18.5	17.0	63.5	19.3	17.2
Samara	45.0	29.2	25.8	71.7	15.6	12.7	63.7	20.0	16.3
Penza	21.3	45.8	32.9	60.5	26.7	12.8	57.4	28.2	14.4
Simbirsk	25.3	44.9	29.8	72.5	17.9	9.6	76.5	16.1	7.4
Kazan	20.4	35.4	44.2	72.2	15.6	12.2	73.0	17.0	10.0
Viatka	31.8	39.2	29.0	74.1	15.2	10.7	74.8	15.9	9.3
Ufa	23.3	58.7	18.0	66.7	25.1	8.2	75.5	17.7	6.8
IV. Eastern Agricultural	34.6	39.6	25.8	78.0	14.4	7.7	78.6	14.0	7.5
Ural	34.6	39.6	25.8	78.0	14.4	7.7	78.6	14.0	7.5
Perm	21.0	47.4	31.6	82.0	10.6	7.4	81.5	11.3	7.2
Orenburg	48.2	31.8	20.0	73.9	18.2	7.9	75.7	16.6	7.7
Average Passport Term in 43 Provinces	15.9	43.3	40.9	48.8	25.6	25.6	52.3	24.5	23.2

Source: Adapted from L. E. Mints, *Otkhod krest'ianskogo naseleniia na. Zarabotki V SSSR* (Moscow, 1925), p. 29.

In four districts of Tula Province, for instance, where peasant agriculture was more extensive, passports were issued and renewed regardless of fulfillment of fiscal obligations, because here it was believed that "Land serves as a sufficient guarantee of payment."[64] In Smolensk: "Since the peasant workers, who leave by passport on the side, usually leave at home members of their own families, who are responsible for the punctual payment of duties, or give up their land to the mir or to individual fellow-villagers, then the village communes in a large proportion of the districts do not inhibit them in receiving passports."[65] In effect, communal members were usually satisfied if at least part of an *otkhodnik's* family remained hostage in the village.

In such cases, pressure was applied on migrants' families as a means of extorting earnings from absent members. In Danilov District, Iaroslavl Province, the absent delinquent's family was subjected to arrest, and the movable property was distrained.[66] Distraint—the seizure of peasant property pending payment of taxes or arrears—was one of the most common mechanisms for coercing villagers to fulfill obligations.[67] Generally, the threat of distraint

[64] *SP*, II, p. 38.
[65] *SP*, II, p. 110. Also, see *SP*, II, pp. 44, 88.
[66] *SP*, II, p. 68.
[67] *SP*, II, pp. 38, 44, 53, 60–61, 66, 75, 78, 87, 89, 99, 104.

was the first step. This gave households with arrears the opportunity to raise the needed money—either by pressuring household members working on the side, selling off property on their own (for a better price than public debt auctions), or borrowing from relatives, neighbors or local tradesmen. The second step, the actual seizure of property, usually consisted of the distraint of unessential movable property first—samovars, holiday or town clothing, watches—and only later moved to livestock, sheds, and farm equipment.[68] In most cases, the temporary seizure of property led to payment of at least part of a household's arrears. The overwhelming numerical disparity between cases of distraint and actual sales of property reveals the degree to which seizure and the threat to auction movable property were used to *coerce* cooperation in the payment of obligations. The data from Tver Province is typical for most of the Central Industrial Region. Between 1889 and 1892, peasant movable property was seized for arrears in 6,595 villages of Tver Province for a general sum of arrears of 148,158 rubles. Yet, sales were eventually held in only 811 villages—that is, in approximately 10–15 percent (per year) of all villages in which property was seized. Of all the money collected toward arrears during this period, more than two-thirds (59,895 rubles) was paid by peasants to release property prior to sale, while less than one-third (24,895 rubles) was collected as a result of the public sale of the seized property; together, the two procedures brought in almost 60 percent of the total arrears.[69]

The relative effectiveness of community strategies which exerted pressure on *otkhodniki* through family members was powerfully illustrated in an exchange of letters between a peasant-worker in St. Petersburg and his wife who lived in a village in northwest Kostroma Province. The effectiveness of passport manipulation as an instrument of control is evident in the husband's initial pleading:

> You did not write, my dear Anna Zinov'evna, whether you received the money. I sent 15 rubles on 21 August. You wrote [asking whether I would be returning] to the village, but I don't think so because money is short and it is bad to be without money in the village, but I thank you for the intention. If there is not great hardship, then write and I will come to the village. I remain alive and well. I inform you dear wife Anna Zinov'evna, I beg you: would it be impossible to send an annual pass-

[68] See *SP*, II, pp. 66, 77, 98. Certain items, such as icons, were generally excluded from distraint. See V. V. Tenishev, *Administrativnoe polozhenie Russkogo krest'ianstva* (St. Petersburg, 1908), pp. 100–101.

[69] Data drawn from *SP*, II, p. 89. For similar data in other provinces, see *SP*, II, pp. 38, 44, 60–61, 66, 75, 99, 104. Also, see A. M. Anfimov, *Ekonomicheskoe polozhenie i klassovaia bor'ba krest'ian Evropeiskoi Rossii, 1881–1904* (Moscow, 1984), pp. 98–99. Only in Vladimir Province did the threat and actual sale of peasant property cease to be an effective mechanism for coercing payment of peasant arrears. See *SP*, II, p. 53.

port, because I don't have much time left. My brother had to pay 4 rubles for an expired passport. And if you send an annual passport so that I won't need to get one in the spring, then I will come to the village. I will winter [here] reluctantly, as I would rather [come back] to the village. Please, tell me about everything in detail. How is the horse now, since she had the colt? I think my coming home would be impossible. I could move timber on the water for household expenses, but I don't think I could winter there. Send a passport because I don't have much time. An expired passport is too costly. A passport is not to be wasted even in spring. Please write soon about everything. Farewell. To your health. You never write. Send a letter soon.[70]

The wife—who was illiterate—dictated a letter to a fellow-villager in response, which included this passage:

Dear husband Polien Petrovich, you have written that I should send you an annual passport. I will not send a passport [because] I have no money and the village elder won't issue a travel permit. He is asking about the taxes. If you send money I will send you the passport.[71]

Such were the coercive forces applied when the distance between workplace and village prevented frequent visitations by family members. In the majority of cases, however, such distances were not prohibitive: mothers, fathers, children or wives would visit the workplace often "to make sure her husband doesn't drink or gamble away all of the earnings."[72] It should not be surprising that a high proportion (28.6 percent) of women's passports in Iaroslavl Province at the turn of the century were issued so that wives could check up on their husbands at work.[73]

Village leaders were keenly aware of the importance of family ties as a channel for regulating peasant-workers, a fact that had a telling impact on regional demographic patterns.[74] Ultimately, marriage became the link through which households united the village base with earnings from migration. The challenge of integrating the dual economy into a relatively stable single household was accomplished through bifurcation, or splitting the family between farm and non-farm workplace. The bifurcated household pooled

---

[70] Written by his own hand. Zhbankov, *Bab'ia storona*, pp. 113–14.

[71] Ibid., pp. 114–15.

[72] *Otkhozhie promysly krest'ianskogo naseleniia Iaroslavskoi gubernii*, p. 54.

[73] K. I. Vorob'ev, *Otkhozhie promysly krest'ianskogo naseleniia Iaroslavskoi gubernii: Statisticheskii ocherk* (Iaroslavl, 1903), pp. 5–7.

[74] For two excellent recent studies of the impact of migration on peasant family life, see Barbara A. Engel, "The Woman's Side: Male Out-Migration and the Family Economy in Kostroma Province," *Slavic Review* 45, no. 2 (Summer 1986): 257–71; B. N. Mironov, "Traditsionnoe demograficheskoe povedenie krest'ian v XIX–nachale XX v.," in *Brachnost', rozhdaemost', smertnost' v Rossii i v SSSR*, A. G. Vishnevskii, ed. (Moscow, 1977), pp. 83–104.

the resources of the agricultural and wage-income sectors while also creating a bridge that facilitated the integration of subordinate family members into the village community. Thus—in a very real sense—bifurcation was the mechanism that sustained and upheld traditional village relations by bolstering the capacity of the elder generation to live off the labor products of the young. As one elder put it, the younger generation would abandon the rural world "if there isn't the restraining influence of elders and a wife."[75] Or, as an observer in Tver Province explained, "peasants regard marriage as a way of attaching a person to the household."[76] In fact, in most villages, *odinochki*— those without families—were not permitted to leave for earnings: in Bronnitsy District, Moscow Province, "Those who migrate for earnings are persons from large (*mnogie rabochie*) families exclusively; *odinochki* (lone workers) all remain in the village."[77] In this way, villages regulated the demographic behavior of individual households.[78]

The experience of a peasant-worker from Moscow Province, S. I. Kanatchikov, provides us with one last illustration of the power of family ties when combined with passport manipulation. As he became more outspoken in his views, Kanatchikov came into conflict with employers and began to move from factory to factory, first in Moscow then in Petersburg, where a distant relative from his native region helped him get settled. Still unable to hold down a job, the young Kanatchikov received two anxious letters from his father in the village. The first exhorted him to remember the vows he had made on his departure: to attend church, obey his superiors, and above all, honor his family responsibilities. Soon after, another letter arrived.

> The second letter was even more ominous. This time my father categorically demanded that I mend my ways: ". . . and if you don't settle down, you scoundrel, I won't renew your passport. I'll have you brought home by the police, and when they've brought you home, I'll whip you with a birch rod myself, in the district administrative office, in the presence of honest people. . . ." This threatening letter seriously disturbed me, especially because my passport was about to expire. True, I knew that my father would not carry out his threat, although in those days he definitely had the authority to do so, and I remembered several instances of that kind.[79]

[75] Quoted by Zhbankov, *Bab'ia storona*, p. 63.

[76] Quoted by Engel, "The Woman's Side," p. 262.

[77] *Statisticheskii ezhegodnik Moskovskoi gubernii za 1889 g.* pt. III (Moscow, 1889), p. 7.

[78] See Zhbankov's observation on marriage, *Bab'ia storona*, p. 63; and Zhbankov, "Vliianie otkhozhikh promyslov," p. 638. Also, see *Otkhozhie promysly krest'ianskogo naseleniia Iaroslavskoi gubernii*, pp. 26–27, 73.

[79] S. I. Kanatchikov, *A Radical Worker in Tsarist Russia: The Autobiography of Semën Ivanovich Kanatchikov* (hereafter, *Autobiography*), trans. and ed. Reginald E. Zelnik (Stanford, 1986), p. 94.

Even for a "conscious" worker like Kanatchikov, such overt threats were a source of tremendous anxiety. More often, the family position was presented in the form of a gentle, parental exhortation: "We beg you, our dear son, don't waste money, we have no rich relations, so help no one; don't play cards, don't smoke tobacco or drink wine, and live virtuously."[80] Such steady prodding was usually sufficient. "Typically, such workers send to the village 60–80 rubles and up to 200 rubles per year. Several send money only for the payment of taxes, although they neglect the land. Adolescents who earn in a day 40–50 kopecks send 10–15 rubles in a year 'so that father will not summon [me back] to the village.' "[81]

In the event that an *otkhodnik* ignored various efforts to exact the payment of taxes and family support, he could be arrested and returned by force to his native village. This return could be accomplished by issuing an order—ordinarily by resolution of the communal assembly—that the "careless member" be brought back to the village under guard (*po etapu, vytrebovanie,* or *vysylka*). The incurred cost (about 12 rubles in Kostroma during the 1880s) was added to the accumulated fiscal debt of the *etapnik* or returnee. Zhbankov summarized the myriad cultural, economic and legal pressures that came into play.

> Coming home as a prisoner in transit is considered a disgrace in the village. . . . The community indiscriminately looks upon every *etapnik* as a person guilty of drunken behavior, not zealous toward his household, and as such he is usually sentenced by the *volost'* court to punishment or arrest or "the birch." All this has a demoralizing effect on young out-migrants. Shame from punishment, the decline of the household, and the impossibility for 1–3 years of going on the side, until payment of the forced-transit fee and arrears, puts the young migrant in an exitless position, the more so as at home he is a poor helper: he doesn't know agricultural work and such workers are not hired. After the light work [of the city or at the factory] he must willingly or unwillingly get accustomed to the heavy field work of the village.[82]

Vytrebovanie was a classic and compelling instrument to uphold the aura of patriarchal authority in the village, and to encourage obedience and responsibility among *otkhodniki*. In the context of the village community, it was only the family—injured directly by the delinquent's irresponsibility—that could wield the support of community opinion to such a degree as to warrant so extreme a measure without provoking community defiance against authority. *Etapniki* were not just scofflaws, they were corrupt and immoral individ-

---

[80] Zhbankov, *Bab'ia storona*, p. 116.

[81] P. Maslov, *Agrarnyi vopros v Rossii: uslovie razvitiia sel'skogo khoziaistva v Rossii* II (St. Petersburg, 1908), p. 72.

[82] Zhbankov, *Bab'ia storona*, p. 55. On the escalation of such procedures, see *SP*, II, p. 60.

uals who had grossly deviated from community norms: ". . . they summon
for return only those delinquents who are leading a dissolute life."[83] As B. V.
Tikhonov observed in his fascinating study of passport manipulation in Moscow Province, the greatest factor in the refusal to renew passports or the
arrest and return of *otkhodniki* to the village was "the failure to send to the
native village money for the payment of taxes and for the livelihood of disabled or aged parents."[84] In Riazan Province, by far the greatest number of
cases of *vytrebovanie* were initiated by such family members.[85] Likewise, in
Smolensk, those with high arrears were summoned back to the village "in
large part at the desire of the parents or wife."[86] In Moscow Province, there
were even cases of the forced return of wives ordered by husbands living in
the village.[87]

For obvious reasons, *vytrebovanie* was more a deterrent to inspire obedience and fear among village members, and was not a procedure that could
be used often. The *myth* of control was more effective for everyone—both
those dependents in the village needing money and those away from the
village earning it. Such forceful intervention was of necessity an instrument
of last resort, used to make a public example of extreme cases. For instance,
only 1.8 percent of all passports issued in the two highest-migration districts
of Kostroma Province during the 1880s actually involved *etapniki*. Ultimately,
the community's need for earnings was the overriding concern that set definite limits on the coercive power of the passport system. *Volost'* authorities
"do not issue passports to tax delinquents, but this relates only to those adult
workers who have accumulated arrears exceeding 1–2 years of apportioned
taxes, and [who] lead 'on the side' a wild life. In general, this measure . . .
is used by . . . authorities with great care, more as a threat to the rest with
small arrears accumulated, with the goal of extracting from them some part
of the debt.[88]

Efforts to extract taxes, redemption payments and arrears were designed
to *coerce*, not to destroy. Fines, imprisonment, and revocation or non-re-
newal of a passport all represented procedures that were best used rarely, as
examples for the rest. The procedure most often applied against flagrant delinquents was corporal punishment, limited by law to a maximum of twenty
blows with a birch rod. The birch spared the delinquent and his family the
hardship of fines, imprisonment or—worst of all—an invalid passport, and
the outward appearance of vigorous efforts to collect arrears regularly spared
the community from having to cover the accrued debt from its own coffers.

[83] *SP*, II, p. 53.
[84] Tikhonov, *Pereseleniia v Rossii*, pp. 122–23.
[85] *SP*, p. 44.
[86] *SP*, II, p. 23. Also, see *SP*, II, p. 88.
[87] Tikhonov, *Pereseleniia v Rossii*, pp. 119, 123.
[88] Zhbankov, *Bab'ia storona*, p. 34.

The use of the birch was designed both as a *moral* lesson for the delinquent, and as an exercise in public shaming. As a village elder in Kostroma Province noted: "Flogging is little imposed but always feared."[89] In the vast majority of cases, the sentence of corporal punishment was expressed in terms that emphasized the character flaw which had induced the negligent member to deviate from the norm—his drunkenness, profligacy, "blatant stubbornness," or lack of zealousness which had led to his negligence of responsibilities to his family and the community.[90]

Data from districts throughout European Russia suggest that the use of corporal punishment declined during the last quarter of the nineteenth century. Nonetheless, it tended to be applied more frequently in high-migration districts. According to official statistics on the use of corporal punishment in *volost'* court sentences during 1896, flogging was proposed in 2 percent or more of all cases in fourteen of forty-nine provinces of European Russia. Five of these fourteen provinces were located in the Central Industrial Region, and ten of the fourteen were northern Non-Black-Earth provinces with high rates of migration.[91] In one *volost'* of Kineshma District, Kostroma Province, the birch was used rarely, maybe three times per year, "only to frighten [delinquents] and put them to shame in front of the people." Or, as a *volost'* elder from Uglich District in Iaroslavl province explained: "You don't really always [have to] flog them. Often, it's enough to just strip them and scare them a little."[92]

CREDIT AND HIRING: PEASANT COMMUNES AND MARKET BROKERS IN THE CENTRAL INDUSTRIAL REGION

In their efforts to coerce fulfillment of obligations without disabling a delinquent's productive capacity, communes had to find ways to override the strict insistence among the majority of *volost'* authorities on the preliminary payment of taxes and arrears prior to the release of passports. There was also need to mitigate against the potentially catastrophic effects posed by distraint and public sale of peasant property, which usually began with the seizure of tax delinquents' property and then moved "to the distraint of the property of the rest of the community in the event that the arrears are not covered by the value of the delinquent's property alone."[93] Two options were commonly used in villages of the Central Industrial Region: credit, and active intervention in the hiring process. Both practices had a far-reaching impact on the

[89] Quoted in V. I. Semevskii, "Neobkhodimost' otmeny telesnykh nakazanii," *Russkaia Mysl'*, no. 2 (1896), sec. II, p. 20.

[90] Ibid., pp. 15, 19–20.

[91] Ibid., p. 77.

[92] Ibid., pp. 12, 16.

[93] *SP*, II, p. 53.

evolution of the rural system in the region, and each will be discussed in turn.

The issuing of loans to assist those in arrears with partial and temporary fulfillment of dues was practiced extensively—almost always in place of *krugovaia poruka*, the "mutual responsibility" of all villagers for fiscal obligations, and always coupled with strict passport restrictions. *Krugovaia poruka* and *dopol'nitelnye raskladki* (supplementary apportionments) were used rarely, and only in special cases when the solvency of one or a few households was affected—usually following catastrophic destruction by fire, a household chief's death, or other calamity.[94] In 1900, for instance, *krugovaia poruka* was invoked on the initiative of the peasant commune in only *.22 percent* (139 villages) of all communes in European Russia in which the statute applied; in just 142 additional instances that year, local tax inspectors ordered compulsory reapportionments.[95] The unifying element in all community affairs was opposition to behavior that would provoke the interference of state agents and the police: for solvent households, loans to delinquent fellow-villagers often involved less risk than outsider intervention.[96] And, in most cases, borrowing—even at usurious rates—was a delinquent household's only defense against complete failure of the peasant household due to expropriation by district police and *volost'* authorities. This convergence of interests among community members—the need for the collective defense of village autonomy—set the context for a rural credit and financial system which developed, in the words of a Vladimir tax inspector, "in order to avoid police intervention."[97] In this sense, the commune acted as a buffer to preserve local arrangements and hierarchies against inroads by state agents and other community "outsiders."

Poorer village members, on their part, showed a marked preference for indebtedness to village insiders rather than running the risk of invoking the intervention of arbitrary and "energetic tax collectors." For most peasants, the prevailing issue was that of finding alternative sources of local credit. A Ministry of Finance study noted in 1894:

---

[94] The practice of *krugovaia poruka* was rare or nonexistent in all provinces of the Central Industrial Region. For examples of rare exceptions, see *SP*, II, pp. 36, 43, 49–50, 73, 97. The emergent pattern suggests that aside from obvious cases of isolated catastrophe, *krugovaia poruka* was applied most frequently in Old Believer villages and in wealthy, highly stratified villages where community members perceived a direct threat to local interests if outsider intervention were provoked by non-payment of taxes. Typical on the non-use of "mutual responsibility" guidelines are: *SP*, II, pp. 37, 43, 50, 58, 65, 73, 84, 102, 107.

[95] See Anfimov, *Ekonomicheskoe polozhenie*, pp. 100–103.

[96] On village insecurity in dealing with tax agents and other authorities, see Terner, "Krest'ianskie platezhi," pp. 454–59. For descriptions of police intervention, see *SP*, II, pp. 37, 43, 58, 74, 86. State officials rarely considered peasant well-being when imposing obligations (II, p. 99).

[97] *SP*, II, p. 50.

There is for the large mass of the population no other means for satisfying their urgent needs, if they do not have any resources on hand, other than turning to the kulaks, lenders and various money-lender-benefactors (*rostovshchiki-blagodeteli*), as they are called now and then according to need. The power of the money-lenders is founded precisely on the fact that except for them, poor people frequently have nowhere else to turn.[98]

For most, a usurious loan was preferable to the total failure that often followed outside intervention. Such loans of expediency were made widely in every province of the Central Industrial Region, carrying interest charges (in cash, goods, or labor) ranging from non-interest loans (in very few cases) to average rates amounting to 20–36 percent interest annually. Usurious rates from private sources often reached as much as 60–100 percent per year! The main source of loans was usually the communal treasury, with the new debt added to the delinquent's accrued household debt, to be repaid before all other arrears.[99] Inevitably, the collection of such loans was much more strictly enforced than efforts expended toward the recovery of tax arrears.[100] In the best cases, communes managed to get low-interest loans through nearby banks and lending cooperatives, at an average of 8 percent per year, then re-lending the money to communal members, sometimes at higher rates.[101] Just as common were loans from private sources—in particular, well-to-do fellow villagers and rich peasants, but also local tavern- and storekeepers, tradesmen, rural priests and monasteries, and local merchant-industrial interests and their agents. In some cases, the lenders were rural officials (village and *volost'* elders) who were also owners of small business establishments.[102] Intended by the debtor to be a short-term expedient during a moment of particular need, opponents charged that instead such loans formed the basis for a new form of debt servitude: "Once made, the debt is usually passed on year after year," with the principle growing at an enormous rate, eventually dwarfing the size of the initial loan.[103] The scale and impact of

[98] Quoted by M. Ia. Gertsenshtein, "Melkii kredit," in *Nuzhdy derevni po rabotam komitetov o nuzhdakh sel'skokhoziaistvennoi promyshlennosti* II (St. Petersburg, 1904), p. 405.

[99] The village commune was the main lender to assist peasants in the payment of dues in all but three provinces. See *SP*, II, pp. 37, 42, 65, 73, 84, 102, 109. Communal loans were rare in three provinces: Moscow, Nizhnii Novgorod, and Vladimir. A study of 1,247 communal loans in Moscow Province revealed, however, that the communes had been the main lenders to peasant households during the period 1876–1878. *Statisticheskii ezhegodnik po Moskovskoi gubernii za 1889 g.*, pt. IV (Moscow, 1889), pp. 54–75.

[100] *SP*, II, pp. 37, 43, 50, 58, 65, 73, 84. For a description of the use of *samosud* or "unofficial" and usually coercive peasant methods for debt collection, see V. V. Tenishev, *Pravosudie v Russkom krest'ianskom bytu* (Briansk, 1907), pp. 45–46.

[101] *SP*, II, p. 65.

[102] *SP*, II, pp. 41, 43, 50, 58, 65, 73, 84, 97, 102, 109.

[103] *SP*, II, p. 58.

such rural credit patterns on local peasant economy were enormous, affecting both rural and urban hiring markets, agriculture and land use, and the hierarchy of village relations in general.

Of course, peasant credit transactions rarely involved the exchange of cash for cash. And, in fact, peasants were notorious for their failure to fulfill such transactions. Instead, credit in the village was most often issued as part of a transaction involving the sale of access to communally controlled resources: cash advances were issued during the peasant's time of greatest need (in fall and winter, when most of the taxes were due, or in spring, for food supplies or new seed) and forward contracts were signed which stipulated the transfer of land, labor, and raw materials (usually produce, livestock, etc.) for a fixed period. It is difficult to exaggerate the role of personal contacts in village credit networks. In the words of an investigator in Smolensk Province in 1887:

> every peasant has his own "benefactor" ("blagopriiatel' "), "merciful"-creditor ("milostivets"-kreditor) with whom he is connected by numerous "indestructible" bonds. "Out of friendship" (po druzhbe), "because of [the borrower's] connections"(po znakomstvu), the creditor does not take a large [cash] percentage in making a loan. In the name of this "friendship," the borrower pays with numerous small services, which sometimes amount to a large rate of interest.[104]

Numerous observers reported that credit relations were often closer and infinitely more complex in villages situated in the vicinity of factories: "peasant [families] with workers on the side take products on credit from shop-keepers, who wait 'do poluchki' (until receipt)" of cash sent home by peasant-workers.[105]

Often, to reduce the burden on community members, the right to use communal lands was sold to outsiders. Usually, such access was granted as part of a credit agreement between communes and local tradesmen or merchant-industrial interests, thereby circumventing the protective communal umbrella which, since 1861, was intended to guarantee "the inalienability of peasant allotments." In Riazan and Kaluga, for instance, the interest charge on merchant loans to communes was paid heavily, not in cash, but in kind, with concessions for the use of common pastures or arable fields.[106] In addition, some communes rented shares of ceded or confiscated peasant allotments on the open market to interested outside buyers: access to village com-

---

[104] Sbornik statisticheskikh svedenii po Smolenskoi gubernii I, pt. 2: Viazemskii uezd (Moscow, 1886), p. 161.

[105] V. M. Kolobov, compiler, and P. A. Vikhliaev, ed., Sel'skii kredit v Moskovskoi gubernii (Moscow, 1914), pp. X–XI, 9. On the interrelationship between village credit and migrant earnings, see Sel'skokhozianistvennyi obzor Tverskoi gubernii za 1897 god, pt. II, pp. 56–57.

[106] SP, II, pp. 43, 104.

munal lands or those allotments given up or seized by the community was sold (in single-soul parcels) for one or more seasons at local bazaars. This transformation of restricted peasant allotments into public rental land—usually offered at a bargain price by communes desperate for funds—had a powerful downward effect on rental prices in the local land markets. In Vladimir Province, for instance, "Owing to the growth in peasant departures for side work, rental prices for [arable] land have fallen with each year."[107] Depending on the quality of land resources, official rental prices of individual parcels were three to four times higher than the rate of large parcels rented over long terms by communal resolution to outsiders. In such arrangements, the interests of the commune were met because state obligations on the land were covered, thereby freeing community members to pursue a livelihood in wage-earning positions elsewhere. The long-term character of such transactions lent a degree of stability to an otherwise unpredictable land market in which the peasantry's fiscal obligations were constant and inexorable, while incomes varied enormously from year to year, depending directly on the strength of the industrial economy. Such rentals of communal and allotment lands to outsiders were particularly common in villages located close to urban and industrial centers.[108]

Another local innovation which often went hand-in-hand with efforts to issue loans to delinquent households was the commune's role in the Central Industrial Region as labor broker in the hiring process. Three official and unofficial elements enhanced this control: the police; group-hiring under the artel principle; and *zemliachestvo*, whereby workers used kinship and fellow-villagers' contacts to find work outside the village.

First, there was the role of the Russian police, who could be called upon for assistance in locating, pressuring and even forcing the return of negligent migrants. Integral to the police role was the requirement that all *otkhodniki* register with local address bureaus (in the towns) or turn their passports over to employers until the termination of the hiring contract. In both urban and non-urban employment, hiring contracts generally stipulated that workers' passports be surrendered until the termination of work: employers held wages and passports in order to exercise control over workers. Such procedures facilitated the regulation of migrants and greatly enhanced the effectiveness of the internal passport system. For instance, in parts of Tver Province where the cobbler's trade was particularly common, delinquent taxpayers working and living in Moscow or Petersburg were personally visited by their village elders during late November or early December, with an

---

[107] Smirnov, "Zemledelie i zemledelets," p. 176. Also, see *Otkhozhie promysly krest'ianskogo naseleniia Iaroslavskoi gubernii*, p. 25; Terner, "Krest'ianskie platezhi," pp. 480–81.

[108] L. V. Make-ov, "Arendnaia sdacha nadel'noi zemli," *Ekonomicheskii Zhurnal*, no. 4 (1889): 27–28, 33. Also see Bulgakov, *Sovremennyia peredvizheniia*, p. 10.

additional assessment of 30–40 kopecks per taxable soul added to their debt for the elders' "traveling expenses."[109]

Aside from keeping tabs on the whereabouts of migrants, the police were also called upon to enforce the payment of arrears, through authorized wage deductions or court-ordered confiscations of property, or even their forced return of negligent *otkhodniki* "under guard" to the village. In parts of Kostroma and Iaroslavl provinces, for example, on being issued a passport, *otkhodniki* were required to sign a special leave-contract which granted village officials explicit rights regarding delinquent migrants. "For those tax delinquents who are absent, [communes] recover [arrears] through the mediation of the police, who lay an injunction on the earnings received by the delinquent workers."[110] In Tver, *volost'* authorities throughout the province required that money be sent for the payment of arrears prior to the renewal of passports, "threatening otherwise [the worker's] forced return to the village. Frequently, [local authorities] communicate with the police . . . about the workers' place of employment, with a request to retain for arrears part of the money earned by them."[111] In this way, the power of village authorities to impose communal sanctions on members away from the village was considerably enhanced; in effect, the police acted as the community's agents at the workplace.

Community vigilance over departing members was further enhanced by *otkhodniki* themselves, who often lived, worked, and socialized together as they engaged in their economic pursuits away from the village. Two principal factors accounted for the high correlation between village origins, skill type, and workplace destination: patterns of hiring and *zemliachestvo*.

Patterns of hiring assisted communities in their efforts to control *otkhodniki*. Unlike the Central Agricultural Region where a labor surplus existed, the Central Industrial Region was a net labor importer, forced by rapid industrial development to bring in workers from an increasingly wider radius of surrounding villages.[112] To tap rural labor resources, outside the cities there sprang up industrial settlements strategically located to exploit local resources in labor, fuel, raw materials, and an intricate network of internal waterways. The comparatively high concentration of industrial development in certain regions of European Russia afforded a hiring process that moved along *established networks*.

[109] *SP*, II, pp. 88–89.

[110] *SP*, II, pp. 77–78. On the use of leave contracts in eight districts of Iaroslavl Province, see II, p. 67.

[111] *SP*, II, pp. 88, 98. See also pp. 52–53.

[112] The wage disparity between regions in European Russia was a direct reflection of the competition for labor. In the Central Industrial Region, average annual wages among *otkhodniki* were higher than any other region, and almost twice those of the Central Agricultural Region. Mints, *Otkhod krest'ianskogo naseleniia*, p. 43.

A typical illustration of how such established networks operated in practice was provided by an employer in Bogorodsk District, Moscow Province, at the end of the nineteenth century:

> For more than 20 years, I have hired workers from two *volosti* [in Mikhailov District, Riazan Province], and the hiring was accomplished in the following manner: I write down how many workers I need and a peasant acquaintance sends for them in the village during Fomin's Week (October 6). . . . On Sunday of Fomin's Week, one of the workers together with my agent proceeds to Moscow, and at the Khitrovo market they negotiate a price, which—as the peasants say—God has set. . . . I must mention that in the course of more than 20 years, I have managed [to hire] workers who are both honorable and not drunkards; there were some lazy ones, but rarely so; only twice did workers come to me to settle up [before the end of the contract].[113]

Because of the intense competition for scarce labor throughout the Central Industrial Region, employers minimized their own risks by binding their potential laborers to their establishments in several ways.

To reduce the likelihood of a worker's abrogation of the hiring contract (and the employer's loss of the advance), most employers followed a dual strategy. First, increasingly after the mid-1870s, they avoided oral contracts, preferring written agreements which were usually accompanied by a resolution from the communal assembly and/or an official seal of approval from the *volost'* clerk. "The pay-books and contract lists, for greater reliability, are sometimes submitted to the *volost'* office, where the elder witnesses them, as a formal contract, with his own signature and affixes them with the *volost'* seal. In the book is a detailed rendering of the term for which the worker has been hired, the pay-rate agreed upon at the completion of the contract, and finally the conditions for work. The latter have sometimes been rendered with very detailed, scrupulous precision."[114] Second, as much as possible, workers were hired collectively—in large labor artels—and held mutually responsible for one another in order to ensure that all workers would fulfill the articles of the agreement.[115] The imposition of the principle of *krugovaia poruka* meant in practice that the workers would be collectively responsible for contract violations of any individual: fines and penalties were usually de-

---

[113] Passage quoted by S. A. Korolenko, compiler, *Vol'nonaemnyi trud v khoziaistvakh vladel'cheskikh i peredvizhenie rabochikh, v sviazi s statistikoekonomicheskim obzorom Evropeiskoi Rossii v sel'sko-khoziaistvennom i promyshlennom otnosheniiakh.* Part V in Russia, Departament zemledeliia i sel'skoi promyshlennosti, *Sel'skokhoziaistvennyia i statisticheskiia svedeniia po materialam, poluchennym ot khoziaev* (St. Petersburg, 1892), p. 268.

[114] N. Dobrotvorskii, "Iukhnovskie zemlekopy," *Severnyi Vestnik*, no. 6 (1887), sec. II, pp. 54–77.

[115] Ibid., pp. 72–73; *Vol'nonaemnyi trud*, pp. 323, 325.

ducted from the entire group of workers, who were issued in exchange a receipt suitable for recovering damages from the guilty party.[116] The fact that workers were hired collectively from the same village or *volost'* made it easier to enforce such contracts, both because it facilitated informal arrangements between hiring agents and local officials, and because peer pressure discouraged the abrogation of contracts.

Such legal controls were often buttressed with personal contacts between employers or their agents and local authorities. Such informal arrangements were the direct consequence of Russia's outmoded tax system, which opened the way for labor brokers familiar with the system and often intimately acquainted with village tax and police officials. The prime conditions for their success were provided by aggressive state officials: "Every autumn 'extraordinary measures' are used for collecting taxes and the replenishment of arrears. . . . Naturally, the peasant tries with all his effort to procure some money for the payment of taxes and arrears."[117] Energetic measures by local officials often coincided with the appearance of "benefactors" who could step in at the proper moment with a cash advance and a printed labor contract.

> Contractors, . . . who treat the hiring of workers as a special profession, come year after year to one and the same place, and are therefore well-acquainted with local conditions and local village authorities, who render them a considerable service in the hiring of workers. Contractors are supplied, according to their trustworthiness, a certain sum of money for use as advances to those who are hired, advances which frequently are very large in relation to the total sum of the earnings. They know well the state of affairs in the region of their activity: where there is a particularly strong need for earnings, the time at which peasants experience greatest hardship, [the period] when efforts to collect taxes and arrears will be intensified, etc. Finally, they can be found to be in the very best relations with *volost'* authorities, who—in the event of [an employer's] need—can intensify their efforts for the exaction of every type of tax.[118]

Incomplete data from 1899 revealed that there were at least 936 such labor contractors operating in just three districts of Kaluga Province.[119]

Despite their legal authority to do so, peasant communities rarely engaged in the forced "hiring-out" of members of delinquent households. More common were prior agreements for deduction of earnings, or the employer's negotiation with *volost'* and village authorities for support in the hiring process. Such labor contractors were especially common in areas where a steady sup-

---

[116] G. P. Sazonov, "Kabala v otkhozhem promysle," *Nabliudatel'*, no. 3 (1889): 37.

[117] Ia. Abramov, "Krest'ianskii kredit," *Otechesvennye Zapiski*, no. 1 (1884), sec. II, p. 7.

[118] P. Chervinskii, "Ekonomicheskiia skitaniia," *Otechestvennye Zapiski*, no. 7 (1880): 71–116. See also Sazonov, "Kabala v otkhozhem promysle," pp. 31–32.

[119] *Statisticheskii obzor Kaluzhskoi gubernii za 1899 god* (Kaluga, 1900), appendix, pp. 86–87.

ply of labor was needed. Local officials benefited directly from such arrangements since usually "the taxes are paid to the village elder every month directly from the factory office."[120] Such arrangements, which usually included advances to assist in both the payment of taxes and family needs, were also widespread in the lumber industry.

> Labor contractors are particularly numerous in north Russia. . . . The contractor . . . gives the peasant a loan both for the payment of taxes and for feeding his family through spring, requiring at the same time that the peasant sign a contract, on the strength of which the peasant is obligated at the contractor's discretion to set out with him for distillation and timber floating in Olonets, Petersburg, Novgorod, Pskov, Perm and other provinces—in a word, anywhere that work is found. . . . Having signed such contracts, peasants at the approach of the spring thaw set out for a hundred kilometers or so to an appointed place—to some river, where timber is stockpiled. Here, the contractor, having arranged for 70–100 workers, resells the right for their labor to a timber merchant or to some other employer, under whose complete command the peasants work.[121]

Peasant-workers were contractually obligated not to set out to find new work on completion of individual jobs; this was the sole responsibility of the foreman, who essentially "rented" peasant labor under his control to outside employers. As the typical labor contract stipulated: "upon completion of the period of work, we, peasants, must present to our *volost'* office a receipt of earnings from the factory, and if this is not done we, peasants, do not have a right to be hired for work at another site."[122] Hiring contractors also protected their interests by maintaining strict hegemony over their specialized information about village labor. The Soviet historian U. A. Shuster found that most of the 19,000 construction workers in St. Petersburg at the beginning of the twentieth century were known to their employers only by skill-classification and the subcontractor's name. For example, a factory record book contained only the following information: "plasterers from Bakhirin, decorators from Sirotkin, stonemasons from Fedorov."[123]

Rural hiring by general contract was especially common among workers in seasonal occupations: sugar refining in the southwest, stevedores on the Volga and along the internal canal system, navvies and unskilled workers throughout the center, light and heavy carriers who conveyed raw materials and industrial goods between station points and factories, lumber workers, peat cutters, brickmakers, railroad workers, miners, and seasonal factory

[120] *Statisticheskii ezhegodnik Moskovskoi gubernii za 1897 god*, pt. II (Moscow, 1897), p. 22.

[121] Abramov, "Krest'ianskii kredit," pp. 20–21.

[122] Passage cited in Sazonov, "Kabala v otkhozhem promysle," pp. 42–43.

[123] U. A. Shuster, *Peterburgskie rabochie v 1905–1907 gg.* (Leningrad, 1976), p. 41.

workers.[124] For instance, "The hiring of [Vladimir] peat cutters takes place in the fall, usually from among the inhabitants of Kaluga and Riazan provinces. For this purpose hiring agents are sent from the factories who settle wage rates with the workers; and then the agent issues to the workers an advance, and the workers, for their part, [give] to the agent a surety—[issued] from the *volost'* office."[125]

The extension of community control over departing members was not limited to those in seasonal skills, however. Similar agreements were reached between village and *volost'* authorities and factory owners as well. Although there were sometimes complaints among local tax inspectors regarding the difficulty of keeping track of *otkhodniki*,[126] village institutions themselves—under the scrutiny of *volost'* authorities, land captains (after 1889), and rural police—managed to exert enormous pressures on migrants to prevent them from relinquishing their village obligations. This was demonstrated by the relatively better position with respect to arrears held by districts in which factory side-earnings represented a high proportion of the incomes of most peasant households. Examples abound of agreements between village officials and outside employers for the direct deduction from peasant-workers' earnings for the payment of fiscal obligations. In Nerekhta District, Kostroma, where most peasant-workers left for factory work on the side, "In factory areas, in agreement with factory and shop owners, [*volost'* and village officials] lay an injunction on part of the wages received by delinquent workers."[127]

There is considerable evidence to suggest that *otkhodniki* themselves actively pursued written hiring agreements. N. K. Brzheskii observed that peasant-workers had begun to demand that contracts be validated by the *volost'* clerk, since the *volost'* authorities had come to expect that "contractors . . . should be answerable for the punctual payment of taxes" of contracted workers.[128] This gave the peasant-worker certain flexibility in the event that a contract was abrogated by the hiring agent. Communal and *volost'* officials likewise favored such agreements, since they could be used—along with corporal punishment—to demonstrate to state officials their own vigilant efforts to collect taxes and arrears.

This pattern of direct deduction from earnings was not unique to the post-Emancipation world, since *obrok* payments which predominated in Non-

[124] Sazonov, "Kabala v otkhozhem promysle," pp. 28–56.

[125] P. A. Peskov, *Fabrichnyi byt Vladimirskoi gubernii: Otchet za 1882–1883 gg.* (St. Petersburg, 1884), p. 66.

[126] See, for example, *SP*, II, pp. 55–56.

[127] *SP*, II, p. 77. For other examples, see pp. 38, 46–47, 52, 77–78, 88, 98, 100. Also, see Robert Eugene Johnson, *Peasant and Proletarian: The Working Class of Moscow in the Late Nineteenth Century* (New Brunswick, 1979), p. 179.

[128] Brzheskii, *Nedoimochnost'*, p. 191.

Black-Earth districts during the pre-Emancipation era were commonly deducted by factory owners and paid directly to magnate landlord-owners. Before 1861, such concessions reduced the difficulty of extracting estate dues from reluctant serfs, and—on the factory owner's part—bought him steady access to a local labor force held in control both by factory authorities and the full coercive apparatus of the estate system. Later in the century, the same logic applied: village communes in the Central Industrial Region gained a partner in meeting high state exactions, while industrialists and other employers found in the village hierarchy an extension of its apparatus for controlling its work force.

Several contemporaries noted the interplay of the rural credit and hiring systems with communal efforts to fulfill state obligations. For instance, G. P Sazonov of the Russian Free Economic Society argued that a considerable proportion of *otkhodniki* entered the labor forces as *kabal'nye rabochie* or *pokruchenniki*—debt or bonded workers—who were given advances prior to their departure in order to cover the "departure fees" imposed by local authorities. In effect, by prior arrangement between hiring agents and local authorities, there was a direct transfer of cash advances from employers to local elders, all or part of the peasant's debt was paid, and only what was left over became available for household use. In such an arrangement, all the forces for social control came into play: seeking a more reliable and docile labor force, employers imposed written contracts on a collective and mutually responsible group of debt-workers from the same general area. With large advances granted when taxes were due in the fall and winter, local authorities managed to satisfy at least part of the state's demands, thereby reducing the likelihood of intervention. The legal character of the agreements brought the full power of the state—through its local judicial and executive agents—to support the arrangements.

The actual degree of collusion between hiring agents and local authorities is, by its very nature, difficult to determine. Inevitably, such collusion between employers and village authorities varied widely from one area to another. The degree of sophistication that could be attained in local schemes is illustrated by this report on the hiring of lumber workers in the north:

> On an autumn day the timber merchant . . . calls upon the elder and proposes that he assemble the peasants for a village meeting. The peasants are assembled; the merchant reminds them that soon the taxes (*sentiabrëvka*) will be expected of them, and asks where they think they will get the money. The peasants scratch the backs of their heads, and are silent. The merchant then offers to hire them to cut and transport logs from his dacha to the pier. For felling and delivering the logs he offers, depending on the amount, from 60 kopecks to 1 ruble 20 kopecks, and an advance of 15 rubles, for a troika with horses. The peasants begin to

make a stir, to haggle [over the terms]. The [village] elder, who had earlier been won over by the merchant, begins to curse the peasants, threatening [to take them to] the *volost'* office, or to the village constable, etc. The peasants, having in perspective the oppressiveness of the *sentiabrëvka*—the distraint of property, [imprisonment in] the "cooler" and other energetic measures—cause a greater stir, even shouting, but eventually they accept the merchant's offer. Then they get drunk on vodka served by the merchant and, tipsy, go to the *volost'* office "to secure the contract." The merchant then distributes the agreed-upon advance, which is immediately used for the payment of state and communal dues. Such a reception is repeated by the merchant in nearly every village of the entire *volost'*.[129]

Often, the large advance would cut into earnings so deeply as to compel peasant-workers to seek further credit, thereby hurling them into a perpetual cycle of debt-servitude. The links between employers, their hiring agents, and village and *volost'* authorities were real, and had an enormous impact on Russian labor history.

Just as hiring agents depended upon established networks and procedures, peasant-workers themselves—when venturing out in search of employment—relied to a great degree on *zemliak* ties and the contacts they provided.[130] With considerable chance for failure, even in good years, peasant-workers relied as much as possible on the guidance and support of their more fortunate or experienced fellow-villagers—*zemliaki* who could supply crucial information and the necessary introductions for finding a job. As the peasant-worker Kanatchikov recalled, "There were, of course, no labor exchanges in those days, but in spite of this we were very well informed about where workers were needed."[131] Particularly among unskilled workers, who often had to " 'shuffle along on their own', 'on the off–chance' " of finding employment, the hazards of job seeking were considerably reduced by relying on the resources of fellow-villagers.[132] This was as much a product of the structure of the hiring market in the Central Industrial Region as of the preferences of prospective employers: hiring agents "in selecting an artel of workers, try always to hire as many as possible from one village or, at least, from one *volost'*. . . . Contractors almost never hire lone workers into large artels; they are selected only by local contractors, and then more *through acquaintances (po znakomstvu), through connections (po znati)*. Fearing abuse, con-

---

[129] Passage cited in Sazonov, "Kabala v otkhozhem promysle," p. 47 [Mogilev Province].

[130] A *zemliak* was a person from one's native village or region. *Zemliachestvo* referred to the friendly "insider" relations—as contrasted with the notorious distrust of "outsiders"—typical among peasants from a particular area.

[131] Kanatchikov, *Autobiography*, p. 64. On the function of *zemliak* networks as an unofficial information bureau for unemployed workers, see Shuster, *Peterburskie rabochie*, pp. 40–41.

[132] *Statisticheskii ezhegodnik Tverskoi gubernii za 1901 god*, pt. II, sec. 2 (Tver, 1902), p. 10.

tractors never hire individual workers who are strangers or newcomers."[133] The typical pattern of hiring and skill acquisition through kinship and *zemliak* networks was observed by a peasant correspondent from Dmitrov District, Moscow:

> As a rule, peasants of an entire village, or even a whole area, leave for one and the same occupation, to one and the same destination, which is explained by the fact that persons going for earnings for the first time are more easily able to settle down and find work there where they have an acquaintance.[134]

Zemliachestvo had a telling impact on patterns of urban settlement, as "urban villages" sprang up in urban and suburban working-class neighborhoods. As an observer in St. Petersburg noted early in this century: "It's enough just for one villager to come to the city before this pioneer drags along his fellow-villagers and helps them get set up. For this reason we have frequently seen apartments inhabited by people of the same village."[135] Observers in Tver Province noted the same high propensity for *zemliak* clustering: "The population of each district has its own favorite place, where it goes for earnings each year."[136] This pattern was reinforced by annual pilgrimage routes which, as the historical ethnographer M. M. Gromyko has demonstrated, were closely associated with peasant economic activity.[137] In short, cultural factors played as significant a role as economic forces in the development of more-or-less stable patterns of migration. As a researcher for the Free Economic Society concluded: "Departing *zemliaki* entice others by their example—with their success, with their stories. Successful migrants are themselves transformed into contractors for their own *zemliaki*, who recruit still more children from their parents."[138]

Patterns of *zemliak* clustering are clearly evident in migration statistics. For instance, 60.4 percent (98,801) of all peasants with passports from Tver Prov-

---

[133] Dobrotvorskii, "Iukhnovskie zemlekopy," p. 72.

[134] *Statisticheskii ezhegodnik Moskovskoi gubernii za 1903 god*, sec. 2A (Moscow, 1904), p. 11. For similar evidence on the role of *zemliachestvo* in labor migration, see Johnson, *Peasant and Proletarian*; and Joseph Bradley, *Muzhik and Muscovite: Urbanization in Late Imperial Russia* (Berkeley, 1985), pp. 103–41.

[135] The passage refers to St. Petersburg in 1902, and was quoted by Bradley, *Muzhik and Muscovite*, p. 116. B. N. Vasil'ev observed *zemliak* clustering in the migration patterns of textile workers in the North Volga region. "K kharakteristike formirovaniia promyshlennogo proletariata v Rossii (Po materialam Vladimirskoi, Kostromskoi, i Iaroslavskoi gubernii)," *Uchenye Zapiski Shakhtinksogo Gosudarstvennogo Pedagogicheskogo Instituta* 2, pt. 2 (1957): 202–54.

[136] *Sel'skokhoziaistvennyi obzor Tverskoi gubernii za 1894-i god*, pt. 88, p. 11.

[137] M. M. Gromyko, *Traditsionnye normy povedeniia i formy obshcheniia russkikh krest'ian* (Moscow, 1986), pp. 99–105.

[138] L. A. Kirillov, "K voprosu o vnezemledel'cheskom otkhode krest'ianskogo naseleniia," *Trudy Imperatorskago Vol'nago Ekonomicheskago Obshchestva*, book 3 (1899): 292.

ince went for work in Petersburg; more than 30 percent (32,316) went to Moscow. Likewise, almost three-fourths (77,322) of Iaroslavl migrants worked in Petersburg.[139] District, *volost'* and village data is even more striking in this regard, with all or almost all local peasant-workers involved in comparable occupations at similar work sites.[140]

The combined effects of distinct regional patterns of hiring and the reliance on established networks for matching peasant-workers to skills and employers was to generate a powerful instrument for social control. Extending the boundaries of the traditional community to the workplace, *zemliak* networks acted as a conduit for information back to the village, providing information about community members, their state of health, their behavior, even their earnings. "I have seen all of my friends and neighbors," wrote one peasant-worker in a letter to his wife, "and all seemed in good health. Everyone greets you. I only did not see Petr Petrov, but I heard he had returned to the village for the winter." Defending himself against rumors of his own dissolute life-style, he continued: "I am now working as a decorator and have completed twenty days' work and through today have drunk no Petersburg vodka and I hope [to live this way] henceforth."[141] *Zemliaki* were the mechanisms by which community norms were projected to urban village life. This included self-policing—to some degree—of village members who deviated from the norms. The overlay of village cultural linkages strengthened the power of institutions that were responsible for regulating the behavior of migrating peasant-workers, so that—as one of the leading contemporary specialists on migration A. A. Bulgakov observed—"Even in migration a peasant remains a peasant."[142]

Two broad observations can be made about the relative effectiveness of communal schemes to redistribute peasant wage income back to the countryside. First, proximity between village and workplace profoundly affected the capacity of villagers to influence out-workers. A number of studies have indicated that an *otkhodnik's* financial connection to the village declined in direct relation to the distance of the workplace from his native village. In one study conducted at the beginning of the century among 9,500 workers in western Vladimir Province, it was found that one-third (36.7 percent) of all workers lived within 7–8 kilometers of the factory, and two-thirds (65.4 percent) lived within 25 kilometers. While 70–72 percent of those workers from villages within 40 kilometers of the factory sent money home, only 30 percent

---

[139] *Sel'skokhoziaistvennyi obzor Tverskoi gubernii za 1894-i god*, pt. II, p. 15. The data on St. Petersburg is based on the 1890 census. Moscow data is based on the 1882 census.

[140] See the comprehensive review of *otkhodnichestvo* in "Svedeniia o vnezemledel'nykh zaniatiiakh krest'ian uezdov Moskovskoi gubernii," *Tsentral'nyi Gosudarstvennyi Istoricheskii Arkhiv goroda Moskvy*, f. 184, op. 10, d. 2699, listy 1–71.

[141] Zhbankov, *Bab'ia storona*, pp. 112–13.

[142] Bulgakov, *Sovremennyia peredvizheniia krest'ianstva*, pp. 3–4.

of those from villages more than 40 kilometers away sent money back to their families in the village.[143] These data suggest that the police system outside of the towns was ultimately less reliable as a means for inducing payment than the coercive mechanisms within the village: as distance grew and direct village pressure dissipated, peasant-workers were more likely to evade fulfillment of their community and family responsibilities.

Second, there was a high correlation between the size of the village allotment and the likelihood that peasant-workers would continue to share earnings with their villages. Throughout the Non-Black-Earth Zone, virtually every peasant household—poor, middle, or wealthy—sent members away for earnings. A study conducted at the turn of the century in Shuia District, in northern Vladimir Province (see Table 2-5), suggests that while most peasant-workers continued to send wages back to their families in the village—a fact that in itself reflects the remarkable persistence of old ways—the proportion of those who did not send wages home was significantly greater among the poorest rural families—those with the least stake in the village economy.[144] These data indicate that the decision to maintain ties to the village was to a large degree influenced by rational economic choice: wages were sent as an investment into a traditional and generally reliable form of social insurance. The fact that three-fourths of all *otkhodniki* from landless households continued to send wages reflects the strength of village and house-

TABLE 2-5.
Proportion of Peasant-Workers Sending Wages Back
to Their Native Villages (Shuia District, Vladimir) 1890s
(in percent)

Rural Holding (1 desiatina = 2.7 acres)	Sent Wages to Their Families	Did Not Send Any Wages to Their Families	Unknown
No sown area	76.0	16.5	7.5
Sown area up to 3 desiatinas	92.4	2.8	4.8
Sown area: 3.1 to 6 desiatinas	92.5	3.1	4.4
Sown area: greater than 6 desiatinas	91.5	5.3	3.2

Source: Prokopovich, "Krest'ianstvo i poreformennaia fabrika," *Velikaia reforma*, VI (Moscow, 1911), p. 272.

[143] Smirnov. "Iz nabliudenii," pp. 2, 6. In the study, 75 percent of all workers came from villages within a 25 kilometer radius of the workplace. Speaking generally, 61 percent of all Russian factories and 59 percent of all factory workers were located in such industrial settlements. In the Central Industrial Region, the proportions were higher: two-thirds (65 percent) of all factories and workers were located outside of the towns. See Bradley, *Muzhik and Muscovite*, p. 16.

[144] See the informative discussion in Maslov, *Agrarnyi vopros v Rossii*, II, pp. 370–73.

hold-based pressures. Two case studies will serve to illustrate the nature of these bonds.

Despite the primitive nature of village financial networks, postal data has left us with a fairly precise record of the flow of cash between workplace and village. Generally, peasant-workers sent money home in specially registered letters (*denezhnye pakety*) by way of the local *volost'* office, a local store- or tavern-keeper, or—in rare cases—directly to the peasant's home. A study of the flow of such parcels was conducted in Tver Province. Table 2-6 contains a detailed breakdown of wage support between migrants and villagers. In 1896, Tver *otkhodniki* sent 446,231 parcels home, at a gross value of 6,381,078 rubles. This reflected an average of 1.3 parcels per migrant (based on passports issued), with an average value of 14 rubles, 29 kopecks each. Data for the years following reflect a steady flow of support. "By virtue of a long-established custom, both the *volost'* office and tradesmen, receiving such cash letters addressed to them, first of all deduct from the received sum a certain percentage for commission, and second the money owed by relatives. *Volost'* authorities deduct all of the sum or part of the arrears for state and *volost'* obligations; tradesmen [deduct] for goods bought on credit in local shops by relatives who have remained at home."[145] Through postal sources alone, peasant-workers transferred receipts which amounted to 150–200 percent of the gross annual burden of all state and local dues imposed on Tver peasants!

In Iaroslavl Province, more than 20 percent of the entire peasant population (nearly 40 percent of adult peasant males) migrated for earnings in 1901. Because of low arrears, more than 90 percent of all passports were long-term (one year or more); 75 percent of the *otkhodniki* had broken entirely from agriculture, with their allotments and personally-owned land left fallow or worked by family members or hired laborers. In some cases, especially in the

TABLE 2-6.
Official Cash Transfers From Peasant-Workers
to Their Villages: Tver Province, 1895–1901

Year	Parcels	Value (in rubles)	Average Value Each Parcel	Average No. Parcels/ Migrant	Average Value per Migrant
1895	402,524	5,830,305	14.48	1.2	17.96
1896	446,231	6,381,078	14.30	1.3	19.41
1897	453,367	6,259,802	13.81	1.3	17.84
1898	448,148	6,621,860	14.78	1.4	20.04
1899	451,514	6,817,401	15.10	1.3	19.79
1900	417,691	6,477,497	15.51	1.2	17.93

Source: *Statisticheskii ezhegodnik Tverskoi gubernii za 1897 [–1901] god* (Tver, 1898–1902).

[145] *Statisticheskii ezhegodnik Tverskoi Gubernii za 1897 god*, pt. II, p. 34.

highest migration districts of Uglich and Rybinsk, fallow land had grown wild with grass or even forests. But even in this case, in which the typical *otkhodnik's* ties to the land seemed most tenuous, the flow of wages to the village were considerable. According to household inventories conducted in Myshkino District—representing the mean for migration in the province— the average annual earnings of an *otkhodnik* were 155 rubles, even higher in a good year. Typically, one-half to two-thirds of an *otkhodnik's* annual earn- ings were sent home. In the entire province, the zemstvo statistician K. I. Vorob'ev estimated, 12–16 million rubles were sent each year by *otkhodniki* back to their families, totalling one and a half to two times the amount taken in from agriculture. This influx of cash into the ailing village economy en- abled peasants to purchase an additional 628,000 *desiatiny* of land between 1861 and the beginning of 1903, bringing peasant landholding to nearly 2 million *desiatiny*. Vorob'ev concluded: "Despite all of the negative influence on agriculture, migrant-laborers at the same time serve as the main support and sustaining force of the peasant farm: without the means which *otkhod* gives to the peasant, the farm would have gradually fallen to ruin and with- ered, and we would have witnessed a stronger impoverishment than is now being observed in the Central Black Earth Region of Russia."[146]

CONCLUSION

This article has traced the responses of village communities throughout the Central Industrial Region to the dramatic growth of "temporary" departures for side-earnings by peasant laborers after 1861. The hybrid apparatus that resulted from Emancipation and in response to commoditization of products and labor consisted of a hodgepodge of local solutions in which a number of interests fought to make their presence felt in the countryside: the state's interminable frustration in its attempts to impose civil discipline and the rule of law; entrepreneurs seeking to exploit the confusion for their own personal gains; peasants and peasant families trying desperately to make ends meet.

State tax authorities, the village commune, and peasant families all com- peted for the peasant-worker's earnings against the myriad enticements that permeated urban, suburban and factory life. The principal task for all three— united by concerns about tax receipts on the one hand, and subsistence sup- port on the other—lay in gaining information about and redistributing the product of the wage labor of migrating peasant-workers from workplace to village.

The state sought to coopt powerful communal forms of social control by more closely aligning its own initiatives with the interests of patriarchal elites in the traditional village hierarchy. In their efforts to enhance the role of com-

---

[146] Vorob'ev, *Otkhozhie promysly krest'ianskago naseleniia Iaroslavskoi gubernii*, pp. 23–24.

munal institutions, state officials, on the one hand, vigorously pursued the collection of taxes and arrears; on the other, they endowed peasant institutions with powerful sanctions for expropriating those obligations from community members.

Communal policy, on its part, was guided by a pervasive sense of insecurity in the burgeoning commodity economy. In their struggle to respond to the dual crises posed by the need for cash to pay excessive tax and redemption dues and imperiled by desertion of their members, village institutions fell back on a number of traditional arrangements. The structures, institutions, and practices that developed under serfdom proved rather well-suited for extension into the post-Emancipation era. Their strength was augmented by several new legislative initiatives. Temporary and limited alliances were forged between *volost'* and village authorities with two agents in particular: (1) the state—which sought to uphold peasant patriarchalism as part of its strategy to maintain internal order and ensure fulfillment of obligations; and (2) market brokers—employers and creditors who exploited village structures to optimize control and reduce wage and resource costs. Throughout the final decades of the Old Regime, the peasant commune lay at the center of these competing forces: it served simultaneously the sometimes conflicting, sometimes harmonious roles as an extension of the state *apparatus*, as *mitigator* defending the interests of villagers, and as *broker* mediating economic relations between peasants and outside agents.

In the Central Industrial Region, in particular, peasant families—severely weakened by household divisions and the increasing and long-term departure of adult male workers for outside earnings—became more dependent than ever on the village commune to ensure family security. Only the village commune could harness the resources necessary to redistribute peasant-workers' wage earnings from the workplace back to the village. And only in the Central Industrial Region did regional-specific conditions support the widespread development of the myriad schemes and arrangements discussed throughout this article. The abundance of non–agricultural job opportunities considerably reduced the distance between village and workplace. The density of the peasant population generated an infrastructure that facilitated the redefinition of peasant conceptions of community to include members who spent the greater part of their adult lives working outside of their native villages. The competition for scarce labor led employers to seek out arrangements with local officials and peasant communes. The competition for scarce regional resources led entrepreneurs to invest heavily in peasant credit schemes, and to assist communes in fulfilling tax obligations. Fears of the instability engendered by proletarianization guided state officials as they upheld peasant patriarchal authority and the imposition of a rule of law in the countryside.

There is a substantial body of evidence which suggests that the *village com-*

munity in the Central Industrial Region remained a cohesive and resilient force perhaps more so than elsewhere in Russia. Numerous forms of communal intervention have been cited: communal control over the distribution of land (and tax) burdens; communal intervention in rental agreements; the communal use of passport constraints; the imposition of departure fees and the preliminary payment of fiscal obligations; the commune as a primary supplier and underwriter of credit for the fulfillment of obligations; collective labor contracts and prearranged wage deductions; the frequent defense of peasant interests in these arrangements; *zemliaki* and the primary role of village contacts in non-village pursuits; cooperation with the police to carry out threats of forced return, corporal punishment, and imprisonment of delinquents.

The evidence from the Central Industrial Region also indicates the need to reinterpret the role of rich peasants or kulaks. In the context of the village "little community," the so-called "kulak" often performed functions crucial to the economic well-being of the *whole* community (by acting as a broker for local produce, as a source of credit for village families and departing *otkhodniki*, as a mediator with outside agents, as a connection with outside employment in certain factories or skills, etc.). In the words of the anthropologist Connor Bailey, wealthy peasants—*blagodeteli* (benefactors) or *pervostateiniki* ("first-class citizens") in the local jargon—emerge as leaders not merely because they are exploiters, but also because they are "brokers, mediators, patrons and kinsmen."[147] From this cultural perspective, wealthy peasants—whose own survival rested to a great degree on the perpetuation of existing conditions of insularity—may by and large be seen as the staunchest upholders of village traditional relations, not—as is so often asserted in the "kulak mythology" presented by contemporary elite sociologists—as the ruthless and "egoistical" (*slastliubivye*) plunderers of hallowed village traditions. In short, kulak exploitation must be understood within its local cultural context, a context fraught with need, and a disproportionate reliance on patronage and personal contacts, or *znakomstvo*, to survive from one season to the next.

Migrant wage labor provoked a profound transformation of peasant subsistence strategies. Throughout the Central Industrial Region, the pattern that developed was one that reflected a strategy of risk reduction through the bifurcation of the peasant household. As in feudal Russia, the *tiaglo*—or conjugal dyad—remained the most basic and viable productive work unit. Conjugality became the nexus that bonded the cash and subsistence economies together in a single household: labor migrants, who persisted in conceiving themselves as "peasants earning income on the side," essentially

---

[147] Connor Bailey, *Broker, Mediator, Patron, and Kinsman: An Historical Analysis of Key Leadership Roles in a Rural Malaysian District* (Athens, Ohio, 1976).

"raided" the cash economy for receipts needed to sustain the wavering village base, while the village economy served as both a "safety net" protecting
all household members and a stay that effectively reduced the rate of di-
vorcement of the non-agricultural work force from its predominantly village
roots. By sending their wages back to their villages (and a large majority of
peasant-workers of the Central Industrial Region continued to do so well into
the twentieth century), migrants were investing in a scheme that could insure them against the insecurities endemic to a commodity economy and the
alienating conditions of their semi-urbanized workplace.

There is perhaps no better testimony of the degree of resilience of "little
community" ties among peasant-workers than the observation made by
A. V. Pogozhev, a contemporary Marxist statistician and one of the foremost
experts on the Russian factory during the late years of the nineteenth century:

> In the majority of cases, Russian workers, when questioned about their
> professional occupation, tend as a rule to label themselves peasant-farm-
> ers, and consider side-earnings as something occasional and inconstant.
> In general, this has nearly always been observed, but especially in fac-
> tory-sanitary investigations in Moscow Province (1880–1902), and even
> in those cases when *otkhodniki* had been working at the factory for a long
> time and were accustomed to continual outside work.[148]

Most peasant-workers before 1905 persisted in upholding their peasant
status: in spite of all the changes that surrounded them, and in spite of their
youthful eagerness to flee the village, they nonetheless continued to perceive
the world from within the parameters of the village *focos* and according to
the norms of the village communal hierarchy.

[148] A. V. Pogozhev, *Uchet chislennosti i sostava rabochikh v Rossii* (St. Petersburg, 1906), p.
xiv.

CHAPTER 3

PEASANT POVERTY IN THEORY AND PRACTICE:
A VIEW FROM RUSSIA'S "IMPOVERISHED CENTER"
AT THE END OF THE NINETEENTH CENTURY

*Elvira M. Wilbur**

THE CONTEMPORARIES who studied the Russian agrarian crisis at the end of the nineteenth century were acutely aware of the many changes going on in the countryside, but their perspectives on the crisis varied significantly. In general, they were outsiders to the village who shared a common worldview that was, however empathetically expressed, fundamentally hostile to the village. They believed social and economic progress was necessary and inevitable; and they looked to Britain for their models.[1] Central to their perspective was the belief that the demise of the peasantry, as a peasantry, was a necessary first step toward progress. Thus they saw all the visible changes in the countryside as evidence of peasant pauperization and failures of the system that prefigured its impending collapse.

These investigators used a number of general and specific methodologies that were seriously flawed.[2] The persistent use of gross averages—empire-wide, regional, and provincial—destroyed almost all sense of the subtle, but rich, variety of peasant life. The use of allotment size and the presence of off-farm and craft earnings as markers for poverty showed they did not understand the workings of the mixed peasant economy;[3] and the presentation of

* I want to thank the National Endowment of the Humanities and the Office of the Provost of Michigan State University for funds that made the research for this work possible. I also want to express my very special thanks to Esther Kingston-Mann and Timothy Mixter for their extensive and patient aid over the years.

[1] Esther Kingston-Mann, "Marxism and Russian Development: Problems of Evidence, Experience, and Culture," *American Historical Review* 86, no. 4 (October 1981): 731–52.

[2] Elvira M. Wilbur, "Was Russian Peasant Agriculture Really That Impoverished? New Evidence From a Case Study From the 'Impoverished Center' at the End of the Nineteenth Century," *Journal of Economic History* 43, no. 1 (March 1983): 137–44.

[3] Teodor Shanin, "The Nature and Logic of the Peasant Economy: Parts I and II," *Journal of Peasant Studies* 1, no. 1 (October 1973) : 63–80 and 1, no. 2 (January 1974): 186–206.

"worst case" studies as typical was all too common.[4] The end result was that outside investigators who used faulty methodologies created a seriously flawed image of a massively impoverished countryside where the peasant was always a victim; and that image became generalized and was accepted as fact. Lenin's classic interpretation, *The Development of Capitalism in Russia* (1899), is the best known and one of the most comprehensive of these formulations. He presented masses of cross-sectional data that demonstrated differences in peasant wealth at a given time, then asserted they proved the differences were increasing over time.

Zemstvo statisticians and Ministry of Agriculture workers provided the chief alternative view. Based in the countryside, they observed peasant life directly; and over time, they developed a considerable understanding of the internal workings of the peasant economy and culture. A. V. Chaianov was one of the best known of these investigators. He demonstrated that peasants faced an economic reality that was objectively different from the one faced by market-oriented capitalists.[5] He showed that an important part of the difference was due to the fact that the independent variable that determined peasant prosperity or poverty was labor, whereas both neoclassical and Marxist economic theory assumed it was land. He also attempted to prove that peasants operated out of noncapitalist economic assumptions that were based on the balance between the family's consumer/worker ratio and its responses to the increasing drudgery of labor. Assuming that the structure of the peasant family was a nuclear one, he argued that the intensity of its labor varied according to the family's cyclical expansion and contraction. When he could not demonstrate the last two points empirically, his concept of a noncapitalist mentality was widely ridiculed as being "romantic" and

[4] Two well-known examples of such misleading representations that deal with Voronezh Province, the object of this study, are A. I. Shingarev, *Vymiraiushchaia derevnia* (St. Petersburg, 1907) and the material on Voronezh Province in V. I. Lenin, *The Development of Capitalism in Russia* (Moscow, 1977), pp. 116–20, 150–90.

Shingarev's work described the villages of Novo Zhevotinnoe and Mokhovatkoi, located on the rail line 25 *versty* from the city of Voronezh, a rail and industrial center of 80,000 that was the capital of the province. Although the conditions described were difficult, they depicted the impact of urban development and industrialization on a surrounding region and did not typify the countryside as a whole. The comparable budget in the data used in this chapter was one at Verkhnoe Boevo, a suburb of Voronezh city. The male head of this household and his son-in-law were/had been town workers more than peasant farmers.

Lenin used data from four of the twelve districts in Voronezh Province as an important part of his overall argumentation. He said he selected them because the data available for these districts were especially suitable for measuring poverty. Whatever the merits of the argument, they represent a highly biased sample. They were the four poorest districts in the province, and the economic and social differences between them and the other eight districts were substantial.

[5] A. V. Chaianov, *A. V. Chaianov on the Theory of the Peasant Economy*, ed. Daniel Thorner, Basile Kerblay, and R.E.F. Smith (Homewood, Ill., 1966; originally published in 1926).

"neopopulist." By the late 1920s, the entirety of his work was rejected; and the interpretation Lenin presented in *The Development of Capitalism in Russia* became the analytical starting point for virtually all investigations of the countryside in the Soviet Union for the next thirty years.

In later decades, Geroid T. Robinson accomplished an almost equally comprehensive codification of the liberal, neoclassical tradition in the United States with the impassioned and ostensibly empathetic *Rural Russia under the Old Regime*.[6] Despite the enormous depth of sympathy both Robinson and Lenin expressed for the peasantry, it was basically a paternalistic and dismissing sympathy for what they saw to be a simple and doomed people. Nevertheless, the combination of their apparent erudition and empathy *and* the fact that the audiences in both the Soviet Union and the West shared the central elements of their worldview—a belief in progress and the conviction that the destruction of the peasantry as a peasantry was the essential first step toward that progress—helped establish and maintain the near-monopoly of their respective positions in the Soviet Union and the United States from the early 1930s to the 1960s.[7] By then, however, interesting new studies in both countries produced evidence that began to challenge the established orthodoxies on both the theoretical and evidential levels.

A study by the Soviet historian A. M. Anfimov in 1961 demonstrated that virtually no Russian peasants hired full-time labor at the turn of the century.[8] This being the case, Anfimov asked how peasant class differentiation could have proceeded to the point Lenin maintained in *The Development of Capitalism in Russia*.

In the West, the debate on the peasantry reopened with the publication of a new edition of Chaianov's *The Theory of Peasant Economy* in 1966, and of Teodor Shanin's "The Logic and Nature of the Peasant Economy" and *The Awkward Class* in the early 1970s.[9] Shanin's article on the peasant economy began with extensive, but *selective*, use of Chaianov. He focused on the peasant small family farm as his unit of analysis, emphasizing the noncapitalistic aspects of both its internal organization and its environment and circumstances. Like Chaianov, he pointed out that although the family farm was primarily an agricultural enterprise, it willingly and regularly used a variety of income sources and activities to survive. He emphasized that it was a production/consumption/reproduction unit, concerned above all with subsistence. But it was willing to sell any available surplus if it had a market.

In *The Awkward Class*, Shanin challenged Lenin's central point: that a rapid polarization of classes was taking place in the countryside under the pressure

[6] Geroid T. Robinson, *Rural Russia under the Old Regime* (Berkeley and Los Angeles, 1969; originally published in 1932).

[7] Kingston Mann, "Marxism and Russian Rural Development."

[8] A. M. Anfimov, *Zemel'naia arenda v Rossii v nachale XX veka* (Moscow, 1961).

[9] Teodor Shanin, *The Awkward Class* (Oxford, 1972).

of massive new market formation. He used a combination of time series data and detailed budget studies to show that the differentiation found in the Russian countryside was the result of a complex equilibrium dynamic shaped by (1) several different kinds of family and random-event mobilities and (2) a variety of macro-level environmental factors.

Responding to the work of Chaianov and Shanin, investigators once again demonstrated that Chaianov's theory of the consumer/worker ratio and the increasing drudgery of labor was not empirically verifiable. Mark Harrison, using these proofs, insisted that Chaianov's formulations could not be separated into their component parts, that they had to stand or fall as a whole.[10] This argument was clearly intended to dismiss not only all of Chaianov, but Shanin as well, despite the fact Shanin *did not* use Chaianov's discredited concepts of the consumer/worker ratio and the increasing drudgery of labor in his analysis.

In a second article on social mobility, Harrison acknowledged both that his own arguments as a whole had a "strongly speculative element" (p. 150) and that the statistical analysis of two different data sets he had offered as proof of his position were, in the one case, "compatible with" either hypothesis tested and, in the other, "ambiguous" (p. 146). These major methodological qualifiers aside, he still asserted in conclusion that: (1) "empirically, the household economy is rarely a unit of production and consumption"; (2) "communal repartition and the 'biological' family life cycle are unsatisfactory explanations for the downward mobility of large farms"; and (3) "Russian Populism" is a "trivial and unscientific construct" (p. 151).[11] In subsequent articles, Harrison and other Neo-Marxists accepted his asserted conclusions as proven. Using the misnomer "neopopulist" as a polemical pejorative, they essentially equated Chaianov, Shanin, and "Russian Populism" and proceeded to dismiss all three out of hand.[12]

At the same time that the debate was raging between the advocates of equilibrium mobility and the proponents of class polarization, a second major set of questions emerged which concerned the economic condition of the peasantry at the turn of the century. Although Shanin[13] continued to argue that at the beginning of the 1890s the peasantry was impoverished and faced a declining situation, a number of studies began to uncover interesting new

[10] Mark Harrison, "Chaianov and the Economics of the Russian Peasantry," *Journal of Peasant Studies* 2, no. 4 (July 1975): 389–417.

[11] Mark Harrison, "Resource Allocation and Agrarian Class Formation: The Problem of Social Mobility Among Russian Peasant Households, 1880–1930," *Journal of Peasant Studies* 4, no. 2 (January 1977): 127–61.

[12] Terry Cox, "Awkward Class or Awkward Classes? Class Relations in the Russian Peasantry Before Collectivization," *Journal of Peasant Studies* 7, no. 1 (October 1979): 70–85; Judith Ennew, Paul Hirst, and Keith Tribe, " 'Peasantry' as an Economic Category," *Journal of Peasant Studies* 4, no. 4 (July 1977): 295–322.

[13] Teodor Shanin, *The Roots of Otherness, 1, Russia as a Developing Society* (New Haven and London, 1985), pp. 151–58.

evidence. Empire-wide studies by Raymond Goldsmith and Olga Crisp indicated that the economic component of the agrarian crisis was apparently not as severe as usually reported; and Paul Gregory's numerous works support their findings.[14] Recent works by Anfimov and Stephen Wheatcroft that reach down to the regional level indicate that even in the "impoverished center," where economic conditions were generally agreed to be the worst in the empire, net population growth by the late 1880s and 1890s was modest; and living standards had apparently largely stabilized.[15]

In the absence of detailed case studies, however, most scholars in the United States still view the major issues raised in both debates as unresolved. My own work and that of scholars like Timothy Mixter and Jeffrey Burds are clearly beginning to provide detailed evidence from different regions of the empire that support a revisionist position.

In this chapter, I examine peasant poverty in a single province in one of the poorest and most backward parts of the Russian empire at the end of the nineteenth century. Using standard minimum resource definitions of poverty, I construct a profile of the typical farm classified as poor, and identify the chief on-farm causes of poverty for the province as a whole. Then I consider the basis for a more limited peasant definition of poverty and examine the most obvious differences between the upper and lower ranks of the poor. Finally, I discuss the evidence of the continued vitality of the primary peasant institutions—the family and the commune.

The data almost without exception, reveal austere but still viable peasant institutions that supported what peasants considered to be "average" or better living standards for almost 80 percent of the households. They indicate a peasant mobility pattern that was cyclical and tended toward equilibrium. It was driven by family partitioning, the biological life cycle, and "random oscillations." No significant culmination of advantages and disadvantages was taking place. The leveling operation of the Great Russian multiple family was strong enough to short-circuit almost completely the culmination of advantages anticipated by Leninist, neoclassical, and Neo-Marxist theory. Com-

---

[14] Raymond W. Goldsmith, "The Economic Growth of Tsarist Russia, 1860–1913," *Economic Development and Cultural Change* 9, no. 3 (April 1961): 441–75; Olga Crisp, *Studies in the Russian Economy Before 1914* (London & Basingstoke, 1976); and Paul Gregory, "Russian Living Standards During the Era of Industrialization, 1885–1913," *Review of Income and Wealth* 26, no. 1 (March 1980): 87–103, "Grain Marketings and Peasant Consumption, Russia, 1885–1913," *Explorations in Economic History* 17, no. 2 (1980): 135–64, and *Russian National Income, 1885–1913* (Cambridge, 1982).

[15] Anfimov indicates that only two other regions had a smaller net population growth between 1883 and 1900 than the Central Agricultural Region; heavy out-migration from the region was the likely explanation for the relatively slow rise in numbers. A. M. Anfimov, *Krest'ianskoe khoziaistvo Evropeiskoi Rossii, 1881–1904* (Moscow, 1980), tables 4 and 6. Stephen Wheatcroft, "Crises and the Peasantry in Late Imperial Russia," this volume. Professor Wheatcroft describes the situation as "stagnating" rather than as "stabilizing." I suggest these terms describe the same phenomena, but evaluate them differently.

munal provision of land to the displaced and extinctions and mergers limited the culmination of disadvantages.

THE PROVINCE TO BE STUDIED

REASONS FOR ITS SELECTION

Voronezh Province (see map 2) was an important economic and political problem site. It was located in the "impoverished center," an area generally agreed to be one of the poorest and most traditional in the empire. About halfway between Moscow and the Black Sea, its access to national and inter-

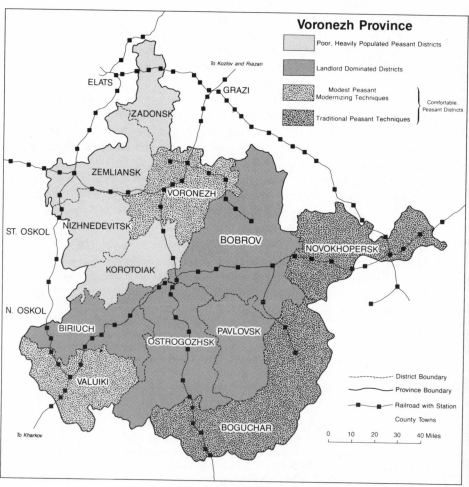

MAP 2.
Regions and Districts of Voronezh Province

national markets was sharply limited. Local jobs were few and pay was low; and departure work and migration rates were locally significant. In some districts, 40 percent of the peasants were poor or nearly poor. Landlord great estates that used sixteen-to twenty-year long-fallow rotations[16] and peasants who had accepted "beggarly allotments" at Emancipation[17] were numerous.

In both 1905–1907 and 1917, revolutionary outbursts in its landlord-dominated districts made Voronezh one of the most disorderly provinces in the empire. In 1906, one of its twelve districts experienced more revolutionary disorders than any other district in the empire. During the Civil War, the major Antonov peasant revolt against the Bolsheviks was centered just across its northeastern border.[18]

The materials available on the province are also very rich. Some of the best, most detailed studies on the peasant economy from the late imperial period are from Voronezh. And the variety of conditions found in the province and their physical distribution provide an almost laboratory-like range of natural, social, economic, and political phenomena that permit one to study each factor in a variety of combinations.

Physical Characteristics

The province was an area of "old settlement," claimed from the Turks by Peter the Great. It was a large province that straddled the Don River; and in 1898 its population was 2,550,000.[19] A historic producer and exporter of grain, its land was uniformly fairly rich. However, rainfall, average crop yields, and population densities all dropped off significantly as one moved from the northwest to the southeast.

---

[16] A crop rotation that took land out of cultivation for sixteen to twenty years to restore fertility. It was typically used on great estates in sparsely populated districts.

[17] When peasants were emancipated from serfdom in the 1860s and 1870s, they were offered land that was to be "redeemed," or paid for, over forty-nine years. "Beggarly allotments" were one-fourth the size of the normal minimum allotment, but they were free and did not have to be redeemed. They were a popular option in sparsely populated districts where lease land was cheap and readily available. As population density increased and lease prices rose, however, they came to be called "beggarly allotments."

[18] Disorders were heavily concentrated in the one-third of the districts dominated by landlords. Landlord-peasant competition triggered by the extension of the railroads, rather than immiseration, was the apparent key to the revolutionary dynamic. See also notes 20 and 21. But detailed examination of this complex topic lies beyond the scope of this work. Elvira M. Wilbur, "The Peasant Economy, Landlords, and Revolution in Voronezh: A Call for a Reappraisal of the Nature of the Russian Revolutionary Crisis at the Turn of the Century" (Ph.D. diss., University of Michigan, 1977), pp. 43–53; Voronezh, Russia (USSR), Universitet, Kafedra istorii SSR, E. G. Shuliakovskii, ed., *Ocherki istorii Voronezhskogo kraia, 1, S drevneishikh vremen do velikoi oktiabr'skoi sotsialisticheskoi revoliutsii* (Voronezh, 1961), p. 368 and William H. Chamberlin, *The Russian Revolution, 1917–1921*, 2 vols., 1 (New York, 1935), pp. 436–39.

[19] Russia, Tsentral'nyi statisticheskii komitet, *Pervaia vseobshchaia perepis' naseleniia Rossiiskoi Imperii 1897 g.*, 9, Voronezhskaia guberniia (St. Petersburg, 1904), tables 1 and 5.

Natural, social, and economic variations divided the province into three economic regions: (1) poor, heavily populated, peasant districts in the north and west[20]; (2) landlord-dominated districts in the middle of the province[21]; and (3) economically comfortable peasant districts. The last "region" was "comfortable," but *not* prosperous.[22] It was made up of two noncontiguous subgroups: (a) districts located between the poor and landlord-dominated districts in the center of the province that had begun the gradual process of modernization;[23] and (b) districts in the east and southeast that still used tra-

[20] The districts were Zadonsk, Zemliansk, Nizhnedevitsk, and Korotoiak. They were peasant dominated and poor. Relatively high population densities were a chief source of their poverty, but other factors also contributed to their economic difficulties. There were few railway stations in these districts and thus little access to the national market. There were also virtually no landlords to provide modernizing models. Thus the peasants had little knowledge of new methods and few market incentives to modernize their rotations, even though living standards were low. The degree of economic want in the districts still had some clear limits, however. Virtually no households in the region were forced to support themselves from their garden plots. And even with the growing subsistence problems, revolutionary activity in the region was limited. This was probably because there were few landlords in the districts with whom to fight. Wilbur, "The Peasant Economy," pp. 15–16, 35–36, 41–42, 46, 49–52.

[21] The landlord-dominated districts were Bobrov, Pavlovsk, Ostrogozhsk, and Biriuch. They were part of an arc of districts dominated by market-active great estates that began in northwest Saratov and Samara provinces and finally ended in Kiev and Podol'ia. The revolutionary confrontation in the countryside in both 1905–1907 and 1917 was heavily concentrated in this arc of districts. See Timothy Mixter, "Peasant Collective Action in Saratov Province, 1902–1906," in Rex A. Wade and Scott J. Seregny, eds., *Politics and Society in Provincial Russia: Saratov, 1590–1917* (Columbus, 1989), pp. 196–98.   In Voronezh Province, most peasants in the revolutionary districts had living standards above the subsistence minimum, so the source of conflict was not simple immiseration. A fairly dense rail network gave the districts good access to the national market. Landlord/peasant competition for land sought for market production seemed to be a primary cause of the revolutionary outbursts in the province. Wilbur, "The Peasant Economy," pp. 31–37, 41–50. However, specific outbursts were frequently fueled by breaches of the peasant moral economy. Two particularly inflammatory examples of such violations were the waste associated with long fallow and landlord unwillingness to fulfill traditional welfare relief roles in difficult years. Elvira M. Wilbur, "The Stolypin Reforms under 'Worst Case' Circumstances: A Case Study" (Paper presented at the Second Annual Seminar on the History of Russian Society in the Twentieth Century, Philadelphia, January 30, 1982) and Roberta Thompson Manning, *The Crisis of the Old Order in Russia: Gentry and Government* (Princeton, 1982), p. 162.

[22] The richest households in the province were in these districts. They had the human and material resources to live comfortably, and they could weather almost any crisis, including the famine of 1891–1892. By peasant standards, they were "rich." But these farms did not become stable, commercialized, capitalistic operations because even the most prosperous of them divided when they reached the size of fifteen to thirty persons. I have chosen the somewhat awkward term "comfortable" to describe the districts to underline the limits of prosperity, even in the most prosperous districts in the province.

[23] The "modernizing" districts were Voronezh and Valuiki. Peasants in these districts were faced with relatively limited competition for land and with good market opportunity. Under these favorable conditions, they modified their cropping patterns modestly within the tra-

ditional peasant techniques and rotations.[24] These two subgroups have been merged under the rubric of "comfortable peasant districts" because of the general equivalency of their living standards.[25] (See map 2.)

Social and Economic Characteristics

Peasants in the province fit Shanin's definition of a peasantry given in "The Theory and Logic of the Peasant Economy." Family farms were primarily agricultural, but both the comfortable and the poor supplemented their incomes with off-farm work; the former, to provide a margin of prosperity; the latter, to ward off material want.[26] Virtually all farms sold into the market, but it took good access to a major market (a railway station or a large regional fair) to stimulate the regular and substantial market activity needed to underwrite relative peasant prosperity.[27]

The large majority of Voronezh's peasants lived in repartitional communes; and their basic land supply came from it. They supplemented the communal base, however, and often heavily, with land rented from large landlords or other peasants. Most of them were middle peasants who had, or could secure, enough land to provide themselves with subsistence, and thus had few pressing needs. But beyond the effective reach of good markets, they also lacked opportunity and thus had limited incentive to change.

What changes peasants were making were within the context of the traditional three-field system; and the limited nature of these changes made them virtually invisible to outside investigators.[28] The outsiders hoped to detect changes that signaled the conversion to a "modern," or commercial, farm economy, but such changes were *not* taking place. And the gross data outsiders typically used did not reveal the changes made in the three-field system in response to market opportunity that were increasing productivity and

---

ditional three-field system to produce a surplus to sell into the national market. Although population density in these districts was beginning to rise, market activity protected living standards. Wilbur, "The Peasant Economy," pp. 31–33, 36–37.

[24] The "traditional" districts were Novokhopersk and Boguchar. They were sparsely populated districts that were subject to wide variations in yields because of uncertain rainfall. Most households in these districts still had enough land to maintain "comfortable" living standards, despite their continued use of traditional rotations. Ibid., pp. 29–34.

[25] In order of relative prosperity, they were Boguchar, Voronezh, Valuiki, and Novokhopersk. Ibid., pp. 20–26.

[26] Ibid., pp. 160–63.

[27] Elvira M. Wilbur, "Peasant Markets, Prosperity and Development: A Case Study From the 'Impoverished Center,' Circa 1890" (paper presented at the Sixteenth Annual National Convention of American Association for the Advancement of Slavic Studies, New York, November 1984).

[28] Elvira M. Wilbur, "Development From the Peasant Perspective: A Case Study From Central Russia at the Turn of the Twentieth Century" (paper presented at the Twelfth Annual National Convention of the American Association for the Advancement of Slavic Studies, Philadelphia, November 7, 1980).

maintaining or improving living standards on a local basis. As a result, Voronezh was viewed as totally backward, stagnant, and poor, that is, as quite typical of the "impoverished center."

PRIMARY SOURCES AND METHODOLOGY

This perception of Voronezh Province made it the focus of considerable attention and study. F. A. Shcherbina's study of peasant budgets,[29] done in conjunction with a province-wide census conducted between 1888 and 1896, was the most important of these studies. He and local zemstvo workers did an in-depth study of a large, representative sample of 230 households. Each budget has 677 statistical entries and an attached narrative; together they provide information on virtually every aspect of the households' resources and operations. Taken collectively, they present a detailed profile of the peasantry for the entire province.

To shape the material, I constructed a ranking of all 230 cases based on land under crops, assets other than land, and gross income per-farm, per-capita, and per-worker.[30] Visual inspection of the ranking reveals that the farms between the twentieth and thirty-third percentiles were distinct from the farms both above and below them in the ranking. The question is: Did these farms constitute the bottom ranks of the nonpoor or were they the upper ranks of the poor?

In Russian peasant studies, authors traditionally use either three or five *desiatiny* of land under crops per-farm to mark off the poor from the nonpoor.[31] On the basis of either of the two conventional measures, the farms in

[29] Fedor A. Shcherbina, *Krest'ianskie biudzhety* (Voronezh, 1900). The material on the budgets is found in a separately paged part II of *Krest'ianskie biudzhety*, pp. 1–271. The budgets are numbered; and material is listed according to number in both the statistical and narrative sections.

[30] Because a handful of the most prosperous farms were widely separated from most of the other farms in the sample and the ones at the bottom of it were tightly grouped, I used a "scaled" ranking, that is, one that valued the richest farm at 100 and the poorest at zero.

I used multiple measures of the same variable because use of any single measure produced significant bias at the extremes of the ranking. The traditional per-farm measure of resources unduly raised the ranking of well-endowed farms with work forces of ten to eighteen workers and lowered those of some two-worker (especially retiree) farms. Per-worker and per capita measures, on the other hand, understated the resources of the largest farms and overstated those of the smallest ones. When the several measures are used together, the biases generally offset each other. Only one difficulty remains at the lower end of the composite ranking. When per capita and per-worker measurers for a farm become a unity, the correction they provide is overstated and a limited number of individual cases are biased upward.

[31] Shanin, *The Awkward Class* and most of the sources he cited used three *desiatiny* as the break point. Lenin and many of his sources used five *desiatiny*. The average area of land under crops for the farms between the twentieth and thirty-third percentiles was four *desiatiny* or 10.9 acres. More than 70 percent (22 of 31) had less than five *desiatiny* under crops; almost half (15 of 31) had less than three *desiatiny* under crops.

question should be included among the "poor." Peasant and census-worker commentary in the Shcherbina narratives, however, describe the majority of them as "doing tolerably well" or as "average." Given this difference in valuation, it will be useful to examine the groups described by the alternative definitions. Let us begin with the traditionally defined group.

THE TYPICAL FARM IN THE BOTTOM THIRD OF THE RANKING

Seventy-five percent of the farms in the bottom third of the ranking were labor-short farms that were based on a single conjugal couple (see table 3-1). This is the typical profile of the Russian poor peasant farm.[32] However; most of the couples were *not* "typical" nuclear couples beginning or ending a normal nuclear family life cycle. They were couples who had fallen out of, been pushed out of, or opted out of the Great Russian multiple family that was still the "normal" structure for the majority of farms in the province.[33] Some

TABLE 3-1.
Farm Prosperity and Poverty as a Function of Family Size

Percentile Budget Rank Within Province	Households (N = 230)	Conjugal Couples per Household		
		None	One	More Than One
Bottom Third of the Sample				
0–33	78	1%	76%	23%
21–33	31	—	65	35
0–20	46	2	83	15
Total Sample				
34–100	152	3%	27%	70%
0–33	78	1	76	23

Source: Compiled from Fedor A. Shcherbina, *Krest'ianskie biudzhety* (Voronezh, 1900), pt. II, table II, pp. 203–71.

[32] See Lenin, p. 62 and Shanin, *The Awkward Class*, p. 63.

[33] Both Chaianov and Shanin argued that peasant families typically went through the full cycle of a nuclear family. This cycle begins with the marriage of a couple and the establishment of an independent household, proceeds through an expansion phase as children are born, then contracts as the children mature, marry, and establish their own independent households. (*A.V. Chaianov on the Theory of the Peasant Economy*, p. 58, table 1-5; and Shanin, *The Awkward Class*, p. 104, table 6.IV.)

There is evidence to indicate this may have been the pattern for the Ukrainian family. Christine D. Worobec, "Patterns of Property Devolution Among Ukrainian Peasants in Kiev and Kharkiv Provinces, 1861–1900" (paper presented at a Conference on the Peasantry of European Russia, 1800–1917, Boston, August 1986), p. 8.

This was not the pattern in Voronezh Province, however. In Voronezh, a majority of all the farms in the 230-farm sample had multiple families with two or more conjugal units and

had walked away quietly, hoping to improve their situation; others had stomped away in anger; still others had been forcibly ejected. They included the young newlywed pair, and the childless older couple; only sons, those who had married late, and those starting over; and the orphaned and abandoned. Some of the farms were newly created; others were midway through a long struggle for survival.

The future of these farms was dependent on demographic success or failure. Those who had a minimum of two sons in a timely manner (i.e., the number needed to reestablish a viable labor supply of four healthy adults—the sons and their two wives) probably could escape the ranks of the poor. For those facing a partial demographic failure (one son, or only a daughter[s]), another generation of struggle was likely. For the total demographic failures and the sick and the lame, however, the only probable escape from poverty was death.

The remaining 25 percent of the group had a full work force of two or more conjugal units. They were about equally divided between (1) families who were "about to make it" after some long struggle; (2) those who were relatively recent victims of a catastrophe such as a major fire, the great famine of 1891–1892, or a migration that failed; and (3) those who, because of location, landlord presence, and/or population pressure, lacked access either to the land or markets necessary to utilize their available labor supply effectively. The latter accounted for only about 8 percent of the total, and were heavily concentrated geographically in the four landlord-dominated districts located in the middle of the province.

Clearly in Voronezh Province, nuclear couples who had fallen out of the multiple family strongly dominated the lower economic ranks. Multiple families that depended heavily on leased land for their farming operations just as strongly dominated the upper ranks. (See table 3-1.) This is convincing evidence that, in Voronezh, Chaianov's contention that the independent variable that determined peasant prosperity or poverty was labor, not land, was true.

THE PRIMARY ON-FARM CAUSES OF POVERTY

But what circumstances put a farm into the bottom third of the ranking? An analysis of statements from the Shcherbina narratives permits us to establish the probable on-farm cause(s) of poverty for almost 90 percent of the farms

---

three or four generations resident in the household. Among the nonpoor, 70 percent of the families were still multiple families and 65 percent of them still contained three or four generations. Elvira M. Wilbur, "The Russian Multiple Family After Emancipation: A Case Study From the 'Impoverished Center' " (Paper presented at the Tenth Annual Meeting of the Social Science History Association, Chicago, November 21, 1985).

in the bottom third of the sample.[34] Although thirteen on-farm sources of poverty can be identified (see table 3-2), four accounted for about 60 percent of the total. They were: (1) family demographic failure; (2) chronic illness/ permanent disability; (3) beginning a household without economic resources; and (4) family fights. Family demographic failure was the largest category, accounting for almost 30 percent of the total. The other three each accounted for 10 percent.

Largest On-Farm Source of Poverty

Peasants almost never mentioned family demographic failure in the Shcherbina narratives. But farms that failed to produce the two sons needed to maintain the minimum labor supply of four adults necessary to sustain a viable peasant farm made up the largest identifiable group of farms in the bottom third of the ranking. Demographic failure was also an important secondary cause (or effect) of poverty.[35]

No children (absolute failure) or no sons, an only son (especially a late-born one), or even two widely spaced sons all constituted forms of family demographic failure. The random nature of normal reproductive patterns,

TABLE 3-2.
Primary On-Farm Causes of Poverty in the Bottom Third of the Shcherbina Sample

	Households	Percent of All Poor
Demographic failure	23	30%
Illness/disability	8	10
Beginning a household without resources	8	10
Family fights	8	10
Other (less than 10%)[a]	23	29
Unknown	8	10
Total	78	99

Source: Compiled from Fedor A. Shcherbina, *Krest'ianskie biudzhety* (Voronezh, 1900); pt. II, table II, pp. 203–71.

[a] The other nine on-farm causes of poverty included: voluntary departure, 8 percent; not farmers (i.e., a statistical effect), 5 percent; fire, 4 percent; failed immigrations, new farms, debt, early/multiple deaths, 3 percent each; and retirees, famine, 1 percent each.

[34] It was possible to identify a source(s) of poverty for sixty-seven of the seventy-eight farms, or 86 percent of the total. When a farm had multiple factors that contributed to its economic distress, I placed it in the single category that seemed to be the most important cause of its problems.

[35] For example, farms formed after family fights were frequently demographically weak; and the orphaned were often late-born, only sons. In the lowest 10 percent of the ranking, 56 percent of all the farms were full or partial demographic failures, as discussed later.

late marriages, and the consequent delay and reduction in number of births they produced were apparently the most frequent causes of such failures.

No children or only daughters were the most severe forms of failure. A. V. Aksenov's life history illustrates the problem. He had three daughters, aged thirteen, ten, and two, but no sons. He had already lost two allotments of communal land because of "the lace of the male element," and was worried he would lose his last allotment for the same reason.[36] At ages thirty-seven and thirty-six, the Aksenovs still had perhaps ten years to produce a son or accept a son-in-law, but they were old enough that one or both was likely to die or become dependent before mature grandsons and their wives could provide the minimum adult labor force needed to secure the future of the household.

Such units might survive on the basis of a merger with some other individual or unit, but the evidence suggests that mergers were often made under deprived economic circumstances or delayed until the burden of dependent older workers was a relatively near-term reality. This meant that although the merger might permit the unit to survive, the combination of limited resources and the burden of aged dependents often prevented a full-blown recovery. When such farms did recover, it often took decades.

Partial demographic failure such as a single, late-born son or two widely spaced sons also left farms economically weak for extended periods. For example, G. S. Iakimenko's father had been thirty-eight when he was born, and Iakimenko's only son was born when he was forty. At the time of the census in 1896, Iakimenko was forty-seven years old and burdened by his dependent eighty-five-year-old father. His son was only seven years old and still at least thirty years away from the possibility of full-grown, productive grandsons. Obviously, the second generation into the problem, the long-term future of the Iakimenko farm was still in question.[37]

Two widely spaced sons also produced unsatisfactory results. For example, N. S. Sosonskii's sixteen-year-old brother was twenty-three years his junior. Sosonskii and his wife, aged thirty-nine and thirty-five, had been liable for the support of his widowed, sixty-five-year-old father, their seven-year-old daughter, and the younger brother for some years. In 1894, the brother was not yet a mature worker or ready for marriage. And because the Sosonskiis had failed to produce a son of their own by their mid-thirties, there was a question whether the brother's approaching maturity and future marriage were going to secure the farm's future.[38]

The Next Three Largest Categories

Farms With Permanently Disabled or Chronically Ill Family Members.   Permanent disability or chronic illness, especially when combined with one or more

---

[36] Budget no. 21, Nizhnedevitsk District.

[37] Budget no. 70, Ostrogozhsk District.

[38] Budget no. 149, Biriuch District.

other major problems, had a catastrophic impact on a farm.[39] Disability and chronic illness often appear to have preceded or followed an open or "disguised" expulsion. For example, Ia. A. Zukov was driven out by his father when he was thirty-five years old with only private property valued at twenty-five rubles. At forty-five, Zukov was "constantly sick in the head"; and his family survived on the earnings of his wife and three daughters, aged seventeen, nine, and six. The only son was a six-month-old infant.[40] P. V. Lapin, on the other hand, seems to have been the object of a "disguised expulsion." Five years after he was lamed and with a pregnant wife, he reportedly "divided" with his brother. In 1889, fifteen years after the division, they were still so poor they could not keep their only son, a fourteen-year-old, at home with them.[41]

Multiple chronic illnesses or chronic disabilities were the ultimate disaster, however. For example, T. A. Efimenko had a blind wife and an eighty-year-old father-in-law who was described as a "decrepit old man who had been lame since infancy." His farm was only two years old; and the two disabled adults and four small children, aged eight, five, three, and six months, were dependent on Efimenko and his one seventeen-year-old son. His was the poorest household in the sample.[42]

Beginning a Household Without Economic Resources. These households[43] shared the fact that they all began without economic resources, but they were a composite group that included orphans, those expelled, and those both orphaned and expelled. Despite their similar economic circumstances, however, their perception of their own individual situations was very different. The angriest were those who considered themselves victims of injustice. Forty-year-old E. Prokhorenko's bitter story was that of an "orphaned"[44] nephew expelled by an uncle when he was fifteen years old. He had managed to establish an independent farm by the time he was twenty-one; and he and his wife began having children in a timely fashion. However, twenty-five years after the original expulsion, the household was still burdened by multiple dependencies: his sixty-four-year-old mother; a widowed, thirty-year-old sister; two sons, aged fourteen and ten, and daughters, aged twelve, seven, and four. The two sons offered good hope for the future, but

[39] Farms with permanently disabled or chronically ill members accounted for five of the nine poorest farms in the province.

[40] Budget no. 29, Novokhopersk District.

[41] Budget no. 32, Boguchar District. Such disguised expulsions apparently were not rare. See also budget no. 50, Pavlovsk District.

[42] Budget no. 4, Boguchar District.

[43] Budgets no. 118, Pavlovsk District; no. 56 and no. 148, Ostrogozhsk District; no. 25, Bobrov District; no. 16, no. 81, and no. 83, Zadonsk District; and no. 23, Korotoiak District.

[44] A boy was considered orphaned if his father died. Note below that Prokhorenko's mother was still alive and living with him in 1895, twenty-five years after the "orphaning."

they were still four to eight years away from marriageable age. In the meantime, Prokhorenko looked back with anger, rather than forward with hope.[45]

Orphans faced material conditions similar to those of the orphaned and
expelled, but they confronted their situation with surprising energy and optimism.[46] Nikita Donchenko, a late-born, only son from Ostrogozhsk District,
exemplified them. He was "orphaned" at fourteen when his sixty-six-year-
old father died. Without an adult male in the household, he had hired a
substitute head of household, sold the paternal horse and cow, and leased
out the communal allotment, while he worked as a farm laborer to earn
money to reestablish the farm. As a fourteen-year-old, he earned only eighteen rubles a year; but after his sixteenth birthday, his earnings averaged fifty
rubles a year. He earned enough in six years to recover the household land,
secure a horse, and marry. At the time of the census, he and his wife, aged
twenty-two and twenty-three, were the farm's only workers. Although he
had a dependent seventy-year-old mother and the farm still had no cow or
tools, he planned to buy a steel plough on shares with a neighbor and use
their two horses to pull it. With two young sons, aged two years and nine
months, he expected his economic situation to improve. The census-taker,
impressed by his energy, also expected him to succeed.[47]

Those expelled from their paternal home occupied something of a psychological middle ground between the orphans and those both orphaned and
expelled. They had been expelled from two to thirty years before the census.
They told their life histories in a matter-of-fact way that had neither the bitterness of Prokhorenko nor the confidence of Donchenko. An investigator
has to be cautious about interpreting the significance of their neutral tone,
however. The evidence suggests it reflected more their relative acceptance of
their situation than their actual economic circumstances. Half of them lacked
the minimum of two sons essential for the eventual economic stabilization of
a farm; hence the long-term future for these households was problematic.[48]

Farms Formed After Family Fights.   Drunkenness, the pressures caused by ab-
sences associated with army service, or a combination of the two accounted
for over 80 percent of the farms still in the bottom third of the ranking that
had been formed after family fights. Only one of them had emerged after a
fight among the women.[49] The accounts of the fights were laconic, but fights

[45] Budget no. 148, Ostrogozhsk District.

[46] Also see below, budget no. 56, Ostrogozhsk District and no. 81, Zadonsk District.

[47] Budget no. 56, Ostrogozhsk District.

[48] Two of the four farms lacked the requisite number of two sons. None of the four orphaned or orphaned and expelled householders had this problem.

[49] Four involved fights during, or soon after the return from, army service; a fifth involved
drunkenness; and a sixth involved a combination of the two. Budgets no. 71, Valuiki District;
no. 69, Ostrogozhsk District; no. 27, Bobrov District; no. 15 and no. 18, Zemliansk District;
no. 139, Zadonsk District; no. 39, Nizhnedevetsk District; and no. 98, Korotoiak District. A

seemingly threatened the long-term security of a household more than or-phanings, expulsions, or even a combination of the two.

Four pivotal factors contributed to the greater risk. Virtually all the fights took place much later in the life of the householder than the orphanings and expulsions. Second, they involved couples who, at the time of the fight, were only marginally successful in demographic terms. Third, the demographic failure visible at the time of the fight was predictive of continuing relative failure.[50] Finally, almost two-thirds of the recorded fights (63 percent) oc-curred in the poor, heavily populated, peasant districts, where the resources essential to recovery were very limited.

The four primary causes of on-farm poverty just described are rather sur-prising. All four were types of random oscillation or chance events; and they all included a complex mix of "natural," structural, and "willed" phenom-ena. Family demographic failure resulted either from the physical failure to produce sons, or from delays in marriage that were related to growing pop-ulation pressure. Permanent disabilities/chronic illnesses were natural "acts of God," but they were often complicated by willed acts of open or disguised expulsion. Instances of beginning without economic resources stemmed both from acts of God that created full orphans and from willed acts of expulsion that ejected sons and nephews. Even family fights, when looked at closely, shared this dual quality. The fights themselves ostensibly were acts under human control; but the combatants frequently were also demographic failures.

THE PEASANT PERSPECTIVE ON POVERTY

To this point, we have discussed "the poor" as defined by the traditional measures of a minimum of three to five *desiatiny* of land under crops. In Voronezh Province, this basically amounted to the bottom third of the rank-ing. As mentioned above, however, the farms between the twentieth and thirty-third percentiles were distinct from the farms both above and below them in the ranking. The question still is: Did these farms constitute the bot-tom ranks of the nonpoor or were they the upper ranks of the poor?

THE "AVERAGE" OR "TYPICAL" FARM

The evidence from the Shcherbina narratives indicates that both peasants and census-workers believed the great majority of these farms (75 percent)

---

seventh case involved a fight between the women; and the cause of the fight in the eighth case is not indicated.

[50] Seven to ten years after the initial fights, seven of the eight farms (87 percent) were still demographically vulnerable. Four had only one son; two had one daughter. The seventh couple was childless. These couples were still young enough that their demographic fate was not yet sealed, but they were no longer young. Four were couples in their thirties; and in the other three cases, the wives (the younger spouses) were in their late twenties.

were not poor. Some were upwardly mobile or stable and relatively secure. They were characterized in relatively positive terms as "having been created by their own will" or as "doing tolerably well." Others were described as "average," "typical," or as "having nothing that distinguished [them]" by census-takers or as "neither leasing nor leasing out land" or "neither buying nor selling grain" by peasants. Still others were not characterized at all.[51]

These descriptions indicate the peasant definition of the "average" or "typical" farm was a self-sufficient unit that balanced both consumption and production and available labor and land. Such a balanced condition was relatively unstable, and characterization of it was likely to be influenced by the probable direction of its economic evolution. Therefore, the fact that significant numbers of these farms had a full labor force of four or more adults and were likely to be upwardly mobile probably contributed to peasant and census-taker perceptions that they were not poor.[52]

Only 25 percent of the group were characterized in negative terms. They were fairly equally distributed between the landlord-dominated districts and the poor, heavily populated, peasant districts. Most of them were demographic failures that had no, or only one, late-born son.

This peasant definition of "average'" suggests that traditional statistical markers, at least for Voronezh Province, put almost one-third too many farms into the ranks of the poor. The misplaced ones included farms with (1) a relatively stable and adequate subsistence; (2) an "average" profile; and/ or (3) a significant potential for future upward mobility. If other studies show similar numbers, the finding suggests that the quasi-apocalyptic tone of many traditional presentations may have been, at the very least, somewhat overstated.

THE POOR

By peasant definitions, the poor in Voronezh were roughly equal to the bottom 20 percent of the ranking. Considered in the aggregate, these farms seemed like an undifferentiated mass that the census-takers described in phrases like "lives poorly"; "is extremely poor"; and "cannot escape need." If the budgets are disaggregated geographically and considered region by region, however, it becomes clear the causes of poverty and the potential for upward mobility differed significantly between the subregions of the province.

The Upper Half of the Poor.   The farms in the upper half of the poor were fairly evenly distributed between and concentrated almost entirely within, the sub-

[51] Nine farms were about to become upwardly mobile or were economically stable. Eight others were characterized as "typical"; and another seven were not characterized. Ten of the twenty-four farms (43 percent) had a full labor force.

[52] See below, the section titled "The Upper Half of the Poor."

sistence plus, landlord-dominated districts and the poor, heavily populated peasant districts. In the landlord-dominated districts, the problems were typical of the bottom third of the sample as a whole. Some were partial demographic failures; others had begun with nothing. Still others had suffered the combined problem of the premature death of a worker and a major catastrophe.[53] Despite their difficulties, however, 90 percent of them still had a sufficient labor supply or enough young sons that they had the potential for upward mobility.

In the poor peasant districts, however, the problems reflected more straitened circumstances. They included (1) divisions that permitted the householder or his brother to exit farming (33 percent); (2) crippling debts incurred in connection with major life ceremonies like weddings and funerals (33 percent); and (3) divisions precipitated by chronic illness or drunkenness that were designed to ensure the survival of one of the resulting units (25 percent). These farms also faced a more problematic future. Over half of them (seven of twelve) were demographic failures, either without children or sons.[54] They, in particular, probably faced long-term hardship or extinction.

A closer look at the demographic failures also provides surprising information on the deceptive "nonrole" divisions played in causing impoverishment in the poor districts.

All seven of the demographic failures had "divided," but the evidence clearly indicates the divisions were not the primary cause of their poverty. Four of the divisions had taken place twenty to thirty years before the census, under economically viable circumstances. Subsequent demographic failure had weakened two of the farms. The other two were formed by childless couples who had opted for (or been encouraged to accept) reliable nonfarm occupations at the age of forty. Twenty years later and still childless, however, they both faced a precarious old age in a society where the only provision for old age was the family.[55] Two other "divisions" were disguised

[53] Budgets no. 57, Ostrogozhsk District, and no. 149 and no. 59, Biriuch District, were partial demographic failures. Budgets no. 25 and no. 44, Bobrov District, and no. 148, Ostrogozhsk District, involved expulsions/departures; and budgets no. 33 and no. 52, Pavlovsk District, and no. 61, Biriuch District, had experienced premature deaths in combination with failed migrations or fires. The cause of poverty for the tenth farm (budget no. 143, Bobrov District) is unknown.

[54] There were twelve farms in the group. Those with two or more sons and those whose demographic success or failure was not yet determined were budgets no. 37 and no. 160, Zadonsk District, and no. 97, Nizhnedevitsk District; and no. 15, Zemliansk District, and no. 36, Zadonsk District.

The demographically weak farms were budgets no. 38, Zemliansk District, and no. 39 and no. 95, Nizhnedevitsk District; no. 1 Zadonsk District, no. 20, Nizhnedevitsk District, and no. 98, Korotoiak District; and no. 12, Zemliansk District.

[55] The two that had divided thirty years before were budgets no. 95 and no. 20, Nizhnedevitsk District; and the two that had opted out of farming were budgets no. 38 and no. 12, Zemliansk District.

expulsions designed to protect one of the units. Ia. I. Mitrofanov had "voluntarily divided" with his widowed, mentally ill brother and the brother's three-year-old daughter. And nephews had divided with the Khodykins, probably because of the Khodykins' drinking problem. Only one farm had been involved in a straightforward division precipitated by a fight among the women.[56] And this farm was poor enough before the fight that it seems unlikely staying together would have secured it economically.

The Bottom Half of the Poor.   The distinguishing mark for the poorest farms[57] was that many of them had experienced two or more catastrophic disasters. Their poverty was deep and apparently largely beyond recovery. Only 25 percent of them had the minimum number of sons necessary to provide the potential for upward mobility.[58] Even for them, however, the evidence suggests sons were not going to alleviate their situation significantly. The fact that such farms were relatively evenly distributed across all three provincial subregions[59] suggests that the kinds of multiple disasters that had reduced them were fairly random occurrences.

In both the comfortable peasant districts and the landlord-dominated ones, the poorest households were those with one or more chronically ill or permanently disabled dependents. It was only in the poor, heavily populated, peasant districts that the poorest farms fit the stereotypical image of "the poor farm" from the standard sources. In these districts, the poorest farms had begun with nothing or experienced a series of mini-disasters that brought them to bay in a stressed and overpopulated environment.

G. G. Kulikov's life history details how relatively ordinary events became serious threats that could undermine a small farm for years in the poor districts. Kulikov had divided with his brother to permit the brother to migrate. He was thirty-nine years old at the time of the division, and his second son had arrived, so a division seemed viable. Shortly afterward, however, the horse died and the cow had to be sold to pay for two funerals, which cost fifty rubles. Twenty rubles were also lost to a dishonest contractor. In order to cope, Kulikov leased out the family hut for three years at forty rubles per year, while he leased back another dwelling at half the price. He also baked

[56] The last three budgets were no. 1, Zadonsk District; no. 98, Korotoiak District; and no. 39, Nizhnedevitsk District.

[57] The bottom half of the poor (the poorest farms) were those in the bottom 10 percent of the ranking.

[58] This is in contrast to the potential for upward mobility among the upper half of the poor, where 90 percent of the farms in the landlord-dominated districts had the potential, and slightly over 40 percent of them had it in the poor peasant districts.

[59] There were seven impoverished households in both the comfortable peasant districts and the landlord-dominated districts, and nine in the poor peasant ones. They accounted for 10, 8, and 13 percent of the respective samples.

bricks for a contractor in summer at ten rubles per month and made felt boots in winter between jobs.[60]

These data indicate that the poverty of the poor in Voronezh was deep, but they also show there was some limit to it. The proportion of the poor who had a full labor force was small. Half the upper ranks of the poor also retained a potential for upward mobility. In the landlord-dominated districts, 90 percent of the farms had the potential for improvement; and in the poor, heavily populated, peasant districts, slightly over 40 percent. Also, for the most part, even the poorest farms in the province had *not* been forced to move from grain production and consumption to a heavy dependence on potatoes and other vegetables to maintain a subsistence diet.

The Vitality of the Peasantry and Peasant Institutions

The Voronezh data also provide considerable evidence that indicate the traditional view of the peasants as hopeless victims, bound by tradition and the rigidities of outmoded, archaic institutions may have been significantly overstated.

The Family and the Commune as Peasant Coping Mechanisms

The peasant family was a flexible, resilient institution that coped with poverty in a variety of ways. In worst-case circumstances, it might disperse entirely for five to six years to accumulate resources to begin again. An orphan might sell the live inventory and rent out the family plot, while he worked for wages and waited to come of age. Or a wife might return to her family with the children, while the husband worked full-time for others for wages. Alternatively, the basic household might be maintained, but "mouths"—for example, individuals who ate at the table or had to be fed—would be dispersed. Children would be placed out to other families; or workers might work away from the household for all or part of the year. The house could be sold or sublet, while the family moved into a hut. But as (or if) the situation improved, the numbers sent out or the time they were gone was reduced and the original house reclaimed.

The commune's role in confronting poverty was two edged. It was the major enabling agent for resource-short families who needed to establish or reestablish independent households: It gave them the basic land supply necessary to create a new farm. However, it also took land from households that (1) failed to produce sons, (2) lost workers, or (3) fell behind on taxes. The commune's critics believed it discouraged initiative because it redistributed improved land and "leveled down" larger units. Nothing in the Shcherbina sample indicates that was the case. What the commune and the peasants faced was the specific problem of how to secure land for households that had a viable labor force. In Voronezh, evidence from the sample indicates they

---

[60] Budget no. 37, Zadonsk District.

accomplished this by taking land from households that did not have a labor force, rather than by leveling-down large work units.

Peasant Attitudes and Opportunities

Most peasants did not verbalize negative opinions about their economic situation in the Shcherbina narratives. Negative reports came almost exclusively from farms that had suffered (1) a major setback that was seen as *unjust*, such as the expulsion of a young orphan or (2) a *recent and severe* setback, such as a major fire.[61] The tone of the typical report was toughly factual and stoic, or sometimes optimistic. Surprisingly, as one moved into the lowest parts of the ranking, negative self-reports virtually disappeared. One possible explanation for this startling fact may be that under really trying circumstances, angry or bitter self-characterizations had a negative survival value, and therefore were largely abandoned.

The evidence indicates, however, that reasons other than sheer survival mechanisms often underlay the stoic tone of the typical narrative. The reports document the fact that peasant institutions did provide survival protection against potentially catastrophic events. The family's several coping responses were austere, but workable—and even if the family lost its land, the commune would provide the minimum needed to begin again when the family situation improved. Also, if a couple produced two or more sons, the odds were good they could eventually escape the ranks of the poor. The Voronezh materials also remind us that the army, the frontier, and the town were real alternatives that peasants could and did choose, with varying degrees of success.

SUMMARY AND CONCLUSIONS

The Surprising Vitality of the Voronezh Peasantry

The materials presented here provide us with a reasonably comprehensive picture of late imperial peasant society in Voronezh Province from a "bottom up" perspective. It was still a traditional peasant society that used tough, traditional methods to survive difficulties; but from a subsistence perspective, these efforts were still relatively successful.

By peasant and census-worker standards, conventional markers overstated poverty in Voronezh Province by almost 30 percent. By the peasant/census-worker standard, poverty was confined largely to the bottom 20 percent of the ranking. Although hardship below this level was deep, there were still some real limits to it. Few farms with a full labor supply were poor; and 50 percent of the farms in the upper half of the poor still had enough

---

[61] Even when recovery was possible and within apparent reach for such householders, the pain and anger expressed remained stark.

sons to retain the potential for upward mobility. It was only in the poor peasant districts, where increased population density was becoming a significant
problem, and in the bottom 10 percent of the ranking in the other districts,
where the chronically ill and permanently disabled made up the bulk of the
poor, that most farms seemed to have little hope of escaping poverty. *But
even these farms* had not been forced to abandon grain production and consumption to become "potato eaters."

The Great Russian multiple family was still the dominant family structure
in Voronezh. Such families were concentrated in and circulated throughout
the upper two-thirds of the provincial ranking. Only a major catastrophe like
a big famine or fire might temporarily bump them out of the upper ranks.
Labor-short nuclear families dominated the bottom third of the ranking.
They were weak, anomalous fragments of multiple families that had fallen
out of, been expelled from, or walked away from a larger unit. They were
not couples beginning or ending a "normal" nuclear family life cycle, as
Chaianov and Shanin maintained. It was their small size, especially in the
poor districts, that often doomed them to the lower ranks for extended
periods.

Demographic failure, chronic illness/permanent disability, beginning a
household without resources (orphanage and/or expulsion), and family
fights over drunkenness or the tensions associated with army service were
the primary on-farm causes of poverty and near-poverty. The most stereotypical causes—fights among the women and the fairly ordinary events that
became disasters for weak farms in the poorest districts—produced *some* of
the poor units in Voronezh Province, but the evidence indicates that they
were probably over-reported in many standard sources.

The key to peasant coping was tough, flexible peasant institutions. The
peasant family, armed with an arsenal of coping behaviors, was elastic and
flexible. It could disperse entirely or "put out" individual members when
necessary; but it also retained the ability to reassemble itself in better times.
The commune, as a source of land for newly created households, was a major enabling agent for families that needed to establish or reestablish themselves.

Although peasant reporting could be misleading on occasion, the balance
of the evidence suggests the toughly factual and stoic, or sometimes surprisingly optimistic, peasant attitudes expressed in the Shcherbina narratives reflected peasant reality with reasonable accuracy.

Theoretical and Interpretive Implications of the Voronezh Material

The Equilibrium Model of Peasant Mobility Confirmed and Elaborated. Shanin's
model of peasant mobility is a complex five-part model.[62] The Voronezh ma-

---

[62] It included: (1) the culmination of advantages and disadvantages presumed to occur as

terials confirm its broad outlines, but suggest significant modifications and elaborations. First, one dynamic operated in the upper portion of the provincial ranking; another operated in the lower portion of it. Four factors, not five, dominated the process. The three most visible ones were: (1) the partitioning of families; (2) the biological life cycle of the family; and (3) random oscillations/chance events. Communal redistribution of land was also an important factor, but it was less visible and its significance was harder to assess. However, the culmination of advantages and disadvantages resulting from ordinary competition, posited by all major investigators, was virtually nonexistent in Voronezh Province.

A fairly simple cyclical mobility driven by partitions of the Great Russian multiple family dominated peasant household movement in the upper portions of the ranking. However, these divisions usually did not take place until there were at least four adult workers for each new unit. This meant the downward mobility of new units took them only to the middle ranks, not the lower ones, as Chaianov and Shanin maintained.[63]

The dynamic operating at the lower end of the ranking was more complex. It included three major factors. Quantitatively, the dominant one was random oscillations. All four of the major on-farm causes of poverty in the province—demographic failure, chronic illness/permanent disability, beginning without resources, and family fights—were one kind of chance event or another.

Partitionings and the biological life cycle also operated at the lower levels, but they operated quite differently than they did at the upper levels. The typical partition in the upper ranks took place as a matter of course when a large family matured. In the lower ranks, however, partitions typically were intended to deal with economically difficult situations. Some permitted a brother to migrate. Others were disguised expulsions that protected one household unit at the expense of another. They were not economically irrational, as standard sources often imply, but usually they were undertaken under difficult circumstances—and they were not fully successful until

---

a result of "ordinary competition"; (2) communal redistribution of land; (3) partitioning of families and family mergers and extinctions; (4) "random oscillations," such as weather, disease, family fights (especially those by women), etc.; and (5) possibly the biological life cycle. The only element Shanin considered new was the "random oscillations" or chance events factor. He did not speak to the question of the relative weights of the five factors, nor did he insist they would produce an equilibrium. Shanin *The Awkward Class*, figs. I, II, III, and V, pp. 51, 76–78, 118, and ch. 6, pp. 112–21.

[63] Although this point narrowly confirms Mark Harrison's 1977 position that "communal repartitions and the 'biological' family life cycle are unsatisfactory explanations for the downward mobility of large farms." (See above, p. 104.) The balance of the evidence refutes his main argument. Harrison maintained that there was a culmination of advantages and disadvantages taking place in the countryside that was leading to agrarian class formation. (See above, the previous paragraph, and below, pp. 125–26.)

young sons matured and married. This meant the process was almost always a long one, and highly subject to delay, disruption, or failure.

The usual biological life cycle of the family at the lower end of the ranking was that of an isolated nuclear couple in a stressed environment, not that of the multiple family. Demographic failure was often what isolated the couple and dropped them into the ranks of the poor in the first place. A partial failure could be recovered by demographic success in the next generation. However, total failure compensated by a merger was likely to produce another generation of struggle, while uncompensated failure often meant extinction of the unit when the couple forming it died.

Communal redistribution managed, paradoxically, to operate almost entirely as a "leveling up" process. First, the commune gave land to farms with the labor force needed to begin again. It also "leveled up," in a statistical sense, when it accelerated extinctions by removing land from failed or failing farms. There is no evidence in the Shcherbina sample to indicate that redistribution "leveled down" any units that had a viable labor force.

Further, the evidence indicates that the culmination of advantages and disadvantages posited by Shanin and by Leninist, neoclassical, and Neo-Marxist theory alike was *not* taking place in Voronezh Province. The partitioning of large multiple families was sufficient to prevent the culmination of advantages. And the combination of demographic success and communal grants of land to those in need, on the one hand, and extinctions, on the other, limited the culmination of disadvantages in an environment that was more viable than most investigators have thought it was.

Why the True Causes of Poverty Were Historically "Invisible." Shanin was one of the first to consider random oscillations an important independent aspect of the poverty process; and he presented it only as a hypothesis. Yet the Shcherbina sample seems to demonstrate clearly that chance events dominated the *on-farm* causes of poverty in Voronezh Province. If this analysis is confirmed elsewhere, the obvious question is: Why have these particular random oscillations been so totally overlooked? Several factors contributed to the problem.

The incidence and significance of chance events that created isolated multiple family fragments had increased rapidly in the last generation. A key factor in the increase in landlord-dominated districts was probably the elimination of landlord authority over peasant households. Prior to Emancipation, landlords regularly limited the division of peasant households and forced some mergers. Such actions protected the chronically ill/permanently disabled, the orphaned, and those threatened by family fights and expulsion. The sudden ending of this constraint almost certainly increased significantly the number of isolated nuclear couples who ended up in the ranks of the poor in the landlord-dominated districts.

Other broad structural changes also made the situation worse. The emergence of market opportunity that accompanied the building of the railroads seemingly promoted hostile family action against weak or dependent couples. Increases in population density in some districts also reduced both the viability of the multiple family and the ability of the commune to cushion problems. The individual or couple who fell out of a multiple family unit in the poor districts also faced much greater difficulty getting reestablished. The key to the last problem was the extra time needed to collect resources to reestablish a farm. The extra time delayed marriage and children, often until the couple was in its late thirties or early forties. Such a delay usually eliminated the family's chances to reestablish a multiple family household for another generation.

A fourth, more limited, problem was the impact of army service on households. Half the family fights reported in the Shcherbina sample involved incidents with veterans that took place while they were still in service or shortly after they returned. It seems that the separation from the family that military service involved undermined family solidarity enough to increase significantly the likelihood of major family fights.

Outside investigators did not distinguish between the different aspects of the situation. They understood the culmination of ordinary events *cum* disasters that could undermine or destroy a weak farm in the poorest districts to be the general condition. They equated virtually all partitions with the failed and failing ones at the lower end of the ranking, lumped partitions together with family fights, especially among the women, and presented the aggregated mass as evidence of the collective irrationality of the peasantry. Believing the problems were endemic, they could not conceptualize the possibility of amelioration. Instead, they looked to transform the system.

And peasant reports offered no corrective. Even with sources as rich as the Shcherbina narratives, cross-referenced against statistical profiles for the subregions of the province, the on-farm sources of poverty discussed here were difficult to identify. This is because they were often passed over in silence, euphemistically misnamed, or underreported. Reflection suggests these difficulties were probably the result of embedded peasant attitudes, perceptions, and behaviors. For example, demographic failure, chronic illness/permanent disability, and orphanings probably were viewed by peasants as judgments by God against the "victims." The tone numerous expellees used to describe their own expulsions indicates that most of the society, including many expellees themselves, viewed the expulsion of a son by a patriarch as a lawful, if not a righteous, act. Other, more "unspeakable" family behaviors, like the disguised expulsion of an ill, disabled brother with a three-year-old child, or the failure to allot an absent soldier/brother a portion at a division seemingly provoked such guilt that both expeller and expellee frequently used the euphemism "division" to describe the occurrence.

Peasant attitudes operating in the opposite direction were likewise the probable source of the overreporting of women's fights and mini-disasters. Women's fights were, by definition, illegitimate. When they occurred, it is likely no self-respecting peasant could ignore such a terrible breach of community norms. Likewise, a Job-like string of mini-disasters that brought down a weak farm was a human-interest story neither peasants nor outside investigators could resist. Hence these types of stories ended up heavily overreported relative to their actual incidence.

This work has focused on on-farm causes of poverty and province-wide data. It indicates the traditional case for poverty was overstated for Voronezh Province. A closer look at the subregions of the province will reveal the off-farm sources of poverty active in the province and show the different faces poverty assumed in the different regions. But these are tasks for another study.

CHAPTER 4

CRISES AND THE CONDITION OF THE PEASANTRY
IN LATE IMPERIAL RUSSIA

Stephen G. Wheatcroft

PEASANTS in late Imperial Russia were placed in an extremely difficult situation. The terms of the 1861 Emancipation had left them short of land and highly indebted to the government. Their rate of population growth was extremely high, and as Russia entered the demographic transition, it was increasing. The government was intent on a policy of rapid industrialization, which was ultimately to be paid for by large grain exports. This already strained situation was further complicated by three additional factors. Both the changing level of international grain prices and the weather-induced fluctuations in grain yields were external factors capable of applying severe shocks to the peasantry, and little could be done to affect their impact. The third factor was the effectiveness of the tsarist administrative machinery for levying taxes on the peasants and providing them with relief. This was a highly complex factor which was deeply related to domestic politics and ultimately to the revolutionary crisis.[1]

To help understand the complex situation in which the Russian peasantry found itself in the last thirty years of the empire it is useful to make the distinction between (1) agricultural crises, (2) crises in peasant living standards, and (3) agrarian crises. An agricultural crisis as defined.in this study is simply a crisis caused by a decline in agricultural production relative to the level of accepted utilization of agricultural produce. This could be either a sharp conjunctural crisis caused by a temporary fluctuation in either supply or demand, or it could be a more long-term systemic crisis caused by a major imbalance in the factors determining the long-term trends of supply or demand. Such a crisis will normally result in exceptional measures being taken by the government and the individuals concerned. The agricultural crisis

---

[1] The crisis in the tsarist administrative mechanism was mainly the result of domestic political pressures: the rise of the liberation and revolutionary movements. Its timing, however, was partly also the result of such external factors as the Russo-Japanese War and domestic economic problems.

may well turn out to have great social and political consequences, but in itself the agricultural crisis, as defined here, is a purely economic event.

The next category of crisis is a crisis in peasant living standards. It is important to remember that this type of crisis is not necessarily a consequence of a crisis in agricultural production. Peasant living standards would be greatly affected by an agricultural crisis, but in a complex way that would be modified by the role of the market and by government. And these latter two elements were in themselves quite capable of provoking a crisis in peasant living standards irrespective of the existence of an agricultural crisis. The sharp rise in agricultural prices that normally accompanies an agricultural crisis need not necessarily lead to a decline in the living standards of those peasants and producers who still had surplus product to sell. On the contrary, these groups would have much to lose from the fall in prices caused by a glut and overproduction. The sharp rise in market prices would, however, be extremely serious for those peasants and laborers who needed to purchase part or all of their foodstuffs. It is important, therefore, to examine the relative price levels and, in particular, the real rural wage levels of different groups of producers measured in terms of their command over the purchasing power of basic foodstuffs (i.e., their rye equivalent). Similarly, the living standards of those peasants who needed to purchase or rent land would be affected by the relative changes in land prices. Government, having the power either to increase the tax burden on the peasantry or to pursue a policy of tax remissions and relief, would also play an important role in aggravating or moderating the effect of the agricultural crisis on peasant living standards.

Our third category of crisis is an agrarian crisis. This crisis is only partly a consequence of the economic conditions of the peasantry. It is also partly a consequence of the degree of authority (or more precisely lack of authority) and determination of the government. An agrarian crisis is a crisis in the sociopolitical system and is manifested by the peasantry threatening to disrupt the social and political order. It takes a form that is described by the authorities as "agrarian disorders" and that includes: murder of landowners and officials; destruction of property; trespass; theft; land seizures; civil disorder; and, in particular, failure to pay taxes or perform traditional duties. If the government fails to respond adequately to these disorders, the movement will grow and may ultimately become revolutionary.

Although the agrarian crisis, the crisis in peasant living standards, and the agricultural crisis are connected, their relationships are neither simple nor direct. This essay examines some, but by no means all, of these relationships. The first part concentrates on agricultural production data in order to establish some of the main outlines of the chronology, severity and regional incidence of the main agricultural crises of the last thirty years of the tsarist regime. The next part focuses on the impact of real rural wage levels, the burden of rent, the burden of taxation and the effect of relief measures on peasant living standards, and will analyze these in terms of their chronology and regional incidence. The third part analyzes taxation data for the period in order to investigate the chronology and regional dimension of the extent of peasant refusal to accept the burdens placed on it by the government. The conclusions are based on a comparison of the regional and chronological factors discussed above.

In all these sections, the available data will be studied in some detail as regards their chronology (fluctuating annual level), their trends, and their overall regional differentiation. To avoid confusion, a few preliminary points should be made about groupings of data and classifications.

Time series may be analyzed in several ways. The data may be split into subgroups with averages calculated—for example for every five- or ten-year period—or each year may be considered in succession. The latter will be rather cumbersome for large sets of data. The procedure used in this essay is to use both approaches. When looking for crises in a large series of data I have made a grouping into five-year averages in the first instance, but have then gone on to consider the data in more detail at the annual level. Growth rates in the data have likewise been calculated from the average five-year data groupings, in the first instance, but also for the total annual data using the standard statistical procedures.[2]

There are two possible approaches to the problem of regional differentiation: One is to select a series of case studies (often separate administrative provinces, *Uezdy* or even *Volosti*) from the different regions and to analyze them in depth; the other is to concentrate on the full regional division of the data. The problem with the former approach is to determine how typical are the case studies that have been chosen. Since there were 72 different provinces, 777 different *Uezdy* and 17,075 different *Volosti* in the Russian Empire, how do we assess the relative importance of the information that we gain from any one of them? The latter approach is, I think, necessary in order to overcome this problem and to place the individual case studies in some form of perspective.

THE AGRICULTURAL CRISES

Throughout recorded history, grain has been the predominant agricultural product in Russia. As late as 1913, grain comprised over 90 percent of the total sown area. It was the major foodstuff, the major export good, and a major input into the livestock sector.[3] Particular attention will, therefore, be

[2] The procedure used was normally to fit a straight line to the data, which minimized the square difference to the fitted and original points—in other words, the least squares method.

[3] For a more detailed study of the different aspects of Russian agricultural production on the eve of the First World War see Stephen G. Wheatcroft, "Agriculture" in Robert W. Da-

paid to grain production. At the same time, it is worth noting that a part of the problem with Russian agriculture has been the predominance of grain and the weak development of livestock and other non-grain arable sectors. The amount of data on these other sectors is far less than for grain and they tend to be ignored in most accounts, yet the condition of these sectors and in particular the livestock sector provide a most revealing indication of the nature of the crisis. Following the section on grain production I will briefly consider the livestock crisis.

Grain Production

According to the standard interpretation made by Alexander Gerschenkron, toward the end of the nineteenth century Russian agriculture, taken as a whole, was in a serious long-term crisis: "In the last quarter of the nineteenth century Russian agriculture taken as a whole, made a valiant effort to maintain the per capita output constant. *But failed.*"[4] This conclusion of Gerschenkron's is based on the observation that over the period 1870–1874/1896–1900, Russian grain production rose at 1.3 percent per year while the population grew at 1.4 percent per year.

Figure 4-1 presents an indication of the growth in grain production since 1861; the growth in grain exports; and the growth in net grain production exclusive of exports. Figure 4-2 presents an indication of grain production per head of population for gross grain production and grain production net of exports. Figure 4-3 compares the annual data on per-capita gross grain production, the five-year average data, and Gerschenkron's growth indicator based on his calculations for the periods 1870–1874 and 1896–1900.

From the data in figure 4-3 it can readily be seen that Gerschenkron's conclusions are grossly misleading; growth rates are extremely difficult to measure, and they depend on the periodizations used. The 1870–1874 period was a quite exceptional five-year period with a record harvest in 1870, very high harvests in 1872 and 1874, and relatively good harvests in 1871 and 1873. If we were to select any other five-year period by moving our base years either forward or backward a number of years (or even a year), we would be forced to include a more typically bad harvest and that would make the average growth in production rise substantially. A move of just one year would result in the growth rate rising to either 1.4 percent per year or 1.6 percent. These are rates equal to, or slightly above, the population growth rate. The extension of the period into the twentieth century and especially up to the untypically good years 1909–1913 would increase the rate of per-capita growth of grain production even more.

vies, ed., *From Tsarism to the New Economic Policy: Continuity and Change in the Economy of the USSR* (forthcoming).

[4] Alexander Gerschenkron, "Agrarian Policies and Industrialisation, Russia 1861–1917," *Cambridge Economic History of Europe* (Cambridge, 1966), vi, pt. 2, p. 778. My emphasis.

FIG. 4-1. Grain Production and Exports, Russia 1861–1913

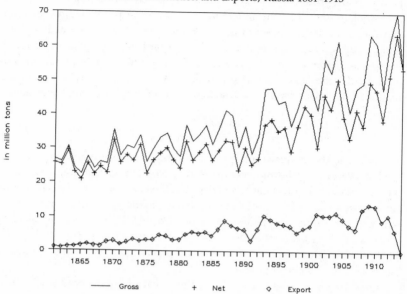

FIG. 4-2. Per Capita Grain Production, Russia 1861–1913

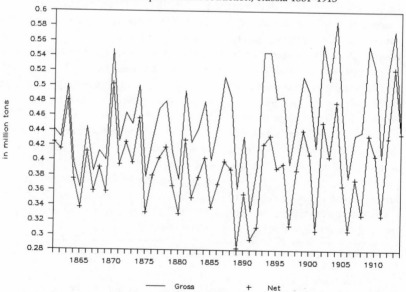

FIG. 4-3. Per Capita Grain Production, Gerschenkron and Others

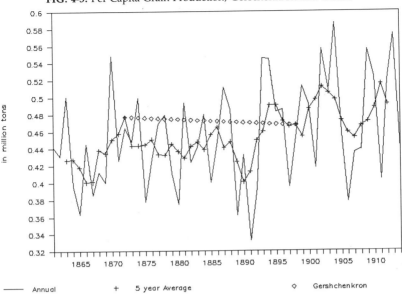

While there does appear to have been some long-term decline in per-capita production from the series of peaks in the 1870s to the series of troughs in the period 1889–1892, subsequently there was a quite distinctive improvement from the late 1880s to 1914, with a partial relapse in the 1905–1908 period. According to the careful calculations made by the distinguished Soviet statistician V. M. Obukhov, the average annual growth rates for the period 1883–1914 are: 2.1 percent per year grain production; 1.5 percent per year population growth and therefore; +0.6 percent per-capita grain production.[5] In other words, grain production was growing at a much faster rate than the rapid population growth.

There can be no doubt that in the last thirty years of the tsarist regime, there was a general trend toward increased per-capita grain production (even excluding grain exports). However, this trend was disturbed by two periods

[5] See V. M. Obukhov, "Dvizhenie urozhaev zernovykh kultur v Evrop. Rossii v period 1883–1915gg.", in V. G. Groman, ed., *Vliianie neurozhaev na narodnoe khoziaistvo Rossii*, pt. 1 (Moscow, 1927). The period 1883–1914 was chosen simply because of the availability of data. The growth rates are based on the method of least squares and so they do take account of values for intermediary dates. A measurement based on a more carefully selected periodization from peak to peak or trough to trough would indicate similar levels. Average growth rates (least squares) for period peak to peak 1895–1914 are 2.4 percent for grain production, 1.6 percent for population, and therefore +0.8 percent in per-capita terms. For trough to trough measurements 1891–1911 the average growth rates for grain production are 2.0 percent, for population 1.6 percent, and therefore in per-capita terms +0.4 percent.

of agricultural crisis: from the late 1880s to early 1890s; and in the middle of the first decade of the twentieth century. These temporary declines covering the years 1889–1892 and 1905–1908 will be considered in more detail below. It should, however, be noted that since some of the data are given for five-year periods the intensity of the decline is registered in the five-year periods 1886–1890, 1891–1895 and 1906–1910. (See table 4-1.)

The cyclical nature of the fairly regular fluctuations in levels of grain production is readily identifiable in figures 4-1–4-3. It will be noted that while most fluctuations have a periodicity of five years, there are two periods when four relatively low harvests follow each other: 1889–1892 and 1905–1908. The level of any one of these years is comparable to other individual low points, such as 1897, 1901, or 1911, but the important thing that makes these periods critical is the concentration of four low points together. Table 4-2 presents the annual data for these two crisis periods.

From the data in table 4-2, it can be seen that the arbitrary division between the late 1880s and the early 1890s masks the close proximity of four low harvest years: 1889, 1890, 1891, and 1892, of which two—1889 and 1891—were extremely low. Any five-year grouping that contained these four years would indicate a much more acute crisis than the five-year groupings mentioned above and in table 4-1. These annual data also indicate that per-capita grain production net of exports was actually lower in 1889 than in 1891. In 1889 the level of grain production exclusive of grain exports was 23.6 million tons, about 9 million tons lower than the 1887 and 1888 levels. But in 1891 it was 25.6 million tons; some 2 million tons higher. In per-capita terms of grain retentions in the country (production net of exports per head of population) the figures were 0.30 tons per head in 1891 but only 0.28 tons per head in 1889.

The reasons why the famine occurred in 1891–1892 and not in 1889–1890 lie not so much in the poor harvest of 1891, which was partly offset by reduced exports, but in the earlier decline in peasant stocks due to the general impoverishment of the peasantry, the large increase in grain prices, and the specific regional problems of the 1891 harvest.

A more detailed analysis of the annual data also indicates that the 1906–1910 five-year grouping tended to mask the concentration of four low-harvest years (1905, 1906, 1907, and 1908). But unlike the 1889–1892 crisis period, only one of these four years was exceptionally low. The 1905–1908 crisis in grain production was therefore relatively more simple than the 1889–1892 crisis. The low point came in 1906 when the level of grain production was 20 million tons below the 1904 peak. The decline in exports by 3.7 million tons could do little to offset this decline, and per-capita grain production (net of exports) fell to 0.3 tons per head, only marginally higher than the 1891 average. In 1907 the rise in grain production by 7 million tons when exports fell by 2 million tons eased the strain on supplies. But supply pressures in-

TABLE 4-1.

Grain Production, Population, Grain Exports and per Capita Production in European Russia in Arbitrary Five-Year Groupings

Year	Production in Millions of Tons	Population in Millions	Export in Millions of Tons	Per Capita Production Gross in Millions of Tons	Net of Exports in Millions of Tons
Koval'chenko's data					
1802/1811	19.51	37.1	0.22	0.525	0.519
1840s	23.69	49.0	0.60	0.483	0.471
1850s	24.43	51.1	0.92	0.479	0.461
Nifontov's data					
1851–1855	25.23	57.8	0.78	0.437	0.423
1856–1860	25.96	60.0	1.19	0.433	0.413
1861–1865	26.09	61.2	1.24	0.426	0.406
1866–1870	27.78	63.3	2.15	0.439	0.405
1871–1875	29.72	67.1	2.87	0.443	0.400
1876–1880	31.14	72.1	3.85	0.432	0.379
1881–1885	34.25	77.0	5.20	0.445	0.377
1886–1890	36.82	82.8	7.26	0.445	0.357
1891–1895	40.00	88.5	7.61	0.452	0.366
1896–1900	43.89	95.2	7.14	0.461	0.386
Obukhov's data					
1883–1887	36.10	79.1	6.17	0.456	0.378
1886–1890	37.01	82.8	7.26	0.447	0.359
1891–1895	40.74	88.5	7.61	0.460	0.374
1896–1900	44.53	95.2	7.14	0.468	0.393
1901–1905	52.36	103.6	10.71	0.505	0.402
1906–1910	52.63	112.6	10.84	0.467	0.371
1909–1913	60.84	118.1	10.66	0.515	0.425

Sources: 1802/1811, 1840s and 1850s data from I. D. Koval'chenko, *Russkoe krepostnoe krest'ianstvo v pervoi polovine XIX veka* (Moscow, 1967), pp. 78, 386; 1850s–1890s data from A. S. Nifontov, *Zernovoe proizvodstvo Rossii vo vtoroi polovine XIX veka* (Moscow, 1974), pp. 187, 200–201, 229, 278–79, 286–87, and V. I. Pronin, "Dinamika urovnia zemledel'cheskogo proizvodstva Sibiri vo vtoroi polovine XIX—nachale XX veka," *Istoriia SSSR* No. 4 (July–August 1977): 63, 74, 75; 1883–1915 data from V. M. Obukhov, "Dvizhenie urozhaev zernovykh kultur v Evrop.Rossii v period 1883–1915 gg.," app. 1, in V. G. Groman, ed., *Vliianie neurozhaev na narodnoe khoziaistvo Rossii*, chast' 1 (Moscow, 1927), pp. 56–108, and *Statisticheskii Ezhegodnik Rossii*, various issues; for calculations, see Stephen G. Wheatcroft, "Grain Production and Utilisation in Russia and the USSR Before Collectivisation" (Ph.D. diss., Birmingham University, 1980), vol. 3 (appendices).

Note: Significant low points have a solid underline; secondary low points have a broken underline.

TABLE 4-2.

Grain Production, Population, Grain Exports and Per Capita Production in European Russia: The Crisis Years in Detail

Year	Production in Millions of Tons	Population in Millions	Export in Millions of Tons	Per Capita Production — Gross in Millions of Tons	Per Capita Production — Net of Exports in Millions of Tons
The Crisis of the Late 1880s and Early 1890s					
1886–1890	37.0	82.8	7.2	0.44	0.35
1888–1892	34.2	85.3	6.1	0.40	0.32
1891–1895	40.7	88.5	7.6	0.46	0.37
1887	41.7	81.5	9.0	0.51	0.40
1888	40.2	82.7	7.6	0.49	0.39
1889	30.5	84.2	6.9	0.36	0.28
1890	36.9	85.3	6.4	0.43	0.36
1891	28.8	86.5	3.2	0.33	0.30
1892	34.5	87.7	6.6	0.39	0.32
1893	48.0	88.1	10.5	0.55	0.43
The Crisis of the second half of the decade of the 1900s					
1901–1905	52.4	103.6	10.71	0.505	0.402
1904–1908	49.9	108.8	9.58	0.459	0.370
1906–1910	52.6	112.6	10.84	0.467	0.371
1904	61.9	105.4	11.4	0.59	0.48
1905	49.1	107.4	9.7	0.46	0.37
1906	41.1	108.8	7.7	0.38	0.31
1907	48.1	110.7	6.6	0.43	0.38
1908	49.5	112.7	12.5	0.44	0.33
1909	63.6	114.6	13.9	0.56	0.43

Sources: See Stephen G. Wheatcroft, "The Agrarian Crisis and Peasant Living Standards in Late Imperial Russia: A Reconsideration of Trends and Regional Differences," Paper Presented to the Conference on The Peasantry of European Russia, 1800–1917, University of Massachusetts at Boston (Boston, August 19–22, 1986) Appendix 1 and 2; Stephen G. Wheatcroft, "Grain Production and Its Utilisation in Russia and the USSR Before Collectivisation" (Ph.D. diss. Birmingham University, 1980), vol. 3, pp. 5–46, where Nifontov and Obukhov data are also given with an annual breakdown.

Note: Significant low points are underlined.

creased again in 1908 as grain exports leaped up by almost 6 million tons with an almost stationary level of production. This second crisis subsided only after the excellent harvest of 1909 and the exceptional five-year period 1909–1913.

REGIONAL CLASSIFICATIONS

In this study I will use a hierarchy of more or less consistent regional classifications which divide the empire into grain-deficit and grain-surplus regions. The former are called the Consumer Regions and are further divided into the Northern Consumer Region (NCR), and the Southern Consumer Region (SCR). The NCR comprises the Moscow and St. Petersburg Industrial Areas, the Baltic provinces and the northern Non-Black-Earth Region, while the SCR comprises the Transcaucasus area and Russian Central Asia. The surplus regions are known as the Producer Regions and are divided into three major groups: the Southern Producer Region (SPR), comprising the Ukraine and North Caucasus; the Central Producer Region (CPR), comprising the Central Black-Earth Region (*Chernozem*) and the Volga; and the Eastern Producer Region (EPR), comprising the Urals, Siberia, and the Steppe. An alternative classification is needed in this study because different groupings of regions are used in the relevant taxation data. For the tax data the NCR and SPR regions were roughly comparable with those used above, but the CPR and EPR Regions differ quite significantly. The CPR (tax data) compresses both the Central *Chernozem* and the East. For the distribution of the separate provinces into these *main* regions see map 3.

In order to make these regional data more readily comparable I have divided them by the appropriate population figures. Table 4-3 and figures 4-4

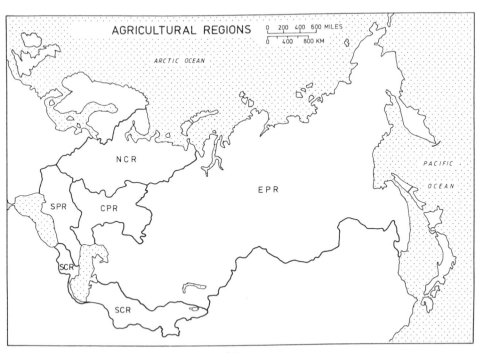

MAP 3.
Agricultural Regions of Russia

through 4-8 provide a very clear indication of some of the fundamental regional changes occurring during this period. There is a very distinct trend for per-capita production to decline in the NCR, which is associated with the increased move into industrial employment and other branches of agriculture. Within the different producer regions we see a remarkable increase in per-capita grain production in the SPR; which is associated with the development of grain exports. In the EPR there is a rather unclear pattern, due mainly to its relatively small size at this time and to the decline of the Urals industrial area. But in the CPR there is a quite distinct decline in per-capita production, which results in the replacement of the CPR by the SPR as the

TABLE 4-3.
Grain Production per Capita by Region in Tons per Head; Data Grouped Arbitrarily into Five-Year Groups

Koval'chenko's data						
Year	NCR (K)	SCR	SPR (K)	CPR (K)	EPR (K)	USSR (K)
1802/1811	0.503		0.430	0.668	0.379	0.525
1840s	0.414		0.370	0.632	0.530	0.483
1850s	0.408		0.374	0.614	0.525	0.479
Nifontov's data						
Year	NCR (N)	SCR	SPR (N)	CPR (N)	EPR (N)	USSR (N)
1850s	0.404		0.396	0.602	0.528	0.449
1860s	0.390		0.392	0.625	0.478	0.477
1870s	0.373		0.459	0.626	0.510	0.493
1880s	0.378		0.513	0.626	0.513	0.497
1890s	0.362		0.578	0.585	0.513	0.511
Obukhov's data						
Year	NCR	SCR	SPR	CPR	EPR	USSR
1883–1889	0.356		0.468	0.597		0.453
1890–1894	0.323		0.580	0.494		0.445
1895–1899	0.325		0.542	0.555	0.443	0.454
1900–1904	0.328		0.639	0.619	0.373	0.488
1905–1909	0.277	0.198	0.641	0.485	0.435	0.453
1910–1914	0.299	0.213	0.715	0.543	0.443	0.496

Sources: 1802/1811, 1840s, and 1850s data from I. D. Koval'chenko *Russkoe krepostnoe krest'ianstvo v pervoi polovine XIX veka* (Moscow, 1967), pp. 78, 386; 1850s–1890s data from A. S. Nifontov, *Zernovoe proizvodstvo Rossii vo vtoroi polovine XIX veka* (Moscow, 1974), pp. 187, 200–201, 229, 278–79, 286–87, and V. I. Pronin, "Dinamika urovnia zemledel'cheskogo proizvodstva Sibiri vo vtoroi polovine XIX—nachale XX veka," *Istoriia SSSR* No. 4 (July–August 1977): 63, 74, 75; 1883–1915 data from V. M. Obukhov, "Dvizhenie urozhaev zernovykh kultur v Evrop.Rossii v period 1883–1915gg.," app. 1, in V. G. Groman, ed., *Vliianie neurozhaev na narodnoe khoziaistvo Rossii*, chast' 1 (Moscow, 1927), pp. 56–108, and *Statisticheskii Ezhegodnik Rossii*, various issues; for calculations, see Stephen G. Wheatcroft, "Grain Production and Utilisation in Russia and the USSR Before Collectivisation" (Ph.D. diss., Birmingham University, 1980), vol. 3 (appendices).
Note: Low points are underlined.

FIG. 4-4. All Empire, per Capita Grain Production

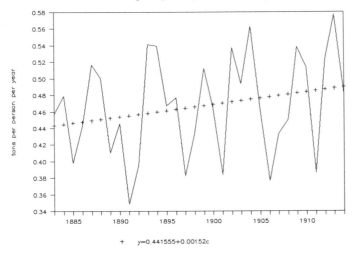

$$+ \quad y=0.441555+0.00152c$$

FIG. 4-5. Northern Consumer Region, per Capita Grain Production

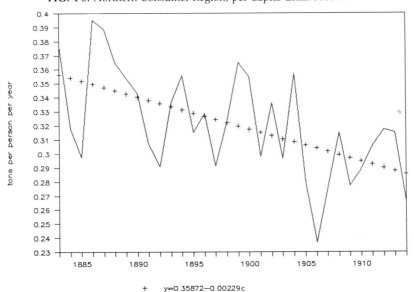

$$+ \quad y=0.35872-0.00229c$$

FIG. 4-6. Southern Producer Region, per Capita Grain Production

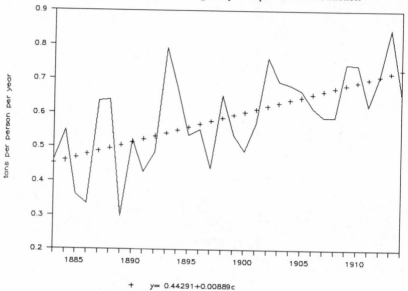

+   y= 0.44291+0.00889c

FIG. 4-7. Central Producer Region, per Capita Grain Production

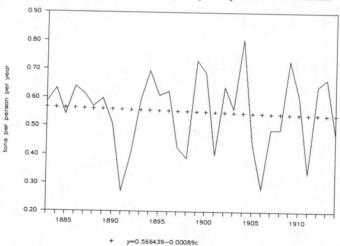

+   y=0.566439−0.00089c

FIG. 4-8. Eastern Producer Region, per Capita Grain Production

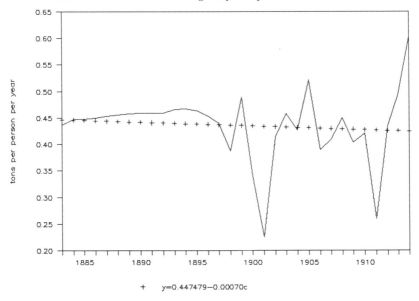

+   y=0.447479−0.00070c

largest producer per capita of grain in the late 1890s. The decline in the CPR continued until 1917. In contrast to the NCR, the CPR's decline in per-capita grain production is not associated with a great increase in industrial activity or with the development of other branches of agriculture. In fact, as will be shown below, a regional analysis of livestock holdings shows a serious decline in livestock numbers per capita, especially in this area.

A more detailed analysis of the regional data with an annual breakdown (table 4-4) indicates an important difference between the two crisis periods of 1889–1892 and 1905–1908. The very low level of grain production in the 1889–1892 period can be seen as being caused by two separate and slightly different regional cycles that coincide to some extent. The decline begins in the Ukraine in the SPR with a very low harvest in 1889, followed by an average harvest in 1890 and two relatively low harvests in 1891 and 1892. The position in the country became especially serious when the decline in the SPR coincided with a relatively low harvest in the CPR in 1890 and an exceptionally low one in 1891.

In the 1905–1908 crisis period the maximum decline in the CPR in 1906 was almost as significant as in 1891 but on this occasion it did not coincide with a fall in the SPR, which on the contrary was developing quite strongly to become the main grain-surplus area at this time. Thus, the recurring stagnation in the CPR was being masked by the growth in the SPR.

From the above analysis it is clear that a crisis in grain production did occur

TABLE 4-4.

Grain Production per Capita by Region in Tons per Head; Data for Crisis Years

	NCR	SCR	SPR	CPR	EPR	USSR
The crisis years 1888–1892						
1888–1892	0.332		0.474	<u>0.470</u>		<u>0.410</u>
1887	0.389		(0.635)	0.613		0.510
1888	0.365		(0.640)	0.570		0.493
1889	0.354		**(0.298)**	0.598		<u>0.401</u>
1890	0.343		(0.522)	0.507		0.435
1891	<u>0.307</u>		(0.428)	**0.270**		<u>0.337</u>
1892	0.291		(0.484)	0.404		0.385
1893	0.337		(0.790)	0.593		0.537
The crisis years 1903–1908						
1904–1908	0.293	0.197	0.628	0.500	0.440	0.458
1904	0.357	0.200	0.683	0.806	(0.427)	0.563
1905	0.280	0.196	0.666	0.437	(0.522)	0.461
1906	0.237	0.192	0.616	0.437	(0.390)	<u>0.377</u>
1907	0.275	0.194	0.588	0.487	(0.410)	0.433
1908	0.315	0.201	0.589	0.488	0.451	0.456

Sources: 1883–1915, data from V. M. Obukhov, "Dvizhenie urozhaev zernovykh kultur v Evrop. Rossii v period 1883–1915gg.," app. 1, in V. G. Groman, ed., *Vliianie neurozhaev na narodnoe khoziaistvo Rossii*, chast' 1 (Moscow, 1927), pp. 56–108, and *Statisticheskii Ezhegodnik Rossii*, various issues; for calculations, see Stephen G. Wheatcroft, "Grain Production and Utilisation in Russia and the USSR Before Collectivisation" (Ph.D. diss., Birmingham University, 1980), vol. 3 (appendices).

Note: Low points are underlined; exceptionally low points are bold-faced.

in the CPR in both 1889–1892 and 1905–1908, that it was the cumulative effect of a series of bad harvest years that was particularly serious and the coincidence of similar declines in other areas. It was this complex of reasons, rather than simple global declines in production, that had the most serious consequences.

LIVESTOCK PRODUCTION

Livestock data were notoriously incomplete, and this has led some commentators to deny their use at all. For example, Paul Gregory claims that because of the unreliability of available livestock data "we cannot determine . . . whether per-capita livestock holdings were rising per capita between the 1880s and 1904"[6]

[6] Paul R. Gregory, "The Russian Agrarian Crisis Revisited," in Robert C. Stuart, ed., *The Soviet Rural Economy* (Totowa, N.J., 1983), p. 27. He then proceeds to refer to his own work: Paul R. Gregory, *Russian National Income, 1885–1913* (Cambridge, 1982), pp. 268–69, which shows a per-capita increase in livestock holdings, and to Arcadius Kahan, "Capital Formation During the Period of Early Industrialization in Russia, 1890–1913," in *Cambridge*

While admitting that there are grave difficulties with these data and that they are certainly incomplete in their coverage of young animals, there is nevertheless no reason for assuming that the level of underreporting changed over this period or that these data cannot provide useful inter-temporal comparisons. The reason that Professor Gregory's data differ so markedly from those of Professor Kahan and everyone else would appear to be due to some discontinuity and non-comparability in the series of data that he is using.[7]

Despite the claims of Professor Gregory to the contrary, there was a very distinct fall in per-capita horse, cattle, and pig numbers between the 1880s and 1904, and a further fall between 1904 and 1914.[8] The crisis in Russian livestock has so far been very little studied. While some of the decline may be accounted for by exogenous livestock epidemics, the sharp fall in numbers in 1891 and 1892, and again in 1902 to 1907, would tend to indicate that it was related to the agricultural crises of these years.

The early decline of 1891–1892 would appear to be associated with the drought of 1891 and the shortage of livestock feed in the famine years. The leading Soviet economic historian Professor P.I. Lyashchenko and the leading émigré expert Professor G. Pavlovsky have both described the effects of overpopulation and the crisis in the three-field system in late-nineteenth-century Russian agriculture.[9]

A slight rise in livestock numbers in the 1880s was followed by a period of stagnation and decline between 1891 and 1895. There was some slight growth in the late 1890s, but further stagnation after 1903. The absolute number of long-horned cattle and pigs registered in 1913 was lower than at the 1902 peak, and for horses it was only 5.5 percent larger, despite the fact that the population had grown by over 21 percent in this period. (See table 4-5.)

The regional data simply reinforces the picture of the very serious decline that was taking place in all regions (with the exception of the EPR). (See table 4-6.) There were, however, some interesting regional differences. The number of horses fell more sharply in the NCR in comparison with numbers of cattle and pigs. Such movements were indicative of the relative decline in arable farming in this area and the relative increase in livestock farming. In the SPR the reverse trend was visible with numbers of horses falling less sharply than those for cattle and for pigs. This was a result of this region switching over to more intensive grain farming. The CPR experienced a se-

Economic History of Europe, VII, pt. 2 (Cambridge, 1978), p. 300, which shows a per-capita decline.

[7] See Wheatcroft, "Agriculture."

[8] Ibid.

[9] See George Pavlovsky, *Agricultural Russia on the Eve of the Revolution* (London, 1930), pp. 84–88, and P. I. Liashchenko, *Istoriia Narodnogo Khoziaistva SSSR*, Tom II (Moscow, 1956), pp. 66–69. (See particularly a section entitled "The Grain Economy and the Three-Field Crisis.")

TABLE 4-5.
Livestock Numbers in European Russia in Millions

	Horses	LHC	Pigs	Sheep
Trends				
1850s	15.5	21.0		
1881–1883	16.1	22.3	9.1	45.4
1887–1888	17.7	24.0	9.5	45.9
1890–1892, 1894	17.6	24.7	9.2	40.8
1895–1899	18.7	29.2	11.8	44.4
1900–1904	20.3	31.9	11.8	45.5
1905–1990	20.7	30.7	11.5	41.6
1910–1913	21.6	31.3	11.6	40.5
Years of Crisis 1891–1894				
1887	15.8	23.1	9.7	47.3
1888	19.7	24.9	9.2	44.5
1889				
1890	19.8	25.5	9.6	46.1
1891	17.3	25.3	9.6	39.8
1892	16.6	24.0	8.8	40.0
1893				
1894	16.7	24.1	8.8	37.3
Years of Crisis 1904–1909				
1903	20.4	31.8	11.4	46.9
1904	20.8	31.9	12.0	46.5
1905	20.8	31.2	11.5	45.4
1906	20.5	30.5	11.9	42.2
1907	20.5	29.7	11.6	40.7
1908	20.6	29.7	11.4	39.9
1909	21.3	30.5	11.3	39.9

Source: *Sbornik statistiko-ekonomicheskikh svedenii po sel'skomu khoziaistvu Rossii i inostrannykh gosudarstv* (St. Petersburg, 1915), pp. 242–43.

rious decline in all livestock branches indicating that the crisis in arable production was not being offset by increased livestock production. The only area showing any signs of increase in livestock per head of the population was the EPR, where numbers were increasing rapidly as the Urals-Siberian dairy- and bacon-farming cooperatives developed, and for those areas around the major cities. For most of Russia the picture of livestock farming was very grim.

The Agricultural Crises in Summary

The data on agricultural production present a rather complex picture. Grain-production data indicate a general trend toward increased production per capita but with a large concentration of unfavorable years in 1889–1892 and 1904–1908 (which were to a very large extent a direct result of the weather).

TABLE 4-6.
Regional Recorded Livestock Numbers per Head of Population

Year	NCR	SCR	SPR	CPR	EPR	50Gub/USSR
Horses						
1850s	0.271		0.141	0.378		
1883	0.194		0.197	0.286		0.226
1891			?	0.306		0.201
1892				0.215		0.190
1895						0.188
1900	0.170		0.207	0.233	0.504	0.201/0.247
1905	0.172		0.197	0.245	0.415	0.193/0.237
1906	0.168		0.200	0.232	0.417	0.234
1907	0.164		0.188	0.209	0.389	0.220
1908	0.162		0.197	0.209	0.394	0.221
1909	0.161		0.193	0.207	0.414	0.223
1910	0.160	0.182	0.193	0.213	0.433	0.188/0.228
1914	0.155	0.155	0.200	0.206	0.428	0.186/0.226
Cattle						
1850s	0.367		0.553	0.326		
1883	0.268		0.452	0.257		0.302
1891				0.254		0.293
1892				0.214		0.273
1895						0.270
1900	0.312		0.457	0.298	0.540	0.322/0.373
1905	0.299		0.368	0.307	0.531	0.290/0.371
1910	0.279	0.480	0.306	0.256	0.544	0.269/0.338
1914	0.272	0.417	0.300	0.242	0.529	0.265/0.326
Pigs						
1850s	0.118		0.233	0.176		
1883	0.076		0.169	0.106		0.118
1891				0.064		0.110
1892				0.046		0.101
1895						0.101
1900	0.101		0.138	0.085	0.064	0.120/0.99
1905	0.083		0.127	0.084	0.068	0.107/0.090
1910	0.074	0.046	0.115	0.062	0.076	0.104/0.081
1914	0.081	0.050	0.127	0.065	0.082	0.093/0.088

Source: Stephen G. Wheatcroft, "Grain Production," vol. 3, pp. 228–69.

Note: Low points are underlined. The absolute reliability of these figures is extremely problematic. It is generally considered that the prewar data underestimate reality by about 16 percent. The data may, however, have greater comparability on an inter-temporal basis.

Grain exports had been rising over this period, but the growth in grain production was sufficient to maintain a long-term rise in per-capita production
even net of exports. However, in the short term large grain exports undoubtedly added to the severity of the crisis in particular years (e.g., 1889, 1901,
and to some extent 1905).

A regional breakdown indicates that this relatively favorable picture of
generally rising per-capita grain production is a result of the predominance
of the dynamic areas of relatively new settlement in the SPR and EPR, which
masked the very serious stagnation in per-capita production in the CPR and
the decline in per-capita production in the NCR. The decline in the NCR was
undoubtedly a natural corollary of increased urbanization and industrialization in this region. But the position in the CPR was very different because
here the stagnation in grain production was not associated with any substantial increase in urbanization and industry—and consequently must be considered extremely serious. There was a crisis in grain production in the CPR,
which became particularly evident in the crisis years of 1889–1892 and 1905–
1908.

As regards livestock holdings the picture is bleak in all regions with the
possible exception of the EPR and parts of the NCR. Particularly serious reductions in holdings followed the early 1890s and most of the decade preceding the First World War.

In summary, there was a somewhat mixed situation with no overall decline in agriculture; some overall growth in per-capita grain production with
problems in some areas and some years; but with a far less favorable position
for livestock farming and great underdevelopment in other sections.

THE CRISIS IN PEASANT LIVING STANDARDS

The crisis in peasant living standards was not purely a result of the crisis of
agricultural production. As I have explained above, the price increases that
normally accompany a decline in production could partially (or totally) offset
the value of the decline in production for those groups holding surplus
stocks. The victims would be the groups needing to purchase the high-priced
grain, but lacking appropriately inflated wage or other exchange entitlement.
Although most peasants labored on their own allotment land[10] some hired
themselves out as farm laborers to work on the landowners' estates, and
some needed to rent or purchase more land. The prices paid to the peasants
for their labor and the price paid by the peasant for additional land were two
additional factors that affected living standards. Apart from these market-
oriented factors we also have to include the impact of the government on the

[10] That is, land alloted to them for their use by their own rural community.

peasant through the burden of taxation and the level of relief given to the peasants. We will consider the data on rural agricultural wages first.

RURAL WAGES

The effective wage rates for rural labor[11] can best be understood by examining their exchange entitlement in terms of the amount of basic foodstuff or the amount of rye that they could purchase with their wages (i.e., the rye equivalent of their wages). (See figs. 4-9 and 4-10 and table 4-7.)[12] Between 1882 and 1914 the rise in wages is largely but not completely offset by the rise in prices of rye. The rye equivalent of the wages rose from 10 to 15 kilograms per day in 1882 to 15 to 20 kilograms per day in 1914. But this trend is very uneven with two major declines: a very sharp decline between 1888 and 1894; and a more gentle long-term decline between 1897 and 1910. During the first sharp decline between 1888 and 1894 the average wage levels fell to 6 to 8 kilograms per day in 1891. This was followed by a period of very high wages in 1894–1896, before the second fall beginning sharply in 1897 and with minor fluctuations continuing through to a trough of 8.6 to 12 kilograms per day in 1907–1909. (See fig. 4-4.) The fluctuations were particularly sharp as wage rates tended to fall in poor harvest years, when less work was available and more peasants were looking for work. Such falls in wages coincided with higher grain prices.

In regional terms money wages in the NCR tended to be much higher (see table 4-8) than in the Producer Regions, but since the price of rye was even higher, the real-wage level was much lower. In the famine year of 1891 the grain prices in the Volga exceeded those in the NCR, as a result of which real wages in the Volga fell considerably more than in the Consumer Regions. The regional data for real-wage rates in the second crisis of 1903–1909 are not so readily available.[13] The conjuncture of high-grain prices with low rural-wage rates in poor harvest years was of particular importance for that part of

[11] It could be argued that (1) relatively few peasants engaged in rural wage labor, and (2) that it tended to be of a rather short duration and should not therefore be equated with annual wage levels—in other words, that wage labor was primarily only a temporary supplement to incomes mainly derived elsewhere. However, I would argue that even these temporary wage rates would be indicative of the value that rural labor could demand on the rural labor market on these occasions and should not be lightly dismissed.

[12] See also table 4-7.

[13] The series of regional data for the 1890s have been taken from a 1903 compendium of data *Svod statisticheskikh svedenii po sel'skomu khoziaistvu Rossii kontsu XIX v.*, vyp. 2 (St. Petersburg, 1903), pp. 22–25, 106–7. No similar compendiums were produced in the final years of the tsarist regime, and the one compendium of prerevolutionary data subsequently compiled by N. D. Kondratiev and N. P. Oganovskii did not contain regional series of wage data. The annual data are available from the original publications . . . *god v sel'skokhoziaistvennom otnoshenii po otvetam, poluchennym ot khoziaev*, SPb 1900–1915, but these are in a highly disaggregated form.

TABLE 4-7.

Rural Daily Wage Labor, Price of Rye in Kopecks per Kilogram, and Daily Rye Equivalent of One Day's Labor, 1882–1916

Year	Average Daily Wage in Kopecks for: Sowing	Hay Making	Threshing	Price of Rye (kop/kgm)		Real Wages in Rye Equivalent (kgs/day) Sowing		Hay Making	
1882	37.4	52.6	56.4	4.9				10.8	
1883	38.3	59.1	61.0	5.0		7.7		11.8	
1884	38.2	53.0	60.2	4.5		7.7		11.8	
1885	37.0	48.4	51.6	3.8		8.2		12.6	
1886	35.9	43.1	51.4	3.5		9.3		12.4	
1887	34.7	47.6	51.5	3.0		10.7		15.9	
1888	36.3	50.1	69.1	3.2		12.1		15.6	
1889	37.3	45.9	50.3	3.8		11.5		12.1	
1890	35.3	45.5	51.6	3.6		9.2		12.6	11.5
1891	33.8	42.8	46.5	7.4	6.3	9.3	8.5	5.7	6.7
1892	33.2	44.0	49.3	5.2	6.0	4.4	5.2	8.5	7.2
1893	34.0	49.3	63.7	3.5	4.8	6.6	5.6	13.9	12.4
1894	37.1	48.7	58.3	2.5	2.8	10.5	9.3	19.5	17.4
1895	37.6	47.0	52.2	2.7	2.3	15.0	13.4	17.5	20.8
1896	37.5	48.3	50.7	2.7	2.1	13.9	16.5	17.5	23.3
1897	38.2	49.9	51.3	3.7	2.8	14.1	18.3	13.4	17.7
1898	40.0	52.2	56.8	4.3	3.8	10.8	14.2	12.3	13.6
1899	40.5	52.6	54.9	4.0	3.8	9.4	10.5	13.3	13.9
1900	43.8	55.0	59.1	3.6	3.0	11.0	11.6	15.2	18.3
1901	45.0	55.2	57.9		3.4	12.5	15.0		16.2
1902	44.5	56.6	60.9		3.8		13.1		14.9
1903	45.4	60.9	67.7		3.5		11.9		17.4
1904	45.1	54.7	60.0		3.7		12.9		14.8
1905	46.4	61.6	60.7		4.5		12.6		13.8
1906	50.4	69.5	66.9		4.8		11.3		14.4
1907	51.8	65.8	69.1		6.0		8.6		10.8
1908	53.3	64.1	66.7		6.0		8.7		10.6
1909	53.8	64.6	72.3		5.3		9.0		12.3
1910	56.9	71.5	76.4		4.3		9.8		16.7
1911	58.4	71.7	74.4		4.8		13.6		14.9
1912	62.1	78.6	86.3		5.5		12.9		14.3
1913	66.8	84.6	96.4		4.6		12.1		18.3
1914	73.2	95.3	92.4		4.9		15.7		19.5
1915	85.9	116.2	131.8		7.1		17.5		16.5
1916	151.6	222.0	250.0				21.5		

Source: Wage rates from S. G. Strumilin, "Dinamika podennoi platy za 1882–1916gg.," in *Izbrannie proizvedeniia*, tom 3 (Moscow, 1964), p. 277 (these data have been reworked by Strumilin and corrected for faulty weighting; rye prices 1882–1900 for fifty provinces of European Russia from *Svod statisticheskikh svedenii po sel'skomu khoziaistvu Rossii k kontsu XIX v.*, tom 2 (St. Petersburg, 1902), pp. 24–25; rye prices 1890–1915 for domestic market from *Svod tovarnykh tsen na glavnykh russkikh i inostrannykh rynkakh za 1915g.* (Petrograd, 1917), p. II; other figures calculated from the above.

Note: Rural daily wage rates refer to a peasant without a horse and are exclusive of food.

FIG. 4-9. Russian Rural Real Daily Wages, Sowing

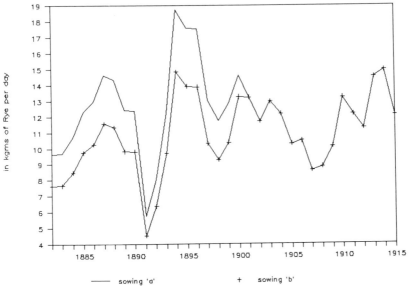

FIG. 4-10. Russian Rural Real Daily Wages, Threshing

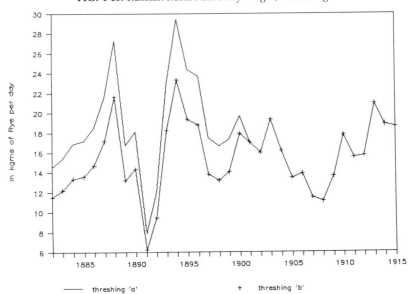

TABLE 4-8.
Rural Daily Wage Labor for Harvesting in Rye Equivalents (kgm rye/day)

Year	NCR C.Ind	SPR MaloR	CPR CChZ	CVolga
Wages for Haymaking (kop/day)				
1882	73	57	61	63
1883	71	63	59	60
1884	77	57	57	59
1885	61	53	49	52
1886	59	50	48	56
1887	63	50	50	51
1888	66	60	53	51
1889	63	47	43	48
1890	63	52	49	47
1891	**64**	**52**	**43**	**36**
1892	63	46	43	45
1893	66	45	53	50
1894	68	62	56	54
1895	72	53	51	50
1896	74	53	53	54
1897	79	50	48	50
1898	82	37	53	54
1899	86	55	57	59
1900	89	62	67	60
Prices of Rye (kop/kgm)				
1881	7.5	2.2	5.7	2.2
1882	5.8	4.1	4.7	4.0
1883	5.1	4.2	3.9	4.9
1884	5.4	3.4	3.9	3.0
1885	4.6	2.9	2.9	2.9
1886	3.7	2.9	2.6	2.2
1887	3.1	2.4	2.3	2.2
1888	3.8	2.7	2.4	2.8
1889	4.3	3.1	3.1	3.4
1890	3.9	3.1	2.7	3.3
1891	**7.8**	**7.2**	**7.6**	**8.3**
1892	5.5	4.5	2.0	4.6
1893	4.3	2.7	2.9	2.6
1894	3.1	1.7	1.8	1.7
1895	3.1	2.0	1.8	1.6
1896	2.8	2.1	2.1	1.6
1897	4.0	3.4	3.8	3.1
1898	4.7	3.8	3.7	4.2
1899	4.0	3.2	3.0	2.8
1900	3.7	3.0	2.8	2.4

TABLE 4-8 (cont.)

Year	NCR C.Ind	SPR MaloR	CPR CChZ	CVolga
Real Wages in Rye Equivalent (kgm/day)				
1882	11.6	15.4	13.3	17.2
1883	13.1	16.5	17.7	13.3
1884	12.0	20.0	15.9	21.8
1885	12.3	20.1	18.5	17.4
1886	15.2	17.4	20.1	15.4
1887	19.0	26.7	23.9	21.8
1888	15.6	33.6	25.9	18.5
1889	13.4	17.7	15.7	14.1
1890	15.6	20.3	22.9	13.6
1891	**7.4**	**8.8**	**5.6**	**4.1**
1892	10.6	13.8	25.6	10.3
1893	14.6	21.3	24.7	22.9
1894	21.3	58.5	39.8	36.2
1895	19.3	38.2	32.8	36.4
1896	22.8	28.0	28.0	32.1
1897	16.7	17.9	12.6	16.7
1898	15.4	15.4	15.6	11.5
1899	18.3	22.3	23.1	20.3
1900	21.0	24.4	27.7	26.7

Source: Calculated from data in *Svod statisticheskikh svedenii po sel'skomu khoziaistvu Rossii kontsu XIXv.* vyp. 2 (St. Petersburg, 1903), pp. 22–25, 106–7.

Note: Data for the famine year of 1891 appear in boldface type.

the rural population that was dependent on the rural labor market. They would find their wages falling precisely at the time when grain prices were rising and when they would need to purchase more grain. The real wages of rural labor in rye equivalent fell by more than 50 percent from 1887–1888 to 1891–1892 and by slightly less than 50 percent from 1900–1903 to 1907–1908. For that part of the population dependent on wage labor to supplement their incomes, 1891–1892 and 1907–1908 were clearly crisis years.

LAND PRICES AND RENTS

The available data on land prices (for either purchase or rent) are unfortunately far less comprehensive than the grain-price or wage-labor rates. The Soviet historian A.M. Anfimov has produced a survey of rent data which only covers the years 1887–1888, 1901, and 1912–1914.[14] We are of course con-

[14] A. M. Anfimov, *Zemel'naia arenda v Rossii v nachale XX veka* (Moscow, 1961). See table 4-9.

cerned to discover whether these three short periods (of six years) were very
indicative of the overall movements: according to the data, the rental price
of arable land fell from 6.92 rubles per desiatina in 1887–1888 to 6.77 rubles
in 1901, before doubling to 13.72 rubles per desiatina in 1912–1914.[15] (See
table 4-9.) From these data and from the figures for grain yields and grain
prices given by Anfimov, it can be calculated that the value of rye produced
per desiatina of rented land exceeded the rent value of the land by 246 percent in 1887–1888 and that this had risen to 354 percent in 1901, but had then
fallen back to an excess of 228 percent by 1912–1914. The data suggest that

TABLE 4-9.
Land Rental Prices

Region	Land rented in 1901 (in thousands of desiatina)	Rent for sown land (in R/des)		
		1887/1888	1901	1912/1914
NCR				
Sev	105.1	4.63	1.79	5.82
Sev. Zap	705.5	7.15	2.66	13.52
Zap	544.9	5.94	6.27	9.82
Prom	2054.3	7.03	3.01	11.05
Baltic	872.8	11.47	7.24	17.48
NCR	4282.6	7.73	4.18	12.58
SPR				
S. ChZem	1004.3	7.94	9.49	19.94
S. West	414.1	8.64	10.27	16.52
S. Steppe	3649.3	5.44	7.77	17.31
SPR	5067.7	6.19	8.30	17.75
CPR				
N. ChZem	1615.8	10.77	11.22	16.07
L. Volga	5715.4	6.45	6.64	11.38
C. Volga	779.1	4.41	2.59	5.34
CPR	8110.3	7.11	7.15	11.72
ALL	17460.6	6.92	6.77	13.72
NCR		100	54	163
			100	301
SPR		100	134	287
			100	214
CPR		100	101	165
			100	164
All		100	98	198
			100	203

Source: Calculated from data in A. M. Anfimov, *Zemel'naia arenda v Rossii v nachale XX veka*
(Moscow, 1961), pp. 199–201.

[15] Ibid., p. 201

the purely financial advantages of renting more land was increasing between 1887–1888 and 1901, but then fell sharply in the last years of the empire. However, the scale of peasant renting of land was increasing particularly in these latter years. In order to maintain the per-capita level of grain production for their households, peasants were being forced to continue renting land, even though it was becoming relatively less advantageous to do so. Such a situation tends to support the argument that the peasantry was likely to be motivated far less by classical economic theories, with their emphasis on individual profit, than by concern for household subsistence needs—as Chaianov and others have argued.[16]

For land-purchase prices a continuous series of data are available for the land sold through the Peasant Land Bank (see table 4-10 and figures 4-11-4-14).

There is a quite sharp disjuncture in the trend of real land prices. A downward trend began in the 1880s and continued reaching a low point in 1891. Thereafter there was a very sharp rise, with the tripling of land prices between 1891 and 1903, before another less sharp fall in prices which occurred between 1903 and 1908. We would expect changes in land purchase price to be similar to those for land rentals. But this does not seem to be occurring. While land-bank prices rose by a factor of almost two and a half between 1887–1888 and 1901, Anfimov's data indicate an overall decline in rentals. Between 1901 and 1912–1914 there is a closer relationship with both indicators showing a rise in prices, but this is by about 50 percent for land-bank purchase price, but by more than 100 percent for rentals.

The regional data on land rentals summarized in table 4-9, indicate that between 1887–1888 and 1901 there was a fall in land prices in the NCR by almost 50 percent while prices rose by 34 percent in the SPR and were stationary in the CPR. There then appears to have been a sharp change in trend as land prices increased everywhere following 1901. Between 1901 and 1912–1914 they increased by 300 percent in the NCR, by 214 percent in the SPR, and by 164 percent in the CPR. This would tend to indicate that in the NCR before the turn of the century there was an easing of pressure on the land by peasants—but that there was an increase in demand in all other areas earlier, and after the turn of the century in the NCR as well.

THE TAX BURDEN ON THE PEASANTRY

The data on the Russian peasantry's tax burden, especially for the period before 1891, are very complex and contradictory and the issue itself was quite politically sensitive. Russian Finance Minister A. I. Vyshnegradsky fell from

---

[16] For a discussion of Chaianov's theory of the peasant economy see Teodor Shanin, *The Awkward Class: Political Sociology of Peasantry in a Developing Society, Russia 1910–1925* (Oxford, 1972).

TABLE 4-10.
Land Prices in Rye Equivalent From Peasant's Land Bank

Year	Land Price (R/des)	Rye Prices (R/ton)		Land Price (tons rye/Des)	
1883	52	50		1.04	
1884	53	45		1.18	
1885	52	38		1.37	
1886	46	35		1.31	
1887	42	30		1.40	
1888	34	32		1.06	
1889	32	38		0.84	
1890	36	36		1.00	
1891	39	74	63	0.53	0.60
1892	45	52	60	0.87	0.70
1893	50	35	40	1.43	1.20
1894	49	25	28	1.96	1.70
1895	52	27	23	1.93	2.20
1896	49	27	21	1.81	2.30
1897	71	37	28	1.92	2.5
1898	76	43	38	1.77	2.00
1899	78	40	38	1.95	2.00
1900	83	36	30	2.31	2.70
1901	91		34		2.6
1902	108		38		2.8
1903	108		35		3.0
1904	112		37		3.0
1905	111		45		2.4
1906	123		48		2.5
1907	129		60		2.1
1908	132		60		2.2
1909	141		53		2.6
1910	132		43		3.0
1911	129		48		2.6
1912	135		55		2.4
1913	133		46		2.8
1914	134		49		2.7

Source: Land prices from data in D. A. Baturinskii, *Agrarnaia politika Tsarskogo pravitel'stva i krest'ianskii pozemel'nyi bank* (Moscow 1925), passim. Rye prices: two series, see table 4-7 above. Land prices in tons of rye per *desiatina* of land are calculated from the other data in this table.

office because it was alleged that he had been overtaxing the peasantry when they were on the point of starvation. His protégé and successor S. Iu. Witte was anxious not to succumb to the same fate, and made sure that the published data presented the best possible picture.

For these reasons, great care is needed in the use of these data. First we

FIG. 4-11. Price of Land in Russia (in rye equivalents)

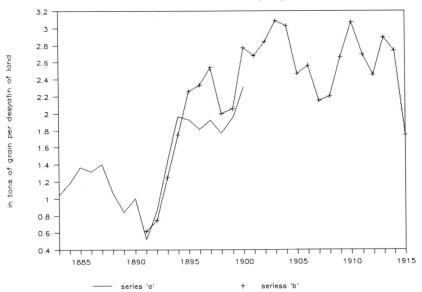

FIG. 4-12. Peasant Land Bank, Sum Loaned

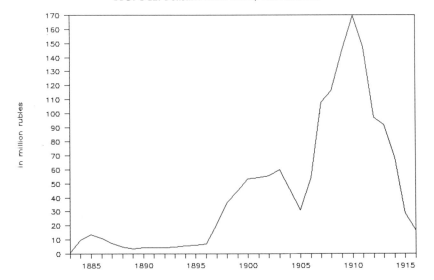

FIG. 4-13. Peasant Land Bank, Land Purchased

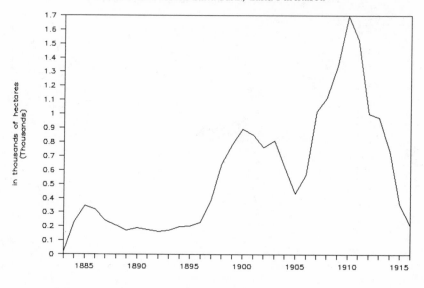

FIG. 4-14. Peasant Land Bank, Price Paid for Land Purchases

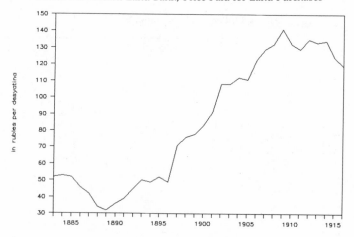

need to distinguish between direct and indirect taxation. Among the former, *kazennii* (central government exchequer) and other locally administered direct taxation must be carefully differentiated. The decline in the former after the 1890s was to a large extent offset by the expansion of the latter. But from the peasants' point of view, both were a burden. The central government's direct taxation covered a large variety of separate taxes which moved in different directions: the soul tax rose until 1877 and fell sharply in 1884 before being phased out in 1887; redemption payments rose enormously in 1885 and again in 1887 before falling sharply during and after the 1905 Revolution; and there were numerous other smaller local taxes especially in the non-European part of Russia, which tended to grow throughout this period. An incorrect or incomplete coverage of all these taxes for all the years could easily have made the data inaccurate and non-comparable.

There is also a need to ensure that we are dealing exclusively with actual tax payments and not with the tax levy (*oklad*).[17] There was a tendency among local officials to include *oklad* figures instead of payment figures in the preliminary taxation reports when no other figures were available, and this would naturally produce misleading and inaccurate statistics.

Many of these statistical problems appear to have been sorted out under Witte, and the series of detailed taxation data for direct tax payments for the period after 1891 appear to be more or less reliable.[18] See tables 4-11 and 4-12.

[17] A comparison between *oklad* and payments will be made in the final section when we also consider peasant indebtedness.

[18] For the period before 1891 there are enormous problems. According to the detailed regional data supplied by N. K. Brzheskii there was a long-term decline in rural direct taxation in the years before the crisis of the early 1890s. (N. K. Brzheskii, *Nedoimochnost' i krugovaia poruka sel'skikh obshchestv*, St. Petersburg, 1897). This decline in rural direct taxation is contrary to all other indicators. See table 4-11. It is not at all clear why Brzheskii's data produces such surprising results, but the most likely reason is the non-comparable coverage of data for different years.

The data for the famine year of 1891 is also problematic. 1891 was the first year of coverage for many of the data series, and there is clearly a discrepancy between the two sets of less detailed long-term series of direct tax data. The series published in 1902 indicate a 20-million-ruble fall in redemption payments in 1891—the year of the famine—while the alternative series published in 1913 shows the fall coming a year later, in 1892. (See tables 4-11 and 4-12.) This clearly makes an enormous difference to the incidence of the tax burden on the peasantry. The more detailed series of data for the post-1890 period would tend to favor the series showing the fall in 1891, which indicates that the peasants responded to their famine by lowering their tax payments.

After 1891 and 1892 there was a recovery of central state direct tax receipts, which was followed by the beginnings of a fall which was gentle in 1901–1903, more marked in 1904 and extremely sharp in 1905 and 1907. However, during this period there was a fairly regular expansion in most forms of non-central-government direct taxation, especially for the zemstvo, mir, and for insurance. (The sole non-central-government tax which failed to expand rapidly was associated with the grain relief system, the "Grain Capital Levy," which

There is less discrepancy between the different series of indirect tax data.[19] The main components of indirect taxation were the liquor tax and vodka monopoly, taxes on tobacco, sugar, oil, and matches, and customs duty. The value of all of these increased by at least fourfold between the late 1870s and 1910–1914.[20] See tables 4-13 and 4-14.

Recently Professor James Simms has challenged the traditional view of the existence of a crisis in peasant living standards. He has argued that the evidence that indirect taxation was rising more sharply than direct taxation is, in itself, an indication that there was no overall agricultural crisis.[21] His argument is that since the peasants were the majority of the population, they would therefore pay the bulk of the indirect taxes and the liquor taxes. If the peasants were prepared to make large and increasing voluntary contributions to these indirect taxes, then their position could not have been as desperate as is often assumed. Professor Simms, therefore, challenges the views of such authorities as Donald MacKenzie Wallace, Geroid Robinson, Lazar Volin, Theodore Von Laue, Petr I. Liashchenko, and George Pavlovsky who all considered the growth in arrears in paying the annual direct tax assessment a prima-facie indication of the existence of distress in the countryside.

It has already been pointed out that Simms's argument is likely to be fallacious since it was quite possible for some groups of the peasantry to be destitute while others were drinking the vodka and paying the tax for it. Hans Rogger has recently summarized the views of G.M. Hamburg and Eberhard Müller, in his well-known recent textbook:[22]

> The most important corrective of [Simms's] view that tax collections denoted an improvement in the peasant economy is the finding that the main source of indirect revenue was not the villages but the burgeoning cities and industrial districts where bigger monetary income gave rise to

---

no longer appears in the central tax records after the late 1890s.) The effect of these additional non-central-government direct taxes was to increase the total direct tax burden on the eve of the First World War to an absolute level above its 1891–1892 level. However, in per-capita terms the direct tax burden was well below the 1891–1892 level.

[19] There are, however, again a number of problems: in particular, concerning the liquor tax receipts, which need to be combined with the income from the state vodka monopoly once the latter had been set up in the 1890s.

[20] The revenue from the liquor taxes and vodka monopoly increased by 4, customs revenue increased by 4.4, and taxes on tobacco, sugar, matches, and oil by 16.

[21] James Y. Simms, Jr., "The Crisis in Russian Agriculture at the End of the Nineteenth Century: A Different View," *Slavic Review*, 36, no. 3 (September 1977): 379–80.

[22] See G. M. Hamburg, "The Crisis in Russian Agriculture: A Comment," *Slavic Review* 37, no. 3 (September 1978): 481-86, Eberhard Müller, "Der Beitrag der Bauern zur Industrialisierung Russlands 1885–1930, Bemerkungen zur Korrektur eines Interpretations Modells," *Jahrbücher für Geschichte Osteuropas*, 27, no. 2 (1979): 197–219, and the survey in Hans Rogger, *Russia in the Age of Modernisation and Revolution, 1881–1917* (London and New York, 1983), pp. 87–88.

TABLE 4-11.

Direct Taxation Paid by the Peasantry and the Rural Population (in million rubles): Trends

| Year | Central Taxation | | | | | | | Non-Central Taxation | | | | | | Total Taxation (7+13) |
	Soul (1)	Redemption (2)	Redemption (3)	Land (4)	(1+[2 or 3]+4) (5)	All (6)	All (7)	Zemstvo (8)	Volost (9)	Selskie (10)	Food (11)	Insurance (12)	All (13)	(14)
1866–1870	40.4	—		0.9	41.3									
1871–1875	48.8		4.8	6.3	59.9	134.5?								
1876–1880	58.9		6.6	13.1	78.6	142.9?								
1881–1885	50.1		16.8	16.3	83.2	137.9?								
1886–1890	5.1	82.0	91.2	20.6	107.7	105.0?	94.4	21.5		27.6	0.5	11.8	61.4	155.8
1891–1895	1.1	87.8	83.9	21.7	110.6	104.4?	95.2	27.0	23.4	20.8		13.4	84.6	179.8
1896–1900	1.0	92.7	82.7	14.5	108.2		83.4	31.2	25.7	23.0		18.4	98.3	181.7
1901–1905		81.1	85.4	14.5	95.6									
1906–1910		7.6	7.5	22.6	30.2		19.7	44.5	25.0	23.8		24.3	117.6	137.3
1911–1912		0.8	0.8	25.3	26.1		11.5	57.1	26.8	26.4		27.1	137.4	148.9

Sources: Columns 1,3,4: *Departament Okladnykh Sborov, 1863–1913gg.* (St. Petersburg, 1913), pp. 260–69; column 2: *Ministerstvo Finansov, 1802–1902gg.*, pt. 2 (St. Petersburg, 1902), pp. 640–41, and *Ezhegodnik Rossii 1910g.* (St. Petersburg 1911), pp. 640–43. Cited in P. A. Khromov, *Ekonomicheskoe razvitie rossii v xix–xx vekhakh* (Moscow, 1950), pp. 448–511; column 6: 1871–1875 / 1891–1895, N. K. Brzheskii, *Nedoimochnosti i krugovaia poruka sel. obshchestvo* (St. Petersburg, 1901), pp. 416–19 (refers to 47 Guberniia only; there is also some uncertainty as to the comparability of the data); columns 7–13: Ministerstvo Finansov, Departament Okladnykh Sborov, *Svod svedenii postuplenii i vzimanii kazennykh, zemskikh i obshchestvennykh okladnykh sborov za . . .* (covers 54 guberniia only); column 11: Food Capital (there were clearly enormous difficulties in collecting funds for this grain reserve system, and it was dropped after the famine years).

TABLE 4-12.
Direct Taxation Paid by the Peasant Population (in million rubles): The Crisis Years

	Central Taxation						*Local Taxation*					
	Soul	*Redemption*		*Land*	*(1+2+4)*	*All*	*Zemstvo*	*Mir*	*Food*	*Ins*	*(7+8+9+10)*	*All*
Year	*(1)*	*(2)*	*(3)*	*(4)*	*(5)*	*(6)*	*(7)*	*(8)*	*(9)*	*(10)*	*(11)*	*(12)*
1889–1895 Crisis												
1889	1.3	99.1	91.9	21.3	121.7							
1890	1.3	98.9	88.2	21.3	121.5							
1891	1.3	98.8	69.0	21.6	121.7	73.3	16.8	22.0	0.5	10.7	171.7	123.3
1892	1.3	74.0	77.1	21.6	96.9	82.7	18.7	23.5	0.3	10.7	150.1	135.9
1893	1.1	77.0	99.0	21.3	99.4	106.6	23.4	25.1	0.5	11.8	160.2	167.4
1894	1.0	82.0	92.8	21.9	104.9	100.0	23.5	26.1	0.8	12.6	167.9	163.0
1895	1.0	87.8	101.3	22.0	110.8	109.3	25.3	41.3	?	13.2	190.6	189.1
1903–1909 Crisis												
1903	0.2	89.2	88.8	14.7	104.1	91.8	33.5	49.9		18.7	206.2	193.9
1904	0.2	86.2	81.6	14.9	101.3	83.7	32.1	49.7		19.5	202.6	185.0
1905	0.1	76.4	55.4	14.3	90.8	57.5	30.2	47.5		19.6	188.1	154.8
1906	0.2	35.0	35.0	21.7	56.7	40.3	30.4	45.6		20.2	152.9	136.5
1907	0	0.5	0.6	21.7	22.2	19.5	39.5	47.5		22.7	131.9	129.2
1908	0	0.5	0.7	21.8	22.3	16.8	46.6	48.7		25.5	143.1	137.6
1909	0	0.6	0.8	22.8	23.4	15.7	51.8	50.9		26.2	168.0	160.3

Sources: See table 4-11; columns 1, 2, 4 from *Departament okladnykh sborov 1863–1913gg.* (St. Petersburg, 1913), pp. 260–70; column 2 from *Ministerstvo Finansov, 1802–1902gg.*, pt. II (St. Petersburg, 1902), pp. 640–41, and *Ezhegodnik Rossii 1910g.* (St. Petersburg, 1911), pp. 640–43, cited in P. A. Khromov, *Ekonomicheskoe razvitie Rossii v XIX–XX vekakh* (Moscow, 1950), pp. 448–511; column 5 = column 1 + column 2 + column 4; columns 6 and 12, *Svod svedennii po postuplenii i vzimanii kazennykh, zemskikh i obshchestvennykh okladnykh sborov za . . .* 1891–1912, St. Petersburg 1898–1914, passim; columns 7–11: same sources as in table 4-11.

> consumption patterns different from those prevailing in the still largely natural economy of the countryside. The amount of goods purchased by the peasantry remained low; about three quarters of trade was concentrated in urban areas (with only 14% of the population in 1912) . . . The off-farm wages of peasants who did not permanently join the industrial labour force, and especially those of agriculture labourers, did not rise enough in real terms to lift their families above the minimum subsistence level.[23]

While I have some sympathy with Rogger's criticism, this account nevertheless presents a rather misleading picture. In my opinion, the peasant economy was not largely a natural economy. There was no persistent and widespread uniform level of minimum subsistence above which the vast majority of the peasants failed to rise. And finally the finding that the main source of indirect revenue was not the villages but the burgeoning cities and industrial centers is far from convincing. It may well be the case, but the budget consumption data are insufficient to provide a reliable rural time se-

[23] Rogger, *Russia in the Age of Modernisation*, pp. 87–88.

TABLE 4-13.
Indirect Taxation (in million rubles): Trends

Year	Liquor (1)	Vodka (2)	Salt (3)	Tobacco and Sugar (4)	Customs (5)	All (6)	Direct (7)
1860–1864	125.4		8.1	4.2	31.8	169.5	
1865–1869	130.2		10.5	7.9	34.8	183.4	
1870–1874	178.9		12.3	12.9	52.0	256.1	134.5
1875–1879	205.0		11.4	17.0	72.6	306.0	140.7
1880–1884	239.9			26.3	94.1	360.3	126.6
1885–1889	253.2			46.1	118.8	418.1	102.6
1890–1894	268.6			77.9	150.1	496.6	155.8
1895–1900	294.5	58.7		120.4	198.9	672.5	179.8
1901–1904	72.9	444.0		158.2	221.6	896.7	181.7
1905–1990	37.9	688.4		202.3	253.6	1182.2	137.3
1910–1914	47.1	755.6		278.9	322.5	1404.1	148.9

Sources: Columns 1–5 compiled from data from *Ministerstvo finansov 1802–1902* (St. Petersburg, 1902), pp. 636–39, and from *Ezhegodnik Rossii 1910g.*, and *Statisticheskii ezhegodnik Rossii 1915g.*, cited by P. A. Khromov, *Ekonomicheskoe razvitie Rossii v XIX–XX vekakh* (Moscow, 1950), pp. 514–29; column 6 = columns 1 + 2 + 3 + 4 + 5; column 7 from table 4-11 above. Figures for 1870–74 to 1885–89 exclude non-Central direct taxation and need to be elevated by about 60 million rubles to be compatible.

ries for this period and very few conclusions can be drawn from the predominantly urban location of the retail outlets. It would be most unwise to assume that peasants did not go to town for their shopping. Urban registered sales include sales to the peasants. For this reason, the urban/rural location of retail outlets is of very little operational significance for gathering evidence on final location of retail consumption and the incidence of indirect taxation. A far better approach is to use a regional division which is far more amenable to analysis.

My presentation of the evidence indicates that the rising trend of indirect taxation was reversed in 1891–1893 and was severely slowed down in 1906–1909. The regional data indicate quite clearly that regions like NCR and SPR, which preserved relatively high levels of indirect taxation in 1891 and 1892, were not the areas that suffered the greatest force of the crisis, and that their direct taxation payments also tended to remain high. (See tables 4-15 and 4-16.) The fall in direct taxation payments in 1891 and 1892 appears to have been particularly severe in the CPR and especially in the Eastern Region. These were the areas that suffered a major decline in indirect taxation.

Figures for the later period indicate a long-term decline in direct tax payment. This was above all a result of a major decline in kazennyi direct taxation with a halving of redemption payments in 1906 and their cancellation in 1907. By contrast, the non-kazennyi direct tax, was increasing but not sufficiently to offset the decline in kazennyi. Within this increasing trend there was a temporary downward reversal in 1905 and 1906. But this temporary

TABLE 4-14.
Indirect Taxation (in million rubles): Crisis Years

Year	Liquor (1)	Vodka (2)	Tobacco and Sugar (3)	Customs (4)	All (5)	All less Customs (6)	All less Customs alt. (7)
1889	274.9		59.9	138.1	472.9	334.8	383.1
1890	268.4		64.7	141.9	475.0	333.1	390.6
1891	247.4		64.3	128.4	440.1	311.7	346.3
1892	269.0		75.3	130.6	474.9	344.3	381.0
1893	260.8		85.1	166.0	511.9	345.9	384.2
1894	297.4		100.2	183.8	581.4	397.6	427.3
1903	34.2	542.3	164.6	241.5	982.6	741.1	741.2
1904	29.8	543.5	170.0	218.8	962.1	743.3	743.1
1905	29.8	609.4	166.1	212.8	1018.1	805.3	805.4
1906	39.4	697.5	213.5	241.3	1191.7	950.4	949.0
1907	41.1	707.1	208.2	260.5	1216.9	956.4	957.1
1908	39.1	709.0	207.9	279.3	1235.6	956.3	955.9
1909	40.2	718.9	215.3	274.3	1248.7	974.4	974.8

Sources: Columns 1–5: See sources for table 4-13; column 6 = column 5 − column 4; column
7: alternatvie series from Glavnoe Upravlenie Neokladnykh Sborov, . . . g. Otchet Glavnogo
Upravleniia Neokladnykh Sborov i Kazennoi Prodazhei Pitei (St. Petersburg), 1885–1915, passim.

reversal in the growth of direct taxation was not reflected in a reversal or
even a slowdown in gross indirect taxation receipts in these years, although
there was a slowdown in the later period from 1906–1908.

All regions and in particular the NCR gained from the sharp reduction in
kazennyi taxation. Local government and insurance taxes appear to have
been rising more sharply in the CPR than in the NCR, as a result of which
the overall direct taxation burden in the CPR increased by 73 percent from
1891 to 1912 while it fell in the NCR.

OTHER RELIEF MEASURES

Very little work has been carried out on tsarist relief efforts, with the exception of Professor Richard G. Robbins's fine study of the 1891 famine measures.[24] Professor Robbins has demonstrated the enormous scale of tsarist
relief measures in 1891–1892—a level of operations that greatly ameliorated
the immediate effects of the agricultural crisis of 1889–1891. It was the failure
to accompany these relief measures with tax remissions, rather than any failure in these relief measures themselves, that was to lead to the accumulation
of tax arrears and later problems.

[24] Richard G. Robbins, Famine in Russia, 1891/1892: The Imperial Government Responds to a
Crisis (New York, 1975).

TABLE 4-15.
Direct Taxation Paid by the Peasantry (in million rubles): Payment of Central,
Zemstvo, Mir, and Insurance Taxes (crisis years by region)

Year	NCR	SPR	CPR	(CChZ)	(East)	Total
1891	45.6	37.9	39.8	(25.9)	(13.9)	123.3
1892	48.7	35.5	51.6	(31.9)	(19.6)	135.9
1893	50.3	40.0	77.1	(49.4)	(27.8)	167.4
1894	50.1	40.6	72.2	(46.1)	(26.1)	162.9
1895	56.7	44.5	88.9	(55.1)	(32.9)	189.1
1896	56.8	42.4	79.7	(50.0)	(29.8)	178.9
1897	59.4	43.6	69.3	(39.4)	(29.9)	172.3
1898	59.1	45.0	66.5	(44.6)	(21.9)	170.6
1899	61.1	42.6	84.0	(53.0)	(31.0)	187.7
1900	60.7	44.7	84.7	(52.4)	(32.3)	190.1
1901	61.5	45.6	78.9	(49.5)	(29.4)	185.9
1902	60.6	47.1	80.9	(50.8)	(30.2)	188.6
1903	61.1	48.0	84.0	(51.9)	(32.1)	193.1
1904	57.9	45.4	81.8	(50.7)	(31.1)	185.0
1905	49.2	44.7	60.9	(34.1)	(26.8)	154.9
1906	47.8	41.0	47.7	(29.4)	(18.2)	136.5
1907	38.3	34.0	57.0	(37.4)	(19.6)	129.3
1908	41.4	35.4	60.8	(37.9)	(22.9)	137.5
1909	41.3	38.4	64.8	(41.2)	(23.6)	144.5
1910	41.6	39.9	65.9	(41.3)	(24.6)	147.3
1911	42.1	40.4	57.8	(38.2)	(19.5)	140.2
1912	44.7	44.0	68.8	(42.3)	(26.5)	157.5

Source: Ministerstvo Finansov, Departament Okladnykh Sborov, *Svod svedenii po postuplenii i vzimanii kazennykh, zemskikh i obshchestvennykh okladnykh sborov za* . . . 1891–1912 (St. Petersburg, 1898–1914), passim.

Note: (CChZ) Central Chernozem, and (East) are the two constituent parts of CPR, as defined by the tsarist taxation office.

In subsequent years relief operations were carried out regularly under the Tsarist Ministry of Internal Affairs[25], but have been very little studied.[26]

The domestic food relief scheme was undoubtedly complex and had become highly dependent on central state subsidies. A food capital relief scheme set up in 1868 was intended to be financed by the local community,

[25] See *Prodovol'stvennaia kampaniia 1906–7 po dannym otchetnykh materialov MVD* (St. Petersburg, 1908), and similar volumes for 1907–1908, 1908–1911, 1911–1912, 1914–15.

[26] The major recent work on the prerevolutionary grain trade—T. M. Kitanina, *Khlebnaia torgovlia Rossii v 1875–1914gg. (Ocherki pravitel'stvennoi politiki)*, (Leningrad, 1978)—pays considerable attention to grain purchases by the intendantstvo for the army, but totally ignores the far more extensive and complex operations of the Economic (Khoziaistvennii) Department of the Ministry of the Interior (MVD) aimed at peasant relief operations.

TABLE 4-16.
Indirect Taxation by Region (in million rubles)

Year	NCR	SCR	SPR	CPR	(CChZ)	(East)	All	
1886	140	5	96	53	(23)	(29)	382	
1887	153	5	105	59	(27)	(32)	414	
1888	164	7	120	61	(29)	(32)	449	
1889								
1890	185	25	128	63	(29)	(35)	516	391
1891	186	29	127	59	(26)	(33)	509	346
1892	211	13	132	57	(26)	(32)	541	381
1893	222	13	143	62	(26)	(35)	581	384
1894	244	12	164	69	(30)	(39)	654	437
1895								458
1896								465
1897	/154	/16	/167	/100	/(59)	/(41)		/489
1898	187	16	188	100	(60)	(90)		557
1899	200	16	205	108	(65)	(98)		602
1900	204	15	199	120	(71)	(106)		612
1901	208	16	204	132	(81)	(120)		630
1902	218	19	229	147	(95)	(145)		688
1903	228	20	249	162	(105)	(158)		741
1904	231	16	248	162	(103)	(155)		743
1905	243	14	265	186	(114)	(170)		805
1906	283	13	317	209	(128)	(192)		949
1907	293	16	311	210	(128)	(191)		957
1908	296	17	302	215	(132)	(197)		956
1909	294	18	312	220	(130)	(194)		975
1910	303	21	359	239	(141)	(212)		1059
1911	330	23	366	229	(141)	(208)		1086
1912	356	25	381	241	(148)	(218)		1148

Sources: 1886–1894 data calculated from Ministerstvo Finansov, Departament Okladnykh Sborov, *Svod Dannykh o postuplenii okladnykh sborov . . . za 1888–1890gg.* (St. Petersburg, 1894), pp. 385–89, and ibid., *za 1891–1893gg.* (St. Petersburg, 1897), pp. 465–69; 1897–1912 calculated from Glavnoe Upravlenie Neokladnykh Sborov, . . . *g. Otchet Glavnogo Upravleniia Neokladnykh Sborov i Kazennoi Prodazhi pitei*, 1885–1915.

Note: The 1886–1894 data are inclusive of customs receipts; 1895–1912 data are exclusive.

which was to make periodic contributions in money or grain, to be lent out in periods of strain. Once aid was granted, the grain or capital would have to be returned, but no interest was charged. In 1868, the food capital relief system possessed a capital of 885,172 rubles; this was regularly increased until in 1880 its value reached 7.4 million rubles. However, with the enormous harvest failures of 1881, withdrawals from the capital fund totalled the whole of this 7.4 million, as well as an additional 3.2 million supplied by the central exchequer. Between 1881 and 1906 a further 300 million rubles was expended: 146.5 million rubles in the famine of 1891–1892; 35 million rubles in 1897–1898, 39 million in 1901–1902 and 71 million in 1905–1906.[27] On the eve of the 1906–1907 campaign the food reserve consisted of only 73.5 million puds (1.2 million tons) and 37.9 million rubles, instead of the required 161.6 million puds (2.6 million tons) and 62.4 million rubles. By the end of the 1906–1907 campaign the government was forced to expend over 170 million rubles from the central exchequer on relief measures.[28] The scale of relief expenditure in 1906–1907 consequently appears to have exceeded the very high level for the 1891–1892 famine.

The detailed data on the scale of food loans also indicate that at the height of the 1906–1907 relief operations in March 1907 almost 15 million people were receiving food loans: 2.6 million in the NCR (1 million in Nizhnii Novgorod and 0.74 million in Tula); 0.6 million in the SPR (predominantly in Khar'kov and the Don Oblast); 0.6 million in the EPR (primarily in Orenburg and Akmolinsk); and almost 11 million in CPR (predominantly in the Volga: Samara 1.9 million, Kazan 1.5 million, Saratov 1.3 million and over a million each in Penza, Simbirsk and Ufa; the numbers in the Central chernozem were almost 2.5 million with over a million in Tambov). By contrast, at the height of the 1891–1892 campaign in April 1892 almost 11.9 million people were receiving food loans: 1.9 million in the NCR (0.6 million in Nizhnii Novgorod and 0.7 million in Riazan); 0.1 million in SPR; 1.2 million in EPR (Orenburg, Tobol'sk, Perm). Again the bulk of food loans were 8.7 million in CPR (predominantly in the Volga: over a million in Kazan and Samara, 0.9 million in Saratov and Simbirsk, 0.8 million in Penza; in the Central Chernozem there were 2.8 million: a million in Voronezh and 0.9 million in Tambov).[29]

This scale of relief operation in both 1891–1892 and 1906–1907 is most impressive and certainly needs to be taken into consideration in evaluating peasant living standards during periods of crisis.

Peasant Living Standards in General

The price/wage data clearly indicate two periods of crisis for wage laborers: the sharp but short crisis of 1889–1893 and the gentler but longer crisis of 1896–1908. This applies especially to the CPR. The latter crisis in living standards was less severe but of much longer duration than the earlier one.

Land-price data indicate that it was more difficult for peasants to rent or purchase land in the period after the late 1890s and particularly in 1902–1903 and 1910.

The taxation burden was undoubtedly very severe in the late 1880s and

[27] *Prodovol'stvennaia Kampaniia 1906-7g. po dannym otchetnykh materialov MVD* (St. Petersburg, 1908), 1, p. 47.

[28] Ibid., p. 58

[29] See R. G. Robbins, *Famine in Russia*, pp. 186–87.

increased greatly in the 1890s. There *was* a temporary decline in the tax burden at the time of the famine of 1891–1892 due to peasant defaults in tax
payment. Contrary to Simms's suggestion that they indicate unwillingness
rather than inability to pay, these defaults *can be* accepted as an indication of
peasant desperation and were associated with a fall in indirect peasant taxation. The subsequent growth in zemstvo, mir, and insurance payments increased the tax burden on the peasantry until a large part of it was slashed
at the time of the agrarian revolution of 1905–1906. This relief in kazennii
direct tax burden was not totally passed on to the peasantry since it coincided with a large increase in non-kazenni payments (zemstvo, insurance,
etc.) These changes resulted in an overall regional relocation of the direct tax
burden that further depressed the position of the peasantry in the CPR in
comparison with those in the NCR and SPR. However in per-capita terms
the fall in living standards would not have been as great as in 1891–1892.

The government food relief system for the peasantry was very extensive
and did provide relief on an enormous scale, particularly in the CPR in 1891–
1892 and 1906–1907.

In summary, the situation was very complex and mixed. But when the real
incomes of rural wage labor were in a critical condition, relief measures and
the many defaults on direct tax payment offered a greater degree of compensation than is often realized. However, the relief and tax defaults of 1889–
1893 were only temporary and would ultimately contribute towards greater
peasant indebtedness later. The relief and tax defaults of 1904–1906 were
non-recoverable.

AGRARIAN UNREST AND PEASANT REVOLUTION

In 1905–1906 and again in 1917 the Russian countryside was engulfed in
peasant revolution. While the agricultural crises and the crises in peasant
living standards were undoubtedly extremely important factors in producing
these movements, it would be extreme reductionism to attempt to explain
these movements directly or exclusively in terms of these factors. As noted
in the introduction, we need to consider both the attitudes and authority of
the government as well as the desires and circumstances of the peasantry.
The political crisis came when the government was seen to lack the determination and the authority to ensure that the dissatisfied peasantry fulfilled
the societal and political obligations that the authorities placed on them.

In this section I have emphasized the difference between the government
taxation system's response to the condition of the peasantry in the 1890s and
in the first decade of the twentieth century. Although taxes were deferred in
the late 1880s and early 1890s there was an extremely tough response by the
government to the question of repayment of most of these debts. In the beginning of the twentieth century, following the peasant disturbances in

Khar'kov and Poltava in 1902, there was an abrupt reversal in government policy on repayment of debts, with a "soft" line on concessions to the peasantry beginning in 1903–1904. This soft line contributed to the collapse of state authority in the countryside from 1904, which was reinforced by the revolutionary events of 1905. From the end of 1905 the government decided to abandon the collection of redemption payments and the old debts related to it, but this new policy was combined with harsh disciplinary measures, and the agrarian reforms associated with Stolypin.

The data presented below suggest that the untimely and unprepared changes in the taxation system in 1903 and 1904 probably contributed to the agrarian and political crisis of 1905–1906.

GOVERNMENT RESPONSE TO PEASANT INDEBTEDNESS IN THE 1890s

Peasant indebtedness increased rapidly in the last decades of the nineteenth century. According to N.K. Brzheskii's data peasant indebtedness on the payments of direct taxation rose from a sum equal to 22 percent of tax assessment in 1871–1875 to just under 100 percent in 1890–1895. Most of the increase came between the late 1880s and the early 1890s and was particularly concentrated in the CPR. In 1886–1890, the level of indebtedness of the Volga peasantry was already equivalent to 114 percent of their assessments, in 1890–1895, it rose to more than 200 percent. See table 4-17.

Within this period it was specifically during the famine years of 1891 and 1892 that there was a sudden and rapid growth of indebtedness. The bulk of the debt came from defaults on redemption payments, particularly among former state peasants, who had only recently been incorporated into this redemption tax system.

The data for the individual years from 1888–1897 indicate that the level of annual defaults in tax payment was as high as 14 to 15 percent of annual tax assessments in the eastern part of the CPR in 1888 and 1889, and rose to 34 percent in this region in 1890 and well over 50 percent in both the East and Central Chernozem regions in the famine year of 1891. In 1892 it was still over 40 percent in both these regions, and it was only after 1893 that tax receipts returned to a level in close proximity to the amount levied. The level of fulfillment of tax obligations was much higher throughout in all the other regions.

In absolute terms the level of peasant indebtedness on kazennii tax increased from 52 million rubles in 1891, to 81 million in 1892, to 103 million in 1893, and was still roughly in this order at the turn of the century. However these figures exclude the debts on the food capital which had risen from over 5 million to over 50 million rubles over this period.[30]

---

[30] See *Svod svedenii o postuplenii i vzimanii kazennykh, zemskykh i obshchestvennykh okladnykh sborov*, for the appropriate years.

TABLE 4-17.
Indebtedness per Level of Annual Taxation Assessment for the Rural Population in
the 47 European Provinces of the Russian Empire (in million rubles)

Region	1871–1875	1876–1880	1881–1885	1886–1890	1891	1896
Annual Assessment						
NCR	43.8	46.5	45.8	32.8	31.4	31.9
SPR						
Ukraine	31.4	33.6	33.2	22.7	23.0	23.5
CPR						
CChZem	37.8	40.6	39.1	32.1	31.9	31.1
Volga	21.7	22.2	20.8	17.4	17.1	17.7
All	59.5	62.8	59.9	49.5	49.0	48.8
Total	134.7	142.9	137.9	105.0	104.4	104.2
Indebtedness						
NCR	15.9	12.3	15.4	9.7	15.1	17.5
SPR						
Ukraine	4.8	5.2	5.8	6.9	4.5	4.0
CPR						
CChZEM	3.9	6.4	12.4	13.4	39.9	39.3
Volga	5.4	8.0	14.6	19.8	40.4	35.7
All	9.3	14.4	27.0	33.2	80.3	75.0
Total	30.1	31.9	48.2	48.9	99.9	96.5
Indebtedness as Percentage of Assessment						
NCR	36.3	26.5	33.6	29.6	48.1	54.9
SPR						
Ukraine	15.3	15.5	18.0	30.4	19.6	17.0
CPR						
CChZEM	10.3	15.0	32.0	42.0	122.0	127.0
Volga	24.9	36.0	71.0	114.0	236.0	201.0
All	15.5	22.9	45.1	67.1	163.9	153.7
Total	22.3%	22.3%	35.0%	47.4%	95.7%	92.6%

Sources: 1876/1880–1896 calculated from data in *Issledovanie ekonomicheskogo polozheniia tsen-tral'no-chernozemnykh gubernii, Trudy osobogo soveshchaniia 1899–1901gg.*, compiled by A. D. Polenov (Moscow 1901), p. 6, cited in N. A. Egiazarova, *Agrarnyi krizis kontsa XIX veka v Rossii* (Moscow, 1959), p. 171; 1871/1875–1891/1895 calculated from data in N. Brzheskii, *Nedoimochnosti i krugovaia poruka sel. obshchestv*, pp. 416–19.

Note: This regionalization is slightly different from the other ones used in this study due to the inability to get disaggregated data.

During the 1890s the government responded to this large scale of peasant taxation defaults with a series of harsh measures designed to recover the debt. The procedure was to threaten the defaulting peasants, to take an inventory of their property, and forceably to sell it off. Alternatively, attempts were made to reallocate the debt among the rural society or the *volost'*, and to press the defaulters into forced labor. Finally there was the infamous procedure of threatening and ultimately arresting and fining the local officials: *volost'* elders, rural elders, local tax officials, and others, as well as the defaulting peasants. All these procedures were systematically recorded in the tax accounts in the volumes published before 1903. See table 4-18 for a stark indication of the level of pressures applied by the central government to the localities.

Faced with these kinds of pressures the local authorities and tax collectors

TABLE 4-18.

Measures Taken by the Government to Enforce the Payment of Direct Taxes and of Debts on Payments

	1891	1892	1893	1894	1895	1896	1897	1898
Inventorization of Property of Defaulting Peasants								
No. of villages	17,985	24,421	26,112	28,964	22,321	22,329	18,200	12,971
Forced Sales of Property								
No. of villages	2,861	2,960	3,152	3,987				
No. of households					64,029	43,208	17,953	13,823
Indebted sum (in millions of rubles)								
	0.802	0.662	4.042	5.693	2.76	1.76	0.59	0.65
Sum realized (in millions of rubles)								
	0.174	0.193	0.556	0.672	0.446	0.321	0.136	0.074
Reallocation of Debt								
Supplementary reallocation of debt								
to *obshchestva*	823	745	988	415	804	693	313	560
to *volost'*					259	2,026	220	32
Forced labor	768	1,336	1,613	1,285	?			
Other Measures								
Arrests								
Volost' elders	465	953	905	666				
Village elders	4,679	10,066	11,584	9,993				
Tax collectors	284	622	644	729				
Other officials	109	48	42	95				
Debtors	2,270	9,422	12,257	14,945				
Others	1,331	227	444	299				
All	9,138	21,338	25,876	26,731				
Fines								
Volost' elders	416	1,318	1,235	1,157				
Village elders	4,679	10,066	11,584	9,993				
Tax collectors	161	539	638	658				
Other officials	84	74	109	142				
Others	660	495	112	57				
All	2,925	6,145	6,706	6,952				

Sources: Ministerstvo Finansov, Departament Okladnykh Sborov, *Svod svedenii o postuplenii kazennykh, zemskikh i obshchestvennykh okladnykh sborov po Imperii, za 1891* (St. Petersburg, 1898), p. 413 (covers 50 Provinces of European Russia); *za 1892–4* (St. Petersburg, 1902), p. 725 (covers 49 provinces excluding Lifland); *za 1895-9* (St. Petersburg, 1902), p. 446 (covers 42 provinces & 3 oblasts only; no data given for arrests or fines).

naturally turned to brutality in order to save themselves from arrest and punishment. The system was notoriously harsh, and it was only by means of
such repressive methods, backed up by the strength of the police and army,
that the taxes were collected and the debts kept within order.

RESPONSIBILITY FOR TAXATION AND FOR PAYING OFF
INDEBTEDNESS, 1903–1904

After 1903 the tax records fail to provide further detail on repression against
tax defaulters or any form of record of food capital indebtedness. In February
1903 an imperial manifesto concerning plans for perfecting the political order
had foreshadowed the abolition of the mainstay of this repressive system of
tax enforcement.[31] It was announced that the institution of joint responsibility for peasant direct taxation was to be abolished. And a month later a decree was passed which did make the payment of current direct taxes and of
accumulated arrears the responsibility of the individual peasant household.
The following year on the occasion of the birth of the heir apparent (August
11, 1904), the tsar issued another Manifesto which went much further. The
tsar ruled that all debts on redemption payments and other central state direct taxes were to be canceled from January 1, 1904, and that the peasant
population was in future to be exempt from corporal punishment. As a result
of this magnificent (but politically inopportune) gesture 130.6 million rubles
of debt were immediately wiped away, mostly from the peasantry, and predominantly (98.3 million) from the CPR.

In his survey of these events Professor Gerschenkron noted that the cancellation of debts and the abolition of corporal punishment were closely related to each other, "inasmuch as administration of whipping had been very
widely used by the police in its efforts to reduce the amount of accumulated
arrears."[32] However, he failed to note that this change in policy left the authorities in an extremely difficult position as regards collecting the 1904 and
subsequent direct taxes. Did the government really think that the peasantry
would continue to pay the hated redemption tax, once the government had
foresworn the use of violence, and group pressure, and once it had forgiven
those who had earlier refused to pay? Given the historical animosity over
this issue, the response of the peasantry should not have been in doubt.

LOSS OF CENTRAL AUTHORITY IN 1905–1906 AND THE
STRUGGLE TO REGAIN IT

From the political point of view, as regards the security of the state, the 1904
concessions to the peasantry were made at the worst possible time. It was
sheer folly immediately to remove the repressive machinery, to forgive de-

---

[31] This was probably a response to the mass peasant disturbances of 1902 in Poltava and
Khar'kov.

[32] A. Gerschenkron, "Agrarian Policies," p. 786.

faulters, and then to expect the peasants to keep on paying their taxes. It could not have worked in normal times, and 1904 was a particularly unfortunate time to dabble with this kind of machinery. The government was soon suffering from a series of defeats in the Russo-Japanese War that lowered morale and limited the effectiveness of the central government in policing the villages.

The result was that the level of defaults in direct tax payment rose sharply (threefold) in 1904, especially in the NCR. In the following year as the government's authority fell further, the level of defaults tripled again to levels well in excess of the early 1890s. The level of defaults in the NCR more than doubled, and those in the CPR and especially the Central Chernozem rose eight-fold.

The government was losing control over rural taxation in the countryside in 1904, before the dramatic urban revolutionary events of 1905 and the beginning of the agrarian disturbances of 1905.[33] Following these events peasant disturbances increased, and the government was unable to rely on the army to restore order. Immediately following the October Manifesto in which the tsar promised to introduce a more constitutional system, another manifesto was published on November 3, 1905, which announced that all redemption payments were to be cut by 50 percent in 1906 and totally abolished by January 1, 1907. However, even after the reduction of the peasants' tax bill in 1906 by 40 million rubles, the peasants still managed to default in their tax payments by over 25 million rubles. By 1906 the bulk of the default had shifted from the NCR to the CPR, the traditional defaulters.

Unlike the situation in the 1890s, these defaults were clearly a result of reluctance to pay, rather than the inability to pay. As we have explained above, the most serious decline in peasant living standards came in 1906–1908 rather than in 1905–1906. The concessions granted in 1904, at an inopportune moment, did little to ease peasant living standards and simply increased the pressures for more concessions when the crisis came in the following years.

CONCLUSIONS: PEASANT UNREST, THE AGRICULTURAL CRISIS, AND LIVING STANDARDS

The growth in peasant unrest over this period was probably more a consequence of the decline in governmental authority, regional problems, and the specific problems of wage laborers, than any increase in overall peasant destitution. There was, in fact, a long-term improvement in the major indicator reflecting the living standards of peasant producers—namely rising per-capita grain production even net of exports. The indicators of real crisis are re-

[33] For a fine survey of the chronology and the nature of the 1905–1907 peasant disturbances, see Teodor Shanin, *Russia, 1905–07: Revolution as a Moment of Truth* (Houndmills, Basingstoke, Hampshire 1986), pp. 83–99.

lated to specific areas, specific groups, and specific times. In certain areas, particularly the CPR, the per-capita grain-production indicator was certainly showing signs of long-term crisis. Livestock farming was in a general long-term crisis. And the position for rural wage laborers indicated a long-term decline in wage-labor rates in rye equivalents from the mid 1890s to 1907–1908; the recovery by 1913 was relatively minor. On the whole, the position as regards trends was therefore mixed.

However, within these trends there were two particularly serious periods of crisis in peasant living standards which can be identified for 1891–1893 and 1905–1908. In both cases the position was particularly severe in the CPR. And in both cases the government responded with enormous amounts of relief in the form of food loans. In 1891–1892 the government attempted to keep track of the increased level of peasant indebtedness and to recover it by means of harsh repression. There was no immediate increase in peasant unrest in response to these harsh measures until the 1902 disturbances in Khar'kov and Poltava. In 1903 and 1904, following these disturbances, there was a major softening of the policy on pressing for debt payments. Although well intentioned, the concessions were not carefully planned, and their timing appears to owe more to the personal life of the tsar's family (celebrating the birth of a male heir) than to interests of state. The results of these measures were disastrous from the government's point of view, inasmuch as they encouraged further peasant resistance, led the peasants to expect more concessions, and provided a demonstration of the real benefits to be gained by flouting tsarist authority.

The limited peasant disturbances of 1902 may have been associated with the government's inflexible response to a temporary regional decline in peasant living standards, but the much greater level of disturbances in 1905–1907 appears to have been encouraged by the inopportune manner in which necessary concessions were granted. The temporary relaxation of the pressure on the peasantry in 1904 and 1905 coincided with a period of government political weakness, during which time peasant reluctance to pay taxes was greatly increased. Encouraged by their success on this score, and with the apparent loss of government authority, the peasants moved on to larger-scale disorders which were largely aimed at the landowners. Order was restored only after the tsar had been forced to announce the phasing out of the disastrous redemption tax, and when mass repression was again applied to the peasantry in martial-law circumstances. The bungling of the belated cancellation of taxes and debts and the subsequent change in agrarian policy failed to remove the pressure for further peasant insurrection and may well have contributed to the peasants' psychological readiness for revolt.

9. LOG HOUSES, WATER WELL, AND BASKET-MAKERS IN A CENTRAL INDUSTRIAL REGION VILLAGE (JOHN FOSTER FRASER, *RED RUSSIA* [NEW YORK: THE JOHN LANE COMPANY, 1907], BETWEEN PP. 70 AND 71).

10. THATCHED-ROOF, PLASTERED, AND WHITEWASHED PEASANT HUT IN POLTAVA PROVINCE, UKRAINE (P. P. SEMENOV AND V. I. LAMANSKII, EDITORS, *ROSSIIA: POLNOE GEOGRAFICHESKOE OPISANIE NASHEGO OTECHESTVA*, VOL. 7: *MALOROSSIIA* [ST. PETERSBURG: A. F. DEVRIEN, 1903], P. 116).

PART II

Peasant Culture

As WE have already seen, the behavior, values, and institutions that are fundamental to the culture of the peasantry of European Russia do not lend themselves to easy classification. In the Central Black Earth Zone, peasants supported themselves by their farming activities; in the Central Industrial Region, where the soil was less fertile and the growing season much shorter, they depended less on farming and more on proto-industrialization or on work as migrant laborers. Communal tenure prevailed in most regions of the empire, but not in the west and some regions of the south. The look of houses and villages and the dress of peasant men and women varied considerably in the forested north and the steppe-lands of the south. It is in this disparate context that the essays by Christine Worobec and Samuel Ramer provide a rich and complex picture of some of the common values and attitudes that prevailed among peasant men and women in widely differing regions of European Russia.

In Worobec's ground-breaking essay on Russian peasant women, the rigidity of village patriarchy is everywhere manifest. Separate "spheres" of male and female activity and clear patterns of subjugation were enforced in work, ceremonial duties, and in the allocation of space within the home, church, and communal assembly. At the same time, women were granted a measure of respect for their labor, and the spheres of male and female activity were themselves part of a system of communal norms of "appropriate" behavior. Thus, if a male peasant failed to fulfill his obligations, women were often able to assume them, and peasant courts would on occasion recognize their rights to do so. In the course of the nineteenth century, as husbands went into labor migration, wives often took over many of the farming chores that had traditionally been the province of the male. As Worobec sees it, these changes were implemented in ways that reinforced many aspects of the traditional peasant economy, with women holding fast to traditional, patriarchal forms of family and community which gave them a measure of security and definition of purpose.

The search for well-being in a world pervaded by the threat and the reality of physical, economic, and material disaster is illuminated by Samuel Ramer's essay on the role of traditional healers in peasant society. Ramer indicates that the peasant healer—often a women—was a purveyor of spiritual counsel, a sort of lay "therapist" and a family adviser as well as the hoped-for source of cures for physical ailments. In the late nineteenth and twentieth centuries, as physicians and feldshers arrived in the countryside in ever increasing numbers, peasants did not reject their services. Instead, they eagerly sought professional medical help, but they did so without ever abandoning their traditional belief that the concerns of a "healer" should go far beyond the treatment of narrowly defined medical problems. For their part, when the traditional peasant healers (*znakhari*) were faced with the competition of physicians, they did not rigidly reject the use of "modern" remedies; they modified their practices by emulating physicians in their treatment and medications, particularly in the case of syphilis and malaria.

—E. K.-M.

CHAPTER 5

VICTIMS OR ACTORS? RUSSIAN PEASANT WOMEN AND PATRIARCHY

*Christine D. Worobec**

They are making me marry a lout
With no small family
Oh! Oh! Oh! Oh dear me!
With a father, and a mother,
And four brothers
And sisters three.
Oh! Oh! Oh! Oh dear me!
Says my father-in-law,
"Here comes a bear!"
Says my mother-in-law,
"Here comes a slut!"
My sisters-in-law cry,
"Here comes a do-nothing!"
My brothers-in-law exclaim,
"Here comes a mischief-maker!"
Oh! Oh! Oh! Oh dear me![1]

A BETROTHED Russian peasant girl viewed her future life as wife, daughter-in-law, and mother with trepidation. She did not rejoice at the prospect of leaving her natural family and taking on the responsibilities that awaited her in a new home with a husband and, in many cases, in-laws. Rather, in the presence of girlfriends and married village women, she lamented the loss of her maidenly freedoms in exchange for a life in which it was said that "nei-

* For elaboration of the ideas presented in this paper, see Christine D. Worobec, "Family, Community, and Land in Peasant Russia, 1860–1905" (Ph.D. diss., University of Toronto, 1984), chap. 7–8; and its revised form, *Peasant Russia: Family and Community in the Post-Emancipation Period* (Princeton, forthcoming).

[1] Translated in William Ralston Shedden-Ralston, *The Songs of the Russian People, as Illustrative of Slavonic Mythology and Russian Social Life* (London, 1873), p. 289.

ther father-in-law nor mother-in-law, / Neither brother-in-law nor sister-in-law . . ." would love her. Or worse still, "Your good-for-nothing husband will bring all his weight / down to bear on [you]. / [He] will scoff at you. / . . . [He] will taunt, / [And] abuse me for everything.[2]

Marriage marked the greatest upheaval in a young girl's life in post-Emancipation Central Russia. With patrilocal residence the norm, marriage celebrations constituted a rite of passage during which a bride made the transition from the security of her natal family to the insecurity of her new husband's family. It is little wonder that as a intruder into the established rhythms of a tightly knit family household, a girl was anxious about her new life. She bemoaned her unenviable situation in ritual songs. Akin to funereal laments, these songs mourned the sacrifice of maidenhood in exchange for all the burdens of a married woman. No longer could a woman count on the understanding of a loving father and mother. Instead she had to cultivate potentially hostile in-laws who might harass her verbally, physically, and sexually. Bonds would be created very slowly through labor, obedience, and, most importantly, bearing and raising children.

A wife's responsibility to produce offspring underscored the fact that weddings transferred more than an individual between families. They also transferred, as in other Eastern European peasant cultures, "rights to the bride's reproductive powers."[3] These rights gave a conjugal family ultimate authority over a bride. In an extended family she was directly subordinate to household patriarch, husband, and mother-in-law and subject to physical punishment if she disobeyed her superiors or failed to live up to their expectations. A wife was obliged to love and respect her husband. This meant, above all, that she render him unquestioning obedience, fulfill her numerous domestic duties, and do fieldwork, as well as bear and raise children.

In addition to accepting a new family and obligations, a bride had to alter her social relationships and assume guardianship of her conjugal family's honor. She could no longer associate with her unmarried girlfriends in work and play. Instead she had to abandon her maidenly single braid for the two braids of a married woman and don a traditional headdress and kerchief that completely covered the hair.[4] Visually undifferentiated from other married women, the young novice joined her new peers in gossip across the yards,

---

[2] V. N. Debrovol'skii, comp., *Smolenskii etnograficheskii sbornik*, 4 (St. Petersburg, 1894), p. 308; and quoted in O. P. Semenova-Tian-Shanskaia, *Zhizn' 'Ivana': Ocherki iz byta krest'ian odnoi iz chernozemnykh gubernii* (St. Petersburg, 1914), p. 44

[3] See Gail Kligman, "The Rites of Women: Oral Poetry, Ideology, and the Socialization of Peasant Women in Contemporary Romania," in *Women, State, and Party in Eastern Europe*, ed. Sharon L. Wolchik and Alfred G. Meyer (Durham, 1985), p. 327.

[4] For a discussion of the regional variations in headdresses worn by married women in the Great Russian, Belorussian, and Ukrainian provinces, see D. Zelenin, "Zhenskie golovnye ubory vostochnykh (russkikh) Slavian," *Slavia* 5 (1926–1927): 303–38, 535–56.

at laundry sessions at the rivers, and local festivities. She did not, however, have the right to complain to them about her treatment in her new life or cast aspersions on any family member. "When you are melancholy [and] sad," a folk song from Poshekhon'e District, Iaroslavl Province, advised, "Go to a virgin field, / Fall down and pour your soul out to a hot stone. / The hot stone will not gossip, / The damp mother earth will not tell."[5] Social protocol demanded that a women not wash her conjugal family's "dirty linen in public."[6] Rather it was a wife's duty to protect and enhance her family's honor.

Yet, at the same time, marriage and the responsibilities of wife, mother, and in-law that accompanied that stage of life endowed women with respect and status within the Russian peasant community. A mother-in-law and household head's wife, the *bol'shukha*, held the most coveted position. As manager of domestic tasks, she supervised the work of her daughters-in-law, sisters-in-law, and children. In addition, she had the major duty of acculturating her children in village mores. The community rewarded a woman for fulfilling her parental obligations by permitting her to arrange her offsprings' marriages. Married women could also assume the important role of *svakha* (matchmaker). The community further buttressed wives' positions by accepting women as household heads when their husbands died and left behind small children, when husbands and adult sons left the village for work elsewhere, or when husbands were incompetent household managers. It obligated women, as a group, to seek out and punish publicly communal members who committed moral improprieties.

A woman outside marriage, on the other hand, did not enjoy community status. As a relatively unproductive member in terms of labor and reproduction, she was a burden on her family and community. The uncomplimentary nomenclatures of "privateers," "old maids," "wolfish women," and "hypocrites" that were applied to spinsters underscore that burden.[7] The social organization of an agriculturally based society in which real property was reserved for men was not equipped to provide for unmarried women and childless widows. Spinsters, childless widows, and soldiers' wives (whose husbands were in active service) were marginal members of their community

[5] I. Il'inskii, "Svadebnye prichety, detskiia pensi i pr., zapisannyia v Shchetinskoi, Khmelevskoi i Melenkovskoi volostiakh Poshekhonskago uezda," *Zhivaia Starina* 6, no. 2 (1986): 235, no. 33.

[6] Cited in G. L. Permyakov, *From Proverb to Folk-Tale: Notes on the General Theory of Cliché* (Moscow, 1979), p. 41.

[7] Only *chernichki*, unmarried women who had taken religious vows, were accorded community respect for fulfilling various family and community services. They taught children how to read and washed, dressed, buried, and mourned the dead. A. V. Balov, S. Ia. Derunov, and Ia. Il'inskii, "Ocherki Poshekhon'ia," *Etnograficheskoe Obozrenie* 10, no. 4. (1898): 88; V. N. Bondarenko, "Ocherki Kirsanovskago uezda, Tambovsk. gub.," *Etnograficheskoe Obozrenie* 2, no. 4 (1890): 2–5, and M. M. Gromyko, *Traditsionnye normy povedeniia i formy obshcheniia russkikh krest'ian XIX v.* (Moscow, 1986), p. 103.

and were sometimes forced to leave the village to eke out a livelihood else-where.[8]

Russian peasant women both coveted and feared marriage, two diametri-cally opposed reactions which reveal the complexities of Russian peasant so-ciety and the patriarchalism that shaped that society. Domination of men over women, parents over children, and in-laws over affines was part of the hierarchy of relations within family and community, facilitating management of peasant households as economic and social welfare units. Women found themselves subordinated to men on the misogynist grounds that they were inferior to men and, as temptresses, prone to sexual impropriety.[9] Accord-ingly, they had few property and overt political rights and were liable to beatings from their husbands.[10] Nonetheless, it is impossible to speak of the complete subordination of women to men and to view women as purely vic-tims of the patriarchal system.

While accepting male authority in the family, community, and state be-cause their families' survival depended on that power, Russian peasant women used the functions and honor that patriarchy accorded them to as-sert their will and mitigate some of the worst features of their subordination. A household head's wife may ultimately have been under her husband's au-thority. Nonetheless, she wielded considerable power because of her indis-pensable role in maintaining the household as a social and economic unit and presenting it in a favorable light to the larger community. As reflected in the complementary nomenclatures of *khoziain* and *khoziaika*, male and female "householders," respectively, a complementary and interdependent ex-

[8] The fate that awaited such women in large cities was not necessarily a desirable one. Arriving with only the clothes on their backs and at the mercy of male employers, these defenseless women were sometimes forced into prostitution. Richard Stites has estimated that approximately one-third of the Russian empire's prostitutes were soldiers' wives. See Richard Stites, "Prostitute and Society in Pre-Revolutionary Russia," *Jahrbücher für Geschichte Osteuropas* 31, no. 3 (1983): 351. The soldier's wife has received attention in Beatrice Farns-worth, "The Soldatka: Folk Lore and Court Record," *Slavic Review*, 49, no. 1 (Spring 1990).

[9] For a discussion of the belief in woman as temptress among post-Emancipation Ukrai-nian peasants of the Russian empire, see Worobec, "Temptress or Virgin? The Precarious Sexual Position of Women in Post-Emancipation Ukrainian Peasant Society," *Slavic Review* (forthcoming).

[10] Women were not allowed to assume local administrative posts. For a depiction of the negative popular attitude toward women in public office, see the folk tale, "The Mayoress," in *Russian Fairy Tales*, comp. Aleksandr N. Afanas'ev and trans. Norbert Guterman (New York, 1973), p. 41. In a recent article Barbara Engel claims that in northeastern Kostroma Province, an area of heavy male out-migration, women filled the positions of representative and elder. The frequency with which women did so however is unknown. D. N. Zhbankov in his field study of Kostroma Province asserted that male village authorities remained home, suggesting that instances in which women occupied positions of authority were ex-ceptional. See Barbara Alpern Engel, "The Woman's Side: Male Out-Migration and the Fam-ily Economy in Kostroma Province," *Slavic Review* 45, no. 2 (Summer 1986): 268; and D. N. Zhbankov, *Bab'ia storona: Statistiko-etnograficheskii ocherk* (Kostroma, 1891), pp. 2, 33.

change of labor existed between spouses.[11] Although unequal to men, women were highly valued as laborers and mothers, and in these roles wielded power indirectly. Control over the domestic hearth, the ability to affect social relationships, the functions of matchmaker, mother, mother-in-law, midwife, and herbalist provided women with power bases extending beyond the household. Through these channels women were very much actors in as well as victims of the patriarchal system. As much, they supported a hierarchical system of relations that at times rewarded and at other times oppressed them. Their accommodation to patriarchy can best be understood if it is remembered that that system gave women some authority and protection and ensured their families' welfare.[12]

In order to unravel the complexities of Russian women's position, it is necessary to examine their economic roles, traditional beliefs about women, courtship practices, and abuse of women. This essay concentrates on the central agricultural and central industrial provinces of European Russia, at times drawing upon material from other European Russian and Ukrainian provinces for comparative purposes. Unlike many articles in this collection, this one takes a macro rather than a micro approach. It is based on a variety of economic, folklore, demographic, and juridical sources, which demonstrates a general cultural pattern of patriarchy over diverse economic regions without, however, masking regional differences and nuances.

The sources concerning Russian peasant women are bountiful. Women as keepers of Russian popular culture left behind an extremely rich storehouse of songs and ritual. With a couple of exceptions, their oral cultural has not been studied systematically.[13] The current quantitative bias of some social historians in part explains this lacuna. It is sometimes argued that folklore materials provide only an impressionistic picture of reality. The uneven quality of sources also poses a problem for a methodical examination of oral culture.[14]

[11] S. V. Pakhman made this important observation in his *Obychnoe grazhdanskoe pravo Rossii: Iuridicheskiia ocherki*, vol. 2 (St. Petersburg, 1877–79), p. 30. Greek peasants also have complementary nomenclatures for male and female householders—*nikokyris* and *nikokyra*. See S. D. Salamone and J. B. Stanton, "Introducing the *Nikokyra*: Ideality and Reality in Social Process," in *Gender and Power in Rural Greece*, ed. Jill Dubisch (Princeton, 1986), p. 98.

[12] Russian peasant women were not unique in supporting a patriarchal society that both oppressed them and provided for their family's survival. For a discussion of Greek peasants, see Dubisch, "Introduction," in *Gender and Power*, pp. 16–27.

[13] The Russian lullaby has received some attention in the past decade. See Sheryl Allison Spitz, "The Russian Folk Lullaby in the Nineteenth Century" (Ph.D. diss., Stanford University, 1977) and Antonina Martynova, "Life of the Pre-Revolutionary Village as Reflected in Popular Lullabies," in *The Family in Imperial Russia: New Lines of Historical Research*, ed. David L. Ransel (Urbana, 1978), pp. 171–185.

[14] In the first half of the nineteenth century the first attempts to preserve the Russian national epos were unscientific. I. P. Sakharov, a pioneer in Russian ethnography, compiled five volumes of collected songs. The songs are not regionally differentiated and are marred

Folklore materials, in spite of their limitations, overcome the tendency of quantitative methods to reduce the peasantry to a faceless mass without individual concerns and tastes.[15] Russian peasants were, after all, creators of folk songs, proverbs, folktales, embroidery patterns, and clothing. Through such media they conveyed their fears, expectations, and worldview. The contradictions that these cultural expressions sometimes contain demonstrate the peasants' flexibility in reacting to ever-changing circumstances and the options they had in gaining some control over their lives. Women's active participation in the patriarchal system and also their ambivalence toward it are documented in their songs, clothing, and rituals.

Other materials, among which *volost'* court cases figure prominently, substantiate the impressions conveyed by folklore sources. In the wake of Emancipation, peasant-administered cantonal courts were established throughout rural European Russia to safeguard customary law and provide uniform justice for peasants. Uniformity proved impossible to achieve as jurists quickly learned that customary law practices varied not only from region to region, but from village to village as well. Nevertheless, general patterns of customary law do emerge. *Volost'* court records, published in the 1873–1874 Liuboshchinskii Commission reports, are a superb source for studying peasant

---

by textual inexactness. The subsequent ethnographic projects of A. V. Tereshchenko, V. I. Dal', and Petr Kireevskii were more scientific. The authors gave some attention to authenticity of textual material, regional differentiation, and variations in dialect. The foundation of the Imperial Russian Geographical Society in 1845 and its division of ethnography made the systematization and coordination of ethnographic studies throughout European Russia possible. Programs set project goals, defined methodoligies, and established scholarly standards, while journals under the auspices of the Imperial Russian Geographical Society provided a forum for ethnographic collections. Censorship controls, however, prevented the publication of national oral poetry that threatened virtuous morals, evoked evil superstitions, or touched such sensitive issues in Russian history as peasant rebellions, social poverty, and suffering. See I. P. Sakharov, *Pesni russkago naroda*, 5 vols. (St. Petersburg, 1838–1839); Sakharov, *Skazaniia russkago naroda*, 2 vols. (St. Petersburg, 1841–1849); A. V. Tereshchenko, *Byt russkago naroda*, 7 vols. (St. Petersburg, 1848); V. I. Dal', *Poslovitsy russkago naroda: Sbornik poslovits, pogovorok, rechenii, prislovii, shistogovorok, pribautok, zagadok, poverii, i proch.* (Moscow, 1862); Dal', *Povesti, skazki, i raskazy kazaka Luganskago*, 4 vols. (St. Petersburg, 1846); Dal', *Tolkovyi slovar' zhivago velikorusskago iazyka*, 4 vols. (St. Petersburg, 1903–1914; first published in 1863–1866); and Petr Kireevskii, *Pesni* (Moscow, 1929; first published in 1860). The Imperial Russian Geographical Society's ethnographic publications include the journals and serials *Etnograficheskii Sbornik* (1853–1864), *Zapiski po otdeleniiu etnografii* (1867–1917), and *Zhivaia Starina* (1980–1916). The influential *Etnograficheskoe Obozrenie* (1889–1916) was published by the Imperatorskoe obshchestvo liubitelei estestvoznaniia, antropologii i etnografii.

[15] For excellent studies of French peasants and American black slaves in which ethnographic materials figure prominently, see Eugen Weber, *Peasants Into Frenchmen: The Modernization of Rural France, 1870–1914* (Stanford, 1976); Martine Segalen, *Love and Power in the Peasant Family: Rural France in the Nineteenth Century*, trans. Sarah Matthews (Chicago, 1983); and Eugene D. Genovese, *Roll, Jordan, Roll: The World the Slaves Made* (New York, 1976).

customary law and Russian peasant women's position in family and community.[16] Women turned to the local courts to complain about inheritance and division of property, encroachment of other peasants on their property, broken engagements, wife beating, alcoholic husbands, treatment they received from other family members, and co-villagers who publicly slandered them. And in so doing, women were actors in their society. Through an examination of cases involving wife beating, this essay reveals women's expectations, perceptions of themselves, on what occasions they chose to defy village assembly decisions, and their place in the larger community.

The picture presented here is largely static. Culture generally changes at a much slower pace than economic and political relations. Thus, while economic conditions in the post-Emancipation Russian village were to varying degrees altered by the intrusion of a money economy, an all-national market, and urbanization, peasant mores, worldview, social relationships, and institutions were not immediately transformed. Despite the fact that peasants in the Central Industrial Region were increasingly forced into artisanal pursuits and migrant labor, the commune and patriarchal family remained the focal point of peasant life. Several historians have charted how post-Emancipation Russian peasants succeeded in subverting external agencies of change and protecting the moral fiber of their daily lives. The late-nineteenth-century and early-twentieth-century army, village school, urban culture, and Stolypin agrarian reforms were all unable to transform the Russian peasant into a modern citizen who controlled his or her environment and embraced the ideals of a national rather than parochial culture.[17] By the end of the nineteenth century Russian peasants may have been attracted by the trappings of urban living. Nevertheless, the carrying of a parasol, the wearing of retail clothing, the playing of the urban accordion, and the shortening of a wed-

---

[16] *Trudy Kommisii po preobrazovaniiu volostnykh sudov; slovesnye oprosy krest'ian, pis'mennye otzyvy razlichnykh mest i lits i resheniia: volostnykh sudov, s''ezdov mirovykh posrednikov i gubernskikh po krest'ianskim delam prisutstvii,* 7 vols. (St. Petersburg, 1873–1874). Hereafter cited as *Trudy Kommisii.*

[17] See John Bushnell, "Peasants in Uniform: The Tsarist Army as a Peasant Society," *Journal of Social History* 13, no. 4 (Summer 1980): 565–76; Ben Eklof, "The Myth of the Zemstvo School: The Sources of the Expansion of Rural Education in Imperial Russia, 1864–1914," *History of Education Quarterly* 24, no. 4 (Winter 1984): 561–84; Eklof, *Russian Peasant Schools: Officialdom, Village Culture, and Popular Pedagogy, 1861–1914* (Berkeley, 1986); Anthony Netting, "Images and Ideas in Russian Peasant Art," *Slavic Review* 35, no. 1 (March 1976): 48–68; Julie Brown, "Peasant Survival Strategies in Late Imperial Russia: The Social Uses of the Mental Hospital," *Social Problems* 34, no. 4 (October 1987): 311–29; George Yaney, *The Urge to Mobilize: Agrarian Reform in Russia, 1861–1930* (Urbana, 1982); and Judith Pallot, "*Khutora* and *Otruba* in Stolypin's Program of Farm Individualization," *Slavic Review* 43, no. 2 (Summer 1984): 242–56. Post-Reform Russian peasants were not at the same stage of development as French peasants, who by the First World War had become modern French citizens subscribing to a national French culture. See Weber's brilliant study, *Peasants Into Frenchmen.*

ding celebration were insufficient in themselves to change the village's patriarchal structure. Right up to the turmoil of the First World War and Russian Revolutions peasant women found themselves subordinate to men and secondary citizens.

WOMEN'S ECONOMIC ROLES

In order to understand the position of post-Emancipation Russian peasant women within family and community and the contradictory images of victim and actor, it is essential to begin with the economic underpinnings of the peasant household. Women were able to exert some control over their lives within the confines of a a restrictive and at times abusive patriarchal system in part because they played an indispensable role in the household economy. They carved out their own spheres within the household and family.

In European Russia husband and wife shared responsibilities in maintaining their largely self-sufficient, family-based household. A sexual division of labor delineated the spouses' respective duties. The wife bore full responsibility for the home, surrounding garden, small animals, and fowl, while her husband concentrated energies on farming the household's allotment strips. At times men and women crossed the line separating the domestic and agricultural spheres. During peak periods of the agricultural calendar, especially harvest time, women joined their fathers, fiancés, or husbands in heavy field labors. At such times agricultural tasks were once again divided according to gender. Women harvested rye, winter wheat, and oats with the sickle, tied grain into sheaves, loaded hay, and gleaned the harvested fields for precious leftover grain. The heavier tasks of plowing, harrowing, cutting hay, and harvesting with the scythe were left to the men. In both the pre- and post-Emancipation periods a partnership of husband and wife or *tiaglo* was essential for a household's ecomonic well-being[18] in part because of the multitude of tasks during the short growing season.

During the winter when peasants engaged in non-agricultural tasks, the division between home and fields disappeared as men were forced to spend a good deal of time indoors. Husbands shunned domestic work as typically women's responsibility and pursued instead such male tasks as mending agricultural implements and making tools, leaving the women to spin and weave cloth for family clothing. Husband and wife might also complement each others' work in auxiliary industries, the profits from which supplemented their agricultural income. In the poor-soil areas of the central industrial provinces these profits relegated meager agricultural income to second-

---

[18] Steven L. Hoch, *Serfdom and Social Control in Nineteenth Century Russia: Petrovskoe, a Village in Tambov* (Chicago, 1986), pp. 91–92.

11. MAKING WOODEN LOOM REEDS (N. A. FILIPPOV, COMPILER, *KUSTARNAIA PROMYSHLENNOST' ROSSII: PROMYSLY PO OTRABOTKE DEREVA* [ST. PETERSBURG: TIPO-LITOGRAFIIA "IAKOR'," 1913], FOLLOWING P. 244).

12. THE PRODUCTION OF SMALL WOODEN PIPES INSIDE A PEASANT HOUSE IN THE NON-BLACK-EARTH ZONE (NOTE THE PORTRAIT OF THE TSAR AND TSARINA, THE ICON, AND THE SAMOVAR) (MINISTERSTVO ZEMLEDELIIA I GOSUDARSTVENNYKH IMUSHCHESTV, *OBZOR KUSTARNYKH PROMYSLOV ROSSII*, ED. D. A. TIMIRIAZEV [ST. PETERSBURG: SKOROPECHATNAIA M. M. GUTZATS', 1902], BETWEEN PP. 28 AND 29).

ary importance.[19] Consequently men's and women's nonagricultural activities took on the added importance of meeting subsistence needs.

The industries that men and women engaged in varied according to location and availability of raw materials. In central industrial Nizhnii Novgorod
Province, for example, women worked side by side with men making spoons
in Semenov and Balakhna Districts, gloves in Gorbatov District, finishing
nets in Nizhnii Novgorod District, and bast matting in several districts.[20]
Sometimes tasks were delineated along gender lines. In the spoon industry
of Semenov and Balakhina districts, for example, a complicated division of
labors ensured that all family members, from young children to the eldest,
were employed. The patriarch left the village in search of birch, which he
purchased at a reduced rate by felling the trees himself. Upon his return to
the village he split the wood into pieces. Then nine- and ten-year-old boys
squared the ends of the wood pieces and turned them over to their adoles-
cent brothers to hollow out with adzes. An experienced male adult cutter
finished tooling the spoon. Then women cleaned and polished each spoon,
passing it, in turn, to their adolscent daughters who with paint in hand
added the decorative touches.[21] In the bast-matting trade women did the
same jobs as men, separating fibers, working the shuttle, or doing the actual
basting.[22] Other domestic industries, such as cooperage, blacksmithing, and
metalworking, were strictly male occupations while lace making, knitting,
rolling cigarette tubes, and, naturally, wet-nursing were women's work.[23]

Similar gender delineations of labor occurred in merchant trades. In the
Ukrainian village of Belovod, Starobel'sk District, Khar'kov Province, where
peasants derived more income from selling wares and animals than from
farming, both men and women sold goods in such faraway places as the Don
Oblast, the Caucasus, and Astrakhan and Saratov provinces. Women sold
only small items connected with their domestic sphere, including produce
from their gardens and orchards, eggs, chickens, and handicrafts. The men,

[19] See, for example, "Zhurnaly nizhegorodskago gubernskago statisticheskago komiteta,"
Nizhegorodskii Sbornik 8 (1889): 602–03 and V. Borisov, "Kustarnye promysly Sergievskoi vo-
losti, Tul'skago uezda," in *Trudy Kommisii po izsledovaniiu kustarnoi promyshlennosti Rossii*, 7
(St. Petersburg, 1881), pp. 894–95, 938.

[20] V. F. Mukhin, *Obychnyi poriadok nasledovaniia u krest'ian: K voprosu ob otnoshenii narodnykh
iuridicheskikh obychaev k budushchemu grazhdanskomu ulozheniiu* (St. Petersburg, 1888), pp. 18–
19; M. A. Plotnikov, *Kustarnye promysly Nizhegorodskoi gubernii* (Nizhnii Novgorod, 1894), pp.
138–47; and F. I. Marakin et al., "Kustarnye promysly nizhegorodskoi gubernii: Nizhegorodskii uezd," *Nizhegorodskii Sbornik* 7 (1887): 69–70.

[21] Plotnikov, *Kustarnye promysly*, p. 141.

[22] Mukhin, "Kustarnye promysly," pp. 18–19.

[23] For an excellent discussion of women's domestic industries, see David L. Ransel, *Mothers of Misery: Child Abandonment in Russia* (Princeton, 1988), and Pallot, "Women's Domestic
Industries in Moscow Province 1880–1900," in *Russia's Women: Accommodation, Resistance,
Transformation*, ed. Barbara Evans Clements, Barbara Alpern Engel, and Christine D. Worobec (Berkeley, forthcoming).

on the other hand, dealt with more lucrative sales of horses, cattle, and fish.[24]

In areas of heavy male out-migration, such as Soligalich, Chukhloma, and Kologriv districts of Kostroma Province, Poshekhon'e District, Iaroslavl Province, and Arzamas District, Nizhnii Novgorod Province, where the soils did not sustain full-time farming, the delineation between male agricultural tasks and women's domestic activities did not exist. Gender division of labor applied instead to the agricultural and wage domains. In these localities the burdens of maintaining the household and farming the land both fell heavily upon women. Their husbands, on the other hand, left the village for considerable lengths of time to pursue trades in towns and cities as far afield as St. Petersburg. Women were responsible for feeding their families, and their husbands for meeting the tax and redemption payments levied on the land. The functions of both spouses were accordingly indispensable for their families' survival. Clearly married women in areas of heavy out-migration enjoyed greater control over their lives and independence than women in nonmigratory village economies. Nevertheless they still depended on their husbands' wages and deferred to their husbands' authority when the men returned home, however short the stay.[25]

Women also enjoyed greater independence in areas where they hired themselves out as agricultural laborers. In Right-Bank Ukraine, for example, where land allotments were too meager to sustain a family, women worked on commercial sugar plantations, leaving the men behind in the village to farm. Married and unmarried female (with the latter predominating) agricultural laborers were also to be found in New Russia, the Kuban Oblast, and Saratov provinces. In documenting active female participation in 1905 strike movements on gentry estates in Right-Bank Ukraine, Robert Edelman has recently argued that wages provided women with a newfound independence that challenged traditional patriarchal authority. Nevertheless, he is quick to point out that elsewhere in Ukraine and European Russia women did not form a substantial part of the wage-labor force and consequently did not figure as prominently in the strikes of 1905. Instead they deferred to the rules of patriarchalism and urged caution rather than confrontation.[26]

[24] P. Ageeva, "S. Belovodsk," *Khar'kovskii Sbornik* 12 (1898), sec. 2, pp. 157–186.

[25] Zhbankov, *Bab'ia storona*, pp. 2, 19–20. See also Engel, "The Woman's Side," pp. 257–71.

[26] Timothy Mixter agrees with Edelman's conservative assessment of collective women's actions in areas outside right-bank Ukraine. Mixter points out that women generally confronted their employees and husbands when their families' welfare was at risk. Thus women might pester a landowner on payday after a harvest or keep a watch on their husbands' activities in order to ensure that they did not squander their wages on drink. When women did confront the authorities in a strike, such as occurred in 1906 in Arkadak, Saratov Province, they may have believed that they "had more immunity from retaliation than peasant men," a belief that held steady as late as the 1930s in Stalin's collectivization program, as

WOMEN'S WORLDVIEW

Despite the complementary and interdependent labors of husband and wife, Russian peasant women were subordinate to men. How does the historian uncover the complexities of their lives? How were Russian women treated? Did they uphold the patriarchal system? Did they enjoy community support? What was their worldview? What choices of action were available to women within their communities? Space limitations and the embryonic state of scholarship in the field of Russian peasant women studies prohibit the examination of all these questions. However a brief exploration of available primary cultural and legal sources can illustrate the channels that the study of Russian peasant women must take to achieve a well-rounded picture.

Lullabies, marriage and funereal lamentations, and many of the songs and tales that punctuated festivals and family events were outlets for women to express their fears, concerns, relations to other people, expectations, and worldview.[27] The marriage lamentations introduced in the opening pages illustrated the anxieties that young women felt toward marriage. Maidens sang them in the presence of girlfriends, married female kin, and married village women. These women shared in the bride-to-be's fears and offered their sympathy. At the same time they helped her understand that accepting her new burdens in life was part of the natural order. In fact, married women continually acted as support groups for young women, acculturating them in the responsibilities they would assume as wives, mothers, and daughters-in-law. Even before the bethrothal stage they interpreted the fortune-telling practices that younger women indulged in in order to have some fleeting control over their destinies and the many songs and stories that punctuated the *posidelki* or working bees.[28] While encouraging the acceptance of patriar-

---

described by Lynne Viola. See Robert S. Edelman, "Rural Proletarians and Peasant Disturbances: The Right Bank Ukraine in the Revolution of 1905," *The Journal of Modern History* 57, no. 2 (June 1985): 248–77; Timothy Mixter, "Women Migrant Agricultural Laborers in Russia, 1860–1913" (unpublished paper), especially pp. 1–2, 3–10, 20–23; and Lynne Viola, "*Bab'i Bunty* and Peasant Women's Protest During Collectivization," *The Russian Review* 45, no. 1 (January 1986): 23–42.

[27] For important ethnographic collections, see note 15 and especially, Afanas'ev, *Russian Fairy Tales*; Aleksandr Evgen'evich Brutsev, *Narodnyi byt velikago severa: Ego nravy, obychai, predaniia, predskazaniia, predrazsudki, pritchi, poslovitsy, prosloviia, pribautki, perequdki, pripevy, skazki, priskazki, pesni, skorogovorki, zagadki, schety, zadachi, zagovory i zaklinaniia*, 3 vols. (St. Petersburg, 1898); Dobrovol'skii, *Smolenskii etnograficheskii sbornik*, 3–4 (St. Petersburg, 1894–1903); P. V. Shein, *Velikoruss v svoikh pesniakh, obriadakh, obychaiakh, verovaniiakh, skazkakh, legendakh i t.p.*, 2 vols. (St. Petersburg, 1900).

[28] For descriptions of fortune-telling practices and *posidelki*, see Mikhail Dmitrievich Chulkov, ed., *Slovar' russkikh sueverii* (St. Petersburg, 1782), pp. 119–25; A. V. Balov, "Ocherki Poshenkhon'ia," *Etnograficheskoe Obozrenie* 9, no. 4 (1897): 67–81; N. Dobrotvorskii, "Krest'ianskie iuridicheskie obychai: Po materialam, sobrannym v vostochnoi chasti Vladimirskoi gubernii (Uezdy Viaznikovskii, Gorokhovetskii, Shuiskii i Kovrovskii)," *Iuridicheskii*

chalism, married women also explained the complexities of the system and ways in which prospective brides could gain some control over their lives. That control came within the conjugal family, the focal point of a married woman's life.

A woman's primary obligations to her husband and children sometimes conflicted with the interests of the extended household in which she often lived. Under her mother-in-law's ever watchful eye and having to compete with sisters-in-law for the mother-in-law's favor, a daughter-in-law sometimes felt isolated and constricted in the ways she could meet her immediate family's needs. She might choose to encourage her husband to leave his father's home and set up a separate household. In an independent nuclear family a wife enjoyed complete authority over domestic affairs and ensured that her family's needs were fulfilled without sacrificing them to the interests of a larger family network. In fact, Russian peasants often blamed the breakup of extended households on the quarrels among women. In areas of Vladimir Province they noted that "sisters-in-law are cunning when it comes to tricks, while the daughters-in-law seek revenge." In 1873–1874 in Serenov *Volost'*, Iaroslavl Province, peasants attributed 22.3 percent of 112 household divisions to arguments among women.[29] Systematic study of Russian family songs by region would reveal local variations in and general patterns of women's sentiments, loyalties to their families, and expectations for their children.

The rich and colorful embroideries with which women adorned their clothing and linens supplement the themes and worldview of women's songs and tales. During the idle winter months unmarried girls wove and embroidered the numerous items that made up their trousseaus. The trousseau included clothing for a bride and her husband in their family life and various towels, shirts, and kerchiefs which a bride presented as wedding gifts to her new conjugal relatives and honored guests. A young woman's "diligence, abilities, and tastes were judged by the number of articles prepared, the perfection of patterns woven and embroidered, and the harmony of colors she used."[30] She had to select carefully colors and intricacies of embroidery pat-

---

Vestnik 23, no. 11 (November 1891): 355–57; Gromyko, *Traditsionnye normy povedeniia*, pp. 222–50.

[29] Quoted in Dobrotvorskii, "Krest'ianskie iuridicheskie obychai," *Iuridicheskii Vestnik* 21, no. 5 (May 1889): 284 and Andrei Isaev, "Znachenie semeinykh razdelov krest'ian: Po lichnym nabliudeniiam," *Vestnik Evropy* (July 1883): 336–38. For a general discussion of household fissions among post-Emancipation Russian peasants, see Cathy Frierson, "Razdel: The Peasant Family Divided," *The Russian Review* 46, no. 1 (January 1987): 35–52. Russian peasant women were not unique in disrupting multiple family households in favor of smaller family units over which they gained better control. For a discussion of behavior among Chinese peasant women, see Kay Ann Johnson, *Women, the Family and Peasant Revolution in China* (Chicago, 1983), p. 20.

[30] Nina T. Klimova, *Folk Embroidery of the USSR* (New York, 1981), pp. 10–13, 22.

terns in tandem with local variations. Bright red threads characterized the embroideries of northern Russia. In south Central Russia brilliant colors of scarlet, blue, green, gold, and violet blended together in a panorama of exquisite beauty. One generation of women passed on to the next stylized embroidery patterns of geometric and floral motifs, and depictions of birds, animals, goddesses, and men on horseback. Each added her signature to those patterns by telling her personal story and interpretation of the world. Consequently no two patterns were ever exactly the same. Yet "the harmonious balance between man and woman" and men's reverence of women remained dominant themes. On the one hand, they reflected the living union of husband and wife and re-creation of life and, on the other, reversal of the painful reality of female subordination in a male-dominated society.[31]

This worldview reflected Russian peasant women's collective definition of the importance of their sex to their society's survival, a reality that the patriarchy had to accept and reward. From an economic and spiritual standpoint some were vital links in the perpetuation of Russian peasant society by carrying on the family name, looking after elderly parents and unmarried and disabled siblings, and evoking the memory of deceased relatives through memorial services and prayers. They were all the more coveted because of high infant mortality rates. More than 25 percent of infants died within the first year of life, another 25 percent in the next four years.[32]

While expressing their understanding of the world in embroidery patterns, women graphically portrayed their different life stages in their clothing. Upon reaching the age of marriageability in her late teens, a young woman entered a new phase of life. The title "*nevesta*" (prospective bride or bride-to-be) announced that she was ready to participate in the traditional customs and rituals of various holidays and evening work and social gatherings (*posidelki*) that were reserved for marriageable females and suitors her age. She was not allowed to abandon the simple full-length shirt for good quality sarafans, embroidered shirts, beads, and special headdresses.[33] On her wedding day and in the first year or so of her marriage the young bride could take pride in wearing the most beautiful and colorfully embroidered shirt in the village. The shirt symbolized the transition that she would soon make between wife and mother. Once she gave birth to her first child, she had to abandon that article of clothing. "After the birth of each child, the number of patterns and colors gradually decreased and the fabrics used for the head-

---

[31] Netting, "Images and Ideas," pp. 63–64.

[32] Infant mortality rates were highest in the Ural region, south central industrial provinces, and mid-Volga provinces. See Peter Gatrell, *The Tsarist Economy 1850–1917* (London, 1986), pp. 31–37 and Ransel, *Mothers of Misery*, p. 264.

[33] T. A. Bernshtam, "Devushka-nevesta i predbrachnaia obriadnost' v Pomor'e v XIX—nachale XX v.," in *Russkyi narodnyi svadebnyi obriad: Issledovaniia i materialy*, ed. L. V. Chistov and T. A. Bernshtam (Leningrad, 1978), pp. 51–55.

dress got simpler." As a woman approached old age the white of her linen shirt became predominant.[34]

The ways in which a woman's hair was dressed also symbolized different stages of her life. A maiden always wore her hair in a single braid and adorned it with colorful ribbons, usually red to symbolize her virginity. Depending on regional variation, hair accessories ranged from elaborate headdresses to wreaths of fresh flowers which marriageable girls could wear both at home and on holidays. Maidens, as opposed to married women, were allowed to have some or all of their hair exposed. The transition from maidenhood to wifehood was so dramatic that the abandoning of the single maiden's braid for a married woman's double braids and new head coverings was highly ritualized.

The final ritual plaiting of a maiden's hair in a single braid occurred on the eve of her wedding. During the *devishnik* (literally, "an evening for maidens") the bride-to-be, in short lamentations, beseeched her mother, sister, aunt, and godmother, in turn, to remove her maidenly beauty or purity, which her maidenly braid entwined with red ribbons symbolized, and to conceal her in a grave. With her hair loose, the bride-to-be was led to the ritual bath at the bathhouse, after which her female peers ceremoniously plaited her hair in the maidenly braid for the last time.[35] The bride's brother, the keeper of his sister's purity and symbol of the sexual prowess of men who deprived women of their purity, usually performed the final unplaiting of the bride's hair on her wedding day prior to the wedding ceremony.

After the wedding ceremony, the bride's *svakha*, or married female sponsor, braided the bride's hair, which had hung loose during the ceremony, in the two plaits worn by a married woman. The braids were wound round the head and covered with a *provoinik, kokoshnik,* or *kichka*—a ceremonial headdress which again varied in ornamentation and style from region to region.[36] A kerchief was often worn over the headdress. The ritual was performed in the refectory, out of men's sight, because a woman without a head covering was believed to be unprotected, susceptible to evil spirits and plausibly to the attractions of other men. A married woman's head covering represented her total submission to her husband.[37]

---

[34] Klimova, *Folk Embroidery,* p. 11.

[35] For descriptions of the ritual plaiting, see I. M. Kolesnitskaia and L. M. Telegina, "Kosa i krasota v svadebnom fol'klore vostochnykh slav'ian," in *Fol'klor i etnografiia: Sviazi fol'klora s drevnimi predstavleniiami i obriadami,* ed. B. N. Putilov (Leningrad, 1977), pp. 113–16; and P. Pevin, "Narodnaia svad'ba v Tolvuiskom prikhode Petrozavodskago uezda, Olonetskoi gubernii," *Zhivaia Starina* 3, no. 2 (1893): 235.

[36] In some areas of Perm and Kostroma provinces the braiding of the bride's hair occurred after the wedding ceremony at the groom's parents' home. See A. Smirnov, "Obychai i obriady russkoi narodnoi svad'by," *Iuridicheskii Vestnik* 10, no. 7 (July 1878): 1003.

[37] V. Iu. Leshchenko, "The Position of Women in the Light of Religious-Domestic Taboos Among the East Slavic Peoples in the Nineteenth and Early Twentieth Centuries," *Soviet*

13. GREETING OF BREAD AND SALT FOR A PEASANT BRIDE AND GROOM (JOHN FOSTER FRASER, *RED RUSSIA* [NEW YORK: THE JOHN LANE COMPANY, 1907], FOLLOWING P. 174).

The varied styles of women's clothing and ways in which maidens and married women wore their hair illustrated women's body image and symbolically expressed the contradictions that Russian peasants believed women's characters to exhibit. The uneasiness and ambivalence that Russian peasants felt toward women are common to other Christian associates that associate women with the images of two diametrically opposed figures: the tender, merciful, devoted Virgin Mary, on the one hand, and the temptress Eve, on the other. Women's reproductive capacities inspire both fear and awe in men.[38] The Russian Orthodox Church accordingly reinforced ancient Middle Eastern and Old Testament taboos concerning menstruating women by suggesting that they were polluted and in danger of fornicating with the devil. It barred all women from the church sanctuary and from approaching the high altar, allowing only postmenopausal women to bake communion bread.[39] At the same time, Russian peasants permitted maidens and brides,

Anthropology and Archeology 17, no. 3 (Winter 1978–1979): 33 and D. B. Chopyk, "The Magic of a Circle: Ceremonial Attire, Food and Dance Symbolism in Slavic Weddings" (Paper presented at the Annual Meeting of the Canadian Association of Slavists, University of British Columbia, Vancouver, Canada, June 5, 1983). For other interpretations of the double braid and head covering that married women wore, see E. Vsevolozhskii, "Ocherki krest'ianskago byta Samarskago uezda," *Etnograficheskoe Obozrenie* 7, no. 1 (1895): 20 and N. I. Gagen-Torn, "Magicheskoe znachenie volos i golovnogo ubora v svadebnykh obriadakh Vostochnoi Evropy," *Sovetskaia Etnografiia* (1933), nos. 5–6, pp. 75–88.

[38] Segalen, *Love and Power*, p. 125.

[39] See Leshchenko, "The Position of Women," p. 31; Dorothy Atkinson, "Society and the Sexes in the Russian Past," in *Women in Russia*, ed. Dorothy Atkinson et al. (Stanford, 1977), p. 14; and Worobec, "Temptress or Virgin."

as the most sexually enticing women, to exhibit their sexuality in elaborate clothing and uncovered hair. As these women came under the domination of husbands and had children, they progressively lost the right to advertise their sexuality. Indeed, uncovering a married woman's hair in public was a punishable offense as an insult to the woman and her family's honor.

Peasant women of European Russia shared many of the fears associated with their bodies. In Ukrainian Poltava Province and Belorussian regions women avoided working in gardens and orchards during menstruation for fear of adversely affecting the growth of fruits and vegetables.[40] Peasant women all over European Russia gave birth in isolated places, such as the bathhouse, believing that upon delivery they were both vulnerable and dangerous. Forty days after giving birth they had to undergo the ceremony of churching, or ritual purification, before they could reenter their church and community.[41]

As a woman gradually lost her sexual powers with age and increasingly became identified as a mother, she gradually lost the pejorative association with Eve and assumed the traits of undying love and self-sacrifice of the Mother of God. In contrast to a menstruating woman's supposed adverse effect on crops, a postmenopausal woman was believed to possess powers beneficial to a harvest. In a ritual ceremony on the eve of harvesting elderly women were sent out in the fields to cut the first stalks of grain.[42]

PREMARITAL CHASTITY

Women's sexual propriety was an issue of importance to Russian peasants. While women were believed to have uncontrollable sexual urges, they were not to act upon them. Peasants expected a maiden to retain her virginity until marriage. A male suitor's family placed great store in a bride's reproductive capacity and the purity of the bloodline. By producing male heirs a woman perpetuated "the family and its honor."[43] The amulets, decorative belts, and geometric designs in the embroidered clothing that a bride-to-be wore before

[40] V. Miloradovich, "Zhit'e-byt'e Lubenskago krest'ianina," *Kievskaia Starina* 80 (February 1903): 188; and Leshchenko, "The Position of Women," pp. 25–26.

[41] See Balov, "Rozhdenie i vospitanie detei v Poshekhonskom uezde Iaroslavsloi gubernii," *Etnograficheskoe Obozrenie* 2, no. 3 (1980): 93; V. Stepanov, "Svedeniia o rodil'nykh i krestinnykh obriadakh v Klinskom uezde Moskovskoi gubernii," *Etnograficheskoe Obozrenie* 18, nos. 3–4 (1906): 226–31; Leshchenko, "The Position of Women," pp. 27–29; and Worobec, "Temptress or Virgin." For similar beliefs among other Orthodox peasants, see Dubisch, "Culture Enters Through the Kitchen: Women, Food, and Social Boundaries in Rural Greece," in *Gender and Power*, p. 196 and Kligman, *Căluş: Symbolic Transformation in Romanian Ritual* (Chicago, 1981), p. 124.

[42] Gromyko, *Traditsionnye normy*, p. 121.

[43] Kligman's observations about Romanian peasant beliefs apply also to Russian folk beliefs. See her "The Rites of Women," p. 329.

the wedding and on the wedding day safeguarded her chastity and reproductive abilities from evil spirits and the ever-present threat of the evil eye.[44]

Community and family supervision of courting rituals and relations between marriageable adolescents complemented the precautions that maidens
took in wearing amulets. While community values could not be entirely de-
terminant, they effectively constrained individual behavior. Relations between marriageable girls and boys varied depending upon the customs of
individual communities. However, there does not appear to have been any
clear-cut difference in supervision of courting adolescents between the more
advanced mixed economies of the central industrial provinces and the more
backward central agricultural provinces. A degree of controlled intimacy was
permitted courting couples in both regions. For example, in Poshekhon'e
District in Iaroslavl Province, Soligalich and Chukloma districts of Kostroma
Province, all in the Central Industrial Region, older women and men customarily frequented the fall and winter *posidelki* or evening socials as spectators.
They sat at the back of the huts while the young folk played various
games, including kissing games, and sang songs.[45] In Kirsanov District in
central agricultural Tambov Province, it was taboo for young people at spring
and summer round dances (*khorovody*) to caress one another in public, but
permissible for them to do so at *posidelki*, specifically designed for greater
intimacy.[46]

In some areas of northern and central Russia and the southern Ukrainian
provinces, the relationships between boyfriends and girlfriends were more
intimate as couples were permitted to become acquainted in private. In Novgorod and Pskov provinces, for example, an eyewitness reported that when
the socializing at *posidelki* came to an end, the "fellows abducted their girlfriends." This is presumably a reference to bundling. Nocturnal intimacy between courting couples becomes clearer in an account of courtship practices
in Perm Province. There an outside observer noted that during the warm
summer months young marriageable girls were allowed to sleep in unheated
granaries or small huts, separate from the family residence. The physical separation of young girls from the collective family room, which served as both
eatery and bedroom, confirms that girls and their boyfriends were encouraged to court one another in private.[47]

Contemporary accounts of nineteenth-century Russian peasant life are virtually silent on the question of whether bundling led to premarital sex. In

---

[44] Described by Chopyk, "The Magic of a Circle."

[45] Balov, "Ocherki Poshekhon'ia," p. 72; and Zhbankov, *Bab'ia storona*, p. 76.

[46] Bondarenko, "Ocherki Kirsanovskago uezda," p. 79.

[47] Smirnov, "Ocherki semeinykh otnoshenii po obychnomu pravu russkago naroda," *Iu-
ridicheskii Vestnik* 9, nos. 1–2 (January–February 1877): 58–59; Zelenin, "Sbornik chastushek
Novgorodskoi gub. (Po materialam iz bumag V. A. Voskresenskago)," *Etnograficheskoe
Obozrenie* 17, nos. 2–3 (1905): 190.

fact, there is little information about peasant sexual practices in general.[48] Low illegitimacy rates for the second half of the nineteenth century suggest that premarital sex in the village was not a common phenomenon.[49] Early ages at marriage for women, particularly in the central agricultural provinces, may in part account for low illegitimacy. In the 1880s the average age for women in the central agricultural provinces was 19.4 and in the central industrial provinces of European Russia was 21.8.[50] "When women marry young, the code of honor can be more easily sustained, the breaches being both less frequent and more serious."[51] On the other hand, it is also true that the late onset of the age of menarche (ages fifteen through seventeen) among Russian peasant women may have maintained a low illegitimacy rate and masked the frequency of premarital sexual activity.[52]

In both Russian and Ukrainian provinces a premarital pregnancy might

[48] In a recent article Laura Engelstein suggests that zemstvo doctors avoided attributing the virulence of syphilis to extramarital and homosexual relations among peasants. See her "Morality and the Wooden Spoon: Russian Doctors View Syphilis, Social Class, and Sexual Behavior, 1890–1905," *Representations* 14 (Spring 1986): 169–208. Reprinted in *The Making of the Modern Body: Sexuality and Society in the Nineteenth Century*, ed. Catherine Gallagher and Thomas Lacqueur (Berkeley, 1987), pp. 169–208.

[49] In the towns and countryside of the Central Russian provinces (minus Moscow) illegitimacy rates ranged between 0.76 in Riazan to 4.02 in Iaroslavl. Moscow Province, including the city of Moscow, had a much higher rate of 16.55. See *Statistika Rossiiskoi imperii*, 18 (St. Petersburg, 1891), pp. 28–29; and *Statisticheskii vremennik Rossiiskoi imperii*, series 3, 7 (St. Petersburg, 1887), p. 22.

[50] Data on average ages at marriage may be found in *Statistika rossiiskoi imperii*, 18. Resources accumulation as a prerequisite for marriage was discouraged in the agricultural belt of the center where equal partible inheritance, the apportionment of full communal land allotments to married men alone, the incorporation of new conjugal units into existing patriarchal multiple-family households, and supplementary incomes from local trades encouraged early ages at marriage for both men and women. The highest ages at marriage for women characterized those districts of Vladimir, Kostroma, Moscow, Tver, Nizhnii Novgorod, and Iaroslavl province, where auxiliary local trades became increasingly important in the second half of the nineteenth century as the returns on land allotments were insufficient to meet a family's subsistence needs. Since daughters were essential laborers in household economies engaged almost exclusively in local trades, parents either discouraged early marriages or enlarged their labor force by adopting a son-in-law.

[51] Jack Goody found this to be a general pattern in his examination of various European societies. See his *The Development of the Family and Marriage in Europe* (Cambridge, 1983), p. 212.

[52] B. N. Mironov, "Traditsionnoe demograficheskoe povedenie krest'ian v XIX-nachale XX v.," in *Brachnost', rozhdaemost', smertnost' v Rossii i v SSSR: Sbornik statei*, ed. A. G. Vishnevskii (Moscow, 1977), p. 94 and Engelstein, "Morality and the Wooden Spoon," p. 179. In Tula Province, where the average age at marriage for a woman was 18.7, a physician noted that over 20 per cent of marrying women were not yet menstruating. See V. Smidovich, "Nabliudeniia na fiziologicheskii proiavleniiami zhenskoi polovoi deiatel'nosti," *Sbornik Sochinenii po Sudebnoi Meditsine* 2 (1877): 71–88, cited in Engel, "Peasant Morality and Rural Illegitimacy in Late Nineteenth Century Russia" (unpublished paper), pp. 7, 35. I am grateful to Barbara Engel for sharing the results of her research in the Tenishev archive with me.

have advanced the marriage date. Young women expected that young men with whom they had had sexual intercourse would marry them.[53] A promise of marriage and exchange of tokens to symbolize that promise may have enticed them into engaging in sex in the first place. When such a deception on the suitor's part became public knowledge, community members sometimes pressured the young man to marry his pregnant girlfriend. The village priest might refuse to marry him to another.[54]

Normally, however, premarital sex resulted in the ostracism of a young girl from the collective of eligible maidens through ritual shaming or charivaris. In the second half of the nineteenth century the harsh pre-Emancipation practice of cutting an unchaste girl's braid, covering her head with the kerchief worn by married women, and parading her naked to the waist about the village appears to have died out.[55] Young men and women who wished to draw attention to a girl's sexual impurity chose instead to tar the gates and break the windows of her parents' home and bar her from the *posidelki* and other social gatherings.[56] A sexually promiscuous bachelor, on the other hand, would not have been ostracized from his peer group.

A girl falsely accused of sexual impurity did have the right to confront her accuser at a village assembly. Once she underwent a humiliating physical examination and was declared chaste, the eligible bachelors of the village publicly asked her for forgiveness. The prankster who tarred her gates had

[53] Examples of such cases came before cantonal courts in Uman, Berdichev, and Lipovets districts, Kiev Province, in the decade after emancipation. In each case pregnant girls or their fathers brought charges against men who had broken their promises to marry them. According to the Liuboshchinskii Commission materials, cases of this kind did not come before *Volost'* courts in the central Russian provinces. Presumably they were under the jurisdiction of other courts. Ukrainian peasants, unlike Russian villagers, also brought rape cases before the *Volost'* courts. See the *Trudy Kommisii*, 5:155 (27 April 1871); 317 (1872); 325 (13 October 1865); 348 (13 February 1869); 24 (16 November 1870); 69 (25 April 1871); 125 (2 August 1870); 172 (28 May, 7 July 1872); 282, (24 March 1870). Other examples of *Volost'* court cases in Kiev and Podol'ia provinces in which rape charges were heard can be found in *Trudy etnografichesko-statisticheskoi ekspeditsii v zapadno-russkii krai*, comp. P. P. Chubinskii, 7 vols., 6 (St. Petersburg, 1872), p. 186 (25 May 1864, 26 April 1865); 207 (12 January 1869); 244 (15 April 1868).

[54] Gromyko, *Traditsionnye normy*, p. 224

[55] For a description of public shaming practices in various areas of the Russian Empire and the difficulties that disgraced girls had in finding suitable marriage partners, see St. fon-Nos, "Pokrytka," *Kievskaia Starina* 1, no. 2 (February 1882): 427–29; V. V. Tenishev, *Pravosudie v russkom krest'ianskom bytu* (Briansk, 1907), pp. 46–47; Vsevolozhskii, "Ocherki krest'ianskago byta," p. 6; and I. N. Shmakov, "Svadebnye obychai i prichitaniia v seleniiakh Terskogo berega Belogo moria," *Etnograficheskoe Obozrenie* 15, no. 4 (1903): 56. In 1873 peasants in Taganchev *Volost'* Kanev District, Kiev Province, noted that the last recorded public shaming of an unchaste girl had occurred there in 1870. *Trudy Kommisii*, 5:161.

[56] Gromyko, *Traditsionnye normy*, p. 224.

to pay a fine and was at the mercy of the girl's relatives who might choose to seek retribution by beating him up.[57]

It is not surprising that in this patriarchal system with a double standard, young peasant women found themselves at the mercy of male suitors. Males who generally did not have to answer publicly for engaging in sexual intercourse were not averse to pressuring their girlfriends for sexual favors and then shunning them as undesirable marriage partners. An observer of courting practices in the northern village of Maripchelki in Velikoluts District, Pskov Province, noted that suitors were sometimes allowed to spend winter and summer nights with girlfriends with the tacit approval of the girls' parents. He added, however, that suitors did not consider unwed mothers to be acceptable marriage partners.[58] In several areas of central industrial Moscow Province young men also purposely avoided young women who had sullied reputations as prospective wives.[59] Boys in Poshekhon'e District, Iaroslavl Province, were in full control of determining a girl's reputation. They required girlfriends to cast rye kernels in a nearby river as a test of their sexual purity. If the grain remained afloat they were certified virgins. One may assume that young men cast aside young women whose rye kernels sank.[60] Further south, in Elat'ma District in agricultural Tambov Province, a young woman who continuously fell in and out of love fell victim to her own capriciousness as she became the object of scorn among her friends and the entire community. If she went so far as to have sexual intercourse with a man, all men, including widowers, refused to consider her a prospective spouse.[61]

The threat of public humiliation and community censure suggests that sexual taboos were strong enough to control bundling and prevent sexual intercourse among courting couples in the majority of cases. This conclusion is further substantiated by night courting practices which were undertaken not by individuals but by peer groups who carefully monitored their members'

---

[57] We find this happening as late as 1899 in the village of Meshkovo, Orel District and Province. Cited in ibid., p. 98. For other examples of false accusations and punishment of the perpetrators, see *Trudy Kommisii*, 1:51, no. 5, 322, no. 85; 2:12, no. 23; 3:280, no. 14, no. 25; and "Obrashchik krest'ianskago suda," *Moskovskiia Vedomosti*, 19 July 1887, p. 2, col. 6. The latter is also cited in E. I. Iakushkin, *Obychnoe pravo: Materialy dlia bibliografii obychnago prava*, 3 vols., 2, no. 610 (Moscow, 1875–1908), p. 66.

[58] M. Uspenskii, "Maripchel'skaia krest'ianskaia svad'ba. (Bytovoi ocherk)," *Zhivaia Starina* 8, no. 1 (1898): 81.

[59] Smirnov, "Ocherki semeinykh otnoshenii," *Iuridicheskii Vestnik*. 9, nos. 5–6 (May–June 1877), p. 93.

[60] Balov, "Ocherki Poshekhon'ia," p. 71.

[61] A. P. Zvonkov, "Sovremennye brak i svad'ba sredi krest'ian Tambovskoi gubernii Elatomskago uezda," in *Sbornik svedenii dlia izucheniia byta krest'ianskago naseleniia Rossi*, ed. Nikolai Kharuzin, 3 vols., 1 (Moscow, 1889–1891), pp. 67–68.

behavior and punished delinquents.[62] In Cherepovets District, Novgorod Province; Melenki District, Vladimir Province; and Egor'ev District, Riazan Province, it was acceptable for lads to fondle maidens' breasts and in Melenki to clutch at their genitals.[63] Sexual intercourse, however, was taboo and its occurrence easily became common knowledge in these tightly knit rural communities. Rumor that she committed some impropriety made a young peasant woman anxious as evidenced in the following ditty: "I was sitting in the shack, / People said that I was with Jack; / I thought of life and all I missed, / People said we sat and kissed; / I leaned against the window pane, / People said with Jack I'd lain."[64]

Russian peasant women also banded together as a collective to seek out sexual promiscuity in their midst. They were virulent in punishing a female co-villager who dared exhibit her sexual powers by engaging in premarital sex or adultery. Throwing soot at a disreputable woman and parading her about the village were not uncommon.

During wedding festivities married women were guardians of a bride's virginity until the marriage could be comsummated. On the wedding night specially designated women prepared the nuptial bed which was located in an unheated hut (klet') or cold-storage room attached to the main residence. To protect the newlyweds against evil spirits and the evil eye and to ensure fecundity, the bed custodians placed flax seed on the bed or rye sheaves or fishing net under the bed. Sometimes they placed a container of harvested rye or wheat in a corner of the room, adding to it the candles that the newlyweds had held during the wedding ceremony.[65]

When the bride and groom entered the nuptial chamber, the svakha changed the bride's shirt to a nightshirt, which went on public display once the marriage had been consummated. The bloodied nightshirt or kalina (viburnum opulus) attested to a bride's virginity, the object of public celebration.[66] In Voznesensk suburb and its neighboring villages in industrial Vladimir Province female wedding guests walked through the village streets carrying symbolic wares decorated with colored ribbons and banging screens and pans. They announced to all residents the bride's chastity and invited them to pay tribute to the comsummation of the marriage.[67]

---

[62] A. A. Titov, Iuridicheskie obychai sela Nikola-Perevoz Sulostskoi volosti, Rostovskogo uezda (Iaroslavl', 1888), p. 26 and Engel, "Peasant Morality," pp. 15, 46.

[63] Engel, "Peasant Morality," p. 13.

[64] Translated in Alex E. Alexander, Russian Folklore: An Anthology in English Translation (Belmont, Mass., 1975), p. 394.

[65] I. V. Kostolovskii, "Iz svadebnykh obriadov i poverii Iaroslavskoi gubernii," Etnograficheskoe Obozrenie 23, nos. 1–2 (1911): 106–7, 249; and Smirnov, "Obychai i obriady," p. 1004.

[66] Evgenii Vasil'evich Anichkov, "Pesnia," Istoriia russkoi literatury, 1 (Moscow, 1908), p. 200.

[67] Zelenin, Opisanie rukopisei uchenago arkhiva Imperatorskago russkago geograficheskago obshchestva, 3 vols., 1 (Petrograd, 1914–1916), p. 174. For a comparative analysis of the rituals

WIFE BEATING

Songs, attire, and a variety of courtship and wedding rituals thus permitted women to express themselves within the security of a collective of women. They acknowledged their general fears and anxieties, but did so at the price of accepting their subordination to men and all the beliefs justifying that subordination. Did Russian women ever act independently of one another? The answer to this question may be seen in women's litigious activities in local courts. Lack of space prohibits an examination of all types of cases that involved peasant women. The problem of wife beating, which figures prominently in the written record, nonetheless, illustrates the complex position of Russian peasant women.

Russian peasants believed that a woman, having inherited her character from Eve, was prone to excessive behavior. Force, they reasoned, was necessary to contain it. A husband had the right to beat his wife because, according to popular proverbs and sayings which have a decidedly male voice: "A husband is the law for his wife." "Beat your wife like a fur coat, then there will be less noise." "The more you beat the old woman, the tastier the soup will be." "There is no court for women and cattle." "If the man sins, his sin is outside the house; if the woman sins, she brings her sin home."[68]

It is much more difficult to assess women's own feelings about the physical abuse that they received from their husbands. In a rare post-1905 letter peasant women from three villages in Tver Province, in protesting their lack of the vote to the First Duma, voiced their ambivalence to beatings:

> Our men are quite ready to entertain themselves with us, they refuse to talk to us about the land and the new laws. . . . *Before now they admittedly beat us at times, but serious matters were decided together.* Now they say that we are not partners any more, for only they elect the Duma.[69]

These women suggested that beatings, although not coveted, did not adversely affect their importance within the domestic unit and the interdependence of husband and wife in the household economy. According to the populist ethnographer Aleksandra Efimenko Russian peasant women re-

---

attesting to a bride's virginity among all Slavs, see Ján Komorovský, "The Evidence of the Bride's Innocence in the Wedding Customs of the Slavs," *Ethnologia Slavica* 6 (Bratislava, 1976): 137–46.

[68] I. I. Illiustrov, *Sbornik Rossiiskikh poslovits i pogovorok* (Kiev, 1904), pp. 144–46; Maxim Gorky, "On the Russian Peasantry," *The Journal of Peasant Studies* 4, no. 1 (October 1976): 17; A. A. Sukhov, "Bytovyia iuridicheskiia poslovitsy russkago naroda," *Iuridicheskii Vestnik* 6 (September–October 1874): 65; and Permyakov, *From Proverb to Folk-Tale*, p. 41.

[69] Quoted in Teodor Shanin, *The Roots of Otherness: Russia's Turn of Century*, 2: *Russia, 1905–07: Revolution as a Moment of Truth* (New Haven, 1986), pp. 132–33. (My emphasis.)

garded physical punishment as an integral part of the patriarchal order.[70] Be that as it may, they certainly did not actively seek out beatings and, in fact, took precautions against them by chanting incantations.[71] In extreme cases they temporarily left violent husbands.

Volost' courts heard many cases in which wives had run away to their parents' homes to escape their husbands and others in which parents had overturned rules of propriety to encourage daughters to leave their husbands. In both the central industrial and central agricultural regions it was unacceptable for parents to meddle directly in a marital squabble or accept a runaway daughter into their home. The husband, according to custom, was a wife's sole guardian. In his absence, if he were a migrant laborer, the father-in-law assumed full control. Interfering parents had to be properly punished. Thus cantonal courts usually punished both the runaway wife for disobeying her husband and her parents for harboring her.[72]

The unspoken law of noninterference by outsiders in the private domain of married life did not, however, condone a husband's criminal action. The village assembly and the *volost'* court apparatus set limits on a husband's authority by providing women with an avenue of redress against a husband's undue cruelty. The community ethos accepted controlled wife beating as a proper way for a man to curb a wife's willful character and ensure her obedience. Excessive beatings, however, threatened anarchy within the village community and disrupted a household's productive function.

Nonetheless, the traditions of a wife's complete subordination to her husband and the community's nonintervention in marital and household quarrels were difficult to overcome. Villagers had to decide when it was appropriate to ignore those customary strictures and defend a woman against a husband's excessive violence. Their responses were invariably conditioned by the husband's social and economic status in the village, the power his kin wielded in the community, the wife's character, and so on. Community action regarding an abused woman was, accordingly, inconsistent.

In the 1880s the inhabitants of a small village in Simbirsk Province became split along gender lines in the public shaming of a woman who had disobeyed her father-in-law. Here, as in other areas of heavy male out-migration, daughters-in-law in extended families were subject to their in-laws' authority. At times fathers-in-law abused their power by making sexual demands on daughters-in-law. The title of the newspaper article that reported the incident suggests that *snokhachestvo*, or incest between father-in-law and daughter-in-law, was at issue in this quarrel. The daughter-in-law

[70] Aleksandra Efimenko, "Zhenshchina v krest'ianskoi sem'e," in her *Izsledovaniia narodnoi zhinzi*, 1: *Obychnoe pravo* (Moscow, 1884), pp. 81–82.

[71] See A. N. Minkh, *Narodnye obychai, obriady, suerviia i predrazsudki krest'ian Saratovskoi gubernii sobrany v 1861–1888 godakh* (St. Petersburg, 1890), p. 82.

[72] For examples, see *Trudy Kommisii*, 2: 214–15, no. 3; 3: 15–16, no. 14; 1: 342, no. 43.

must have repelled her father-in-law's sexual advances, causing the in-law to charge her publicly with disobedience. Male villagers, in accordance with the father-in-law's wish, armed the unruly woman with a broom and led her through the village, forcing her to sweep under the windows of every home and village school. Meanwhile, several women intervened in the public punishment, demanding that they and their children be spared this distasteful spectacle. The male leaders of the procession nonetheless completed the circuitous route through the entire village.[73] The women's action in this case suggests that they did not believe in the public shaming's legitimacy because *snokhachestvo* was a sinful act and not to be condoned. Their collective action against male villagers thus reasserted, rather than challenged, behavioral norms. It is unclear why the men readily came to the father-in-law's aid. Perhaps they felt that the maintenance of the patriarchal power structure of the family was more important than protecting a daughter-in-law in the face of rumors of *snokhachestvo*.

In another case in the early 1870s, villagers in Tambov Province interfered more directly in an unjust shaming incident. After withstanding two years of daily beatings from her husband, a peasant woman, Maria Miniushina, had on several occasions run away from her in-laws' home. This last time when her husband and father-in-law has discovered her whereabouts, they tied her to a cart and forced her to run alongside the horse as they proceeded from village to village whipping both her and the horse. Inhabitants of one village halted the cart and freed the unfortunate woman. Clearly they viewed this punishment as exceeding accepted wife beating and as shamefully displaying the household's dirty linen in public. They were, however, unable to do more because tradition dictated that a woman belonged with her husband. Indeed, once the cart had proceeded a safe distance from the village the sadistic husband and father-in-law had again tied the woman to the cart and resumed the beatings.[74]

When all else failed to stop an abusive husband, his wife could appeal directly to the village assembly or *volost'* court.[75] *Volost'* court records are re-

---

[73] "Publichnoe posramlenie zhenshchiny za nepochtenie k svekru: Snokhachestvo," *Russkiia Vedomosti*, 1883, p. 330, cited in Iakushkin, *Obychnoe pravo*, 2:175, no. 1164. For a discussion of the greater incidence of *snokhachestvo* in villages of heavy male out-migration, see L. P. Vesin, "Znachenie otkhozhikh promyslov v zhizni krest'ianstva," *Delo* 20, no. 5 (May 1887): 187–88.

[74] Iakushkin, *Obychnoe pravo*, 1: xxvii.

[75] An observer noted, however, that community members in Novgorod Province considered it improper for a woman to take her husband to court and belittled women who did so. That sentiment was not peculiar to peasants in Novgorod Province. In several cantons of Kiev District and Province, peasants noted that village and *volost'* courts did not permit women to make charges against their husbands, or at least, women did not bring cases against their husbands to the cantonal court for fear of being chastised in the community. In Taganchev *Volost'*, Kanev district, Kiev Province, on the other hand, peasants and judges

plete with cases of women launching legal suits against their husbands. While the community obliged a wife to refrain from airing her household's domestic squabbles, it countenanced her right to complain to the authorities when her husband threatened her life, beat her without cause, abandoned her and her children, or threatened the household's economic viability. A woman's complaints against her husband in such cases gained even more strength if an in-law or village elder represented her in court.[76]

Unfortunately, we know less about what happened in this regard in the village assemblies than in the cantonal courts, for which records are extant. The village assembly's role in protecting women against violent husbands can be discerned only indirectly when women appealed village assembly decisions to the cantonal court.[77] In other instances women turned to cantonal courts when their husbands, having already been admonished or punished by local authorities, repeated their offenses. Usually judges treated a repeated offender with severity. In still other cases wives used the *volost'* court as the first court of appeal, perhaps because they were skeptical of receiving justice at a village assembly meeting attended by their husbands' kinfolk.

In all such cases, the *volost'* judges examined the spouses' character to determine the guilty party. Community members did not hesitate to attest to a woman's upright character when they believed that her husband had treated her unjustly. Thus, for example, on December 14, 1871, in Kukarin cantonal court in Mozhaisk District, Moscow Province, a village elder supported a peasant woman's claim that her husband repeatedly mistreated her and validated a village assembly document (dated February 25, 1866) that attested to her exemplary character and mistreatment at her husband's hands. On the basis of this evidence the judges sentenced the defendant to the maximum penalty of twenty lashes for his repeated offenses against his wife and his father to three days in jail for perjury and participation in his son's cruel behavior toward his wife. In a similar case in 1869, heard before

---

told the Liuboshchinskii commissioners that the *volost'* courts heard many cases between husbands and wives. Since husbands and wives were usually able to reconcile their differences, the *volost'* scribe did not record such cases. See Dobrotvorskii, "Krest'ianskie iuridicheskie obychai," *Iuridicheskii Vestnik* 21, no. 5 (May 1889): 265 and *Trudy Kommisii*, 5:3, 33, 141, 161.

[76] See, for example, *Trudy Kommisii*, 3: 141, no. 10; 53, no. 11; 237, no. 15; "Pis'mo mirovago posrednika iz Riazanskoi gubernii," *Den'*, 25 November 1861, p. 14; and Pakhman, "Ocherk narodnykh iuridicheskikh obychaev Smolenskoi gubernii," in *Sbornik narodnykh iuridicheskikh obychaev*, 2, ed. Pakhman (St. Petersburg, 1900), p. 67. (*Zapiski Imperatorskago Russkago Geograficheskago Obshchestva po Otdeleniiu Etnografii*, 18.)

[77] In 1871, for example, a peasant woman of the village Goliada in Klin District, Moscow Province, complained that the village assembly had unjustly sentenced her to confinement in jail on account of her request that her drunken husband be removed from his position as household head. The assembly had apparently found her action to be a case of insubordination to her husband. *Trudy Kommisii*, 2: 609–10, no. 23.

the Bol'sheselsk *volost'* court in Iaroslavl Province, a repeated offender was given twenty lashes for his drunkenness and cruelty toward his wife and threatened with expulsion from his commune if he did not mend his ways.[78]

Wife-beating cases at the *volost'* court level were not confined to the central industrial provinces where women played an important role in both local crafts and agriculture and might have been expected to take more forthright action against their abusive husbands. In a case of 1872, heard before the Gorel' *volost'* court in agricultural Tambov Province, four male peasants had witnessed an unjust beating. They testified that on June 4 they heard female screams outside the home of the defendant, Sergei Antonov Betin. Shortly thereafter they saw Betin and his brother-in-law parading the plaintiff, with her hands tied behind her back, through the village in the direction of the elder's quarters. They added that the husband and his family were evil people who frequently indulged in fights. On the basis of this incriminating evidence, the judges sentenced Betin to seven days in jail and his brother to three days.[79]

Women who complained about their husbands at village assemblies or *volost'* courts received the most sympathetic hearing when their spouses were drunkards and squandered away their household economies. On October 15, 1871, the Shulets *volost'* judges of Rostov District, Iaroslavl Province, responded to a wife's complaints about her husband's alcoholism and wild behavior by charging the village elder with keeping an eye on the husband's activities. They were concerned with not only the defendant's treatment of his wife, but also his ability to pay taxes since he already had arrears. A month earlier, in the same *volost'*, a wife made a legitimate complaint against her husband for beating her and squandering the family property by exchanging twenty-five pounds of peas, ten pounds of field peas, six pounds of rye flour, and scissors for vodka at the local tavern. The judges sentenced the defendant to twenty lashes and ordered the elder to recover the household items from the tavern proprietor. In some areas the village community even sanctioned the transfer of a household headship from husband to wife if the drunken husband was incapable of properly managing the household economy and there were no adult males to assume that position. A woman as household head could represent her household at village assembly meetings, an honor generally reserved for men.[80]

---

[78] Ibid., 2:274–75, no. 24; 3:183, no. 12.

[79] This was a particularly harsh sentence in the eyes of peasants. Seven days in jail meant seven precious days away from work in the fields. Ibid., 1:37, no. 1.

[80] Ibid., 3:261, no. 102, no. 118. Communications in Karachev, Orel, and Bolkhov districts in Orel Province and Poshekhon'e and Iaroslavl districts in Iaroslavl Province did not, however, condone the transfer of household management from husband to wife. See P. S. Tsypkin, "Opeka v krest'ianskom bytu," in *Administrativnoe polozhenie russkago krest'ianstva*, comp. Tenishev (St. Petersburg, 1908), pp. 162–63. For an account of how peasant males felt

The above-mentioned *volost'* court decisions against delinquent husbands, however, present only one facet of the court in its rulings regarding domestic improprieties. Wronged wives often did not win their legal battles. Furthermore, cantonal court decisions in the post-Emancipation period do not suggest any fundamental change in a woman's position vis-a-vis her husband within the Russian peasant family.[81] Male peasant judges supported the patriarchal system. They sided with a woman only when her husband exceeded community norms and plunged a household into economic chaos. Otherwise, they generally upheld the behavioral norm whereby women were to be subservient and obedient to their husbands. If a wife's charge against her husband could not be substantiated, she was punished for lying and disobeying her husband. *Volost'* court judges arrested women for stubbornness, rudeness, coarseness of language, and disobedience toward their husbands in the courtroom.[82]

The *volost'* courts further upheld the sanctity of marriage and a wife's subordination to her husband by expecting an abused wife to resume her marital life in her husband's household. Even if judges had a guilty husband swear on paper that he would refrain from beating his wife or appointed the village elder to keep the husband under surveillance,[83] the wife had no guarantee that her humiliated husband would not seek vengeance against her. If married life proved intolerable for an abused woman, separation remained her final recourse. Separation, however, had its own burdens. A woman's op-

---

threatened by a village woman's assuming her drunken husband's responsibility for working the land, see G. I. Uspenskii, "Krest'ianskie zhenshchiny," in his *Sobranie sochinenii* 8 (Moscow, 1957), pp. 515–16.

[81] For a different assessment of similar sources, see Farnsworth, "The Litigious Daughter-in-Law: Family Relations in Rural Russia in the Second Half of the Nineteenth Century," *Slavic Review* 45, no. 1 (Spring 1986): 49–64. Some changes, on the other hand, occurred in the area of Russian women's property rights. In a multiple-family household widows were entitled only to sustenance and shelter from their in-laws unless their husbands had bequeathed them property in a testament. A widow in a nuclear family had a right to a share of her deceased husband's property. Normally she received between one-seventh and one-quarter of her late husband's real and moveable property. The partial property rights that a widow came to enjoy in the nuclear family did not remain without effect upon the multiple-family household. While a women's position usually remained closer to the customary norm, according to which she should not receive a portion of her husband's property, cantonal judges sometimes awarded daughters-in-law one-seventh of their husbands' share of the patrimony if they departed from their fathers-in-laws' households. This created a precedent for women to appeal to the legal system to redress the injustices of customary law and their dependence on the goodwill of in-laws. For more information concerning Russian peasant women's inheritance rights, see Worobec, "Customary Law and Property Devolution Among Russian Peasants in the 1870s," *Canadian Slavonic Papers* 26, nos. 2 and 3 (June–September 1984): 220–34.

[82] See, for example, *Trudy Kommisii*, 3: 89 (28 January 1870); 56, no. 18; 2: 103, no. 73; 108, no. 2; 151–52, no. 24; 348, no. 8.

[83] Ibid., 2:68, no. 7; 531, no. 13; 3: 260, no. 87.

tions were limited in a peasant economy. She could either return to her parents' home with only her dowry or trousseau or leave the security of the village for employment in a nearby town, factory, or gentry estate where she would surely by exploited.

CONCLUSION

In spite of their oppressive treatment, Russian peasant women did not set up a diametrically opposed ethos to patriarchalism. Indeed, they had little to gain by combating male authority and erecting a different power structure. Women were an integral part of the patriarchal system which was at the foundation of their agricultural and proto-industrial economies. They were both actors in and victims of a system that provided them with rewards and punishment. Although Russian peasant women did not generally have rights to land use, they were vital laborers in household economy. They managed all domestic affairs and aided males in their agricultural and artisanal pursuits. Economic necessity permitted them to assume traditional male roles as tillers of the soil or household heads either when men left the village for migrant work or defaulted in their responsibilities as household heads. By virtue of their indispensable role in the peasant economy and their charge of perpetuating the family through bearing and raising children, Russian peasant women were able to carve out their own spheres of activities within the household and community. Patriarchalism in the Russian countryside did not imbue women with substantial property rights or political authority, but relegated to them important roles in acculturating their children in the mores of village society, affecting power relations indirectly through kin networks and the collective of women, arranging their children's marriages, and maintaining their society's moral foundations. In extreme cases the patriarchy provided some safeguards against intolerably abusive husbands.

Women were the guardians of Russian peasant culture and ritual which reinforced hierarchical political, social, and gender relationships, the belief in women's natural propensity toward sexual promiscuity, and the importance of the family in Russian peasant society. The collective of married women guided future brides through various rituals which at one and the same time underscored their acceptance of their unequal and at times unenviable lot in an extended family and demonstrated to them how they might achieve some control over their lives through child rearing and influencing family decisions. Folk songs and ritual sometimes depicted the fears and frustrations that women faced within an oppressive system that justified wife beating. Nevertheless, most Russian peasant women rejected sexual freedom and individual rebellion as possible avenues of control over their lives because they threatened the very existence of Russian peasant society.

Russian peasant women chose not to rebel because the survival of their families and community depended upon the balancing of the finely tuned patriarchal system. Despite its oppressive nature, that system gave peasants some control over their daily lives and management of their economies in a precarious environment. To tinker with that mechanism would have been to court disaster.

CHAPTER 6

TRADITIONAL HEALERS AND PEASANT CULTURE IN RUSSIA, 1861–1917

*Samuel C. Ramer**

DURING the nineteenth century, most observers with a Western, secular education who ventured into the Russian countryside were struck by the peasantry's belief in magic, or in what might be called the spiritual possession of the world. Nowhere was this belief more manifest than in peasant attitudes toward disease and healing. Physicians, ethnographers, and almost everyone else who took the trouble to record their impressions were unanimous in their observation that for the vast majority of the peasantry disease, injury, and misfortunes affecting one's livestock, crops, or family relationships were all phenomena that could have their origin in some specifically spiritual or magical dimension.[1]

This paper seeks to illuminate this magico-religious aspect of the Russian peasantry's worldview by studying the place that traditional healers occupied in peasant society. The paper will address four general questions. First, what kinds of traditional healers existed in the Russian countryside, and what was the nature of their practice? Second, what was the character of the medical culture that they shared with their peasant clientele, from beliefs

* I would like to thank the International Research and Exchanges Board, the Fulbright-Hays Fellowship Program, and the Tulane University Committee on Research for their generous support. I am grateful to Ben Eklof, Steven L. Hoch, Esther Kingston-Mann, David Landy, Richard B. Latner, and Timothy Mixter for their thoughtful comments and helpful bibliographical suggestions. I want to express particular appreciation to Jeffrey Burds and Stephen P. Frank for the generosity with which they shared ideas and materials from their own research.

[1] On the character of this magical world view see Vladimir Dal', *O pover'iakh, sueveriiakh i predrassudkakh russkago naroda*, 2d ed. (St. Petersburg-Moscow, 1880); S. V. Maksimov, *Nechistaia, nevedomaia i krestnaia sila* (St. Petersburg, 1903); S. A. Tokarev, *Religioznye verovaniia vostochnoslavianskikh narodov XIX-nachala XX v.* (Moscow-Leningrad, 1957); Linda J. Ivanits, *Russian Folk Belief* (Armonk, N.Y., 1989); Jeffrey Brooks, *When Russia Learned to Read: Literacy and Popular Literature, 1861–1917* (Princeton, N.J., 1985), pp. 246–68; and Moshe Lewin, *The Making of the Soviet System: Essays in the Social History of Interwar Russia* (New York, 1985), pp. 63–71.

about disease to the appropriate choice of a healer? Third, in what ways did peasant attitudes toward these healers change as modern physicians became more accessible in rural areas? Finally, how can we account for the continuing popularity in rural Russia of both traditional healers and their methods?

"What peasants believed" or "how peasants thought" are notoriously difficult questions to answer, particularly since most of what we know about peasant attitudes and behavior is based upon the reports of literate outsiders whose analysis and actual choice of material were shaped by their own cultural perceptions. In answering such questions about the Russian peasantry one also encounters numerous other methodological difficulties. The most important is that there was no single Russian peasant culture either in location or in time. Local and regional variations in popular medicine and reliance on traditional healers were considerable.[2] Moreover, peasant culture itself, whatever it was in a particular area, underwent an accelerating process of change and adaptation as peasants came into increasing contact with urban, secular culture in the late nineteenth and early twentieth centuries.

Finally, there is the problem of adequate source material on a subject as inaccessible and diverse as that of popular medicine. Although the sanctions against traditional healing were not generally enforced in the countryside, it was nevertheless an illegal activity. While traditional healers might practice relatively openly with their peasant clientele, their actual treatment was usually carried out in private, and they were not anxious to discuss their work with physicians or other urban outsiders. Most peasants appear to have been equally reticent with outsiders on the subject.

The difficulty of finding precise answers to the kinds of questions posed here does not make the questions themselves any less compelling. Fortunately for the historian, there are materials that can serve as a basis for study. G. A. Popov's pioneering and encyclopedic study of Russian popular medicine, in which he used eyewitness information provided by 350 informants scattered throughout twenty-three Great Russian provinces, provides an invaluable starting point.[3] Contemporary physicians and ethnographers also wrote extensively on popular healers. There is a rich literature on peasant societies in Western Europe which provides an important comparative dimension in studying these questions.[4] Finally, this paper has drawn numer-

---

[2] If one considers the Russian Empire as a whole, of course, national variations in medical beliefs and practices were also important. This paper treats only the Russian peasantry.

[3] G. A. Popov, *Russkaia narodno-bytovaia meditsina* (St. Petersburg, 1903). Popov based his work on ethnographic materials collected by Prince V. N. Tenishev. Tenishev's correspondents included priests, teachers, landowners, *zemskie nachal'niki*, feldshers, and in some instances peasants themselves. For a description of the Tenishev archive see N. Nachinkin, "Materialy 'Etnograficheskogo Biuro' V. N. Tenisheva," *Sovetskaia Etnografiia* 1 (1955): 159–63.

[4] A good example of this is Judith Devlin, *The Superstitious Mind: French Peasants and the Supernatural in the Nineteenth Century* (New Haven and London, 1987), ch. 2.

ous comparative insights from the stimulating literature on social and medical anthropology that has appeared in recent decades, including the work of historians who have been influenced by this literature.[5]

THE SPECTRUM OF RURAL HEALERS

PHYSICIANS, FELDSHERS, AND TRAINED MIDWIVES

One must recall at the outset that modern medicine only began to penetrate the Russian countryside in the late nineteenth century. Until then, traditional healers of some kind were the only medical personnel to whom most peasants had any sort of regular access. Even at the height of the zemstvo era, the number of physicians in rural practice in most provinces was not remotely sufficient to meet the needs of Russia's widely scattered and burgeoning peasant population.[6] Feldshers (paramedics) and midwives were modern practitioners with more limited medical training than a physician who ideally extended the latter's reach in rural areas. But feldshers' qualifications were so diverse and inadequate that, in many physicians' view, their independent rural practice was no better than that of traditional healers, and in some ways even worse.[7] Trained midwives found it more difficult than feldshers to develop a peasant clientele, and most eventually abandoned the countryside altogether.[8]

When a Russian peasant of the nineteenth or early twentieth century suffered either illness or injury, therefore, it was natural for him or her to turn for help to a traditional healer, who could usually be found either in his or her own or in a neighboring village. There was a great diversity of these traditional healers in the Russian countryside, whether one measures this by

[5] The outstanding example of a historical work that has benefited from this anthropological literature is Keith Thomas's magisterial *Religion and the Decline of Magic* (New York, 1971).

[6] In 1910 the zemstvo provinces, which had the best rural health networks in the country, employed only a few more than 3,000 rural physicians. In 1880 the average zemstvo physician's bailiwick (*uchastok*) encompassed 58,000 persons scattered over an area of 1,200 square miles. By 1910, the average bailiwick still included a population of 28,000 persons dispersed over 400 square miles. Z. G. Frenkel', *Ocherki zemskogo vrachebno-sanitarnogo dela* (St. Petersburg, 1913), pp. 121, 125.

[7] On the diverse qualifications feldshers possessed see Samuel C. Ramer, "Who Was the Russian Feldsher?" *Bulletin of the History of Medicine* 50, no. 2 (Summer 1976): 213–25. Physicians' arguments that feldshers were less desirable than traditional healers were based on the notion that traditional healers tended to be less reckless and intrusive in their therapy than feldshers, "who had the whole Latin kitchen [i.e., strong drugs] at their disposal." K. Tolstoi, *Vospominaniia zemskogo vracha* (Moscow, 1876), p. 95.

[8] By most estimates trained midwives attended only about 2 percent of all peasant births well into the Soviet period. On the difficulty they experienced in developing a rural practice see Samuel C. Ramer, "Childbirth and Culture: Midwifery in the Nineteenth-Century Russian Countryside," in *The Family in Imperial Russia: New Lines of Historical Research,* ed. David L. Ransel (Urbana, 1978), pp. 218–35.

the diseases they treated, the therapies they employed, the extent of their practical knowledge, or the purported source of their power. They were known by many names, some of which indicate the specific nature of their activity, but these names in themselves offer no very precise description of their abilities or even their methods.

ZNAKHARI

The most common and all-encompassing name applied to traditional healers was that of *znakhar'* (f. *znakharka*). The word itself shares the same root as the verb "to know" and can best be translated as "cunning man (or woman)" or "wise man (or woman)," terms used to describe their English counterparts of the sixteenth and seventeenth centuries.[9] Peasants viewed *znakhari* as persons who had a special healing gift which was usually (although not always or exclusively) rooted in magic or the occult. Closely related to the *znakhar'* was the *vorozheia*, who was a healer and fortune-teller. *Vorozhit'* was, in fact, a popular verb for folk healing, and the terms *znakhar'* and *vorozheia* were used as synonyms.

Znakhari were common figures in the Russian countryside. There was a *znakhar'* of some sort in virtually every village, and at some point almost all peasants sought their help. Although any effort to describe them is impressionistic at best, several observations that contemporary sources repeatedly mention are worth noting. They were generally older people, many of whom were widowed.[10] A large number of rural *znakhari* were women. Many *znakhari* had "inherited" their practice from a parent or other close relative who had taught them whatever skills and magical charms that they knew.[11] Others were landless peasants (*bobyli*) who had turned to healing in search of a meager living. Although they were marginal figures in the economic life of the village, *znakhari* commanded unusual respect because of their age and experience as well as their purported ability to heal. Some were viewed with

[9] Thomas, *Religion and the Decline*, ch. 7.

[10] In 1898 Dr. N. A. Kogan made a statistical survey of the *znakhari* in his district of Samara Province. The information he obtained is understandably incomplete, since many healers refused to cooperate with the district police who carried out the survey. The results nevertheless tend to confirm the fact that most *znakhari* were older persons. Of the fifty-nine male *znakhari* in his sample, forty-three (or almost 75 percent) were over forty-five years old. Of the thirty-two *znakharki* respondents, twenty were over forty-five. Of the ninety-one *znakhari* surveyed, only seven of either sex were under thirty-five. N. A. Kogan, "O znakharstve v Novouzenskom uezde," *Vrachebnaia Khronika Samarskoi Gubernii* 5, no. 7 (July 1898): 1–11. For an excellent portrait of a younger man who inherited his calling as a *znakhar'* from his father see I. N. Zakhar'ina (Iakunina), *Liudi temnye. Ocherki i kartinki iz narodnogo byta* (St. Petersburg, 1890), pp. 203–13.

[11] Asked how she had become a healer, for example, a *znakharka* named Aksinia recalled: "I had an aunt, my father's sister, who healed, and I imitated her; I also copied my grandfather, who had been a soldier but then worked as a healer." Petr Bogaevskii, "Zametka o narodnoi meditsine," *Etnograficheskoe Obozrenie*, no. 1 (1889): 101.

awe and gratitude by peasants who saw them as their only protection against sorcerers and evil spirits.[12] To some extent they inspired fear as well, since the power to heal through magic was so closely related to the potential to cause harm. They tended to be observant, and were armed with a detailed knowledge of peasant life. Many were clearly imposing personalities who projected an image of power, authority, and mystery.[13]

Although unusual features or a physical deformity might serve as an external sign of the znakhar's magical powers,[14] znakhari were on the whole undistinguished in their appearance. A skeptical writer who managed to interview a znakhar' in the 1850s found him at first glance to be "an ordinary Russian muzhik." Upon looking closer, however, he found his appearance and demeanor both unusual and impressive: "When he sat with his eyes downcast, his face had a thoughtful, almost sad expression, but when he suddenly looked up at me, I felt some confusion. It seemed to me that he could see what was in my soul. I noticed that he had a special way of looking at you in order to produce a stronger effect, and that he always looked you directly in the eye. This was obviously in part charlatanism, and in part his genuine belief in the power of his gaze."[15]

Some znakhari had reputations that extended far beyond their own village or even its surrounding area, and it was not unheard of for them to treat patients who lived more than a hundred miles away. The znakhar' Ivan Kapitonych of Kostroma Province was often called to visit patients who lived more than thirty miles from his village. (In such cases the patient's family provided the transportation).[16] Other well-known znakhari were swamped with patients who had come from far and wide to be healed. During the 1880s a znakhar' named Kuzmich in Buzuluk District of Samara Province treated an average of 150 patients a day, people who had come to him from throughout the lower Volga region.[17]

As a rule, znakhari treated patients without specifying any fee, simply taking whatever was offered in return for their services. Peasants generally rewarded them with gifts in kind, although token cash payments were also common. When they were called to treat richer merchants, or even land-

---

[12] For an illustration of this see Mikhailov, "Narodnye predrassudki," *Biblioteka Dlia Chteniia* 150 (July 1859): 15–27.

[13] Maksimov, *Nechistaia, nevedomaia i krestnaia sila*, pp. 173–85; Nikolai Rudinskii, "Znakharstvo v Skopinskom i Dankovskom uezdakh Riazanskoi gubernii," *Zhivaia Starina* 6, no. 2 (St. Petersburg, 1896): 169–201; and M. K. Gerasimov, "Materialy po narodnoi meditsine i akusherstvu v Cherepovetskom uezde, Novgorodskoi gubernii," *Zhivaia Starina* 8, no. 1 (1898): 158–59.

[14] E. Ia. Zalenskii, *Iz zapisok zemskogo vracha* (Pskov, 1908), p. 66.

[15] Mikhailov, "Narodnye predrassudki," p. 27.

[16] Zakhar'ina (Iakunina), *Liudi temnye*, p. 212.

[17] A. A. Levenstrim, *Sueverie i ugolovnoe pravo* (St. Petersburg, 1899), p. 105.

lords, the cash remuneration could be enormous.[18] While the gifts that they were given in kind might constitute a considerable income, the general refusal of most *znakhari* to charge was interpreted by most peasants as generosity and lack of greed, traits that only enhanced their popular authority.[19]

While not primarily a healer, the *iurodivyi* or "holy fool" was another figure to whom peasants occasionally turned with medical problems. According to popular belief the *iurodivyi* was one chosen by God—literally a *"bozhii chelovek"*—and as such had the power to heal such disorders as insanity, hysteria, epilepsy, and alcoholism. One physician described these "holy fools" as "popular neuropathologists."[20]

Traditional Midwives, Bloodletters, and Bonesetters

Physicians tended to use the word *znakharstvo* to describe all unlicensed healing. Although this paper will concentrate on rural *znakhari* and their practice, it is important to recognize that there were numerous other traditional healers in the countryside who figured prominently in the popular medicine of the nineteenth century. The most important of these was the *povitukha*, or traditional village midwife, who remained the predominant obstetric practitioner in the Russian countryside until well into the 1930s. (Peasant women traditionally preferred to give birth alone, but some obstetric help was often required.) Most *povitukhi* were older peasant women, known to their fellow villagers, who not only assisted in childbirth but cooked meals and ran the household during the mother's confinement and recovery.[21]

Other commonly encountered specialists were the *rudomet*, or bloodletter, whose therapy the peasantry deemed essential for almost every ill; the masseuse, who rubbed her patients down on top of the stove or in the heat of the *bania* or peasant bath; and the *kostoprav*, or bonesetter, who often displayed real dexterity in setting fractures and sprains.[22] Whatever their abilities, the traditional midwife, the bloodletter, the masseuse, and the boneset-

[18] The *znakhar'* whom I. N. Zakhar'ina (Iakunina) describes was paid twenty-five rubles for such visits. I. N. Zakhar'ina (Iakunina), *Liudi temnye*, p. 212. (A zemstvo feldsher was paid about thirty rubles a month.)

[19] Evgenii Markov, "Derevenskii koldun," *Istoricheskii Vestnik* 28 (1887): 17; I. N. Zakhar'ina (Iakunina), *Liudi temnye*, pp. 211–12.

[20] Rudinskii, "Znakharstvo," p. 193. For a comparison of "holy foolery" and shamanism see Ewa M. Thompson, *Understanding Russia: The Holy Fool in Russian Culture* (Lanham, Md., 1987), pp. 97–123.

[21] The predominance of older persons was, if anything, even greater among *povitukhi* than it was among *znakhari*. Almost 90 percent of the 451 *povitukhi* whom Dr. N. A. Kogan surveyed in his district of Samara Province in 1898 were over forty-five years old.

These 451 *povitukhi* assisted in 14,542 births in 1897, compared to the 406 attended by all the physicians, feldshers, and trained midwives in the district. Kogan, "O znakharstve," p. 4.

[22] Gerasimov, "Materialy," p. 159.

ter were all more narrowly defined and secular technicians than the *znakhar'*. Although traditional midwives in particular might call upon the Lord in the case of a difficult delivery, their activity was also less directly connected to the world of magic than that of the *znakhar'*.

Sorcerers, Witches, and the Therapeutic Functions of Magic

Finally, although this paper cannot pretend to treat all aspects of witchcraft and magic in the Russian countryside, one cannot overlook the critically important place that sorcerers and witches occupied in the peasantry's medical culture.[23] The peasant conception of disease and healing was intimately bound up with a magical conception of the universe in which evil and misfortune occurred through the specific agency of human beings who had made a pact with "dark forces" or "devils." The sorcerer's or witch's power was thus spawned from evil.

In the peasant's eyes, the sorcerer or witch had real power. For the most part this was the power to do harm, to inflict *porcha* ("spoiling" or *maleficium*) on one's neighbors. While peasants for the most part accepted the secular origin of such things as colds, fatigue from overwork, or the feebleness of old age, almost all other diseases or misfortunes—particularly those that seemed unusual in some way—could be and often were seen as the results of the "spoiling" inflicted by a sorcerer or a witch. (The "evil spirits" or "devils" in which the peasantry certainly believed had to act through human agents.)

In nineteenth-century Russia there were numerous instances in which those suspected of witchcraft were beaten or murdered by members of their community, usually with a great deal of brutality.[24] For the most part, however, sorcerers and witches were an accepted part of the community whose potential to inflict damage one tried to ward off through preventive action.[25]

[23] For the sake of convenience I have used only the English words "sorcerer" and "witch" in the text. Both sorcerers and witches in Russia could be male as well as female, although the latter were almost exclusively female. While most anthropological studies make a strict distinction between sorcerers and witches, the terms in Russian were used interchangeably. The most common term for sorcerer was *koldun* or *koldun'ia*; a witch was most often called a *vedun* or *ved'ma*. The terms *volkhva, charodei, kudesnik, chernoknizhnik*, and simply *babka* were also widespread. In some areas of northern Russian sorcerers were known as *eretiki*, or heretics. For an excellent discussion of Russian sorcery see Ivanits, *Russian Folk Belief*, pp. 83–102.

[24] For the most comprehensive survey of this kind of violence against sorcerers and witches see Levenstrim, *Sueverie*, pp. 26–58. Two recent analyses of the significance of the broader phenomenon of peasant *samosud* are Stephen P. Frank, "Popular Justice, Community and Culture Among the Russian Peasantry, 1870–1900," *The Russian Review* 46, no. 3 (July 1987): 239–65 and Cathy Frierson, "Crime and Punishment in the Russian Village: Rural Concepts of Criminality at the End of the Nineteenth Century," *Slavic Review* 46, no. 1 (Spring 1987): 55–69.

[25] On the comparatively mild view of witchcraft in Russia in the seventeenth century when

(One could propitiate sorcerers by buying them off, or else turn to a *znakhar'* or a more powerful sorcerer to undo whatever damage the witch or sorcerer might have done.)

When we look at the kinds of people who were sorcerers and witches, we find a portrait remarkably similar to that of *znakhari*. They were almost always older people, usually landless peasants who lived alone. Like *znakhari*, they were generally poor. Most reports suggest that they were marginal persons who were withdrawn, unsociable, and outside the normal ranks of village life. Some were evidently misanthropes. A few appear to have been mentally deranged. Any deformity they might have—a humped back, a withered arm, or a face disfigured by syphilis—only tended to confirm their sorcerer or witch status in the popular mind. Generally unkempt, many appear to have dressed and behaved in a fashion calculated to instill fear and respect in their neighbors.[26] Unlike *znakhari*, they were persons who had become outsiders even in their own village.[27]

In many cases sorcerers were simply village extortionists, demanding gifts or money and threatening to damage one's crops, livestock, or family should they not be forthcoming. Peasants took these threats seriously, and tended to pay sorcerers off, flatter them, and defer to them out of a genuine fear of their power. The stereotype that one gave witches and sorcerers a prominent place at the wedding and fed them well was rooted in peasant reality: the consequences for failing to do so were seen as severe, ranging from impotence or infertility to the married partners' physical disgust for each other.[28] Outraged peasants occasionally responded to a sorcerer's blatant extortionist threats by killing him or her.

According to popular belief, one could become a sorcerer or witch in several different ways. One could first be born a sorcerer or a witch, in which case one would have a small tail.[29] It was generally thought that people consciously chose to become sorcerers or witches and did so by studying with an older sorcerer, who shared the secrets of his craft before dying. But one had to make one's own pact with the "dark forces," since this was the indispensable source of the sorcerer's power. The nature of this pact could vary,

---

compared with the experience of Western Europe see Russell Zguta, "Witchcraft Trials in Seventeenth-Century Russia," *American Historical Review* 82, no. 5 (December 1977): 1187–207, and the literature he cites.

[26] Tokarev, *Religioznye verovaniia*, p. 25.

[27] Peasants occasionally regarded everyone from a particular neighboring area as a likely sorcerer or witch. See Aleksandra Efimenko, "Zhenshchina v krest'ianskoi sem'e," in *Issledovaniia narodnoi zhizni*, vyp. pervyi: *Obychnoe pravo* (Moscow, 1884), p. 107.

[28] Popov, *Russkaia narodno-bytovaia meditsina*, p. 33. For English translations of a variety of sources on Russian sorcerers and witches that emphasize the respect and fear with which the peasant population regarded them see Ivanits, *Russian Folk Belief*, pp. 190–205.

[29] Ibid., pp. 29–30.

as could the circumstances under which it was concluded, but it involved an explicit renunciation of God.[30]

There may have been those who underwent this sort of rite in choosing to become sorcerers or witches. For the most part, however, it was the community that decided that someone was a sorcerer or a witch. Something about an older person in the community caused him or her to be viewed as such. Old age, physical deformities, or the begging in which older peasants frequently engaged may have increased the believability of witchcraft accusations, but they do not in themselves seem to have provoked them. Such charges most commonly arose when someone in the community perceived a causal connection between a given individual and a misfortune or series of misfortunes that had affected either another person or the community at large.[31] Once the community had labeled someone as a sorcerer or a witch, the older person thus categorized usually had little choice but to play the role the community had assigned to him or her.[32] However much that role may have isolated one socially, it gave one a position of respect and power, and was a potential source of income.

Some witches came by their name as a result of disputes within the village, and frequently within a peasant family. Labeling a woman a witch was a common weapon in situations of family strife. Thus we find frequent instances of witch accusations made against wives, mothers-in-law, or daughters-in-law. A. A. Levenstrim argues that women—mothers-in-law and daughters-in-law or simply village rivals—were particularly prone to use witch accusations against one another. Those accused were often subject to terrible tortures, and occasionally murdered.[33] The number of sorcerers or witches in rural areas is impossible to calculate, but it seems to have been large.[34] Violence against them was thus the exception rather than the rule, and usually precipitated by a community or family tragedy for which the person charged with witchcraft was blamed.

As ideal types, *znakhari* and sorcerers represented opposite poles in a field

---

[30] Ibid., pp. 24–26.

[31] Evgeniia Vsevolozhskaia, "Ocherki krest'ianskogo byta Samarskogo uezda," *Etnograficheskoe Obozrenie* 24, no. 1 (1895): 30. A fictional portrayal of just this process can be found in A. I. Kuprin's "Olesia," in A. I. Kuprin, *Sochineniia v dvukh tomakh*, vol. 1 (Moscow, 1981), p. 23. For excellent discussions of the complexity of this phenomenon in England see Thomas, *Religion and the Decline*, ch. 17 and Alan Macfarlane, *Witchcraft in Tudor and Stuart England: A Regional and Comparative Study* (London, 1970).

[32] Tokarev, *Religioznye verovaniia*, pp. 24–26.

[33] Levenstrim, *Sueverie*, pp. 35–39.

[34] G. V. Zavoiko indicates that the number of sorcerers and witches in Vladimir Province on the eve of 1914 was "relatively great." The peasants he talked with estimated that there were anywhere from ten or fifteen to fifty per *volost'*. G. K. Zavoiko, "Verovaniia, obriady i obychai velikorossov Vladimirskoi gubernii," *Etnograficheskoe Obozrenie* 53–54, no. 3–4 (1914): 113.

of magic. The healing and protective *znakhar'* or *znakharka* represented the forces of good, and the magical elements of his or her healing were often couched in religious terminology. The malevolent and threatening sorcerer was a mirror opposite. In actual practice, however, these distinctions were not nearly so clear. Sorcerers engaged in healing much as the *znakhar'* did, even if they were claiming to heal an affliction that they took credit for causing. The *znakhari*, on the other hand, were understandably feared by their neighbors since they were believed capable of using their curative powers, which were most clearly manifested in the magical charm, to cause the same kind of *porcha* which was theoretically the exclusive domain of the sorcerer and the witch. Most important, both sorcerer and *znakhar'* enveloped their practice in an aura of magic and secrecy. Whatever their original meaning, by the beginning of the twentieth century the labels "*znakhar'*" and "sorcerer" had begun to be used virtually interchangeably.[35]

The sorcerer, the witch, and the *znakhar'* were all part of a magical worldview whose specifically medical functions are important to understand. For the Russian peasantry as well as for primitive societies, magic was in the first place a cosmology that offered some cause for what had happened. First, it provided patients who in many cases had no other plausible explanation for their disease or misfortune, with a reason for their affliction that they could understand. Second, it held out the possibility of hope. Its function, as Bronislaw Malinowski put it, was "to ritualise man's optimism, to enhance his faith in the victory of hope over fear."[36]

The hope that magic offered in medicine was not an abstract concept, but a specific set of prescriptions as to whom one should consult and what one should do in order to improve one's situation. It thus transformed patients from passive and fatalistic observers of their own ills into active combatants in fighting them off. Jeffrey Burton Russell is correct in his observation that magic is essentially a homocentric worldview which exalts man's power. Within that worldview all the elements in the universe are amenable to the force of one's own actions. Through magic, one could be a conqueror rather than a victim.[37]

SPECIALIZATION WITHIN ZNAKHAR' PRACTICE

Znakhari tended to specialize according to the maladies they treated. Over time, individual *znakhari* developed a reputation in their own village and the surrounding area for their effectiveness in curing specific ailments.[38] Some

[35] Ibid., p. 25; Levenstrim, *Sueverie*, p. 104; Tokarev, *Religioznye verovaniia*, pp. 30–31.

[36] Bronislaw Malinowski, "Magic, Science, and Religion," in *Science, Religion, and Reality*, ed. Joseph Needham (London, 1925), p. 83.

[37] Jeffrey Burton Russell, *Witchcraft in the Middle Ages* (Ithaca and London, 1972), p. 5.

[38] Gerasimov, "Materialy," pp. 158–59.

were known for their ability to relieve headache or toothache pain, or handle such emergencies as snakebites. Many specialized in treating malaria or syphilis, both of which were endemic among the peasant population; still others were known for their skill in healing a broad variety of internal disorders. Individual *znakhari* were frequently called upon to treat such chronic conditions as epilepsy, and a large number specialized in the treatment of emotional problems, including hysteria and depression. Although *znakhar'* surgeons were rare, they did exist, and there were even rural hospitals run by *znakhari* for those suffering from syphilis.[39]

In contemplating *znakhar'* specialization, it is essential to recall that for the peasantry the word *znakhar'* was a descriptive term rather than a title that conferred status or authority in itself. In our own society, in which the principles of modern medicine dominate medical discussion, we tend to assume—with differing amounts of skepticism—that all physicians possess the requisite degree of medical knowledge and skill by virtue of their title. This notion that a title could guarantee such knowledge or ability was entirely foreign to the Russian peasantry. On the contrary, knowledge and ability were qualities that peasants attributed only to persons who had demonstrated them.

Peasants believed in the therapeutic gifts of individual *znakhari* (or physicians) either because they knew them, and had seen or experienced what appeared to be the positive results of their healing, or else because they were recommended to them by people whose judgment and experience they considered reliable. Although peasants had a greater predisposition to believe in magical healing, and had little regard for a formal degree or title, the actual way in which they decided to consult healers was thus not radically different from that of better-educated and wealthier Russians, or for that matter from ourselves.

Just how *znakhari* chose their specialization is a question that is impossible to document. Sometimes the answer was simple: "apprentice" *znakhari* acquired their skills from an older *znakhar'*, often a parent or relative, who was already a specialist in a particular area. Those who had not inherited any specialty seem to have developed one gradually based on the pattern of their initial success in treating a broader set of problems. To some degree, choice of specialization thus depended on chance. Where a *znakhar'*'s therapy actually yielded positive results, or else seemed to because it so closely coincided with improvement in the patient's self-limiting condition, both patient and

---

[39] On *znakhar'* surgery see V. F. Demich, "Ocherki russkoi narodnoi meditsiny: khirurgiia u russkogo naroda," *Vestnik Obshchestvennoi Gigieny, Sudebnoi i Prakticheskoi Meditsiny* 47, no. 11 (November 1911): 1603–27 and 47, no. 12 (December 1911): 1739–94. On *znakhar'* hospitals for syphilitics see Tolstoi, *Vospominaniia*, p. 74, and Grigorii Kovalenko, "K narodnoi meditsine malorussov," *Etnograficheskoe Obozrenie* 11, no. 4 (1891): 176.

znakhar' would be impressed by these results and attribute them to the latter's intervention.

Having achieved numerous successes in dealing with a particular condition, the *znakhar'* had every reason to specialize in its treatment. On the one hand, his clientele began to identify such practitioners with a particular expertise and seek them out selectively on this basis. More important was the fact that one could maintain one's reputation as a healer—and, incidentally, belief in one's own therapeutic gifts—only through a certain level of perceived ability based on apparent results. Where *znakhari* believed themselves unable to treat a particular affliction successfully, it was in their interest to refuse treatment altogether, even if it meant referring a patient to another *znakhar'*.

ZNAKHAR' *THERAPEUTIC TECHNIQUES*

The therapies that individual *znakhari* employed depended on their own training, skills, and beliefs as well as the patient's particular complaint. They were best known for healing through ritualistic magical charms (*zagovory*). Charms, in the words of one zemstvo physician, were the "cornerstone of popular medicine."[40] They generally incorporated some elements of prayer, were accompanied by the sign of the cross, and were sometimes known simply as prayers. (Sorcerers and witches also healed as well as inflicted *porcha* through charms, but abstained from any reference to God in doing so.) The charm itself was the *znakhar'*'s professional secret, and retained its efficacy only as long as it remained so. The only circumstances in which charms could be communicated without destroying their power was for older *znakhari* to pass them on to younger persons studying with them.[41]

Russian charms were an interesting mixture of magic and religion in which

[40] Zalenskii, *Iz zapisok*, p. 66. Of the ninety-one *znakhari* whom Kogan surveyed in his district of Samara Province, forty-seven described themselves as psychic healers specializing in charms. The remainder were for the most part bloodletters and bonesetters. Kogan, "O znakharstve," p. 4.

[41] The secrecy that surrounded charms makes it difficult to comprehend the exact meanings that peasants and healers invested in their performance. Even as subtle and informed an observer as the physician and lexicographer Vladimir Dal' expressed trepidation at the task. See Dal', *O pover'iakh*, p. 32. Their central importance in peasant life has attracted the attention of literary scholars and historians of culture as well as that of folklorists and ethnographers. In addition to Dal' see A. Vetukhov, *Zagovory, zaklinaniia, oberegi i drugie vidy narodnogo vrachevaniia, osnovannye na vere v silu slova. (Iz istorii mysli)* (Warsaw, 1907); V. J. Mansikka, *Über russische Zauberformeln: Mit Berücksichtigung der Blut- und Verrenkungssegen* (Helsingfors, 1909); N. Poznanskii, "Zagovory: opyt issledovaniia proizkhozhdeniia i razvitiia zagovornykh formul," *Zapiski Istoriko-Filologicheskogo Fakul'teta Petrogradskogo Universiteta* 86 (Petrograd 1917); and Elena Eleonskaia, *K izucheniiu zagovora i koldovstva v Rossii* (St. Petersburg, 1917).

the magical elements were clearly predominant.[42] Whatever their religious trappings, they called upon the power of magic to control or transform reality.[43] There were certain characteristic introductions and conclusions that many charms shared, but the body of the charm voiced a specific wish. There were charms to stop bleeding, to reduce fever, to relieve minor ailments such as earaches, toothaches, and stomachaches. Charms existed to combat impotence, prevent seizures, ease emotional trauma, deworm cattle and horses, and ward off potential ills such as those associated with the "evil eye."[44]

Nor did charms serve exclusively medical purposes. Indeed, the encyclopedic range of specific charms strikes the modern observer as nothing short of astonishing. Some were intended to bring one luck, whether in fishing, hunting, commercial endeavors, or fistfights. Others provided assistance in such everyday matters as finding stolen goods, cultivating bees, or making sure that one's rifle did not misfire. Still others buoyed the courage of those summoned by the authorities, promised luck to those going to court, protected one from the wicked, or watched over young soldiers going off to war. Particularly common were "love charms" through which znakhari—or more likely sorcerers or witches—endeavored either to win the love of a third party for their client, or else to satisfy their client's jealousy and desire for revenge by spoiling whatever rival relationship that third party had chosen.[45]

The time, place, and manner in which the charm was uttered were all important in assuring its validity. Because the charm had to remain secret, it was customarily whispered.[46] (The term sheptun, or whisperer, was a syno-

---

[42] While recognizing the close relationship between religion and magic, William Goode has emphasized the greater "concrete specificity of goal" and "manipulative attitude" that tended to characterize magic, together with the magician's more explicitly professional relationship toward his client and his greater freedom to choose when and even if any magical process is to take place. See William J. Goode, Religion Among the Primitives (New York, 1951), pp. 53–54.

[43] On the relationship between charms and the magical world of fairy tales see Elena Eleonskaia, "Nekotorye zamechaniia po povodu slozheniia skazok: zagovornaia formula v skazke," Etnograficheskoe Obozrenie 42–43, no. 1–2 (1912): 189–99.

[44] Belief in the "evil eye" was almost universal in Russia, as in most peasant societies. Nor was this belief confined to the peasantry. Vladimir Dal', for example, argued that the popular belief in the evil eye "is without doubt based in truth," and went on to discuss the kinds of individuals who were capable of inflicting it. Dal', O pover'iakh, p. 48.

[45] The most extensive literary compilations of charms are I. P. Sakharov's early Skazaniia russkago naroda (St. Petersburg, 1836); M. Zabylin, Russkii narod: ego obychai, obriady, predaniia, sueveriia i poeziia (Moscow, 1880), pp. 289–417; and L. Maikov, Velikorusskie zaklinaniia (St. Petersburg, 1869). Maikov's extensive collection illustrates the extreme variety of charms and their explictness of purpose, and further indicates the geographic source of his information about particular charms together with the rites that were to accompany them. For excellent but more limited selections see Dal', O pover'iakh, pp. 36–38 and Popov, Russkaia narodno-bytovaia meditsina, pp. 224–49.

[46] Dal', O pover'iakh, p. 36.

nym for a *znakhar'* who employed charms.) The patient in this setting was asked to assume the attitude of one in prayer or meditation, while the *znakhar'* uttered the charm in a rapid and barely audible whisper. Charms were usually accompanied by some kinds of ritualistic activity on the part of the *znakhar'*, whether burning incense or blowing on water. Often these rituals included acts that the patients themselves would later have to perform on their own. Nowhere was the peasant belief in magic, and particularly in the magical power of spoken words and gestures, more clearly expressed than in the conviction that the charm, if uttered correctly in letter as well as spirit, would be effective.[47]

Many peasants believed that small rituals and charms were indispensable in performing everyday tasks. Studying popular life in northern Russia, for example, S. A. Priklonskii encountered shepherds who were convinced that the right charms and rituals had to be performed before releasing livestock into open fields in order to protect them against wolves, snakes, epidemic diseases, or an evil person's hex. They were willing to pay *znakhari* whatever they asked for this "science." In their view, as a local priest reported, the main thing was that "you have to know the *word*." Priklonskii concluded that "the peasant is happy to give the shirt off of his back to any fraud who will teach him this word. No matter how I tried to convince peasants that magical charms were useless, nothing came of it."[48]

In addition to using charms, some *znakhari* were genuine experts in herbal medicine. Those who specialized in herbal remedies were assiduous students of plant life, and they regularly collected supplies of roots and grasses that contained therapeutic ingredients.[49] When patients boiled these natural products and drank or bathed in the resulting potion, they often experienced at least temporary relief from their suffering. If recovery ensued, the remedy would be given credit no matter how irrelevant its consumption.

The best of these herbal healers were skilled native pharmacists whose armory of medicines in any given case might be every bit as therapeutic as anything a trained physician could provide. This is in part reflection on how poorly supplied rural pharmacies were in Russia during the nineteenth century (and twentieth century, for that matter). Given the fact that some knowledge of *"travki"* was fairly widespread among the peasantry in general, it is somewhat surprising that *znakhari* as herbal healers appear to have

[47] Ibid., p. 34. For two thoughtful discussions of the magical power of words in other contexts see Stanley Jeyaraja Tambiah, *Culture, Thought, and Social Action: An Anthropological Perspective* (Cambridge, Mass., and London, 1985), pp. 1–86; and Jeanne Favret-Saada, *Deadly Words: Witchcraft in the Bocage* (Cambridge, 1980).

[48] S. A. Priklonskii, *Narodnaia zhizn' na Severe* (Moscow, 1884), pp. 285–88 (emphasis in original).

[49] For a description of how one *znakhar'* gathered and prepared herbal remedies see I. N. Zakhar'ina (Iakunina), *Liudi temnye*, p. 204.

been more the exception than the rule. In his exhaustive study of popular medicine, for example, Popov gives only a footnote to *znakhari* as herbal healers.[50] Although accounts of *znakhar'* practice by contemporary physicians often mention herbal healing in passing, it is never emphasized.

A large number of rural *znakhari* specialized in treating syphilis and malaria. Syphilis was rampant among the peasantry, often afflicting whole families, and in many areas *znakhari* were known principally for treating this one disease.[51] There was no cure for syphilis in the nineteenth century. The methods that *znakhari* used to combat it did not differ in kind from those employed by physicians, who for the most part treated syphilis with some variety of mercury therapy. Mercury could be employed in a variety of ways. Most often peasants mixed it with vodka and drank it. It could also be rubbed undiluted directly into the chancre, or the patient could absorb vaporized mercury through the skin in a process known as fumigation.[52]

In analyzing the ways in which the treatment of syphilis by *znakhari* differed from that of physicians, it is useful to look at the process from the afflicted peasant's point of view. Lacking any understanding of the true nature of syphilis, the peasant suffering from it was primarily concerned to get rid of the external signs of primary or secondary syphilis. Most peasants wanted a quick cure, since visible infection with syphilis quickly became known in the village and subjected one to ostracism. For this reason peasant syphilitics usually demanded large doses of mercury—the more painful the better—in the belief that such doses would hasten the cure. (The smaller doses physicians administered did not produce dramatic results.)[53] For their part, *znakhari* were more than willing to comply, and these large, intensive doses were what distinguished their treatment from that of physicians. In many cases, *znakhari* gave large doses of mercury to patients who did not have syphilis at all, but only suspected that they did. *"Mercury is the znakhar's first medicine,"* Dr. Nikolai Rudinskii insisted. "Every therapy begins and ends with it."[54] One should note here that European and American physi-

---

[50] Popov, *Russkaia narodno-bytovaia meditsina*, p. 53 n.

[51] For a stimulating discussion of the Russian medical profession's attitude toward syphilis see Laura Engelstein, "Morality and the Wooden Spoon: Russian Doctors View Syphilis, Social Class, and Sexual Behavior, 1890–1905," in *The Making of the Modern Body: Sexuality and Society in the Nineteenth Century*, ed. Catherine Gallagher and Thomas Laqueur (Berkeley and London, 1987), pp. 169–208.

[52] V. F. Demich, "Sifilis, venericheskie i kozhnye bolezni i ikh lechenie u russkogo naroda," *Russkii Arkhiv Patologii, Klinicheskoi Meditsiny i Bakteriologii* 11, no. 4 (1901): 357–64. On the clinical aspects of syphilis see William J. Brown, James F. Donohue, Norman W. Axnick, Joseph H. Blount, Oscar G. Jones, Neal H. Ewen, *Syphilis and Other Venereal Diseases* (Cambridge, Mass., and London, 1970), p. 12.

[53] Rudinskii, "Znakharstvo," pp. 171–73.

[54] Ibid., pp. 174–75 (emphasis in original). Rudinskii's observations were based on his practice as a zemstvo physician during the 1880s.

cians also prescribed mercury (calomel) almost as a panacea for a broad spectrum of ailments well into the twentieth century.[55]

The results of this intensive use of mercury by *znakhari* were frequent instances of mercury poisoning with side effects ranging from ulcerated gums and palates to gastrointestinal disorders and deterioration of the bones.[56] For the physician who encountered such patients the question was what to treat first, the syphilis or the mercury poisoning, with the latter being more immediately devastating.[57] Toxic dosages of mercury resulting in death were not uncommon. It is interesting that such fatal cases of mercury poisoning do not appear to have marred the *znakhar'*s reputation among the peasantry. The reaction of survivors was rather to attribute the patient's death to his own weakness, which seemed to be proved by the fact that "he couldn't survive the medicine."[58]

Znakhari treated malaria with quinine, just as physicians did.[59] Both syphilis and malaria furnish interesting evidence of the ways in which *znakhari* "modernized" their practice as they came into contact (and competition) with physicians and feldshers. Through this contact they witnessed the apparent effectiveness of mercury compounds in healing syphilis, and of quinine in alleviating the effects of malaria. They were quick to emulate these practices, and appear to have learned how to use mercury and quinine from the large number of retired military feldshers living in the countryside, many of whom practiced the same therapies.[60] However different the dosages they prescribed, *znakhari*'s use of mercury and quinine blurred the distinction between modern and traditional medicine that physicians sought to inculcate in the peasantry and made it difficult for the peasant to perceive that modern medicine was substantially different, let alone superior, to that practiced by traditional healers.

ZNAKHARI *AS "GIFTED PERSONS" IN THE VILLAGE*

It is important to recognize that the *znakhar'* was not only a healer in the eyes of his fellow peasants, but rather a person to whom one could turn for a wide

[55] I am grateful to Professor David Landy for this insight.

[56] Brown, Donohue *et al*, *Syphilis*, p. 12.

[57] Rudinskii, "Znakharstvo," p. 176.

[58] Tolstoi, *Vospominaniia*, p. 73.

[59] Rudinskii, "Znakharstvo," p. 177. According to Rudinskii, the major reason why malaria patients turned to *znakhari* was that zemstvo physicians did not have enough quinine because it was so expensive. How *znakhari* obtained quinine, and at what price, he does not say.

[60] For a comparative study of the adapations that traditional healers made as they came in contact with modern medicine see David Landy, "Role Adaptation: Traditional Curers Under the Impact of Western Medicine," in *Culture, Disease, and Healing: Studies in Medical Anthropology*, ed. David Landy (New York, 1977), pp. 468–81.

variety of services. The enormous variety of magical charms with no relationship to medical problems makes this clear. Even the *znakhar'*s explicitly medical skills might be required for tasks other than healing. A peasant woman
seeking an abortion, for example, might turn to a *znakhar'* or *povitukha* for
assistance. A young man hoping to avoid the draft might seek a *znakhar'*s
help in acquiring a disease.[61]

Telling fortunes was one of the *znakhar'*s or *vorozheia'*s most important roles
in the village. While not strictly speaking a medical task, it could serve to
allay the peasant client's anxiety and was an important part of the peasantry's daily life and beliefs. Girls contemplating marriage would seek the *zna-*
*khar'*s opinion as to whether the boys they liked would have them. (Once
again, the *znakhar'* was a figure through whom one might hope to influence
this reality through charms.) Young wives whose husbands were either serving in the army or away for lengthy periods at work turned to the *znakhar'* or
vorozheia to learn how their husbands were getting along, whether they
missed their wives and children, and whether they were faithful. Older
mothers asked whether their sons would be drafted. These were not idle
inquiries, but efforts to exercise some control not simply over fate, but over
family members who were far away.

Znakhari and *vorozhei* were also consulted frequently for help in finding lost
or stolen objects.[62] They were on occasion so skillful at doing this that, as one
Kostroma source suggested, it might have been worthwhile for the police to
investigate whether such *znakhari* were actually working in partnership with
thieves.[63] Maksimov suggests, quite reasonably, that *znakhari* tended to be
observant persons who kept a close hand on the community pulse. Their
success in ferreting out thieves often resulted from their ability to make sen-
sible guesses from the limited evidence they picked up while eavesdropping
on their neighbors.[64]

The roles that *znakhari* played in the village were so numerous and varied
that they were almost always in demand. As E. L. Markov observed in 1887:

> Those who don't know the life of the village well cannot imagine what
> an important role the *"babka"* or sorcerer plays, not only in family affairs,
> but in the peasant's economic life. One needs him at every step. Peas-
> ants call upon him to guess who stole their horse, to rid their pigs of
> worms, to cure their cow of plague, to heal those bitten by mad dogs, to
> stop bleeding or toothache, to remove *porcha* from a person, to lift the

[61] For examples of both these kinds of activity see Levenstrim, *Sueverie*, p. 108.

[62] A. Kolchin, "Verovaniia krest'ian Tul'skoi gubernii," *Etnograficheskkoe Obozrenie* 42, no.
3 (1899): 53.

[63] V. N-bekov, "Krazhi i bor'by s nimi," *Izvestiia Kostromskogo gubernskogo zemstva* (October
6, 1916), sec. 2, p. 16. I would like to thank Jeffrey Burds for sharing this obscure note with
me.

[64] Maksimov, *Nechistaia, nevedomaia i krestnaia sila*, p. 182.

charm of the evil eye from a child, to turn a young man's attention toward a girl or vice-versa.[65]

The *znakhar*'s or sorcerer's advice was sought before any major step such
as building a mill, digging a well, or undertaking a new endeavor.[66] In short,
for most peasants the *znakhar*'—and often the sorcerer as well—was seen as
a "gifted person" whose talents, insight, and magical powers were indispensable in a variety of activities, some of them entirely unrelated to healing.
This generally "gifted" status was an important reason for the lasting nature
of the *znakhar*'s authority.

PHYSICIANS AND ZNAKHARI

When significant numbers of physicians first began to be assigned to rural
areas in the 1860s and 1870s, they knew that there were traditional healers
in the countryside with whom they were in competition. Overwhelmed by
their own duties, they had little direct contact with these healers, whose
practice was anyway quasi-secret. However, many of their patients consulted traditional healers, often for the same maladies that eventually
brought them to a physician. Over time, physicians thus learned something
about these healers from their peasant clients' laconic descriptions of their
methods.

Confronted with a world of disease and suffering that derived in large part
from the conditions and habits of peasant life, physicians were understandably more interested in changing peasant culture than in merely studying it.
While they recognized that the two processes were interrelated, the predominant sentiment of many who went directly from medical school to the countryside was often a frustrated resentment of peasant attitudes and beliefs,
including the peasantry's attachment to traditional healers.[67] When they
wrote about traditional healers, it was generally to bemoan what they saw as
the superstitious and occasionally barbaric nature of their practice, and even
more so the peasantry's belief in their therapeutic powers. What one finds
lacking in most of these early physicians' considerations is any explicit recognition that the peasantry's reliance on traditional healers was part of a cultural system of beliefs about the origin and nature of diseases and their appropriate treatment which was both complex and deeply rooted in peasant
consciousness.[68]

[65] E. L. Markov, "Derevenskii koldun," p. 11. Markov indicates that the term "*babka*" was
used to apply to *znakhari* and sorcerers alike, even those who were male.

[66] Ibid., pp. 11–13.

[67] Tolstoi, *Vospominaniia*, pp. 2–3.

[68] One early exception to this was Vladimir Dal's sympathetic study of popular beliefs. A
later generation of rural physicians such as Popov and Zalenskii would undertake the study
of popular medicine with a less exclusively manipulative attitude than their predecessors.

Ascribing this reliance instead to the peasantry's overall superstition and benightedness, most early rural physicians tended to dismiss traditional healers as an unfortunate but passing legacy which would gradually disappear as rural schools dispelled the peasantry's superstition and as increasing numbers of physicians in rural practice provided all but the most remote peasants with ready access to a physician's help, or at the very least to that of a well-trained feldsher.[69] This vision reflects their belief not only in the superiority of modern medicine as a system of medical beliefs and practices, but also their confidence that—given time—the superiority of modern medicine *as a system* would be apparent to the peasantry as well.[70]

This confidence that modern medicine would eventually cause *znakhar'* practice to die out seemed justified on many grounds. Most important was the fact that, whenever physicians actually took up residence in the countryside, nearby peasants eagerly sought their help. By the early twentieth century, however, it was clear that this initial confidence that *znakhar'* practice would simply fade away had been excessive, or at the very least that the time required for it to do so would be much longer than originally anticipated. Despite the real inroads that physicians, feldshers, and zemstvo medicine in general had made in the countryside, traditional healers remained an important factor in rural medicine well into the twentieth century. Early rural physicians had underestimated both the tenacity of peasant beliefs and the resilience *znakhari* would display in adapting their practice in the face of competition. Before turning to the evolution of peasant beliefs and *znakhar'* practice during the period under study, let us consider the reasons for the *znakhar'*'s continuing appeal.

THE SOURCES OF THE ZNAKHAR'S APPEAL

According to most physicians, the most important factor in sustaining *znakhari*'s practice was their proximity and easy availability when compared to

---

Zalenskii was particularly explicit about the need to study *znakhar'* techniques and peasant medical beliefs (Zalenskii, *Iz zapisok*, pp. 69–71). On the general problem of the cultural dimension of healing see Arthur Kleinman, *Patients and Healers in the Context of Culture: An Exploration of the Borderland Between Anthropology, Medicine, and Psychiatry* (Berkeley, 1980), pp. 24–25.

[69] Most physicians thought the overall enlightenment of the peasantry through schools and contact with the intelligentsia more important in undermining traditional healing than anything physicians themselves could do. Demich, "Ocherki," p. 1792; Rudinskii, "Znakharstvo," pp. 200–201; Zalenskii, *Iz zapisok*, p. 103.

[70] Belief in the superiority of modern medicine was not confined to physicians or even to the educated elite. Jeffrey Brooks cites fascinating examples of the way in which *lubok* (popular literature) writers toward the end of the century made an explicit distinction between traditional healers and physicians, urging the superiority of the latter. Earlier in the century they had tended to extol the traditional healer's ability. See Brooks, *When Russia Learned to Read*, pp. 260–62.

that of the physician.[71] Every village had its *znakhar'*, and a peasant could consult him on the spur of the moment without traveling any great distance. The nearest physician, on the other hand, was often miles away, and one could not be sure of finding him or her at home even if one made the journey. In this regard it is important to remember not only how difficult and time-consuming travel was over country roads, but also how reluctant peasants were to take time off from work. (Physicians typically had the largest number of patients on market days, when peasants could combine such a visit with other work.) By the time most peasants actually traveled any distance to consult a physician in anything other than an emergency, whatever illness they were suffering from was usually so advanced that the physician could do little to help. The enhanced failure rate that resulted from treating serious illnesses in their advanced stages tended to damage the physician's prestige in the peasantry's eyes.[72]

The peasantry's impression that the physician's abilities were limited was not inaccurate, of course, since there was a host of diseases in the nineteenth and early twentieth centuries that a physician could do nothing to cure. A clear distinction between modern and traditional medicine was thus not something that could be clearly and consistently demonstrated on the basis of results.[73] Physicians recognized medicine's limitations, but were frustrated by the fact that the circumstances of rural practice did not allow them to demonstrate modern medicine at its best. They saw most peasants only for a few minutes, and they had little or no opportunity to provide follow-up examinations or therapy for peasants who lived at any distance from them. Even more frustrating for physicians was their powerlessness to bring about any substantial overall improvement in rural public health, which they recognized would only be possible when one improved peasants' diet, clothing, and the sanitary conditions in which they lived.[74]

It would be a mistake to attribute *znakhari*'s popularity exclusively to the handicaps under which the inadequate numbers of rural physicians labored, no matter how important these were in limiting modern medicine's reach in the countryside. Peasants frequently turned to *znakhari* first even when physicians were readily accessible. In short, both *znakhari* and the therapies they

---

[71] Popov, *Russkaia narodno-bytovaia meditsina*, p. 101; Zalenskii, *Iz zapisok*, p. 75; I. Molleson, "Ocherk narodnoi meditsiny v Rossii," *Arkiv Sudebnoi Meditsiny i Obshchestvennoi Gigieny* 4, no. 12 (December 1869): 2–3.

[72] Molleson, "Ocherk," pp. 2–3; Popov, *Russkaia narodno-bytovaia meditsina*, p. 102. Popov emphasizes that zemstvo medicine served a disproportionately large number of well-to-do peasants, since they were the ones most able to afford to seek out a remote physician's help.

[73] Eliot Freidson, *Profession of Medicine: A Study of the Sociology of Applied Knowledge* (New York, 1970), pp. 15–16.

[74] Popov, *Russkaia narodno-bytovaia meditsina*, pp. 47–48.

employed exerted their own positive appeal. In order to explain the *znakhar'*s persistent popularity, it is essential to understand the nature of this appeal.

In part, this appeal rested upon the status *znakhari* held as valued members of the community whose advice peasants respected. Unlike physicians, rural *znakhari* were for the most part peasants, and thus not outsiders. They shared a world of beliefs and mental concepts with their peasant clientele, understood their lives, and spoke their language. The role of tradition was also important here. Nineteenth-century peasants turned to *znakhari* for all kinds of help in part because that was what peasants with problems had always done. Moreover, when a peasant believed that his affliction had a magical origin such as the "evil eye," it was natural for him to consult a healer who could not only accept this general diagnosis, but who also had the magical power to do something about it.[75]

These explanations by reference to social and cultural kinship, although important, are not in themselves sufficient, since we know that physician "outsiders" quickly developed huge peasant clienteles once they had demonstrated an ability to heal. *Znakhar'* therapy itself had a number of intrinsic qualities that were important in sustaining its popularity. In the first place, *znakhari* actually listened to their patients' complaints. Physicians understood that it was important to do this, but they were so overwhelmed with patients that it was difficult for them to do so. The zemstvo physician S. Ia. Elpat'-ievskii, for example, recalls treating 250 patients in one exceptionally long day that began at six in the morning and ended at two o'clock the next morning. He thus averaged less than five minutes with each patient, assuming he took no breaks at all. Obviously he did not have time to hear each patient out at length, but made a quick diagnosis, prescribed some treatment or medication, and passed the patient along to his feldsher.[76]

Peasants liked to talk about their illness or troubles, no matter how obvious the diagnosis might appear to the physician or the *znakhar'*.[77] *Znakhari* had time to listen, and were often better listeners than physicians because of the fact that they had a better intuitive understanding of the kind of life that the patient led. (In many cases this understanding was more than intuitive. *Znakhari* who lived in the same village as their patients knew a great deal about the latter's past life and family.) Listening, in short, was part of the *znakhari'*s therapy and one of the greatest sources of their appeal.

In addition to listening, *znakhari* were skilled in saying the right things when they talked. This was particularly important in the case of patients who confronted serious disease. In the course of his examination the *znakhar'* might speak at length about the multitude of similar cases he had seen, and

[75] Ibid., p. 49.

[76] S. Ia. Elpat'ievskii, *Vospominaniia za 50 let* (Moscow, 1929), p. 15.

[77] Popov, *Russkaia narodno-bytovaia meditsina*, p. 50.

how successfully most of these patients had recovered. This kind of talk tended to be soothing in a number of ways. Originally isolated and fearful in their pain, patients became aware that others shared their condition, and that many had recovered. This assurance, together with the promise of the *znakhar'*s magical therapy, tended to generate hope. However unwarranted, such hope could only enhance the *znakhar'*s reputation as a healer.[78]

But by far the most important factor in explaining the popularity of *znakhari* as healers was their perceived record of success. Certainly the colorful descriptions physicians penned of their failures, of the absurdity of many of their remedies, and of the real damage some of their therapies caused are grounded in truth (although they should be read critically). *Znakhari* were not infallible, but they were protected from a critical evaluation of their effectiveness in any given case by the possibility of placing the blame elsewhere.[79] A *znakhar'*s failure thus tended to be less damaging to his or her reputation than a physician's. It is also true that much of what peasants perceived as success in healing was in fact the coincidence of an irrelevant therapy with a self-limiting disease.

What is more difficult to recognize or adequately explain in a secular and skeptical age is that many *znakhari* were genuinely gifted healers. The ways in which they accomplished this healing varied. Often they were experienced in using purely somatic therapies such as massage or herbal remedies whose operation and reasons for being effective a modern physician would readily understand. Their use of magical charms in treating physical as well as emotional disorders often seems to have produced a marked improvement in the patient's condition, if not an outright cure. (Their success in stopping bleeding, for example, was both indisputable and highly visible.) In charm therapy, including the rituals that the *znakhar'* asked the patient to perform, the *znakhar'* was working in part through the power of suggestion, and more broadly through what medical anthropologists refer to as "sympathetic healing."

"Sympathetic healing" was made possible by a number of factors. Most important was the fact that *znakhari* believed in their power to heal and communicated that belief to their patients.[80] Their patients, in turn, also believed in the *znakhar'*s therapeutic gifts, as did the bulk of the surrounding com-

---

[78] A. Makarenko, "Materially po narodnoi meditsine Uzhurskoi volosti, Achinskogo okruga, Eniseiskoi gub.," *Zhivaia Starina* 7, no. 3–4 (1898): 384.

[79] *Znakhari* were occasionally prosecuted for injuring a patient, although peasants on the whole were reluctant to give evidence against them. Demich cites one case in which a *znakharka*'s treatment of an abscess resulted in the need for a skin graft. In the court proceeding her village *skhod* presented a document testifying to her "useful" activity. She was arrested for one day.

[80] Popov, *Russkaia narodno-bytovaia meditsina*, p. 49.

munity.[81] Beyond this mutual belief in the *znakhar*'s ability was a shared cultural perception of the nature of a specific illness and how it could be combated. In anthropological terms, skilled *znakhari* located the patient's affliction in a cultural myth whose symbols, together with the patient's emotions, they could then manipulate. The result, depending on the nature of the affliction and the *znakhar*'s skill, was often a genuinely effective healing process. The remedy would be no less valid even if a modern researcher were to attribute it to the placebo effect.[82]

THE EVOLUTION OF ZNAKHAR' *PRACTICE AND PEASANT MEDICAL BELIEFS*

The experience of zemstvo medicine suggests that peasant faith in *znakhari* was by no means either fanatical or exclusive. When physicians and feldshers became more numerous and accessible in the countryside, peasants eagerly sought their help, and thus the "conversion" of the Russian peasantry to modern medicine would appear to have been at least under way. But such an expansion of physicians' rural practice did not necessarily imply a wholesale rejection of older peasant medical beliefs. Peasants could turn to physicians in increasing numbers without abandoning their more traditional notions of the origin and nature of disease. They could even acquire some conception of modern medicine without entirely giving up the magical worldview that had characterized medical practice in the village for centuries.

Peasants could integrate modern and traditional practices in several ways. First, they frequently adopted a pattern of seeking help selectively, consulting a physician about certain kinds of problems and a *znakhar'* about others. Equally reasonable in the peasant's view was to see both a physician and a *znakhar'* about the same problem. This peasant eclecticism, which struck an outsider in 1902 as "remarkable," made it difficult to prove that the physician's efforts had anything to do with whatever healing occurred. It also

[81] Observing the practice of popular medicine during the 1850s, a secular-minded priest conceded that "empty and insignificant means" could bring about real healing. The source of this healing, in his view, was "a firm belief, on the part of the patient as well as the *znakhar'*, in the immediate efficacy of the given means." See M. Dobrozrakov, "Selo Ul'ianovka, Nizhegorodskoi gubernii Lukoianovskogo uezda," *Etnograficheskii Sbornik* 1 (1853): 53. On the importance not only of the beliefs of the healer and the patient, but also of the community, which serves as a kind of "gravitational field" mediating the relationship between the two, see Claude Lévi-Strauss, "The Sorcerer and His Magic," in *Magic, Witchcraft, and Curing*, ed. John Middleton (Garden City, N.Y., 1967), p. 23–24.

[82] On "sympathetic healing" see Daniel E. Moerman, "Anthropology of Symbolic Healing," *Current Anthropology* 20, no. 1 (March 1979): 59–80; idem., "Physiology and Symbols: The Anthropological Implications of the Placebo Effect," in *The Anthropology of Medicine: From Culture to Method*, ed. L. Romanucci-Ross, D. Moerman, and L. Tancredi (New York, 1983), pp. 156–67; and James Dow, "Universal Aspects of Symbolic Healing: A Theoretical Synthesis," *American Anthropologist* 88, no. 1 (March 1986): 56–69. For an enviably intelligent discussion of the role of faith in healing see Thomas, pp. 207–11.

meant that "*znakhari* in the countryside get along fine side by side with zemstvo medicine."[83] Finally, where an individual physician inspired respect as an exceptional healer, the peasant might simply transfer to him or her the same unquestioning faith that had earlier been bestowed on the healing power of the *znakhar'*. For the peasant it was the result of the treatment he received that counted most; the growing authority physicians enjoyed in the countryside derived primarily from the positive results they were able to show in treating particular kinds of diseases.[84]

The selective use of physicians and *znakhari* made eminently good sense to most peasants, who had simply expanded their original choice of healers to include physicians, feldshers, and (less frequently) trained midwives. Such a pattern, however, which implied the continued popularity of *znakhar'* practice in the countryside, was frustrating to physicians who were determined not only to win the peasantry's confidence in their abilities as individual healers, but to persuade them of the superiority of modern medicine as a system. Rural physicians, however, were so burdened with their everyday practice that their efforts to instruct the peasantry concerning modern medicine were rarely anything more than a few sanitary maxims. This was just as well, since most peasants would have found theoretical explanations of scientific medicine either incomprehensible or irrelevant.

As rural physicians became more plentiful and their reputation as healers spread, *znakhari* modified their own practice in a number of ways.[85] One response which we have already discussed was that of emulating physicians or feldshers in their treatment, medications, and even vocabulary.[86] This kind of adaptation, which was most obvious in the treatment of syphilis and malaria, could guarantee a sustained practice only in those provinces where the numbers of rural physicians was inadequate. (*Znakhar'* treatment of syphilis in Moscow Province, the showcase of zemstvo medicine, had almost disappeared as early as the 1870s.)[87]

Another tactic that *znakhari* employed was to avoid competing with a neighboring physician altogether by retreating to a rural area where physicians were still relatively inaccessible.[88] But this again was only a temporary

---

[83] A. V. Balov, "Ocherki Poshekhon''ia," *Etnograficheskoe Obozrenie* 51, no. 4 (1902): 114.

[84] Elpat'ievskii describes how quinine and mercury virtually established his reputation as a healer. Elpat'ievskii, *Vospominaniia*, p. 19.

[85] Popov, *Russkaia narodno-bytovaia meditsina*, p. 84.

[86] A. Lozinskii, a physician, argued that "a *znakhar'*s popularity depends entirely on how skillfully he can diagnosis each patient's condition with a word he has heard somewhere, for example, from feldshers." A. Lozinskii, "Psikhologiia znakharstva," *Severnyi Vestnik*, no. 8 (August 1896), sec. 1, p. 63.

[87] Tolstoi, *Vospominaniia*, p. 82.

[88] Elpat'ievskii recalls how his feldsher had begged him to bring legal proceedings against the local *znakhar'*. Like most zemstvo physicians, Elpat'ievskii was reluctant to drive *znakhar-*

solution (although, given the slow progress that zemstvo medicine made, it might guarantee an individual *znakhar'* many years of relatively undisturbed practice).

The most characteristic adaptation *znakhari* made was to specialize in the treatment of disorders that physicians could do nothing about, but in whose treatment the *znakhar'* could claim an expertise and therefore offer hope. Many of these were either emotional or chronic disorders such as impotence, hysteria, madness, or epilepsy.

The clientele that sought help from *znakhari* seems to have evolved in a number of ways during the period under study. Leaving aside the problem of access to a physician, which was always an important factor in peasant medical choice, the bulk of *znakhar'* patients at the turn of the century was composed of either middle-aged or older people.[89] The younger generation, which had a higher rate of literacy, was more likely to seek a physician's help when it was available. Almost all observers note that women, who had always constituted a disproportionate number of *znakhar'* patients, were an even more predominant portion of the *znakhar'*'s cientele by the turn of the century. Explanations for this vary. Peasant women were on the whole less literate than peasant men.[90] They had had less exposure than men to the world beyond the village, and were thus more attached to traditional ways. The intense interest that women had in fortune-telling was another factor that attracted them to *znakhari* and *vorozhei*. Beyond this, the lot of women in the countryside—and especially that of sick women—was so difficult in most respects that one suspects that the *znakhar'*, or in this case most likely the *znakharka*, served as a sort of village psychotherapist. By listening, consoling, and providing support, they could help women who were terrorized by their husbands or frightened for their future somehow to cope with their reality.

In evaluating the materials at his disposal, Popov concluded that physicians and *znakhari* at the turn of the century probably treated about an equal number of patients. Despite the continued popularity of *znakhari*, one could nevertheless conclude from contemporary materials that their practice was slowly yielding to that of physicians. By 1914, *znakhari* seem to have been most successful in maintaining their practice either in remote rural areas (of which there were still many), or else among the older and less literate portion of the peasant population. This general trend was radically altered by the First World War and Civil War, which decimated the ranks of physicians and even trained feldshers that had been working in the countryside prior to

---

stvo entirely underground, and patiently waited until the success of his own practice caused the *znakhar'* to leave. Elpat'ievskii, *Vospominaniia*, pp. 14–15.

[89] Popov, *Russkaia narodno-bytovaia meditsina*, pp. 85–86.

[90] For a breakdown of 1897 literacy rates by age, sex, and urban/rural residence patterns see Gregory Guroff and S. Frederick Starr, "A Note on Urban Literacy in Russia, 1890–1914," *Jahrbücher für Geschichte Osteuropas* 19, 4 (December 1971): 520–31.

1914. The new Soviet regime encountered great difficulty not only in training cadres of physicians, but also in persuading them to go into rural practice.[91] The result of these catastrophic events, which virtually stripped the country-side of modern medical care, was a reinvigoration of *znakhar'* practice which lasted well into the 1930s, and which has never been entirely eliminated.[92]

[91] Samuel C. Ramer, "Feldshers and Rural Health Care in the Early Soviet Period," in *Social Medicine in Revolutionary Russia*, ed. Susan Gross Solomon and John F. Hutchinson (Bloomington, Ind., 1990), pp. 121–45.

[92] An excellent local study of peasants which stresses the prominence of traditional healers and magical thinking during the 1920s is Helmut Altrichter, *Die Bauern von Tver: Vom Leben auf dem russischen Dorfe zwischen Revolution und Kollektivierung* (Munich, 1984), pp. 118–22. Contemporary *znakhar'* practice in the Soviet Union, particularly in such forms as psychic healing, is a fascinating subject which lies beyond the scope of this article.

PART III

Peasant Politics

IF THE ISSUE of politics is interpreted as the power relationships that prevail among different persons and different groups, then it can be said that many of the studies in this book confront the issue of politics—in patriarchal relations, in the role of kulaks and the behavior of peasant communes, and in the struggle among state officials, labor contractors, employers, communes, and household members over the information needed to appropriate a share of the income earned by migrant laborers. In the peasant world, where the division of labor was not very advanced, politics was most often local, personal, and embedded in cultural symbolism as well as economic relations. The role of the peasantry's "moral economy" (see introduction) which has been stressed throughout our collection, is at least equally important in the essays that follow. However, in this section, politics is discussed in relation to the wide range of factors that contributed to outbreaks of collective action directed, for the most part, against outsiders. While recognizing the multiple causes of such actions, all five authors have emphasized four factors as particularly significant in generating the tactical mobility and opportunity that facilitated mobilization. They are: (1) splits in the elite; (2) the influence of outside actors and events; (3) the creation of independent spaces, or "turf" and (4) peasant maintenance of their unique culture and ways of seeing.

In his study of the liquor boycott campaign of the pre-Emancipation period, David Christian emphasizes the role of splits in the elite, as evidenced by contradictory government orders and hints given by some members of the gentry which suggested that peasants could count on tacit support if they protested the practices of the liquor trade. On the other hand, Timothy Mixter suggests that outsiders played a relatively minor role in the protest of migrant laborers in hiring markets. The independent space of the hiring market created by both employer organization of production and the efforts of workers themselves gave migrant laborers enough anonymity, information, resources, and tactical mobility so that they could engage in collective action without much outside assistance. Although Scott Seregny's description of the emergence of the All-Russian Peasant Union recognizes the important role of outsiders and splits in the elite in peasant protests in Vladimir and Khar'kov provinces, he also highlights the efforts made by peasants themselves in the period 1900–1905. In his discussion of the Civil War which followed the Bolshevik Revolution of 1917, Orlando Figes suggests that as a result of the power struggle among several contending groups in the country and the weakness of repressive forces, peasants had less need of allies from beyond the village. They were to a certain extent left alone and had enough power themselves to define who was an outsider and determine the terms of contacts with the outside world deemed favorable to peasant interests. In contrast to the claims advanced by many modernization theorists, our contributors suggest that in the course of the nineteenth and early twentieth centuries, the degree of peasant contact with outsiders fluctuated rather than grew inexorably.

In this section, we are presented with much evidence demonstrating the way that peasants carved out independent social spaces and organizations that provided them with information and knowledge, while either preserving or creating ways of seeing that were different enough from the elite to allow for the generation of protest. What was often remarkable in this process were the ways that information and knowledge were obtained, spread, and contested. According to Rodney Bohac, the correspondence between the absentee lord and his serfs was itself a terrain of struggle; it was interpreted, reinterpreted, distorted by "middlemen" or purposely misunderstood in ways that revealed, for example, that the lord wanted rigidly punctual rental payments while peasants wanted flexible rent adjustments that reflected weather and harvest fluctuations, poor soil conditions, and God's justice. The serfowner responded to serf resistance by trying to control the flow of information and impose his way of seeing by ordering more inspections, reports, household censuses, debt ledgers, use of nonlocal estate managers and even introduction of *barshchina* supervision. All this took away some of the serfs' tactical mobility and spatial autonomy, making covert actions the only feasible and somewhat effective means for serfs to protest given the absence of outside assistance. In his essay, David Christian demonstrates the vital role played by the spread, censorship, or selective interpretation of information contained in newspapers, rumors, boycott oaths, and government circulars in the emergence and decline of liquor protests in Lithuania and the Volga region that were organized in village meetings, churches, or marketplaces. Timothy Mixter describes how migrant agricultural laborers tried to turn the space of the hiring market into their turf by publicly supervising the behavior of employers, petty entrepreneurs, and "middlemen" who attempted to control information. Like Bohac, who has introduced the concept of "everyday forms of peasant resistance" into Russian historiography,[1] Mixter demonstrates that besides occasional overt and covert protest, peasants engaged in an ongoing struggle to implant their own definitions of "true" information, morality, and progress, by fighting to preserve their mobility and spatial autonomy. In his essay, Scott Seregny gives evidence of how peasants created, used, or took over the organizational space of peasant unions, zemstvo economic councils, agricultural societies, and mini-republics to gain more power and prevent elite deception by attempting to ensure greater equality, public accounting (*glasnost'*), and peasant local control. From within these and other social spaces they elected or sought out messengers, orators, and readers and composed their own letters, communal resolutions, newspapers, and laws to generate information and definitions of morality; in 1905, they often went on to choose as leaders members of the rural intelligentsia whom the conservative clergy had tried to define as Japanese spies and anti-Christs. According to Orlando Figes the power vacuum at the national level in the period 1917–1921 permitted peasants to destroy manor houses—the old seats of power— and to protect the spaces of the village assembly and sometimes the church. His evidence from the mid-Volga region suggests that village concepts of democracy often differed from those being enforced by Soviet authorities. Village communes redefined property relations according to their own standards; they refused compensation to those from whom land was expropriated, distributed it to those who worked it, and prohibited its sale.

—T. M.

[1] This is a phrase popularized by James Scott in *Weapons of the Weak: Everyday Forms of Peasant Resistance* (New Haven, 1986).

CHAPTER 7

EVERYDAY FORMS OF RESISTANCE: SERF OPPOSITION TO GENTRY EXACTIONS, 1800–1861

Rodney Bohac

HISTORIANS have long recognized that Russian peasants did not turn solely to rebellion to protest serfdom. Serfs also used dissimulation, petty theft, work slowdowns, and flight to counter the demands of their owners and overseers. Most scholars have not emphasized these practices, because they appeared to be ineffective or to lack political sophistication. Behavior of this sort has been characterized by Russianists as the "only way" to express discontent, as "primitive protest," and as "hedonistic rather than political,"[1] But scholars who have studied peasant societies elsewhere have argued that these techniques of everyday resistance effectively counter pressures imposed by elites and act as an important part of the peasant arsenal of weapons against a variety of masters, supervisors and officials.[2]

[1] Richard Pipes, *Russia Under the Old Regime* (New York, 1974), pp. 153–56 best displays this attitude. Jerome Blum, *Lord and Peasant in Russia* (Princeton, 1961), p. 552, also downplays peasant resistance by characterizing flight as "the only way" to manifest peasant discontent along with "sporadic outbursts of disobedience and violence." Steven L. Hoch, *Serfdom and Social Control in Russia: Petrovskoe, a Village in Tambov* (Chicago, 1986), pp. 184–86 takes an ambiguous view of these acts, pointing out that noncooperation comprised part of the basic serf "response" to servitude and compares serfs to prisoners who are "constantly trying to beat the system at its own game." Geroid T. Robinson, *Rural Russia Under the Old Regime* (Berkeley, 1969), pp. 48–50, mentions peasant resistance reflected in spirituals and flight. He also argues that "stubborn shirking and sabotage of the villagers sometimes so clogged the economy of an estate" that the proprietor had to sell it. Robinson, however, does not develop this concept and explore its relationship to peasant rebellion. Peter Kolchin, *Unfree Labor: American Slavery and Russian Serfdom* (Cambridge, Mass., 1987), pp. 242–43, 278–84, sees "silent sabotage" such as shoddy work, slowdowns, and minor acts of disobedience as "primitive protest" in which it is difficult to separate deliberate resistance from deliberate malingering. However, he considers flight an important form of resistance, evidently because in this form of resistance it is easier to discern the difference between resistance and malingering.

[2] James C. Scott, *Weapons of the Weak: Everyday Forms of Peasant Resistance* (New Haven, 1985); James C. Scott and Benedict J. Tria Kerkvliet, eds., "Everyday Forms of Peasant Resistance in South-East Asia," Special Issue of *Journal of Peasant Studies* 13, no. 2 (January 1986): 1–149.

This article explores the validity of the concept of everyday resistance as a way to understand Russian serfdom, by examining the actions of serfs living on an early-nineteenth-century Russian estate. Petitions and managerial reports sent from the estate to the absentee owner document forms of resistance used to mitigate the effects of money rent (*obrok*). The peasant repertoire included flight, illegal lumbering, and evasion of work details. The correspondence itself on occasion formed part of the material for resistance, as serfs used it as a means of anonymous protest and footdragging.[3] The reports and petitions affected rent collections during the crop failures of the 1810s and served to postpone rent collections during crop failures in the 1820s. But despite such successes, everyday resistance did not prevent the owner from establishing work details and a new labor rent (*barshchina*) in 1828. Although everyday resistance could not prevent the serf owner from redefining the amount of rent due and the means of payment, it did help to maintain an ideology of resistance that contributed to the serfs' persistent efforts to resist even after suffering repeated and costly defeats.

THE CONCEPT OF EVERYDAY RESISTANCE

The scholars who developed the concept of everyday resistance believe this tactic counters and reshapes the demands of the ruling elites. In their judgment, peasants challenge elite demands with their own perceptions of elite responsibility toward them. Elite demands for cheap, available labor are thus countered by peasant demands for loans, charity, and just treatment. The failure of elites to adhere to the peasant interpretation of their relationship can generate peasant protest in the form of everyday resistance. Concealing part of the harvest, work slowdowns, tax evasion, and poaching all function to reduce the elites' power and income and the peasants' burdens.[4]

Everyday resistance brings several advantages to peasants who challenge the elites' demands. It provides a channel for resistance, when the instruments of repression make outright rebellion dangerous. It does not require peasants to organize or coordinate their activities. Acts of everyday resistance also generally remain anonymous, greatly reducing the risk of reprisal.[5] With these acts peasants, perhaps unwittingly, maintain an ideology of resistance, a belief in their own rights and privileges, that facilitates sudden

---

[3] Kolchin, p. 275, mentions the frequent petitions to *pomeshchiki* but does not explore the petitions' effectiveness. The petition does form the first stage of the *volnenie*. He may exaggerate the proportion of collective protests due to the nature of his sources.

[4] Scott, *Weapons of the Weak*, pp. 296, 306–7.

[5] Scott, *Weapons of the Weak*, p. 296; Benedict J. Tria Kerkvliet, "Everday Forms of Peasant Resistance," p. 108.

outbursts of rebellion. Peasants do not swing from acquiescence to rebellion. Instead they are in constant struggle with local elites.[6]

This depiction of tax evasion, pilfering, and sabotage as positive acts of resistance assumes that ideological views motivate the peasants. As critics and adherents point out, these acts could also arise out of simple laziness or criminal intent. The acts could, furthermore, be defensive measures, designed not to challenge the elites, but simply to ensure survival. To discover the peasants' motivations is difficult, because they have mixed motives and rarely reveal their thoughts.[7] James Scott circumvents this dilemma by suggesting that the acts' motives do not matter as much as their results. In 1917, for example, desertion by thousands of Russian soldiers arose for many reasons, but clearly contributed to the revolution. Scott classifies selfish acts by individuals as resistance when they combine with similar acts to form a consistent pattern and affect the behavior of governing elites. When the acts have such an impact, they deserve as much weight in the study of resistance as does rebellion.[8]

Scott's definition serves as a guideline for this paper in evaluating everyday resistance among Russian serfs. My sources rarely hint at the motives of individual peasants, because the writers couched the correspondence in deferential terms. They permit the reader, on the other hand, to judge the peasants' portrayal of the landlord's responsibilities toward them, because the peasants bring up these responsibilities to sway the owner to their point of view. The sources also allow the reader to evaluate the effectiveness of everyday resistance and its usefulness in preparing the ground for collective protest.

OWNER-SERF CORRESPONDENCE

The obrok serfs under study lived on the Manuilovo Estate in Rzhev District of Tver Province (see map 1). The estate's nine villages lay scattered along a road that linked the county seats of Staritsa and Rzhev, a Volga river port. The estate's over one thousand serfs provided for their households by farming.[9] They employed the traditional three-field system to grow rye and oats

[6] Scott, *Weapons of the Weak*, pp. 302–3.

[7] Kerkvliet, "Everyday Resistance of Injustice," pp. 116–20; Michael Adas, "From Foot-dragging to Flight: The Elusive History of Peasant Avoidance Protest in South and South-East Asia," *Journal of Peasant Studies* 13, no. 2 (January 1986): 76–96; Christine Pelzer White, "Everyday Resistance, Socialist Revolution, and Rural Development. The Vietnamese Case," *Journal of Peasant Studies* 13, no. 2 (January 1986): 54.

[8] Scott, *Weapons of the Weak*, pp. 293–94.

[9] Gagarin Family Papers, *Tsentral'nyi Gosudarstvennyi Arkhiv Drevnikh Aktov*, fond (collection) 1262, *opis'* (inventory) 2, 1861 Household Economic Census, *delo* (item) 7338. All Gagarin documents are from the same *fond* and *opis'* and these will no longer be cited in the notes.

and smaller amounts of buckwheat and barley. In an average year the serfs could feed their families and market some of their harvest.[10]

Other economic activities provided a degree of autonomy from the estate economy. The serfs supplemented their agricultural income with work off the estate as carters, bucket makers, and carpenters.[11] They also supplemented the land allotted to them by the landlord with land they purchased themselves. The purchased land brought the average household landholdings to well above the Tver provincial average. The land also intensified socioeconomic differentiation among estate households.[12] The purchased land and the nonagricultural by-employment enabled the peasants to develop sources of income divorced from the system of serfdom and to maintain separate spheres of limited autonomy. The peasants' autonomy extended to estate management as well, because neither the landlord nor his officials acted as direct, "on-the-spot" supervisors or managers. Nikolai Sergeevich Gagarin administered the estate from Moscow and St. Petersburg. A wealthy nobleman, Gagarin spent most of his time pursuing other activities. He also owned a number of other larger and more profitable estates, so he probably did not devote much time to Manuilovo.[13] He depended on a large number of hired clerks or officials in his Moscow home office to analyze reports, inspect or supervise the estates, and carry on correspondence. A Manuilovo serf served as Gagarin's representative on Manuilovo Estate. The estate manager (*burmistr*) was elected by and from the local peasants and approved by Gagarin. The estate manager reported to Gagarin and the Moscow officials on estate business and carried out their orders. Other elected officials, the treasurer (*vybornyi*), scribe (*zemskii*), and elders (*stariki*), assisted him.

The correspondence exchanged between Manuilovo and Moscow comprises the basic source material for this study. The local Manuilovo authorities sent reports, financial ledgers, peasant petitions, and household eco-

[10] V. A. Preobrazhenskii, *Opisanie Tverskoi gubernii v sel'sko-khoziaistvennom otnoshenii* (St. Petersburg, 1854), pp. 268–71; V. I. Pokrovskii, ed., *General'noe soobrazhenie po Tverskoi gubernii izvlechennoe iz podrobnogo topograficheskogo i kameral'nogo po gorodom i uezdam opisaniia, 1783-1784 gg.* (Tver', 1873), pp. 119, 128; Rodney D. Bohac, "Family, Property, and Socioeconomic Mobility: Russian Peasants on Manuilovskoe Estate, 1810–1861" (Ph.D. diss., University of Illinois, 1982), pp. 20–28.

[11] Rodney K. Bohac, "Agricultural Structure and the Origins of Migration in Central Russia, 1810–1850," in *Agrarian Organization in the Century of Industralization: Europe, Russia, and North America*, ed. George Grantham and Carol S. Leonard, *Research in Economic History*, supp. 5, pt. B (Greenwich, Conn., 1989), pp. 369–87.

[12] Excerpts from Land Survey Books, March 22, 1828, delo 7236, listy (sheaves) 7 ob.–8; 1842 Household Economic Census, delo 7263, listy 35–36 ob. Villages, small groups, and individuals began to purchase this land in the early eighteenth century. Although this land was purchased in the name of the landlord, the peasants referred to it as their own and treated it separately from the alloted land. Much of the purchased land, located on the estate's periphery, served as pasture or lay unused until needed.

[13] Hoch, *Serfdom and Social Control in Russia*, pp. 13–14.

nomic censuses to Moscow. Gagarin and the Moscow office returned directives confirming local decisions, settling disputes, or outlining new policies. Through this correspondence the serfs defined their relationship with Gagarin and engaged in everyday resistance.

The correspondence presents an incomplete view of the dialogue between lord and serf, because neither party wanted to express his private views of the situation publicly. Scholars studying other peasant societies have found that peasants play several roles in their relationship with the landlord. Peasants in Malaysia showed deference toward local landlords when in public places and when face-to-face with the landlord. Privately, the peasants criticized and challenged the landlord's conception of themselves and through gossip belittled the landlord's status.[14] The Manuilovo documents do not reveal the serfs' informal, private thoughts. They instead reflect the serfs' public posture, infused with caution and deference. As a landlord, Gagarin could publicly take a bolder stance than the peasants, but he had to appear to understand his obligations to the peasants as lord and patron. Not to do so might intensify peasant resistance to his orders and lower his status.

Despite the public, incomplete nature of the estate documents, they provide a sense of each party's expectations of the other. As an absentee landlord, Gagarin rarely, if ever, talked face-to-face with his serfs. The correspondence served as the primary form of interaction between lord and serf. The documents themselves became part of a ritual or "theater of power" in which each party tested and developed their interpretation of the proper relationship between the two parties.[15]

Each party consisted of many different voices, and the documents do not always identify who is speaking. When writing reports, the estate manager usually opened with the words "from the estate manager and all the mir. (commune)" At other times he noted that the mir assembly (skhodka) decided the course of action.[16] The mir encompassed all male household heads who held the right to attend mir assemblies and be elected to mir offices. A variety of conflicts divided these men. The heads contended with younger men in their own households, with households in other socioeconomic strata, and households within their own stratum.[17] In his reports the estate manager could at his discretion represent a variety of different groups or his own

[14] Scott, *Weapons of the Weak*, pp. 286–89.

[15] E. P. Thompson, "Patrician Society, Plebian Culture," *Journal of Social History* 7, no. 4 (Summer 1974): 396–97; Gerald M. Sider, "The Ties That Bind: Culture and Agriculture, Property and Propriety in the Newfoundland Village Fishery," *Social History* 5, no. 1 (January 1980): 24.

[16] 16 October 1820 Report from Estate Manager, delo 7213, list 14. The estate sent most reports and the notes from here on will simply read "Report."

[17] Hoch, *Serfdom and Social Control in Russia*, pp. 186–89 argues intragenerational disputes accounted directly or indirectly for community tensions.

opinion. The estate managers came from a variety of socioeconomic levels, but members of four wealthy households most often occupied the post. These men participated in local agricultural markets and developed new economic activities such as a blacksmith shop and a dyeworks.[18]

The reports contained another important point of view. The illiterate estate managers dictated their reports to the estate scribe. Two local peasants filled this position from 1810 until 1843. They could alter the estate manager's message or at least provide the ritual terms of deference. The multiplicity of voices allowed the estate manager to distance himself from positions taken in the reports. He and the rest of the peasants could hide in the anonymity of the term "mir" or could shift responsibility to others. Masking responsibility became a technique of everyday resistance.

Gagarin could also hide behind the ambiguous authorship of his directives. The estate managers acknowledged his authority by addressing most correspondence to him and by referring to him as "Your Majesty." Gagarin's Moscow employees, however, wrote at least the final drafts of the directives. Peasant and landlord alike could complain that Moscow officials misinterpreted Gagarin's orders. One peasant, for instance, complained that the list of candidates for military conscription on which he was listed was drawn up incorrectly. The officials, he claimed, did not know His Majesty's wishes.[19] Because Gagarin and the estate manager held formal responsibility for the reports and directives, this paper refers to them as the authors unless the source suggests otherwise.

COMMON FORMS OF EVERYDAY RESISTANCE

The correspondence and the everyday resistance centered on a fundamental aspect of serfdom, which was the money rent, or obrok. Because obrok was Gagarin's chief source of income from the estate and the largest duty owed by the serf's, it was crucial to the two-party relationship. The assessment and collection of rent also symbolized the lord's dominant position and drained peasant income. To resist this dominance and save their income, serfs chose several forms of everyday resistance. This paper will first discuss commonly analyzed forms of resistance, including flight, concealment of harvests, and pilfering. It will then turn to the efforts of Manuilovo serfs to resist payment of part of the obrok through their manipulation of reports and petitions.

Although successful in other peasant societies, flight did not prove effective for Manuilovo serfs, and they rarely attempted it. Too many obstacles hindered the successful escape to freedom. There were no nearby frontier

---

[18] Bohac, "Family, Property, and Socioeconomic Mobility," pp. 273–75.

[19] 13 December 1811 Petition from Grigorii Fedorov, delo 7189, list 69–69 ob. For a full elaboration of this strategy see Daniel Field, *Rebels in the Name of the Tsar* (Boston, 1976), pp. 208–14.

regions to offer a safe and profitable haven, and there always seemed to be enough police to capture runaways. The estate archive contains references to only six runaways, most of whom were not fleeing serfdom but were attempting to escape the military draft or the aftermath of family disputes.[20] When protesting the distant national government's military draft, the serfs usually employed other techniques of everyday resistance. One serf cut off a finger. Others may have bribed county officials. In 1827, county officials declared eight candidates from wealthy households physically unfit for service. The ninth and tenth candidates, who came from poor households and presumably suffered from a poor diet, were declared fit for military service.[21] Most peasant resistance to the draft surfaced in the form of petitions sent to Gagarin by individual households. The petitioners complained that either the draft would take away a valuable worker or that their household was taken out of turn. Such petitions often pitted peasant against peasant, and encouraged more intervention by Gagarin.[22] Even when resisting the military draft, the peasants turned to the written word.

Neither individually nor collectively did the Manuilovo peasants use concealment of harvests as a form of everyday resistance. None of the many household economic censuses or peasant petitions hint at any form of concealment. Because the mir assessed each household's rent primarily on the basis of the number of married couples and not the amount of grain harvested, hiding the harvest did not affect the households' tax burden.[23]

Peasants compensated for the burden of rents by pilfering firewood and lumber from the lord's forests. This illicit activity indirectly challenged serfdom, first, by contesting the lord's right to determine land usage and, second, by using the lord's property to provide necessary income for obrok payment. Strict rules regulated the quantity and types of lumber the Manuilovo

[20] Adas, "From Footdragging to Flight," pp. 73–75 discusses the impact of widespread flight. 18 August 1826 Report, delo 7228, list 38; 23 June 1830 Report, delo 7235, list 99; 20 November 1836 Report, delo 7251, list 41.

[21] 26 January 1835 Report, delo 7249, list 35; 23 October 1827 Report, delo 7232, list 62–62 ob.

[22] Examples include 27 October 1813 Petition from Donna Fedoseev, delo 7197, list 11; November 1831 Petition from Egor Afonasev, delo 7243, list 35–35 ob. See also Rodney D. Bohac, "The Mir and the Military Draft," *Slavic Review* 47, no. 4 (Winter 1988): 652–66. Disobedient sons about to be punished by their fathers or the mir were a common source of runaways. Only one runaway was successful.

[23] Brian Fegan, "Tenants' Non-Violent Resistance to Landowner Claims in a Central Luzon Village," *Journal of Peasant Studies* 13, no. 2 (January 1986): 97–103, describes several methods used by tenants to conceal part of the rice crop from landlords. See also James C. Scott, "Resistance Without Protest and Without Organization: Peasant Opposition to the Islamic *Zakat* and the Christian Tithe," *Comparative Studies in Society and History* 29, no. 3 (July 1987): 417–52. Samuel Popkin, *The Rational Peasant: The Political Economy of Rural Society in Vietnam* (Berkeley 1979), p. 41, stresses the peasant need to find criteria for tax assessment that are highly visible in order to avoid struggle over fairness in assessment.

serfs could use for construction and fuel.[24] The peasants clearly did not obey these rules. An overseer sent to supervise the estate in 1828 promised that the "useless" lumbering done in the past would be stopped, and that no one would enter the forests without permission.[25] When the estate manager and other local peasants reported illegal lumbering, they used the reports to gain political or economic advantage. In 1811 the mir noted that one small tract of forest land was too far away from the estate and too close to a main road and outside villages to be easily protected against illegal activities. They asked permission to cut it down, probably because they wanted to use the lumber and to extend nearby fields.[26] Peasants also accused unpopular estate managers of illegal lumbering in order to justify the managers' ouster.[27] Although this type of everyday resistance denied the lord some of his resources, peasants also used Gagarin's disapproval of the practice as a political weapon against one another.

Flight, illegal lumbering, and concealment of holdings failed to alter significantly the peasants' burden or to weaken the landlord's ability to drain off peasant surpluses. The peasants had to direct their efforts toward rent assessment and payment. To do so meant negotiating with Gagarin and his officials through the correspondence, which became a most effective tool of resistance.

THE BATTLE OVER INFORMATION: THE ORIGINS

The mir could use its reports to lessen the rent burden at two points; first, when Gagarin set the original rate per soul and, second, when it was time for households to pay. Gagarin assessed the rent according to the number of male souls living on the estate. He determined the amount to be paid per soul and multiplied it by the number of souls. Moscow officials relayed the total to the mir. The mir assembly then determined the amount each household was to pay. The mir did not use the male soul as its tax unit, but instead calculated the rent on the basis of the number of *tiagla* in each household.[28] One *tiaglo* consisted of a married couple of working age. The mir would assess an unmarried young man or a widower a fraction of a *tiaglo*. Once the mir assessed the household, the household and not the mir held the responsibility for debts.

During the 1810s Manuilovo serfs resisted the rent at both points. Resistance took individual and collective forms, but in all cases serfs cited labor

---

[24] 22 January 1811 Report, delo 7189, list 9.

[25] 30 January 1829 Report from Overseer Ivan Ivanov, delo 7240, list 21 ob.

[26] 27 March 1811 Report, delo 7189, list 13.

[27] 22 December 1818 Petition, delo 7211, list 73.

[28] The dual system of rent assessment units reflects the efforts of the Manuilovo peasants to retain their autonomy.

shortages and economic problems as causes of the inability to pay rent. Struggle against obrok began in 1810, when Gagarin started to supervise the estate more closely. The correspondence began in that year, and it was between 1810 and 1814 that the most precipitous nineteenth-century increase in obrok assessments occurred. Whereas in 1810 peasants paid Gagarin 2,500 rubles a year, in 1814 they paid 10,000 rubles. A rise in the number of male souls, a sudden drop in the value of the paper ruble, and Gagarin's desire for more income contributed to the increase.[29] When the assessment doubled between 1810 and 1813, Manuilovo peasants initially managed to pay the obrok. Only once did the proportion of households in arrears creep over 10 percent. Most households paid promptly within one or two months of the January and August due dates.[30] The size of the arrears and the timing of payments did not indicate any footdragging.

When in 1814 the obrok assessment doubled again from 5,000 to 10,000 rubles, arrears began to mount. In February 1815, almost half of the estate's households still owed rent for 1814. Three months later in May, a smaller but still significant 20 percent suffered arrears. The next month the proportion of households in arrears dropped to the pre-1814 levels.[31] The arrears for 1816 follow a similar pattern. In February 1817 a little over 40 percent could not pay rent. These households cleared their arrears only after the October harvest.[32]

Petitions from individuals and the mir explaining the rent arrears emphasize the debtors' economic distress. At least two reports sent by the estate managers refer to those peasants with arrears as "poor" (neimushchie) peasants. In 1814 the estate manager pointed out that these needy peasants were widows who headed households with only one male worker and several small children.[33] One woman petitioned Gagarin directly. "I am a widow with small children," she pleaded. "I had two sons and four daughters and this year the eldest son died. The surviving son is five years old and I have three souls or one half tiaglo of obrok." She wanted rent relief until her young son grew up. To the mir an easily verifiable labor problem such as the lack of male workers warranted a rent reduction.[34]

[29] 10 March 1810 Report, delo 7187, list 16; 6 February 1815 Report, delo 7200, listy 14; N.K. Brzheskii et al., eds. Ministerstvo finansov, 1802–1902, 1 (St. Petersburg, 1902), pp. 61–69.

[30] 27 December 1810 Report, delo 7189, list 2; 2 May 1811, delo 7189, list 24; March 1814 Report, delo 7199, list 13; 13 August 1813 Report, delo 7197, list 23.

[31] 6 February 1815 Report, delo 7200, listy 15–16; May 1815 Report, delo 7200, listy 24–25 ob.; 2 June 1815 Report, delo 7200, list 31.

[32] 26 February 1817 Report, delo 7206, listy 85–87; December 1817 Report, delo 7199, list 13.

[33] 2 April 1813 Report, delo 7197, list 10; 4 March 1814 Report, delo 7199, list 13.

[34] 5 February 1811, delo 7189, list 28. For the importance of finding easily verifiable standards such as age and marital status to judge need see Popkin, p. 41. The mir closely evaluated tax relief petitions. It gave Iakov Petrov tax relief only at the insistence of Gagarin.

The estate managers turned to problems affecting the whole mir, when trying to lower total obrok assessment. Inadequate labor resources and unfavorable agricultural conditions formed the core of the mir's defense. In late 1810 and early 1811 two estate managers argued that most serfs could not handle proposed rent increases due to the quality of the estate's soil and the need to purchase lumber for construction and firewood. Their arguments lowered proposed rates of 12.50 rubles and 9.00 rubles to a rate of 7.50 rubles per soul.[35] Gagarin, however, continued to press for rent increases. In 1813 he ordered a household economic census which provided information on household labor resources as well as some economic data. He used the demographic data to determine the number of tax units and found 295 *tiagla*. With that number of tax units, Gagarin believed rent could be raised to twenty rubles per soul. The mir claimed that 33 of the 295 *tiagla* found in the 1813 register could not pay, because the bearers of these *tiagla* were too young or too old to work. Gagarin then lowered the rate to 17.80 per soul.[36] Attempts to lower the rent the next year, when frosts damaged spring crops, were unsuccessful.

In the 1810s individual peasants and several estate managers argued that local economic conditions limited the justifiable amount of rent. These shared justifications imply that the peasants adhered to the principles of a moral economy, in that they believed the landlord should acknowledge limits to his demands. Manuilovo serfs also used these principles against one another. In the early 1810s rising rents and arrears were not the only problem confronting the community. Eighteen men were lost in the war against Napoleon, the hay crop was expropriated by the Iaroslavl militia without compensation, and inflation added to already existing material burdens. These problems weakened the political stability of the community, which elected eight different estate managers between 1810 and 1820. Peasants claimed that estate managers had not protected them from the loss of hay, spent too much on church remodeling, embezzled mir funds, and lumbered illegally.[37] In internal community affairs, the mir blamed the inability to pay rent on the estate manager.

Gagarin attempted to fulfill his role in the moral economy as the paternal protector of his children, the serfs. He tried to defend poor peasants who

Petrov claimed an injury prevented him from working. He was the only male in the household, but owned two horses, and the estate manager argued that Petrov possessed enough property to pay arrears. 6 October 1815 Report, delo 7200, list 41; 3 November 1815 Report, delo 7200, list 45.

[35] 27 December 1810 Report, delo 7189, list 6; 12 February 1811 Report, delo 7189, list 11; 2 May 1811 Report, delo 7189, list 24.

[36] 1813 Financial Ledger, delo 7193; 14 January 1814 Report, delo 7199, list 3.

[37] Examples include 20 February 1813 Report, delo 7197, list 1–2; 19 January 1814 Report, delo 7199, list 1; 4 May 1819 Report, delo 7211, list 104.

had to pay too much rent or exorbitant interest on loans to the mir's wealthy peasants. He also tried to insure fair procedures in the selection of military conscripts. Throughout his lifetime, Gagarin further worked to prevent political conflicts among the peasants, because he evidently believed the mir ought to be a community that worked together for the common good.[38]

Gagarin, however, wanted to maintain his income, so he tried to circumvent the peasant claims based on poor agricultural conditions. In order to ensure rent payments, he ordered the mir to send peasants to work on his other estates in nearby provinces. The migrants were to go to Nikolskoe Estate in Moscow Province or Butskoe and Petrovskoe estates in Tambov Province to work as lumberers and carpenters. The men worked for wages, but instead of receiving the wages directly, Gagarin officials credited the money they earned toward the obrok owed by each worker's household. The program began in 1812 when the mir sent three groups of twenty men to Nikolskoe. The men earned enough money to pay a quarter of the year's rent.[39]

To counter these demands, peasants resorted to everyday resistance. Seven of the fifty whom they chose to send on an 1814 work detail were either too young or too old to do the work demanded. An 1815 list of thirty workers shows that the mir sent a fourteen-year-old boy and four men over fifty years old who had able-bodied sons at home. Six other peasants hired substitutes.[40]

Clearly, peasants were attempting to prevent the loss of labor during the agricultural season. An 1812 work detail left on April thirtieth and returned in October after the harvests.[41] The peasants obviously resented the work details and feared they would harm agriculture, the traditional source of their subsistence.

Unsurprisingly, the estate managers defended the peasants' delaying tactics on the basis of labor needs. In 1814, the manager said the mir sent the seven young and elderly men on the work details because the households needed the able-bodied men to stay at home and sow the fallow fields. In 1815 the new estate manager claimed that fever kept many men at home and also that only large families were able to send a worker.[42] His statements implied that he was only reporting the decisions made by individual households. The estate manager had generalized individual everyday resistance into collective protest and retained much of the element of anonymity found in everyday resistance.

[38] 2 May 1811 Report, delo 7198, list 21; 24 November 1811 Directive from N. S. Gagarin, delo 7189, list 40; 22 June 1812 Report, delo 7190, list 18.

[39] Financial Ledger: Obrok Payments, 1812–1815, delo 7201; 2 September 1813 Report, delo 7197, list 36; 19 October 1813 Report, delo 7197, list 40.

[40] 3 June 1814 Report, delo 7199, list 28; 15 June 1815 Report, delo 7200, listy 34–37.

[41] Financial Ledger: Obrok Payments, 1812–1815, delo 7201.

[42] 3 June 1814 Report, delo 7199, list 28; 15 June 1815 Report, delo 7200, listy 34–37.

Gagarin attempted to unmask peasant recalcitrance by ordering lists of men to be sent on the work details and by gathering information on the men once they arrived at the assigned work sites. The paperwork did not stop the footdragging; approximately the same number evaded service in 1815 as in 1814. The Manuilovo archive also contains no record of work details between 1818 and 1820. The temporary end to the migrations does not imply victory for the peasants. The migrations, for instance, may have continued without being recorded. Or Gagarin's new policy may have shown the peasants that they could manage to pay the higher rents by using traditional sources of income. Throughout the 1810s the peasants had used both individual and collective acts of everyday resistance based on their public argument that local agricultural conditions and labor problems prevented increases in taxes. Their tactics forced delays in rent increases and the possible end to work details. Peasant concerns had partially shaped Gagarin policy. However, the serfowner's response indicated that the desire to guarantee a constant flow of income concerned him as much as carrying out any paternalistic role.

CRISIS AND RESISTANCE: THE 1820S

The 1820s brought a new economic crisis which placed further peasant demands on Gagarin's paternalism and, in turn, increased Gagarin's pressure on the peasants to pay their rent on a regular basis. The crisis also intensified the volume of correspondence as both parties attempted to control the flow of information.

A crop failure in the fall of 1821 prevented many households from paying rent. The crop failures continued in 1822 and 1823, when the rye crops suffered extensive damage due to drought and frosts. The fourth consecutive crop failure occurred in 1824.[43] Due to these crop failures the majority of the peasant households did not have enough grain to feed themselves, let alone pay the rent. In January 1822, just three months after the first crop failure, Gagarin sent 146.5 *chetverti* of grain to feed almost two-thirds of the households. After the 1824 crop failure the peasants owed 7,232.87 rubles for grain loaned by Gagarin, 2,179.41 rubles for rent from past years, and would in two months owe another 10,800 rubles for the 1824 rent. Earnings of 8,705.08 rubles from the work details covered part of the debt, but the peasants still owed 12,592.80 rubles.[44]

Villagers responded to the subsistence crisis by reminding Gagarin of his

[43] 27 August 1823 Report, delo 7214, list 168; 12 August 1824 Report, delo 7220, listy 62–63.

[44] 8 January 1822 Report, delo 7214; 6 February 1822 Register of Debtor Households, delo 7214, list 55; 30 May 1822 Report, delo 7214, list 87; January 1823 List of Households Receiving Grain Loans, delo 7214, list 137; 12 July 1823 Debt Register, delo 7217; 12 August 1824 Report, delo 7220, listy 62–63; 1 November 1824 Register of Manuilovo Wage Earnings and Debts, delo 7216.

responsibility toward them in their time of need. In the spring of 1822 three peasants "with comrades" explained that the 1821 rye crop had not matured due to drought. They had nothing to plant or to buy and pleaded for a grain loan, so they could plant this year's crop. The peasants promised to pay for the borrowed grain in installments after the next harvest.[45] They implied that they were not shirking obligations and would pay for the borrowed grain.

Stepan Romanov, the estate manager, sent a formal report which supported the three peasants' petition. He had repeatedly flogged peasants to get them to pay, but the poor peasants said there was no grain. He looked in their granaries and they were empty. The only way to get the rent, Romanov claimed, was to sell the peasants' property and livestock. He could not carry out such a step without orders from Gagarin.[46] Romanov's report reiterated that material circumstances, not unwillingness, prevented compliance with Gagarin's demands. By asking for Gagarin's support, he further confirmed the existence of serious peasant distress, and delayed taking further action toward collecting the arrears. Peasant requests, which in the 1810s stressed that general agricultural conditions made higher rents impossible, now explained that natural climatic problems led to the inability to keep up with their obligations. Interestingly enough, the peasants never blamed the rent increases of the 1810s for their problems. They even worked to pay off their rent debts first and then the grain loans. Perhaps they believed that the loans did not need to be paid back.

Gagarin reacted to the crisis by fulfilling his responsibilities. He answered peasant requests by arranging for the purchase of grain and flour which he shipped to the peasants. To make certain that wealthy peasants did not end up with the grain, he warned that the loaned grain should not be sold on local markets. Twice in 1824 he cautioned Romanov to treat the rich and poor alike when assigning men to the work details. In the same year he also directed the mir to pay the obrok debts of households no longer assessed rent due to a lack of male workers. The money was to come out of community funds (obshchestvennye summy). When he ordered work details in 1825, he commanded the mir to plow the fields of households who had sent their only male worker.[47]

Paternalistic duties shaped his response, but legal requirements and the need to protect his property also could have played a role. His terse directives do not reveal his motives. The documents only reflect his belief that peasants had to pay him for the loaned grain as quickly as possible. He demanded that men be sent on work details and intensified his use of reports,

<hr />

[45] May 1822 Petition from Vasilii Efimov, Zakhar Gerasimov, Tikhon Zakharov with comrades, delo 7214, list 91.

[46] 18 October 1822 Report, delo 7214, list 106.

[47] 1 November 1824 Directive, delo 7218, list 4; 29 November 1824 Directive, delo 7218, list 6 ob.; 24 March 1825 Directive, delo 7218, list 33.

ledgers, and censuses. In 1823 he ordered Romanov to compile a household economic census, the first taken in a decade. The census described in detail the households' demographic composition, a broad range of economic indicators, and total debts.[48] Instead of requiring a list of those persons sent, Gagarin now wanted to know who *could* be sent. In a master-serf relationship shaped through exchanging paperwork, Gagarin countered growing arrears by demanding more precise and frequent record keeping.

When in 1824 Romanov reported the 12,592 ruble debt, Gagarin stepped up the pressure on the estate. Gagarin first emphasized the enormity of the problem by calculating a much higher debt of over 32,000 rubles. He reached that figure by ignoring income earned on the work details and adding the rent due for the next year, 1825.[49] In the coming year, he was warning the peasants, they would be not just paying off past debts, but that year's rent as well.

To pay off these high debts Gagarin reemphasized the belief that poor agricultural activity should be no excuse for slow payment of arrears. He first ordered Romanov to collect as much from the peasants as he could from normal sources of income. Then the estate manager was to compile another household economic census which listed household members and debts. From this census Romanov was to find debtors "wishing" to go to clear land for cultivation in Butskoe. Gagarin assured the peasants they would be paid the same as non-Gagarin laborers. At the end of 1825 the peasants were to be "not one kopeck" in debt.[50] If the debts remained, Gagarin threatened harsher measures. Romanov would have to send 100 men each to the Gagarin estates of Nikolskoe and Petrovskoe.[51] The number of men demanded was double or triple those sent in the previous decade.

Less than a month later Gagarin used the newly compiled census as the basis for a more intimidating directive. Any household that had not sent someone on a work detail, he argued, must be wealthy enough to pay their debts by the end of the next year. He told Romanov to place a mark by their names and collect the rent from them "without fail." If these households "suddenly" found themselves unable to pay, he cynically remarked, Romanov was to collect only half of the rent. A family member ought to be sent out on a work detail to pay the other half. It often happened, Gagarin observed, that peasants did not fulfill their promises and carried them out only when assigned and "out of fear (*izapushannost*)."[52] When in January no progress had been made in clearing up the debts, Gagarin no longer gave the

[48] 1823 Household Economic Census, delo 7215.

[49] 1 November 1824 Directive, delo 7218, list 4.

[50] Ibid.

[51] Ibid.

[52] 29 November 1824 Directive, delo 7218, list 6 ob.

peasants until the end of the year to erase their debts. He called for two hundred workers to work on his other estates.[53]

As Gagarin increased his demands, Romanov and the mir heightened their depiction of the peasants' misery. Separating himself from his report, Romanov passed on the "testimonies" of peasants departing for the work details. The peasants, he said, had no grain at home, "not a single kernal and there is nothing to feed the elderly and the young." "Your Majesty," he continued, show us "your own fatherly mercy (otecheskago miloserdiia), otherwise we should die as a result of the famine (golodnoiu smertoiu)." Twenty families wanted to be freed from the work details. The men wanted to "remain with us in their own home" to help with the work there.[54] Romanov emphasized the intense suffering and Gagaarin's paternal responsibilities, rather than the large debts.

Gagarin remembered the debts, and responded to Romanov by again noting the enormous sum due. Then, despite Romanov's attempts to distance himself from the request, Gagarin attacked Romanov's trusteeship of the debt collection. Gagarin claimed that due to Romanov's activities, the peasants were thrown into "considerable confusion" about the debts they owed and the ways they were supposed to erase them. In such circumstances the peasants suddenly found they could not pay the debts. To counter this problem Gagarin ordered the estate manager to supervise the debt collection "more strictly" and to send without fail the 160 men still needed for the work details. He wanted these orders carried out "without the tiniest of excuses on the part of the mir."[55] The serfowner now suspected the abilities and loyalty of his record keeper. These suspicions would eventually lead to a new level of coercion. Despite his criticism of Romanov, Gagarin a week later reduced the number of men still needed for the work details from 160 to 120.[56]

With this small victory the peasants continued to emphasize their plight. Later the same month two poor peasants with "seventy-five comrades" reminded Gagarin that they had not had a rye harvest for four years. They had sold all their nonessential wealth (dostatki) and had nothing left to sell. During the winter the mir had sent 160 men to work to feed their families. Therefore they pleaded to "Your own fatherly Mercy" for more grain loans. If not helped, they would die as a result of the famine or would have to leave their agricultural work and find other employment to feed their families. The peasants, while trying to show their cooperation and willingness to work, still clung to their belief that at this difficult time it was better to be home. Gagarin agreed to send the flour.[57]

---

[53] 15 January 1825 Directive, delo 7218, list 20.

[54] 26 January 1825 Report, delo 7220, listy 93–94.

[55] 28 February 1825 Directive, delo 7218, listy 23–24.

[56] 10 March 1825 Directive, delo 7218, list 27.

[57] 7 March 1825, Petition from Mikhail Ivanov and Tikhon Zakharov with 75 Comrades, delo 7223, list 21–21 ob.; 15 March 1825 Directive, delo 7218, list 28–28 ob.

The rest of 1825 and 1826 saw more pleas for help as the peasants' situation worsened. Gagarin continued to admonish Romanov to be more vigilant and to assign all the able men to the work details. The policy of work on other estates suffered a setback in late March and early April, when eight men on the work detail died from an illness. In August, however, Romanov had some good news for Gagarin. He wrote that the rye crop "praise God" was excellent. The spring grains, on the other hand, were not doing well, because the poor peasants had to use low-quallity seed purchased from nearby land-lords. Despite the impending good harvest, the peasants needed to purchase more rye flour for food.[58] The long-term effects of the crop failures, Romanov was warning, would not be easily overcome. While the peasants vividly de-scribed their economic woes, they minimized successes.

At the same time that Romanov, the mir, and Gagarin were negotiating loan and work requirements, political struggles within the mir continued. Dissatisfied peasants targeted Romanov as the source of the mir's troubles. As early as June 1825 a peasant accused Romanov of not allotting him the proper share of grain loaned by Gagarin. The peasant claimed he received only a third of the grain due him, but Romanov charged him for the full portion. Six months later, in January 1826 the mir treasurer and other mir elders sent a petition listing eight offenses committed by Romanov. The mis-deeds included illegal lumbering, drunkenness, misuse of mir carts, and the unjust beating of a peasant woman. Romanov answered accusations in a sep-arate report, but the trouble continued.[59]

The accusations against Romanov confirmed Gagarin's suspicions of his estate manager. Believing that village turmoil weakened the effort to pay off debts, and wanting another, first-hand view of his estate's political and eco-nomic problems, Gagarin sent two inspectors to investigate. One came from the Moscow office and the second worked as an overseer on another Gagarin estate.[60]

The inspectors added a new dimension to the struggle for control over information by adding on-site inspection to the detailed paperwork. The two inspectors arrived on Manuilovo Estate in late October and less than a week later filed their reports. They completely vindicated Romanov, finding that a small minority of seven men had forced the scribe to send false accusations in January. The seven men included two former estate managers who had competed with Romanov in the 1810s. The wealthy Romanov had replaced

---

[58] 16 June 1825 Petition from Scribe Kirila Mironov, delo 7223, list 32–32 ob.; 10 December 1825 Directive, delo 7218, list 42; 4 March 1826 Petition from Stepan Romanov and All the Mir, delo 7228, listy 16–17; May 1826 Excerpt from Ledger of Manuilovo Carpenters Sent to Moscow Province, delo 7225; 18 August 1826 Report, delo 7228, list 14.

[59] 25 June 1825 Petition from Vasilii Nikonov, delo 7223, list 29; 18 January 1826 Petition from Treasurer Afonasei Mikhailov with All the Mir, delo 7228, list 203 ob.; 3 February 1826 Petition from Stepan Romanov, delo 7228, list 12.

[60] No Manuilovo record describes information about these men or other Gagarin officials.

the poorer Erafei Vasilev as estate manager in 1817 and then two years later was replaced by Moisei Konstantinov. Romanov then succeeded Konstantinov in 1822. Vasilev and Konstantinov joined with other political veterans to use the economic crisis to challenge their political foe. They accused him of failure to fulfill his paternal duties, of preying on the weak, and taking advantage of his position.[61]

The two inspectors' report cleared Romanov but created other problems for the serfs. Tackling the arrears problem by compiling a household economic census and a detailed debt ledger, they exhaustively inventoried each household, listing everything from the number of poultry to the deportment of each male worker. The debt ledger recorded how much each household owed for 1825, 1826, and previous years. It also noted how many men the household sent on work details and how much they earned. The inspectors then went around the estate collecting the money on hand in the households and recorded the payment in the ledger. This exhaustive effort garnered 4,152.15 rubles, the largest sum collected in months. Yet this sum and a credit of 8,555.81 rubles for work detail wages still left a debt of 22,252.66 rubles.[62]

The inspectors concluded their stay by reporting on general conditions on the estate. The two agreed with the peasants' claims that they were "poor (bednyi)" due to the crop failures. However, the rest of the report confirmed Gagarin's deepest suspicions. Several peasants, they claimed, were poor from "not trying and laziness," because they lived at home without engaging in any kind of by-employment at home or off the estate and centered their hopes on future harvests. With this attitude, the inspectors concluded, it would hardly be possible to get the outstanding arrears from them. There were several peasants of excellent deportment, the two assured Gagarin, but they were a minority.[63]

The inspectors then contested the peasants' long-standing argument that poor soil quality lowered agricultural productivity and made it difficult to handle rent increases. The gray soil was mixed with "black earth (chernozem)" and was "fertile (khleboroden)." It was a pity, the two men observed, that the peasants did not sow all the available land, but instead kept it empty or in grasses. Grain yields were also low, because the peasants manured very little

[61] Bohac, "Family, Property, and Socioeconomic Mobility," pp. 273–74. In 1813 Vasilev owned two horses, Konstantinov owned three, and Romanov, seven. In 1826 the three men possessed two, five, and eight horses, respectively. The allies of Vasilev and Konstantinov owned four, three, three, three, and two horses. 18 August 1826 List of Disobedient Peasants, delo 7228, listy 39–43.

[62] 1 November 1826 Report, delo 7228, list 52–52 ob.; 1 November 1826 Household Economic Census, delo 7226; November 1826 Investigation of Peasant Request, delo 7228, listy 59–68; 1 November 1826 Ledger of Manuilovo Arrears, delo 7227.

[63] 3 November 1826 Report from Overseer Eremei Afonasev and Clerk Mikhail Karpov, delo 7228, list 66.

of the seeded land.[64] The inspectors had shifted the cause of the estate's economic woes from poor soil and weather to laziness and incompetence. In fact, their report reflected their preconceptions more than it did the reality of Manuilovo agriculture. The peasants clearly understood the importance of manuring, for instance, but simply did not have the laborers or livestock to cover all the land.[65] Nevertheless, the inspectors confirmed Gagarin's suspicions by uncovering the footdragging he had always suspected.

The inspectors' report resulted in a drastic alteration of the peasants' work regimen. The next spring the estate manager reported eighty-five men being sent on work details. The men were not being sent to other Gagarin estates, but to St. Petersburg. Romanov appointed foremen to find employment and lodging, collect the pay, and transfer their earnings to a Gagarin official in St. Petersburg.[66] The long journey made the work details more inflexible. The peasants had to wait for the Volga river ice to thaw in order to take barges to the capital, where they generally stayed for six months. The long journey meant the peasants could now work only during the agricultural season and could not send the young and physically unfit.

After initiating the St. Petersburg migration, Gagarin turned to the second phase of his campaign to ensure rent payments. The inspectors had shown him the importance of having his own representatives on the estate. In August he sent a clerk from the Moscow office to be the estate's new scribe. Within two weeks after his arrival, the scribe, Semen Semenov, sent a report lamenting the poor use of arable land, just as the inspectors had previously done.[67] The new scribe quickly fulfilled his duties by confirming Gagarin's suspicions.

With the scribe's arrival, Gagarin entered the final phase of his campaign. From 1 December to 30 December 1827, there were no reports from Manuilovo estate, only silence. On the thirtieth Semenov wrote up a final ledger listing everyone's debts. Someone had noted in the margin the fate of each. Twenty-one households were to be deported to Nikol'skoe Estate in Moscow Province. Two-thirds of the remaining households were placed on barshchina. Four days later Romanov reported on the resettlement process. The households' fates, he went on, had been verified "after His departure."[68] The capitalized pronoun suggests Gagarin may have come to the estate to end rent and grain arrears, although the title could have also referred to a high Gagarin official. Over the last five years the struggle between master and

---

[64] Ibid., list 67–67 ob.
[65] Bohac, "Family, Property, and Socioeconomic Mobility," pp. 36–39. Peasants distinguished between manured and unmanured land in land sales and inheritance disputes.
[66] 5 May 1827 Report, delo 7232, list 26; 26 April 1827 Report delo 7232, listy 32–33.
[67] 29 August 1827 Report, delo 7232, list 54; 14 September 1827 Report from Semen Semenov, delo 7232, list 57 ob.
[68] 30 December 1827 Debt Ledger, delo 7231; 3 January 1828, delo 7237, list 1 ob.

serfs over the payment of arrears had escalated. A campaign that began with a new wave of paperwork now perhaps ended with a face-to-face meeting.

The only recorded resistance to Gagarin's drastic measures is an updated petition sent by the households assigned for deportation. "Do not send us to be destroyed," they pleaded. "Prepare yourself always to pray to God." The peasants for the first time used God's justice to combat the injustice committed against them. They asked why they had to suffer before all the other peasants. They explained that the debts were a result of crop failures and vainly promised to pay all debts and future assessments. The peasants concluded on a defiant note. "We are sorry how much we inconvenienced you, that we had nothing to feed our families."[69]

Gagarin selected these twenty-one households to demonstrate what he expected from his serfs. The thirty-five households that remained on obrok enjoyed arrears that averaged less than fifty rubles. Most of these wealthy households never suffered serious financial problems throughout the whole crisis. The twenty-one deported households carried much larger debts. All but five owed more than 150 rubles. Many of these households either never sent a worker or sent only one worker on the work details despite having large families.[70] Gagarin had decided these households had not tried to pay their debts. Other households were deported because they used land that was to be incorporated into the demesne.

Gagarin's reasons for deporting a final small group of households are unclear. Grigorii Ivanov, for instance, lived in one of the villages whose field land was earmarked for the demesne. His small household had worked hard to lower its debt to 110 rubles. Another village household, headed by Evdokim Anafrev, sent no one on the work detail and owed 269 rubles. Ivanov was deported and Anafrev stayed home. In another perplexing case, Danila Ivanov was deported despite living far from the demesne and owing only seven rubles. No documents reveal the rationale for sending the two Ivanovs' households, but their deportation clearly showed the Manuilovo serfs that their conception of what was just no longer mattered to Gagarin. He had demonstrated the extent of his power.

THE BARSHCHINA EXPERIMENT AND RESISTANCE

Gagarin also displayed his ability to define the burdens of serfdom to the peasants who remained on the estate. The new labor rent or barshchina meant they no longer controlled their work regimen. Under this system of labor rent, the serfs paid their dues by working in fields designated as the lord's demesne. The harvest from the demesne went to Gagarin and took the

[69] 1827 Petition from 17 Peasants, delo 7232, list 53.

[70] Data from 1 November 1826 Ledger of Manuilovo Arrears, delo 7227; 30 December 1827 Debt Ledger, delo 7231.

place of the money rent. The serfs had to work on the demesne when ordered and had to find time to work in the fields left to them.

Barshchina also increased the level of supervision over Manuilovo serfs. Romanov had to set up the demesne and organize the fieldwork. He complained that he had too many important tasks to supervise, including the surveying of the fields, the manuring, and the planting. Gagarin thought better of thrusting all that responsibility on Romanov. In early May an overseer, Ivan Ivanov, arrived from another estate to supervise the planting. After he completed that task, a top Gagarin official came and appointed Ivanov the permanent overseer and Romanov as his assistant. The official admonished them to "cultivate the fields with the greatest vigilance . . . to receive for the pomeshchik income (*dokhod*) . . . and to make certain that the well-being of the *pomeshchik* (would) not in any way be neglected."[71] The peasants' inability to pay the arrears had ended with the loss of their autonomy.

Manuilovo peasants also lost control of composing and sending reports. Ivanov took up that duty. With a handful of exceptions, Ivanov limited his reports to recitals of figures and observations directly relating to agriculture and the lord's income. He reported little about the peasants' work or conduct and instead described grain sales and the weather. His reports do not refer to any form of everyday resistance. The overseer took seriously the Gagarin philosophy that producing an income came first, paternal responsibilities second.

On the basis of that philosophy Ivanov intervened in the important peasant institution of marriage. In the only characterization he made of the estate peasants, he described single women as living "for their own pleasure" and not being of any use to their households. He then "invited" these women to marry. If they did not voluntarily marry, Ivanov threatened to send them to Nikol'skoe or a Iaroslavl paper factory. The marriages, Ivanov calculated, would add twenty work teams (*tiagla*).[72]

To resist, the peasants turned again to the use of documents. They demanded a written directive from Moscow. This demand implied Gagarin's officials were not obeying the lord's true wishes. But after the recent deportations, the peasants could not take any stronger actions. In late October, after the harvests, the marriages took place. Five girls and two widows married bachelors from Nikolskoe who came back to their former estate to find brides. Twenty-one other girls and widows married local boys. Six more marriages were pending. All twenty-seven couples, Ivanov explained, were married without coercion.[73] The overseer ignored his original threats in order to make the case that peasants were voluntarily cooperating.

---

[71] 25 March 1828 Report, delo 7237, list 23; 20 May 1828 Report, delo 7237, list 47; 15 June 1828 Instructions from Ivan Kappel, delo 7237, list 90.

[72] 5 September 1828 Report from Ivan Ivanov, delo 7240, listy 17–17 ob.

[73] 23 October 1828 Report from Ivan Ivanov, delo 7237, list 204.

Early the next year Gagarin officials won another battle. The rent assessment for those still on obrok rose from just over twenty rubles to twenty-five
rubles per soul.[74] The estate archives do not reveal any resistance. Despite
the high arrears, no increases in the level of productivity, and little inflation,
the peasants had to accept the same type of increase they had previously
resisted.

The peasants concentrated their efforts on slowing down the payment of
arrears. At the end of the first year of barshchina, the total debt stood at
14,781.90 rubles, a drop of about 8,000 rubles from the total owed two years
earlier in November, 1826.[75] About 5,000 rubles of this payment may have
come from the deported peasants whose debts were probably transferred to
Nikolskoe Estate. Another 3,700 was paid soon after the deportation. Since
that last payment, the peasants had done little to take care of the debt. The
1828 rent paid by the thirty-five obrok households went to buy livestock and
supplies for the demesne.[76] Gagarin never credited income from the demesne toward payment of past debts.

Working on the demesne made it difficult for the peasants to earn money
to pay off the debts. They realized they could not erase the debts in the two-
year period Gagarin had stipulated and asked for an extension. The request
came through Ivanov. His plea echoed the peasant petitions from the last
two decades. It is not clear if he was merely describing the mir's opinion, or
if he had come to accept the mir's point of view. A sufficient number of peasants, he argued, were in the poorest of conditions and could not pay. This
year, he concluded, the harvest was inadequate, and the peasants feared
they could not meet their obligations.[77]

Ivanov proposed to solve the peasants' difficulties by returning all of them
to obrok. He asked Gagarin to show his "goodwill" and release the peasants
back to "traditional rent (*pervobytnoe ikh obrochnoe sostoianie*)." Gagarin
agreed. A March 14th directive ordered Ivanov to inspect the estate one final
time, leave instructions for taking care of the demesne fields and livestock,
and return to his home estate. Ivanov carried out his orders in just three days
and left the estate, leaving his wife and children behind to follow him later.[78]

In his final instructions Ivanov cautioned Romanov and Semenov to "supervise for the good (*vygody*) of Your Majesty without any kind of neglect."[79]
For his good or profit, Gagarin had instituted the labor rent and deportations. Now for his good, he had decided to return his serfs to money rent.

[74] 20 February 1829 Report, delo 7240, list 92.
[75] 26 August 1828 Obrok Ledger, delo 7240, listy 84–85.
[76] January 1829 Obrok Ledger, delo 7240, listy 61–62.
[77] 30 January 1829 Report from Ivan Ivanov, delo 7240, list 21–21 ob.
[78] Ibid., 16 March 1829 Letter from Ivan Ivanov, delo 7240, list 178–178 ob.
[79] 16 March 1829 Instructions from Ivan Ivanov to Stepan Romanov and Semen Semenov,
delo 7240, listy 179–180; 21 March 1829 Report, delo 7240, list 178–178 ob.

The estate records offer no clues explaining Gagarin's decision to end bar-shchina. I have no document listing the total gross income from the de-mesne. The income at best could probably have only matched the previous obrok payments. This small amount did not warrant the added expense and trouble of supervising a barshchina estate. Manuilovo obrok in previous years brought only one-sixth of the profits from a barshchina estate in Tam-bov province.[80]

In any case, Gagarin had taught the peasants a lesson. He had deported twenty-one households, twice changed the type of rent, initiated the St. Pe-tersburg migration, increased the number of tax units, arranged for mar-riages, and raised the rent. The modest flow of income from the estate would resume, and he could devote his resources to other ventures.

STALEMATE

When Ivanov left, the peasants slowly began to assert themselves, but more than ever stressed their willingness to cooperate with Gagarin. Two weeks after the overseer departed, Romanov asked Gagarin to return a piece of land the mir had given to Gagarin to use in the demesne. The peasants had ex-changed their land for a less fertile plot. They reminded Gagarin that they had willingly agreed to exchange the strips. Now, however, they had re-turned to obrok and needed the better land. The lord's land was also cross-stripped with their own, and so it was difficult for peasants to move their livestock on and off their own land. In order to prevent harming a good relationship, the peasants argued, they needed to have their former land back.[81] The mir had learned its role was to act for the "good" of Gagarin. Its petition emphasized peasant cooperativeness and the economic importance of the transfer.

A request sent a month later reiterates the peasants' willingness to play their subservient role. The mir wanted aid for the purchase of substitutes for the military draft. Romanov reminded Gagarin of the hard work the serfs were doing in the lord's fields and told him an infectious disease had killed many cattle. "All our children are your slaves," he concluded, "and pay their duties."[82]

Other requests show more assertiveness. Romanov complained that the mir could not afford to send the former overseer's wife back to her estate. She wanted to leave in the middle of the planting season, when labor and carts were difficult to find and expensive. He proposed that her entourage be routed through other Gagarin estates, so they could pay part of the ex-

[80] Hoch, *Serfdom and Social Control in Russia*, pp. 13–14.
[81] 28 March 1829 Report, delo 7240, list 177–177 ob.
[82] 16 April 1829 Report, delo 7240, listy 172–173.

penses. Gagarin turned down Romanov's plan, but delayed the woman's departure until after the planting.[83]

Romanov and some of the other peasants moved aggressively to capitalize on the losses of the twenty-one deported households. Four wealthy households obtained permission to partition, an act denied during the 1820s. The new branch households formed by the partitions moved onto farmsteads abandoned by the deported peasants and purchased the farmsteads' buildings. Other peasants, including Romanov, used other abandoned buildings.[84] Romanov also asked to use one of the horses still left in the demesne's stables to ride when inspecting the lord's rye fields.[85]

Romanov's self-aggrandizement was stopped less than a year later. Political opponents claimed that he and the scribe had stolen rye worth almost 140 rubles from the lord's granary. Romanov explained that he was borrowing the grain and had planned to replace it. He had wanted to report his actions to Gagarin, but the scribe did not want to bother the prince. The peasants were angry, Romanov claimed, because they blamed him for the barshchina, the deportations, and the arrears collection. Romanov's defense failed and in 1830, with Gagarin's approval, the mir replaced him. The scribe was sent to another assignment.[86]

The mir had cast off many reminders of the last three years' misery. The demesne had been broken up and the last of the lord's rye harvested and sold. The estate manager who had failed to avert the disaster had been ousted. The overseer had been gone for a year, and now the scribe whose arrival had signaled the beginning of their time of troubles was expelled.

The peasants still had to send men to St. Petersburg, pay the debts, and keep up with current rent payments. The St. Petersburg migration continued without much resistance. The peasants may have come to enjoy the higher wages and the relative independence they had in St. Petersburg. The wages were high and in good years paid the estate's obrok. Only once did a Manuilovskoe peasant on assignment in St. Petersburg run away to find better work.

The peasants may never have paid off the debts from the 1820s. In 1830 and 1831 the peasants paid the current rent and the scheduled installment for the past years' debts. In 1832, poor weather gravely damaged the rye crop, and cholera prevented the men from migrating to St. Petersburg. The crop failed again in 1833, and peasants could not pay the last two installments of the debt accrued before the barshchina experiment. They also had to ask for more grain loans. In 1835 they owed 12,225.87 rubles for part of the

---

[83] 23 May 1829 Report, delo 7240, list 165; 13 June 1829, delo 7240, list 163.

[84] 16 May 1829 Register of Households Requesting Partition, delo 7240, listy 167–168.

[85] 16 April 1829 Report, delo 7240, list 172.

[86] 11 February 1830 Report, delo 7238, listy 60–61 ob.; 20 April 1830 Petition from Stepan Romanov, delo 7238, list 69; 15 April 1830 Report, delo 7238, list 71–71 ob.

1834 rent and other debts. In 1840, two years before Gagarin's death, the debt had dwindled to 2,063.15 rubles, but 41.9 percent of the estate's households still owed money.[87]

The Gagarins never found a completely satisfactory method to ensure rent payments. Periodic crop failures and ensuing arrears presented problems again in the early 1850s. Rent arrears, unpaid grain loans, and political turmoil led the Gagarin family to appoint another overseer from outside the estate. He lasted no longer than Ivanov in the late 1820s, and was replaced by a local peasant who had worked as an overseer on another Gagarin estate. Gagarin supervision through record keeping also intensified. Detailed ledgers recorded changes in *tiagla* assessment, and ten household economic censuses were compiled between 1851 and 1861.[88] The struggle over the control of information continued until Emancipation.

CONCLUSION

Manuilovo serfs never quit their struggle to lessen the burden of serfdom. They continually argued that Gagarin ought to follow certain norms in assessing the money rent. In their opinion, labor shortages, infertile soil, and a poor climate should limit the amount of rent and taxes demanded. Crop failures obligated the owner to send grain loans which did not need to be paid back quickly. These shared norms formed an ideology that could be used by individual petitioners or the mir acting as a collective. Manuilovskoe serfs even used the concept of reciprocal duties against one another by accusing political opponents of taking advantage of the poor and defenseless, of pilfering wood, or embezzling.

When Gagarin tried to circumvent this interpretation of duties by increasing rents or demanding that the men go on work details, the peasants used everyday resistance to erode the serfowner's orders. They employed flight and illegal lumbering on a limited basis, but foot dragging served as the most common and effective form of resistance. The serfs tried to avoid the work details by sending the elderly instead of the able-bodied or by hiring substitutes. The most effective form of footdragging, however, became the use of the deferential petition or report. A petition pleading poverty or a report declaring the estate manager's inability to carry out a policy slowed down the implementation of Gagarin orders. A shrewd estate manager could make the public report a covert act by implying he had no direct knowledge of an action or was merely reporting the wishes of the mir. The foot dragging de-

---

[87] 3 September 1833 Report, delo 7246, list 1; September 1833 Report, delo 7246, list 20; 7 March 1835 Report, delo 7249, listy 40–43; 20 March 1840 Debt Ledger, delo 7259, listy 1–4 ob.

[88] 17 July 1851 Report, delo 7282, list 43; April 15, 1852 Report, delo 31.

layed increases in rent and led to smaller work details. It could not prevent Gagarin from changing the type of rent or from establishing the work details.

The concept of everyday resistance broadens our awareness of the variety of weapons Russian peasants could use against serfdom. A wide range of individual and collective acts of resistance fill the space between submissiveness and violent outbursts of rebellion in our conception of the peasants' reaction to serfdom. On the Manuilovo Estate these collective acts played off of one another, reinforced one another, and sometimes coalesced into a resistance that appears to have been greater than the sum of its parts. As the crisis of the 1820s showed, the level of resistance could intensify, as could the serfowner's counterattacks. On the Manuilovo estate, resistance never escalated into rebellion. The lack of a rebellion is not explained well by the concept of everyday resistance. Perhaps the small deeds of everyday resistance needed the support of external circumstances, such as the perceived weakening of the power of the landlord or local authorities, in order to widen into direct conflict. But the possibility of rebellion, nevertheless, remained. And in the meantime, everyday resistance sustained both the rhetoric and practices necessary to challenge the bonds of serfdom.

CHAPTER 8

THE BLACK AND THE GOLD SEALS: POPULAR PROTESTS AGAINST THE LIQUOR TRADE ON THE EVE OF EMANCIPATION

David Christian

> Local people [in Spassk, a district town in
> Tambov Province] claim that there appeared
> amongst them an unknown person, called
> "towndweller" (*meshchanin*) Kochkin, who
> had two seals: one gold, proclaiming
> freedom for all landlords' serfs, and
> the other black, and proclaiming the sale of
> vodka at 3 rubles a bucket.[1]

VODKA AND EMANCIPATION

HISTORIANS are generally agreed that the abolition of serfdom in 1861 marks a major turning point in modern Russian history. But why did the government undertake a reform that was bound to undermine the economic position of its most reliable supporters—the landed gentry? For Soviet historians, who have long classified the 1861 reform as the point at which a whole mode of production (feudalism) was abandoned, the problem is particularly acute. And it has been a matter of slight embarrassment that so momentous a transition occurred in the absence of a revolution. However, Lenin's writings offered a neat solution to this dilemma by arguing that the tsarist government acted under the threat, if not of a revolution, then at least of a "revolutionary situation." Lenin first offered the concept of a "revolutionary situation" to describe social and political crises in which revolution was averted by timely concessions; and he regarded mass popular protest as one of the

---

[1] *Pod Sud. Supplement to the Bell*, 1 April 1860, in A. I. Gertsen, and N. P. Ogarev, *Kolokol*, vol. 10 (facsimile ed.; Moscow, 1962), pp. 45–46.

three distinguishing features of a "revolutionary situation."[2] Lenin's plausible idea provided the theoretical basis for the research program of Soviet historians, led by M. V. Nechkina, which aimed to document in detail the "revolutionary situation" preceding the abolition of serfdom.[3] Not surprisingly, Nechkina and her colleagues had little trouble in identifying a widespread popular movement of protest in the period they examined. They could even claim the authority of Marx, who wrote in January 1860: "In my opinion, the greatest events in the world at present are, on one hand, the American slave movement . . . and, on the other hand, the Russian slave movement."[4]

But there is a surprising, and long-neglected, difficulty with this theory. Soviet historians have identified three waves of popular protest in this period. Of these, however, only one preceded the promulgation of the emancipation act, and therefore counts as a possible cause. This wave peaked in 1859. But of the 938 separate reports of peasant insubordination listed during this year, as many as 636 (68 percent) involved either boycotts of vodka sales or attacks on taverns.[5] Numerically, therefore, protests against the liquor trade were the most important single element in the movement of popular protest which preceded the promulgation of the emancipation statute.[6] As Ia. I. Linkov wrote in 1952: "In terms of scale, the first place in the peasant

[2] The other two were: increased pressure on working-class living standards and a crisis within the ruling classes. "The Collapse of the Second International" (May–June 1915), *Collected Works*, 4th ed. (Moscow, 1963), vol. 21, pp. 213–14. Lenin explicitly cited the 1859–1861 crisis as an example of what he meant.

[3] Its results are summarized in M. V. Nechkina, ed., *Revoliutsionnaia situatsiia v Rossii v seredine XIX veka* (Moscow, 1978). Recent Soviet accounts are more skeptical of this theory. See L. G. Zakharova, *Samoderzhavie i otmena krepostnogo prava v Rossii. 1856–1861* (Moscow, 1984), also available as "Autocracy and the Abolition of Serfdom in Russia, 1856–61," trans. and ed. G. M. Hamburg, *Soviet Studies in History*, 26, no. 2 (Fall 1987): 11–115; and G. Popov, "Fasad i kukhnia 'velikoi' reformy," *Ekonomika i Organizatsiia Promyshlennogo Proizvodstva* no. 1 (1987): 144–175.

[4] Cited in Nechkina, ed., *Revoliutsionnaia situatsiia*, p. 133.

[5] V. A. Fedorov, "Krest'ianskoe trezvennoe dvizhenie, 1858–1859 gg.," in *Revoliutsionnaia situatsiia v Rossii v 1859–1861 gg.*, 2 (Moscow, 1962), p. 125; S. B. Okun', ed., *Krest'ianskoe dvizhenie v Rossii v 1857–1861 gg.: Dokumenty* (Moscow, 1963), p. 736. The common Russian word for "vodka" at this time was *vino*, but as the word *vodka* was often used as a synonym and is, in any case, the familiar English translation, I will translate both Russian words as "vodka" in what follows.

[6] One hundred and ninety-two instances of peasant insubordination were reported in 1857; 528 in 1858; 938 in 1859; 354 in 1860; and 1,370 in the first half of 1861, the year in which emancipation was officially proclaimed. Okun', ed., *Krest'ianskoe dvizhenie*, p. 736. The extent of the unrest in 1859 was long masked by the inflation of figures for 1858. See Daniel Field, *The End of Serfdom: Nobility and Bureaucracy in Russia, 1855–1861* (Cambridge, Mass., 1976), pp. 52–53 and A. S. Nifontov, "Statistika krest'ianskogo dvizheniia v Rossii v 50-kh gg. XIX veka," *Voprosy istorii sel'skago khoziaistva, krest'ianstva i revoliutsionnago dvizheniia v Rossii* (Moscow, 1961), p. 186.

movements of the years before the reform is held by the so-called 'temperance protests.' "[7] Indeed, so crucial are the liquor protests to the theory of a "revolutionary situation" that many Soviet historians have felt obliged to claim that the protests were not directed merely at the liquor trade but were, in fact, an expression of a general movement of protest against serfdom. Thus, Ia. I. Linkov adds that: "the temperance protests . . . represented a distinctive (*svoeobraznoi*) form of anti-feudal protest on the part of the broad popular masses."[8] And the major Soviet study of the liquor protests concludes: "The temperance movement was a manifestation of the fight against the feudal-serf system as a whole. In many cases . . . it linked directly with the fight of the enserfed peasantry for 'land and freedom.' "[9]

But what had protests against vodka traders to do with "land and freedom"? Or (to return to our initial quotation) what was the connection between the gold and black seals carried by "towndweller" Kochkin? This essay will explore these questions by examining the liquor protests of 1858 to 1859.[10] It attempts to explain the real meaning of "towndweller" Kochkin, whose gold and black seals announced the simultaneous arrival of freedom and of cheap vodka. It will argue that there were, indeed, links between the issues of liquor and emancipation, but they were far less direct than Soviet interpretations imply.

THE LIQUOR PROTESTS: THREE PHASES

PHASE 1: THE LITHUANIAN VODKA BOYCOTTS, 1858–1859

The liquor protests went through three distinct phases. They began in the Catholic provinces of Lithuania (see the map on p. 267), with disciplined and peaceful boycotts of vodka sales. In September 1858, with support from the local Catholic clergy, consumers in the townships and villages of Lithuania began to take oaths of abstention from vodka. The first report in a national paper appeared in *Moskovskiia Vedomosti* in December.

[7] Ia. I. Linkov, *Ocherki istorii krest'ianskogo dvizheniia v Rossii v 1825–1861 gg.* (Moscow, 1952), pp. 176–77.

[8] Linkov, *Ocherki*, 176–77.

[9] Fedorov, "Krest'ianskoe trezvennoe dvizhenie," p. 112.

[10] Apart from Dobroliubov's contemporary account, which retains its value, there are only two modern accounts. See N. A. Dobroliubov, "Narodnoe delo: rasprostranenie obshchestv trezvosti," in *Sobranie sochinenii v 9-ti tomakh*, ed. B. I. Bursov et al. (Moscow-Leningrad, 1962), 5, pp. 246–85; first published in *Sovremennik*, no. 9 (September 1859), sec. 3, pp. 1–36, and signed N. T-nov; Fedorov, "Krest'ianskoe trezvennoe dvizhenie"; and G. Lur'e, "Piteinye bunty 1859 goda i P.P. Linkov-Kochkin," in *Zven'ia*, nos. 3–4 (1934): 426–69. In addition, the following account uses Russian newspapers and journals for 1858 and 1859. It is part of a larger study of the vodka trade in this period: David Christian, *"Living Water": Vodka and Russian Society on the Eve of Emancipation* (Oxford, 1990).

Three months ago, peasants from Kovno Province made solemn under-takings in their churches (without outside interference) to drink no more vodka. To this day, they have kept their promise with remarkable stub-bornness, despite cunning attempts by the Jews to attract them back to the taverns, and in spite of the fact that as a result of these events there has been a temporary fall in the price of vodka in certain localities.[11]

Despite the disclaimer, the initiative seems to have come from the Catholic clergy of Kovno. Inspired by the tsar's visit of September 6–9 (according to the police, they even claimed the tsar's blessing for their project)[12] they had founded a local branch of the "Brotherhood of Sobriety," originally estab-lished by Pius IX.[13] In Vilnius, a book was published in Lithuanian to publi-cize the society's aims.[14] This explained procedure for enrolling members af-ter they had taken solemn oaths of abstention in church. The oaths demanded total abstention from hard liquor (except for "medicinal pur-poses"), though they allowed the consumption of beer, mead, and wine, but never to the point of drunkenness. (As this clause shows, it was vodka that was the target of the movement rather than alcohol in general.) Members were instructed to watch one another's behavior, and those who broke the oath were to be expelled from the society and cut off from contact with other members. But those who persisted were promised a full pardon both for sins already committed and for those in contemplation.

But while the clergy were important, the movement spread so rapidly and had such an impact that it clearly met with popular approval. As one com-mentator put it, "the words of the priests fell on fertile ground."[15] In Vil'no Province it was reported that the slowness of the clergy in organizing similar movements led to "complaints and criticisms of the local parish clergy on the part of the common people."[16] There is even evidence that in Vilnius some local artisans spontaneously formed their own temperance societies.[17] By De-cember, the movement was spreading beyond Kovno Province, to Vil'no and Grodno.[18] And by May 1859, it was claimed that three-quarters of the popu-lation of Vil'no Province had joined.[19] The degree of popular enthusiasm for

[11] *Moskovskiia Vedomosti*, no. 145, 4 December 1858.

[12] *Svedeniia o piteinykh sborakh*, 5 vols. (St. Petersburg, 1860–1861), 2, p. 232.

[13] *Ekonomicheskii Ukazatel'*, 12 February 1859, pp. 177–79, letter of A. Rudzskii.

[14] *Ekonomicheskii Ukazatel'*, 24 January 1859, pp. 43–44, review of "O bratstve trezvosti ili vozderzhaniia."

[15] "Sovremennaia khronika,"*Otechestvennye Zapiski*, no. 3 (1859): 22.

[16] "Zapiska o prichine upadka vinnykh otkupov v Kovenskoi gub. 1860," cited in S. A. Lazutka, *Revoliutsionnaia situatsiia v Litve 1859-1862 gg.* (Moscow, 1961), p. 90.

[17] *Ekonomicheskii Ukazatel'*, no. 11, March 1859.

[18] *Svedeniia*, 2, p. 232.

[19] Dobroliubov, "Narodnoe delo"; Dobroliubov's source was *Russkii Dnevnik*, no. 22, 28 January 1859.

the movement is also suggested by the fact that it was the consumers themselves, rather than the priests, who insisted on punishing those who broke
their oaths.[20]

> In Lukniki, in Shavli District, one state peasant got drunk, in spite of
> having taken the pledge. When they found out about this, the whole
> village seized the traitor (izmennik), this slave of habit, attached to his
> back a sign saying "drunkard," and, with a drummer in front, led him
> twice around the village.[21]

The judicial methods used in such cases reflected, not upper class judicial
rituals, but the rural tradition of charivari, with the one significant difference—that a boycott movement did not permit the traditional ritual of reconciliation, in which the victim purchased vodka for the rest of the community.[22]

The staying power of the Lithuanian boycott movement also indicates the
depths of support for it, for in this region the movement survived for four or
five years.[23] Further, it cut deeply into liquor sales. In February, the Kovno
tax farmer attempted to renegotiate his contract with the government on the
grounds that "circumstances had arisen which had not been foreseen when
the contract was concluded."[24] By the middle of 1859, the liquor tax farmers
in Kovno and Vil'no Province were bankrupt, and the government had to
take direct charge of liquor sales.[25] Liquor sales had fallen by 40 percent in
Vil'no Province, 33 percent in Grodno Province, and an astonishing 70 percent in Kovno Province.[26]

By February, newspaper correspondents sympathetic to the movement
were claiming that drunkards could no longer be found in Kovno Province,
that taverns were empty, distilleries were closing, and grain prices had
fallen, while in Kovno town itself:

> The beneficient fruits of this happy change amongst the people are strik-
> ing: the price of consumables has fallen, there is much less begging, and
> the population of the region is in the best of health. It is remarkable that
> during this time there has appeared in Kovno Province not one of the
> epidemic diseases which used to be customary visitors at this time of
> year.[27]

[20] Lazutka, Revoliutsionnaia situatsiia, p. 93.

[21] Dobroliubov, "Narodnoe delo," p. 274.

[22] On charivari, see Stephen P. Frank, "Popular Justice, Community and Culture Among
the Russian Peasantry, 1870–1900," Russian Review 46, no. 3 (July 1987): 239–65.

[23] Lazutka, Revoliutsionnaia situatsiia, p. 93.

[24] Ekonomicheskii Ukazatel', no. 178, 1859.

[25] Svedeniia, 2, p. 240.

[26] Svedeniia, 4, pp. 2, 3, 184–214, 362–63.

[27] Ekonomicheskii Ukazatel', 28 February 1859.

PHASE 2: THE GREAT RUSSIAN VODKA BOYCOTTS, JANUARY–MAY 1859

During the second phase of the protests, which began in December, boycotts spread to the Orthodox Great Russian provinces (see map 4). In village after village, peasants took public oaths of abstention from vodka in the churches. The first report appeared in a letter to *Moskovskiia Vedomosti*, written by a serfowner from Balashov District in the Volga province of Saratov, on December 16, 1858.

> This is what I heard from a Serdobsk serfowner. In Serdobsk District there is a village of modest size; in the village there is, of course, a tavern; the owner does not live on the estate, and the peasants are managed by a baliff or clerk. . . . In the autumn, the peasants gathered together in the mir (commune) and decided to abstain from vodka, and they held firm until the trustee [of the local tax farmer] came to the village. "Eh!, Peasants!", he said. "Your beards may be large but your minds are small. Don't you know that one ruble of the price of each bucket goes towards the purchase of your freedom?" [This, of course, is the first link between freedom and cheap vodka.] The peasants believed him and by evening almost all the tavern's liquor was consumed. Ruin for the peasants; profits for the tavern; and honor and glory to the trustee for his cunning.[28]

The trustee's attempt to link vodka drinking with emancipation was not pure improvisation. In December 1857, the famous tax farmer, Vasilii Kokorev, had proposed that tax farmers should contribute ten million rubles to the redemption of serf land.[29] But this was one of the few occasions on which the linking of the issues of emancipation and vodka favored the liquor traders.

Soon other, more successful, boycotts were organized. A report from Severki village in Balashov District (Saratov Province), recounted how,

> the villagers agreed not to drink vodka. At the first bazaar, rumors about this spread and other peasants began to follow their example so that at present [mid February 1859] in Balashov, Serdobsk, and Kirsanov Dis-

---

[28] *Moskovskiia Vedomosti*, no. 1, 1859, pp. 2–3; a bucket (*vedro*) was about 12.3 liters.

[29] "Sovremennaia letopis," *Russkii Vestnik*, book 2 (December 1857): 212–17. The manager of the Balashov tax farm, Ogurtsov, may have read of Kokorev's proposal in *Russkii Vestnik*; but he probably also read of it in Alexander Herzen's *Kolokol*, copies of which were supplied to him throughout 1858, for *Kolokol* made no less than five enthusiastic references to Kokorev's proposal between March and September 1858. See V. N. Shablin, "Obshchestvennaia zhizn' Saratova v otrazhenii periodicheskikh izdanii 50–60 godov XIX v.," in *Sbornik nauchnykh rabot studentov* (Saratov, 1968), p. 31. (My thanks to Tim Mixter for this reference.)

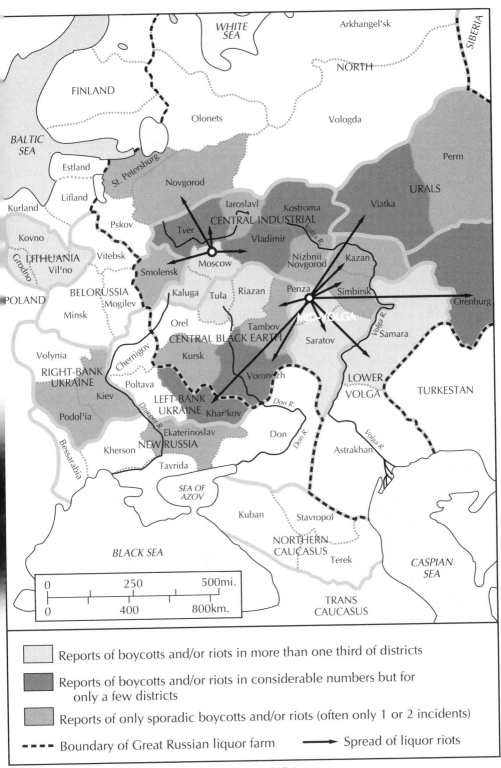

MAP 4.
Geography of Temperance Movement and Liquor Riots, 1859

tricts (the latter in Tambov Province) the majority of the peasants no longer drink vodka.[30]

In Tula Province, to the East, the first reported oath of sobriety was taken in the state peasant village of Khomut in Kashira District on December 6. Here the local state peasants agreed: to drink vodka only at home; to drink it only in quantities permitted by the commune; and to fine offenders 25 rubles for each bucket consumed illegally, or, if they were short of cash, to subject them to corporal punishment.[31]

From these provinces, the movement spread rapidly, particularly after the beginning of the new tax farm period on January 1, 1859, which was accompanied by a sharp rise in the retail price of vodka. In January and February, pledges of abstinence were reported from Saratov and Tula provinces, and also from several provinces in between—Riazan, Nizhnii Novgorod, Vladimir, Penza, and Tambov—as well as from Ekaterinoslav Province in the South. In March, there were were reports from Kaluga, Vladimir, Voronezh, Kursk, Novgorod, Samara, Tver, Iaroslavl, Moscow, Khar'kov, and Orel provinces. By the end of April, there had been reports of boycotts from eighteen provinces in Great Russia and five in the western provinces.[32] Altogether, reports of boycotts have been counted from ninety-one districts of thirty-two provinces during the entire history of the boycott movement.[33]

The Great Russian boycotts did not significantly affect the amount of vodka sold during 1859, though they may explain some of the shortfall of almost 8 percent in liquor revenues for that year.[34] And they certainly affected sales temporarily in particular areas.[35] The traditionally busy tavern of Galits village, in Tula Province, provides a sad symbol of the commercial drought endured by many tavernkeepers in the spring of 1859.

The green fir tree, emblem of the Russian Bacchus, sways and creaks in the wind. The temple is empty. The God is forgotten, and sacrificial offerings are no longer brought to him. The tavernkeeper sits sadly, arms folded, waiting, waiting for guests. But none appear. The *shtof* (see Glossary) bottles are covered with dust, and cobwebs are appearing. Very

---

[30] *Moskovskiia Vedomosti*, no. 43, 19 February 1859.

[31] *Russkii Dnevnik*, no. 35, 13 February 1859.

[32] In order of the first reports, these were, in the west, Kovno, Vil'no, and Grodno, then Podol'ia (early 1859) and Khar'kov (March 1859); in the Great Russian provinces, Saratov, Tula (late 1858), Riazan, Penza, Nizhnii Novgorod, Vladimir, Tambov, Kaluga, and Ekaterinoslav (January and February), Voronezh, Kursk, Novgorod, Samara, Tver, Iaroslavl, Moscow, Orel, and St. Petersburg (March).

[33] Fedorov, "Krest'ianskoe trezvennoe dvizhenie," p. 115.

[34] *Svedeniia*, 4, p. 70; but these shortfalls also reflected the exceptionally high prices bid for the tax farms in 1858.

[35] See, e.g., Fedorov, "Krest'ianskoe trezvennoe dvizhenie," p. 117.

pleasant this must be to the high priest of the God of *sivukha* [low-grade, unfiltered, vodka]. Where 40 buckets were sold, now they barely sell 2, and that to passing trade.[36]

PHASE 3: THE GREAT RUSSIAN LIQUOR RIOTS, MAY–JULY 1859

The third phase of the movement began in May 1859 when the protests turned violent, as consumers took the law into their own hands. The first liquor riot (*piteinyi bunt*) took place on May 12 in the district town of Nizhnii Lomov in Penza Province. It was led by one Fedor Kiselev, who claimed that his aim was to ensure the sale of cheap vodka.[37] We know little about this riot except that it introduces the name of Linkov-Kochkin, who was to feature in police reports as the mythical leader of several vodka riots, appearing in some rumors as the tsar's emissary bearing gold and black seals.

Six days later, on May 18, there was a riot in the neighboring town of Verkhnii Lomov.[38] The police reported that "state peasants from the village of Murovki sacked the main tavern, smashed the glasses, utensils and windows, and wounded the tavernkeeper, who was saved from extreme danger by troops stationed in the town. . . ." A guard was put on the tavern, and the fifteen rioters inside were handed over to the local police."[39]

During the next ten days, there were ten such riots in Penza Province alone. According to the police, large groups, consisting mainly of state peasants, surrounded the taverns,

demanding the sale of *polugar* [ordinary, unfiltered vodka] at 3 silver rubles a bucket [its official price], or of all drinks at that price, and when this demand was refused on the grounds that no *polugar* was held on the premises, . . . they looted the taverns, dragged away everything they could find, broke the vessels and even damaged the buildings.[40]

Over the next few weeks the police claimed that fifty taverns were attacked in Penza Province in seven of its ten districts; many local government officials were attacked; one army officer was wounded; and one army unit was attacked with pikes.[41] Financially, the riots were threatening enough to persuade the managers of the province's tax farms to ask the local Treasury of-

---

[36] *Moskovskiia Vedomosti*, no. 94, 22 April 1859.

[37] A. F. Dergachev, *Krest'ianskoe dvizhenie v Penzenskoi gubernii nakanune reformy 1861 goda* (Penza, 1958), p. 109.

[38] In 1843 this had 5 churches, 675 buildings (of which only 2 were brick), 5 taverns, 5,360 inhabitants, and trades in wax, honey, and tallow. Kn. S. M. Gagarin, *Vseobshchii geograficheskii slovar'*, 3 vols., 1 (Moscow, 1843), p. 318.

[39] Okun', ed., *Krest'ianskoe dvizhenie*, p. 198.

[40] Okun', ed., *Krest'ianskoe dvizhenie*, pp. 197–98.

[41] Okun', ed., *Krest'ianskoe dvizhenie*, p. 187.

fice to assume control of liquor sales, a virtual admission of bankruptcy.[42] Politically, the government took the riots seriously enough to send in the army to repress them. This the army did, under a general Iafimovich, with ruthless and terroristic efficiency. Ninety of those arrested in Penza Province were eventually sent before military courts, and twenty-eight were ordered to run the gauntlet of 300–800 blows and exiled with hard labor, while the rest were exiled to Siberia, sent to punishment battalions, or sent to prison. Of these ninety, thirty-six were state peasants, fifteen were landlords' serfs, thirty-six were retired soldiers or soldiers on leave, and three were townspeople.[43] These figures support the claim of the more liberal Ministry of State Domains, that the riots were not just the work of state peasants (as more conservative ministries had claimed), but that "landlords' serfs, townspeople, *raznochintsy* (people of indeterminate estate), retired soldiers and soldiers on leave, and even on some occasions priests" were all involved.[44]

On May 30, the liquor riots spread west to neighboring Tambov Province, and then east to the Volga provinces of Samara (June 5), Saratov (June 24), Simbirsk (July 2), Orenburg (July 9), and Kazan (July 20), as well as to Viatka in the Urals (July 20), and Voronezh Province to the South (July 5). Meanwhile, on May 31, riots broke out further to the West in Moscow Province. From there they spread more slowly and generally in a more subdued form to Tver (July 1), Smolensk (September 8), Novgorod (September 27), Arkhangel'sk (November 1), and Vladimir (November 29).[45] But the most important areas of protest were the Volga provinces of Penza, Samara, and Saratov, where memories of the great Pugachev revolt still circulated among a population of migratory workers attracted by the commercial transport routes along the Volga.[46]

In contrast to the boycotts, which were mainly a rural phenomenon, most of the riots took place in towns or large villages, and mainly on market days when large crowds were present.[47] This difference is reflected in the legal status of those arrested for "inciting" the urban riots: these included landlords, priests, town dwellers (*meshchane*), and several ex-soldiers or soldiers on leave, as well as state and landlords' peasants.[48]

In the middle of July, all newspaper discussion of vodka protests ceased, presumably at the instructions of the government censors. After July, the protests began to die away, though there were to be minor outbreaks even into the first months of 1860. Altogether, attacks were reported on 260 liquor

---

[42] Okun', ed., *Krest'ianskoe dvizhenie*, p. 534; and *Russkii Dnevnik*, no. 141, 5 July 1859.

[43] Dergachev, *Krest'ianskoe dvizhenie*, p. 115.

[44] Dergachev, *Krest'ianskoe dvizhenie*, p. 107.

[45] Dates from Lur'e, "Piteinye bunty," pp. 428–36.

[46] Fedorov, "Krest'ianskoe trezvennoe dvizhenie," p. 123.

[47] Okun', ed., *Krest'ianskoe dvizhenie*, p. 187.

[48] Okun', ed., *Krest'ianskoe dvizhenie*, p. 188.

outlets in 200 settlements in 38 districts of 15 provinces during 1859, and troops were called out in 8 provinces. According to the police, 400 people were arrested for offenses committed during liquor riots, though the figure may be as high as 780.[49]

EXPLAINING THE "LIQUOR PROTESTS"

Disagreements about the meaning of this complex movement of popular protest begin with assessments of its aims. Those who have written on the protests have described them variously as a temperance movement, as a form of anti-feudal protest, and, more mundanely, as an attempt to force down the price of vodka.

The first attempts to explain the liquor protests were made by the progressive-minded observers from the gentry class who reported on it to national newspapers and journals in the early months of 1859. Almost all the early reports portrayed the protests as a temperance movement, and by March several newspapers were running regular columns headed, "On the Spread of Sobriety." On the whole, these early reports were enthusiastic. As the economist Ivan Vernadskii argued: "For us, what is important is not so much the act of refusing to drink liquor, but the moral impulsion towards self-improvement, the recognition of the harm caused by liquor, which began this movement."[50] It is this view of the protests that has survived to the present in the label "The Temperance Movement" (trezvennoe dvizhenie), which is still frequently applied to it.

But the view that this was a temperance movement did not go unchallenged. The social and literary critic N. A. Dobroliubov wrote the first detailed analysis of the liquor protests in Sovremennik in September 1859, (though he had had to wait for two months, and to delete one third of his original draft before the censors would pass his article).[51] As a committed materialist, Dobroliubov insisted that the aim of the movement was not moral but economic: its aim was to force down the price of vodka. To Vernadskii's analysis, he replied: "We differ somewhat from Mr. Vernadskii in that we see in the spread of sobriety a phenomenon whose character is purely economic, rather than sentimental or romantic."[52]

Soviet historians have tended to agree with Dobroliubov on this.[53] But they

---

[49] Fedorov, "Krest'ianskoe trezvennoe dvizhenie," pp. 122–23; Okun', ed., Krest'ianskoe dvizhenie, pp. 187–88.

[50] Ekonomicheskii Ukazatel', no. 22, May–June 1859, cited in Dobroliubov, "Narodnoe delo," p. 268.

[51] Dobroliubov, "Narodnoe delo," pp. 580–81.

[52] N. A. Dobroliubov, "O trezvosti v Rossii: Sochineniia Sergeia Shipova, Sanktpetergurg, 1859," review in Sovremennik, no. 9 (September 1859), sec. 3, pp. 135–38; cited from Sobranie sochinenii, 5, p. 295.

[53] Most clearly in Fedorov, "Krest'ianskoe trezvennoe dvizhenie," p. 125.

have added a further claim that does not fit happily with his interpretation. This is that the deeper aim of the movement was, nevertheless, emancipation. V. I. Krutikov, for example, describes the vodka riots, without more ado, as being "only in appearance an attack on the tax farmers. In fact, they were an expression of the fight of the peasants against the feudal system, of which the tax farm was one manifestation."[54]

Commentators have also disagreed about the extent to which the protests were "spontaneous." Initial reports often stressed the involvement of priests, while police officials, like their colleagues the world over, tended to look for "instigators." On the other hand, many contemporary observers, including Dobroliubov, insisted on the movement's "spontaneity." And Soviet writers have tended to follow Dobroliubov on this as well.

Such disagreements reflect, in part, a failure to draw clear distinctions between different levels of analysis. As I will argue below, it is necessary, first of all, to be clear about the different meanings the liquor protests had for the Russian *narod* (its working people in both town and country) and Russia's *obshchestvo* (or educated high society of officials, nobles, and merchants). Unfortunately, the English language lacks equivalents for the Russian words *obshchestvo* and *narod*. But it is this distinction, for all its crudity, that provides the necessary starting point for any analysis of the liquor protests. So, in what follows, I will use the phrases "educated elite," or "upper classes," as a rough translation of *obshchestvo*; and I will use the phrase "working people," or the Russian word *narod*, to refer to both peasants and "proletarians."

I will discuss, first of all, what the liquor protests meant for Russia's "working people," in both town and country. But this question is quite distinct from the second level of analysis, which explores what the movement meant to the educated upper-class observers who described and tried to manage it. As will become clear, separating these two levels is not easy because the evidence comes, overwhelmingly, from Russia's educated elite. Nevertheless, with care, the two levels *can* be distinguished.

Finally, the two levels have to be brought together again; for upper class assessments of the movement affected the ways in which landlords and government officials reacted to, and tried to influence, the movement; while the protesters themselves knew that the movement's success would depend vitally on the reactions of landlords, police officials, and the government's own officials. As a result, the timing, extent, and outcome of the movement depended, not just on the aims of the participants, or on the reactions of Russia's elite, but on the dialectical relationship between these two levels of involvement.

In what follows, I will analyze each level in turn.

---

[54] V. I. Krutikov, *Otmena krespostnogo prava v Tul'skoi gubernii* (Tula, 1956), pp. 40–41. And see Linkov, *Ocherki*, pp. 176–77.

THE VIEW FROM BELOW: A CONSUMER PROTEST

At the level of immediate objectives, Dobroliubov was right. The liquor protests were an attempt to force down the price and raise the quality of the vodka sold in Russian taverns. In order to see why such an explanation makes sense, it is necessary to understand something of the role vodka played in the life of the Russian *narod* in this period, and of the ways in which its price and quality were regulated.

The first thing that must be stressed is that vodka was not a luxury item; it was, in practice, an item of necessity in the life of the Russian *narod*, for most forms of ceremonial depended on the drink. No marriage, baptism, or funeral could be decently celebrated without it, nor could any of the major church festivals such as Easter or Christmas.[55] Any significant economic transaction had to be sealed with a drink, and peasant justice used vodka as a way of reconciling the village with those it had punished.[56] Given the absence of home-brewed vodka, or *samogon*, before the twentieth century, this meant that there were occasions on which most households simply had to buy the stuff, however outrageous its price.[57]

The fact that vodka was an item of necessity in the households of most Russian working people meant that sudden changes in its price and quality could have a profound effect on their living standards. To protest against such changes was not a frivolous matter. It was a matter of extreme importance.

Yet in the preceding few years, the price of vodka had risen steadily. To understand why and how requires some grasp of the mechanisms through which the trade in liquor was administered in this period. Since the mid-eighteenth century, in the "Great Russian" provinces of the Russian Empire—and since the early nineteenth century, in towns within the "privileged" western provinces—the right to retail liquor had been auctioned off to "tax farmers," who handed over to the government the taxes on sales in return for temporary monopolies over the retail trade. In law, at least, both the price and quality of liquor were controlled by the government: ordinary 80-proof vodka (i.e., 40 percent alcohol by volume), or *polugar*, for example, was supposed to be sold at 3 rubles a bucket, and most liquor outlets were obliged to carry some. But despite these controls, the real price of vodka had steadily risen during the 1840s and 1850s. The basic reason for this was that

[55] See David Christian, "Traditional and Modern Drinking Cultures in Russia on the Eve of Emancipation," *Australian Slavonic and East European Studies* 1, no 1 (1987): 61–84.

[56] Frank, "Popular Justice," pp. 249, 255.

[57] I know of no firm evidence for illegal domestic distilling in Russia before the twentieth century. The history of *samogon* probably dates from the introduction of prohibition in 1914. See R.E.F. Smith and David Christian, *Bread and Salt: A Social and Economic History of Food and Drink in Russia* (Cambridge, 1984), p. 290.

competition between tax farmers led to steady increases in the amounts they bid for the tax farms at the four yearly auctions, while the level of their legal revenues remained static. As a result, they could only cover their costs if they sold vodka at above its official price and watered it down as well, and most local officials had little choice but to collude in this illegal inflation.[58]

During the tax farm auctions for 1859–1863, which were held in the middle of 1858, there occurred a remarkable increase in the amounts bid, caused partly by a sense that this might be the final chance for the tax farmers, and partly by the post–Crimean War boom.[59] As always, larger outlays meant that the tax farmers had to raise more revenue; and their first resort was to raise the price of liquor well above the official prices set by the government, while simultaneously diluting it below its official strength.[60] In Tula Province, prices began to rise right after the auctions, and local landowners protested to the government.[61] (It is probably no coincidence that some of the earliest reports of boycotts came from this province.) But the sharpest price rises came with the start of the new tax farms in January 1859. While we have no direct evidence on the extent of the price rises—since tax farmers and officials colluded to hide the real prices at which liquor was sold—there is plenty of indirect evidence on the extent of the rise.

We know, for example, that the effective tax on vodka in the Great Russian provinces rose from 1.68 rubles per capita in 1855 to 2.41 rubles in 1859.[62] Given the obligatory nature of vodka purchases, such increases were as severe in their impact as a similar rise in the level of any major tax or feudal due would have been. We also have scattered evidence on changes in prices in particular localities. Predictably, prices rose most sharply in districts where bids had been highest the previous year, such as Balashov District in Saratov Province, or Shatsk in Tambov Province.[63] Indeed, Mikhail Golitsyn, a local landlord in Balashov District, reported that prices for *polugar* rose to 6, 7, and 8 rubles a bucket wholesale, and to 10 rubles retail, while the legal price remained as it had since 1843, at 3 rubles a bucket.

---

[58] For a more detailed analysis of these mechanisms, and the corruption they generated, see David Christian, "Vodka and Corruption in Russia on the Eve of Emancipation," *Slavic Review* 46, no. 3/4 (Fall–Winter 1987): 471–88.

[59] On the postwar boom, see S. G. Strumilin, "Promyshlennye krizisy v Rossii: 1847–1907 gg.," reprinted in S. G. Strumilin, *Ocherki ekonomicheskoi istorii Rossii* (Moscow, 1960), pp. 476–83.

[60] On the commercial methods of the tax farmers, see Christian, "Vodka and Corruption," pp. 479–86.

[61] *Svedeniia*, 1, p. 202.

[62] Calculated from figures on gross liquor tax revenues in *Svedeniia*, 4, pp. 70–71, 266–69; and population figures from V. I. Kabuzan, *Narodonaselenie Rossii v XVIII-pervoi polovine XIX v.* (Moscow, 1971), pp. 159–63.

[63] From a report of the Minister of Finance, August 1858, *Svedeniia*, 3, p. 24.

These changes hurt peasant households throughout the empire and from all the different estates of peasants and workers. Prince Golitsyn added that in Balashov District the price rises were particularly galling at a time when, "the peasants of this region, having only just begun to recover from the prolonged war, and having enjoyed the heavenly blessing of two good harvests and good prices for grain, are now forced, as a result of the calculations of profiteers, to bear the value of their labor in tribute to the taverns and drink shops."[64]

Where barter was still common, the significance of such price rises was painfully clear:

> vodka in itself is alright. . . . the real harm is done when it is costly, and of poor quality, when in order to get "carried away" (*dlia togo chtob dushu otvesti*), you've got to give the tavernkeeper your overcoat, hat, axe, and cart as security, and the vodka itself is such that it only makes you feel bad, like poison. . . . This is what the people could not bear. This is why they boycotted vodka.[65]

The tax farmer, Vasilii Kokorev, wrote that:

> in many areas, where grain is cheap, in order to purchase a bucket of vodka at a market it is necessary to take, for example, three cartloads of rye. In other places . . . even 6 *sazheni* of firewood are not enough to purchase a bucket of vodka. Under such circumstances, when the peasant must part with enough grain or firewood to feed or warm himself for a whole winter in order to earn enough to purchase the vodka he needs, then he will, of course, prefer to do without vodka by taking oaths of abstention.[66]

Such comparisons were peculiarly galling in the spring, when food supplies were running low, cattle still had to be stalled indoors, and the harvest remained a long way off. By the spring, poorer households were already having to sell off grain intended for their own use, in order to buy other supplies, including, sometimes, the vodka necessary to celebrate a marriage.[67]

The issue of strength was as sensitive as that of cost, for consumers themselves had many ways of gauging the real strength of what they consumed. They could try to light it; or see how easily it froze. And there was always the direct test:

[64] Prince M. Golitsyn, letter to *Moskovskiia Vedomosti*, no. 76, 29 March 1859.

[65] Dobroliubov, "O trezvosti," p. 296.

[66] *Moskovskiia Vedomosti*, no. 124, 27 May 1859.

[67] On the dietary meaning of this part of the year, see Smith and Christian, *Bread and Salt*, pp. 331–38.

A worker . . . decides to go on the tiles, buys himself a half-*shtof* [1/20th of a bucket, c. 600 mils] and drinks it. Nothing! He buys another and drinks it. Again nothing. "What's going on?" he thinks. "Let's have another," so he has another half-*shtof*. He begins to feel slightly foggy and his belly begins to swell splendidly. Our young hero is beginning to get ripe, and, to encourage things he has another half-*shtof*. . . . A police officer who happened to be in the drink house checking up on things, took note of our wassailer and in order to prevent him from setting himself on fire took him directly to the police station. And how did this finish? As is well known, Russians have tough constitutions. The man lay down, water poured from his mouth, and still he was not drunk. When I told this story in the company of some managers of the old liquor tax farm, they just laughed with self-satisfaction. And of course it is funny. But what is it like for the poor consumers . . . ?[68]

Vodka of this poor quality was, literally, useless, and to charge money for it was seen as the grossest form of cheating.

Equally important, consumers gradually realized during the boycotts that the behavior of the tavernkeepers was illegal as well as immoral; it broke the government's laws as well as those of their own rural "moral economy." For one of the unexpected by-products of the boycott movement was an increasing awareness on the part of consumers of the fact that they did have rights under the tax farm regulations, a fact that they learned during conversations with sympathetic landlords and officials.[69] In this sense, the aim of the boycott movement was conservative, an attempt to protect existing rights. Protesters, like the "Swing" rioters in rural England in 1830, "did not normally want a disruption of the old society, but a restoration of their rights within it, modest, subaltern, but rights."[70] In their conservatism, those who protested about expensive vodka were conforming to a larger pattern of peasant protest. As Peter Kolchin writes in a superb recent study comparing Russian serfdom and American slavery: "Russian serfs resorted to protest when they felt that their collective 'rights' were being violated."[71]

We also have direct evidence to show that the aim of the boycotts was to bring down the price of liquor. Thus, the citizens of Balashov town agreed in February to hold out until the tax farmer agreed to sell vodka at 1 ruble a bucket, "and at the strength at which it is sold from the government's cellars."[72] In March, peasants of Bolkhov District of Orel Province explained

---

[68] *Russkii Dnevnik*, no. 54, 11 March 1859, letter from Perm Province.

[69] *Pod Sud*, 1 April 1860, 10, p. 45.

[70] Eric J. Hobsbawm and George Rudé, *Captain Swing* (London,1969), p. 39.

[71] Peter Kolchin, *Unfree Labor: American Slavery and Russian Serfdom* (Cambridge, Mass., 1987), p. 303.

[72] Okun', ed., *Krest'ianskoe dvizhenie*, p. 189.

that their reason for taking oaths of abstention was "the raising of the price of grain liquor by the owner of the Bolkhov tax farm, which we consider ruinous for ourselves and our families; in avoidance of which, and in order to spread amongst ourselves and our children better moral standards (*dobroi nravstvennosti*), and ensure that we can continue to pay our dues in full, we have agreed. . . ."[73] As a progressive official of the Ministry of State Domains commented later in the year, the boycotts "never had the noble object of abstention, but were always intended to strike a blow at the tax farm for charging excessive prices."[74]

Thus, the immediate object of the protests was to force down the price and improve the quality of an item of necessity in the household budget of Russian working people. This was not a "temperance movement," but a consumer boycott. Its goal was not a permanent ending of vodka consumption, but a reduction in its price; for a sharp rise in the price of vodka hurt all working people. The rise in the price of vodka in 1859 was what the removal of state subsidies on meat and bread may prove for Soviet consumers in the near future; what high bread prices had been for Parisians in 1789; or what rises in the price of salt were to urban Muscovites in 1646—a serious assault on traditional rights and living standards which had to be resisted.

THE VIEW FROM ABOVE: VODKA AND FREEDOM

But was cheap vodka the only goal of the "temperance movement"? As we have seen, Soviet historians, like many upper-class contemporaries, have argued that the protesters linked the issue of cheap vodka with that of emancipation, that their real aim was to break up the traditional social order. Indeed, "towndweller" Kochkin was himself a symbol of the fact that there was a link of some kind between the issues of freedom and of cheap vodka. But how were the two connected?

The evidence for a direct link is of several kinds. First, it has been argued that: "Although the peasants seemed to act not against the government, but against the tax farms, their actions were directed at the policies of the government, for they struck at the fiscal system of Tsarist Russia."[75] This is to confuse effects with causes. The fact that the protests threatened the treasury tells us nothing about motivations.

More important are the fragments of evidence purporting to show more

---

[73] Dobroliubov, "Narodnoe delo," p. 271; from *Moskovskiia Vedomosti*, no. 71, 24 March 1859; see *Russkii Dnevnik*, no. 56, 13 March 1859: consumers in Vladimir Province expressed a "desire not to drink vodka, because of its extraordinarily high price."

[74] *Pod Sud*, 1 April 1860, 10: 45. Herzen's anonymous correspondent was probably one Kidoshenkov, an official of the Ministry of State Domains; see also Okun', ed., *Krest'ianskoe dvizhenie*, p. 186.

[75] Fedorov, "Krest'ianskoe trezvennoe dvizhenie," p. 125.

direct links between the two issues of cheap vodka and emancipation from serfdom.[76] In Samara, for example, it was reported that peasants attacking taverns called out that soon they would do the same to landlords' houses.[77] Another variant had it that men had appeared with black and gold seals: "The Tsar had given them the golden seal in order that they should attack the landlords and demand freedom, which had been delayed only by officials, and the black seal meant that they were to attack the taverns." Once the taverns had started selling cheap liquor, then would be the time to demand freedom.[78]

However, this evidence must be treated with great care. Certainly, emissaries from a "good Tsar" were a familiar feature of popular protest in Russia in this period. They represent fragmentary echoes of the more highly developed legends about "deliverers" which circulated in Russian society from the early seventeenth century right up to the abolition of serfdom in 1861. And it was common practice for these "deliverers" to dispatch emissaries with golden seals.[79]

But in this case, at least, there is good reason to doubt that the reports of "towndweller Kochkin" are as transparent a guide to the aspirations of Russian working people as they might seem. The black seal is plausible enough. As we have seen, a clear understanding of the role of vodka in the life of the Russian *narod* shows that the activities of the tax farmers themselves provided excuse enough for protest. So we can explain the black seal all too easily—mythical emissaries were common, and cheap vodka was a serious matter.

But with the golden seal we run into problems. Why should people smash a tavern as a way of expressing their disgust with serfdom, particularly if, as in this case, most of the rioters were not themselves landlords' serfs? To suppose that state peasants, or ex-soldiers, or "towndwellers" of various kinds should have attacked taverns as a way of expressing their opposition to the continued enserfment of landlords' serfs is simply too farfetched. In any case, the principle of Occam's razor suggests that we have enough explanations already without supposing that the rioters were also attacking serfdom. We simply do not need the golden seal.

How, then, should we explain the persistent reports of an emissary with two seals? The most plausible explanation is suggested by the anonymous correspondent who supplied one of the fullest accounts of a liquor riot to

[76] For some examples, see Fedorov, "Krest'ianskoe trezvennoe dvizhenie," pp. 119–23.

[77] Fedorov, "Krest'ianskoe trezvennoe dvizhenie," p. 120.

[78] Okun', *Krest'ianskoe dvizhenie*, pp. 212, 533, and n. 140; and see Fedorov, "Krest'ianskoe trezvennoe dvizhenie," p. 121.

[79] The best account of these legends is in K. V. Chistkov, *Russkie narodnye sotsial'no-utopicheskie legendy XVII–XIX vv.* (Moscow, 1967). On emissaries with golden seals see pp. 25, 30–32.

Herzen's *Kolokol*. This correspondent pointed out that all reports of Kochkin came from police sources; he knew of no direct reports from other sources of sightings of Kochkin, or even of claims to have seen him. Indeed, attempts by the authorities to follow up such reports found that, though many rioters admitted to having heard of Kochkin, none claimed to have actually seen him. Besides, the riots in Spassk, which Herzen's correspondent described in such detail, involved very few landlords' serfs. He concluded, therefore, that the rumors of an emissary with two seals probably arose first in the minds of nervous landlords and police officials, rather than among the protesters themselves.

> There is far more reason to think that this story is a mere fantasy, and as it came from the local police, one may suspect that it is the product of inaccurate information from some careless informer. . . . As for the rumors about seals granting freedom to landlords' serfs, they were definitely created by the fears of local landlords, and perhaps by the prospect of disorders which might bring peasants together to discuss the issue of freedom.[80]

So, while Kochkin's black seal sounds genuine enough, the attribution to him of a second seal demanding the emancipation of landords' serfs sounds like an embellishment of the original legend—added, consciously or unconsciously, by nervous landlords or police officials.

We have no proof that this interpretation is correct. But it makes more sense and is more economical than the alternative. And it provides a reminder of the danger of assuming, as does K. V. Chistkov, that official or upper-class sources provide a "spontaneous and natural reflection in official written documents of the real existence of [popular] legends."[81] In reality, upper-class accounts of popular ideology are far less transparent than this casual remark suggests. All too often, they tell us more about upper-class fears than about the real aims of members of the Russian *narod*. So, even if Kochkin himself was not a figment of the official imagination, his golden seal may well have been.

As it happens, we do in fact know something about the source of these rumors, for there was a real Kochkin, P. P. Linkov-Kochkin, who had been in jail in Penza almost continuously since 1849—not, it should be noted, for his opposition to serfdom, but for his attempts to denounce the activities of the local tax farm, of which he had briefly been an employee. Linkov-Kochkin was known all too well by the local authorities, for despite his long detention, he never ceased writing petitions against those who had kept him in jail. He had been released, briefly, on March 25, 1859, but claimed that on

---

[80] *Pod Sud*, 1 April 1860, 10: 46.
[81] Chistkov, *Russkie sotsial'no-utopicheskie legendy*, p. 14.

May 12, the day of the first liquor riot in Nizhnii Lomov, he was in Penza, 110 *versty* away, delivering a further petition against the Penza tax farmers and the local authorities. One must assume that the local authorities, to whom he had long been an embarrassment, would be keen to see him behind bars once more. So we should not be surprised that Linkov-Kochkin was soon being blamed for the liquor riots. Nor should we be surprised to find that he was rearrested on May 17 and spent the rest of his life in jail or, from 1861, in exile in Iakutsk Province in Siberia. (It is pleasant to report that he managed one parting shot at his tormentors, in the form of a final denunciation of the police and tax farmers, this time in verse.)[82] Because he was arrested so soon, we know that Linkov-Kochkin cannot have been present at any riot after May 17, and he, himself, insisted that he was not present at the one riot that took place before that date. In any case, he never expressed any general political ambitions, and he submitted his many petitions against the tax farm as a loyal subject of the tsar. Like the boycotters, his aims were essentially conservative, and he claimed that the rumors about his presence during liquor riots in Penza Province were put about by his personal enemies.[83]

With evidence as tenuous as this, it is more reasonable to suppose that the liquor riots were, like the boycotts that preceded them, exactly what they seemed to be—protests against extortionate and illegal prices on an item of necessity. That, at least, was what they were for participants, even if they had a different, and much more ominous, meaning for conservative landlords and officials.

This conclusion provides the first step toward an explanation of the passage cited at the beginning of this paper. Linkov-Kochkin's courageous struggle against the Penza tax farmers made him a natural symbol of popular frustration at corrupt and oppressive tax farm practices, so the black seal carried by his mythical counterpart may well represent a genuine example of popular mythmaking. But the Kochkin who carried both black and gold seals was almost certainly the product of upper-class mythmaking; he was less a projection of popular hopes than of the fears of conservative landlords and officials, to whom the liquor riots inevitably appeared as a threat to the existing social order; and it is these upper-class observers who seem to have equipped the mythical Kochkin with his second, golden, seal.

LINKS BETWEEN PROTESTERS AND UPPER-CLASS OBSERVERS

But though it is vital to distinguish between the objectives of the protesters and upper-class perceptions of the movement, the two levels were never en-

---

[82] On Kochkin, see Lur'e, "Piteinye bunty," pp. 450–69.
[83] Lur'e, "Piteinye bunty," p. 455.

tirely distinct. There were links between protesters and upper-class observers, though they were more complex, ambiguous, and dialectical than is allowed for in the standard accounts of the liquor protests.

Dobroliubov was certainly right to criticize those contemporaries who saw the peasants as passive followers of progressive clergymen or nobles; but he was wrong to discount the role of outsiders entirely, for consumer outrage alone was not enough to explain the liquor protests. Outside encouragement was also necessary: to aid consumers organizationally, to reassure them as to the legitimacy of their claims, and to convince them that their cause was not hopeless by assuring them of the support of influential allies. And in this way, links of a kind were drawn between protesters from the *narod* and Russia's ruling elite.

As we shall see, though, the precise nature of these links changed during the two phases of the Great Russian protests. During the largely peaceful boycott movements which occurred mainly in rural areas, peasants and progressive landlords seem to have acted together against the tax farmers. In the more violent attacks on taverns which occurred mainly in the towns, townspeople and peasants visiting town on business (usually the riots took place on market days), acted on their own initiative—but they did so in response to rumors that suggested that protests against high liquor prices had official, and maybe even imperial, sanction.

V. A. Fedorov uses two main arguments to refute what he describes as the "false" view that the boycott movement in the villages of Great Russia required outside leadership: first, the rapid spread of the movement, and second, the fact that contemporaries themselves recognized that the peasants were actively involved in the movement.[84] Neither argument stands close examination. The first simply ignores chronology in supposing that boycotts emerged in different places simultaneously. In reality, there was plenty of time for news of the Lithuanian boycotts to reach the Great Russian provinces. As we will see, there is direct evidence that it did so, and that news of the Lithuanian boycotts triggered the spread of the boycotts beyond Lithuania. The second argument proves merely that consumers were not passive participants; it does not disprove the claim that outsiders were also involved in some way in the movement.

In Lithuania, the evidence for outside involvement is clear enough; from the start, Catholic priests were directly involved in initiating and spreading the movement. But in the Great Russian provinces this was not true. There is no evidence that Orthodox priests played as active a role as their counterparts in Catholic Lithuania, and, given the conditions under which they were trained and lived, they could hardly be expected to do so.[85]

---

[84] Fedorov, "Krest'ianskoe trezvennoe dvizhenie," pp. 113–14.

[85] On the ignorance, poverty, and drunkenness of the Russian clergy in this period, see

So, it is easy to miss the fact that the boycott movement *was* supported from outside, even in the Orthodox provinces of Russia, though here the outside support came from non-clerical sections of society. Part of the difficulty is that most of the newspaper correspondents on whom Dobroliubov based his study themselves insisted on the movement's spontaneity. However, the police, like police the world over, preferred to look for "instigators," and for once they may have been closer to the truth, despite their occasional descent into melodrama. In Balashov District of Saratov Province, the local police chief reported a "general conspiracy not to drink liquor," and added that these "conspiracies (*zagovory*) arose not by the general agreement of all inhabitants of the villages concerned, but at the instigation of a small number of individuals, some of whom even permitted themselves to ride to other nearby settlements to call them out."[86]

The "incitement" was there, but it was subtler than this account suggests. And noticing it requires noticing the further subtlety that what seem at first sight to be reports by neutral observers of the liquor protests are often, in reality, the reports of committed, though cautious, upper-class participants.

The evidence for outside "incitement" is plentiful even in many reports protesting the movement's spontaneity. Some protested too much. On the estate of Princess S. A. Shcherbatova, in Tula Province, peasants who had already taken an oath of sobriety then took a second oath to the effect that their original oath was *not* imposed on them as local rumors had claimed. And a report from Kaluga Province cited an extremely formal oath of abstinence, obviously drafted by an educated person, which began: "We . . . unanimously and voluntarily have agreed to accept the persuasive proposal and good advice of our landlord. . . ."[87]

Further, a careful reading of newspaper reports shows that progressive local landlords, and even some progressive government officials, had played an important, though discreet, role in initiating the movement. The first letter on the boycott movement in Balashov District was written by a local landlord and serfowner. He remarked that the first report on the Lithuanian movement

> must, of course, arouse general sympathy, particularly amongst the estate of the nobility, which has been summoned by the government to improve the life of their peasants. One may hope that every well-intentioned landlord will read this article not merely in the solitude of his study, but also to his serfs, and will attempt to arouse their sympathy

---

I. S. Belliustin, *Description of the Clergy in Rural Russia: The Memoir of a Nineteenth-Century Parish Priest*, trans. Gregory L. Freeze (Ithaca and London, 1985). On priestly drunkenness, see pp. 114–47.

[86] Okun', ed., *Krest'ianskoe dvizhenie*, p. 208.

[87] *Moskovskiia Vedomosti*, no. 89, 16 April 1859, and no. 64, 15 March 1859.

for their colleagues in Kovno, which, given the present price of vodka, should not be difficult.[88]

The same letter makes it clear that its author was not just reporting these events, but had directly encouraged them.

Success will certainly follow: at least that is what I conclude from the fact that when I read the article in no. 145 of *Moskovskiia Vedomosti* to my peasants they promised to follow the example of the Kovno peasants.[89]

This letter was anonymous. But it seems likely that its author was the same Prince Mikhail Golitsyn who reported on the further progress of the movement a few months later. According to the police, the Saratov boycotts began "on the estate of prince Mikhail Golitsyn [a village called Severki] . . . and the example of his peasants was followed by other peasants, and spread to the village of Turki in Balashov District . . ." while other reports referred to village meetings "at which newspapers were read."[90] In his letter, Golitsyn wrote that:

without any outside compulsion, landlords' serfs agreed amongst themselves, at a meeting, to address themselves in some cases to their landlord, in others to their landord's agent, with a request that they bind the villagers by counter-signing their oath of abstention from liquor.

He adds that all well-intentioned landlords immediately agreed "and began to joyfully spread the news, until it spread with telegraphic speed through the whole of Rus' " (a reference which may explain the police reports of riders carrying the news from village to village).[91] In this, as in other accounts, it is clear that the reading of newspaper reports of other boycotts, by the peasants themselves, or by their progressive minded landlords, played a crucial role in both initiating and spreading the boycotts.[92]

Reports from other regions also reveal, inadvertently, the important role played by progressive landlords in establishing and spreading the movement. In Riazan Province the first reports of boycotts attributed their appearance to the "influence of count K-v."[93] Police reports on the earliest boycotts in Penza and Tambov provinces claimed that oaths were taken and fines

---

[88] *Moskovskiia Vedomosti*, no. 1, 1859.

[89] *Moskovskiia Vedomosti*, no. 1, 1859.

[90] Okun', ed., *Krest'ianskoe dvizhenie*, pp. 189, 208.

[91] *Moskovskiia Vedomosti*, no. 76, 29 March 1859.

[92] There are many examples. See, for example, *Moskovskiia Vedomosti*, no. 148, 24 June 1859.

[93] *Ekonomicheskii Ukazatel'*, no. 2, 10 January 1859; see, for another example, a report from Orel that peasants had taken oaths of sobriety, "on the advice of their landlord"; *Russkii Dnevnik*, no. 92, 3 May 1859.

published for breaking them, in several cases "after asking the permission of their landlords."[94]

The progressive landlords' role in spreading the boycott movement was particularly important because, while popular rumor networks existed, they were nothing like as efficient or wide reaching as the networks of personal contacts and newspaper reports available to the landed gentry. Indeed, the newspapers, in which members of the educated classes had been attacking the tax farm ever since the middle of 1858, provided one of the most important of all forms of incitement. In the town of Balashov, the taking of an oath was preceded, we are told, by the holding of meetings, at which "newspapers were read, concerning the tax farm, and interpreting it in a hostile sense."[95]

But what were the motivations of these progressive landlords? After the extensive newspaper debates on the tax farm in late 1858, many landlords now realized that the extra money paid to the tax farmers as a result of higher prices threatened their own revenues from feudal dues, as well as the peasants' capacity to redeem their land after emancipation.[96] Landlords were also impressed by the prospect of a sober peasantry awaiting the dawn of freedom with patience and responsibility.

> Now [as a result of the boycott movement] it will be easy for the peasant to pay his state taxes, his local dues, and those owned to his landlord. Now we can hope that the rights which are to be granted to the peasants by their landlords, in accordance with the royal will, will be accepted calmly and reasonably.[97]

But many landlords had more specific moral and economic reasons for opposing the tax farm, whose activities had been debated so thoroughly in the press in the second half of 1858. Liberals were shocked by revelations of the massive corruption associated with the tax farm. But they also learned that the tax farm suppressed consumption of vodka by sustaining monopolistic prices; and therefore restricted distilling (which was a monopoly of the gentry) and agriculture in general, by reducing the demand for grain on the part of distillers, and restricting supplies of *barda*, the by-product of distilling used as a cattle feed.

Why should the consumers themselves have sought outside help? Outside "incitement" was important because rural consumers knew that it was extremely difficult to act on their own. To organize a vodka boycott was no easy task given the crucial role of vodka in rural ceremonial occasions (though high levels of adulteration may have made it easier). Besides, in

---

[94] Okun', ed., *Krest'ianskoe dvizhenie*, p. 190.
[95] Fedorov, "Krest'ianskoe trezvennoe dvizhenie," p. 114.
[96] These debates are discussed more fully in chapter 9 of Christian, *"Living Water."*
[97] Prince M. Golitsyn, letter to *Moskovskiia Vedomosti*, no. 76, 29 March 1859.

small communities anyone who engaged in such activities could all too easily be identified and dealt with by local landlords or government officials. So the organization of vodka boycotts was unlikely to succeed unless it had the support of local power brokers, of whom the most important, at least in serf villages, were the landlords. We have already seen an example of these difficulties in the case of the unsuccessful boycotts that began in Serdobsk District in December 1858.

Most peasants were well aware of the advantages of acting with the support of local landlords. In a casual conversation with a professed drunkard who claimed he was eager to reform, E. Protas'ev asked:

"Why do you not meet together and petition the Tsar to abolish vodka, and say that you are willing to pay the treasury so much?"

"But master how can we send in a petition; the Tsar is far from us. It's the business of you nobles to worry about such things."

"But the Tsar would not believe us if we said that you would prefer to be without taverns and would even pay for their abolition; but if you asked yourselves, things would work much better."

"But how can we write a petition; the authorities will punish us if we do. So it looks as if it really is true that God himself wants us to drink," concluded Fedot, shrugging his shoulders sadly.[98]

The fact that the rural boycotts relied on a temporary alliance between peasants and local landlords may also explain why they remained peaceful, except where individual peasants were punished for breaking them.

Of course, to argue that upper-class "incitement" was important in explaining the timing and nature of the rural boycotts is not to imply that consumers played a passive role. That they were actively involved in the movement is shown by the enthusiasm with which even state peasants took up the idea of boycotts, and by the fact that in Great Russia, as in Lithuania, it was often consumers who took the initiative in punishing those who broke the boycotts.[99] Nevertheless, it seem clear that outsiders played as vital a role in Great Russia as in Lithuania in both starting the boycotts, and spreading them.

"Instigation" from above can also be demonstrated in the case of the more violent urban protests against the liquor trade that began in May. Here, crowds of townspeople and visiting peasants attacked taverns on their own initiative, while the anonymity, size, and transience of the market-day crowds freed protesters from the restraints that had operated in the villages. But a close examination of the evidence shows that urban protesters also

[98] E. Protas'ev, "O poroke, svoistvennom krest'ianam i prepiatstvuiushchem uluchsheniiu ikh byta," *Zhurnal Zemlevladel'tsa*, no. 9 (1858), sec. 6, pp. 6–7.

[99] Fedorov, "Krest'ianskoe trezvennoe dvizhenie," p. 116.

acted in the belief that influential outsiders were on their side. In this case, though, the "incitement" came mainly from progressive officials, trying to apply contradictory policies to deal with the contradictory problems posed by the boycott movement.

Ultimately, it was the government's own inept handling of the boycott movement that provided the necessary "incitement" for the liquor riots. In March, the Committee of Ministers (*Komitet ministrov*) decided that the vodka boycotts had to be taken seriously, as they seemed to threaten both the public order and the government's finances, for in 1859 taxes on vodka yielded over 40 percent of the government's income. It was decided, therefore, to try to limit the spread of the boycotts, while simultaneously encouraging tax farmers to reduce the retail price of vodka. The three ministries most directly involved in the matter—the Ministry of Finance, which managed the liquor trade; the Ministry of State Domains, which supervised the lands settled by state peasants; and the Ministry of Internal Affairs, which was responsible for the maintenance of order—were instructed to issue circulars to this effect to their local officials. However, the precise wording of the circulars was clearly a delicate matter, for the government could hardly be seen to oppose the formation of societies aimed at encouraging sobriety; and at the same time, the Ministry of Finance was embarrassed at the prospect of appealing to the tax farmers, for it had secretly requested as late as January 19 that local government officials should overlook rises in the price of vodka.[100] The government faced a real dilemma.

The Ministry of State Domains issued its circular on March 19. This argued that drunkenness was indeed harmful and should be dealt with by the legal authorities. On the other hand, it cautioned that no one should persecute those "who consume liquor in moderate quantities and even on occasion *need* it to sustain their strength and health."[101] Consequently, it instructed its local agents to punish anyone who organized boycotts without first securing official permission. Then it turned to the tax farmers. The ministry's local representatives were advised that officials of the Ministries of Finance and Internal Affairs had instructions to ensure "that the tax farmers fulfilled exactly the obligations they had assumed, that they did not raise the retail price of drinks, and that they sold ordinary and improved *polugar* at the prices fixed in the tax farm conditions, and at the correct strength."[102] The circular also suggested that if tax farmers "permitted breaches of the law" and refused to sell at official prices, consumers should report this to the local au-

---

[100] The Ministry of Finance probably deserves our thanks, for documents as deliciously corrupt as this are rare, and can do much to brighten the sometimes humdrum life of the working historian. To the embarrassment of the government (but presumably to the delight of his readers), Alexander Herzen received a leaked copy which he promptly reproduced in his émigré journal, *Kolokol*, in its issue for 1 November 1859, 2: 454–55.

[101] *Kolokol*, 22 June 1859, 2: 382.

[102] *Svedeniia*, 1, p. 207.

thorities, who would in turn report to the governors who would "punish (*vsyskat' s*) the tax farmers" for breaking the law.[103] In the context, this last clause, despite its careful wording, was bound to be interpreted by some consumers as an invitation to protest. Meanwhile, the Ministry of Finance had issued an equally confusing circular on March 5, and the Ministry of Internal Affairs issued its instructions on March 22.[104]

The three ministerial circulars created confusion, first among the tax farmers and officials to whom they were directed, and second among the consumers who soon got to know about them. The tax farmers and their employees were confused because the circulars demanded strict enforcement of regulations whose real meaning was not easy to establish, because of the poor drafting of the tax farm regulations. Under the tax farm regulations tax farmers were obliged to sell ordinary *polugar* at 3 rubles; improved *polugar* at 4.50; *pennoe* (or "foamy" vodka) at 4 rubles a bucket, and better-quality vodkas at free prices. However, there were also complex rules on what had to be sold in what kind of institution, and in what forms. Article 69 of the 1850 regulations (which were still in effect in 1859) read: "Tax farmers are obliged to sell ordinary *polugar* as well as *pennoe* vodka in towns only from bucket shops, and in rural areas in all types of liquor outlet, except for vodka stores, depending on the wishes of the consumer, either in a sealed container . . . or by the glass. . . ."[105] These rules were complex enough, and their wording was ambiguous enough, to allow for genuine confusion.

Even more confusing for both tax farmers and local officials was the fact that the ministerial circulars contradicted long-established practice in relations between government officials and the tax farm, as for years it had been assumed that bribes protected the tax farms from official interference. And this convention had been reinforced in a Ministry of Finance circular of January 19 encouraging officials not to harass tax farmers if they were forced to raise vodka prices. Tax farmers must soon have realized that the traditional "broad" interpretation of the tax farm regulations was now under threat. But they cannot have found it easy to guess precisely what the government *did* expect of them as they knew that the *goverment* knew that the whole system might collapse if a strict interpretation of the regulations were to be enforced. In practice, many government officials simply continued protecting the tax farm as they had in the past, until they received explicit orders to the contrary.[106]

[103] Okun', ed., *Krest'ianskoe dvizhenie*, p. 533 and 140n, based on archives of the Committee of Ministers.

[104] Herzen published summaries of the last two circulars in *Kolokol*, 22 June 1859, 2: 382; the State Domains circular was printed in *Moskovskiia Vedomosti*, no. 105, 5 May 1859.

[105] *PSZ*, no. 24058, article 69, 6 April 1850. *Pod Sud*, 1 September 1860, p. 10, summarized these regulations.

[106] See, e.g., *Pod Sud*, 1 September 1860, 10, p. 74: "Without orders from their superiors in the province, it is quite possible that many district officials, accustomed for years to look on

Equally damaging for the government was the fact that muddled summaries of the various circulars soon leaked out to consumers. The police were later to see in this the main explanation for the outbreak of the liquor riots. "The peasants, having found out about these orders, interpreted them as attacks on the tax farm and began to demand cheap liquor from the taverns; and it was the refusal of these demands that provided the motivation for the violent actions of the people."[107]

Sometimes the incitement was due to more than muddle. The clearest example of what progressives saw as a defense of the rule of law, and conservatives as little less than subversion, was the behavior of K. K. Grot, the governor of Samara Province. Grot had long been an opponent of the tax farm, and since his appointment in 1853 had made a special effort to build up a group of young, well-educated, and well-paid officials who were not corrupted by the bribes of the tax farmers.[108] In 1859 he took the opportunity provided by the ministerial circulars to launch a more serious attack on the tax farm. He issued orders on April 6 and again on May 18 that police officials were to ensure that tax farmers sold liquor at the correct price and strength.[109] The order of May 18 was particularly inflammatory for it appeared in the official provincial gazette and included the official price list for liquor, together with a request that breaches of the regulations should be reported to the governor.[110] This circular was reprinted in full in *Russkii Dnevnik* of June 5, with an editorial encouraging other governors to follow Grot's example, and branding failure to do so as collusion with the tax farm.[111]

Though his behavior was quite legal, Grot must have known that it would be regarded with hostility, first by the tax farmers (who complained that it would ruin them), and second by the Minister of Finance. And indeed the minister, Alexander Kniazhevich, told Grot that his actions were almost criminal and suggested that he be removed from his post.[112] Grot, however, had influential friends among a group of liberal officials in the capital who had the support of the emperor's brother, Grand Duke Constantine. So Grot held his ground. Indeed, early in June, he published a third circular in the provincial gazette. In this circular he complained that the tax farm regulations were still not being observed, and he promised to enforce them to the

---

the abuses of the tax farmers as a normal lawful affair, were afraid to breach such well-established arrangements concerning the sale of vodka at high prices."

[107] Okun', ed., *Krest'ianskoe dvizhenie*, p. 187.

[108] [K. K. Grot,] *Konstantin Karlovich Grot kak gosudarstvennyi i obshchestvennyi deiatel': Materialy dlia ego biografii i kharakteristiki* (Petrograd, 1915), 1, pp. 7–8.

[109] The June order, printed in the *Samarskiia Gubernskiia Vedomosti*, no. 24, is reproduced in *Russkii Dnevnik*, no. 136, 27 June 1859.

[110] *Samarskiia Gubernskiia Vedomosti* no. 21, reprinted in full in *Russkii Dnevnik*, no. 117, 5 June 1859.

[111] It may be no coincidence that the *Russkii Dnevnik* was closed down in July.

[112] From Grot's own account in [K. K. Grot], 1, p. 9.

letter—for, as he added with heavy sarcasm, "all instructions from supervisors have equal force in law for all subordinate individuals and institutions, even those concerning the liquor tax farm."[113] (Eventually, Grot himself was to play the leading role in the abolition of the tax farm, thereby becoming Kniazhevich's nemesis, a turn of events which provoked from Alexander Herzen the ghastly pun: "This old man [Kniazhevich] will perish in a *grotto*.")[114]

Grot's behavior was bound to be inflammatory. Subsequently, Grot was to claim that his prompt action had checked the spread of riots in Samara Province by persuading tax farmers to lower prices so that there were only two outbreaks of violence; but there were in fact at least fifty vodka riots in the province in June and July, which suggests that his actions were quite as provocative as the Ministry of Finance feared.[115]

What made rumors of the government's instructions to the tax farmers particularly dangerous was the fact that the boycott movement had already prepared consumers to interpret such instructions as an invitation to demand what, by now, they knew to be their rights. Accounts from Samara show how hard some consumers tried to find out what the laws really said before acting, and how hard it was for them to get an unambiguous answer from local officials.[116]

But despite their vagueness, there were certain things that seemed clear enough from the regulations, and of these the most important was that consumers ought to have been able to get hold of ordinary *polugar* at 3 rubles a bucket, both in rural areas, from taverns, and, in towns, from "vodka stores." In fact, as every consumer knew perfectly well, these drinks were simply never available at the official prices or strengths.

It was in this confused and tense atmosphere that consumers drifted toward confrontation with the tax farmers. As rumors of the government circulars leaked out in April and May, consumers seized on them as confirmation of what they had already come to believe—that the behavior of the tax farmers was both oppressive and illegal. In challenging them, therefore, they believed that they had the law and the government on their side, as well as their own sense of economic justice.

That rioters believed they had the authorities on their side is clear from the detailed accounts of the riots which have come down to us.[117] In most cases, the riots began on market days, and were sparked by rumors about

[113] *Russkii Dnevnik*, no. 136, 27 June 1859, from *Samarskiia Gubernskiia Vedomosti*, no. 24.

[114] *Kolokol*, 15 February 1862, 5: 1020.

[115] [K. K. Grot], 1, p. 9, and Okun', ed., *Krest'ianskoe dvizhenie* (Khronika); and Fedorov, "Krest'ianskoe trezvennoe dvizhenie," p. 120.

[116] See, for example, Okun', ed., *Krest'ianskoe dvizhenie*, pp. 203–5.

[117] The fullest accounts were sent to Herzen (probably by officials of the Ministry of State Domains, which had long opposed the tax farm). See *Pod Sud*, 1 April and 1 September 1860.

the ministerial circulars or other liquor riots. Thus, in Spassk, in Tambov Province, rumors spread at a bazaar that in neighboring Penza Province vodka was being sold at 3 rubles a bucket. These rumors merged with other, vaguer, rumors about the arrival of "towndweller" Kochkin, though no one actually admitted to having seen what our major source describes as "this symbolic figure."[118]

Despite the rumors, the bazaar proceeded normally until lunchtime, when people began drifting into the town's drinking establishments. One group of six (two state peasants, two towndwellers and two soldiers on leave) demanded *polugar* from a vodka store in the market square, at 3 rubles. they were refused, swore at the manager, and set off to complain to the head office of the tax farm, which was on the same square as the bazaar and the vodka store. Here, they became involved in a fight with employees of the tax farm. This spread to the square where the petitioners were soon supported by the crowd, which then turned to a nearby "bottle stall" (*shtofnaya lavochka*), and looted it, pouring out most of the drink.

A similar sequence of events was repeated in town after town in May and June of 1859. The accounts suggest that two elements were necessary, in combination, to explain the outbreak of the protests. The first was a motive: this was provided by the sharp rise in the price of vodka. The second was some signal that the protests were not entirely hopeless, that they had made progress elsewhere, or that they might attract support in high places. These two conditions mark two out of the three preconditions that Lenin claimed were necessary for the existence of a "revolutionary situation": that the "suffering and want of the oppressed classes have grown more acute than usual"; and that the "masses . . . are drawn both by all the circumstances of the crisis *and by the "upper classes" themselves* into independent historical action."[119] As in so many modern-day surrogate wars, it was the combination of bitterness from below and support from above that was explosive, rather than either element on its own.

Such conclusions tend to reinforce Daniel Field's arguments about the nature of Russia's deeply rooted tradition of "naive monarchism." But perhaps "naive monarchism" was not so much a product of naïveté, as of a certain brutal realism. For a member of the Russian *narod* to engage in protest was to do something extremely dangerous. Only where there was evidence of outside support was it worth taking this risk. And this suggests that it may have been the existence of signals seeming to promise outside support that provided the trigger for many movements of popular protest, rather than changes in the level of popular discontent. This may explain why so many

---

[118] There is an extremely detailed account of this particular protest in *Pod Sud*, 1 April 1860, 10: 45–56.

[119] "The Collapse of the Second International," p. 214. (Italics in the original.)

leaders of popular revolts in Russia were keen to find or manufacture evidence of support from above, and why their followers may have occasionally taken on the myth of a Godlike "Tsar Deliverer," even when it was spread by emissaries as unlikely as "towndweller" Kochkin. As Daniel Field has pointed out, figures like Kochkin could be useful (whether or not anyone believed in them), both in gaining support for violent action, and in excusing one's actions once a riot had failed.[120]

But of course, in order to do this, mythical leaders had to set appropriate goals; and to promise the emancipation of landlords' serfs to a crowd consisting mainly of town dwellers, state peasants, and ex-soldiers engaged in the smashing of taverns was simply not appropriate. The "naïveté" of peasants (like that of historians), has its limits; the mythical Kochkin needed only one seal to play the role of tsar's emissary, in which his original audience, drawn from Russia's working people, had first cast him.

Kochkin acquired his second seal because such mythical figures were also useful to the members of Russia's upper classes who reported on their existence. But for this very different audience, they were required to act a very different role: that of bogeyman. And this brings us full circle. In order to play the role of bogeyman, a single seal was just not enough. The golden seal of emancipation was the extra prop Kochkin needed to play the part assigned to him by the authorities. And this, unfortunately for the historian, is the role in which he appears in the records available to us, for the obvious reason that those records were set down by members of Russia's educated elite.

CONCLUSION

What, then, was the aim of the liquor protests? And what was the real significance of "towndweller Kochkin"?

The answers should by now be clear. Those who took part directly in the liquor protests saw them as a form of consumer boycott—a way of forcing down the price of an item of necessity in the households of Russian working people. The protests did not constitute a temperance movement. Nor were they a covert form of protest against serfdom or the feudal system, so they cannot be regarded as part of a larger anti-feudal movement of protest. But despite this, there *were* links between the two issues of cheap vodka and emancipation, for members of Russia's educated elite inevitably interpreted the liquor protests in the light of the government's plans for the abolition of serfdom. And while progressives welcomed the protests (in their peaceful early phases at least) as a healthy sign of the peasantry's maturity and readiness for freedom, conservatives interpreted them as part of a wider move-

---

[120] Daniel Field, *Rebels in the Name of the Tsar* (Boston, Mass., 1976), pp. 209–10.

ment of protest against the entire traditional social order. Finally, though, what educated observers thought about the movement had a profound impact on its actual timing and outcome, for the protesters themselves took action only after making their own assessments of the likely reaction of the government and its officials.

As for the mythical "towndweller Kochkin," he appears as a complex and contradictory symbol of the aspirations and fears of different layers of tsarist society. His black seal expressed the frustrations of Russian working people at the rising price of vodka. But the golden seal of emancipation, which he acquired at some indeterminate stage between his first appearance and his eventual incarceration in the records of the tsarist police, expressed the fears of Russian landlords and officials at any display of popular aggression at this delicate turning point in Russia's history.

The complexity of the symbolism surrounding "towndweller Kochkin" raises a further, methodological conclusion. This is that the evidence available to us only yields its real meaning once one distinguishes clearly between upper-class and popular objectives. And this is peculiarly difficult because almost all of the evidence available to us on the liquor protests is provided by members of Russia's upper classes who, though posing as neutral observers, were often direct or indirect participants in the movement they described. As with the reports of "towndweller Kochkin," the available documents often tell us more about the educated Russians who generated them than about the popular movements they claim to describe. So, in interpreting the movement, very clear distinctions have to be drawn between the objectives of Russia's working people and those of Russia's educated elite. But, once these distinctions have been made, the two levels must then be reintegrated—for it is the interaction of popular and upper-class goals and objectives that really explains the timing and outcome of the movement. I suspect these methodological principles apply to many forms of social protest in which the evidence is supplied almost entirely from above.

There is a final point to be made concerning the connection between vodka and emancipation. We have seen that it is incorrect to claim that those who protested against the liquor trade were in fact engaged in an attack on serfdom. But we have also seen that there were subtler links between the issues of cheap vodka and emancipation, and they were made, mainly, in the minds of members of Russia's upper classes. I would like to end by pointing out a final, and even less obvious, link between the two issues. There is a sense in which those who protested against serfdom and those who protested against high-priced vodka were, unwittingly, attacking similar phenomena. Serfdom and the tax farm were both typically precapitalist forms of tribute taking.[121] Both allocated extensive fiscal powers to non-government

---

[121] I have borrowed the category of "tribute-taking states" from Eric Wolf's magnificent work, *Europe and the People Without History* (Berkeley, 1982), ch. 3.

estates: to the landed gentry in the first case, and to the merchantry in the second. In the capitalist world, direct tribute taking tends to be a monopoly of the state, and other revenue-raising groups raise wealth primarily through commercial means, in the form of rents or profits. By attacking the high prices and arbitrary methods of the tax farm, consumers were, unwittingly, attacking the very principle that merchants could simply levy tributes, even if those tributes were disguised as commercial profits. In this sense, the demand for cheap vodka, sold at commercial (rather than monopoly) prices, was as potent an attack on the Russian ancien régime as was the demand that labor be paid for at commercial rates rather than being mobilized through the monopoly rights of serf-owning landlords. Viewed in this light, the liquor protests do provide support for the claim made in Soviet historiography that the Great Reforms, despite their many limitations, mark a fundamental turning point in modern Russian history.[122]

[122] This point is developed further in David Christian, "A Neglected 'Great Reform': The Abolition of Tax Farming in Russia," in *The Great Reforms in Russia,* ed. L. G. Zakharova, John Bushnell, and Ben Eklof (Bloomington, Ind., forthcoming).

CHAPTER 9

THE HIRING MARKET AS WORKERS' TURF: MIGRANT AGRICULTURAL LABORERS AND THE MOBILIZATION OF COLLECTIVE ACTION IN THE STEPPE GRAINBELT OF EUROPEAN RUSSIA, 1853–1913

Timothy Mixter

OTKHOZHIE PROMYSLY (labor migration or literally "going-away trades") in European Russia did not only occur when peasants of the Central Industrial Region sought work in factory districts or urban centers such as Moscow or St. Petersburg. An equally important but inadequately studied phenomenon was the seasonal migration of peasants from the Central Black Earth Zone and northern Ukraine to the south and southeast. While some went to mining and urban areas as well as to Black Sea ports such as Odessa, the vast majority of peasants leaving villages in the center were agricultural workers intent on hiring out in one of about one hundred and fifty Sunday or holiday markets in the commercial grainbelt which stretched across the steppe from Kherson, Tavrida, and Ekaterinoslav provinces in the west through the Don and Kuban oblasts and up to Saratov and Samara provinces in the Volga River Basin to the east.[1] The commercially oriented farms in this area owned by nobles, merchants, peasants, and foreign colonists had gradually begun to switch from sheep and livestock raising to wheat production beginning in the 1830s, as the export market, tied largely to European city growth, expanded. When after Emancipation a railroad network began to link inland farms and Black Sea ports, the amount of acreage under grain crops grew rapidly. In response, the number of migrant agricultural laborers that came yearly into the sparsely settled steppe to toil during the harvest season increased as well, reaching about one and one half million by the mid-1880s, in part because mechanization made relatively slow headway before 1885.

While provincial zemstvos, beginning in the 1890s, eventually set up as

[1] I would like to thank Jeffrey Burds, Robert Edelman, Steve Frank, Heather Hogan, Esther Kingston-Mann, Ron Suny, Kathy LeMons Walker, and Christine Worobec for their comments on an earlier draft as well as IREX and Fulbright-Hays for their generous support.

many as sixty relief stations (literally medical-food supply stations (*lechebno-prodovol'stvennye punkty*) designed specifically for migrant agricultural laborers, the conditions that workers faced on the road and in the hiring markets were still often appalling.[2] The annual May 9 fair at Kakhovka, Tavrida Province (see Map 1), for example, set wage rates for summer term work in much of New Russia and was the largest market in the entire country. Before it began to decline in the 1880s with the advent of the railroad in the region, the hiring market attracted as many as 50,000 agricultural workers. The migrants, mostly peasants from Kiev and Poltava provinces, quickly dwarfed the town's population of about 10,000 people when they arrived by foot, steamboat or, in over one-third of the cases, by boats called *duby*, which they had fashioned themselves out of rough-hewn boards and wooden nails. These, usually overladen with from ten to eighty people, drifted up to three hundred plus miles down the Dnieper River, barely floating above the surface of the water. Every year several people lost their lives when one or two of these craft participating in the annual flotilla swamped or were smashed to pieces in the course of running the Dnieper rapids during the trip to the fair.

When they finally settled on one of Kakhovka's hiring market squares, migrant agricultural laborers were apt to confront an environment not unlike that etched in the following evocative passage:

There are several such squares and on them are arrayed mainly foot-travellers with their wagons, packed so tightly, that at night it is impossible to wend one's way through the carts, since sleeping people cover the earth almost without interval. Those who come by *duby* usually remain below on the river bank and find themselves in much better conditions than those who settle on the squares. The fact is that if during the fair a good rain does not fall (and this, by the way, occurs very rarely), then these few days which one has to spend in Kakhovka are a positive torture: very fine sand, crushed into particles by the tred of tens of thousands of people, oxen, and horses, rises up in whole clouds with the very slightest breeze. It eats away at eyes, becomes lodged in the nose and mouth, covers the face with an utterly gray mask, pierces through clothing, and penetrating into the pores of the skin, causes an unpleasant itch. There is no refuge from it anywhere, even in a room with doors and windows closed. Over Kakhovka hangs something like an arid fog through which the merciless scorching sun appears as a purplish-red ball. And meanwhile thousands of people in an unbroken mass move in all directions, music resounds at various touring circuses,

---

[2] N.I. Teziakov, *Rynki naima sel'sko-khoziaistvennykh rabochikh na iuge Rossii v sanitarnom otnoshenii i vrachebno-prodovol'stvennye punkty*, vol. 1 (St. Petersburg, 1902), pp. 1–4, 14–31; Boris Veselovskii, *Istoriia zemstva za sorok let*, vol. 1 (St. Petersburg, 1909), p. 319.

booths, and "comedies," [and] hawking done in a thousand different ways by all sorts of merchants is heard.[3]

Laborers already tired out by long journeys from home which lasted an average of about six to eight days were likely to encounter conditions that were even worse in smaller markets serving anywhere from 500 to 5,000 of those who hoped to wield a scythe on one of the southern estates. It was in such dusty and frequently unsanitary environs that migrant agricultural workers sought to defend their interests, in many cases returning week after week to hire anew and occasionally engaging in collective action.

The hiring market was a place where peasants who went out into agricultural labor migration first had to negotiate between two worlds that in many ways operated on different assumptions. They left the confines of a world of subsistence-oriented agriculture in the Central Black Earth Zone and the northern Ukraine, by and large based on considerations of collective eco-

14. MIGRANT AGRICULTURAL LABORERS ON THE JOURNEY ACROSS THE STEPPE (1890) (USING SCYTHE HANDLES AS STAFFS TO WALK WITH; SCYTHE BLADES ON THEIR BACKS WRAPPED WITH STRAW) (THOMAS STEVENS, *THROUGH RUSSIA WITH A KAMARET* [BOSTON: J. S. CUSHING & CO., 1891], P. 15).

[3] Aleksandr Iaroshko, *Rabochii vopros na iuge, ego proshedshee, nastoiashchee i budushchee* (Moscow, 1894), pp. 28–29, 30 n.*; Teziakov, *Rynki naima*, vol. 1, pp. 93–94. See also *Ekaterinos lavskiia Gubernskiia Vedomosti*, no. 47, 14 June 1872, p. 260.

nomic security, for work on great estates located in the steppelands of European Russia that were geared around production for the market, risk, and
individual profit. Moreover, the types of relations were representative of capitalism and the modern world at their least regulated. For many workers the
experience must have been disorienting.

While the term "workers" shall be used throughout the essay, it does not
convey the complexity of the temporary migrants' position and concerns.
While many of them supported themselves more through wage work than
farming their own plots, most migrant laborers were not landless and store
buying like classic rural proletarians. Usually only around 15 to 20 percent
had no tillable land, though this figure might fluctuate between 5 and 40
percent depending on the *volost'* from which they left. In many ways much
of their lives and outlook were peasant in character. They often spent as little
as one month a year away from the village in labor migration and rarely more
than six months. Every year approximately 15–30 percent of the workers
went out for the first time. Sixty percent or more of the workers were under
30 in New Russia with 40–55 percent of the males and 78–93 percent of the
females single (with women making up 18 to 40 percent of the work force in
the period 1890–1913). Many of those who were married were also under the
age of 30 since the mean age of female marriage was usually between 19.5
and 23 years old in areas that sent out migrants into New Russia. Thus labor
turnover here must have been considerable, especially for women. This
meant that many peasants experienced agricultural *otkhod* (labor migration)
during their lives and that it often represented more a stage early on in the
life cycle, as did farm servanthood in other countries, rather than a permanent yearly occupation that might facilitate the development of class consciousness. Many laborers were concerned to accumulate enough money for
a dowry or a house so that they could marry and set up a separate household
as a full member of the peasant community. In this sense, through raiding
the cash economy, labor migration often could and did serve to keep village
life viable and helped perpetuate a peasant mentalité and culture.[4]

Nevertheless, social and economic trends did not always lead in one direction and it was often the case that, instead of buttressing a peasant's ties to
the land, *otkhod* could be a step on the path of proletarianization. The amount
of land held by workers was often paltry and likely to remain so. The soil
was in many cases poor and working livestock nonexistent. Thus frequently

---

[4] For figures mentioned see: A. O. Fabrikant, *Rabochii vopros v sel'skom khoziaistve Novorossii*, vol. 1 (Petrograd, 1917), pp. 38–41; Timothy Mixter, "Migrant Agricultural Laborers in
the Steppe Grainbelt of European Russia, 1830–1913" (Ph.D. diss., University of Michigan,
1991), passim and esp. Appendix K; Teziakov, *Rynki naima*, vol. 1, pp. 34–35, 52–53; N. V.
Shakhovskoi, *Zemledel'cheskii otkhod krest'ian* (St. Petersburg, 1903), pp. 47–57, 95–105; Ansley
J. Coale, Barbara A. Anderson, and Erna Härm, *Human Fertility in Russia Since the Nineteenth
Century* (Princeton, 1979), p. 152.

the family cycle did not lift *otkhodniki* (migrant laborers) out of poverty and they often remained part of a permanently poor stratum. Land, rather than being farmed by other family members, was sometimes rented out to other peasants before a migrant set out to work. It is also probably not an accident that permanent migration to Siberia in 1900–1913 was highest from Poltava, Kiev, and Chernigov provinces which had contributed many migrant agricultural laborers in the past. The rate of permanent migration most likely picked up because the earnings brought home from migrant labor, particularly after 1900, were no longer sufficient, mainly due to the way machinery cut into the length of employment and led to the hire of more lower-paid women and adolescents. Finally in the Volga area only about 9–22 percent of the male and 11–33 percent of the female migrant laborers were single. Even though the mean age of first marriage for females in regions sending out migrants was much lower here than in the Ukraine—18 to 21—it was still likely that for migrant agricultural laborers in the Volga area life as a worker on large estates would be a more permanent profession.[5]

Thus the whole identity of migrant laborers was a complex and slippery one. They worked as both farming peasants and wage earners. While many thought like traditional peasants, something like a new youth culture sometimes developed among certain workers during *otkhod*. As this essay will show, hiring decisions and collective action in hiring markets revealed the complexity of this peasant-worker mentalité.

Recently Robert Edelman has demonstrated how it is best to characterize the poor, but not landless, who engaged in collective action most frequently in the Right-Bank Ukraine as proletarian peasants or, in Lenin's terms, semiproletarians. In many ways such a term captures the ambiguous position of most migrant agricultural laborers who, though far from being as conscious or as leading an element in protest as the proletarian peasants Edelman writes of, were not passive and did mobilize for collective action. They often employed a wider repertoire of protest forms in the steppe grainbelt than did the villagers of the Central Black Earth Zone who are usually seen as the peasants who were most restive in 1861–1907. While landless laborers who lived on estates in the Right-Bank Ukraine may have been too dependent on estate owners to mobilize for collective action, migrant agricultural laborers in the steppe grainbelt did have enough tactical mobility through their use of the hiring market and engaged in protest just like poor landed "proletarian peasants" in the Right-Bank Ukraine and middle peasants elsewhere in Russia.

Edelman also has shown how the complex nature of such peasant-work-

---

[5] Fabrikant, *Rabochii vopros*, vol. 1, pp. 38–41; Ia. Ia. Polferov, *Sel'sko-khoziaistvennyia rabochiia ruki* (St. Petersburg, 1913), pp. 5–7, 39–43; Teziakov, *Rynki naima*, vol. 1, pp. 10–13, 34–35, 52–53 and note 4, above.

ers—and for that matter, all peasants—requires a multiple approach. As he demonstrates, neither a cultural approach in the manner of A.V. Chaianov stressing internal village factors, nor an economic approach emphasizing external factors are *alone* appropriate to the task of analyzing the reasons for the outbreak of rural revolt. In this he is correct, and an effort has been made here to take as wide a view as possible. It takes into account the external economic factors of the organization of wheat production by growers from above and the way the moral outlook, peasant cultural rituals, and economic decision-making of migrant laborers from below together helped shape the hiring market and labor relations. But the view here is that economics, culture, and politics in the peasant world were closely bound up, difficult to disentangle and influenced one another in complex fashion. An emphasis, therefore, is put on showing this interaction, not on separating out economic or cultural factors as paramount—as some historians, including even Edelman, are wont to do. In fact, less stress is put here on the economic strata which migrant laborers belonged to back in their home village, in part because it is so complex and difficult to sort out. In any case, as Edelman and others have shown, cases of poor, middle, and rich peasants, rural proletarians, sharecroppers, migrant agricultural laborers, and slaves protesting or being quiescent can be found in different times and places. Overt protest often depended less on immediate economic position back in the home village than on the opportunities and relationships shaped by the organization of production, the cultural perceptions of the rural dweller in question, and the creation of independent social spaces. Here we shall stress the role played in the fostering of collective action by the creation and perpetuation of the hiring market and the tactical mobility it provided.

I have found over eighty cases of collective action by migrant agricultural laborers in 1830–1913, although the number is undoubtedly higher.[6] If their smaller number and the shorter period possible for protest is taken into account, migrant laborers probably engaged in collective action as much as more traditional peasants in European Russia in this period, in part by using the tactical mobility afforded by the hiring market and not available to most other peasants. As Edelman's book and this essay show, protest did not take place only in the Central Black Earth Zone and only among middle peasants, as is sometimes implied. Furthermore, beyond occasional overt collective action, almost endemic conflict was often evident between migrant workers

---

[6] Government censorship, the paucity of provincial newspapers before 1880, the difficulty for Western historians of procuring local press as well as court records, and the unlikelihood that strikes before hire and other such nonviolent activity would be recorded in the first place all complicate the search for additional cases of protest. The brief, two-month period of the hiring season must also be taken into account when comparing market disturbances with other forms of peasant protest. See discussion in Mixter, "Migrant Agricultural Laborers," passim.

and employers both inside and outside the changing contours of the hiring market, which itself was often fought over. Ongoing conflict can be seen in: worker attempts to use their mobility as a weapon, relatively frequent cases of contract breaking, the spread and interpretation of rumors and information, as well as efforts to implant worker definitions of morality and truth.[7]

Worker collective action continued to be evident even after the turn of the century when labor shortages became less frequent due to increased use of sophisticated harvest machinery and population growth. Demand might still exceed the supply of labor in individual markets as a result of labor maldistribution and the sudden changes of weather and crop outlooks, all of which occurred quite frequently on the steppe. Given such circumstances, workers often had a golden opportunity to contest the power of employers to define relations as the latter frantically tried to avert loss of their crop. In the hiring markets, migrant agricultural laborers negotiated on a *relatively* equal footing with potential employers—a situation at variance with the social norm of unequal *soslovie* (legal estate) relations holding sway elsewhere in Russian society. Thus the hiring market, unlike most other institutions in tsarist Russia, at times provided peasants with the opportunity and power to say what they thought. Moreover, it allowed them to develop their independence and a sense of self-esteem. Within this space they could even dare to denigrate their supposed social betters. According to a report in the journal *Sel'skii Khoziain*, one worker in the Kakhovka market, taking advantage of the abundant harvest of 1893, got revenge for the humiliation of past lean years, not only by refusing to answer an employer's questions, but even refusing to turn around, instead proferring him a foot on the sole of which was affixed a scrap of paper with a designation on it as to the amount of pay wanted for this or that term of hire.[8]

However, once outside the hiring market the worker had to be cognizant that the employer held virtually all the power to define morality and the general tenor of relations. The question of the articulation of "true" worker feelings was thus one mainly of opportunity. The different behavior of workers in the hiring markets and on the estate, based largely on differences of opportunity, resources, and power, is tellingly suggested in the following description of a hiring market near Taganrog in the Don Oblast in the early 1860s:

---

[7] For all the references to Edelman, see: Robert Edelman, *Proletarian Peasants: The Revolution of 1905 in Russia's Southwest* (Ithaca, N.Y., 1987), pp. 9–34, 169–77. For the importance of separating out an analysis of ongoing conflict from occasional overt protest, see Mick Reed, "Social Change and Social Conflict in Nineteenth-Century England: A Comment," *Journal of Peasant Studies* 12, no. 1 (October 1984): 112–13, and esp. 109–11, 119–21.

[8] D. V. Fedorov, "Iz Novorossii," *Sel'skii Khoziain*, no. 34, 20 June 1987, p. 548; E. Varb (pseudonym of Iakov Fedorovich Brave), "Skitaniia sel'skokhoziaistvennykh rabochikh," *Russkaia Mysl'*, no. 8 (August 1898), sec. 2, p. 35.

Usually negotiations are conducted with the uncle (*s diad'koi* [the artel head]; the others all lay on the ground in very free and easy poses, and only rarely, in chorus, interfere in the conversation, [which is] of extreme interest to them. Their half crude and even insolent treatment of the employer during negotiations represents a strange and funny contrast with their deferential and even servile behavior with regard to that same employer, if, by mutual consent, they become his *batraki*. The rude treatment before hire is, as if, a farewell to freedom, which they sell for four whole months to their employer. The tone of the employer likewise changes somewhat, but in inverse ratio: before hire, he is mainly exhorting (*uveshchatelen*), fawning and to the highest degree kind (*dobr'*), especially when he contends to the workers, that it is [more] advantageous for them to hire cheaply to him than to another more expensively. After hire he adopts a tone imperious and strict and no longer talks with them amicably, but limits himself to orders.[9]

By their different "tones" employers implicitly acknowledged the power of workers in the hiring markets. It was the structural space there that not only helped provide laborers with the "freedom" necessary to see their common interests reasonably often, but also allowed for the mobilization of the self-confidence and resources for collective action in defense of these interests. In addition, workers did not attempt just to extract higher wages in the hiring fairs, but to some extent sought to implant their own culture and definitions of morality as well. In the process they tried to shape the behavior of employers and regulate agrarian capitalism from below.

The market was also the site of worker interaction with many other people besides employers and was thus something of a microcosm of Russian society. It attracted a number of groups and people who by the 1880s were increasingly important in the countryside. These were usually either the representatives of petty capitalism—labor and machine contractors, estate managers perhaps educated in agricultural science, peasant commercial farmers, and the purveyors of leisure, food, or crime such as swindlers, vagrants, prostitutes, and townspeople—or the representatives of the state—the police, zemstvo activists, third element (zemstvo-employed) doctors, demobilized soldiers, relief station managers, and railroad officials. A number of historians have noted the connection between the intrusion of capitalism and the state and the mobilization of collective action. In places where labor

---

[9] Dmitri Alferaki, "Zametki o vol'nonaemnykh rabochikh v Novorossiiskom krae, a imenno vozle Taganroga," *Trudy Imperatorskago Vol'nago Ekonomicheskago Obshchestva* 2, no. 2 (1863): 105. For other evidence of such switches in tone, see K. D. Kavelin, "Pis'ma iz derevni," in *Publitsistika: razsuzhdeniia, stat'i i zametki K. D. Kavelina*, vol. 2 (St. Petersburg, 1898), col. 668, and L. Tmutapakanskii, "St. Abinskaia (melochi stanichnoi zhizn')," *Kubanskiia Oblastnyia Vedomosti*, no. 107, 4 August 1901, pp. 1–2.

recruitment took place, these representatives of emerging market relations and the expanding state were frequently deemed outsiders by migrant laborers and their actions seen as immoral intervention in traditional hiring relations. By their occasional control of information and resources, these "professional" middlemen at times made it more difficult for *otkhodniki* to exercise their power in the hiring markets, although in the case of relief station managers, vagrants, and soldiers who were on leave or recently retired, they may have assisted mobilization. It was often to regain control of threatened resources crucial to bargaining leverage that migrant laborers protested. The threat or actual loss of control, though, was relative. Migrant laborers did not engage in collective action because they were uprooted and disoriented or suffered deprivation per se. It was precisely because they still had enough resources in the hiring market to mobilize and were concerned about attempts to deprive them of these resources that they rebelled.[10]

Markets for hire, trade, and other purposes have also often been locales where a conflict of values between different social groups took place in both Russia and elsewhere. Over time such groups contested the resources and boundaries of markets and other social spaces. The struggles were not just over physical space but what it represented. Often the confrontation involved two or more cultures or ways of life, as well as different conceptions of "progress."[11] Since the conflicts were also frequently about the power necessary to enact such conceptions, they were one of the few areas where lower-class "politics"—in the broad sense of power—can be ascertained. The outcomes of the strife in the market served to articulate social relations and arrangements of power.[12]

In the markets and other social spaces lower classes were occasionally able to fashion subcultures—"Satan's strongholds" and "unsteepled places"—that were independent enough from outside hegemony to allow for the promotion or perpetuation of "other ways of seeing".[13] The retention of values

[10] Charles Tilly, *From Mobilization to Revolution* (Reading, Mass., 1978), pp. 4, 48, 73, 141–42, 233, 239; Charles Tilly, "Proletarianization and Rural Collective Action in East Anglia and Elsewhere, 1500–1900," *Peasant Studies* 10, no. 1 (Fall 1982): 5–34.

[11] Battles over enclosure, urban renewal, shantytowns, the factory shop floor, busing, turf, and even park use are all examples of this clash of values. See, for instance, Heather Hogan, "Industrial Rationalization and the Roots of Labor Militance in the St. Petersburg Metalworking Industry, 1901–1914," *The Russian Review* 42, no. 2 (April 1983): 163–90, esp. 178–81; Joseph Bradley, "Once You've Eaten Khitrov Soup You'll Never Leave! Slum Renovation in Late Imperial Russia," *Russian History* 11, no. 1 (1984): 1–28, esp. pp. 18–20.

[12] Sidney W. Mintz, "Internal Market Systems as Mechanisms of Social Articulation," in *Intermediate Societies, Social Mobility, and Communication: Proceedings of the 1959 Annual Spring Meeting of the American Ethnological Society*, ed. Verne E. Ray (Seattle, 1959), p. 20; E. P. Thompson, "Patrician Society, Plebian Culture," *Journal of Social History* 7, no. 4 (Summer 1974): 382–84.

[13] E. P. Thompson, *The Making of the English Working Class* (New York, 1963), pp. 51–52, 55–76, 397, 403; James Scott, "Hegemony and the Peasantry," *Politics & Society* 7, no. 3

that were often in conflict with those held by employers as well as by the representatives of the state and capitalism was crucial to the mobilization of collective action. Independent social spaces and the cultures that developed within them enabled the poor to exchange information which kept these values alive and provided the "tactical mobility" necessary to enforce them. The conflict was often over different priorities that tended to pit: (1) local versus national interests; (2) community welfare and subsistence versus the right of individual profit; (3) personal, face-to-face negotiation versus abstract, mystified, and mediated relationships; (4) public supervision of information and transactions versus deception and a monopoly of knowledge; (5) retention of lower-class culture and leisure in connection with work versus elite imposition of work discipline; and (6) social leveling and turning the world upside down versus maintenance of traditional social hierarchies. The poor often tried to put limits on the behavior of employers, merchants, and professional middlemen by insisting on "just" prices and a "moral economy."[14] In order to ensure such morality and dependable social relations, they at times engaged in public supervision, participated in collective action, or imposed a web of cultural and symbolic restraints aimed at regulating economic transactions and preserving visible market boundaries.[15] These actions were taken against the attempts of state officials, nonlocal merchants, and professional middlemen to obliterate boundaries and create a "free," unsupervised, national market in which they would have the advantage.[16]

This essay will set forth three major themes in elaboration of some of the issues raised so far. They are: (1) the way the hiring markets in the steppe grainbelt of Saratov, Samara, Tavrida, Ekaterinoslav, Kherson provinces and the Kuban and Don oblasts provided agricultural laborers with the opportunity and tactical mobility necessary to protest openly; (2) the ambivalence of employers and agricultural laborers toward the development of agrarian capitalism; (3) the participation of migrant laborers in a wide repertoire of collec-

(1977): 267–96; Jean-Christophe Agnew, *Worlds Apart: The Market and the Theater in Anglo-American Thought, 1550–1750* (Cambridge, 1986), pp. 1–56, 149–61, esp. 1–7, 26–27, 31–46.

[14] E. P. Thompson, "The Moral Economy of the English Crowd in the Eighteenth Century," *Past & Present*, no. 50 (February 1971): 76–136, esp. 83–85, 98, 100–3, 115, 126, 134–35; Louise A. Tilly, "The Food Riot as a Form of Political Conflict in France," *Journal of Interdisciplinary History* 2, no. 1 (Summer 1971): 23–57; Robert W. Malcomson, *Popular Recreations in English Society, 1700–1850* (Cambridge, 1973), passim and esp. 75, 103–4, 149–51.

[15] Guild rules, state law, religious ceremonies, and popular collective action, all had the intent at various times and places to prevent deception.

[16] Jean-Christophe Agnew, "The Threshold of Exchange: Speculations on the Market," *Radical History Review*, no. 21 (Fall 1979): 108–10. Agnew points out that as capitalism developed, the word "market" no longer only referred to a specific occasion or place demarcated by clear boundaries and a market cross, but began to connote the "act of buying and selling regardless of locale" and the "price (or exchange-value) of goods and services." As this process of abstraction and capitalistic expansion occurred and middlemen appeared, deception became easier.

tive action which frequently sought to assert worker definitions of moral social relationships in opposition to the behavior of employers.

THE RISE AND PERPETUATION OF THE HIRING MARKET

Both employers and workers created and shaped the hiring market—the former by the way they organized production in response to crop, weather, and harvest fluctuations, grain prices, and labor supply, the latter by their sabotage of other forms of hire, their collective action, and their frequent return to the markets. Like migrants, employers wanted economic security and dependable, just social relations on the one hand as well as profits and freedom of action on the other—the best of both the pre-Emancipation "feudal" world and the emerging capitalistic one. Steppe grain growers wanted control, but not at too great a cost. Reaching these goals, however, proved difficult since they were often contradictory and a number of factors dictated that the organization of production had to proceed in a certain fashion. Given the fragility of wheat and volatile weather conditions on the steppe, growers needed a large labor force nearby that could be called on immediate notice to work for only the short period of the harvest. The possibility that grain might spill out if overripe or be lost in the event of a hailstorm or drying wind, meant that many workers were needed at once. On the other hand, since one out of three years at minimum was likely to be a poor harvest in the steppelands, farmers were reluctant to hire too many workers before harvest outlooks were clear, even though this precaution might ease their anxiety and provide security. Since there was little work to be done before the hay and grain harvests, the costs of maintaining a large labor force could easily be ruinous, particularly if there was a subsequent crop failure. The migrant labor system came into being partially because it threw the costs of labor reproduction elsewhere.[17]

In the middle of the nineteenth century, steppe grain producers tried to hold down labor costs by engaging in the state-supported, coercive winter hiring system. Under the latter arrangement employers sent their stewards during the winter to villages in central Russia. There they would frequently bribe state authorities as well as village clerks and elders to make an agreement to coerce peasants into migrant labor in order to pay off state tax ar-

[17] N. V. Shakhovskoi, *Sel'sko-khoziaistvennye otkhozhie promysly* (St. Petersburg, 1896), p. 108; K. Bunitskii, "O zatrudneniiakh, vstrechaemykh pri proizvodstve letnykh polevykh rabot v stepnykh khoziaistvakh iuzhnago kraia Rossii, s predlozheniem nekotorykh sredstv protiv takogo nevygodnago polozhenii," *Zapiski Imperatorskago Obshchestva Sel'skago Khoziaistva Iuzhnoi Rossii* (1857): 269–70; Eric J. Hobsbawm and George Rudé, *Captain Swing* (New York, 1975; originally published in 1968), pp. 34, 42, 44–45, 47, 50–51, 72; Michael Burawoy, "The Functions and Reproduction of Migrant Labor: Comparative Material From Southern Africa and the United States," *American Journal of Sociology* 81, no. 5 (March 1976): 1050–87; Sharon Stichter, *Migrant Laborers* (Cambridge, 1985), passim.

rears. The workers did receive an advance for this purpose, but the wages paid the following summer were invariably below the market rate.

Workers were to a certain extent ambivalent about the winter hiring system. A few laborers liked the certainty of employment and the money advances of winter hire. Nevertheless, most were upset that they had little say in the way employers and wages were determined. They became angry that wage rates were invariably below those that could be garnered right before the harvest. They began to sabotage the coercive winter hiring system, thus giving rise to the "free" negotiation of the hiring markets. Migrants at times stole advance money and did not appear when needed. They would go south and then hire out elsewhere when they *saw* higher wages offered in the hiring market. If they did show up to "honor" the winter hiring contract, they often malingered, hurting labor productivity. Increasingly migrant laborers acknowledged the way the hiring market helped them defend their interests by avoiding winter hire altogether. They began to bargain for themselves in the dusty town squares of the steppe grainbelt. Already in the 1850s observers noted the decline of the winter hiring system, and by the early 1890s winter hiring contracts covered no more than about 8 percent of the workers recruited by steppe farmers.[18]

Gradually employers became won over to the new system. The markets gave farmers some security in that an available labor force was now close at hand while allowing them to escape the costs of labor reproduction and procurement. Stewards did not have to travel so far to recruit labor, and the welfare costs of worker maintenance could not only still be thrown on the peasant communes and households of Central Russia, but also on the worker who could be sent back to the nearby town square when not needed and on the zemstvo rate payers who financed the relief stations for migrant laborers in the hiring markets. As increased use of machinery gave employers more confidence that crops could be harvested quickly, as food costs rose, and as the international grain market became more competitive, the incentive of the employer probably grew as well to use the hiring market to recruit labor and to "maintain" field hands at little expense when they were not needed.[19]

However, there were disadvantages for the employer in this new arrangement. While the hiring market provided a certain amount of security and usually helped raise profits by lowering maintenance costs, if not wages, em-

[18] K. Bunitskii, "O zatrudneniiakh," pp. 266–67; Timothy Mixter, "Of Grandfather-Beaters and Fat-Heeled Pacifists: Perceptions of Agricultural Labor and Hiring Market Disturbances in Saratov, 1872–1905," *Russian History* 7, pts. 1–2 (1980): 143, 152, 159; Ia. Ia. Polferov, *Sel'sko-khoziaistvennyia*, pp. 12–13; Stichter, *Migrant Laborers*, pp. 93–121, 190–95, esp. 192–93.

[19] A. Trutovskii, "Stolovaia dlia rabochikh v m. Berezovke Anan'evskago uezda," *Vrachebnaia Khronika Khersonskoi Gubernii* (hereafter, *VKh Kherson*), no. 18 (15 September–1 October 1893): 14–15, 16–17; *VKh Kherson*, no. 12 (15 June–1 July 1893): 14–15; Hobsbawm and Rudé, *Captain Swing*, pp. 34, 47, 50–51, 72.

ployers lost a degree of control over their work force. The temptation to throw the worker back into the hiring market when not needed led to short-term hire, making it difficult to influence and discipline the work force. Employer countenance of the hiring market helped create a social space mostly outside employer control, where a worker subculture could flourish during "free time" and collective action could be mobilized. Commercial grain producers, in fact, recognized some of the loss of their ability to shape dependable social relations in the hiring market by complaining about the immoral behavior of workers there. Estate owners were appalled by the disorderly culture of the labor markets replete with drunkenness and strikes. They often preferred to blame individual worker immorality for their problems rather than themselves or abstract, systemic economic forces. For instance, they redefined as wanton idleness the enforced unemployment created by grower short-term hiring practice, even though it was unlikely that peasants would travel 300 to 1,500 miles just to remain idle.[20] Thus employers continued to worry about control, even as they willingly gave it up—thereby exposing their ambivalence toward market relations.

One of the main responses to the perceived "disorder" of the hiring market system and worker behavior were attempts to "regulate" the worker question from above through the drafting of new laws. P. A. Krivskii, the Saratov Province marshal of the nobility, instigated much of the nationwide discussion concerning the issue when he wrote a draft law project that was reviewed by government officials in 1884–1886 and by a government commission in 1897–1898. In his various commentaries on the agricultural worker question he acknowledged worker power in the hiring markets by expressing outrage at the way laborers virtually took over the market on his property by organizing strikes, swimming in his pond, lighting fires, playing pitch and toss, as well as singing and yelling the whole night through. He felt that the enforced mobility of short-term hire was a two-edged sword that weakened elite control. He sought to return to what seemed to approach a state of serfdom by limiting labor mobility through the institution of worker booklets and penalties for employers who hired already contracted workers. By 1904, frustrated by government inaction and irate at news of a worker strike and disorderly conduct in a neighboring hiring market, Krivskii decided to take matters into his own hands. Almost symbolically he tried to get rid of the vagaries of market capitalism on the steppe by literally plowing up one-third of his hiring square.[21]

---

[20] A. Trutovskii, "Stolovaia," pp. 13–14.

[21] Mixter, "Of Grandfather-Beaters," pp. 152–67, esp. 166; Mixter, "Migrant," passim. In the above instance Krivskii wanted worker booklets instituted because they would have records in them of the laborer's past behavior and would make it difficult for a new employer to claim that he did not know that a worker was already under contract to someone else. In

It is perhaps instructive that Krivskii did not plow up all his market. Generally, employers did not want to abolish the markets since they were enough to their advantage, providing access to labor nearby and cutting maintenance costs. The majority of employers did not support Krivskii's restrictive legislation and his attempts to curtail worker mobility. It may well be that the very lack of permanent worker organization actually dissuaded employers from abolishing the market as well, no matter how effectively workers may have mobilized there in any one year. Given the near certainty of labor turnover and a changed harvest outlook, farmers felt that they might well come out ahead the next time workers negotiated. Later mechanization for the most part obviated the need to resort to more repressive and violent vigilante tactics. Instead of attacking the hiring market outright, employers chose to chip away at worker resources there. In this sense the market was not static, but continuously fought over. Thus employers might organize police sweeps of *rynki* (markets), shut down relief stations as promoting idleness, "spongers," and higher pay, and float false rumors about good wages in order to attract an excess of laborers into a market, hoping in the process to cause labor prices to drop. They also might lie outright, while negotiating. Outside the market they tried to get the zemstvo to help them purchase machinery or tried to induce the state to enact laws, control labor migration, release soldiers for fieldwork, or import foreign labor. Only when the disturbances in the hiring markets became acute, such as in the Kuban Oblast in 1902–1906 or in Saratov Province during 1904–1906 did employers think about forsaking market hire completely by either resurrecting the winter hiring system or by relying on machine and labor contractors only.[22]

Workers, like employers, were also to some extent ambivalent about the short-term relationships fostered by agrarian capitalism in the steppe grainbelt. While they liked the noncoercive nature of the market with its free choice of employer and potentially higher wages, they too were concerned about the lack of security and dependable relations between employer and laborer. As the threat of labor shortage decreased after 1890, employers became less concerned with retaining worker loyalties by engaging in any type of paternalistic practices meant to ensure a reliable yearly labor supply. Bad food, abandonment and discharge of sick workers, welching on promises, beatings, lying, and money fines, which appear to have been common employer tactics on the steppe, all tended to make migrant laborers believe that employers were not concerned with their welfare and looked upon them

---

this way he hoped to control the morality and the mobility of agricultural laborers. See also Stichter, *Migrant Labor*, pp. 139–40.

[22] Mixter, "Migrant," passim; notes 45 and 47, below; *Lechebno-prodovol'stvennye punkty na rynkakh naima sel'sko-khoziaistvennykh rabochikh v Saratovskoi gubernii v 1908 g.* (Saratov, 1909), pp. 2–3, 51.

only in economic terms, as field hands, not as whole human beings.[23] Farmers often lavished better treatment on their machines and would throw workers off their estates and into the markets whenever the latter were sick or not needed. In response, workers would try to use their resources in the hiring market in an effort to regulate the moral behavior of employers and create more dependable relationships. There is evidence, in fact, that some workers preferred to return there weekly to prevent employer deceit.[24]

Worker ambivalence about the vagaries of agrarian capitalism can also be seen in their decisions about how long they would hire out. Hiring markets occurred weekly, usually on Sundays or holidays, and thus workers had the opportunity to choose their term of employment and play one employer off another. Large landowners who could afford maintenance costs more easily were usually more interested in ensuring a labor force for the harvest by offering longer contracts, usually of a month or more, often at a slightly reduced rate. Petty employers wanted weekly or day hire so that they would not have to absorb maintenance costs any longer than absolutely necessary. They would offer higher wages but shorter-term employment, longer hours and harsher labor discipline. Thus there were advantages and disadvantages to each form of hire.[25]

It is difficult to determine whether long- or short-term hire predominated. Day and week terms appear to have been more common in the Volga area and North Caucasus than in New Russia. In the latter region migrant labor seems to have catered to the needs of single Ukrainian adolescents of both sexes. These youths had more free time and wanted longer, dependable employment so that they could accrue dowries and money to set up separate households after they married as well as relieve parents of extra mouths to feed. In the Volga area workers were more likely to be married and have their own plots back home which needed care. Thus they may have preferred shorter-term employment.[26] Overall, though, with increased use of machin-

---

[23] V. V. Khizhniakov, "Sel'skie rabochie na rynkakh naima Khersonskoi gub.: Statisticheskii ocherk)," Zhizn', no. 2 (February 1900), sec. 2, pp. 162–63, 169–70; A. V. Panov, "Sel'sko-khoziaistvennye rabochie v Samarskoi gubernii," Russkoe Bogatstvo, no. 7 (July 1899), sec. 2, p. 73.

[24] Iv. Kondorskii, "O sanitarnom polozhenii sel'sko-khoziaistvennykh rabochikh Ekaterinoslavskoi gubernii," Russkaia Mysl', no. 9 (September 1905): 87.

[25] Bunitskii, "O zatrudneniiakh," p. 265; Polferov, Sel'sko-khoziaistvennyia, p. 24; D. Fedorov, "Anti-Nemetskii bunt," Nedelia, no. 26, 28 June 1898, col. 839; Shakhovskoi, Sel'sko-khoziaistvennye, pp. 115–16, 123–29.

[26] Shakhovskoi, Sel'sko-khoziaistvennye, pp. 102–3; Mixter, "Of Grandfather-Beaters," p. 147 and 147 n. 26; P. F. Kudriavtsev, "Sel'sko-khoziaistvennye rabochie na Nikolaevskoi iarmarke v M. Kakhovke, Tavricheskoi gubernii, i sanitarnyi nadzor za nimi v 1895 godu," in XIII s"ezd vrachei i predstavitelei zemskikh i gorodskikh uprav Khersonskoi gubernii v g. Khersone (10–18 Oktiabria 1895 goda): Doklady, otchety o zasedaniiakh i pr., vypusk 1 (Kherson, 1896), p. 365.

ery and growing numbers of petty employers, hiring terms became more abbreviated.

Workers, as well as employers, however, often played a role in shaping the trend toward shorter hire. Laborers in many cases felt that they could garner higher wages if they took the risk of returning to the hiring market weekly. They learned from experience that if they waited until just before the harvest when petty employers began to recruit and pressure on farmers mounted, wages would often go up. As much could be made in three weeks as in three months, if they only held out in the hiring market where their power usually resided. Sometimes jobs with long-term contractual periods were abandoned and some migrants were known to change employers three or more times in search of a higher price.[27]

Thus at times workers adopted a strategy of staying in the markets and withholding their labor as long as necessary and, after initial hire, using their *mobility* to return to the market as often as possible. By these actions they acknowledged and re-created the power of the hiring market.

Other observers also noted how migrant laborers willingly took risks and failed to accord with the popular stereotype of peasants being conservative in their behavior. According to one member of a state commission, migrants went "directly into day work, since the chance for the very largest, most fabulous pay is linked primarily with day labor, even though with this is tied the prospect of the most complete failure for the worker."[28] A journalist likewise noted that in the Kuban Oblast migrant laborers preferred weekly hire for both economic and cultural reasons:

> The hiring of workers takes place on Sundays and holidays. For day workers, settling of accounts [payday] occurs on the eve of holidays, after which both proprietor and worker head off to the labor markets in the *stanitsa* [cossack settlement] for the concluding of new terms. It sometimes occurs that the farmer hires his previous workers, but not to go into the stanitsa on a holiday—is something inconceivable for a farmer-employer and for a worker. For both it is necessary to know the tenor of the market, having established the price for work hands, it is necessary of course to wet the bargain as sanctified by custom. Farmers, by the way, say this wetting of the bargain is one of the collateral reasons for the reluctance of workers to hire out by the term.[29]

In this way, peasants showed themselves, in a number of cases, not only as unafraid of the free market but also as masters of playing and perpetuating

---

[27] *Vrachebno-Sanitarnaia Khronika Ekaterinoslavskoi Gubernii* (hereafter, *VSKhEG*) (1912): 339; no. 3 (March 1900): 97; no. 6 (June 1900): 303; Shakhovskoi, *Sel'sko-khoziaistvennye*, p. 119.

[28] Shakhovskoi, *Sel'sko-khoziaistvennye*, p. 102; Polferov, *Sel'sko-khoziaistvennyia*, pp. 21–22.

[29] A. Beloborodov, "Prishlye rabochie na Kubanshchine," *Severnyi Vestnik*, no. 2 (February 1896), sec. 2, p. 4.

it. By their mobility and unwillingness to hire out quickly, workers to some extent deprived employers of access to labor—their biggest concern—at a time when much money was already tied up in the crop. Grain needed to be harvested immediately if the farmer was to avoid ruin. The constant complaints of employers about labor shortage, their enticement of workers from one another, their withholding of passports, and their attempts to organize and "regulate" labor migration through the zemstvos, especially before 1890, all testify to the effects of worker mobility and the anxiety it caused. The fact that such fairs occurred only occasionally, combined with the pressure put on employers by an approaching harvest, also allowed migrants to save up and pool their meager resources for the moment when they could be used most effectively. Because most markets in a region occurred on the same day, workers had more incentive to remain united for one price in one place, since they knew if they broke ranks, they would have a degree of trouble securing employment at a decent wage in another market the next day.

Weekly hire also meant that workers never took anything for granted, as the constant effort needed to supervise the market and to protect their interests kept the spirit of resistance alive. Frequent experience in a relatively independent social space and the self-confidence gained from knowing one could partially define one's own life were crucial both to the development of any type of worker consciousness and to the perpetuation of "other ways of seeing." Workers had, in fact, shown their willingness to control their own destiny by helping create the hiring market through their sabotage of winter hire and their return to town every seven days. Through repeated hiring they could learn the repertoire of successful bargaining techniques and collective action. Experience provided in this way during a summer or over the course of several summers taught workers that conditions altered drastically from year to year and even moment to moment and that they had a large role to play in the eventual shape of labor relations.

These relations were to a large degree determined during bargaining in the markets. Information on the actual hiring process there is scarce, nevertheless a number of sources suggest that the following was a common pattern. Most hiring markets occurred on Sundays and holidays. Workers usually arrived sometime the day before. The next morning, bargaining might begin as early as 6 A.M. In some cases a flag was raised signaling the start of negotiations—perhaps also signifying that haggling over wages was to take place only within the designated area and not on the sly.[30] It appears that elected artel leaders usually represented the members of their traveling groups. Often one price was set by the workers, which apparently all the artel spokespersons had agreed to hold out for. The price was sometimes

[30] *Saratovskii Dnevnik*, no. 101, 14 July 1902, p. 4.

determined during meetings the night before.[31] According to one report, artel leaders tied crossed sickles together and held them aloft to indicate that they represented workers who wanted to hire out.[32] Once a general market price had been agreed upon, employers negotiated with artel representatives to satisfy specific requirements. Labor procurement in some markets may well have been less organized with no one market price set—each artel defending its own interests by itself. Usually transactions were complete by mid-afternoon, often consummated by the employer standing the workers to a ruble advance and a drink at the local tavern. Newly hired harvesters handed over their passports, sickle, or an article of clothing as a visible pledge of good faith.[33] Sometimes, especially during good harvest years, workers would hold out on strike for two or three days even selling scythes if necessary to maintain themselves. Employers were known to leave en masse in despair.[34] Nevertheless, in most cases the outcome of the hiring process was difficult to predict. Workers faced numerous obstacles before they could utilize the space and resources of the market to their advantage.

OBSTACLES TO THE MOBILIZATION OF PROTEST

Once in the market, one of the major obstacles workers faced in mobilizing for collective action was their poverty. Most migrant laborers came from poor families, and the food produced from their tiny plots had in some cases run out by the spring, when migrant laborers went out. Various reports concerning migrant laborers on the road, in the market, and on the estates frequently refer to workers starving and having to resort to begging. Leon Trotsky,

[31] For one such possible meeting, see: Vl. Arkhangel'skii, "Otchet o deiatel'nosti Balandinskago lechebno-prodovol'stvennago punkta dlia prishlykh sel'sko-khoziaistvennykh rabochikh v 1911 godu," *Lechebno-prodovol'stvennye punkty Saratovskago Gubernskago Zemstva na rynkakh naima sel'sko-khoziaistvennykh rabochikh v g. Petrovske, s. Balande, g. Khvalynske i Elani i sudovykh rabochikh v g. Tsaritsyne v 1911 g.* (hereafter, *LPP Saratov [1911]*) (Saratov, 1912), p. 12. For holding out for one price or for several different prices, depending upon the work, see Shakhovskoi, *Sel'sko-khoziaistvennye*, pp. 103–4; L. Tmutapakanskii, "St. Abinskaia," pp. 1–2.

[32] Z. P. Solov'ev, "Otchet o deiatel'nosti Borkovskago vrachebno-nabliudatel'nago punkta s 1 iiunia po 15 avgusta 1903 g.," *Vrachebno-Sanitarnaia Khronika Saratovskoi Gubernii* (hereafter, *VSKh Saratov*), no. 11 (November 1903): 703. Around 90 percent of the workers came in artels, 10 percent alone.

[33] Solov'ev, "Otchet," pp. 703–4; Kavelin, "Pis'ma," col. 666; Iaroshko, *Rabochii vopros*, p. 118; notes 29 and 95 of this essay.

[34] A. N. Vol'tman, "Ocherk predvaritel'nago izsledovaniia sanitarnago polozheniia sel'sko-khoziaistvennykh rabochikh v Samarskoi gubernii, Talovyi khutor, Nikolaevskii uezda," in *Opyt predvaritel'nago izsledovaniia i sanitarnago nadzora za prishlymi rabochimi v Samarskoi gubernii—leto 1897 goda*, ed. M. M. Gran (Samara, 1898), pp. 58–59; Mixter, "Of Grandfather-Beaters," p. 165; *Otchet Ekaterinoslavskoi Gubernskoi Zemskoi Upravy po sanitarnomu otdeleniiu za 1901 god*, Chast' chetvertaia: *Otchet o deiatel'nosti vrachebno-prodovol'stvennykh punktov dlia prishlykh sel'sko-khoziaistvennykh rabochikh* (Ekaterinoslav, 1902), p. 28.

whose father hired migrant laborers for his farm in Kherson Province, re-membered how they protested their food rations—vegetable soup or millet that lacked any meat—and noted that one summer because of the poor diet that prevailed on most farms in the vicinity "all the laborers fell ill in an epidemic of nightblindness" and "moved about in the twilight with their hands stretched out before them." According to one author, there were 1,493 cases of night blindness reported at Kherson Province relief stations in 1895 alone.[35]

Caught far away from home with few material resources and in many cases facing starvation, migrant laborers were often unable to hold out for higher wages in the hiring market. They at times rushed toward employers the moment they appeared and if despondent enough might just hire out for the cost of maintenance. In Kherson Province, migrant laborers in one hiring market during a bad harvest year were so desperate to hire out that they attached their passports to long poles in order to pass them over the heads of other workers standing in a ring around a grower just about to hire.[36]

Conditions in general deteriorated after the late 1880s. Although wages were higher in the steppe grainbelt, accounting for the willingness of peas-ants to participate in migrant labor, real wages on average held steady at best from 1889 through 1913. Wage rates do not tell the whole story, however, for there was something of a crisis for migrant agricultural laborers at the turn of the century, as they tended to bring less money home due to the replace-ment of higher-paid male labor by women and adolescents, the increase in the supply of labor, the growing use of machinery particularly in New Russia and the Kuban Oblast, shorter terms of hire and consequent greater periods of unemployment.[37] In addition, as a result of the intensification of work, especially on the smaller estates, and a greater reliance on the use of agricul-tural machinery that was outfitted with few safety features, both the psychic and physical terror of the workplace increased. The number of accidents, for instance, rose substantially at a rate exceeding that in industry, as the crude contraptions lopped off various worker limbs.

Mobilization against employers was impeded not only by worker poverty and declining conditions but also by some of the attitudes workers brought to the market. While social space was a crucial factor promoting collective

---

[35] Leon Trotsky, *My Life: An Attempt at an Autobiography* (New York, 1970), p. 25; Khizhni-akov, "Sel'skie rabochie," *Zhizn'*, no. 2 (February 1900), sec. 2, pp. 160–61.

[36] Khizhniakov, "Sel'skie rabochie," *Zhizn'*, no. 2 (February 1900), sec. 2, p. 167.

[37] On wages, see Mixter, "Migrant." On deteriorating conditions, see Teziakov, *Rynki naima*, vol. 1, pp. 10–12, 19, 34–35, 37, 39, 46, 49, 55–56, 73; Khizhniakov, "Sel'skie rabochie na rynkakh Khersonskoi gub." *Zhizn'*, no. 1 (January 1900), sec. 2, p. 131 and no. 2 (February 1900), sec. 2, pp. 160, 164, 170–71; Iaroshko, *Rabochii vopros*, pp. 31–33, 37, 43–44, 50–51, 123, 127 and 127 n.*, 129, 132, 171–72, 178–79.

action, ultimately human agency, not structures, determined whether it was used for good or ill purpose.

Conflicts along ethnic and regional lines were one of the major ways the energies of agricultural laborers were diverted from total concentration on defending their interests against employers. Even the names migrant laborers gave to those from different provinces sometimes reflected a local community, rather than a class consciousness and evince a different way of seeing things than the cultural elite of the time. The manager of the Bogopol relief station for migrant agricultural laborers in Kherson Province in 1898 reported:

> Among workers there exists their own appellations according to province: *Poltavtsy*—"dumplings" / *"galushniki"* (they travel in wagons—on the road they, for the most part, cook dumplings for themselves in pots), *Chernigovtsy*—"the bast shoe people" / *"lapatsony"* (*lapotniki*), *Khar'kovtsy*—"trunk carriers" [thieves?] / *"cheimodanshchiki"* (a historical explanation - they cut off the baggage for [y—from?] the travelling Catherine the Great), *Kievliane*—"broomstick-fliers" / *"trubolety"* (as a result of the wealth in witches), *Podol'iane*—"those who danced the *trepak"* [folk dancers] / *"trepachki"*, *Khersontsy*—"the unmarried ones" / *"nevenchany"*, *Vladimirovtsy*—"icondaubers" / *"bogomazy"*, *Moskvichi*—chicory addicts" / *"tsikorniki"*.[38]

Strife in which local laborers drove migrants from local markets and estates was even more common than ethnic or regional conflict.[39] Those who lived in the vicinity of markets tried to uphold a "moral economy" which was based on the principle that outsiders should not be allowed to profit from local resources and jobs until all local peasants had been given the opportunity to take care of their subsistence needs.

Besides ill-feeling among themselves, agricultural workers also had to contend with the machinations of an assortment of people who wanted to live parasitically off the earnings of field hands when they entered the hiring market. Local townspeople at times tried to exploit migrants by selling them such delicacies as kvass swimming with little worms, an unnamed drink served in unwashed bottles with a ghastly yellow liquid inside, and rotten, fly-infested fish that had been sitting in the sun too long. Laborers lost money to these vendors and were not infrequently laid low with gastraintes-

---

[38] P. Nazorov, "Lechebno-prodovol'stvennyi punkt v s. Golte-Bogopole," in *Deiatel'nost' lechebno-prodovol'stvennykh punktov dlia prishlykh rabochikh v Khersonskoi gubernii za 1898 g.: Otchety zaveduiushchikh punktami* (hereafter, *LPP Kherson [1898]*) (Kherson, 1899), p. 48 n.*

[39] For cases of ethnic, regional, and migrant-local conflict, see Varb, "Skitaniia," sec. 2, pp. 30–31; Teziakov, *Rynki naima*, vol. 1, p. 13; *Revoliutsionnaia Rossiia*, no. 32, 15 September 1903, p. 19; G. I. Uspenskii, "Koi pro chto," in *G. I. Uspenskii: Sobranie sochinenii v deviati tomakh*, vol. 7 (Moscow, 1957), p. 66.

tinal diseases and food poisoning.[40] Prostitution was also rampant. There were even reports of mobile houses of ill repute being set up by women, especially soldier wives, who went "on tour," arriving just in time for the hiring markets, such as the one held in Talovoi, Samara Province. In some cases employers even provided prostitutes for their work force, ensconcing them among a welter of pillows in tents set up in the fields.[41] Vagrants and tramps were also known to fleece callow field hands. They became the "gentry of the market square" by enticing migrants into rigged games of chance and engaging in pickpocketing, swindles, and theft.[42]

Another problem were the illegal taverns that were common in many markets. According to one observer, "drunkenness is widespread. They drink to seal bargains, they drink to good wages, they drink on account of sorrow and joy. They drink not only vodka, but eau-de-Cologne, kinder-bal'zam, 'fau-aromatique'—by the bucketful, as the commerce of the local shops testifies."[43]

However, the main threat to worker interests was not their own prejudices and squandering of resources, but evolving employer strategies. As we have seen, most grain growers were ambivalent about the hiring market system. At times employers hoped to weaken the effect of worker strength there by imploring police to interfere in the bargaining process to protect grower interests. Farmers also might try to get around worker supervision of the market by hiring a group of laborers on the sly on the fringes or outside of town squares, keeping their wage offers secret from other laborers.[44]

When they felt particularly vulnerable to the mobilization of workers inside the market, though, they sometimes tried to take procurement of labor power outside it. They increasingly hired professional labor and machine subcontractors who in most cases never set foot in the markets in their efforts to furnish labor power. Persons who leased their own agricultural harvest machines to large estate owners began to appear at least as early as the 1890s. At times peasants would pool together resources to purchase the machines and, after harvesting their own crops, if they had any, would offer their services elsewhere. Some became virtual migrant laborers themselves going from farm to farm. After the turn of the century employers, particularly in Kuban Oblast and Tavrida and Samara provinces, increasingly resorted to

---

[40] Solov'ev, "Otchet," p. 708; Khizhniakov, "Sel'skie rabochie," *Zhizn'*, no. 1 (January 1900), sec. 2, pp. 137–38; *Saratovskii Listok*, no. 163, 31 July 1896, p. 2.

[41] Vol'tman, "Ocherk," pp. 52–53.

[42] *VSKhEG* (1913): 345–46, 361–62, 365; Mixter, "Of Grandfather-Beaters," pp. 145–46, 165.

[43] N. Chebotaev, "Vrachebno-prodovol'stvennye punkty dlia prishlykh sel'sko-khoziaist-vennykh rabochikh v Samarskoi gub. za leto 1900 goda (otchety zaveduiushchikh punkt-ami): Vrachebno-prodovol'stvennyi punkt v kh. Talovom za leto 1900 goda," *Vrachebnaia Khronika Samarskoi Gubernii* (hereafter, *VKh Samara*), no. 2 (February 1901): 27.

[44] *Revoliutsionnaia Rossiia*, no. 55, 20 November 1904, p. 20; *Privolzhskii Krai*, no. 132, 25 June 1906, p. 2; Mixter, "Of Grandfather-Beaters," pp. 153, 160, 166 n. 100.

such contractors. They felt that fragile grain was harvested more quickly if the services of these contractors were used. Growers also escaped the costs of purchasing and repairing these machines and to some extent shunted the costs of increasing worker unrest and machine breaking onto these professional middlemen.[45]

A system whereby a contractor hired, paid, and traveled with workers as well as supervised them barely existed in Russia. Migrant laborers helped make sure that labor contracting was a rare phenomenon in Russia by using labor markets and their own ingenuity to provide themselves with the information, welfare, and recruitment services that in other countries were often mobilized by professional middlemen.[46] Nevertheless, the use of labor contractors did increase after the turn of the century in at least one region. Following a series of hiring market disturbances in the Kuban Oblast in the period 1900–1902, employers found it preferable to utilize the services of these professional middlemen who recruited their laborers at the latter's home village rather than in the markets. The use of such intermediaries led to more impersonal relations between employers and workers and deprived migrants of much of the information necessary to protect their interests. Workers recruited by contractors often became angry when they were unable to determine whether the farmer or labor contractor should be held accountable for bad food and poor work conditions. Other laborers waiting to hire out in markets often only learned at the last moment that they would not be employed when they saw machine convoys or groups of earlier hired laborers making their way to the estates. Thus when the procurement of labor power took place outside the market through the use of contractors, workers had fewer ways of gathering needed information, supervising hire, and influencing employer behavior. Contractors took employment away from many of those who looked for jobs in hiring markets. As a result, migrants were occasionally threatened with starvation far from home.[47]

[45] Stud. Gelikonov, "Otchet o deiatel'nosti vrachebno-prodovol'stvennago punkta v s. Rovnom za leto 1900 goda," *VKh Samara*, no. 2 (February 1901): 11; V. I. Lenin, *The Development of Capitalism in Russia* (Moscow 1974; originally published in 1899), pp. 227 n.**, 262; *Tsentral'nyi Gosudarstvennyi Istoricheskii Arkhiv g. Moskvy*, fond 419, op. 1, delo 2126 ("Otvety na tsirkuliary po voprosu o peredvizhenii rabochikh na iug Rossii"), list 141 ob.; *Tsentral'nyi Gosudarstvennyi Istoricheskii Arkhiv* (hereafter, *TsGIA*), fond 1405, opis' 108, god 1906, ed. khr. 6855 ("O kr-skikh bezporiadkakh v Kubanskoi Oblasti letom 1906 g."), list 1.

[46] Robert J. Thomas and William Friedland, "The United Farm Workers Union: From Mobilization to Mechanization?" (Center for Research on Social Organization Working Paper no. 269, University of Michigan, 1982), pp. 14–15. Labor contracting was also a risky undertaking in Russia because of the fluctuations in the grain harvest. Few were willing to assume such risks.

[47] *TsGIA*, fond 1405, god 1902, opis' 103, delo 6657 ("O bezporiadkakh v stanitse Tiflisskoi proizveden. tolpoi prishlykh rabochikh"), listy 2ob.–3, 29, 30, 30ob.–31, 50; *Tsentral'nyi Gosudarstvennyi Arkhiv Oktiabr'skoi Revoliutsii* (hereafter, *TsGAOR*), fond 102, DPOO, no. 4,

Worker poverty, the increased use of agricultural machinery, the overall decline in the conditions of the agricultural *otkhozhie promysly*, the presence of regional and ethnic rivalries, the squandering of resources to food vendors, tavern owners, vagrants, and prostitutes, and the intrusion of machine and labor contractors were at times extremely difficult obstacles for migrant agricultural laborers to overcome. The wonder is that migrant agricultural laborers could mobilize for collective action at all. While they were often passive and overt protest was not especially frequent, migrant agricultural laborers nevertheless did engage in a myriad of protest forms. By dint of their own ingenuity and the tactical mobility provided by the hiring market, they often proved to be quite adept at openly defending their interests.

THE MARKET AS WORKERS' TURF

THE RESOURCES OF THE MARKET

Workers not only created and acknowledged the power of the hiring market by sabotaging winter hire and returning to the market frequently, they also mobilized in defense of their interests there by: (1) using market resources; (2) exchanging information; and (3) engaging in collective action, which often drew on memories of customary village routines and attempted to raise wages, shape employer behavior, or create more dependable labor relations.

Despite the lack of permanent organization, agricultural workers found ways to apply pressure on employers. Because of the likelihood of grain spilling out if left too long and the farming practice on the steppe whereby estate owners tended to risk all on just one crop, workers could generally rely on the anxiety of employers wanting to avoid losses by hiring quickly. In essence, in a good harvest year, laborers did not need the artificial pressure of a union, which the state had banned in any case, nor did they have to hold out for long periods given the onset of the harvest. By withholding their labor through strikes before hire, by returning weekly to the hiring market, and by insisting on the celebration of their own popular holidays, they could increase employer anxiety still more.[48]

The very lack of organization also had one important advantage. Since large crowds gathered in the hiring market legally and many of the workers were migrants, police had a difficult time figuring out whom to arrest if there

---

chast' 21, 1904 g., list 3; *Severnyi Kavkaz*, no. 77, 7 July 1905, p. 3; *Kuban*, no. 96, 27 May 1906, p. 3.

[48] K. Bunitskii, "Vychislenie dnei prazdnuemykh, v techenii goda, rabochimi liud'mi v Aleksandrovskom uezde Ekaterinoslavskoi gubernii," *Zapiski Imperatorskago Obshchestva Sel'skago Khoziaistva Iuzhnoi Rossii* (May 1866): 306–11; *Novorossiiskii Telelegraf*, no. 157, 19 July 1872 and note 54, below.

were disturbances.[49] Heated bargaining was the norm so that by the time law-enforcement officers were called in it was often too late. Almost invariably, troops to assist undermanned police arrived on the scene well after worker collective action had occurred and the participants had dispersed. Thus the large mass of workers in the markets and their relative anonymity acquired as they negotiated the space of migration, gave *otkhodniki* a degree of tactical mobility when they chose to mobilize for collective action.[50]

It is important to note that the market tended to be geared toward workers. It combined several resources cheaply in one place as those with goods to sell and services to render found they were more likely to reap a profit by catering to the needs of numerous workers than those of a few employers. Thus the environment of the market was often more suitable to worker than employer cultural hegemony. Workers had access to inexpensive food, leisure, information, and tools and did not have to lose time and money searching for them. They could husband these resources, which could be better used to generate collective action.

While in the hiring market, workers sought to overcome the alienation and segmentation of their lives which the migrant labor system and employers tended to promote. Migrant laborers had to a large degree left behind their family life and a village culture, which may have afforded them prestige and a sense of dignity.[51] On the estate employers tended to look at harvesters in economic terms only as work "hands," sending them back to the hiring market during nonwork periods. In the hiring market, however, laborers would recombine resources and recover their human dignity by indulging in other aspects of the human experience besides work. Thus they tended to dress up for the hiring fairs to express their equality and independence on what usually was regarded as a holiday and "free" time.[52] With this heightened sense of self-dignity they may have been more truculent in their negotiations with employers, which now took place on a more equal footing than on the estate. They also had the opportunity to implant their own lively culture of singing, game playing, and book reading in the market.[53] Unlike employers,

[49] *Moskovskiia Vedomosti*, no. 282, 12 October 1885, p. 4; Khizhniakov, "Sel'skie rabochie," *Zhizn'*, no. 2 (February 1900), sec. 2, p. 163.

[50] Eric Wolf, *Peasant Wars of the Twentieth Century* (New York, 1973; originally published in 1969), p. 203.

[51] Burawoy, "The Functions," pp. 1050–87; Harvey J. Kaye, "Another Way of Seeing Peasants: The Work of John Berger," *Peasant Studies* 9, no. 2 (Winter 1982): 96.

[52] G. I. Uspenskii, "Pis'ma s doroga," in *G. I. Uspenskii: Sobranie sochinenii v deviati tomakh*, vol. 7, p. 328; N. Chebotaev, "Vrachebno-prodovol'stvennye punkty," p. 27; *VSKhEG* (1913): 368; Mixter, "Of Grandfather-Beaters," p. 156. In England, workers often wore ribbons as a sign of solidarity. See: Michael Roberts, " 'Waiting Upon Chance': English Hiring Fairs and Their Meanings From the 14th to the 20th Century," *Journal of Historical Sociology* 1, no. 2 (June 1988): 132–33, 137, 140, 143, 147.

[53] *VSKhEG*, no. 3 (March 1900): 97, 110; no. 6 (June 1900): 303.

then, who tended to value the market only for its economic function of labor procurement, migrant laborers liked the way it combined economic exchange, leisure, information, food, and medical service as well as provided a place for workers' culture to flourish and potential allies and even marriage partners to be found. Employers clearly saw the combined resources of the market as a potential threat as their outrage at the "rowdy" worker culture there attests. They were particularly outraged when in years of labor shortage migrants through their power in the hiring market tried to get employers to pay heed to their culture. As workers insisted that unofficial popular holidays celebrated back home be recognized on the estates and even demanded that orchestras to entertain them be ensconced amid the wheat, while they worked, employers decried the weakening of labor discipline.[54]

The Exchange of Information

For migrants far from home in a strange environment, knowledge truly was power if they were not to be deceived by unscrupulous employers. In the hiring markets of the European Russian steppe, migrant laborers could physically see and publicly oversee labor procurement and hope to prevent deceptive employer tactics as well as immoral treatment of laborers on the "private" estates. While in winter hiring agricultural laborers had often been forced to accept a private deal negotiated between a *volost'* official and an employer representative about which they had little information or say, in the market workers were "free" to conclude their own contract and had a choice of employers. They could compare wages and employers and by swapping information with migrants from elsewhere they were more likely to perceive common class interests, as they could see that it was not just one employer who treated workers badly. Finally, unlike in winter hire, workers could gain a sense of their own collective strength and could forge a measure of dignity and self-confidence by relying on their own ability to negotiate rather than be subordinate to a middleman.

The concentration of laborers in the hiring market brought about by large-scale capitalist agriculture replete with its factorylike machinery also brought with it outside scrutiny and supervision. The information contained in the reports of the relief station managers and particularly the numerous books and articles by Dr. N. I. Teziakov and Dr. V. V. Khizhniakov concerning the conditions of migrant agricultural labor, which Lenin and others read and further publicized, helped sway public opinion in the 1890s sufficiently to defeat the passage of legislation even more detrimental to workers than the

---

[54] *Krymskii Vestnik*, no. 143, 8 June 1906, p. 4; Iaroshko, *Rabochii vopros*, pp. 48, 55 n.*; *Moskovskiia Vedomosti*, no. 222, 15 August 1894, p. 2; Roberts, "Waiting Upon Chance," pp. 129–30.

15. DR. NIKOLAI IVANOVICH TEZIAKOV, ORGANIZER OF RELIEF STATIONS FOR MIGRANT AGRICULTURAL LABORERS IN KHERSON AND SARATOV PROVINCES (*NIKOLAI IVANOVICH PIROGOV I EGO NASLEDIE*, ED. M. M. GRAN, Z. G. FRENKEL', AND A. I. SHINGAREV [ST. PETERSBURG: TOVARISHCHESTVO R. GOLIKE AND A. VIL'BORG, 1911], FOLLOWING P. 253).

16. THE CONSERVATIVE SARATOV PROVINCE MARSHAL OF THE NOBILITY, PAVEL ALEKSANDROVICH KRIVSKII (SERGEI ALEKSEEVICH PANCHULIDZE, *SBORNIK BIOGRAFII KAVELERGARDOV, 1826-1908*, VOL. 4 [ST. PETERSBURG: EKSPEDITSIIA ZAGOTOVLENIIA GOSUDARSTVENNYKH BUMAG, 1908], P. 165).

17. MIGRANT AGRICULTURAL LABORERS, DOCTORS, MEDICAL STUDENTS, AND FELDSHERS AT THE MEDICAL-FOOD SUPPLY STATION NEAR THE HIRING MARKET AT BERISLAV, KHERSON PROVINCE, 1896 (UKRAINIAN YOUTHS IN STRAW HATS ON RIGHT SIDE OF PHOTOGRAPH) (VSESOIUZNYI NAUCHNO-ISSLEDOVATEL'NYI INSTITUT SOTSIAL'NOI GIGIENY I ORGANIZATSII ZDRAVOOKHRANENIIA IM. N. A. SEMASHKO [MOSCOW], ARCHIVAL *FOND* 9 OF DR. N. I. TEZIAKOV).

1886 statute on agricultural labor relations.[55] Student relief station managers were often populist-oriented and were more likely to defend worker interests than engage in the sort of compulsion and supervised control of laborers in the market that employers in Russia and elsewhere sometimes wanted incorporated into welfare arrangements.[56] The relative lack of social control and the anonymity of most migrant laborers allowed them the tactical mobility to engage in collective action visible to the targets of protest and accompanied by discernible demands. They were not restricted to the drawbacks of covert acts carried out by individuals too scared to join together to face their opponents openly.

Relief stations also provided both an independent source of food and a locale where information could be exchanged and allies found—a circumstance unlikely to occur if labor procurement took place back home or on the estate. The hiring market allowed for a greater choice of skilled leaders as well as allies. Workers or artisans (e.g., cobblers) having knowledge of local conditions, ex-soldiers versed in elementary organization, out-of-work miners, relief station managers, vagrants, and even revolutionaries were at times candidates for such roles. So, for instance, in Tavrida Province in 1906 a Bolshevik rallied unemployed migrants to protest their plight and call for the release of political prisoners. As a result a commission was set up to assist workers.[57]

Most often, though, migrant workers relied not on outsiders but on themselves and their past experience. Artel organization and leaders usually assisted mobilization at the most basic level. The artel heads had frequently gathered much experience, having come into the markets over the course of a number of years. They informed others of successful bargaining techniques and proper employer behavior towards workers. Employers involved in production for the market tended to redefine old relations and language trying to destroy memory and affirm the legitimacy of their ways of seeing things.[58]

---

[55] Lenin, *The Development*, pp. 232–52, 238, and 249–51; Mixter, "Migrant." Teziakov was an important figure in the Society of Russian Physicians in Memory of N. I. Pirogov, while Khizhniakov was the son of the Chernigov zemstvo activist V. M. Khizhniakov as well as secretary of the Free Economic Society and an activist in the Liberation Movement. Their efforts were similar to those of William Cobbett in England in the 1820s and 1830s and John Steinbeck, Woody Guthrie, and Carey McWilliams in California in the 1930s. Such publicity and outside support, which were also manifest in the UFW informational product boycotts of the 1960s and 1970s, proved in many cases crucial to the success of farm worker movements and the articulation of new questions and discourses for the public agenda. See Thomas and Friedland, "The United Farm Workers Union," pp. 34–36, 48–54.

[56] Mixter, "Of Grandfather-Beaters," pp. 164–65; Mixter, "Migrant," passim.

[57] *Revoliutsionnoe dvizhenie v Tavricheskoi gubernii v 1905–1907 gg: Sbornik dokumentov i materialov* (Simferopol, 1955), pp. 180–81; *Zhizn' Kryma*, no. 110, 21 May 1906, p. 2; no. 118, 1 June 1906, p. 4.

[58] The new vocabulary included such terms as *risk, speculation, self-help, saving for the future, and discipline over immediate gratification*. Worker communities were redefined as slums, cus-

Migrant laborers in turn tried to keep alive their alternative visions of what constituted moral labor relations, not only by insisting that employers relate to them as whole human beings, instead of just work hands, but by recalling past experiences in labor migration. The perpetuation of information that relations were different in the past was crucial for the mobilization of collective action; for otherwise, workers would passively accept employer versions of the truth. According to one relief station manager, older Ukrainian workers talked about the old days, recalling the "beautiful" past when they had been paid royally, before the arrival of the machines and the "butchers" (peasants from the Russian provinces).[59] Thus even though they experienced rapid labor turnover from year to year, migrant harvesters were able to spread the knowledge that their status was in decline through their stories and songs. Collective action sometimes resulted from the consciousness that conditions were deteriorating.

There is evidence that youths went out with expectations of striking it rich due to the true or false information contained in stories and songs. Migrant laborers at times acted more upon illusions than upon the basis of actual structural possibilities. Rumors, of course, have been one of the prime causes of agrarian protest in Russia and elsewhere.[60] Youths going out into migrant labor, soon to be laden with family responsibilities when they married and set up a separate household, were perhaps frantic to earn a lot of money quickly for a dowry or to build a house, perhaps hoping in the process to win a marriage partner from a prosperous household. They were ready to press hard to realize their dreams.[61]

In other cases, workers were said to be certain that it was worthwhile going out after a year of fruitless wandering in search of work, because a good harvest was sure to follow a bad one.[62] One of the songs sung by peasant youth in the Ukraine bespoke the incurable hope with which migrant boys began their journey into farm work:

The lads were boasting as they set out for Tavrida that they would soon be wearing leg wrappings of taffeta, leg wrappings of taffeta and boots

---

tomary-use rights as illegal trespassing on private property, unemployment as idleness and vagrancy, gift collection as extortion, gleaning as theft. On this type of redefinition and mystification, see E. P. Thompson, "Eighteenth-Century English Society: Class Struggle Without Class?" *Social History* 3, no. 2 (May 1978): 150.

[59] *VSKhEG*, no. 6 (June 1900): 300, 303; Iaroshko, *Rabochii vopros*, p. 7 and 7 n.*.

[60] Hobsbawm and Rudé, *Captain Swing*, pp. 86–87; Roberta Thompson Manning, *The Crisis of the Old Order in Russia* (Princeton, 1982), pp. 146–47, 150.

[61] Iaroshko, *Rabochii vopros*, pp. 39, 205–7; Shakhovskoi, *Sel'sko-khoziaistvennye*, p. 104; Maxim Gorky, "Chelkash," in *A Sky-Blue Life and Selected Stories*, trans. George Reavey (New York, 1964), pp. 48–50; Cathy Frierson, "Razdel: The Peasant Family Divided," *The Russian Review* 46, no. 1 (January 1987): 42.

[62] Iaroshko, *Rabochii vopros*, pp. 38–39.

of morocco leather; they came back after the frost had set in, their toes sticking out [of their old footwear][63]

Other traditional songs, stories, and rumors made wanderers heroes and pointed to the frontier and specifically the faraway south as a land of bounty and freedom. Thus songs and stories raised the expectations of young migrant laborers in particular when they headed southward and may have made them more truculent in their dealings with employers in the hiring markets.

As with most expressions of peasant mentalité, the songs of migrant laborers were ambivalent. Songs of hope were counterbalanced by cynical laments which contained warnings about the plight of former *otkhodniki* and, according to one observer, rarely ended without the singers in tears.[64] The lyrics of one such song, for instance, described a young girl's arduous journey to the south which involved traipsing along mud roads shivering in the early spring frost. Later she prayed that God would give her the endurance to make it through her grueling term of work. Other songs warned of the deception petty employers often practiced and in the following case may have conveyed information that young women would not normally have learned otherwise since they experienced such high rates of labor turnover. The words of one tune told of how German employers had written Kievan peasants telling them to come "to us" and we shall feed you pike and other good fish, but that the peasants so approached had written back telling the Germans not to lie.[65]

Peasants also asserted their largely oral culture in hiring markets by insisting on oral contracts. They were in fact generally successful in this endeavor, as only 5 to 15 percent of the hiring agreements between employers and agricultural workers were written down.[66] To be sure, employer deception was often easier without written documents, but oral contracts had advantages for workers too. Many laborers were illiterate and were scared that the employer would have the upper hand if disputes based on written contracts were taken to court.[67] Harvesters also knew that one of their few weapons

[63] Teziakov, *Rynki naima*, vol. 1, p. 10; Iaroshko, *Rabochii vopros*, p. 11.

[64] Iaroshko, *Rabochii vopros*, pp. 10–11.

[65] For both songs, see Iaroshko, *Rabochii vopros*, p. 11; Teziakov, *Rynki naima*, vol. 1, p. 10. Bothy ballads in the feeing markets of Scotland and the songs of Woody Guthrie and Cisco Houston in the migrant camps of California contained similar information and warnings. See Ian Carter, "Class and Culture Among Farm Servants in the North-East," in *Social Class in Scotland: Past and Present*, ed. A. Allan MacLaren (Edinburgh, 1976), pp. 110–13.

[66] Iakov Fedorovich Brave, *Naemnye sel'skokhoziaistvennye rabochie v zhizni i v zakonodatel'stve* (Moscow, 1899), p. 195; Polferov, *Sel'sko-khoziaistvennyia rabochiia ruki*, p. 23.

[67] They were to a large extent correct in their suspicions since employers who concluded written contracts received greater protection. According to the 1886 agricultural labor law, worker contract violations often entailed criminal prosecution and penalties, while employer transgressions merited only civil sanctions.

against employers was their mobility and the threat that they might leave in the middle of the harvest. They did not want to be tied down.

Instead of abstract law, often-illiterate peasants chose to see visible evidence of good faith. In the hiring market workers preferred to receive tangible acknowledgment of an employer's goodwill, such as a drink of vodka or a ruble or two advance. They also sometimes made the employer swear an oath, so sacred in peasant culture. According to one observer, agreement was "not managed without oaths [and] assurances that the grain [was] easy to harvest and the food 'fit for a king' [barskie], all this not rarely seasoned with pearls of the Russian dialect. The reputation of the employer has an influence on the tractability of the workers."[68]

Another aspect of oral culture, besides songs and oaths, actually might determine an employer's reputation. Rumors spread inside the market were used to punish employer immoral behavior outside the confines of the hiring square. K. Bunitskii, a member of the Society of Rural Proprietors of Southern Russia, writing about migrant laborers in New Russia during the pre-Emancipation period, claimed that employers rarely treated workers badly because:

> If about some estate an unfavorable rumor (*molva*) breaks out in public among the crowds of workers, then a very dangerous situation imperils this estate: in the nearest market it [the estate] can not hire them, and it must send into more places [for workers], where the bad rumor about it might still not have reached and from such delayed hire the estate may suffer a significant loss in the harvesting of hay or grain.[69]

Public supervision within the market thus attempted to rectify employer covert action and deceit. Workers were even heard to say that on peasant estates "there is no truth" (i.e. only deception).[70] On the other hand, migrant laborers went to Kakhovka, the largest hiring market in the south, precisely because they invested the market there with moral authority, acknowledging that "Kakhovka does not deceive, it reveals the true price" (i.e., wage rate).[71] Workers learned from experience that employers might and often did lie, that labor contractors might resort to ruses, and that even their own rumors, dreams, and expectations might deceive, but that they could rely on the social space of the hiring market for the truth, partially because they insisted

[68] Solov'ev, "Otchet," p. 704; Shakhovskoi, *Sel'sko-khoziaistvennye*, pp. 105–6; Michael Roberts has compared it to the exchange of sacred marriage vows and tokens in church. See Roberts, "Waiting Upon Chance," pp. 135–36.

[69] K. Bunitskii, "O zatrudneniiakh," pp. 273–74. See also: Kavelin, "Pis'ma," col. 669. On the labeling of employers and market intelligence in Africa, see Charles Van Onselen, *Chibaro: African Mine Labour in Southern Rhodesia* (London, 1976), pp. 232–36, 244.

[70] Iaroshko, *Rabochii vopros*, p. 44.

[71] Polferov, *Sel'sko-khoziaistvennyia rabochiia ruki*, p. 12.

on enforcing a moral economy and values by overseeing recruitment and information there.

Dr. V. V. Khizhniakov has summed up some of the above themes by showing how the expectation wrought by peasant mentalité, folklore, dreams, rumors, and memories of past experience both blinded and informed, encouraging *otkhodniki* to take risks, use their mobility, and put their faith on *seeing* the hiring market rather than rely on the word of an employer or outsider:

> In their search for seasonal work, laborers are guided by memories of previous hirings and also by accidental rumors, continually arising in their midst, not having any basis in them; these rumors usually promise mountains of gold (*zolotnyia gory*) ahead and drive workers from one place to another. The manager at Kherson (in 1896) wrote in his report: "None of the workers up till now can be convinced about the state of markets unless they were personally in them."[72]

Another way migrants showed their allegiance to the market was by refusing to take employment very far from it. In general, migrants stayed close to the market so that they could easily find out if wage rates jumped and so that they would not lose money traveling or be stranded if an employer deceived them. This loyalty is confirmed by the relief station manager at Ruditsyn's tavern in Grushevka, Ekaterinoslav Province, who noted as well that workers were willing to let the price established there hold for the entire region, because they had a say in determining this wage:

> the voice of this market is so authoritative and despotic, if it is possible to put it so, that—[it is] an interesting fact—the worker does not want to hire himself out beyond two *versty* from the station, even if they would give to him a fully satisfactory wage. The apprehension of taking less than the prevailing wages sometimes forces him to take a loss, but, all the same, he stubbornly stands by his own [belief]: "We are going to Rudytsa, we shall hire there."[73]

Even if artels went straight to estates to hire out, they might well send one or two scouts to the market to verify wage rates.[74] What was said in the market was supposed to be the truth, and so it is hardly surprising that many of the disturbances that occurred on estates were the result of misrepresentation of work conditions earlier at the time of recruitment in the nearest town. In one such case where workers felt compelled to uphold the sanctity of the market, a drunken steward had hired more workers than needed; in another, a steward had not told laborers that the oats to be harvested had been beaten

---

[72] Khizhniakov, "Sel'skie rabochie," *Zhizn'*, no. 2 (February 1900), sec. 2, p. 163.

[73] *VSKhEG*, no. 6 (June 1900): 301–2. See also Shakhovskoi, *Sel'sko-khoziaistvennye*, p. 104.

[74] *Materialy dlia otsenki zemel' Khersonskoi gubernii*, vol. VI: *Khersonskoi uezd* (Kherson, 1890), p. 264.

down by hail thus making the piecework laborers had been hired for more difficult and less remunerative.[75]

THE TRANSFORMATION OF VILLAGE ROUTINES IN MARKET COLLECTIVE ACTION AND THE SUPERVISION OF NONWORKER BEHAVIOR

Migrant worker use of the lexicon of truth and deception with regard to supervision in the hiring market and employer behavior outside it conjures up the idea of a "moral economy." Agricultural laborers often waited until they returned to the hiring square, where they felt they had more resources to draw on, before they attempted to punish the "immoral" deeds perpetrated by employers on the estates. When mobilized for such retribution they usually tapped, not only the information networks in the market, but also the organizational knowledge gained from collective action learned in their home villages. Traditional village repertoires of collective action were tapped largely because they were familiar. As we shall see, in the hiring market they were sometimes partially transformed, as they tended to be aimed at employers instead of other peasants and were directed toward upholding a code of proper labor relations instead of village community norms.

The *charivari* in Russia was one such village custom and involved the organized public mocking of someone who had violated community values such as an adulterer, a suitor from another village, a thief, or a witch. The banging of oven doors and hooting in a public place, such as a street or market, was intended to tarnish a transgressor's reputation. At times offenders might be driven out of the community as morally unfit, if they were unwilling to accept the judgment rendered. Other village rituals also involved the defining of a commune's boundaries.[76]

Youths in rural Russia were often given a leading role in the organization of such customs as *charivaris*, group courtship practices, fist-fighting matches, caroling, and sewing circles, all of which taught community norms. These seem to have had an effect on the types of repertoires relied on in the hiring markets—where after all, the majority of the workers often were between the ages of fifteen and thirty. Village experience was a substitute for organizational experience in the hiring markets.

Youths also sometimes formed rival street gangs who defended their turf and women, throwing nonlocal suitors out of the village or designated area when they came calling. Migrant agricultural labor, in fact, like farm ser-

---

[75] *Volzhskoe Slovo*, no. 66, 21 July 1907, p. 4; *TsGAOR*, fond 102, D-vo III, no. 1 ch. 33 LV, 1900 g. ("Krest'ianskie bezporiadki po Saratovskoi gubernii"), listy 32A–32Bob.

[76] Stephen Frank, "Popular Justice, Community and Culture Among the Russian Peasantry, 1870–1900," *The Russian Review* 46, no. 3 (July 1987): 239–65; Tilly, *From Mobilization*, pp. 144–45; Anthony Netting, "Images and Ideas in Russian Peasant Art," *Slavic Review* 35, no. 1 (March 1976): 58; Stephen Frank, "Cultural Conflict and Criminality in Rural Russia, 1861–1900" (Ph.D. diss., Brown University, 1986), pp. 106, 109–11.

vanthood in other countries, served as an integral part of youth culture. The meeting of single people in the hiring market as well as courting, pairing off, and sleeping together in straw huts on the estates, appear to have been a regular feature of agricultural *otkhozhie promysly*.[77]

Charivaris were often ambivalent events as well. While usually upholding community values, at times, like marketplace carnivals, they could also serve to criticize and briefly overturn traditional authority, parental or otherwise, in an attempt to bring about social leveling. Over time, the *charivari* became increasingly applied to people outside the village and to nonpeasants, with violence sometimes replacing symbolic ritual.[78] Social leveling manifested in such acts was one of the main desires of peasants and workers during the 1917 revolution and was reflected in the demand for polite address—*vy* rather than *ty*.[79] Agricultural workers at times also insisted that employers address them respectfully.

Migrant laborers adapted the *charivari* to use against outsiders. They, too, publicly punished immoral behavior through collective action—the hiring market taking the place of the village community. They would sometimes boot employers out of the market who refused to offer "just" wages, just as during *charivaris* back home they threw out of the village those who had committed moral offenses. So in Taganrog in the early 1860s:

> Sometimes during bargaining, a terrifying cry of several hundred people is suddenly heard and a gentleman, with the most pitiful expression on his face, rides out of the crowd on horseback or racing carriage. They drove him away *(otiukali)*. *Otiukivanie* consists of this—they all yell *Tiu, Tiu*, and laugh loudly: this is a kind of scandal, administered to an employer whom they don't like and who, probably, offered a price too low.[80]

[77] A. Ia. Porits'kyi, *Pobut sil's'kohospodars'kykh robitkyniv Ukrainy v period kapitalizmu* (Kiev, 1964), p. 123; *The Village of Viriatino*, ed. Sula Benet (Garden City, N.Y., 1970), p. 139; Alferaki, "Zametki," p. 108; *Five Sisters: Women Against the Tsar*, ed. Barbara Engel and Clifford Rosenthal (New York, 1975), pp. 108–11; Frank, "Cultural," pp. 84–89, 101, ch. 5.

[78] Natalie Zemon Davis, "The Reasons of Misrule," in *Society and Culture in Early Modern France*, ed. Natalie Zemon Davis (Stanford, 1975), pp. 97–123; Neil B. Weissman, "Rural Crime in Tsarist Russia: The Question of Hooliganism, 1905–1914," *Slavic Review* 37, no. 2 (June 1978): 228–40, esp. 235–40; Frank, "Cultural," pp. 89–93, chap. 5. Educated society, which had by and large supported the retention of peasant customary law for dealing with peasant problems, quickly redefined the *charivari* as hooliganism, when such an act was aimed at mocking the authority of nonpeasants and asserting social equality.

[79] Richard Stites, "Utopias in the Air and on the Ground: Futuristic Dreams in the Russian Revolution," *Russian History* 11, no. 2–3 (Summer–Fall 1984): 252 and n. 21; Heather Hogan, "Conciliation Boards in Revolutionary Petrograd: Aspects of the Crisis of Labor-Management Relations in 1917," *Russian History* 9, pt. 1 (1982): 64–65.

[80] Alferaki, "Zametki," p. 112; *Krymskii Vestnik*, no. 113, 25 May 1906, p. 3; *VSKhEG* (1913): 364. Driving an "immoral" employer outside the boundaries of the market not only resem-

Tiu was the Ukrainian way of driving away an unwanted beast or of expressing disgust at it. Used in the hiring market versus employers, it was an interesting attempt to assert worker definitions of morality.

Collective action could not always be classified as violent. Some of the acts were symbolic, aimed at supervision of morality and besmirching a reputation through hooting and noise rather than inflicting permanent injury. The spread of rumors in order to blacklist an employer also had a similar intent. This action and others like it resembled the *charivari* and other village rituals, which were often nonviolent.[81] Nevertheless, there were a number of cases in which employers, even from the gentry, were violently beaten up in the hiring market.[82] In 1898 in Voznesensk, Kherson Province, there were ten such cases alone of workers pummeling employers in the hiring square, usually for withholding passports or not paying out what was owed.[83] But as these incidents suggest, violence was not wanton. In almost all the cases the physical abuse came *only* as a response to an *earlier* immoral act on the part of the employer that had usually been committed on the estate. As in other cases in which peasants took the law into their own hands (*samosud*), peasants in the markets may have felt that the penalties employers faced for deceit in courts of law were insufficient. Employer "theft" of worker wages through deceit was apparently deemed to have a similarly grave impact on the family economy that horse theft did. And the latter crime usually warranted the most violent response in the arsenal of popular justice.[84] The fact was that in Elisavetgrad District, Kherson Province, in the early 1890s a sample of court cases showed that out of 50 cases brought by workers against employers only 8 were decided in their favor. On the other hand, judges acquitted just 32 out of 967 laborers that employers had accused of wrongdoing. Even when workers won, it cost them time and money, while they remained in the steppe before and during court proceedings, which employers often purposely tried to drag out.[85] Nor were the police likely to side with them. Thus, the summary justice of the clenched fist often offered more immediate results. Even when they were unable to get the abuse rectified—a

---

bled the village charivari, it also mirrored the actions of factory workers who carted supervisors who had treated them disrespectfully off the space of the shop floor in a wheelbarrow and dumped them "unceremoniously in unpleasant places" outside the factory. See: Diane Koenker, "Collective Action and Collective Violence in the Russian Labor Movement," *Slavic Review* 41, no. 3 (Fall 1982): 446; Hogan, "Industrial," pp. 180–81.

[81] Koenker, "Collective Action," p. 446; E. P. Thompson, " 'Rough Music': Le Charivari Anglais," *Annales ESC* 27, no. 2 (March–April 1972): 293–306; Frank, "Popular Justice," pp. 239–65.

[82] See e.g., Mixter, "Of Grandfather-Beaters," pp. 152–68; Teziakov, *Rynki naima*, vol. 1, p. 14; *VSKhEG*, no. 6 (June 1900): 313, *Krymskii Vestnik*, no. 120, 2 June 1906, p. 3.

[83] Khizhniakov, "Sel'skie rabochie," *Zhizn'*, no. 2 (February 1900), sec. 2, p. 163.

[84] Frank, "Popular Justice," pp. 257–60.

[85] Iaroshko, *Rabochii vopros*, pp. 59–80, esp. pp. 63 and 73.

passport returned or pay given out—the thrashing served as a warning, placing limits on employer behavior and perhaps raising worker self-respect. One worker in Saratov Province, for instance, told his employer, whom he seems to have viewed in class terms: "It would be surprising not to receive it [full wages], surely you know that they beat your brother for bad settling of accounts—in the past year the peasants beat Polenov unmercifully in the village of Arkadak and all the same remained unpunished."[86] During the Revolution of 1905–1907 workers sought revenge for even more distant immoral acts and as, in other cases, migrants who had had no previous dealings with the employer even joined in on giving the lesson. According to one author, in Tavrida Province if a worker turned to his comrades for assistance it was "never" refused. He noted that agricultural laborers dredged up memories of past injustice and publicized the consequences of employer malfeasance in the following way:

> Two days ago such violence rained down upon Mr. B. who several years ago deducted 5 rubles from the salary of a worker for the smothering of an ox. Now on account of 5 rubles Mr. B. was beaten mercilessly by workers, standing up for their comrade. Only owing to the fact that a police officer sensibly hurried to pay the worker 5 rubles, further beating of Mr. B. was stopped and the crowd dispersed.[87]

Here clearly laborers thought they had enough power in the market to be "judges," even if they declined the role on the estate.

The fistfights and turf battles between two different streets back in the home village also may have informed the actions of local and migrant laborers when they fought each other for supremacy in the hiring market. Often these scuffles ended with one side, usually migrant laborers, being forced to quit the market.[88] Nevertheless, physical strength may have been used to uphold strike solidarity just as it was used to uphold community control of courting practices back home. According to a newspaper reporter in Ekaterinoslav Province, for instance, "whole civil wars" occurred "if some party of workers hires itself out to someone more inexpensively than that price which they had defined jointly." These same workers, though, also tried to protect the sanctity of their turf by defaming the reputation of an immoral employer who threatened to pollute the market by his presence:

[86] Mixter, "Of Grandfather-Beaters," p. 162 and 162 n. 84. See also *Krymskii Vestnik*, no. 100, 4 August 1905, p. 3. In D. Fedorov, "Anti-Nemetskii bunt," *Nedelia*, no. 26, 28 June 1898, col. 839, it is noted that the threat of beating left a strong impression on employers in Voznesensk not to cheat their workers.

[87] M. G. "Korrespondentsii (ot korrespondentov): 'Svoim sudom,' " *Krymskii Vestnik*, no. 126, 9 June 1906, p. 3.

[88] See note 39, above; Porits'kyi, *Pobut*, p. 123; *The Village of Viriatino*, pp. 127–44.

The steward of Mrs. Kuzmitskii arrived here for hiring people and went into the inn. Some of the workers, seeing this and wanting to take revenge on him because he ostensibly had settled accounts with them incorrectly, went up to the doorway and waited for his exit. When he came out, one hundred people surrounded him and began to yell "tiu!" (*tiukat'*), hoot (*gikat'*), and tug him by his clothes. Then seeing that things were going bad, he mounted his horse and wanted to leave, but, some [of the workers] ran in front of him, stopped his horse and others threw at him caps taken from their heads and clods of earth and thus accompanied him for a distance of a half-*versta*.[89]

If tarnishing the reputation of an employer often involved throwing him outside the boundaries of the market, strike solidarity entailed keeping labor power within the confines of the hiring square. The student manager of the relief station at the town of Kherson wrote in June of 1898:

The third event was in the end of June when prices for day field work began to rise, and workers took heart. At this time exactly, some landowner arrives and offers the workers a lower price, than that, which was at the market on this day. The workers hold out firmly and do not go out to him. But several persons break down and agree [to terms]. Then the rest, surrounding the dray cart, on which the employer sat with the just-hired *batraki*, began to induce their comrades not to go, [but] remain, while some of them unperceived unscrew the lugs from the wheels. Those departing do not heed their pleas, the employer whips the horses, the horses move, but the wheels fly off and together with them, to general laughter, fly the riders.[90]

In 1906 in such places as Kurman, Simferopol', and Dzhankoi in Tavrida Province, groups of migrant laborers formed "illegal" committees "for the hire of laborers into field work," which the police even termed "revolutionary." They too threw workers and their property out of wagons, if the latter attempted to hire out for a price lower than designated. They yelled, "*Tiu!*" at employers offering too low a wage and collected twenty kopeks from each laborer to serve as a strike fund, although the police and newspaper reports suggest that they kept this money for themselves.[91]

Collective responsibility, unanimous decision-making in the *mir*, artel organization, and full participation in *samosud* actions and petitions to author-

---

[89] *Ekaterinoslavskii Listok*, no. 77, 13 July 1883, p. 3. I learned of this source through O. I. Luhova, *Sil's'kohospodars'kyi proletariat pivdnia Ukrainy v period kapitalizmu* (Kiev, 1965), pp. 176–77.

[90] S. N. Khlebnikov, "Lechebno-prodovol'stvennyi punkt v g. Khersone," in *LPP Kherson* (1898), p. 101.

[91] *Krymskii Vestnik*, no. 113, 25 May 1906, p. 3; *Revoliutsionnoe dvizhenie v Tavricheskoi Gubernii v 1905–1907 gg.*, pp. 166–67.

ities all may have helped prepare migrants for the mobilization of strike solidarity before they reached the point of hire.

At the market near Stanitsa Tiflisskaia, Kuban Oblast, in 1902 a group of activist workers tried:

> to create a certain organization and to talk over together and thrash out the question about hiring and working pay, for which the workers gathered in groups and about which they conferred.

> Those employers who came to the bazaar square of Khutor Sheremet'evskii could no longer obtain workers, since, if separate people or parties contracted to go out to mow for a certain pay, then the leaders of the movement forbade them to follow after their employer, and, in case of disobedience, beat [them] with sticks, saying "we will all sit together," and moreover one party of mowers, of thirty persons, having been hired by the *pomeshchik* Petrik and having gone three *versty* out of the *khutor*, was brought back by force and threats.[92]

Those employers or workers who attempted to hire out deceitfully on the fringes of the market—"on the sly" or "around the corner"—were at times beaten if caught red-handed in the act, just as horsethieves might have been back home. Threats that those who hired out below the established price would be beaten were probably more common than actual beatings.[93]

Another village ritual that migrant laborers adapted for use in the hiring market was the custom of "wetting a bargain" in order to acknowledge that the labor contract was equitable. In the village, sharing a drink signified that an equal economic transaction had been negotiated face-to-face in good faith or that a defendant acknowledged that community justice and courts had reached a fair verdict.[94] It promoted a type of social leveling. In the hiring market, migrants transformed the old peasant custom to suit new purposes, at times even making nonpeasants pay homage to peasant culture:

> Settling accounts with workers is weekly on Saturday evening or Sunday or on the eve of holidays. After payment both worker and employer head off to the market [a bazaar square in a settlement or stanitsa]: here among these and others, terms are concluded again, always accompanied by "wetting of the bargain," without which it is impossible to hire the worker. This "entertainment" and also the hope of receiving a large

[92] *TsGIA*, fond 1405, god 1902, opis' 103, delo 6657 ("O bezporiadki v stanitse Tiflisskoi proizveden. tolpoi prishlykh rabochikh"), listy 29–32ob.

[93] Mixter, "Of Grandfather-Beaters," pp. 153, 159–60; *Privolzhskii Krai*, no. 132, 25 June 1906, p. 2; note 44, above.

[94] *Privolzhskii Krai*, no. 168, 9 August 1906, pp. 2–3; Frank, "Popular," pp. 248, 250, 255.

wage is the reason that workers reluctantly hire themselves out for terms on an estate.[95]

The face-to-face toast to a newly negotiated contract symbolized the equality of migrant laborers in the market. The relationship was in contradiction to the norms that prevailed outside this social space, which were built into state law. By getting the employer to share one's table and company and even to pay for the drink, laborers forced employers to recognize the status and human dignity of the worker—a fact that employers had frequently struck from their memory when they attempted to see the worker as only an "economic man" to whom they had few obligations. Through repeated return to the market and cultural rituals such as the wetting of a bargain, migrants forced employers "to see" things differently—to remember older, more personalized patterns of work relations and to conceive of new more moral ways to treat their hired help. Thus those hiring out put curbs on the supposedly free market and supervised as well as restrained the behavior of employers.

Migrant laborers also tried to supervise the culture of the hiring market and police the petty entrepreneurs of food, leisure, and other services. They often successfully prevailed upon relief station managers to hand complaints to the police and by this action got vendors closed down and card gambling as well as pitch-and-toss curtailed. Workers in many cases trusted the managers so completely that they asked them to mail money home for them or to keep passports and wages under lock and key so that they would not fall prey to vagrants.[96]

Laborers occasionally took more direct action, shutting down local stores and taverns as well as banning games of chance if they seemed to threaten worker unity or strike solidarity.[97] Migrant laborers were also known to ransack shops and beat up merchants who had tried to cheat them.[98] In essence workers knew that the amount of money they could contribute to their household economy was affected as much by consumption prices as it was by wages. In the revolutionary years of 1905–1906 workers became even bolder, feeling that when facing unemployment and starvation they had a moral right to live parasitically off the local townspeople, just as the latter had for years done to them. Here they adapted yet another village ritual whereby peasant youths in order to organize courting parties or help for the poor went around homes in the vicinity and offered entertainment in return

[95] TsGIA, fond 1291, op. 38, god 1898, ed. khr. 221, ch. II ("Po voprosu ob uregulirovanii otkhozhego zemledel'cheskago dvizheniia rabochikh"), list 197–197ob.

[96] VSKhEG, no. 2 (February 1901): 46; no. 7 (July 1900): 394; no. 10 (October 1902): 1163–64; (1913): 365.

[97] Saratovskii Dnevnik, no. 140, 2 July 1906, p. 2.

[98] Boris Trekhbratov, Bor'ba sel'skokhoziaistvennykh rabochikh v period obrazovaniia pervykh organizatsii RSDRP na Kubani (Krasnodar, 1972), pp. 15–16; V. Maslovskii, "Vrachebno-prodovol'stvennyi punkt v s. Balakove," VKh Samara, no. 7 (July 1900): 18.

for small amounts of money or treats. Those who refused to support this community effort were often mocked for their affront.[99] Migrant laborers adapted this practice for use in the hiring markets. Thus in towns like Novomikhailovskoe in the Kuban Oblast and Biiuk Onlar, Seitler, and Ichki in Tavrida Province, they demanded alms from passersby and shopkeepers and, if refused, mugged them or plundered stores.[100] Such a tactic did not always work, though. So in the settlement of Ichki twenty workers, recently dismissed from the Black Cat estate nearby, attempted to destroy some shops. The townspeople, however, quickly organized a self-defense unit for their police-short town and chased the workers away, severely wounding three of them in the process.[101] Thus a custom workers saw as ensuring subsistence and proper social relations was redefined by townspeople as a criminal act.

Agricultural workers also occasionally attempted to assert control over the hiring market turf against state authorities. While they sometimes appealed to police to help get employers to stop using machines and labor procured outside the market, workers deemed police interference inside the market as immoral, believing both sides in the bargaining process should be on an equal footing: "What business is it of the police to interfere in affairs with the employers? This is a friendly matter: if we want to hire out—we hire out, if not—we don't hire. Let them keep order, but as to what wages we hire out for—that's not any of the police's business." When the police did interfere workers were at times known to drive them from the market, and troops had to be assembled before police could safely return.[102]

Migrant laborers tried to defend themselves from machine and labor contracts as well, organizing resistance against them in the hiring markets. In June of 1902 in response to increased use of machinery and contractors by farmers, up to 10,000 agricultural workers engaged in a wave of machine breaking in the Kuban Oblast, in a few cases directed by leaders blaring prearranged signals on horns. The protest was widely scattered and mostly uncoordinated, sparked in part by knowledge of the Poltava-Khar'kov revolts earlier that spring. In some cases heavy harvest machines and threshers were taken from warehouses near hiring markets, hoisted aloft by the crowd

[99] Frank, "Cultural Conflict," pp. 86–89; *The Village of Viriatino*, pp. 132–33.

[100] V. Geiman, "Feodosiia," *Krymskii Kur'er*, no. 154, 26 July 1906, p. 3; no. 129, 24 June 1906, p. 3; *Krymskii Vestnik*, no. 136, 21 June 1906, p. 3; no. 140, 25 June 1906, p. 3. Compare Hobsbawm and Rudé, *Captain Swing*, pp. 61, 67.

[101] V. Geiman, "Feodosiia," p. 3. When one employer in the Northern Caucasus neglected to feed his workers for two days running, migrants went to the nearby town of Armavir and insisted that townspeople feed them and remove, as well as no longer rent out, their harvest machines, if they did not want their settlement turned upside down. See Pylyp Kapel'horods'kyi, "Sil's'kyi proletariat v Kuban'shchyni," *Nova Hromada*, no. 8 (August 1906): 38.

[102] For the quotation see *Revoliutsionnaia Rossiia*, no. 55, 20 November 1904, p. 20. See also *Privolzhskii Krai*, no. 136, 1 July 1906, p. 3; *Saratovskii Listok*, no. 137, 1 July 1906, p. 2; Gelikonov, "Otchet," pp. 11–12.

of workers, and paraded by them to nearby bridges from where the contraptions were dumped into rivers. Workers also insisted that they would not stop their protests until use of machine and labor contractors was halted. This collective action suggested that migrant laborers were at times able to overcome their regional and ethnic differences as the twenty leaders arrested came from nineteen towns and villages in some ten provinces.[103]

While local laborers usually had a greater sense of the hiring market as their turf and sometimes viewed migrants as outsiders and as representatives of expanding capitalism, immoral competitors, migrant laborers themselves were also known to invoke a version of the moral economy argument against parvenu contractors by basing their claims on a type of long-term local residence and right to subsistence. An incident occurred in 1904 in Novomikhailovskoe in the Kuban Oblast which reflects the attitudes of migrant laborers well. A number of migrants while taking a morning swim in a river near the hiring market, spied a convoy of machines on the opposite bank. They quickly gathered the other workers (and presumably their clothes) and took off for the bridge in order to block the convoy's passage across it. There they attempted to throw one of the machines off the bridge and into the river. Unable to cope with all this, the convoy was forced to retreat. It returned to try again later, though, aided by a squadron of cossacks. At this point, two of the elders of the labor artels told the authorities, as paraphrased in a police report:

> Mowers are starving, they had eaten all their supplies, and the estates did not want to hire them or give them money, that there is no way to subsist, that they have been here year in, year out, coming from the distant homeland, and now appear outsiders (*postoronnye liudi*) with mowing machines and with these they take away earnings [or seasonal work—*zarabotki*] and daily crusts of bread. Therefore they will not for any circumstances let the mowing machines onto the far side of the Kuban and will smash them.

When the cossack officer in charge promised to do something about these mechanical harvesters if the workers calmed down, a few of the women assumed what seems to have been a customary role as judges of morality, by upbraiding their fellow male workers: "For what reason do you listen to them! Do you really not see that they are deceiving you: they took a bribe from the owner of the mowing machines and now want to let the mowing machines through." In response to this insolence and distrust of authority, the officer ordered his cossacks to fashion whips from a nearby willow

[103] *TsGIA*, fond 1405, god 1902, opis' 103, delo 6657 ("O bezporiadkakh v stanitse Tiflisskoi proizveden. tolpoi prishlykh rabochikh"), listy 16ob., 20ob., 29–32ob., 35–35ob., 49–56ob.; Trekhbratov, *Bor'ba*, p. 13; *Osvobozhdenie*, no. 4, 2 August 1902, p. 63; no. 4 (28), 2 August 1903, p. 62; *Iskra*, no. 23, 1 August 1902, p. 5.

thicket to punish the women. When the cossacks entered the crowd, whips in hand, the women shrieked and a general free-for-all ensued. The officer was struck by a stone to the head even after he allegedly fired warning shots. He then gave an order to shoot, but although wounded fell as a result of the volley, the crowd became so enraged that it drove the cossacks to the end of the bridge. At this point the officer exchanged his revolver for a hunting rifle and fired, killing one peasant outright. This act "sobered" the attacking crowd and it began to disperse. Seven workers including two women were wounded—two of them severely. Among those who escaped there were likely a number who had been injured as well. Twelve persons were arrested.[104]

In general, worker collective action in or near hiring markets failed to halt the spread of machines and machine contractors. By and large employers had discovered a successful strategy. They contracted for machinery outside the markets and machine convoys stayed clear of these places if possible. Workers were forced to leave the hiring square in order to defend their interests. Only the beginning of agrarian disturbances in 1902 and the increasing inability of the police to deal with the revolutionary upsurge gave workers enough courage to attempt new forms of collective action that often took place outside the market. From 1902 on their repertoire expanded, and performances were now frequently staged on the estates where workers in the past had felt themselves relatively powerless. Among the new forms were "extortion" or "alms" processions from estate to estate, food riots, hijacking of trains, marches on neighboring estates to protest treatment of laborers there, and a wave of work stoppages at the place of production where laborers demanded such things as higher pay, daily settling of accounts, shorter workdays, polite address, compensation for rainy days, and a daily treat of meat or vodka. Laborers also went out to the estates and demanded work and, if refused, sometimes smashed agricultural machines.[105] Nevertheless, once the revolutionary situation passed, employers were able to stop worker assaults on their estates and much to the chagrin of migrants were able to employ with relative impunity machinery procured outside the market.

CONCLUSION

This essay has attempted to show how the social space of the hiring market provided the opportunity for the articulation of conflicting values which in other cases often remained below the surface when peasants and outsiders interacted with one another. Within the boundaries of the recruitment fairs,

---

[104] *TsGAOR* fond 102, DPOO, no. 4, chast' 21, 1904g ("O volneniiakh i stachkakh sredi rabochikh—Po Kubanskoi Oblasti"), listy 3–6 (quotations listy 4ob. and 5); Trekhbratov, *Bor'ba*, p. 14; L. Efimovich, "Kosilki," *Russkoe Bogatstvo*, no. 7 (1905), sec. 2, pp. 32–36.
[105] On these practices, see Mixter, "Migrant."

employers and workers both expressed ambivalence towards the development of agrarian capitalism in the steppe grainbelt. Migrant agricultural laborers also contested employer definitions of moral social relations and values by exchanging information and engaging in collective action in the hiring markets.

THE IMPORTANCE OF THE SOCIAL SPACE OF THE MARKET

Historians have noted how different forms of hire have had different advantages and disadvantages for workers, which affected their ability to protect their interests.[106] In Russia, the independent space, opportunity, exchange of information, and tactical mobility afforded by the hiring market helped workers mobilize for collective action. In other countries, social spaces created by employer organization of production and farm worker actions played a similar role—namely, feeing markets in Scotland, open villages and statute fairs in England, government-sponsored migrant camps as well as UFW hiring halls and farmworker communities in California, the agro-towns and Federterra labor union employment offices in Italy, and the hobo jungles migrant laborers inhabited in the midwestern grainbelt of the U.S.[107]

In Russia, migrant laborers knew that they had some power inside the hiring market and little outside of it. They acknowledged the power of the hiring market in a number of ways. They helped create it by sabotaging the winter hiring system when they learned that through the recruitment fairs they could get higher wages. They perpetuated the market by being reluctant to hire out to estates that were far from it and returned to the *rynok* frequently to hire anew and check on the latest wage rates and information. Laborers dressed up for the occasion and used the space to celebrate their free time. They stayed in the hiring markets during strikes before hire and kicked immoral employers out. Workers waited until they returned to the town squares to punish the unethical behavior of farmers on the estates. They also tried to supervise the activities there of petty entrepreneurs, ped-

---

[106] Thomas and Friedland, "The United Farm Workers Union," pp. 13–21, 41–42, 59–64; Linda C. Majka and Theo J. Majka, *Farm Workers, Agribusiness and the State* (Philadelphia, 1982), pp. 136–66, 212–24, 281–85 (especially 216–17, 281–82, 285).

[107] Carter, "Class," pp. 110–13; J. P. D. Dunbabin, *Rural Discontent in Nineteenth-Century Britain* (New York, 1974), passim; Roberts, "Waiting Upon Chance," pp. 119–60; Ann Kussmaul, *Servants in Husbandry in Early Modern England* (Cambridge, 1981), pp. 62, 189 n. 58; Hobsbawm and Rudé, *Captain Swing*, pp. 34, 42–51, 58–59, 72; Andrew Charlesworth, "The Development of the English Rural Proletariat and Social Protest: A Comment," *The Journal of Peasant Studies* 8, no. 1 (October 1980): 101–3; Carey McWilliams, *Factories in the Field* (Santa Barbara, 1971; originally published in 1939), pp. 299–300; Majka and Majka, *Farm Workers,* pp. 216–17, 281–85; Anthony Cardoza, *Agrarian Elites and Italian Fascism* (Princeton, 1982), pp. 104–5, 141–43, 163–64, 222–25, 353, 364–73; Allen Gale Applen, "Migratory Harvest Labor in the Midwestern Wheat Belt, 1870–1940" (Ph.D. diss. Kansas State University, 1974), pp. 126–29, 157–59.

dlers of leisure, as well as labor and machine contractors. *Otkhodniki* treated both the police and the employers differently inside and outside the market. Finally, they equated the market with the truth and acted to uphold its sanctity there.

By their actions migrant laborers helped create their own opportunities from below. Although some historians have seen the creation of opportunity to be largely a result of factors over which peasants had little control—splits in the elite, weakening of government authority, and the pattern in which repressive forces were deployed—in this essay we have seen how peasants helped create opportunities themselves by carving out independent social spaces, just as did many other groups in the period 1861–1905 that were more directly engaged in the creation of a more independent political framework for action in Russia.[108]

The manufacture of such independent social spaces as hiring markets, which allowed for tactical mobility and the perpetuation of other ways of seeing, was thus crucial to the mobilization of collective action. Such an assertion should not be construed as an attempt to construct a monocausal theory of collective action, however. Rural protest tended to be the product of a complex web of factors, such as demographic and environmental influences, the intrusion of the state, market and other outside factors as well as people, splits in the elite, peasant cohesion, peasant culture and other ways of seeing, and the organization of production.[109] Nevertheless, opportunity and the creation of independent social spaces, which themselves were not fixed but contested over time, were as important for the mobilization of agrarian unrest as the shared interests of a particular economic stratum (i.e., kulaks, middle peasants, poor peasants and in this case proletarian peasants)—the factor that has tended to dominate the debate in Western and Soviet historiography.

AMBIVALENCE CONCERNING AGRARIAN CAPITALISM

Recently in the historiography concerning peasants, a debate has broken out over whether peasants tried to perpetuate the security of a moral economy based on subsistence norms and cultural restraints or if they were willing to take risks and act on the market incentives of higher profits as true "eco-

---

[108] In another essay I have shown how peasants in large villages in particular were able to carve out independent social spaces—cooperatives, parks, temperance societies, etc., that were often crucial in keeping alive alternative ways of seeing necessary for the mobilization of protest. Timothy Mixter, "Peasant Collective Action in Saratov Province, 1902–1906," in *Politics and Society in Provincial Russia: Saratov, 1590–1917,* ed. Rex A. Wade and Scott J. Seregny (Columbus, 1989), pp. 192–94, 206–7, 217, 227–29, 231–32.

[109] Mixter, "Peasant," pp. 192–209. For a review of the historiography of Russian peasant protest see Ben Eklof, "Ways of Seeing: Recent Anglo-American Studies of the Russian Peasant (1861–1914)," *Jahrbücher für Geschichte Osteuropas* 36, Book 1 (1988): 59–61, 64–72, 76–79.

nomic men."[110] With regard to the peasantry examined in this essay, it is clear that migrant agricultural laborers, like their employers, felt ambivalent about the rise of agrarian capitalism. Like most people, migrant laborers, poised between two worlds, wanted the best of both even if this might not be possible. Migrants wanted a free market but one regulated by their definitions of morality. They wanted the security of dependable relations and in the hiring market insisted that the employers be moral and not deceitful. For themselves, though, they often rejected the tenets of a moral economy which they had in some ways tried to impose on employers. They wanted freedom of action so that they could use their mobility to play on employer anxieties and possibly garner higher wages by playing the market. They rejected the coerced but dependable relations of the winter hiring system and often chose short-term relations by their insistence on returning to the hiring market frequently. In many cases they lost out in this gamble, but their expectations, fired by what old-time laborers had to say, still pushed them to wander farther.

Their ambivalence was clear from the type of collective action they chose. Much of it was defensive and reactive.[111] Frequently it came only in response to previous, unethical behavior by an employer perpetrated on the estate. Workers tried to regulate such behavior when they returned to the market, hoping to create a more moral economy and dependable personal relations through boycotts of individual landowners, rumors, hooting out of markets, beatings, and cultural rituals such as "wetting the bargain." On the other hand, the strike before hire was usually more pro-active in intent. New claims were made on employers, and through this tactic workers tried to preserve their freedom of action until the last possible moment by refusing to commit themselves to dependable relations with employers. They knew that if they could wait until the last possible moment before the harvest began, wages would often go up.

Ambivalence about agrarian capitalism was also manifest in other ways. Both employers and workers often were unsure if they preferred long or short terms of hire since both had advantages. Some employers, though participating in market hire, showed nostalgia for serfdom and the winter hiring system. Some worker songs were full of hope and expectation concerning the riches to be made in labor migration. Others, however, were pervaded

[110] Scott Evan Guggenheim and Robert P. Weller, "Introduction: Moral Economy, Capitalism, and State Power in Rural Protest," in *Power and Protest in the Countryside*, ed. Robert P. Weller and Scott Evan Guggenheim (Durham, 1982), pp. 3–12; Michael Peletz, "Moral and Political Economies in Rural Southeast Asia," *Comparative Studies in Society and History* 25, no. 4 (October 1983): 731–39; Robert Edelman, *Proletarian Peasants*, pp. 13–25, esp. 22–25.

[111] Reactive collective action consisted of efforts to reassert established claims when someone else challenged or violated them. Pro-active collective action asserted claims not previously exercised. See Charles Tilly, *From Mobilization*, pp. 144–47.

by despair and warnings about the deception and the unreliability of employers.

THE CONFLICT IN VALUES

While it is important to emphasize the real ambivalence in worker attitudes and actions, there were certain deeply held beliefs on which migrant laborers tended not to waver, even though the opportunity to express them was occasional at best. One of these attitudes was a persistent mistrust of employers. Even when they were literally brawling with each other, the opinions of workers concerning those who hired them usually did not change. The pre-1905 hostility was a result of the constant contract breaking, lying, and mystification that each saw the other engaging in in pursuit of the almighty ruble. The quick shift in relative power and opportunity allowed each side the chance to overtly vent its anger at past treatment, thus only adding fuel for the next round of combustible confrontation between employer and worker, both tied to the stake of virtually untrammeled capitalism. The distrust and conflict of values may have contributed to the unbridgeability of relations between different legal estates and different classes in the 1905 and 1917 revolutions.

In order to close this distance between employer and worker and stop employer deception, workers tried to re-personalize relations in the market. Through their insistence on direct, public negotiation, their attempts to assert their own dignity and denigrate that of an immoral employer, regardless of background, workers continuously demonstrated their insistence on greater social equality and even a reversal of roles. Workers used the relative equality of employer-laborer relations inside the market to protest the traditional subordination and deference landowners expected outside it. This was but one example of the conflict in values articulated in the hiring squares. Another was manifest in the way migrant laborers hoped to ensure the attachment of a human face and a mind, which embodied certain moral cultural values, to the invisible hands of labor economics on the steppe. They did not want to let employers create a division between the two.[112] They returned to the hiring market, which had cultural as well as economic functions, in order to reaffirm their humanity in a leisure culture that contrasted sharply with employer conceptions of time and discipline. Like members of guilds in times past, they used cultural rituals, such as wetting the bargain, to regulate market behavior, stress social equality, and try to recombine work to leisure and culture that employers attempted to separate. Finally, through collective action within the market, workers tried to correct employer morality on the estates, in some cases even beating up people who had cheated

[112] E. P. Thompson, "Folklore, Anthropology, and Social History," *The Indian Historical Review* 3, no. 1 (January 1977): 263–64.

them in the past. They also protested the morality of some petty entrepreneurs in the market. In all this, they often drew on their past peasant experience and village routines for their initial ideas on how to mobilize for protest, but they also flexibly adjusted these repertoires to meet their needs as workers. Indeed at times they fashioned forms of protest rarely seen back home in their villages.

Workers not only contested definitions of morality, they also fought to control information on which to some extent the construction of these values depended. They understood the way the exchange of information in the hiring markets helped them defend their interests. Through songs and stories of past times they articulated warnings against deception and relayed memories of successful bargaining techniques. Migrants also equated the hiring market with the truth—"Kakhovka does not deceive, it reveals the true price"—and tried to prevent employer deceit there through collective action, which often was shaped by information culled from participation in collective cultural routines back home. The perpetuation of other ways of seeing was crucial if collective action was to be mobilized in the market space in a way that would help workers defend their interests. Subjective perceptions and human agency were as important as the creation of structures and spaces.[113] Knowledge was power, and the animus motivating migrant laborers was not much different from that spurring the Petrograd Soviet to check the Provisional Government or industrial laborers to institute workers' control over the space of their factories in 1917. All tried to prevent deception by supervising the flow of information. It was for this reason that migrant laborers tried to sabotage the winter hiring system and labor contractors. Both

[113] On the ongoing struggle over information, the Foucaultian connection between space, knowledge, and power, the interrelationship between structure and human agency/consciousness, as well as the way society shapes space and in turn space shapes society, see Frederick Cooper, "Urban Space, Industrial Time, and Wage Labor in Africa," in *Struggle for the City: Migrant Labor, Capital, and the State in Urban Africa*, ed. Frederick Cooper (Berkeley, 1983), pp. 8–11, 15, 23–38, esp. 23–27; Sara M. Evans and Harry C. Boyte, *Free Spaces: The Sources of Democratic Change in America* (New York, 1987), pp. 17–25, 187–202; James Green, "Populism, Socialism and the Promise of Democracy," *Radical History Review*, no. 24 (Fall 1980): 30–32; Agnew, "The Threshold," pp. 99–118; Reed, "Social Change," pp. 109–23; Thomas and Friedland, "The United Farm Workers Union," pp. 13–21, 34–36, 46, 48–54, 62; *The Foucault Reader*, ed. Paul Rabinow (New York, 1984), pp. 239–56; Agnew, *Worlds Apart*, pp. 1–7, 26–27, 31–46; Philip Cooke, ed., *Localities* (London, 1989); Joan Neuberger, "Stories of the Street: Hooliganism in the St. Petersburg Popular Press," *Slavic Review* 48, no. 2 (Summer 1989): 177–94, esp. 189–94; Van Onselen, *Chibaro*, pp. 227–47, esp. 232–36, 244; Stichter, *Migrant Labor*, pp. 108–12, 114-15, 120, 123, 125, 137, 139–40, 143, 191–94; Robert Eugene Johnson, *Peasant and Proletarian* (New Brunswick, 1979), pp. 77–79, 94–98, 152–62; Jeffrey Burds, "The Social Control of Peasant Labor in Russia: The Response of Village Communities to Labor Migration in the Central Industrial Region, 1861–1905," in *Peasant Economy, Culture, and Politics of European Russia, 1800–1921*, ed. Esther Kingston-Mann and Timothy Mixter (Princeton, 1990), chap. 2, passim.

involved middlemen whose power rested on their monopoly of information to the detriment of workers. These people tried to take the procurement of labor outside the supervised confines of the hiring market, just as professional middlemen in Western Europe had tried to take grain out of the market to the detriment of local villagers who wanted to ensure their subsistence needs over the individual profit of outsiders and engaged in "food riots" to ensure such an outcome. When in Russia machine and labor contractors succeeded in accomplishing their tasks, however, workers in the 1902–1906 period went outside the markets and again contested employer values.

Despite ultimately losing the struggle to the machines, migrant laborers had been able to keep real wage rates, if not income, from falling. They also were able to influence and occasionally place limits on employer behavior by controlling the hiring market through repeated return there, cultural restraints, and the actuality or threat of collective action, especially to punish employer misdeeds. Employers acknowledged worker influence by their different tone in the hiring market, their attempts to order the worker question in state commissions, their increased use of machine and labor contractors after 1900, and the temporary return to the winter hiring system that some employers resorted to after the labor disturbances of the 1902–1906 period. The determination of labor relations was not a one-way street.

CHAPTER 10

PEASANTS AND POLITICS: PEASANT UNIONS DURING THE 1905 REVOLUTION

Scott J. Seregny

WHILE recognizing the importance of revolutionary upheavals, scholarly debates on the patterns of Russian history have emphasized the fundamental continuities in Russia's political culture and social relations. These include the famous isolation of the peasantry from the wider society and from national politics. From the Emancipation of the serfs through the Civil War and 1920s several features stand out. One is peasant particularism, or absorption with a single *peasant* issue, land. Related to this particularism is a second reality: Russian peasants seem to have evinced little interest in or comprehension of national politics or shared interests with other social groups. Peasants were often keenly suspicious of nonpeasants, whether privileged elites or intelligentsia. Despite their good intentions and selfless idealism, even the Third Element professionals employed by the zemstvos remained in peasant eyes "outsiders," suspected and kept at arm's length.[1]

The political consequences of peasant isolation are well known. Since the 1870s, urban *intelligenty* more often than not failed in their attempts to link up with a peasant mass movement or ignite a popular rebellion against the autocracy. During World War I Russian peasant-soldiers failed to identify with national objectives, with the result that the Russian army found itself at a comparable disadvantage with armies that exhibited a greater degree of modern nationalism.[2] In 1917–1918 peasants acted spontaneously and independently to realize their dreams of a Black Repartition of private lands, while peasant communities became more cohesive in facing the outside world, shunning urban Russia and its political conflicts.[3]

---

[1] Terence Emmons and Wayne S. Vucinich, eds., *The Zemstvo in Russia: An Experiment in Local Self-Government* (Cambridge, 1982).

[2] Allan K. Wildman, *The End of the Russian Imperial Army: The Old Army and the Soldiers' Revolt, March–April 1917* (Princeton, 1980), p. 93.

[3] Leopold H. Haimson, "The Problem of Social Identities in Early Twentieth Century Russia," *Slavic Review* 47, no. 1 (Spring 1988): 13–17.

Peasant isolation, however, should not be overstated. Peasants, of course, preferred to be left alone. By definition, however, peasant societies cannot escape economic relations with the urban sector, the demands of state and towns, or penetration by bureaucracy and other urban institutions—except in times of a breakdown of state authority and of the social order in the towns, as occurred in 1917–1921. Indeed, in the late imperial period the outside world impinged dramatically on the Russian village. Under the impact of industrialization, the spread of railways and markets, literacy and military conscription, as well as the expansion of zemstvo services and contacts with the Third Element intelligentsia, peasant communities were increasingly enmeshed in a web of complex relations with the wider society.

While peasants have commonly been characterized as the passive objects (or victims) of such modernizing forces, this was far from the case. A more persuasive model is one that recognizes peasants as active and flexible in relations with the outside world, muting or deflecting external forces deemed inimical to local interests, while opportunistically exploiting shifts in the correlation of political and social forces or the appearance of nonpeasant allies. Recent research in the area of peasant schooling and literacy demonstrates that peasants actively promoted education, while pursuing a strategy to limit its corrosive effects on village cultural norms and traditional patterns of deference and authority.[4] Similar peasant responsiveness, not isolation, can be found in the realm of politics and rural protest during the Revolution of 1905.

Peasant revolution in 1905 was a complex phenomenon. On the one hand, it often seemed focused on local social conflicts, followed its own rhythms, and expressed itself most dramatically in spontaneous actions against gentry property, in "short outbursts of accumulated frustration and rebellious feeling."[5] Such agrarian revolts failed to generate long-term goals or structures designed to pursue them. Peasant monarchism remained strong and there appeared to be little organized support in the village for the political goals of educated society. Contemporaries bemoaned what they saw as an essentially premodern, isolated, and apolitical peasant movement. Government spokesmen drew relative comfort from the same events.

There is considerable evidence, on the other hand, that peasants were far from being passive observers of the political storms raging in 1905–1907. Peasant interest in politics quickened during 1905 as measured by rural interest in the press, communal petitions to the government, participation in

[4] Ben Eklof, *Russian Peasant Schools: Officialdom, Village Culture and Popular Pedagogy, 1861–1914* (Berkeley, 1986).

[5] Teodor Shanin, "Peasantry as a Political Factor," in *Peasants and Peasant Societies*, ed. Teodor Shanin (Harmondsworth, Eng., 1971), pp. 257–58 and Henry A. Landsberger, "Peasant Protest: Themes and Variations," in *Rural Protest: Peasant Movements and Social Change*, ed. Henry Landsberger (New York, 1974), pp. 21–22.

elections to the Duma, and the relative success of liberals and revolutionaries in penetrating the countryside.[6] The most dramatic evidence of peasant political mobilization in 1905 was surely the organization of the All-Russian Peasant Union (*Vserossiiskii krest'ianskii souiz*). In a matter of months local unions mobilized hundreds of thousands of peasants around a program of radical social and political change, pursued organized tactics, and helped link the peasant movement with the demands of Russian society at large.[7] The Peasant Union was arguably the most successful attempt to set up a mass peasant organization during the late imperial period, eclipsing even the Socialist-Revolutionary (SR) party in the Russian and Ukrainian countryside.[8]

Teodor Shanin has recently emphasized the Peasant Union's importance in the peasant protest of 1905–1906. Better than any other, this mass organization embodied the "peasant dream," not only of land, but also of local power and civil rights; and it demonstrated the peasantry's ability to organize as a political "class for itself," able to create its own national organization and ideology and to produce leaders from within.[9] In stressing the Russian peasantry's political autonomy, however, Shanin reinforces the traditional picture of isolation. John Bushnell has rightly pointed to the impact of national events and peasants' perception of the shifting contest between government and urban opposition on both the timing and forms of peasant rebellion in 1905–1906.[10]

[6] François-Xavier Coquin, "Un aspect méconnu de la révolution de 1905: Les 'motions paysannes,' " in *1905: La Premiere Révolution Russe*, ed. François-Xavier Coquin and Celine Gervais-Francelle (Paris, 1986), pp. 181–200; Terence Emmons, *The Formation of Political Parties and the First National Elections in Russia* (Cambridge, Mass., 1983); Timothy R. Mixter, "Peasant Collective Action in Saratov Province, 1902–1906," in *Politics and Society in Provincial Russia: Saratov, 1590–1917*, ed. Rex A. Wade and Scott J. Seregny (Columbus, 1989), pp. 191–232; Michael Melancon, "Athens or Babylon? The Birth of the Socialist Revolutionary and Social Democratic Parties in Saratov, 1890–1905," in ibid., pp. 73–112.

[7] E. I. Kiriukhina, "Vserossiiskii Krest'ianskii Soiuz v 1905 g.," *Istoricheskie Zapiski*, no. 50 (1955): 95–141 and idem., "Mestnye organizatsii Vserossiiskogo Krest'ianskogo Soiuza v 1905 godu," *Uchenye zapiski Kirovskogo pedagogicheskogo instituta* 10 (1956): 83–157.

[8] *Protokoly vtorogo (ekstrennago) s"ezda Partii Sotsialistov-Revoliutsionerov* (St. Petersburg, 1907), reprint, ed. Christopher Rice, Publications of the Study Group on the Russian Revolution, no. 10 (Millwood, N. Y., 1986), pp. 81–82. According to one estimate only 18,466 peasants had joined the SR "peasant brotherhoods" in twenty provinces: V. N. Ginev, *Bor'ba za krest'ianstvo i krizis russkogo narodnichestva, 1902–1914 gg.* (Leningrad, 1983), pp. 138–39. Even in Saratov Province, which boasted the strongest SR rural organizations in the country, these were quite thin at the village level: S. Anikin, "Za 'pravednoi zemlei' (pamiati I. M. Igoshina)," *Vestnik Evropy*, no. 3 (1910): 97–98.

[9] Teodor Shanin, *Russia, 1905–07: Revolution as a Moment of Truth* (New Haven, Conn., 1986), pp. 99–100; and idem., "Peasantry as a Political Factor," p. 257.

[10] John Bushnell, "Peasant Economy and Peasant Revolution at the Turn of the Century: Neither Immiseration nor Autonomy," *The Russian Review* 47, no. 1 (January, 1988): 82–86 and idem., *Mutiny amid Revolution: Russian Soldiers in the Revolution of 1905–1906* (Blooming-

Both authors' generalizations, however, suffer from neglect of the local context. What Shanin says about the Peasant Union as a genuine expression of peasant aspirations is true, but in emphasizing autonomy he gives a one-sided and simplistic view of social and political relations in the countryside. Closer examination of union activity at the local level provides a clearer picture of reality, while affirming Shanin's general arguments about peasants' creative potential. The experience of local peasant unions demonstrates that not only were peasants able to transcend a narrow particularism on issues, but they were also able to respond flexibly to events and opportunities outside the community (locally and nationally), and sought alliances with other groups on the basis of tactical convenience and shared interests. While unions focused on issues of land reform and democratization of local institutions, they recognized the need to situate these demands within a framework of national political reform and build local coalitions with nonpeasants. The union movement further shows that relations between peasants and outsiders (intelligentsia, local elites) were fluid and very much shaped by national and local political conflicts.

Bushnell's generalizations about the peasant movement, drawn from his close study of peasants in the army in 1905, would be more plausible if the national conflicts he discussed were reflected at the local level. Examination of local union activity, indeed, indicates that local conflicts, some predating 1905, played a critical role in providing peasants with information, tactical mobility, and nonpeasant allies. They were probably more important in generating and shaping peasant protest than national events, not least because it was through the prism of local conflicts that national politics reverberated into the countryside. What follows is an attempt to provide a picture of this interplay between local and national contexts during 1905 as well as the complexity of local politics that helped shape the peasant movement of that year by looking at Peasant Union activity in two locales: the black-earth province of Khar'kov, specifically the remarkable events in Sumy District, and in the central-industrial province of Vladimir, specifically Iur'ev and Pokrov districts (see map 1).

PEASANT UNIONS IN SUMY DISTRICT, KHAR'KOV PROVINCE

Sumy District lay in the northwest corner of Khar'kov. The rural population of more than 200,000 was dense and largely Ukrainian. The town of Sumy was a substantial commercial and administrative center, with a population in 1897 of 27,575 (approaching 40,000 in 1905). Grain production dominated, but the district also specialized in the cultivation of sugar beets, which were

ton, Ind., 1985) and "The Dull-Witted Muzhik in Uniform: Why Did He Smash the Revolution?" in 1905, ed. Coquin and Gervais-Francelle, pp. 203–23.

processed in refineries on local estates and in town. With the addition of local machine-building works Sumy's working class approached four thousand, the highest for any district town in the province. Furthermore, in the years leading up to 1905 Sumy was the scene of strike activity, abetted by SR and Social Democratic (SD) organizations.[11]

Peasant land hunger in Sumy was intense. Unlike neighboring Poltava and Chernigov provinces, most of the land (78 percent) was held under communal tenure. Allotments had shrunk considerably since Emancipation, averaging 2 2/3 *desiatiny* (see Glossary) per household by 1902, and peasants lacked access to forest and pasture ("even chickens could not find a place to roost," they complained). To secure more arable and pasture, households entered exploitative leasing arrangements with local estates, most commonly by sharecropping (*arenda ispolu*), or in exchange for labor on estate land (*otrabotka*). With the appearance of the railway and spread of commercialized agriculture, especially beet cultivation, land prices and rents rose dramatically during the decade before 1905, as was the case in other parts of southern Russia and the Volga region. Estates decreased the amount of land available for lease, which peasants viewed as a violation of a "moral economy" of traditional economic and social relations that supported peasant welfare and subsistence. Peasants also found it increasingly difficult to compete with the large latifundia in land purchases. Agrarian relations were thus strained between peasant communities and large estates in Sumy like those of the Shcherbatovs who owned over 12,000 *desiatiny*, Countess A. D. Strogonova who held 15,000 and P. I. and N. M. Kharitonenko, the "Sugar Kings" of Sumy, who held over 80,000 *desiatiny* of land in addition to eleven sugar refineries in Sumy and bordering districts Lebedin and Akhtyrka.[12]

Despite an accumulation of rural grievances and frustrations, external events stimulated protest in Sumy's villages in early 1905. Peasants were bombarded by news of political opposition and strikes in the major cities, as well as agrarian disorders which began in early February in neighboring Kursk and Chernigov provinces. Locally workers in the Belgian and Vulcan machine works (330 and 160 workers) and at the large sugar refinery in the village of Pavlovka (1,800 workers) went on strike in late February, and stu-

[11] V. P. Semenov, ed., *Rossiia: Polnoe geograficheskoe opisanie nashego otechestva*, 19 vols., 7 (St. Petersburg, 1899–1913), pp. 162–63, 202–4, 327–29; A. G. Mikhailiuk, "Krest'ianskoe dvizhenie na Levoberezhnoi Ukraine v 1905–1907 gg. (Khar'kovskaia, Poltavskaia i Chernigovskaia gubernii)," *Istoricheskie Zapiski*, no. 49 (1954): 195. On the workers' movement in Sumy, see I. Glazman, "Robitnychyi rukh v Sumakh v pershyi revoliutsii 1905 roku," in *1905 rik na Sumshchyni* (Sumy, 1930), pp. 13–17 and A. E. Getler, "Poperedniky 1905 roku v m. Sumakh," in ibid., pp. 28–34.

[12] Semenov, *Rossiia*, 7: 130–34, 140–41, 329–32, 338; N. Onats'kyi, "Selians'kyi revoliutsiinyi rukh na Sumshchyni 1950 roku," in *1905 rik na Sumshchyni*, pp. 42–45; *Trudy mestnykh komitetov o nuzhdakh sel'skokhoziaistvennoi promyshlennosti*, 58 vols, 45 (St. Petersburg, 1903), pp. 358–60, 377.

dents in secondary schools organized political demonstrations. Peasant interest in national events had already been sparked by concern over military
reversals in the war with Japan and the fate of local husbands and sons on
distant battlefields.[13] Political conflicts at the national level resonated in
Sumy where local supporters of the autocracy and its opponents each initiated efforts to mobilize the rural masses in support of the old order or for
reform, a process that unfolded throughout provincial Russia during the first
half of 1905. Sensing that the peasantry might well tip the balance of forces,
the two sides offered peasants competing explanations for Russia's current
crisis.

The conservatives' strategy was twofold. On the one hand, local officials
appealed to peasant monarchism and blamed urban unrest and military defeats in the Far East on educated society. Clerics and officials launched a full-
scale campaign against the rural intelligentsia employed by the local
zemstvo. The Sumy Agricultural Society responded by urging the government to take firm action against this "agitation," warning that in every
church throughout the land appeals were read summoning the population
to violence against "internal enemies." Teachers and medical personnel were
branded as "Japanese agents" and "antichrists."[14] At the same time the Im-

18. PEASANTS BEING LED AWAY BY POLICE AFTER ARREST FOR PARTICIPATING IN AGRARIAN UNREST
IN THE VILLAGE OF PAVLOVKA, SUMY DISTRICT, KHAR'KOV PROVINCE (*ISTORIIA SELIANSTVA
UKRAINS'KOI RSR*, VOL. 1 [KIEV: "NAUKOVA DUMKA," 1967], P. 454).

[13] A. Ovcharenko, "Spogady pro revoliutsiiu 1905 roku na Sumshchyni," in *1905 rik na
Sumshchyni*, p. 81; Glazman, "Robitnychyi rukh," pp. 18–20; *Revoliutsiia 1905–1907 gg. v Rossii: Dokumenty i materialy* (hereafter *RvR*), 15 vols. (Moscow, 1955–1963): *Nachalo pervoi russkoi
revoliutsii, ianvar'-mart 1905 g.*, pp. 459–60, 463.

[14] *Pravo*, no. 18, 8 May 1905, cols. 1501–2; *Nizhegorodskii Listok*, no. 113, 30 April 1905, p. 2.

perial Decree of February 18, 1905, invited rural communes to address petitions, in the form of *prigovory* (resolutions), to their "little father," the tsar. Officials sought to provide a safety valve for peasant grievances and at the same time hoped to tap a reservoir of peasant monarchist support to counterbalance the urban opposition of intelligentsia and militant workers.

Conservative agitation helped galvanize both the Third Element intelligentsia and their liberal patrons in the zemstvo. The February Decree, ironically, facilitated a political dialogue between peasants and nonpeasant opposition elements as zemstvo employees seized upon the decree to carry their own agitation for political reform to the village. Peasants were hardly passive objects in this process, since communes frequently demanded that teachers and others help draft their petitions and serve as literate "decoders" of concepts and terminology that peasants had gleaned from the press. Indeed, peasant requests that teachers perform a new service of "political education" was an important factor in the teachers' own mobilization during 1905. By June 1905 teachers in Sumy had organized a chapter of the All-Russian Union of Teachers, an organization dedicated to bringing the Liberation Movement to the village and which worked closely with the peasant unions.[15] What seems clear in Sumy, and elsewhere, is that in peasant eyes the rural intelligentsia acquired a new utility and the status of teachers and others in the local community improved as a result.

Third Element initiatives found strong support from some of their zemstvo employers. A group of liberal gentry led by P. M. and G. M. Lintvarev and S. D. Velichko had dominated the Sumy District Zemstvo since the mid-1890s. Under the chairmanship of Pavel Lintvarev the zemstvo had expanded educational and other services for the peasant population, and in the process the zemstvo liberals had established close ties with the radical Third Element. Here Sumy reflected a broader liberal-radical alliance which underpinned provincial opposition in many locales during the decade before 1905.[16] Furthermore, the Sumy Zemstvo leaders were inclined to move beyond the patronizing framework that had traditionally encompassed zemstvo-peasant relations. In 1902–1903 when Witte's "local committees on the needs of agriculture" convened throughout Russia, participation was

---

Anti-intelligentsia agitation occurred in many provinces, most notably Saratov: see Scott J. Seregny, *Russian Teachers and Peasant Revolution: The Politics of Education in 1905* (Bloomington, Ind., 1989), ch. 7.

[15] *Syn Otechestva*, no. 120, 6 July 1905, p. 3; *Russkiia Vedomosti*, no. 176, 1 July 1905, p. 2.

[16] B. B. Veselovskii, *Istoriia zemstva za sorok let*, 4 vols. (St. Petersburg, 1909–1911), 1: 724; 4: 327; N. M. Pirumova, *Zemskoe liberal'noe dvizhenie: Sotsial'nye korni i evoliutsiia do nachala XX veka* (Moscow, 1977), pp. 276–77; I. Saloid, "Skalky spogadiv," in *1905 rik na Sumshchyni*, pp. 84–85. As in many locales, one can discern a strong correlation between zemstvo liberalism and Third Element activism in Sumy, which had, for example, the strongest Teachers' Union organization in the province during 1905 (100 members): *Tsentral'nyi Gosudarstvennyi Arkhiv Oktiabr'skoi Revoliutsii* (hereafter *TsGAOR*), f. 6862, op. 1, d. 54, listy. 166–67.

generally limited to gentry landowners and officials. But in Sumy and a handful of other districts, peasant "experts" were invited to attend. At the meeting in Sumy, a peasant from the village of Stepanovka, Iakov Shevchenko (a union activist in 1905) delivered a report on peasant grievances while Pavel Lintvarev and others concurred that local peasants needed economic relief.[17] This event prefigured the Sumy liberals' support for the Peasant Union program in 1905; and, indeed, on the eve of 1905 a loose coalition uniting zemstvo liberals, Third Element, and peasant activists was already taking shape.

In summary, peasants in early 1905 were offered two competing analyses of Russia's present crisis, and the content of rural *prigovory* suggests that the opposition's calls for political reform were at least partly persuasive. Peasants in Sumy, as elsewhere, took advantage of the February 18 Decree in large numbers. Above all, their petitions addressed economic issues (land hunger, high taxes), but also echoed the political demands of educated society for democratization of education, civil freedoms, an end to the war, popular control over police and officials, reform of local zemstvo government, abolition of land captains, and even a constitution. A fierce struggle was under way in Sumy for the hearts and minds of the rural masses; local officials moved to halt the ongoing political discussions, dismissing peasant political demands as the work of "outsiders," and in some cases arresting local teachers. In the village of Lokhnia a teacher, L. N. Skrynnikov (subsequently a peasant union activist), was arrested for simply reading the text of the decree at peasant request, after *volost'* officials had tried to conceal it.[18] Such behavior by local authorities played a significant role in politicizing the peasant movement in Sumy and making more credible the intelligentsia's argument that an arbitrary government was the major obstacle to satisfaction of peasant aspirations.

Reform of local government would constitute a major concern of the peasant unions, and when the union assumed effective control in Sumy District after October 1905, peasant officials deemed subservient to the administration would be thrown from office. The very tensions generated by the petition campaign, no doubt, permitted peasants and rural intelligentsia to find common ground in demands for civil freedoms and legal guarantees against the depredations of officialdom. What is striking about these events is not the isolation of the countryside, but rather the way the national struggle between autocracy and society found sharp reflection in local political conflicts between zemstvo and bureaucracy, teachers and priests, and thus pene-

---

[17] M. S. Simonova, "Zemsko-liberal'naia fronda (1902–1903 gg.)," *Istoricheskie Zapiski*, no. 91 (1973): 187; I. P. Belokonskii, *Zemskoe dvizhenie* (Moscow, 1914), pp. 221–22. On the proceedings in Sumy, attended by twelve peasants, see *Trudy mestnykh komitetov* 45: 358–77.

[18] *Nasha Zhizn'*, no. 104, 28 May/10 June 1905, p. 4. On other petitions, see K. V. Sivkov, "Krest'ianskie prigovory 1905 goda," *Russkaia Mysl'*, no. 4 (1907), sec. 2, pp. 24–42.

trated the village, confronting peasants with choices and alliances. That these conflicts gave birth to a mass peasant movement organized to support reform also owed much to the appearance of a charismatic leader from America.

Anton Petrovich Shcherbak had been born, probably to a gentry family, in Sumy in 1863. After an early career of student radicalism that included expulsion from gymnasium, an imperial pardon, expulsion from Khar'kov University, and service in a punitive battalion, he later boasted that he had "lived under three tsars and under all three had been arrested and exiled." Shcherbak emigrated in the 1890s with his wife and seven children to southern California. He bought an orange grove near San Bernardino and described himself as a "farmer of two hemispheres." Collaborators described him as an epic figure who looked as if he had stepped out of Ilia Repin's huge canvas *Zaporozhian Cossacks*.[19] Police reports noted that peasants in

19. ANTON PETROVICH SHCHERBAK,
PEASANT UNION LEADER FROM
KHAR'KOV PROVINCE (PETER N. MALOV,
*DUKHOBORTSY, IKH ISTORIIA, ZHIZN' I
BOR'BA* [THURMS, BRITISH COLUMBIA:
PETER N. MALOFF, 1948], P. 352).

[19] Tan (V. G. Bogoraz), "Vtoroi s"ezd," in his *Krasnoe i chernoe: Ocherki* (Moscow, 1907), p. 244; N. Stroev, *Istoricheskii moment. Vypusk 2: Krest'ianskii s"ezd* (St. Petersburg, 1906), p. 53; Petr N. Malov, *Dukhobortsy, ikh istoriia, zhizn' i bor'ba* (Thurms, B. C., 1948), pp. 352–66; Ethel M. Dolsen, "Planning a Russian Revolution in a California Orange Grove: The Thrilling Life Story of Antoine Cherbak, Exile," *San Francisco Call*, 30 May 1909, p. 3. Shanin claims that Shcherbak was a well-to-do peasant (*Russia*, p. 112) which would seem to support his argument about peasant political autonomy; there is little evidence to support him and in any

Sumy referred to him with great reverence as *bat'ko* or *pan*, a man who "speaks well with the simple folk in the Little Russian dialect and who by virtue of his anti-state ideas and undoubted sway over the peasants can lead them wherever he wishes, including armed insurrection." Authorities dated the beginning of serious trouble in Sumy to Shcherbak's return from America at the end of January 1905 when he settled on seventy-three *desiatiny* which he inherited near the village of Solodko, seven *versty* from town.[20]

Shcherbak, who claimed to belong to no political party, planned to rally the local peasantry around a program of social and political reform utilizing the February Decree, given "the high regard and traditional awe with which the Tsar was held in the village." As he saw it the peasant movement should steer clear of direct assaults on the person of the monarch and reject demands for a democratic republic. At first Shcherbak waged a petition campaign along these lines in the vicinity of Solodko, stressing peasant land hunger and the depredations of the bureaucracy, but with a vague formulation of hope that the tsar would resolve them with the aid of representatives trusted by the people. Peasants gravitated to Solodko in increasing numbers and from greater distances. The local zemstvo aided these efforts by distributing copies of the decree and encouraging its employees to wage political agitation in the villages.[21]

By May, the Liberation Movement had deepened and Shcherbak, aided by P. M. Lintvarev, radical Third Element personnel, and activist peasants like Iakov Shevchenko, had decided to mobilize the entire population of Sumy District around a more radical program and use the Sumy Agricultural Society to that end. Shcherbak and his associates succeeded in having the society's charter amended to open its doors to all comers, regardless of whether they were able to pay the regular membership fee. Overnight the formerly staid society became the scene of mass peasant meetings, scheduled on market days (Sundays) and attracting a growing audience from seven *volosti* surrounding the town. The fact that the society was a legal and prestigious entity, according to officials, only enhanced its authority in the eyes of the population.[22]

---

case Shcherbak was clearly more than a "peasant," regardless of his legal status. His own reference to fellow unionists as "comrade-peasants" would seem to indicate that Shcherbak came from a different social background: *Materialy k krest'ianskomu voprosu: Otchet o zasedaniiakh delegatskago s"ezda Vserossiiskago Krest'ianskago Soiuza 6-10 noiabria 1905 g.* (Rostov-on-Don, 1905), p. 42.

[20] Svidzins'kyi, "Selians'ki spilky na Ukraini v revoliutsii 1905 r.," *Litopys Revoliutsii* (Khar'kov), no. 6 (1928): 158; N. Karpov, ed., *Krest'ianskoe dvizhenie v revoliutsii 1905 goda v dokumentakh* (Leningrad, 1926), pp. 249–50, 252.

[21] Anton Shcherbak, "1905 god v Sumskom uezde," *Proletarskaia Revoliutsiia*, no. 7 (54) (1926): 123–26.

[22] *Khar'kov i Khar'kovskaia guberniia v pervoi russkoi revoliutsii 1905-1907 gg: Sbornik dokumen-*

This phenomenon—opening the doors of local institutions to the masses—was a common one during the heady days of summer 1905. After the debacle at Tsushima Straits, Nicholas II's rebuff to zemstvo moderates, and reports of agrarian disorders, gentry liberals made an unprecedented attempt to "go to the people" in hopes of steering the peasant movement into peaceful channels and linking up with a mass base in the village to apply pressure on the government and ultimately prepare for national elections. Zemstvo economic councils and agricultural societies in various provinces were transformed into open assemblies where peasants and intelligentsia discussed reforms that went well beyond the agenda of zemstvo moderates. In many districts of Russia and the Ukraine these meetings served as the nuclei for the organization of peasant unions.[23]

In Sumy the mounting petition campaign, tapped by Shcherbak and others, culminated in a huge meeting outside the agriculture society on May 29, 1905. Ignoring a ban by Governor Starynkevich, 5,000 peasants gathered to hear speeches by Shcherbak and others critical of the government. Shcherbak urged the crowd to request the tsar to order the expropriation of gentry and church lands for equal distribution among the laboring masses. If the regime failed to consider their appeal peasants should cease paying taxes or performing military service. According to police reports, Iakov Shevchenko called for a republic, which was echoed by SR and SD speakers; in most instances, however, peasant unions avoided criticism of the monarchy. All were bitterly critical of the war with Japan and bureaucratic rule.[24] A petition to the tsar was drawn up along lines originally laid down by Shcherbak at Solodko. The meeting then approved a resolution calling for a constituent assembly to deal with the following questions: (1) the war; (2) expropriation of private lands; (3) political amnesty; (4) civil freedoms; (5) abolition of land captains and rural police. Failing to secure an audience with Nicholas II, Shcherbak personally delivered the petition to Count Sergei Witte in St. Petersburg. The legal journal *Pravo* agreed to publish both documents, which received wide circulation and helped to stimulate the birth of peasant unions in other provinces.[25]

---

tov i materialov, comp. M. P. Avdusheva et al. (Khar'kov, 1955), pp. 106–7; Shcherbak, "1905 god," pp. 126–27.

[23] Kiriukhina, "Vserossiiskii," pp. 129–31; P. Olenin, "Krest'iane i intelligentsiia (K kharakteristike osvoboditel'nago dvizheniia v Malorossii)," *Russkoe Bogatstvo*, no. 2 (1907): 135–69; Roberta T. Manning, *Crisis of the Old Order in Russia: Gentry and Government* (Princeton, 1982), pp. 119–27; B. B. Veselovskii, *Krest'ianskii vopros i krest'ianskoe dvizhenie v Rossii, 1902–1906 gg.* (St. Petersburg, 1907), pp. 45–46.

[24] *Khar'kov i Khar'kovskaia guberniia*, pp. 100–101, 106–7, 154–55; Shcherbak, "1905 god," pp. 126–27; Karpov, *Krest'ianskoe dvizhenie*, pp. 251–52; Ovcharenko, "Spogady," pp. 81–82; "Krest'ianskoe dvizhenie 1905 goda," ed. S. Dubrovskii, *Krasnyi Arkhiv*, no. 2 (9) (1925): 74.

[25] *Pravo*, no. 22, 6 June 1905, cols. 1810–12; Shcherbak, "1905 god," p. 128. The Sumy peti-

In their petition the Sumy peasants noted that in other provinces agrarian disorders (*bunty*) had already broken out, and they asked the tsar to forgive those involved since these misguided peasants were also "your children." Disorders occurred in neighboring Lebedin District (Khar'kov) in May and June 1905 while relative calm prevailed in Sumy; only individual cases of trespassing were reported. Officials explained this by the fact that many peasants in Sumy derived part of their income from work in the town's refineries and distilleries, while the peasants of Lebedin were wholly dependent on agriculture. In Lebedin relations between peasants and landowners had become tense. Arson and looting were often directed against those estate owners who had exacted particularly harsh leasing terms from local peasants. One example was a certain Mme. Bulatovich who refused to lease uncultivated estate land and "never left her home without a sword and revolver" trying to intimidate local peasants.[26]

Officials were of two minds as to the impact of the political ferment in Sumy on the agrarian movement at this stage. Some insisted that the agitation of Shcherbak, Shevchenko, and others was at least partly responsible for the destruction of private property in Lebedin. Others grudgingly admitted that the activities of the Sumy Agricultural Society had exercised a moderating influence on the mood there.[27] Nevertheless, 200 Cossacks were posted in Sumy, General A. P. Strukov toured local villages, and Governor Starynkevich admonished peasants to remain calm, reading Nicholas II's statement of 1902 that his government would never violate the sanctity of private property. Public sessions of the agricultural society were banned, zemstvo statistical work in the district was halted, and finally in mid-June Shcherbak was arrested and incarcerated in the Khar'kov prison where he would languish until the amnesty of October 21, 1905.[28]

By this time, however, the political movement had dug a deep furrow in the black soil of Sumy, and the peasant union movement had taken root. Meetings continued. In Tereshkovka *Volost'*, Lintvarev, local peasant activists and zemstvo employees used a demonstration of iron plows to attract a crowd of over one thousand peasants out into the fields where political speeches were made and proclamations distributed.[29] In July peasant dele-

tion was read at the founding meeting of the Kursk provincial peasant union in early July: *Russkiia Vedomosti*, no. 185, 11 July 1905, p. 2.

[26] Karpov, *Krest'ianskoe dvizhenie*, pp. 227, 252–53; Onats'kyi, "Selians'kyi revoliutsiinyi rukh," p. 39; Mikhailiuk, "Krest'ianskoe dvizhenie," pp. 170–71; N. Lavrov, "Krest'ianskie nastroeniia vesnoi 1905 goda," *Krasnaia Letopis'*, no. 3 (14) (1925): 40–42.

[27] Karpov, *Krest'ianskoe dvizhenie*, p. 252.

[28] *Pravo*, no. 29, 24 July 1905, col. 2402; *Syn Otechestva*, no. 131, 20 July 1905, p. 3; *Russkiia Vedomosti*, no. 172, 28 June 1905, p. 2; no. 182, 8 July 1905, p. 2.

[29] *Agrarnoe dvizhenie v Rossii v 1905–1906 gg.* (*Trudy Imperatorskago Vol'nago Ekonomicheskago Obshchestva*), 2 vols, 2 (St. Petersburg, 1908), p. 302; Onats'kyi, "Selians'kyi revoliutsiinyi rukh," p. 39.

gates from various *volosti* gathered at the home of the zemstvo doctor Aleksei Agishevskii in the village of Iunakovka to select representatives to the first national congress of the Peasant Union scheduled for July 31–August 1 in Moscow. Lintvarev and various Third Element people were closely involved in this affair, as was the estate manager of the zemstvo liberal Prince Peter D. Dolgorukov in neighboring Sudzha District (Kursk). Andrei T. Ovcharenko, a peasant employed as a clerk in the Sumy trade school, played a prominent role. He was typical of a significant group of young peasant activists who had some education and employment experience in cities or in zemstvo institutions as nonprofessional "fourth element" specialists. Socially and culturally, these "conscious" peasants remained more closely tied to the village than many teachers of peasant origin and as such occupied a strategic position as intermediaries between the rural community and outsiders.[30]

Ovcharenko led a delegation of six peasants to the union congress in Moscow where they helped pass resolutions in favor of universal schooling and reform of local self-government. Radical land reform headed the agenda. One unidentified Sumy delegate expressed the general view: "Land is the mother of us all. It is not the product of human hands, but of the Holy Spirit and therefore must not be bought and sold." A majority of delegates endorsed abolition of private landholding with distribution on the basis of family labor. Bearing in mind lands purchased by peasants, they left room for some compensation for expropriated holdings. The congress repudiated violent tactics such as forceful land seizures in favor of boycotts of officials, a continued petition campaign to pressure the regime into summoning a national assembly, and intensified organizational efforts.[31]

Back in Sumy the pace of union organizing quickened under the impact of the October general strike and government concessions announced in the October 17 Manifesto. Bushnell has underscored the importance of these events in the timing of peasant protest and, indeed, the organization of peasant unions throughout the country accelerated in the following weeks, as did political activism among the rural intelligentsia. The regime's capacity for repression seemed diminished, and the manifesto appeared to provide legal cover for dissent.[32] In Sumy District the local union met in Solodko on Oc-

---

[30] TsGAOR, f. 102, DP OO, op. 233 (1905), d. 1800, ch. 21, listy 50–51ob; *1905 god na Ukraine: Khronika i materialy*, ed. M. I. Mebel', I (Khar'kov, 1926), pp. 359–60; Ovcharenko, "Spogady," p. 82. On the term "conscious" peasants, see Shanin, *Russia*, p. 100.

[31] *Protokoly uchrezhditel'nago s"ezda Vserossiiskago Krest'ianskago Soiuza* (Moscow, 1905), pp. 9–10, 27–28. For accounts of the congress, see Kiriukhina, "Vserossiiskii," pp. 102–10; Geroid T. Robinson, *Rural Russia Under the Old Regime* (New York, 1932), pp. 160–63; Maureen Perrie, *The Agrarian Policy of the Russian Socialist-Revolutionary Party from its Origins Through the Revolution of 1905–1907* (New York, 1976), pp. 108–11.

[32] Bushnell, *Mutiny*, pp. 65–76; Seregny, *Russian Teachers*, ch. 8; Kiriukhina, "Vserossi-

tober 29 to welcome back Shcherbak and elect delegates to the second Peasant Union congress scheduled for early November in Moscow. Representatives from twelve *volosti* rejected the idea of compensation for private lands and endorsed the transfer of factories, like land, to local communes, a resolution that probably reflected the influence of the SR socialization program. Maksim Gorky and Leo Tolstoy were elected honorary members of the Sumy District union and urban workers were invited to join. The meeting demanded that a constituent assembly be summoned no later than January 1906 and then dispatched Shcherbak, Ovcharenko, Shevchenko, and the peasants I. V. Letvinov and I. V. Arshinov to Moscow.[33]

When the Peasant Union convened from November 6 to 10, 1905, the delegates were in a somewhat more militant mood. By this time agrarian disorders had become widespread, especially in the Central Black Earth and Volga regions, and the government applied military force to restore order. Some delegates—particularly those from Saratov where the agrarian movement was strong and violent, government repression savage, and where peasant unions were dominated by SRs—called for revolutionary land seizures and armed insurrection, not waiting for the problematical convocation of a constituent assembly. But the majority still hoped for a nonviolent solution to peasant land hunger. Holding out the threat of insurrection as a last resort, they argued that local *bunty* were counterproductive and instead favored a stepped-up campaign of political organization, agricultural strikes, and refusal to pay taxes or provide army recruits as means to counter official repression.[34]

Shcherbak and other Sumy delegates were particularly vocal in this regard. They still put their faith in an imminent constituent assembly elected on a four-tail franchise (including female suffrage), "where our deputies will number 1,200 against 200–300 gentry and merchants." In the meantime they urged agricultural strikes and boycotts, nonpayment of taxes, and a temperance campaign aimed at denying the government the excise tax on vodka. One of the Sumy delegates (unidentified) went so far as to predict that "by March [1906] all of the police will have evaporated into the air and on one day we will quietly divide all the land." Despite the angry retorts from Saratov delegates (mainly Socialist Revolutionary intelligenty) that such tactics were naive, Shcherbak insisted that "the peaceful path means a *peaceful assault* on landowners and officials."[35] These were precisely the tactics pursued

iskii," p. 133; P. I. Klimov, *Revoliutsionnaia deiatel'nost' rabochikh v derevne v 1905–1907 gg.* (Moscow, 1960), pp. 166–70.

[33] *Volzhskii Vestnik*, no. 11, 19 November 1905, p. 3; Kiriukhina, "Mestnye," p. 122; *Materialy k krest'ianskomu voprosu*, p. 43.

[34] Shanin, *Russia*, pp. 115–17, 122–226; Tan, "Vtoroi s"ezd," pp. 241–44; Robinson, *Rural Russia*, pp. 170–73; Perrie, *Agrarian Policy*, pp. 114–17.

[35] *Materialy k krest'ianskomu voprosu*, p. 43 (italics in the original), and pp. 40–45, 56–58, 66–71.

by the Peasant Union in Sumy in late 1905. The union directed successful strikes on the estates of Countess Strogonova and the landowners Lishin-skaia and Kharitonenko. According to Shcherbak, all field hands and domestics refused to work and the landowners, faced with early rains and the loss of the sugar beet harvest, were compelled to offer better terms. Such victories only enhanced the union's prestige. Peasants refused to pay taxes, withdrew savings from banks, and in Tereshkovka and elsewhere closed liquor shops and refused to drink so as to deny the state an important source of revenue and to maintain discipline.[36]

Most dramatic were peasant attempts to assert local control or "peasant rule." Here they aspired to a radical restructuring of local government. Specifically, peasants targeted the powerful land captains (*zemskie nachal'niki*), who embodied in peasant eyes an oppressive bureaucratic rule and gentry tutelege, as well as *volost'* elders (*starshiny*), whom peasants properly perceived as being less responsible to the local community than to officials like the land captains. Peasants boycotted local officials and refused to deal with land captains. This movement was particularly well organized in Khoten *Volost'*, encompassing five villages, interspersed with the Strogonova lands. In the village of Iastrebennoe, where nearly all peasants labored in estate fields, a strike committee was set up. Peasants reelected the *volost'* administration, drove out rural police, and closed the state liquor shop. The new administration, composed of peasant unionists, withdrew 5,000 rubles of local deposits from the state savings bank and, perhaps in retribution for earlier clerical agitation, drew up plans to convert the church into a mill. When rumors reached the *volost'* that "black hundreds" were organizing in Sumy, Iastrebennoe peasants sent an armed militia to town to protect the revolutionary movement. In late December 1905 the Iastrebennoe "republic" was crushed in armed confrontation with troops.[37]

In Sumy *Volost'* the old rural administration was deposed and replaced by a revolutionary one headed by Andrei Ovcharenko. Police were unable to leave town since they were refused horses and the Peasant Union organized a worker-peasant militia to keep order.[38] A gendarme report summed up these remarkable events: "Shcherbak's ideas stirred the people with the result that entire peasant communes put them into effect, refusing to acknowledge police and other authorities, driving out officials and choosing new

[36] Shcherbak, "1905 god," pp. 129–30; Onats'kyi, "Selians'kyi revoliutsiinyi rukh," pp. 44–45; Glazman, "Robitnichyi rukh," pp. 27–28; *Agrarnoe dvizhenie v Rossii*, 2: 300–302; on the importance of the anti-alcohol campaign in union tactics, see Shanin, *Russia*, p. 101.

[37] Onats'kyi, "Selians'kyi revoliutsiinyi rukh," pp. 40–43; *Agrarnoe dvizhenie v Rossii*, 2: 302; *RvR: Vysshii pod"em revoliutsii 1905–1907 gg. Vooruzhennye vosstannia, noiabr'-dekabr' 1905 goda*, pt. 3, bk. 1, pp. 474–75; *RvR: Vserossiiskaia politicheskaia stachka v oktiabre 1905 goda*, pt. 2, p. 163; on the prevalence of boycott and reelection of local officials, see Shanin, *Russia*, pp. 113–14.

[38] Ovcharenko, "Spogady," p. 83; Shcherbak, "1905 god," pp. 131–34.

ones, demanding their money from savings banks and, finally, compiling *prigovory* adhering to the Peasant Union." The only official who did not lose his head during this period of "incipient revolutionary administration," and continued efforts to uphold state authority in Sumy was the assistant to the district police chief (*ispravnik*), I. D. Kryzhanovskii.[39]

Kryzhanovskii must have received a promotion after the government restored "order" in Sumy and crushed the Peasant Union. For the union had, in effect, assumed administrative functions in the district. Working closely with the Railwaymen's Union, organized in spring 1905, the Peasant Union made efforts to supply the town with basic necessities, and even published three issues of its own newspaper, *Krest'ianskaia gazeta*, edited by Shcherbak and M. N. Serdiuk.[40] Sumy was the scene of frequent mass meetings in November and early December, and the union was able to extend its influence into neighboring districts of Khar'kov and Kursk provinces. On November 20 a meeting in Sumy attracted Peasant Union representatives from Lebedin, Bogodukhov, and Akhtyrka (Khar'kov), and Sudzha, Ryl'sk, and L'gov (Kursk). In response to the recent arrest of the Central Bureau of the Peasant Union in Moscow on November 14, those in attendance declared the government in violation of the October Manifesto and outside the law.[41] Shcherbak, aided by railway workers, made speeches to peasant crowds at stations in Sudzha, urging them to pursue strikes and boycotts instead of plundering estates. Evidence indicates that in the southern part of Sudzha where the Peasant Union struck root such tactics were pursued, while in the northern half where organization was weak peasants resorted to more traditional methods.[42]

The Sumy Peasant Union held its last meeting, attended by 350 delegates, on December 18, 1905. A week later the government declared martial law, and as it reasserted control the Sumy union—as was true of the movement in general—was suppressed. Shcherbak was arrested in mid-December and, in the face of a huge rock-throwing crowd, troops managed to transport him to Khar'kov City. During the First Duma sessions, liberal and radical deputies continually pressed the government for his release. In late 1906 he was permitted to leave Russia and return to California, where he edited a Russian-language socialist newspaper until 1917. He returned in 1917 to play a

[39] P. V. Zamkovyi and L. Ia. Demchenko, "Novi dokumenty z istorii revoliutsiinoi borot'by selian Sumshchyny u 1905 r.," *Arkhivy Ukrainy*, no. 1 (1986): 42; *Khar'kov i Khar'kovskaia guberniia*, p. 343.

[40] Shcherbak, "1905 god," pp. 134–39. Serdiuk was employed at the zemstvo board as a technician.

[41] TsGAOR, f. 518, op. 1, d. 22, list 11–11ob; Svidzins'kyi, "Selians'ki spilky," p. 161; Shcherbak, "1905 god," p. 135.

[42] *1905 god v Kurskoi gubernii: Sbornik statei* (Kursk, 1925), pp. 52–53; *Agrarnoe dvizhenie v Rossii*, 1: 57–58; Kn. P. D. Dolgorukov, "Agrarnaia volna," *Pravo*, no. 1, 9 January 1906, cols. 25–28; *Gosudarstvennaia Duma. Stenograficheskie otchety, 1906* (hereafter *GDSO*), 2 vols., 2 (St. Petersburg, 1906) pp. 1365–67.

modest role in Ukrainian politics and died in the Soviet Union in the early
1920s.[43] Large numbers of union activists, including P. M. Lintvarev, were
arrested and exiled. He and other liberals were removed by the governor
from the zemstvo board. When the zemstvo met in emergency session in
early 1906 rank-and-file zemstvo men repudiated their leadership, specifically charging them with helping Shcherbak organize the peasant union.
Conservative zemstvo men then aided state officials in carrying out a full-
scale purge of Third Element employees in Sumy.[44]

Undoubtedly, the Sumy union was a radical enterprise; indeed its usur-
pation of power in the district in autumn 1905 could be characterized as revolutionary. Minister of the Interior P. N. Durnovo and other police officials
charged in addition that it, and other peasant unions, incited the masses to
violent insurrection and destruction of property. At the same time, and
somewhat paradoxically, they alleged that the union movement did not have
genuine peasant support and was really a machination of the intelligentsia
and urban opposition. Events in Sumy call into question both allegations.
There is little evidence that Shcherbak and his associates promoted agrarian
violence and spontaneous *buntarstvo*. It is abundantly clear that the union
enjoyed great authority among the population (some sources claim that the
entire population of the district followed it), and that it was thus able to pursue organized, nonviolent means of struggle, with some success, before it
was crushed by military force. Indeed, serious agrarian disorders began in
Sumy only after the union was crushed.[45] In what sense was Sumy typical of
peasant union activity in 1905? The movement in the non-black-earth region,
Vladimir Province in particular, provides a useful point of comparison. Here
officials also claimed a direct link between union activity and peasant *bunt*
and—of direct interest to the historian—tried to prove this charge in publicized trials of union activists.

PEASANT UNIONS IN IUR'EV AND POKROV DISTRICTS, VLADIMIR PROVINCE

As in the Left-Bank Ukraine, peasant protest in 1905 in the non-black-earth
provinces centered on issues of economic resources and land relations as
well as on the question of local power. The demand for "peasant rule," for

[43] *Khar'kov i Khar'kovskaia guberniia*, pp. 302–4, 322; *Budushchee* (Khar'kov), no. 5, 8 February
1906; *Khar'kovskaia Zhizn'*, no. 7, 16 February 1906, p. 2; *GDSO* 2, pp. 1210, 1122–25. On
Shcherbak after 1906, see Malov, *Dukhobortsy*, pp. 352–65; *San Francisco Chronicle*, 16 February
1918, p. 2.

[44] *Budushchee*, no. 1, 4 February 1906, p. 4; no. 13, 25 February 1906, p. 4; *Zhurnaly Sum-
skago uezdnago zemskago sobraniia* (Sumy, 1906), pp. 213–24, 233–43; Veselovskii, *Istoriia zemstva*, 4: 45–47, 327; *Russkiia Vedomosti*, no. 33, 3 February 1906, p. 3; no. 60, 3 March 1906, p.
3; V. P. Obninskii, *Polgoda russkoi revoliutsii* (Moscow, 1906), pp. 76, 115, 145; *Pravo*, no. 2, 17
January 1906, col. 142. Kiriukhina ("Vserossiiskii," p. 140) notes that 1,100 peasants and
intelligenty were arrested and/or exiled in Sumy District.

[45] Tan, "Vtoroi s"ezd," pp. 242–44.

reform and democratization of local institutions to enfranchise peasants and to remove a legacy of nonpeasant control and tutelage over rural society, occupied a prominent place in nearly all peasant statements during the revolution. It proved to be a central issue for the mobilization of peasants around the program of the Peasant Union.

Economic and political demands were tightly wound together, and in the non-black-earth provinces—even more than elsewhere—these often focused on inequitable tax assessments, fiscal accountability, and the peasantry's taxation burden. According to Veselovskii, peasants in at least sixty-six districts in European Russia refused to pay taxes on a massive scale during 1905–1906, mainly in the non-black-earth provinces. Peasant protest was often specifically directed against zemstvo levies, especially where peasants perceived zemstvo assessments on allotment, as compared with private land, as inequitable and unjust.[46] Very often the tax issue served as a lightning rod for wider protest and organization, helping peasants define themselves in a political sense in relation to other social groups and local institutions, forge alliances, and pursue coherent tactics. The issue was central to the peasant movement in this region. On the one hand, it underscored peasants' economic grievances: inadequate (or inconvenient) allotments, lack of access to resources (forests, meadows) vital to the peasant economy, and exploitative relations with private landowners. On the other hand, taxation also raised the issue of democratization of local institutions (zemstvo, *volost'*) and assertion of "peasant rule" unhampered by bureacratic controls.

The taxation question played a key role in peasant political mobilization in Novgorod, Moscow, Iaroslavl, and Nizhnii-Novgorod provinces. In Cherepovets, Beloozersk, and other districts of Novgorod zemstvo teachers raised the issue of zemstvo taxes and fiscal control to make common cause with peasants, channel protest into the peasant unions, and challenge the estate nature of local government.[47] These issues and conflicts, as well as the process of rural political mobilization in 1905, stand out in especially stark relief in Vladimir Province, particularly in Iur'ev District, where the union movement struck deep roots in 1905. Participants were put on trial here in 1906, an unusual occurrence which allowed Peasant Union activists to defend themselves against charges of inciting agrarian riots and which permits the historian to balance the picture presented in official sources.

Iur'ev District lay in the Central Industrial Region. Rural handicrafts were well developed among the local peasantry, and there was a long tradition of

---

[46] Veselovskii, *Istoriia zemstva* 4: 26–31; Dorothy Atkinson, "The Zemstvo and the Peasantry," in *The Zemstvo in Russia*, ed. Emmons and Vucinich, pp. 108–10; A. M. Anfimov, *Ekonomicheskoe polozhenie i klassovaia bor'ba krest'ian evropeiskoi Rossii, 1881–1904 gg.* (Moscow, 1984), pp. 75–77. (I would like to thank Jeff Burds for the latter reference.)

[47] See *Agrarnoe dvizhenie v Rossii* 1: 265–73; Klimov, *Revoliutsionnaia deiatel'nost'*, pp. 166–67; Seregny, *Russian Teachers*, pp. 191–93.

migrant labor (*otkhod*). Peasants worked as carpenters and stonemasons, in local textile factories, and farther afield in industrial centers like Ivanovo-Voznesensk, Orekhovo-Zuevo, and Moscow. Local peasants, predominantly males between the ages of fifteen and thirty-five, routinely sought supplementary earnings in local factories. The Kol'chugin factory, located in Il'insk *Volost'* near the border with Pokrov District, was the largest metalworks in Vladimir Province with 1,700 workers in 1905, most from surrounding villages. There were also textile factories in the district center of Iur'ev-Pol'skoi, employing 1,430 workers out of a population in 1897 of only 5,640.[48]

As in Sumy District, peasant economic frustration sharpened on the eve of 1905. Evidence compiled by the Vladimir Zemstvo statistician Aleksei Smirnov indicated that the Russo-Japanese War adversely impacted nonagricultural opportunities for peasants in Iur'ev and other districts by depressing wages and demand for labor in local factories. Local officials reported acute dissatisfaction with the war among domestic craft workers (*kustari*) and peasants laboring in factories. And despite the fact that only 16 percent of working-age males were involved mainly in agriculture, peasants complained about the size and location of their allotments and especially about a dearth of economic resources like meadows, pasture, and forests—which strained relations with estate owners. The issue of forests, owned mainly by gentry or other private concerns (often leased to merchants and wealthy peasant entrepreneurs), proved particularly vexing inasmuch as peasants often lacked access to these vital resources and saw increased commercial exploitation of forests as contrary to their views of a "moral economy."[49]

Peasant economic grievances in Iur'ev were exacerbated and politicized by local political conflicts outside the village, particularly in the zemstvo. Iur'ev was typical of zemstvo politics in Vladimir Province, where a small number of gentry families dominated zemstvo affairs and where district zemstvos had proven relatively inert in sponsoring services for the rural population during the 1890s, a period of dramatic upsurge in zemstvo education and other measures in many provinces. Liberal zemstvo activists, who often pushed such projects, tended to be concentrated in the Vladimir provincial assembly and in the Kovrov District Zemstvo before 1905.[50] Only in Kovrov can one detect the liberal *zemtsy*-radical Third Element alliance, which was

[48] Semenov, *Rossiia* 1: 268–70; Aleksei Smirnov, "Iz nabliudenii zemskago statistika," *Russkoe Bogatstvo*, no. 4 (1904), sec. 2, pp. 1–20; *RvR: Revoliutsionnoe dvizhenie v Rossii vesnoi i letom 1905 goda, aprel'-sentiabr'*, pt. 1, pp. 405–6.

[49] Lavrov, "Krest'ianskie nastroeniia," p. 30; Vl. Voznesenskii, "Krest'ianskoe dvizhenie vo Vladimirskoi gub. v pervuiu revoliutsiiu (1905–1906 g.g.)," in *O rabochem dvizhenii i sotsialdemokraticheskoi rabote vo Vladimirskoi gubernii v 900-kh godakh*, vypusk 1, ed. A. N. Asatkin (Vladimir, 1926), pp. 133–36; Aleksei Smirnov, "Voina i promyshlennaia derevnia (Iz Vladimira-gubernsk.)," *Obrazovanie*, no. 11 (1904), sec. 2, pp. 47–55; idem., "Zemledelie i zemledelets tsentral'noi, promyshlennoi gubernii," *Russkaia Mysl'*, no. 7 (1901), sec. 2, pp. 173–86.

[50] Veselovskii, *Istoriia zemstva* 4: 481.

so important to local politics in places like Sumy, or a pattern of activism in primary education and other fields (including attempts to meet employees' professional demands). It is not surprising, therefore, that in 1905, aside from the provincial zemstvo, only the Kovrov Zemstvo promoted political discussion among peasants as well as the organization of peasant unions through the medium of the zemstvo's economic *sovet* (council) during the summer of 1905.[51] Here, Kovrov followed a pattern observable in other provinces where zemstvo liberals helped further politicization in the countryside by supporting employees' political activity and opening the doors of zemstvo institutions and agricultural societies to the rural masses.

In other districts in Vladimir such activism was largely absent, except for isolated individuals like A. P. Gresser, a zemstvo deputy and future Kadet organizer from Sudogda. In Iur'ev zemstvo affairs had long been dominated by a conservative gentry faction, led since the 1890s by the brothers A. I. and S. I. Krasenskii, respectively chairman of the district zemstvo board and district marshal of the nobility, and Prince A. B. Golitsyn who in 1901 became provincial marshal of the nobility and acted as the conservative standard-bearer in the provincial zemstvo. This group had proven singularly inactive; management of the zemstvo's fifty schools was left largely to the local school board, a sure sign of inertia and conservative hegemony.[52] In contrast to Sumy, neither the configuration of the Iur'ev Zemstvo nor its record seemed conducive to the kind of Third Element and peasant mobilization discerned elsewhere.

Nevertheless, local zemstvo affairs were enlivened, and elite solidarity jeopardized, in the late 1890s with the appearance of a new zemstvo deputy, Sergei Viktorovich Bunin. Bunin was a hereditary noble, aged forty to forty-five years in 1905, who settled down on his estate near the village of Vlas'evo in Nikul'sk *Volost'*. Information on his background is scant, though police reports noted that he sometimes wore a pince-nez, and the Soviet historian N. M. Pirumova has described him as having a university education and participating in informal national zemstvo meetings in Moscow. He was also affiliated with the Moscow Agricultural Society and was a sharp critic of the state's fiscal and industrialization policies, which he saw as ruining both gentry and peasantry alike.[53] Bunin immediately established himself as a maverick and gadfly in local zemstvo affairs, first by opposing the conservatives'

[51] *Severnyi Krai*, no. 161, 29 June, p. 2 and no. 179, 22 July 1905, p. 3; A. Smirnov, "Ekonomicheskii sovet pri kovrovskoi zemskoi uprave," *Russkiia Vedomosti*, no. 240, 4 September 1905, pp. 3–4; TsGAOR, f. 102, DP, OO, d. 2250, ch. 49, list 60; A. I. Ivanov, *Krest'ianskoe dvizhenie vo Vladimirskoi gubernii v 1905-1906 gg.* (Vladimir, 1923), pp. 5–6.

[52] Veselovskii, *Istoriia zemstva* 4: 479–80.

[53] TsGAOR, f. 102, DP, OO, op. 233 (1905), d. 1800, ch. 43, list 2ob; Pirumova, *Zemskoe liberal'noe dvizhenie*, pp. 232–33; *Trudy mestnykh komitetov o nuzhdakh sel'skokhoziaistvennoi promyshlennosti* 6: 184–86.

continued support for church schools (a kind of political litmus test in zemst-vos around the turn of the century), and then, most powerfully, with a sustained critique of zemstvo tax assessments and peasant disenfranchisement.

Peasant communes, Bunin contended, paid a disproportionate share of zemstvo levies due to tax rates fixed in the 1860s, soon after the establishment of the zemstvos, on peasant allotment land (mostly arable) and private holdings (much of it in forest). The original assessments, carried out hurriedly and without adequate expertise (only in 1897, at Bunin's prodding, did the Iur'ev Zemstvo establish a statistical bureau), were inequitable. In subsequent decades, they became grossly unfair given the skyrocketing market value of forests spurred on by construction and urbanization. Half of the 104,212 *desiatiny* held by private owners in the district was forest, assessed at a rate ten times lower than peasant arable. Peasants held only a fraction of the 63,260 *desiatiny* of forest in Iur'ev, a fact that led to dependence on local gentry or leaseholders for fuel and other necessities.[54] The question of zemstvo assessments thus had considerable explosive potential.

Bunin lobbied within the zemstvo assembly for a reevaluation of property in the district to account for changes in productivity and market value—a move resisted by the conservatives. In 1902 he raised the issue in the press at both the local (*Severnyi Krai*) and national (*Russkiia Vedomosti* and *Russkaia Mysl'*) levels. In 1903 and 1904 in the district zemstvo assembly he again criticized a situation in which private owners, who dominated the Iur'ev Zemstvo, had shifted the burden of zemstvo levies onto the peasantry. In 1903 Bunin was easily thwarted by the Krasenskiis and Golitsyn, all owners of considerable tracts of forest (Golitsyn, with over half of his 10,066 *desiatiny* in forest, was the largest owner in the district). At the 1904 meeting Bunin managed to get a proposal to raise assessments on forests put to a secret ballot, but found himself in the minority.

Most of the peasant deputies had voted with the gentry faction, a curious outcome which, as Bunin explained, underscored peasant disenfranchisement. The 1890 Zemstvo Law (or counterreform) had paralyzed peasant elections to the zemstvo, with the result that nearly all the peasant deputies in Iur'ev were *volost'* elders, directly dependent on the marshal of nobility, land captains (appointed from local gentry), and other officials. One can appreciate the quandary of these *volost'* officials who, on the one hand represented local peasant communities but who, on the other hand, served as the lowest link in the Ministry of Interior's chain of control in rural Russia. Indeed, some of them approached Bunin after the vote, apologizing for their actions and thanking Bunin for his defense of popular interests. One can also appre-

---

[54] S. Bunin, "Neravnomernost' zemskogo oblozheniia v Iur'evskom uezde," *Russkaia Mysl'*, no. 7 (1902): 115–19; Veselovskii, *Istoriia zemstva*, 4: 479–80; *Vladimirets*, no. 75, 21 October 1906, p. 3.

ciate the central place demands for reform of zemstvo and *volost'* government would occupy in peasant politics in 1905.[55]

Bunin also charged that gentry self-interest had prevented the zemstvo from providing vital services and threatened the well-being of zemstvo employees who often left the district for posts elsewhere. Because the zemstvo's coffers were depleted, teachers often had to wait three to four months to receive their salaries. Bunin related a heartrending scene he had witnessed in Iur'ev-Pol'skoi on August 20, 1904. A zemstvo teacher, unable to secure his salary on time, ran through the town with tears streaming down his face, soliciting four rubles for the burial of his son; he had pawned his only possession of value, a pocket watch. In this context it is worth pointing out that in 1903 in the Vladimir Provincial Zemstvo it was namely Prince Golitsyn, the mentor of gentry conservatives in Iur'ev, who led the attack against summer courses for zemstvo teachers. Relations between the Second and Third elements in Iur'ev District were strained on the eve of 1905.[56]

In raising the zemstvo taxation issue, Bunin had touched important issues—peasant poverty, estate privilege and local power, the status of the Third Element—and it is tempting to speculate that already before 1905 he was working to build the coalition of forces that would eventually seek to channel peasant protest into the Peasant Union movement. If so, local officials in early 1905 (March–April) discerned few signs of such agitation or politics in Iur'ev, outside the normal run of "undesirable" relations between individual landowners and peasants.[57] But political ferment there was. Given relatively high rates of literacy and seasonal migratory labor (*otkhozhie promysly*), peasants in Iur'ev were not isolated from outside events. In addition, the war with Japan, which had summoned local peasants to the fields of Manchuria, had dramatically increased peasant interest in newspapers, a phenomenon evident in many locales throughout European Russia. The Imperial Decree of February 18, 1905, and official notice of elections to a consultative Duma enhanced peasant interest in politics and, as elsewhere, sparked a petition campaign and discussion of political questions in the villages; one press report from Iur'ev noted that peasant *politiki* (political activists) warned that land captains would have to be abolished before fair elections to a national assembly could be held.[58]

[55] In general, see Atkinson, "The Zemstvo and the Peasantry," pp. 117–19.

[56] S. V. Bunin, "Otkrytoe pis'mo k vladimirskomu gubernskomu predvoditeliu dvorianstva kniaziu A. B. Golitsynu," *Russkaia Mysl'*, no. 5 (1905): 208–13; *Russkaia Shkola*, no. 7–8 (1903), sec. 2, p. 100. Golitsyn was outvoted in the zemstvo, but the government refused to sanction the summer courses.

[57] *TsGAOR*, f. 102, DP OO, d. 2250, ch. 49, list 1–1ob; Lavrov, "Krest'ianskie nastroeniia," p. 30.

[58] *Severnyi Krai*, no. 97, 12 April 1905, p. 2; Aleksei Smirnov, "Manifesty v derevne," *Istina*, no. 2 (January 1906): 23; *Russkiia Vedomosti*, no. 112, 27 April 1905, pp. 3–4. In Sudogda District peasants noted in *prigovory* how they had read about the war in newspapers and

Bunin took advantage of this situation and launched a campaign of agitation among peasants neighboring his estate (probably soon after the February 18 Decree, which was widely viewed as legalizing political activity). In a dramatic gesture Bunin granted one *desiatina* of his best land to each household in Vlas'evo, "given the inadequacy of allotments provided by his ancestors," and notified the zemstvo that this land should immediately be enrolled in the village's name. More important, he drafted an "Open Letter to the Vladimir Provincial Gentry Marshal, Prince A. B. Golitsyn," in which he again raised the question of zemstvo assessments, and, naming names, charged the conservative leadership of the zemstvo with blocking any reevaluation of property. He and a former zemstvo employee Anton K. Flerov (then working as a clerk in the Kol'chugin factory), distributed one thousand copies of the letter among the population (very likely these were printed by the Moscow Agricultural Society, which in May 1905 helped launch the national organization of the All-Russian Peasant Union).[59] Bunin was also aided by Fedor P. Gerasimov, a peasant agriculturalist from Vlas'evo. Gerasimov, about thirty years of age, had attended a rural school; though little is known about his experience beyond the village, he appears to have been fairly typical of those younger literate peasants who played significant roles in the rural politics of 1905. Throughout 1905 he was an active Peasant Union agitator in Iur'ev District; in 1907 the local peasantry elected him to the Second Duma as a Socialist Revolutionary deputy.[60]

Bunin's letter touched off an explosion in the district. According to police reports, it struck a responsive chord among the peasant population, stirring a deep reservoir of accumulated hostility to the zemstvo. Peasants had complained about wasteful outlays of zemstvo money, including private use by zemstvo officials and employees of zemstvo horses; long delays in receiving treatment at the zemstvo hospital, causing peasants lost workdays; the zemstvo board's careless disregard in making sure that soldiers' wives were provided the subsidies due them while their husbands were fighting in the Far East; and a general "coarse and inattentive attitude" displayed by zemstvo officials toward peasants. A subsequent investigation (*reviziia*) of the Iur'ev Zemstvo carried out by the governor's office revealed that there was substance to peasant complaints that the zemstvo board chairman Krasenskii showed little interest in day-to-day business and that board member E. D. Koritskii had treated peasants arriving on business in a "coarse" manner.

---

came to realize that "the Japanese beat us because their soldiers are literate, can read a map and even use a compass. We are humiliated!" They petitioned that more zemstvo schools be built: Voznesenskii, "Krest'ianskoe dvizhenie," p. 137.

[59] *Severnyi Krai*, no. 127, 19 May 1905, p. 3; no. 108, 26 April 1905, p. 2; the letter appeared in May in the thick journal *Russkaia Mysl'*.

[60] *Tsentral'nyi Gosudarstvennyi Istoricheskii Arkhiv SSSR* (hereafter *TsGIA*), f. 1327, op. 2 (1907), list 64; *Chleny 2-oi Gosudarstvennoi Dumy* (St. Petersburg, 1907), p. 10.

The demand for humane treatment was common in the popular protest of 1905, from peasant and worker alike, and helped to orient peasants toward issues of civil rights and legal equality and thus find common ground with other groups.[61]

Local officials countered with their own agitation. At communal assemblies land captains and *volost'* elders read a special appendix of *Sel'skii Vestnik* explaining the Goremykin Commission's rescript outlining government plans to improve peasants' condition, Siberian migration, and reaffirming the inviolability of *pomeshchik* property. It also called on peasants to resist internal enemies, a clear appeal to peasant monarchism against the liberation movement. Press reports noted that peasants reacted to this message with distrust, and even warnings from the governor that zemstvo employees and other outsiders not participate in rural *skhody* (assemblies) had little effect in stemming the tide of popular protest.[62]

By early summer 1905 Bunin had helped organize an extensive petition campaign. On June 9 peasant delegates (*upolnomochennye*) from eight villages, and on June 10 from another five villages, gathered at his estate to hear him read the now famous "letter" and offer advice that rather than resort to "force" peasants should compile *prigovory* addressed to the zemstvo and government. According to police reports, Bunin circulated copies of a model *prigovor*, concentrating on zemstvo taxes and peasant enfranchisement. From 100 to 150 petitions were adopted by rural communes (in other words, the entire district).[63] Peasants demanded that a special meeting of the zemstvo be convened to deal with the tax issue and that each of Iur'ev's thirteen *Volosti* send a representative, with the proviso that these be freely chosen, without official pressure and in no case be selected from among peasants holding rural administrative posts. Peasants demanded that the zemstvo provide a strict public accounting of its budget so "we may know just how our hard-earned peasant kopeck is spent." Finally, those who signed the petitions resolved to ask the government to increase peasant representation in the zemstvos and free peasant deputies from bureaucratic pressure.[64]

Rumors circulated that on Sunday, June 19, 1905, peasants would gather in Iur'ev-Pol'skoi to present their demands to the zemstvo (or in one variant destroy the zemstvo building, causing some townspeople to flee or insure

---

[61] *TsGAOR*, f. 102, DP OO, d. 2250, ch. 49, listy 25–27; d. 1800, ch. 43, listy 4ob–5; see also Ivanov, *Krest'ianskoe dvizhenie*, pp. 6–7.

[62] *Severnyi Krai*, no. 136, 29 May 1905, p. 2; *Russkiia Vedomosti*, no. 240, 4 September 1905, p. 3.

[63] *TsGAOR*, f. 102, DP OO, d. 2250, ch. 49, list 45–45ob; *Protokoly delegatskago soveshchaniia Vserossiiskago Krest'ianskago Soiuza 6–10 noiabria 1905 g. v Moskve* (Moscow, 1906), pp. 16–17.

[64] Voznesenskii, "Krest'ianskoe dvizhenie," pp. 158–59; Veselovskii, *Krest'ianskii vopros*, pp. 50–51.

their property). The peasants received only partial satisfaction when the
zemstvo voted in September to shift 8,000 rubles (by another account 15,000)
in taxes from peasant allotments to private lands and promised that in future
a reevaluation would be made and peasant delegates invited to consult in
the process. These tactics were viewed suspiciously (a Iur'ev delegate to the
November Congress of the Peasant Union described them as a "mockery")
and did little to dampen peasant discontent in the district.[65] News of the
October general strike and the Manifesto of October 17, combined with a
poor harvest, only intensified local agitation and peasants' sense of imminent victory. Iur'ev peasants thirsted for information, in some cases offering
to pay a stipend to "orators," and in one locale agreeing to help a literate
fellow villager work his land in exchange for reading aloud from the newspaper. The district police chief (*ispravnik*), von Grote later recalled that in
October and November rural meetings sprang up like mushrooms after a
spring rain, encompassing an entire village or even *volost'*. Peasants eagerly
discussed issues of land, taxes, *volost'* elders, and rural administration, the
promised Duma elections, and the "inevitable question" of abolishing land
captains.[66]

In Glumovsk *Volost'*, "meetings" began on Sundays, during the general
strike and communications breakdown. Peasants from five to six villages,
constituting a parish (or *votchina*), gathered after religious services. In the
village of Berezhka (Glumovsk) a large meeting was held on October 22. At
first, according to an eyewitness account, the older *stariki* reacted with suspicion to news of the October Manifesto's "freedoms," but the mood shifted
when younger peasants with factory experience talked about the importance
of the Duma for solving the land question and about the agrarian programs
of the revolutionary parties. Peasants agreed that all land should revert to
the toilers (with provision of 3 1/2 *desiatiny* per soul), rejected compensation
to *pomeshchiki*, and drew up a communal decision including these demands.

Meetings continued in this area through autumn, stimulated in part by
inter-village rivalry: "Are we any worse than the people from Skomovo?"
they asked and then decided to send horses to fetch an "orator," either a
local *intelligent*, or a "conscious" peasant, understood as one who was independent of officialdom, literate, and of progressive sympathies. Some 100 to
150 people then crowded into a large, nine-*arshin* (see Glossary) log home
(*izba*), with the guests ensconced in the icon corner (*krasnyi ugol*), or met outside in the case of larger meetings. On local issues of land and peasant con-

[65] S. Dubrovskii and B. Grave, comps., *Agrarnoe dvizhenie v 1905–1907 g.g.*, 1 (Moscow-Leningrad, 1925), p. 60; Veselovskii, *Istoriia zemstva*, 4: 480; *Protokoly delegatskago soveshchaniia*, p. 17; *Vladimirets*, no. 75, 21 October 1906, p. 3. Communal petitions were also sent to the Vladimir provincial zemstvo on this issue: *Russkiia Vedomosti*, no. 249, 13 September 1905, p. 2.

[66] Voznesenskii, "Krest'ianskoe dvizhenie," pp. 162–63.

trol participants at these meetings inclined toward the left, but on the issue of the tsar versus a republic they remained conservative, a fact that led Peasant Union activists here, as elsewhere, to tread warily around the issue of monarchy and generally not support the call of the revolutionary parties for a democratic republic.[67]

In the *volosti* around Iur'ev-Pol'skoi Bunin decided to provide a firmer organizational foundation for local peasant protest. He was aided in Peasant Union organization by a group of Third Element people, many of peasant origin, and "conscious" peasants: N. N. Ottenberg, son of local *pomeshchiki* and a student at the Moscow Agricultural Institute; A. I. Agapov and A. I. Doronin, both local teachers of peasant origin (Doronin had recently been dismissed for political unreliability); N. V. Tikhomirov, son of a priest; a doctor Orlov and the above-mentioned Flerov; the peasant Seleznez who had been delegated by his commune as a messenger (*khodok*) to attend political meetings in Vladimir and elsewhere in late 1905; Nikon Fedorov, a peasant from Sleptsovo (Nikul'sk *Volost'*) elected as a delegate to the November Peasant Union congress in Moscow; the above-mentioned peasant Gerasimov from Vlas'evo; and finally Ivan S. Morozov, who was one of the most important local union organizers and who also represented Iur'ev at the Moscow Congress. Morozov was a peasant from the village of Ozertsy. Educated in a church primary school, from adolescence he had left home to work in factories and other urban jobs, finally becoming a skilled metalworker. Active in radical workers' circles, Morozov joined the SR party, was exiled to Arkhangel Province for four years, and returned home in 1905 where he was an energetic union activist.[68]

These and others helped organize a series of daily mass meetings in villages beginning on October 22 and culminating in large gatherings, drawing 1,500 to 2,000 people in Iur'ev-Pol'skoi at the end of the month. Reports throughout Vladimir Province indicate that local officials and priests often tried to conceal the October Manifesto, perhaps instinctively sensing that any shift in authority at the center would undercut their positions locally. Peasant Union organizers, by contrast, obviously wanted to give the "freedoms" maximum publicity, which granted a kind of legitimacy to their efforts. Meetings were held in El'tsy (Nikul'sk *Volost'*) on October 22, in Zagor'e on October 23, and in a field outside town on October 24. Bunin, the teacher Agapov, and the peasant V. A. Petrov spoke at these as well as in Berezhka (Glumovsk). In the village of Skomovo (Parshinsk *Volost'*), Agapov and Tikhomirov led a demonstration with red flags and peasants singing rev-

---

[67] Ivanov-Razumnik, "Chto dumaet derevnia? (vpechatleniia ochevidtsa)," *Sovremennost'*, no. 2 (1906), sec. 2, pp. 51–53, and *Russkoe Bogatstvo*, no. 5 (1906), sec. 2, pp. 9–10.

[68] *TsGAOR*, f. 102, DP OO, op. 233 (1905), d. 1800, ch. 43, listy 7–8; Ivanov-Razumnik, "Chto dumaet derevnia?," *Russkoe Bogatstvo*, no. 5 (1906), sec. 2, pp. 7–8; "Pamiati I. S. Morozova," *Vladimirets*, no. 9, 5 August 1906, p. 2.

olutionary songs. On October 30 Bunin, aided by Morozov, Doronin, and the peasant I. K. Bykov distributed the Peasant Union's leaflet "What Do the People Who March Under the Red Flag Want?" which summarized the union's program and appealed to the population to resist the arguments of black-hundred elements. At a huge meeting in town on October 31, Peasant Union supporters drafted a telegram to Count Witte demanding the removal of Prince Golitsyn as marshal of the nobility and of Governor I. M. Leont'ev, charging them with stirring up black-hundred sentiment.[69] Morozov and Bunin urged peasants to cease paying taxes (police reports allege that Bunin also called for seizures of land and forests, beginning with his own, but testimony at the October 1906 trial of Iur'ev Peasant Union activists failed to support these claims). Bunin declared that "the zemstvo spends, in fact wastes, the people's money, and all because there are few peasant representatives in it, little people's control (narodnyi kontrol')." Morozov and others called on peasants to join the Peasant Union.[70]

The question of the tsar generated a good deal of heated discussion at these meetings. At separate gatherings on November 1 both the peasant Bykov and Bunin bent over backwards to assure peasant audiences that neither they nor the union sought to abolish the monarchy. "I have never been against the tsar, but only against the tyranny of the bureaucrats," proclaimed Bunin, who then went on to urge his listeners to elect trusted representatives to the Duma, rather than the old volost' elders, and to send their communal decisions to the Peasant Union's Central Bureau in Moscow, which would forward them to the Duma when it convened.[71]

This agitation, officials insisted, resulted in unprecedented popular insubordination toward local authorities. At the 1906 trial a land captain, Iz''edinov, complained that Bunin and peasant activists like Morozov had spoiled "my peasants," who no longer were willing to appear before the land captain on any trifling pretext, even under threat of three to four days in jail. When peasants did bother to submit prigovory to the local land captain for confirmation, these proclaimed adherence to the Peasant Union and included demands for increased representation in the zemstvo as well as the right for junior household members to take part in the village assembly (skhod). The latter demand suggests the key role played by younger, literate, and more traveled villagers in the rural politics of 1905. Given the recent poor harvest, which local peasants claimed placed them in "terrible need," a

---

[69] Smirnov, "Manifesty v derevne," pp. 24–27; Voznesenskii, "Krest'ianskoe dvizhenie," pp. 142–44; Dubrovskii and Grave, Agrarnoe dvizhenie, 1: 61–62; Protokoly delegatskago soveshchaniia, p. 17; Ivanov, Krest'ianskoe dvizhenie, pp. 20–22; TsGAOR, f. 102, DP OO, d. 2250, ch. 49, listy 84–87; G. I. Chernov, Stranitsy proshlogo: Iz istorii dorevoliutsionnoi shkoly Vladimirskoi gubernii (Vladimir, 1970), pp. 192–93.

[70] Vladimirets, no. 80, 5 November 1906, p. 3; Ivanov, Krest'ianskoe dvizhenie, pp. 21–22.

[71] Dubrovskii and Grave, Agrarnoe dvizhenie, 1, pp. 65–66.

crowd besieged a meeting of land captains in Iur'ev-Pol'skoi, compelling it to turn over all the emergency relief funds (*prodovol'stvennye kapitaly*), after these officials had temporized on releasing these funds. As for Iz"edinov, he resigned his post, unwilling to continue in a situation where "peasants now displayed a coarse attitude toward the authorities and respect had plummeted."[72] What seems clear is that in 1905 a key demand of peasants in Iur'ev was for humane treatment by officials and privileged society. Not surprisingly, when they asserted themselves and acted on Bunin's exhortation "not to bow and scrape before land captains," the latter balked at relinquishing the traditional patterns of deference and authority.

Refusal to pay taxes became endemic in Iur'ev District in autumn 1905, sweeping all villages in Il'insk and Davydovsk *volosti*. The government's Manifesto of November 3, 1905, canceling redemption payments (which local officials, in contrast to the October Manifesto, bent every effort to circulate), failed to quiet the peasantry and simply reinforced peasants' inclination not to pay any taxes. Peasants in these locales as well as in Simsk and Gorkinsk *volosti* replaced *volost'* and village officials with persons enjoying their trust and deemed independent of officialdom. In some places salaries of *volost'* elders and clerks were cut in half.[73] Iur'ev peasants in late 1905 heeded the advice of union activists and sought to assert greater "popular control" over local affairs.

Peasants in Iur'ev also resorted to economic forms of struggle, mainly the illegal cutting of wood in private forests, trespassing on meadows, and committing arson and theft on estates. In most instances, peasants displayed solidarity in these actions. In December 1905 peasants of Elokh (Gorkinsk *Volost'*), by a two-thirds vote of the communal assembly, carted from the forest of a neighboring *pomeshchik* wood that had already been cut for fuel. Peasants appear to have been motivated by need, but also by an ingrained prejudice against any commercial exploitation of these resources. This movement abated somewhat by the end of the year, but again picked up in spring-summer of 1906. In the village of Aleksino (Gorodishchensk *Volost'*) the entire commune, by decision of the assembly, illegally pastured its herd on local private lands and mowed a tract of waste. Peasants were driven by lack of land as well as by the fact that many of their allotments were located five *versty* away. The owner had refused to sell them the more conveniently located waste. Peasants also refused to lease lands and organized agricultural strikes.[74]

[72] *Vladimirets*, no. 74, 29 October, p. 2 and no. 75, 31 October 1906, p. 3; *TsGAOR*, f. 102, DP OO, d. 2250, ch. 49, list 88.

[73] *Agrarnoe dvizhenie v Rossii*, 1: 17–19; Smirnov, "Manifesty v derevne," pp. 28–30; *RvR: Vysshii pod"em revoliutsii 1905–1907 gg.*, pt. 2, pp. 43–44.

[74] *Agrarnoe dvizhenie v Rossii*, 1: 18–19; Voznesenskii, "Krest'ianskoe dvizhenie," pp. 164–66; Ivanov, *Krest'ianskoe dvizhenie*, pp. 31–32.

As in Sumy and elsewhere, the Vladimir provincial authorities, spurred on by Durnovo's circulars, crushed the local Peasant Union movement in December 1905, arresting many activists throughout Vladimir Province, particularly in Iur'ev and Pokrov districts. True to form, they showed a decided preference for rural intelligenty, particularly teachers, a fact that masks somewhat the genuine peasant support and degree of peasant leadership this organization had enjoyed.[75] In Iur'ev in October 1906 Bunin, the teachers Agapov and Doronin, Tikhomirov, and the peasants I. L. Sazonov and V. A. Petrov were put on public trial. At his arrest in December 1905 the peasant Nikon Fedorov escaped by clever dissembling, playing the simpleton ("What use would I have for illegal literature; you can't farm with it"). Ivan Morozov had been shot and killed in July 1906 in his native village, under cloudy circumstances, when police came to arrest his brother for his involvement in the Moscow Insurrection of December 1905. Indeed, the liberal press contended that Morozov offered no resistance and that the local *pristav* had murdered him in cold blood.[76]

The trial of "Bunin and Co.," held in Vladimir, became a local *cause célèbre*, with some forty-five witnesses called to testify, including thirty peasant members of the union. Onlookers jammed the corridors. The prosecution tried to establish that the accused had incited peasants to seize land and overthrow the existing state order. Although the unionists were represented by defense counsel, Bunin personally cross-examined the peasant witnesses, referring to each of them by name. Press reports stress that all witnesses, with the exception of *volost'* elders and rural police, held him in great reverence. The defendants sought to distance themselves from statements made by more radical delegates at the Peasant Union's November Congress; they admitted that the local union had supported expropriation of all private lands, but *with compensation*, a claim that seems to contradict other evidence. In any case, witnesses asserted convincingly that Bunin and the others (including Morozov) had not called for violent acts, and had, on the contrary, acted to prevent attacks on property, described as pogroms in the testimony. All were acquitted of the charges.[77]

Trials of individual Peasant Union agitators in other districts of Vladimir Province were also held in late 1906, providing some idea of the nature of

[75] Ivanov, *Krest'ianskoe dvizhenie*, pp. 33–38. Local peasant communes sent messengers (*khodoki*) to the tsar asking for Bunin's release: *Pravo*, no. 1, 9 January 1906, col. 51.

[76] *Vladimirets*, no. 14, 11 August, p. 2; no. 109, 13 December 1906, p. 3; *RvR: Vtoroi period revoliutsii, 1906-1907 gody*, pt. 2, bk. 2, pp. 19–20, 459 n. 16; Dubrovskii and Grave, *Agrarnoe dvizhenie*, 1, p. 74.

[77] *Vladimirets*, no. 62, 14 October, p. 3; no. 73, 28 October, p. 3; no. 80, 5 November, p. 3; no. 86, 12 November 1906, p. 3. Like Lintvarev in Sumy, Bunin was repudiated by conservatives in the local zemstvo and left the area, eventually taking a post as secretary to the Tver zemstvo board and setting up his own publishing concern in Moscow: Veselovskii, *Istoriia zemstva*, 4: 480.

the movement outside Iur'ev, particularly in Pokrov. In nearly every instance those brought to trial were rural teachers, not surprising given teachers' strong support for peasant unions as a "conscious" movement, a counterweight to village black-hundreds and officialdom, but also due to the government's desire to portray the movement as an intelligentsia charade.

In Kovrov District the teacher V. G. Amatov was accused of agitating for an overthrow of the existing regime, specifically for distributing the union's "What Do the People Who March Under the Red Flag Want?" which had been sold openly at bookstalls in Vladimir and had been printed in *Syn Otechestva*. Amatov insisted that his agitation was directed not against the tsar, but against violence from the right directed against rural intelligenty and peasant activists who sought to take advantage of the promises of the October Manifesto, particularly rural officials and others who saw their power threatened by the emerging post-October order. Indeed, Amatov's lawyer argued, his activities could hardly be construed as appealing to force, since he had supported the idea of participation in the Duma elections. Amatov was acquitted as was the teacher A. I. Al'bitskaia in Murom District.[78]

In Pokrov District the most intense agitation on behalf of the Peasant Union was waged by the local affiliate of the All-Russian Teachers' Union, boasting more than 100 members in the district. Many of these were close to the Socialist Revolutionary party, but supported the Peasant Union. Teachers urged peasants to compile *prigovory* demanding the following: expropriation of church, state and, in part, private lands (reflecting concern for peasant purchases), and allotment of land to peasants who would work it with their own labor; abolition of existing taxes in favor of a progressive income tax; abolition of land captains and police; free education and access to secondary and higher schools; and ministerial responsibility to a democratically elected Duma.[79]

As in Iur'ev, activists in Pokrov District framed their appeals around the issues of land and local power. In the village of Afanasovo (Zherdevsk *Volost'*) on November 26, 1905, peasants from five villages met to elect a new police official (*sotskii*). The teacher A. M. Sobolev (son of a deacon) argued that rural police were unnecessary and recited the program of the Peasant Union calling for election of officials trusted by the population. As a result, peasants decided not to fill the police post. Peasant witnesses at Sobolev's trial affirmed that there was no talk about violence and that the tsar was not mentioned; rather, discussion centered on the Duma and "how it was nec-

---

[78] *Vladimirets*, no. 60, 12 October, p. 2; no. 61, 13 October, p. 3; no. 69, 24 October 1906, p. 3; Ivanov, *Krest'ianskoe dvizhenie*, p. 22.

[79] *TsGAOR*, f. 102, DP OO, d. 999, ch. 1, tom 2, list 135–135ob; *Syn Otechestva*, no. 19, 1905, p. 5; *Kliazma*, no. 3, 4 January 1906, p. 3; N. Malitskii, "Professional'noe dvizhenie vo Vladimirskoi gub. v 1905–1907 g.g.," in *O rabochem dvizhenii*, pp. 73–80.

essary to diminish (*ubavit'*) officialdom and augment (*pribavit'*) peasant land." Sobolev was acquitted.[80]

In Kopninsk *Volost'*, Peasant Union agitation was waged forcefully in autumn 1905 by the following: I. S. Samokhvalov, a twenty-one-year-old native of the village of Tsepelevo, employed as a teacher in Nizhnii Novgorod Province; I. M. Medvedev, also of peasant origin, who had served as a teacher in Tsepelevo for eighteen years (Samokhvalov had likely been his pupil); and a student A. L. Borisov, son of peasants from neighboring Pernikov. According to the indictment, in mid-November 1905 these three, without permission (*samovol'no*), called together communal assemblies in the villages of Tsepelevo, Pogost, and Bryzgunovo, where they presented a *prigovor* calling for nonpayment of taxes, withdrawal of peasant deposits from state banks, and expropriation of *pomeshchik* lands and forests. Not only did local peasants join the union, but they also moved quickly to put its program into practice. Nearly all savings were withdrawn from the bank at the local post office, tax collections in Kopninsk *Volost'* ceased, and, according to rural police, peasants prepared to divide up private forests. The defendants, who claimed they had acted on the basis of the October Manifesto and considered the Peasant Union a legal organization, received three-month sentences.[81]

In industrial Fillipovsk *Volost'* teachers and other Peasant Union activists (including the exiled student V. I. Pokrovskii) organized a successful strike of 4,000 textile workers, forcing concessions from factory owners, and carried political agitation to remote locales "into which the [political] parties had never penetrated."[82] By all accounts, one of the most active organizers in Pokrov District was the teacher in the village of El'tsino, Efim S. Kamrakov. Twenty-four years old in 1905, Kamrakov was of peasant origin from the industrial settlement of Orekhovo in neighboring Moscow Province. He had graduated from the Kirzhach Teachers' Seminary in 1901 and then taught in several schools in Pokrov District. He belonged to the SR party and was a leading figure as well in the local Teachers' Union organization.[83] Kamrakov and others helped organize huge peasant meetings in Pokrov as well as in Iur'ev District (he helped organize a railway strike near the Kol'chugin fac-

---

[80] *Vladimirets*, no. 72, 27 October 1906, p. 3; also trial of teacher in village of Savel'evo (*Zherdevsk Volost'*), S. V. Dvorianinov: *Vladimirets*, no. 64, 17 October, p. 3; no. 66, 19 October, p. 3; no. 66, 20 October 1906, p. 3.

[81] *TsGAOR*, f. 102, DP OO, d. 2550, ch. 49, list 33; appendix to Voznesenskii, "Krest'ianskoe dvizhenie," in *O rabochem dvizhenii*, pp. 263–66.

[82] *Protokoly vtorogo delegatskago s''ezda Vserossiiskago Soiuza uchitelei i deiatelei po narodnomu obrazovaniiu 26–29 dekabria 1905 goda* (St. Petersburg, 1906), p. 13; Vakhlin, "Narodnoe obrazovanie v Orekhovo-Zuevskom uezde do revoliutsii," in *Orekhovo-Zuevskii uezd, Moskovskoi gubernii: istorikoekonomicheskii sbornik* (Orekhovo-Zuevo, 1926), p. 423; *TsGAOR*, f. 518, op. 1, d. 77, list 19–19ob.

[83] Malitskii, "Professional'noe dvizhenie," p. 101; *TsGAOR*, f. 102, DP OO (1905), d. 999, ch. 1, tom. 3, list 77–77ob.

tory which stopped traffic on the Iur'ev line). At a *volost' skhod* in Korobov-shchina in early December 1905 Kamrakov convinced peasants to cease paying taxes, and his agitation against rural officials was, reportedly, so persuasive that the local *uriadnik* voluntarily resigned his post.

Success did not always come so easily. Conservative forces, stimulated by the growing repression in Russia, still existed in the village. On December 14, 1905, Kamrakov was headed for a political meeting in the village of Dubki where he was to speak. This had already been broken up when a wealthy peasant treated villagers to drink and incited them to attack the meeting held in the local school. Kamrakov was warned of the melée, which included serious beatings of local intelligenty, and turned back. Along the road he was confronted by a member of the zemstvo board and local landowner, M. L. Rumshevich, who was heading to Dubki to investigate. Rumshevich, well known for rightist sympathies, shouted at Kamrakov: "Teachers, the sons of bitches, are all guilty. They refuse to stick to their business and only agitate the people." Kamrakov stood his ground. Although testimony is conflicting, a shootout ensued which left Rumshevich mortally wounded. Kamrakov was forced into hiding and was eventually arrested and executed in February 1909. Fearing that he would become a martyr for the local intelligentsia and "working class youth," the authorities placed Kamrakov's body in an unmarked grave in Vladimir City.[84]

CONCLUSION

By the time of Kamrakov's execution the Peasant Union movement had long disappeared from the scene. What conclusions can be drawn from the experience? In the short run, it seems clear that the unions were able to inject a modicum of political organization into the peasant movement of 1905. This was evident in the elections to the First and Second Dumas where, despite the union's official boycott of the elections, a significant number of peasants, rural intelligenty, and some gentry liberals with union connections were sent to St. Petersburg. In more general terms, it seems logical that the Peasant Union experience served as a kind of political school, facilitating the kind of successful "coalition politics" that allowed peasant electors to ally with others to ensure solid peasant representation in the elections to the first two Dumas. Peasant Union activists played a key role in the formation of the

[84] *TsGIA*, f. 733, op. 175, d. 65, listy 190–92ob; *Russkiia Vedomosti*, no. 326, 21 December 1905, p. 2; N. Malitskii, "Kazn' Ef. St. Kamrakova," *Trudy Vladimirskogo gubernskogo nauchnogo obshchestva po izucheniiu mestnogo kraia*, no. 3 (Vladimir, 1922), pp. 99–106; Malitskii, "Professional'noe dvizhenie," pp. 99–102; *1905 god v Orekhove-Zueve* (Orekhovo-Zuevo, 1925), pp. 191–94.

Trudovik Group, which in terms of its program and peasant constituency was the natural successor to the union movement.[85]

Examination of Peasant Union activity at the local level reveals the existence of an organized peasant movement seeking to effect agrarian reform, civil and political rights, local control, and access to education, through political channels and in concert with other groups. Both the Sumy and Vladimir experiences show a pattern of successful political mobilization during 1905 and indicate that peasant communities were quite capable of responding rationally to outside political stimuli, of sorting out contradictory political explanations, and of entering into broader alliances with nonpeasant groups. If nothing more, the peasant unions reflect the peasantry's diminishing isolation.

None of this should suggest that nonpeasants led the peasant movement, even in its most overt political manifestations. During the 1905 revolution both the government and revolutionary parties took comfort in exaggerating the role of the rural intelligentsia in the Peasant Union movement; the government ascribing its radicalism and the revolutionaries its excessive moderation to nonpeasants. Shanin has helped to set the record straight, recognizing the utility of intelligenty for peasants, but underscoring the limits of their influence when their principles clashed with those of peasants (for example, on a Duma boycott or a republic).[86] His judgments are sound and are strongly supported by what we know about peasant–Third Element relations. Nevertheless, Shanin overstates the case for peasant autonomy and in doing so distorts a complex reality.

Evidence from Khar'kov and Vladimir provinces confirms the peasantry's capacity for autonomous action and self-determination. Peasants in 1905 displayed remarkable creativity and stubbornness in formulating programmatic goals and in organizing for their realization. What is perhaps most impressive was the skill with which peasants were able to maneuver within the complex web of relations that had evolved by the turn of the century between peasant communities on the one hand, and local elites, officials, and other outsiders, on the other. Relations between peasants and outsiders were complex, symbiotic, and, particularly in the heated atmosphere of 1905, fluid. It was precisely the dynamic inherent in this relationship that helped to stimulate and shape the unprecedented politicization of peasant protest

[85] Leopold H. Haimson, "Conclusion: Observations on the Politics of the Russian Countryside (1905–1914)," in *The Politics of Rural Russia, 1905–1914*, ed. Leopold H. Haimson (Bloomington, Ind., 1979), pp. 284–85, 291–92; D. A. Kolesnichenko, *Trudoviki v period pervoi rossiiskoi revoliutsii* (Moscow, 1985); Mixter, "Peasant Collective Action," pp. 200–22; Scott J. Seregny, "Politics and the Rural Intelligentsia in Russia: A Biographical Sketch of Stepan Anikin, 1869–1919," *Russian History* 7, pts. 1–2 (1980), pp. 185–89.

[86] Shanin, *Russia*, pp. 125–26, 139–40, 144–45.

20. PEASANTS LISTENING TO A PROCLAMATION WITH CAPS OFF IN DEFERENCE TO AUTHORITY
(JOHN FOSTER FRASER, *RED RUSSIA* [NEW YORK: THE JOHN LANE COMPANY, 1907], BETWEEN
PP. 28 AND 29).

21. THE LABOR (TRUDOVIK) GROUP (MOSTLY FROM PEASANT ORIGIN) IN THE FIRST STATE DUMA, 1906
(WILLIAM ENGLISH WALLING, *RUSSIA'S MESSAGE* [NEW YORK: DOUBLEDAY, PAGE & COMPANY, 1908],
FOLLOWING P. 284).

that occurred in 1905, particularly in its most dramatic manifestation, the Peasant Unions.

In many ways the peasant unions represented a rural version of the national Liberation Movement of 1905 and can perhaps be best understood as a coalition. This included peasant activists, the "conscious" peasants in contemporary parlance, who were literate and had employment experiences beyond the village through which they had established contacts with nonpeasant groups and institutions. Sumy, Iur'ev, and Pokrov districts all exhibited, to varying degrees, patterns of industrialization and peasant migration which along with supplementary earnings provided local peasants with information and acquaintance with the city. But the presence of peasant activists like Shevchenko and Ovcharenko in Sumy, as well as Morozov, Fedorov, and Seleznev in Iur'ev, appears to have been crucial in the political mobilization of peasants in 1905. They were prominent everywhere as Peasant Union organizers and undoubtedly helped shape a program that, on the one hand, reflected areas of agreement between the peasantry and the urban opposition in 1905 (civil rights, control over officials), and, on the other hand, was sensitive to peasant feelings about the tsar and religion. They often possessed contacts with local elites predating 1905 and as such acted as a strategic link mediating between a mass movement and outsiders during the revolution. Unlike most peasant factory workers, these activists traveled easily between rural and urban worlds and felt comfortable in each. Their presence seems to have been highly significant in peasants' ability to maximize the opportunities for effective organization and protest provided by the revolution.

To a lesser extent Third Element professionals, many of peasant origin, played a similar role in the Peasant Union coalition: first, as sources of information, as literate "decoders" and interpreters of events outside the village; second, by providing links between the village and liberal zemstvo gentry like Lintvarev and Bunin. These alliances flowed naturally from the process of political mobilization in provincial Russia. Questions of peasant disenfranchisement, gentry hegemony in the zemstvos, and unrestrained bureaucracy concerned not only peasants, but also the rural intelligentsia. Teachers and other zemstvo professionals, of course, interpreted the question of local power in broad terms, assuming that in reformed zemstvos and rural administration they would play prominent roles given their education, expertise, and service. The Third Element viewed the Peasant Union as a means to apply organized popular pressure on both local elites and the central government to achieve these changes in a nonviolent manner. Rural intelligenty distrusted spontaneous peasant activism, which might turn against them, and they saw the Peasant Union as a sheet anchor against the inevitable gales of reaction that threatened to sweep them away once they openly sided with peasant protest and challenged local powers. Therefore, it is not surprising that there was a high correlation between strength of local peasant unions and organizations like teachers' unions during 1905 in places like Sumy and Pokrov.[87]

Peasant Union and Third Element political activism also correlate with the strong presence of liberal zemstvo activists, either dominating zemstvo politics in the decade before 1905, as in Sumy, or represented by vocal minorities, as in Bunin's case. For peasants, effective political organization appeared most likely in the context of perceived splits among local elites (mirroring official disarray at the national level), which peasants viewed as offering room to maneuver (tactical mobility) and potential alliances. Such splits could involve a history of conflict between liberal zemstvo activists and the administration, or conflicts among local landowning elites, often reflected in zemstvo politics. In different ways these conflicts were evident in both Sumy and Iur'ev even before 1905, and just as important they were coupled with overt demonstrations that opposition elements among local elites were leaning toward alliance with the peasantry.

What should be stressed is the capacity of peasant communities to respond to and take advantage of the opportunities provided by the presence of sympathetic elites and rural intelligentsia. These outsiders, aided by such transitional figures as the "conscious" peasants, had much to offer a peasant movement struggling to find its political voice. They provided information, political analyses, the language of political protest, and organizational models, which peasants adapted to their own purposes.[88] Underpinning this dialogue was a broad area of common interests and shared goals between peasants and outsiders, in terms of both program (civil rights, education, and political reform) and in terms of tactics.

The tactics of local peasant unions were essentially moderate. In most instances, local unions worked mightily, and often with success, to steer peasant activism into organized, largely nonviolent channels. Union aims were indeed radical, including expropriation of private lands, but the unions exerted a moderating influence on the peasant movement and, as revolutionary critics maintained, helped sow "constitutionalist illusions" among the masses, to the effect that agrarian reform could be attained through a legislative assembly.

Despite this evidence, the government continued to insist that there was a causal link between union activity and peasant insurrection. Such analysis tended to justify indiscriminate and heavy-handed repression of any political

---

[87] Seregny, *Russian Teachers*, pp. 165–69, 181–89.

[88] Recent studies of the Russian labor movement in 1905 also recognize the important role played by liberal elites and the nonrevolutionary intelligentsia in stimulating workers' mobilization and protest. See Gerald D. Surh, *1905 in St. Petersburg: Labor, Society and Revolution* (Stanford, Cal., 1989) and Laura Engelstein, *Moscow, 1905: Working-Class Organization and Political Conflict* (Stanford, Cal., 1982).

activity in the countryside. One has the sense that the regime preferred peasant *bunt*, which it felt capable of containing by traditional pacification measures, to organized peasant struggle in concert with other social groups. Logically, this fit nicely with the government's attempt to take refuge in an essentially premodern analysis of rural social relations and peasant revolution that was consistent with preservation of the old regime: that the peasantry remained isolated, particularistic, and immune to wider political conflicts.

The result was suppression of Russia's first relatively successful attempt to establish a mass political movement in the countryside. The long-term effects of this are difficult to calculate, but one could reasonably argue that repression of this experiment, which seemed sanctioned by the government's own acts of February 18 and October 17, 1905, did little to foster peasant faith in the efficacy of legal norms, political action, or moderate tactics. In this sense the fate of the Peasant Union was one of a number of objective political circumstances that combined after 1907 to reinforce peasant political apathy, isolation, and particularism. Changing political conditions, as Leopold Haimson has suggested, were just as significant in determining political behavior as "more enduring features of peasant attitudes and political culture." Coupled with the subsequent failure of the first two Dumas to resolve the land issue, the failure of local government reform after the 1905 Revolution, and Stolypin's coup d'état of June 3, 1907, which both solidified the gentry's stranglehold over the new constitutional system and hamstrung peasant elections, the fate of the Peasant Union movement cast a cloud over the prospects for reform in rural Russia as well as the integration and reconciliation of the peasantry.[89] Perhaps, in terms of the promise and opportunity they seemed to hold out, the political circumstances of 1905 and its immediate aftermath were unique in the history of late imperial Russia. This, however, should not obscure peasants' ability to seize and, indeed, shape such opportunities.

[89] Haimson, "Conclusion," pp. 280–96.

CHAPTER 11

PEASANT FARMERS AND THE MINORITY GROUPS OF RURAL
SOCIETY: PEASANT EGALITARIANISM AND VILLAGE SOCIAL
RELATIONS DURING THE RUSSIAN REVOLUTION (1917–1921)

Orlando Figes

THE PEASANT farmer was the principal figure in the nineteenth-century Russian village. Small-scale family farming supported the great majority of the
rural inhabitants of Russia. The peasant commune (*mir*), which was governed by an assembly of household farm heads (*khoziaieva*), resolved most
agrarian and social matters within the village. However, the peasant farmer
was not the only figure in the village. There were others who were excluded
from the assembly of household farm elders (*mirskii skhod*) because they
lacked one of the essential qualifications of peasanthood, such as rural craftsmen, agricultural laborers, and immigrants without their own family farm
(*khoziaistvo*), or widows and the wives of soldiers without a male household
head. Then, there were the village schoolteachers, doctors, veterinarians,
and priests who sometimes had a powerful influence in the village; and the
gentry, and state officials who seldom did.

As a class, the peasantry was defined as much by its relations with these
rural groups, as it was by its position in Russian society at large. During the
revolution, when the local agrarian system was turned upside down and the
countryside was dislocated from the rest of Russian society, the peasantry
was defined almost exclusively by these village relations.

The revolutionary period offers the historian of rural Russia a unique van-
tage point from which to survey the class relations of the peasantry in action.
Revolution is a moment of truth, when the class interests that lie dormant
under normal social conditions come to life and express conflicting concepts
of social justice and freedom. The agrarian revolution in Russia brought the
smallholding peasantry to the center of the historical stage. All the main enemies of the peasantry—the state, the gentry, and the urban bourgeoisie—
were weakened or destroyed. The social and political domination of the
peasant family farm and the commune were greatly increased. The communes divided all the private landed property (the estates, the church lands,

and the peasant land enclosures) among their own members, usually on the family labor principle legally established by the Decree on Land of October 1917.[1] As a result of the revolution, the communal system of strip farming in three fields gained a virtual monopoly of land tenure in the central part of European Russia. The communal assembly of household farm heads defined the social criteria and legal norms of land use and regulated nearly all the relations of production within the village (e.g. labor hire, exchange of means of production, utilization of harvests).

If the revolution increased the influence of the peasant commune, how did it affect the position of those rural inhabitants who were excluded from this institution because they were not family household farmers? Did the village soviet democracy of 1917–1918 amount to a dictatorship of the farming peasantry controlled through the communal assembly of peasant household members, or did the smallholders share their power with the other rural groups in political, social, and economic forms that cut across class categories? Did the peasants include their former class enemies in the would-be egalitarian system of the village, or did they seek their revenge on them? How could the peasantry establish equal economic relations with other occupational groups, such as rural craftsmen, in the absence of a stable monetary system?

Hitherto, such questions have not really been asked by students of the revolution. Soviet historians have approached the question of village social relations almost exclusively from the perspective of class differentiation among the peasantry. Yet it is evident that what we require is a *trans-class* analysis of the peasantry and other occupational rural groups. Western historians, on the other hand, have become somewhat fixated with the idea that all the peasants wanted after 1917 was to be left alone. Much—although strictly not all—of the evidence supports this hypothesis. The peasants resisted the heavy tax burdens of War Communism by retreating into subsistence farming and economic autarky; they reduced their field economy and oriented it toward the consumption needs of the family (by cultivating more rye, potatoes, and millet); they developed their cottage industries to manufacture the goods that the cities could no longer supply; they buried their taxable grain in the ground, fed it to their livestock, or sold it on the black market; and they developed networks of barter and exchange to counteract the sharp fall in the official (monetary) value of agricultural goods relative to industrial prices.

---

[1] On the labor principle land was granted to family households according to their ability to cultivate it with their own labor (rather than with hired labor). It was an established principle of land tenure in the commune and was contained in the "peasant mandate," which formed the basis of the Decree on Land. The "mandate" is published in V. I. Lenin, *Polnoe sobranie sochinenii*, 5th ed., 58 vols., 34 (Moscow, 1958–1966), pp. 108–16.

All these measures effectively enabled the countryside to cut itself loose from the economic domination of the towns. The social mechanisms of the land commune enclosed the indigenous inhabitants of the village within a virtually self-sufficient community which excluded outsiders such as urban in-migrants. Many villages and localities declared themselves autonomous republics—separate from the Soviet state and in opposition to the towns—after 1917. Inter-village conflicts were commonplace during the redivisions of the land in 1918. The many different peasant uprisings during the Civil War (1918–1921) held in common their opposition to the urban-based Bolshevik and White regimes.

Against these social currents, however, the younger peasants were beginning to break out of the cultural cocoon that had enveloped their forefathers. Some peasants took part in district and provincial peasant assemblies. Others joined the army, where they learned new skills and ways of thinking. Others used their powers of literacy to join the emergent class of rural bureaucrats. Even the communal assembly of household elders broadened its sphere of political jurisdiction after 1917 in response to the breakdown of government and the need to resolve a widening range of social issues arising from the war and the revolution. The extension of the powers of the communal assembly was paralleled by the widening social base of village representation. The *mirskii skhod* of household farm elders was increasingly rivaled by the general communal assembly (*obshchii skhod*)—attended by all adult peasants (including peasant sons, though rarely women)—and the open village gathering (*sel'skoe sobranie*), which was attended by all the inhabitants of the village (including those, such as landless laborers and craftsmen, without rights at the communal assembly).

This democratization of village politics reflected the obligation of the peasantry to involve a broader range of rural inhabitants in its decision making as the range of its responsibilities grew. The revolution had replaced the *volost'*-level *upravy* (boards) and the zemstvos, dominated by the gentry, the merchants, and state officials, with democratic village committees and councils (soviets), which were equally dominated by the smallholding peasantry. But if the peasant farmers were to sustain the authority of their soviets, they would have to learn how to share power with other elements from the village democracy. The Civil War witnessed the economic collapse and the depopulation of the major manufacturing centers; millions of townsmen migrated into the countryside in the hope of sitting out these hungry years in rural party offices, police organizations, and departments of the Red Army. These outsider plenipotentiaries would be looking to extend their influence to the villages and the *volost'* soviets by mobilizing those on the margins of rural society against the peasant smallholders.

In the following pages we will consider the relations between the peasant farmers and a number of these marginal rural groups: gentry squires; farmers of enclosed household plots; landless agricultural laborers; rural craftsmen; urban in-migrants and refugees; peasant soldiers; parish priests; and village schoolteachers. Then, we will make a number of general points about Russian rural society, and the ways in which the peasantry applied the egalitarian principles that stood at the center of the agrarian revolution.

Most of the materials utilized in this essay are taken from the records of village, *volost'*, and district (*uezd*) soviets in areas bordering the Volga River (Samara, Saratov, Simbirsk, and Penza provinces) in southeastern European Russia. In 1920 the rural population of these four provinces—an area approximately the size of West Germany today—was 8.6 million people.[2]

PEASANTS AND SQUIRES

In its resolutions and mandates to district and provincial assemblies during 1917, the Russian peasantry was certain that the confiscation of private land without compensation was, in principle, just.[3] However, few peasant communities failed to recognize the personal right of their former squire to farm an equal share of the village land with his own family labor—a right formally established by the October Decree on Land.[4] In response to an inquiry of the Moscow provincial land committee in 814 villages around Moscow on the eve of the October Revolution, 79 percent of the peasants in land communes and 92 percent of the peasants in enclosed farmsteads agreed that the landowners and their families should retain a share of their former land according to a local labor norm.[5]

It is not easy to make generalizations about the fate of the squires, but it seems that peasant animosity toward the landowners was strongest in the densely populated black-soil regions, where the majority of the largest estates were concentrated and where peasant farming was highly intensive. The peasant movement was most powerful and the devastation of the manors (pogrom, razgrom) was most common in these regions. In Penza Province one-fifth of the manors were burned or destroyed in September and October 1917, alone. In the following spring it was reported that the manors had been destroyed in 89 out of 152 *volosti*. In February 1919 the Insaro land department in Penza reported that all but two of the manors in the district had been destroyed.[6] Impatience for a resolution of the land question and

[2] *Trudy TsSU: Itogi vserossiiskoi sel'sko-khoziaistvennoi perepisi 1920g. v granitsakh gubernii na 1 marta 1922 g.*, vol. 2, vyp. 8 (Moscow, 1923), pp. 11–112.

[3] See E. A. Lutskii, "Krest'ianskie nakazy 1917g. o zemle," in *Istochnikovedenie istorii sovetskogo obshchestva* (Moscow, 1968), pp. 145ff.

[4] *Dekrety Sovetskoi vlasti* (Moscow, 1957), p. 19.

[5] V. V. Kabanov, "Oktiabr'skaia revoliutsiia i krest'ianskaia obshchina," *Istoricheskie Zapiski*, no. 111 (Moscow, 1984): 124.

[6] *Tsentral'nyi Gosudarstvennyi Arkhiv Narodnogo Khoziaistva* (hereafter *TsGANKh*), f. 478, op. 1, d. 149 and d. 150; op. 6, d. 1015, list 194.

hatred of the large landowners were the most common explanations of the *pogromy*. The peasants destroyed the manor houses to make sure their owners would not return. They rarely harmed the squire in person, but were quick to single out the landowners who had directed previous repressions. In June 1917, for example, the villagers of Bor-Polianshchina (Buturlin *volost'*, Serdobsk *uezd*) broke into the manor of V. V. Saburov and brutally killed the old squire. His son, D. I. Saburov, had been land captain in 1906 and had bloodily suppressed the peasant movement of that year. In the course of the three days following the murder, the villagers destroyed every building on the estate, including a large library. Livestock and grain to the value of 125,000 gold rubles were taken away.[7]

Such acts of violence were generally reserved for the largest and most unpopular squires. Although peasants in the middle Volga region were known to have arrested and humiliated some of the landowners supporting the Whites, they took little part in the systematic persecution of ex-squires by the Cheka during the Red Terror of autumn 1918.[8] Rather, having confiscated their land, the peasantry tended to leave them alone, as one rural delegate suggested at the Saratov Provincial Soviet Assembly in May 1918:

> we worked hard for the landowners and the merchants and by our own sweat and blood made them rich . . . we will not take anything from [them], but will turn our backs on them. While we were working for them, they did nothing but enjoyed themselves; now we will leave them to fend for themselves.[9]

Many of the smaller landowners—especially those whose social origins were among the peasantry—were allowed by the commune to remain in their manors and retain a share of their land and property. John Channon has recently estimated that about 100,000 landowners (400,000 people including their families) remained on the land in Russia during the mid-1920s; that represents 11 percent to 12 percent of the landowners in Russia before the revolution. Most of them were farming on a similar basis to the richest peasant stratum.[10] Whether from fear, timidity, or esteem, many village communes and soviets resolved to leave their former landlord a relatively large amount of property. For example, the Bogdanovka village soviet (Samara *uezd*) left the landowner Kirilin:

---

[7] T. Galynskii, *Ocherki po istorii agrarnoi revoliutsii Serdobskogo uezda, Saratovskoi gubernii* (Serdobsk, 1924), pp. 117, 141, 172.

[8] Ibid., pp. 171–73.

[9] *Protokoly Saratovskogo gubernskogo s''ezda sovetov krest'ianskikh deputatov, proiskhodivshego v g. Saratove s 25-go maia po 2-e iiunia 1918 g.* [hereafter *PS*] (Saratov, 1918), p. 19.

[10] John Channon. "Tsarist Landowners After the Revolution: Former Pomeshchiki in Rural Russia During NEP," *Soviet Studies* 39, no. 4 (October 1987): 584. See similarly V. P. Danilov, *Rural Russia Under the New Regime*, trans. O. Figes (London, 1988), pp. 96–98.

a manor house with barn, stables, and bathhouse
4 horses
1 cow and calf
10 chickens
1 mowing machine and rake
1 iron plough
1 iron harrow
1 winnowing machine
1 seed drill
1 cultivator
several carts and a tarantass with harnesses, collars, and saddles

The following resolution was then passed:

> to grant Kirilin the full rights of a household farmer (*khoziain*) on an equal basis with the other household farmers of the village, and to give him enough seed and grain and to leave him 8 cart-loads of hay for his cattle . . . the agricultural tools should stay with Kirilin for safe-keeping, but other citizens have the right to use them.[11]

That Kirilin was entrusted with the tools (which entered the communal domain) is perhaps a reflection of the peasantry's fears that the revolution might not last. But it also highlights the assimilation of the small gentry farmers into the peasantry. Many squires in the Volga region were registered as "peasant souls," with rights of representation at the communal assembly, during 1918. Some were even given jobs in the soviet and social institutions.[12]

PEASANT SEPARATORS

Together with the gentry estates the peasant agrarian farmsteads and enclosed arable holdings (*khutora, otruba*) fell victim to the movement. If, in 1916, between 27 percent and 33 percent of Russian peasant households farmed arable land in enclosed tenure (outside the land commune), then six years later fewer than 2 percent continued to do so in the major agricultural regions of European Russia, and only in the far northwest were significant numbers of separate holdings still to be found.[13] The communal movement

[11] Gosudarstvennyi Arkhiv Kuibyshevskoi Oblasti (hereafter *GaKO*), f. 81, op. 1, d. 119, list 36.

[12] *Tsentral'nyi Gosudarstvennyi Arkhiv Oktiabr'skoi Revoliutsii* (hereafter *TsGAOR*), f. 393, op. 13, d. 578, list 186; *TsGANKh*, f. 478, op. 1, d. 149, listy 153–54; *PS*, pp. 33–34; T. Galynskii, *Ocherki*, p. 173.

[13] V. P. Danilov, "Ob istoricheskikh sud'bakh krest'ianskoi obshchiny v Rossii," in *Ezhegodnik po agrarnoi istorii*, vypusk VI: *Problemy istorii russkoi obshchiny* (Vologda, 1976), pp. 106–8.

against these peasant separators was most intense in 1917 in the south and southeast, where the Stolypin enclosure movement had gained most ground. From 1916 to 1922, the percentage of peasant land in household enclosures fell from 19 percent to 0.1 percent in Samara Province; from 16.4 percent to 0.0 percent in Saratov Province; and from 24.9 percent to 0.4 percent in the Stavropol region.[14] Although historians of the 1920s estimated that no more than 6 percent of all rural disturbances in 1917 involved the peasant enclosures, recent Soviet historians have raised the percentage to 20 percent in European Russia and to anything between 33 percent and 44 percent in the southeast.[15] The later estimates, which have been used to support the argument that the peasant attacks on separators were part of a socialist struggle against the rural bourgeoisie, may well be too high.

In the middle Volga region, the peasant war against the separators was perhaps even more bitter than the struggle against the gentry landowners. Whereas the peasantry feared the landowners and almost expected them to return (the latter did in the middle Volga region during the summer of 1918), they held the separators in contempt as peasants who had betrayed their social peers by leaving the commune after the suppression of the 1905–1907 revolution. Many communes divided the gentry land separately from the allotments in 1918, lest the squire should return; but the land of the separators was more commonly divided together with the allotments, especially if it had been cut off from them (non-communal land purchased by the separators was sometimes kept apart). Much of the peasantry's resentment toward the separators may be explained by the traditional peasant legal culture of family ownership, which was of course threatened by the separators' rights of private land ownership (and therefore primogeniture). As early as 1906, a correspondent of the Free Economic Society reported from Saratov Province that the peasantry was very hostile to the Law of 9 November, fearing

> that elders will sell up and their children will become paupers. . . . let them trade what they like, but not land. Let him have land who will work it. In this conviction all peasants, both rich and poor, are united in solidarity.[16]

The defense of traditional land rights was often used to legitimize violence against the separators in 1917. Communally organized boycotts and *samosudy*

---

[14] P. N. Pershin, *Uchastkovoe zemlepol'zovanie v Rossii* (Moscow, 1922), p. 8.

[15] A. V. Shestakov, *Sovety krest'ianskikh deputatov i drugie krest'ianskie organizatsii*, vol. 1 (Moscow, 1929), pp. 254–56; S. M. Dubrovskii, *Krest'ianstvo v 1917 godu* (Moscow-Leningrad, 1927), p. 56; T. V. Osipova, *Klassovaia bor'ba v derevne v period podgotovkii provedeniia Oktiabr'skoi revoliutsii* (Moscow, 1974), p. 169; V. I. Kostrikin, "Krest'ianskoe dvizhenie nakanune Oktiabria," in *Oktiabr'i sovetskoe krest'ianstvo 1917–1927 gg* (Moscow, 1977), pp. 33–34; I. V. Igritskii, ed., *1917 god v derevne: Vospominaniia krest'ian* (Moscow, 1967), pp. 70–71.

[16] Cited in *Agrarnoe dvizhenie v Rossii v 1905–1906 gg* (St. Petersburg, 1908), pp. 151–52.

(see Glossary) against farmers refusing to submit their enclosed holdings to a general repartition were widely noted. In Vol'sk *uezd* 160 peasants from Tersa commune marched on a rich *otrubnik* and dragged him to a *skhod*, where, in front of other separators, they tied him to a stake and beat him to death with clubs. A resolution was then passed, which the separators were forced to sign, calling for the liquidation of all enclosed holdings. According to a local police official, it was usual for the peasants to legitimize violence through the *skhod* in this manner: the *skhod* always assembles before an attack and resolves that all *otruba* must return to the commune before the next sowing.[17]

It is very doubtful, however, whether the land communes consciously organized their struggle against the traders in land as a socialist struggle against the rural bourgeoisie, as suggested by Soviet historians. Many enclosed holdings were relatively weak in economic terms and smaller than the neighboring communal allotments (a phenomenon noted in twenty out of forty-seven provinces in European Russia).[18] In the southeastern steppe regions, where many of the enclosed holdings were situated, only 3.1 percent of the peasant enclosures were consolidated in one *khutor*, whereas 38.3 percent were divided into three or more plots.[19] Without advanced agricultural machinery, three or four horses, and the shelter of a village, it was not easy for a single family to farm between twelve and thirty *desiatiny* (see Glossary) of land (the average size of an enclosed holding) on the steppe, which was characterized by a harsh climate, poor soil, lack of water and building materials, and vast distances between markets.

In 1917, many of the smaller *otrubniki* in the southeast voluntarily returned to the land commune in order to share in the division of the estates. A contemporary study of the agrarian revolution in Zadonsk *uezd* (Voronezh Province) noted that in one-third of the villages all the *otrubniki* broke up their holdings voluntarily; 70 percent of the *khutora* followed suit.[20]

The more stubborn *khutoriane* in the steppelands of the southeast should be seen simply as the victims of a strong collective village bonding against outsiders, especially where they were from the Volga German ethnic minority, rather than as the bourgeois targets of some abstract socialist struggle. One statistician from Samara Province noted in 1917 that whereas 58 percent

---

[17] G. A. Gerasimenko, *Nizovye krest'ianskie organizatsii v 1917—pervoi polovine 1918 gg.* (Saratov, 1974), p. 209. An article by Steven Frank confirms that *samosudy* were often sanctioned by the *skhod*. See Stephen P. Frank, "Popular Justice, Community and Culture Among the Russian Peasantry, 1870–1900," *Russian Review* 46, no. 3 (July 1987): 239–65.

[18] *O zemle: Sbornik statei o proshlom i budushchem zemel'no-khoziaistvennogo stroitel'stva,* 1 (Moscow, 1921), pp. 14–15.

[19] P. N. Pershin, *Uchastkovoe,* pp. 14–15.

[20] V. Keller and I. Romanenko, *Pervye itogi agrarnoi reformy. Opyt issledovaniia rezul'tatov sovremennogo zemleustroistva na primere Zadonskogo uezda Voronezhskoi gubernii* (Voronezh, 1922), pp. 103–4.

of the peasants expressed hostility toward the *khutora* in villages less than 25 *versty* (see Glossary) from a market center, 66 percent expressed such hostility in the more remote villages. If this was part of a socialist struggle against rural capitalism, then the reverse correlation would be expected, with peasants expressing greater dislike for the enclosure farmers in areas close to the market centers.[21]

The movement against peasant enclosure-farming was guided by the principles of communal land tenure. The communal principle was a flexible concept of the agrarian revolution, not an axiom of socialist dogma. It entailed the old peasant ideals of brotherhood and equality which were impossible to attain without a certain degree of social conformity. Yet, although it demanded the annihilation of large private farms, the communal principle did not preclude the possibility of separators' hamlets (*vyselki, poselki*) farming a share of the communal land; nor did it prohibit the establishment of independent communes (*kommuny*) with enclosed household land tenure.[22] It called for the freedom of the peasant family farm to choose its own form of land use, as expressed in the Land Code of 1922, but recognized that this in itself depended upon the unity of the village. This complex balance between the ideals of equality and freedom of choice was expressed by the Dubovo-Pobedimov soviet (Samara *uezd*) in March 1918:

> Now in free Russia all should be equal and united and there should be no disputes between citizens . . . and separators. . . . the citizens of the *volost'* should take all the separators into their family on an equal basis and should cease all oppressive measures [against them], since they only play into the hands of the enemies of the people.[23]

AGRICULTURAL LABORERS

In 1917–1918, the Russian peasantry sought an agricultural system based upon the smallholding family labor farm. The peasant mandate, that formed the basis of the Decree on Land, called for the abolition of hired labor and the allocation of all the farmland to peasant households on a family labor norm.[24] Wage labor, which facilitated large-scale capitalist and gentry farming, could play no part in the peasant family farm system. During the redivisions of the farmland in 1918, the peasant communities did indeed allocate allotment land to the resident landless laborers (*batraki*) and provided some of them with horses and tools. Yet, most of the *batraki* who received land in

---

[21] G. I. Bas'kin, *Printsipy zemel'nogo naseleniia v sviazi s otnosheniem naseleniia k raznym formam zemlevladeniia i zemlepol'zovaniia* (Samara, 1917), pp. 16–18.

[22] *GAKO*, f. 81, op. 1, d. 119, listy 65–68.

[23] *TsGAOR*, f. 393, op. 3, d. 359, list 202.

[24] *Dekrety Sovetskoi vlasti*, 1, p. 19.

1918 proved too weak to farm it, and thus became dependent upon neighboring households with extra cattle, tools, and labor. Although the censuses of 1917–1921 noted a decline of long-term (*srokovoi*), money-based wage-labor relations, other sources noted a simultaneous increase of daily (*podennyi*) and contract (*sdel'nyi*) hiring-labor relations without cash payments.[25] Some former *batraki* in the middle Volga region leased out their newly acquired allotments to the middle peasants and turned instead to non-agricultural occupations, such as handicrafts, barge hauling, timber felling, or employment in the soviet. Others sharecropped their land with the more stable peasant households, or rented horses and tools from the latter, often at extortionate rates.

The communes, which themselves employed a large number of wage laborers (e.g., shepherds, watchmen, messengers), did very little to prevent these exploitative relations, since their prime concern was to support the stable peasant farms. The *volost'* soviets, however, did on occasion intervene in the labor market to protect the poor. They fixed the prices and conditions of labor; regulated sharecropping and rental contracts; merged the weakest households with stronger ones; and even allocated means of production to groups of poor peasants for the collective cultivation of the land.[26]

The effect of such policies was bound to be limited within the semi-natural economy of the civil war. Of the 1,119 village respondents in Saratov Province who replied to an inquiry of the Saratov provisions committee in spring 1918, as many as 969 (86.8 percent) testified to the continuation of contract- and day-labor hire. The respondents stressed that inflation, the influx of urban workers, and the general shortage of housing had resulted in the substitution of a natural system of labor hire (with the laborers paid in land or food) for the old cash system of wage labor:

there is no wage-labor, but those who do not have an allotment or a horse work without pay and are given one *desiatiny* of inferior land with seven *pudy* (see Glossary) of seed. (Ekaterinolav-Maza *volost'*, Khvalynsk *uezd*)

to quote a daily price for labor is impossible, because the system has transferred to flour. One man without a horse hired for the whole of the spring sowing will receive 3 *pudy* of flour. A boy with a horse who is hired to do the harrowing will also get 3 *pudy* of flour, as well as food at work. (Bulgakovka and Sinodskoe *volosti*, Vol'sk *uezd*)

[25] *Biulleten' Saratovskogo Gubprodkoma* (hereafter *SGB*), nos. 3–4, 1 July 1918, p. 8; *Otchet Saratovskogo ekonomicheskogo soveshchaniia* (Saratov, 1922), pt. 2, p. 49.

[26] *TsGAOR*, f. 393, op. 3, d. 325, list 417; d. 337, list 228; d. 340, listy 25, 32, 38; *Protokoly i doklady VI-go Atkarskogo uezdnogo s"ezda sovetov 15 oktiabria 1918 goda* (Atkarsk, 1918), p. 138; *Izvestiia* (Balakovo), no. 8, 26 January 1919, p. 3; no. 24, 2 February 1919, p. 4.

Some of the respondents also emphasized that, by combating wage-labor hire, the soviets unavoidably handicapped the weakest peasant households:

The soviet has decreed that you have to work on your own without hired labor, even if you starve as a result: from now on, everyone must be equal! Our comrades have decided to work the land with their own labor, and so many households have no choice but to leave some of the land unsown. (Beguchevka *volost*, Petrovsk *uezd*)

It is possible to find labor, but it is expensive. The rich and the middle peasants are able to sow their own land, but the poor do not have enough labor and can not afford to hire it, so they are going hungry. The landless soldiers go from barn to barn and steal grain. (Kniazevka *volost'* Petrovsk *uezd*)[27]

Only the peasant households of at least average economic strength could expect to maintain the status of an independent family farm. Without a horse or the basic tools, the farms of the former *batraki* and the newly partitioned household farms (established mainly by peasant sons on return from the army[28]) were unable to support themselves through agriculture during the economic crisis of 1917–1921. The number of smallholdings in Saratov Province with less than 2 *desiatiny* of arable land increased by 13.4 percent between 1917 and 1919; the proportion of these households without a horse remained at a very high level (69 percent in 1917 and 54 percent in 1919). Most of these households had a cow (57 percent in 1917 and 62 percent in 1919), from which a small living could be made.[29] But those without a horse must have found life very hard, and many must have been forced into liquidation.

RURAL CRAFTSMEN

Many peasants were, by choice or necessity, engaged in craft industries and trades (*kustarnye promysly*) during the winter months of enforced agricultural inactivity. These crafts were a rich repository of peasant science and peasant art,[30] occupying surplus domestic labor and, to a considerable degree, satisfying local market demand for basic household goods. For obvious reasons, peasant craft industries in the middle Volga region were most advanced in the woodland villages, where tables, chairs, brooms, spades, spoons, clogs, wheels, baskets, icons, and many other simple household objects were man-

---

[27] *SGB*, nos. 3–4, 1 July 1918, pp. 8–12.

[28] Teodor Shanin, *The Awkward Class* (Oxford, 1972), pp. 157–59.

[29] *Trudy TsSU: Ekonomicheskoe rassloenie krest'ianstva v 1917 i 1919 g.* (Moscow, 1922), 6, vyp. 3, pp. 142–43.

[30] Geroid T. Robinson, *Rural Russia Under the Old Regime* (London, 1932), p. 104.

ufactured. However, the southern steppe villages were noted for leather goods, baskets, and German cloth (*sarpinka*). They benefited from easy river transportation to the Caspian Sea and the Don. Craft products from Saratov Province were exported as far as the Caucasus (bentwood chairs), Persia, Bulgaria, and Romania (loom reeds), and Central Asia (*sarpinka*).[31]

The economic role of the peasant craft industries increased in Russia during 1914–1921, when large-scale industrial production collapsed.[32] This retreat into the makeshift and "medieval" world of cottage industry was the result of a number of other factors: the growing rural demand for manufactured household goods caused by the disruption of urban-rural trade and by the increased partitioning of family households after 1917; the influx of unemployed factory workers into the countryside; the relative resilience of small-scale industry in the face of shortages of fuel and raw materials; and the general spread of barter and exchange in the countryside. Narkomzem (People's Commissariat of Agriculture) reported on 20 April 1918: "cottage industry is at present providing the broad mass of the population with all those products which heavy industry is no longer able to produce."[33]

The Kazan authorities agreed in 1920 that in the last few years there had been an extraordinarily rapid development of cottage industries.[34] The same point was made in 1922 by the Tsaritsyn District *sovnarkhoz* (Economic Council), which reported that the rural craft industries had come to life during the Civil War, since they required only small deliveries of raw materials . . . which could be made by private individuals.[35] An advantage of the Volga region in this respect was that the new markets for industrial materials were opening in Kazakhstan and Central Asia. "The entire industrial life of the country," noted one government official in 1918, "has shifted to the east. It is there that the new market centers are situated."[36]

Unfortunately, there are no reliable estimates of peasant household craft production in the middle Volga region (as in most of Russia) between 1913 and the early 1920s. The 1917 census in Saratov Province registered 62,585 rural inhabitants engaged in cottage industries, but in January 1919 Narkomzem put the number somewhere in excess of 150,000.[37] Nevertheless, it

---

[31] E. I. Shlifshtein, *Melkaia promyshlennost' Saratovskoi gubernii* (Saratov, 1923), p. 5; *Nizhnee Povolzh'e* (Nizhne-Volzh'skoi oblastnoi i Saratovskoi gubernskoi Planovykh Komissii), no. 6 (13) (June 1925): 40.

[32] A useful discussion of the role of cottage industry under War Communism may be found in: Silvana Malle, *The Economic Organization of War Communism 1918–21* (Cambridge, 1985), pp. 77–88.

[33] *TsGANKh*, f. 478, op. 10, d. 164, list 24.

[34] *TsGAOR*, f. 532, op. 1, d. 65, list 160.

[35] P. A. Barashevskii, ed., *Istoricheskii ocherk Tsaritsynskogo uezda* (Tsaritsyn, 1922), p. 15.

[36] A. Biriukov, *Kreditnaia kooperatsiia i kustarnaia promyshlennost'* (Saratov, 1918), p. 9.

[37] *Tablitsy statisticheskikh svedenii po Saratovskoi gubernii po dannym vserossiiskoi sel'sko-kho-*

is possible to distinguish which peasant industries fared better than others during the upheavals of 1914–1920. The worst to suffer were the more mechanized industries requiring expensive inputs (textiles, tar distillation, charcoal burning, brick manufacture, soap boiling, fulling, pottery, etc.), although in some of these industries households survived by forming themselves into production cooperatives and artels.[38] The most successful crafts were those producing household goods no longer available from the city. Craftsmen with access to the raw materials for such products could exploit a captive market (e.g., carpenters, wicker workers, coopers, tool makers, and wheelwrights in woodland areas; leather workers, woolen weavers, and sheepskin traders in the steppeland pastoral regions).[39] Blacksmiths survived by collecting scrap metal and trading it with in-migrant workers from the cities.[40]

Other crafts adapted to the adverse conditions (and sometimes even prospered from them) by substituting homegrown products and materials for commodities no longer available on the market. Cotton, hemp, and flax were grown to maintain the cloth and rope trade; wicker sandals and wooden clogs replaced bast shoes and leather boots; sunflower oil, charcoal, wood, animal fat, alcohol, and dozens of other unlikely materials substituted for kerosene fuel; and sugar-beet and honey production substituted for sugar.[41]

It is impossible to tell how many of these rural craftsmen were simply peasant farmers diversifying their productive activities during the economic crisis, and how many were workers from the industrial regions of Russia. The latter probably represented the majority. There is evidence to suggest

---

ziaistvennoi i gorodskoi perepisei (Saratov, 1919), pp. 144–45; *TsGANKh*, f. 478, op. 10, d. 106, list 21.

[38] *TsGAOR*, f. 532, op. 1, d. 65, listy 157–58; *TsGANKh*, f. 478, op. 10, d. 106, listy 16–18, 20; *Biulleten' Saratovskogo Gubernskogo Soveta Narodnogo Khoziaistva* nos. 2–3, July 1918, p. 10; *Tretii otchet Vol'skogo uezdnogo ekonomsoveshchaniia* (n.p., n.d.), no pages; *Vestnik Kustarnoi Promyshlennosti* (Glavkustprom), no. 6, September 1921, p. 9; *Otchet Pugachevskogo uezdnogo ekonomicheskogo soveshchaniia na 1-e oktiabria 1921 g.* (Pugachev, 1921), pp. 24, 31; *Otchet Serdobskogo uezdnogo ekonomicheskogo soveshchaniia* (Serdobsk, 1921), p. 33.

[39] *TsGAOR*, f. 532, op. 1, d. 65, listy 13, 26–27; *Biulleten' Saratovskogo Gubernskogo Soveta narodnogo Khoziaistva*, nos. 3–4 (14–15), 20 March 1919, p. 6; *Otchet Melekesskogo uezdnogo ekonomicheskogo soveshchaniia* (Melekess, 1921), pp. 18–19, 68–70.

[40] Ibid., p. 68; *Otchet Buguruslanskogo uezdnogo ekonomicheskogo soveshchaniia*, p. 14.

[41] On the role of sugar-beet cultivation and beekeeping see *TsGANKh*, f. 478, op. 1, d. 330, listy 24, 121; *Svobodnyi Zemledelets* (Saratov), no. 10, 1 April 1918, p. 31; *Tri goda raboty otdelov Buguruslanskogo uezdnogo ispolnitel'nogo komiteta sovetov* (1917–20 gg.) (Buguruslan, 1921), p. 32. On the fascinating subject of fuel substitutes see: *SGB*, no. 6, 1 August 1918, p. 10; *Iubileinyi sbornik Saratovskogo gubprodkomiteta 7 noiabria 1917 g. (25 okt.)–7 noiabria 1919 g* (Saratov, 1919), p. 45; *Kooperativnaia Mysl* (Saratov), no. 9 (40), 2 March 1919, pp. 10, 12; *TsGAOR*, f. 532, op. 1, d. 65, list 93; and others. Silvana Malle has pointed out (*The Economic Organization*, p. 78) that shortages of salt were partly overcome by the old methods of evaporation, but it is doubtful whether such techniques were widely mastered in the countryside, where salt deficiency was one of the main reasons for cholera epidemics in 1919–1922.

that a large number of the craftsmen did not have (and failed to gain) an allotment in the commune.[42] Also, many *volost'* soviets deliberately set out to attract craftsmen from the towns. For example, the Chernovka soviet (Buzuluk *uezd*) invited two wheelwrights from Simbirsk to set up a workshop in the village. It fixed the prices for the raw materials and the manufactured wheels, and established two communal workshops (a forge and a tool-repair shop) in the center of the village run by two trade unionists with the help of local workers in the busy summer months.[43]

Other Soviets organized artels and cooperatives and sold the manufactures to the Red Army, Sovnarkhoz, or neighboring soviets and social institutions. In the village of Bol'shie Sestrenki (Balashov *uezd*) a consumer society (*potrebitel'skoe obshchestvo*) organized the transfer of three *desiatiny* of woodland from the state domain to enable the local manufacture of wheels. Expert labor was hired from the town of Penza (noted for its wheelwrights), and the prices for the wheels were fixed at 65 rubles for local inhabitants and 75 rubles for outsiders.[44] Similar arrangements were noted in Ivanovka and Alekseevka (Saratov *uezd*) in the autumn of 1918; there the wheelwrights formed themselves into an artel and sold their wheels to the district *sovnarkhoz* in exchange for woodland rights.[45] Dozens of similar instances could be cited, in which village institutions organized the manufacture, distribution and sale of simple craft goods.

IN-MIGRANTS AND REFUGEES

The military and political upheavals of 1914–1921 uprooted and dispersed millions of people throughout the Russian countryside. The middle Volga, traversed by the Riazan-Ural'sk and Trans-Siberian railways, attracted a multitude of different migrant groups, from the unemployed factory workers of Moscow and Petrograd to political refugees and prisoners of war from Siberia. Thousands of refugees, demobilized soldiers, and prisoners of war encamped in the railway stations in the distant hope of getting on a train toward their destination.[46] Many more lived along the railway sidings, on river banks, and in suburban areas. Some found their way into a camp for refugees, where they might expect to receive a meager ration of food. But others moved into the villages. The 1917 census in Saratov Province registered

[42] *GAKO*, f. 81, op. 1, d. 119, listy 22–23.

[43] *GAKO*, f. 3134, op. 2, d. 21, listy 47, 68, 74, 83.

[44] *Rabochii i Kooperativnyi Mir* (Balashov), no. 3, 30 June 1918, p. 12.

[45] *Kooperativnaia Mysl'* (Saratov), no. 9 (40), 2 March 1919, p. 10.

[46] The transport system had come to a virtual standstill by the autumn of 1918. One government instructor reported in November 1918 that it had taken him nearly three days to travel by train, boat, horse and cart, sleigh, and finally foot from Samara to Syzran, a distance of 136 km. (*TsGAOR*, f. 393, op. 3, d. 323, list 354).

16,302 refugees (*bezhentsy*) in the villages (0.6 percent of the rural population). During the following years the number of registered and unregistered immigrants rose sharply.[47]

What was the attitude of the peasantry toward these people? Of the eighty-five villages in the middle Volga region responding to an inquiry by the Central Statistical Administration (TsSU) in 1922, fifty-three claimed to have given allotment land to in-migrants; all but one of the villages claimed to have included in the land repartition the native peasant families who had returned from the city.[48] It is reasonable to assume that the respondents exaggerated from hindsight the goodwill of the villagers, for the contemporary records of the village and *volost'* soviets suggest that the in-migrants were, for the most part, unwelcome. In land-extensive villages close to major market centers the in-migrants represented a high proportion of the agricultural wage-labor force (up to 6 percent).[49] They also comprised—often as craft workers—a large proportion of the population in the collective and state farms (*kolkhozy* and *sovkhozy*).[50]

This gave them strong connections with the higher soviet organs and the rural party cells, which sometimes pressured the village communities to support the in-migrants and grant them rights in the commune. But the communes and the village and *volost'* soviets were rarely well disposed toward the in-migrants. Most villages refused to house them. Some petitioned the higher authorities to take them away or accommodate them in army barracks and other institutions. Others suggested that the authorities billet the refugees in villages with a high proportion of widows.[51] Villages generally excluded in-migrants from the lists of residents on food rations (supplied from communal and soviet grain stores). For example, at a *volost'* assembly in Voskresenskoe (Samara *uezd*) on 20 April 1918 the local soviet provisions commissar asked the peasants whether in-migrants should be included on the rations list; the peasants' unanimous response was not to include the in-migrants, but only natives (*zdeshnye*).[52] The majority of the communes also refused to give land to the in-migrants, or at best allocated them wasteland on the outskirts of the commune. The Rakovka village *skhod* in Samara *uezd* specified during the spring of 1918 that

---

[47] *Tablitsy statisticheskikh svedenii po Saratovskoi gubernii*, p. 139.

[48] Ia. Bliakher, "Sovremennoe zemlepol'zovanie po dannym spetsial'noi anketu TsSU 1922 g.," *Vestnik Statistiki* 13, nos. 1–3, (1923): 144.

[49] See the investigation of G. I. Baskin in *Chislennoist' sel'skogo naseleniia v Samarskoi gubernii* (Samara, 1920), pp. 9–12.

[50] *TsGANKh*, f. 478, op. 3, d. 1157, listy 44–56.

[51] *GAKO*, f. 185, op. 2, d. 89, list 60; *Izvestiia* (Balashov), no. 48, 8 April 1918, p. 4; no. 56, 30 April 1918, p. 3.

[52] *GAKO*, f. 81, op. 1, d. 119, list 87.

all strangers living in Rakovka village will be thrown out if there is not enough land for the peasants of the village according to the norm; but if there is any surplus land, then the strangers should be moved out onto it. In future, they will not be given land from the commune.[53]

Such attitudes went against the Russian village custom of welcoming visitors with bread and salt. It alienated a stratum of the population who were to play a vital political role in the Committees of the Rural Poor (*kombedy*). During the summer and autumn of 1918 the *kombedy* waged an ill-fated socialist war against the kulaks in the *volost'* soviets and the village communes. Although they attempted to rally the poorest peasant smallholders in this struggle, the *kombedy* succeeded in gaining only the landless groups—especially in-migrants—on the margins of rural society. A study of over 800 *kombedy* in Tambov Province found that 22.7 percent of the village *kombed* members had been urban factory workers before 1914; two-thirds of the *kombed* bursars had been factory workers.[54] The majority of the poor farmers stood by their traditional village community leaders, the powerful *khoziaieva*. The neighborly bonds of the farming community were evidently stronger than the social divisions among the peasantry. The violent and criminal methods to which many of the *kombedy* were reduced in their efforts to trim the economic and political influence of the biggest farmers brought together a broad cross-section of the smallholders in defense of their soviets which had emerged from the traditional institutions of peasant society during the revolution.

PEASANT SOLDIERS

It would not be an overstatement to say that the Russian peasant soldiers who returned to their villages after the First World War carried home the revolution. The ex-servicemen were the natural leaders of the peasantry during 1917–1921. They had youth and energy; a comparatively high level of literacy; a mastery of new technologies; knowledge of large-scale social organization; and understanding of urban political ideologies. They had, in short, "tactical mobility."[55] They formed the first generation of peasant officials in the rural soviets, social organizations, and party cells. They gained a dominant position in the communal assembly (indeed, the rapid partitioning

[53] Cited in E. I. Medvedev, *Oktiabr'skaia revoliutsiia v Srednem Povolzh'e* (Kuibyshev, 1964), p. 111.

[54] V. N. Aver'ev, ed., *Komitety bednoty. Sbornik materialov*, 2 vols., 1 (Moscow/Leningrad, 1933), pp. 21–22, 34.

[55] The term was used by Eric Wolf to describe those groups in peasant society most able to participate in social protest. See his *Peasant Wars of the Twentieth Century* (New York, 1973), pp. 276ff.

of peasant households after 1917 increased the representation of ex-service-men at the *skhod*). Above all, they connected the revolution in the village with the revolution in the rest of Russia. Whereas the peasant mandates of 1917 were unclear about the principles of social land ownership (for example they referred in primitive terms to the land "in the hands of the people"), the mandates of the peasant soldiers revealed a sophisticated understanding of the concept of state land ownership with rights of control by the local democratic organs, as specified in the Decree on Land. Whereas the majority of the peasantry voted in a traditional and unanimous fashion during the elections to the Constituent Assembly, the peasant soldiers proved more par-tisan and sometimes managed to persuade their fellow-villagers to vote for one particular party (most commonly, the Left SRs or the Bolsheviks).[56]

From the beginning, then, the peasant soldiers wielded a powerful influ-ence in the middle Volga villages and their soviets. They established their own organizations and sent delegates to soviet assemblies. In Krasnyi Kut (Novouzensk *uezd*) the Union of Front-Line Soldiers (*soiuz frontovikov*)—a na-tionwide organization—confiscated peasant produce on its way to market and received from the Bolshevik-dominated soviet executive a large endow-ment of land, livestock, tools, seed, and cash.[57] In Chernovka *volost'* (Samara *uezd*) the ex-servicemen had two main organizations. The Soldier's Organi-zation was a sort of soviet revolutionary guard. It confiscated the produce of peasants and traders on the roads to the market; requisitioned surplus grain from the peasant farmers; combated the illegal felling of timber; and even-tually formed an armed detachment (*boevaia druzhina*).

The Union of Wounded Veterans (*soiuz uvechnykh voinov*) was a more con-servative, mainly economic organization. It arranged welfare schemes for the widows of soldiers; organized the collective (communal) cultivation of the plots of absent soldiers; petitioned the higher soviet departments of social welfare for the pensions due to the widows of soldiers; elected a "Commissar for the families of veterans," who sat on the four-man *volost'* soviet executive; and imposed levies on the local shopkeepers (and sometimes confiscated their shops) in order to set up craft workshops for the employment of wounded veterans. The influence of the Union was resented and feared. One shopkeeper, A.S. Fedorov, complained to the soviet on 7 March 1918 that the 20-percent tax on his sales and the confiscation of his shop were unjust, since the central authorities had not passed a decree for the confis-cation of shops from small-scale peasant traders, but only from criminals, speculators, and capitalists. Yet Fedorov dared to request only a reduction of the tax to a level of 5 percent. V. I. Istomin, the former land captain of the

---

[56] E. A. Lutskii, *Krest'ianskie*, pp. 139–141; Oliver H. Radkey, *The Elections to the Russian Constituent Assembly of 1917* (Cambridge, Mass., 1950), pp. 36, 40–42, 56, 58, 60.

[57] *TsGAOR*, f. 393, op. 3, d. 325, listy 244, 251, 255.

volost', was more outspoken in his petition against the confiscation of his typewriter by the Union:

> They call themselves invalids, but . . . if they were invalids they would not treat their peasant brothers with such disrepect; the people have no sympathy for these so-called "invalids."[58]

The ex-servicemen were the most important generational subgroup in the revolutionary village; their influence largely superseded that of the old men (*stariki*) who had dominated the nineteenth-century commune.[59] Their increased influence even began to penetrate the large family household, the most conservative of peasant institutions: during the early 1920s it was noted that in many large households the younger brother became the household elder "if he had served in the Red Army, was literate, and had a good understanding of the law and current affairs."[60] It was characteristic that many ex-servicemen became frustrated by the rigid patriarchal hierarchies of rural society and the dull beastly routines of peasant life which they rediscovered on their return from the war. Some found themselves poverty-stricken or unable to do heavy fieldwork because of injuries. Membership of the new ruling elite within the party organizations, the soviet executives, the Cheka, and the Red Army offered these young men an escape from the confined world of the peasants.

PRIESTS AND TEACHERS

The typical parish priest (*pop*) of prerevolutionary Russia barely rose above the peasantry in his standard of living and social status. As I. S. Belliutsin wrote in his *Description of the Clergy*, "the farmer-priest is just a peasant distinguished only by his literacy; otherwise he has a cast of thought, desires, aspirations, and even a way of life that are strictly peasant."[61] Much of the priest's energy was spent tilling the household garden and arable strips assigned by the commune to the church-house. He was accustomed to negotiating the prices of the Christian and pagan rituals which he performed in the fields and the peasants' huts, as well as the church.

The revolution accentuated the "peasant" nature of the parish priest. In 1917–1918 many village churchmen were granted an allotment of land by their commune along with rights of representation at the communal assembly. Some monasteries avoided the confiscation of their land by declaring

---

[58] *GAKO*, f. 3134, op. 2, d. 21, listy 33, 35, 68–69, 80, 92, etc.

[59] Boris Mironov, "The Russian Peasant Commune After the Reforms of the 1860s," *Slavic Review* 44, no. 3 (Fall 1985): 447.

[60] V. P. Danilov, *Rural Russia Under the New Regime*, p. 231.

[61] I. S. Belliustin, *Description of the Clergy in Rural Russia*, trans. Gregory L. Freeze (Ithaca, N.Y., 1985), p. 126.

themselves independent "communes," *arteli* or *kommuny*.[62] Many local priests followed their church leaders and joined the White movement. Others went with the revolution. Some even became activists in the soviets and the Red Army. The editor of the Balashov *Izvestiia*, Aleksinskii, had been a priest before 1917; a prominent member of the Ardatov district soviet executive, Fonchikov, had also been a priest.[63]

The politics of the rural clergy were put to the test by the legal separation of church and state on 23 January 1918. This deprived the church of its right to maintain schools and—in return for state subsidies—register births, deaths, and marriages. Henceforth, these responsibilities were to be carried out by the soviets, which were to account the property of the church in preparation for its transfer to the state.[64] The effects of the separation were diverse. Some peasant soviets in the middle Volga region resolved that payments for religious services (the priest's main source of income) should be voluntary, according to belief, yet simultaneously raised taxes and collected wood and provisions through the communes for the upkeep of the church and its personnel (priests, deacons, sacristans, and sometimes a choir).[65] Other soviets made no effort to prevent the priest from collecting taxes for his religious services in the traditional manner. In Kliuchi village (Buguruslan *uezd*) the commune paid the priest a monthly fee of 300 rubles and granted him 200 *pudy* of flour per annum. In the nearby village of Novo-Spasovskoe the priest was said to be earning 7,000 to 8,000 rubles per month from marriages, christenings, and burials, for which he charged between 150 and 200 rubles according to the wealth of the client.[66]

Occasionally, tensions arose between the soviet and the church council (*tserkovnyi sovet*) over the accommodation of the clergy. Many village priests lived in a church house which after the separation formally became state property. Soviet and party workers could legally evict the priest from his house and turn it into an office, or their own home, or some form of com-

[62] *TsGANKh*, f. 478, op. 3, d. 1157, list 46; *TsGAOR*, f. 393, op. 3, d. 325, listy 76–77; *Rezoliutsii i tezisy priniatye na 7-om Samarskom gubernskom s''ezde sovetov 10–16 dekabria 1920 g.* (Samara, 1921), pp. 30–31; V. V. Kabanov, "Oktiabr'skaia", p. 125; E. G. Gimpel'son, *Sovety v pervyi god proletarskoi diktatury, oktiabr' 1917 g.–noiabr' 1918 g.* (Moscow, 1967), pp. 266–67.

[63] *Izvestiia* (Kamyshin), no. 85, 29 September 1918, p. 2; *TsGAOR*, f. 393, op. 3, d. 359, list 266. See also *Kommuna* (Samara), no. 112, 27 April 1919, p. 3; no. 138, 29 May 1919, p. 3, etc.

[64] M. M. Persits, *Otdelenie tserkvi ot gosudarstva i shkoly ot tserkvi v SSSR* (Moscow, 1958), pp. 99–103.

[65] *GAKO*, f. 3134, op. 2, d. 21, listy 15, 30, 45; *TsGAOR*, f. 393, op. 3, d. 329, list 64; d. 325, listy 236, 259, 266; d. 337, listy 154–55; d. 333, list 89.

[66] *Luch Kommuny* (Buguruslan), no. 354, 27 May 1920, p. 2; *Kommuna* (Samara), no. 244, 5 October 1919, p. 2; *Nabat* (Kamyshin), no. 36, 30 March 1919, p. 3. There is journalistic evidence to suggest that the higher urban church councils attempted to collect flour from the local rural clergy once they had been deprived of financial support by the state: *Kommunist* (Pugachev), no. 177, 17 October 1920, p. 1.

munal building (*obshchestvennyi dom, narodnyi dom, izba chitatel'naia*, etc.). At this point, the church council, the parishioners (*prikhozhane*), or a communal delegation sometimes interceded to protect the priest. In Durnikino village (Balashov *uezd*) the Communists and soviet executive members were heckled and threatened at a village meeting, when they refused to rehouse two priests in the *narodnyi dom*. An ultimatum was issued by the peasants, and the soviet executive agreed to their demands. In the nearby village of Svinukha a similar conflict occurred when the soviet executive and the post office occupied two church houses. The peasants rallied behind their church council and forced out the soviet executive, which fled to the neighboring village of Iniasevo. A *skhod* was then called, which resolved that "priests are needed in the village more than a post office or a soviet executive."[67]

It is probably fair to say that Russian rural society loosened its attachment and servility to the Orthodox Church in the decade after 1917. Some sources suggest that the influence of the church declined most rapidly among the young men who had been taken out of the village during 1914–1920.[68] However, during the turmoil of the Civil War the traditional bonds of the village community remained tight, and the church and the old patterns of belief for which it stood retained a powerful hold over those who doubted or feared what the new order might bring.

The peasantry's support for the church was reflected in the many petitions which the military authorities received from villages in the middle Volga region requesting the release of their priest from the Red Army. Bekovo village petitioned the Serdobsk district military authorities in December 1918 for the release of its priest, Lepleiskii, and its deacon, Bogdanov, who had been mobilized to perform religious services in the rear units. The petition spoke of them as "good men and excellent churchmen who satisfied all our moral and spiritual demands." Lepleiskii, "knowing our need and strong desire for education," had helped the villagers establish a higher school (*vysshee nachal'noe uchilishche*) in 1917. Yet now the school was running down and there was only one priest left, Vekikanov, who was "not able to cater for the 4,795 inhabitants of Bekovo village and the 1,000 inhabitants of Rogachevka twelve *versty* away."[69]

Religious sentiments were also expressed during peasant uprisings, particularly if the Bolshevik party cell—in abuse of its powers under the Decree of 23 January—confiscated or destroyed church property in a crusade against

[67] *Izvestiia* (Balashov), no. 117, 1 June 1919, p. 4; no. 121, 6 June 1919, p. 4.

[68] See the report of Bishop Chesnokov of Samara, published in *Kommuna* (Samara), no. 134, 24 May 1919, p. 2. See also Ia. Iakovlev, *Nasha derevnia: Novoe v starom i staroe v novom* (Moscow, 1924), pp. 127–31.

[69] *TsGAOR*, f. 393, op. 3, d. 340, list 268. See also d. 337, list 161; *GAKO*, f. 81, op. 1, d. 10, list 109; *Nabat* (Kamyshin), no. 39, 6 April 1919, p. 3.

religion.[70] There were street battles during religious processions, village riots, and *samosudy* in defense of the church. In April 1918, a crowd of more than 500 women in Liubimovka village (Buzuluk *uezd*) set upon a group of party workers with cries of "to hell with the blasphemer-Communists!" The latter had removed icons from the church. The Buzuluk police sent in a brigade which the women tried to disarm and put on trial. There were violent scuffles, from which the brigade managed to flee.[71] Finally, the prohibition of religious instruction in soviet schools also evoked widespread peasant discontent. The provincial departments of education received hundreds of peasant complaints on this matter. Most of the peasant Soviets were forced to ignore the government order. Some instituted compulsory religious instruction and punished teachers who failed to comply. One or two Soviets even offered a choice between religious and secular curricula.[72]

The prohibition of religious instruction was difficult to enforce, since so many village schools were attached to the church and run by the clergy. In 1917–1918, when timber was in great demand for fuel and house repairs, it was virtually impossible for the young soviets to organize a school-rebuilding program. Some teachers fled to the towns or joined the White Army in 1917–1918 on account of their poverty, their political beliefs, or their dwindling influence in the village (the teachers did not generally play the leading political role in the village after 1917 that they had played during the 1905–1907 Revolution). A new cadre of peasant teachers was only slowly emerging. Nadezhda Krupskaia, on her propaganda travels through the Volga region during the summer of 1919, noted that many of the village schoolteachers were young girls, often held in low esteem by the peasantry. They must have been educated since 1914, when their brothers joined the army. It was common for them to be paid in kind—in agricultural produce, peasant craft goods, or a garden allotment near the schoolhouse tilled by the pupils themselves.[73]

The typical village schoolteacher, before and after the revolution, was economically dependent upon the smallholding peasantry. For this reason

---

[70] Such abuses seriously threatened peasant-state relations in 1918–1920 according to a report of NVKD. See *Vlast'Sovetov*, no. 5, April 1919, p. 14.

[71] *Kommuna* (Samara), no. 100, 12 April 1918, p. 3. See also *Samarskie Eparkhal'nye Vedomosti*, nos. 7–8, 14–28 April 1918, p. 285; *Revoliutsionnaia Armiia* (Samara), no. 14, 21 January 1919, p. 4; *Nabat* (Kamyshin), no. 33, 23 March 1919, p. 3; *Sbornik "Ves'Kuznetsk"* (Kuznetsk, 1927), p. 49.

[72] *TsGAOR*, f. 393, op. 3, d. 323, list 245; d. 333, list 87; *Vestnik Komissariata Vnutrennikh Del*, no. 11, 24 April 1918, p. 15; *Protokol Kamyshinskogo uezdnogo s"ezda krest'ianskikh deputatov i predstavitelei razlichnykh politicheskiku grupp, uchrezhdenii organizatii, 10-g. marta 1918 g.* (Kamyshin 1918), pp. 32–34; F. G. Popov, *1918 god v Samaraskoi gubernii, Khronika sobytii* (Kuibyshev, 1972), p. 64.

[73] N. K. Krupskaia, "Po gradam i vesiam Sovetskoi Respubliki," *Novyi Mir* 36, no. 11 (1960): 118, 120–21, 123–24, 128.

alone, many teachers remained in the village after 1917. They were highly valued by the peasantry, who went to great lengths to retain them. Schools were repaired, or rehoused in the manor. If the village did not have a school-house, then lessons were sometimes held in the open fields or in the mar-ketplace. Peasants felled timber to heat the classrooms and raised communal taxes to pay the teacher. The village children (and a good number of their parents) attended school lessons on the days free from agricultural work.[74] After the land, literacy loomed large among the peasantry's aspirations dur-ing the revolution. The white-bearded skeptics in the village might have be-lieved that their sons would not want to work if they learned to read, but the younger peasants understood that literacy was a qualification of freedom, "a badge of equality with the non-peasants."[75] In the words of the Chernovka village soviet (Buzuluk *uezd*), literacy was a "path guiding the peasantry out of the darkness and ignorance in which it has found itself for centuries."[76]

In its dealings with the marginal groups of rural society during the agrarian revolution, the Russian peasantry applied many different moral standards and conceptions of social justice. These standards were used by the peas-antry in a number of different forms, according to the perceived social value of the group in question: craftsmen who manufactured goods demanded by the peasant farmers were given more rights within the village community than in-migrant urban workers and other "free riders," who contributed little or nothing to the community and became a burden upon its social resources (land, housing, surplus grain); village teachers and socially minded parish priests were generally perceived as friends of the peasant class; whereas ex-tsarist officials were seen as class enemies. In this way, the peasantry drew up a social circle of "insiders" wherein each occupational group and social subclass was assigned a certain set of rights and duties within the community.

The interests of the peasant farmers—represented by the communal as-sembly—dominated the village and its institutions (the church, the coopera-tive, the village soviet). Although the new class of smallholders created by the revolution (ex-landless laborers, newly partitioned peasant households, separators who had returned to the commune, and some former squires) acquired a political voice at the communal assembly, this was rarely heard

[74] On the general state of the schools and peasant-schoolteacher relations in 1917 see *Dok-lad Vol'skogo uezdnogo ispolkoma sovetov 15 oktiabria 1919 g.* (Vol'sk, 1919), pp. 6–7; *TsGAOR,* f. 393, op. 3, d. 323, listy 59, 77. *PS*, pp. 40, 43. On the various political beliefs of schoolteach-ers see ibid., p. 33; *Izvestiia* (Balashov), no. 57, 1 May 1918, p. 4; E. G. Gimpel'son, *Sovety,* pp. 250ff. On the measures taken by peasant communities to retain their local teachers after 1917 see *GAKO,* f. 109, op. 3, d. 52, listy 2, 21, 36; *TsGANKh,* f. 478, op. 1, d. 330, list 65; *PS,* pp. 22–23, 36; Ia. Iakovlev, *Nasha derevnia,* pp. 110–16; E. G. Gimpel'son, *Sovety,* pp. 249ff; N. K. Krupskaia, "Po gradam" pp. 113–30.

[75] Teodor Shanin, *Russia, 1905–07: Revolution as a Moment of Truth,* (London, 1986), p. 135.

[76] *GAKO,* f. 3134, op. 2, d. 21, list 42.

above the clamor of the biggest peasant farmers. On the other hand, the influence of the latter was counterbalanced by the democratization of the commune and the increased significance of all-village and open *volost'* meetings during the revolution, which strengthened the bonds of interdependence between the smallholders and other rural groups. This village-based system granted equal rights of political representation to all village residents: peasants; former squires and separators; the rural intelligentsia and the priests; craftsmen; landless laborers; kulaks and merchants; yet not always women. The franchise was more inclusive than it had been during the nineteenth century, but the patriarchal and traditionalist influences of the peasant community remained dominant. This last factor distinguished the village democracy of the revolution from the system of soviet representation drawn up by the Constitution of July 1918, which assigned political rights in the village soviets according to class categories, rather than customary practices; hence, the constitution disenfranchised the kulaks and merchants, but gave full political rights to peasant women.

To what degree was the village democracy of 1918 a stable and cohesive social system? The consolidation of the Soviet state ultimately undermined the autonomy of the village soviets and the communes. During the Civil War the Communist party greatly increased its representation in the *volost'* soviet executives, while the local soviets were—to a certain degree—subordinated within a centralized party-state system.[77] Was this process based upon real changes within rural society, or did it proceed from above? The question is controversial. Soviet historians have underlined the connections between the centralization of Soviet (Communist) power in the countryside and the class tensions and contradictions within peasant society. According to their scenario, the increasing domination of the Communist party in the soviets marked the rise of the poor peasants against their "kulak masters" in the communes and the soviets of 1917–1918.

On the other hand, historians in the West have tended to talk of the Russian peasantry during 1917–1921 as one undifferentiated mass whose social identity and class actions were mainly determined in relation to outsiders (e.g., townsmen). This leads to the view that the soviets were subverted by outsider plenipotentiaries from the Communist party. The truth probably lies somewhere between these two ideas, and is rather more complex than either.[78] The farming peasantry experienced a deep social crisis after 1918; but it did not experience an *internal* class crisis in the manner diagnosed by Soviet Marxists, whereby the smallholders were divided into antagonistic— proletarian and bourgeois—class interests. It experienced a crisis on the mar-

[77] On this see Orlando Figes, "The Village and Volost Soviet Elections of 1919," *Soviet Studies* 40, no. 1 (January 1988): 21–45.

[78] See further Orlando Figes, *Peasant Russia, Civil War: The Volga Countryside in Revolution 1917–1921* (Oxford, 1989).

gins of peasant society where the wider social currents of the war and the revolutionary period gradually eroded the patriarchal traditions and structures of the agrarian community.

These erosive currents were washed ashore by the urban workers who migrated into the countryside and, above all, by the peasant soldiers who returned from the front. The latter were young, mobile, and impatient for a radical social transformation of peasant Russia. They sought to break down the patriarchal hierarchies which had previously held back their generation. They wanted an end to the closed and isolated world of the village, the world of cockroaches and priests dressed in black. Their ideal was the urban-oriented civilization of the twentieth century.

Notes on Contributors

Rodney Bohac is an associate professor of history at Brigham Young University. His research has focused on peasant economic and political protest in the pre-Emancipation era. Publications include "Russian Peasant Inheritance Strategies," *Journal of Interdisciplinary History* 16 (Summer 1985): 23–42 and "Agricultural Structure and the Origins of Migration in Central Russia, 1810–1850," in *Agrarian Organization in the Century of Industrialization: Europe, Russia, and North America*, ed. George Grantham and Carol S. Leonard, *Research in Economic History*, Supplement 5, Part B (Greenwich, Conn., 1989), pp. 369–87.

Jeffrey Burds is assistant professor of history at the University of Rochester. He has recently completed a doctoral dissertation at Yale University entitled "Patterns of Change in the Central Russian Village: Community Relations and the Market Economy, 1840–1914." His current research interests include a study of threats to "little community" cohesion in the evolution of Russian state rural institutions, 1700–1905.

David Christian is a professor of history at Macquarie University in Sydney, Australia. His early work focused on the views of bureaucrats in the early nineteenth century. He is coauthor (with R.E.F. Smith) of *Bread and Salt: A Social and Economic History of Food and Drink in Russia* (Cambridge, 1984). He has also written a high-school text entitled *Power and Privilege: Russia and the Soviet Union in the Nineteenth and Twentieth Centuries* (Melbourne, 1986). In addition, he has recently completed a study entitled *"Living Water": Vodka and Russian Society on the Eve of Emancipation* (Oxford, 1990). His current research deals with the topic of prohibition in Russia between 1914 and 1923.

Orlando Figes is a university assistant lecturer and fellow in history at Trinity College, Cambridge University. He is the author of *Peasant Russia, Civil War: The Volga Countryside in Revolution, 1917–1921* (Oxford, 1989). He is currently writing *Social History of the Russian Revolution 1917–1921* (forthcoming, 1991).

Esther Kingston-Mann is professor of history at University of Massachusetts-Boston. She has written on topics ranging from Tolstoy and Kropotkin to Lenin as well as issues of Westernization and Russian rural development, including *Lenin and the Problem of Marxist Peasant Revolution* (Oxford, 1983) and "In Search of the True West: Western Economic Models and Russian Rural Development, 1870–1906," *Journal of Historical Sociology* (Spring 1990). Current research includes a forthcoming monograph entitled *The Majority as an Obstacle to Progress: Problems of Russian Rural Development*, and *Understanding Peasants, Understanding the Experts: Zemstvo Statisticians and Economists, 1870–1906*.

Timothy Mixter is currently an assistant professor of history at Temple University. He has recently taught in the History and Literature program at Harvard University. He is the author of "Of Grandfather-Beaters and Fat-Heeled Pacifists: Perceptions of Agricultural Labor and Hiring Market Disturbances in Saratov, 1872–1905," *Russian History* 7, parts 1–2 (1980): 139–68. In addition to his University of Michigan dissertation and other forthcoming work on migrant agricultural laborers in Russia, he has been researching peasant collective action in Saratov Province, 1902–1906. An article on this topic is included in *Politics and Society in Provincial Russia: Saratov, 1590–1917*, ed. Rex A. Wade and Scott J. Seregny (Columbus, 1989). His future work will be on the nature of urban space in the post-World War II Soviet Union.

Samuel Ramer is associate professor of history at Tulane University in New Orleans, Louisiana. He has written numerous articles on Russian intellectual and social history. The most recent is "The Transformation of the Russian Feldsher, 1864–1914," in *Imperial Russia, 1700–1917: State Society and Opposition, Essays in Honor of Marc Raeff*, ed. Ezra Mendelsohn and Marshall S. Shatz (DeKalb, Ill., 1988), pp. 136–60. He is presently completing a book on feldshers, midwives, and rural medicine in Russia from the mid-nineteenth century until the early Soviet period.

Scott J. Seregny is associate professor of history at Indiana University (Indianapolis). Author of *Russian Schoolteachers and Peasant Revolution: The Politics of Education in 1905* (Bloomington, Ind., 1989), he has published articles on the Russian rural intelligentsia and peasant politics. In addition, he is co-editor of *Politics and Society in Provincial Russia: Saratov, 1590–1917* (Columbus, 1989).

Stephen Wheatcroft is a senior lecturer in the department of history and director of the Center for Soviet and East European Studies at the University of Melbourne, Australia. Among his publications are *Materials for the Balance of the Soviet National Economy 1928–1930* (Cambridge, 1986), "A Reevaluation of Soviet Agricultural Production in the 1920s and 1930s," in *Studies of the Soviet Rural Economy*, ed. Robert C. Stuart (London, 1983), pp. 32–62 and "Famine and Epidemic Crises in Russia, 1918–1922: The Case of Saratov," *Annales de Démographie Historique* (1983): 329–52.

Elvira Wilbur is associate professor in the department of history at Michigan State University. Her current research is focused on the Russian peasantry and the relationships among population growth, market development, modernization, and revolution. Her publications include "Was Russian Peasant Agriculture Really That Impoverished? New Evidence From a Case Study From the 'Impoverished Center' at the End of the 19th Century," *Journal of Economic History* 43, no. 1 (March 1983): 137–44.

Christine D. Worobec is assistant professor of history at Kent State University. She is author of the forthcoming *Peasant Russia: Family and Community in the Post-Emancipation Period* (Princeton, 1991) and coeditor of the forthcoming *Russia's Women: Accommodation, Resistance, Transformation* (Berkeley, 1991). Her next research project is a comparative study of Russian, Ukrainian, and Belorussian demonology. Her "Horse Thieves and Peasant Justice in Post-Emancipation Imperial Russia," *Journal of Social History* 21, no. 2 (Winter 1987): 281–93, was nominated for the Berkshire Prize.

Glossary

arendu ispolu Sharecropping.

arshin(y) A unit of measure equal to two feet, four inches.

artel'(li) A cooperative association of peasants or workers laboring together by agreement, usually under the guidance of an elected head. Sometimes members pooled resources and shared profits.

babka(ki) Grandmother; also a term used for a traditional healer, midwife, or sorcerer.

barshchina Corvée; labor rent or obligatory work performed by peasants, especially serfs, for the landowner.

batrak(i) Peasant without land; either a wage laborer or a young peasant who had not yet succeeded to an allotment. Sometimes used more loosely to refer to any hired agricultural laborer.

bedniak(i) A poor peasant (*Bednyi* = poor).

bezhentsy Refugees; sometimes used more loosely to refer to any immigrants arriving in a village during the period 1914–1921.

blagodeteli Benefactors.

bol'shak(i) Senior male head of a peasant household.

bunt(y) Agrarian disorder or revolt with the connotation of being unplanned or spontaneous as well as violent.

burmistr(y) Estate manager.

charivari(s) A village custom involving the organized public mocking of someone who had violated community values.

chernozem "Black earth"—rich agricultural soil.

chetvert' (ti) The basic dry measure for grain, equal to 5.95 bushels.

demense Lands retained by a noble landowner for his or her own use.

desiatina(ny) Land measure equal to 2.7 acres or 2,400 square *sazheni*.

Duma The nationwide representative assembly; the State Duma was the lower house in the legislature set up in 1905–1906, lasting until 1917.

etapnik(i) Person brought back under guard (*po etapu*) to the village who had broken the law elsewhere, often during the time spent in labor migration.

fel'dsher(a) Feldsher, paramedic, doctor's assistant.

guliatskii obrok "Wanderer's tax"; a departure fee paid by a person (usually a migrant laborer) leaving the village. Fee was used for the most part to cover future tax obligations.

ispolkom(y) Executive committee of a soviet, both at the national and local level.

ispravnik(i) Chief of police in a district (*uezd*).

iurodivyi(ye) "Holy fool."

izba(by) Peasant hut.

khodok(dki) Literally, a "walker." In general, a representative of peasant communities sent to some government body, often with a village petition or resolution.

khorovod(y) Spring and summer round dances.

khoziain, khoziaeva Male household head, able to vote in the village assembly. Also can refer to a farmer or master, sometimes used loosely as a synonym for an employer or a landlord. *Khoziaika*, (ki)-female head of household, etc.

khutor(a) An independent, enclosed, or consolidated individual farmstead in private possession where a peasant, with his or her family, lived outside the village.

khutorianin(ne) Owner, of a *khutor*.

kolkhoz(y) Collective farm.

kombed(y) Committee of the Village Poor set up by the Soviet government in the summer of 1918.

kommuna(ny) A Soviet collective farm in which all property was held collectively.

korennoi peredel A radical redistribution of the land which involved a change in both the number and size of the strips into which commune land was divided.

krugovaia poruka Collective responsibility, often for the payment of taxes or fulfillment of work.

kulak(i) Literally, a "fist"; often used pejoratively to refer to a rich peasant who exploited others through moneylending or renting of land.

kustarnye promysly Nonagricultural cottage industries, handicraft industries, or proto-industries, particularly common in the relatively infertile Central Industrial Region.

mir(y or e) Village community, also means "world" and "peace."

muzhik(i) Peasant, usually a term used condescendingly or pejoratively by non peasants.

nadel(y) Land allotment.

narod Common people—term mainly referring to peasants and workers.

nevesta(ty) Prospective bride or bride-to-be.

oblast'(ti) A region or territorial administrative division corresponding to a province.

obrok Quitrent or dues paid in cash or kind.

obshchestvo(va) Literally, "society." (1) *sel'skoe obshchestvo*—synonymous with the *mir* or village community. (2) "enlightened society" or the "enlightened elite," often contrasted with the *narod*.

otkhodnichestvo and otkhod Labor migration or seasonal work.

otkhodnik(i) Migrant laborer.

otkhozhie promysly Literally, "going-away trades"; labor migration or seasonal work.

otrabotka Leasing arrangement whereby peasants received land in exchange for labor on estate land.

otrub(a) A peasant farm consisting of one to three or four plots of arable land in different locations and separate from grazing land. The peasant cottage and other farm buildings remain in the core village or some other central location (unlike a *khutor* in this respect).

otrubnik(i) Owner of an *otrub*.

pan(y) Master, lord, especially of serfs used particularly in Polish, Ukrainian, and Lithuanian areas.

pennoe Foamy vodka.

pereverstka(ki) A limited exchange of strips of land which applied only to those households whose size had changed since the last repartition.

pogrom(y) Destruction of estates by peasants. In other cases refers to anti-Semitic attacks on Jewish citizens or other minority groups.

polugar Ordinary unfiltered vodka; 40 percent alcohol vodka.

pomeshchik(i) general name for a noble estate owner.

pomoch' Aid, help.

pood, pud(y) One pud or pood equals 36.113 pounds.

posidelki Social gathering, usually in the winter, sometimes including work such as sewing. Usually a gathering of girls, although often male suitors were invited and courting encouraged.

povitukha(khi) Traditional village midwife.

pravo na trud The unconditional right to land, i.e., to the means of survival.

pravo truda The right to land based upon the investment of labor.

prigovor(y) Petition, resolution, or declaration, usually of the *mir* assembly

prikazchik(i) Steward or bailiff.

pristav(y) A police official with jurisdiction at the sub-district level.

pud(y) A *pood*, basic unit of weight equaling 36.113 pounds.

rynok, rynki Market.

samogon "Moonshine," or home-brewed vodka.

samosud(y) Lynch law; peasants taking the law into their own hands.

sazhen'(ni) A measurement of length equal to 7 feet.

semeinyi razdel Family household division or a division of property belonging to a family which often needed the approval of the village assembly.

shtof Liquid measure equal to 1.23 liters or 1.3 quarts.

skhod, skhodka The village or *mir* assembly.

snokhachestvo Incest between father-in-law and daughter-in-law.

soslovie, (viia) Legal estate; *état* (Fr.), Stand (Ger.).

sotskii, (kie) Village policeman subordinate to a *pristav*.

sovet(y) Soviet or council elected by workers, peasants, etc.

sovkoz(y) State farm.

stanitsa(sy) A cossack settlement composed of one large village or several lesser villages.

stariki Peasant elders who invariably had a right to vote in the village assembly and often controlled it.

starshchina(ny) Peasant elected by villagers in a *volost'* to adminsiter it.

Third Element Employees of the zemstvo such as teachers, doctors, statisticians, etc., who were often from peasant or lower-class backgrounds. Distinguished from the First Element (the administration) and the Second Element (the elected zemstvo deputies), who were largely from the nobility.

tiaglo(la) A work team consisting of a married couple of working age, and a fiscal unit according to which taxes, labor dues, and land were apportioned.

trezvennoe dvizhenie Temperance or sobriety movement.

uezd(y) District.

uriadnik(i) Police sergeant above the level of a *sotskii* but below a *pristav*.

usad'ba(by) Plot usually including the peasant's house and kitchen garden.

verst, versta(ty) Measure of length equal to 500 *sazheni* or .663 miles.

vol'nye shkoly Free schools established by peasants without state aid.

volost'(ti) An all-peasant administrative subdivision of the *uezd*, usually composed of several peasant communes and governed by peasant-elected officials; referred to as a canton or township.

volostnoe pravlenie or volostnaia uprava The *volost'* administration or board, usually the elected leaders of the *mir* from all villages in the *volost'*. Peasants chose village scribes (*pisary*) and judges to help with *volost'* administration. In 1889, placed under the jurisdiction of the *zemskie nachal'niki*.

vorozhei (a) Fortune-teller, sorceress, or traditional healer.

Vserossiiskii Krest'ianskii Soiuz All-Russian Peasant Union, founded in the summer of 1905, by and large suppressed by late 1906.

zadatok(tki) Advances paid by an employer to a worker. Used by worker as a form of credit, often to pay off tax arrears, and by an employer as a way to obtain labor for less than the market wage rate.

zagovor(y) (1) Conspiracy; (2) healing through ritualistic chants or spells.

zemliachestvo(va) regional loyalty or association often of migrant laborers; sometimes the organizational basis for defense of interests.

zemskii nachal'nik (zemskie nachal'niki) Land captain: post created in 1889 by the Ministry of the Interior, in order to supervise peasant activity more closely.

zemstvo(va) Semiautonomous, elective local-government bodies created at the provincial and *uezd* level in most provinces of European Russia after 1864. Usually dominated by the nobility, the *zemstva* provided a number of social services to the peasantry.

zemtsy Deputies to the zemstvo assembly.

zherebëv'ka(ki) Method of peasant land distribution which exchanged previously marked-off strips of land according to a plan determined by lot.

znakhar'(ri, rka) Literally, a knowledgeable one, expert; "a wise man or woman" perceived by their clientele as possessors of a special healing gift, often deemed to be rooted in magic or the occult.

znakharstvo Term used by physicians to describe all unlicensed healing.

Index